INTRODUCTION TO THE
STUDY OF SOCIOLOGY

INTRODUCTION TO THE STUDY OF SOCIOLOGY

BY

EDWARD CARY HAYES, Ph.D.

PROFESSOR OF SOCIOLOGY IN THE UNIVERSITY OF ILLINOIS

D. APPLETON AND COMPANY
NEW YORK AND LONDON
1927

Printed in the United States of America

PREFACE

This is an elementary textbook with the limitations which that fact implies. It is intended for the use of classes and also for general readers who desire a clearer view of the field of thought designated by the much used word "sociology."

Such a book must aim to serve two purposes. First, it must present as much as space permits of the accepted results of study in this field, to the reader who may have no further formal instruction in sociology, and whose further progress will be gained by independent thought and reading. Second, it must afford to the student, who will pursue more intensive courses in subdivisions of sociology, an outline of the entire field, and a sense of the relation of those special topics, which he may later study more intensively, to the subject as a whole. Each of these purposes requires the elementary textbook to be compendious so as to afford a view in perspective. The best books in sociology have been written by men who were contributing actively to the new body of teaching, and who have been too much preoccupied with the original materials, in the production of which their minds were engaged, to give adequate time and space to the contributions of others. As a consequence, it is hardly too much to say of the textbooks in sociology which have thus far been produced, that in proportion to their originality and intellectual excellence has been their failure as compendiums or outlines.

A compendium of sociology must include not only a summary of the chief abstract teachings in all branches of the subject, but also some practical applications, the result of hard experience and of investigation into specific evils and their causes, and of empirical efforts at reform as interpreted in the light of scientific principles. This corresponds with the practice of elementary textbooks in economics, which include practical suggestions on money, taxation, and labor problems along with theoretical discussion. This practice interrupts, to a slight degree, the course of scientific exposition, but is justified by its usefulness.

I have been influenced by the example of the best text-books in economics and psychology to do without a multitude of footnotes, but I have inserted a considerable number of references, (1) when it has seemed especially desirable to call the attention of the reader to some passage that supplements the text, or (2) to some book that should be universally associated with the particular doctrine under discussion, or else (3) to afford opportunity to verify some statement that might otherwise be questioned, and (4) in case of direct quotation.

It might seem more logical to reverse the order of parts 1 and 2. As it now stands, the book presents the conditions which affect the life of society before it presents the inner nature of the life of society. This order has been adopted because it better develops the conception of society as a realm of cause and effect, and also because it places first those matters about which the student already knows something, in many of which he is already interested, which he expects to study when he registers for a course in sociology, and which are more material and easier, postponing those which are more psychological and difficult, which would cause him surprise if not disappointment if first presented, and for the study of which he requires some preparation, but which are the very soul of the subject when really understood. This arrangement is the result of much experimentation during thirteen years of teaching sociology.

Some readers may be inclined to criticize the inclusion of a few pages which might have been omitted if it had been possible to take for granted that all students of this text would have fresh in mind the facts and principles of biology, psychology, and economics. But it is impossible to take that for granted, and sociology, like general biology, requires some reference to facts of antecedent sciences.

In some universities where numerous courses in sociology are offered, it may be thought best to omit portions of the matter which deals with charities, criminology, and social evolution, because these subjects are to be covered by other courses. And an omitted part may be used later in connection with a subsequent course. Even in such universities, however, the brief outline of these topics here given may preferably be retained undiminished as an introduction to more extensive work, and as bringing the parts of the subject into their relations.

The author desires to express his thanks to the following persons who have read portions of the book in manuscript: Professor Felix von Luschan, of the University of Berlin, who read the part on social evolution; Professor E. L. Bogart and Assistant Professor R. E. Heilman, of the Department of Economics in the University of Illinois, who read the part on the necessity for social regulation of the distribution of wealth; Professor Charles Zeleny and Assistant Professor J. A. Detlefsen, of the Departments of Zoölogy and of Genetics in the University of Illinois, who read the parts which utilize biological data. Of course the kindness rendered by these gentlemen involves them in no responsibility for anything here contained.

The book is offered with the hope that it may promote comprehension and insight, and help some of its readers to "find themselves," with reference to the perplexing intellectual problems, the opportunities, and the responsibilities of the life we live in society.

UNIVERSITY OF ILLINOIS.
   October, 1915.

NOTE TO THE NINETEENTH PRINTING.

In this edition the most recent statistics have been inserted at several points in place of older ones.
   May, 1925.

tion, because these subjects are to be covered by other courses. And an omitted part may be used later in connection with a subsequent course. Even in such universities, however, the brief outline of these topics here given may preferably be retained undiminished as an introduction to more extensive works and as bringing the parts of the subject into their relations.

The author desires to express his thanks to the following persons who have read portions of the book in manuscript: Professor Felix von Luschan, of the University of Berlin, who read the part on social evolution; Professor E. L. Bogart and Assistant Professor R. L. Huddian, of the Department of Economics in the University of Illinois, who read the part on the necessity for social regulation of the distribution of wealth; Professor Charles Zeleny and Assistant Professor F. A. Detlefsen, of the Departments of Zoology and of Genetics in the University of Illinois, who read the parts which utilize biological data. Of course the kindness rendered by these gentlemen involves them in no responsibility for anything here contained.

The book is offered with the hope that it may promote comprehension and help some of its readers to "find themselves," with reference to the perplexing intellectual problems, the opportunities, and the responsibilities of the life we live in society.

University of Kansas,
October, 1914.

Note to the Nineteenth Printing.

In this edition the most recent statistics have been inserted at several points in place of older ones.

May, 1925.

CONTENTS

INTRODUCTION

PART I

THE CAUSES WHICH AFFECT THE LIFE OF SOCIETY

I. GEOGRAPHIC CAUSES WHICH AFFECT THE LIFE OF SOCIETY

ix

PART II

NATURE AND ANALYSIS OF THE LIFE OF SOCIETY

PART III

SOCIAL EVOLUTION

CONTENTS

PART IV

SOCIAL CONTROL

CONTENTS

INTRODUCTION

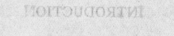

CHAPTER I

THE NATURE OF THE STUDY

Sociology Studies Good and Bad Alike.—Apparently many persons turn to sociology with the idea that it is a study of vice, crime, and poverty, and that the typical sociological exercise is "slumming." It is, however, at least as important scientifically to understand the normal as to understand the abnormal, and at least as important practically to know how to promote the good as to know how to combat the evil. We should at the outset divest ourselves of the one-sided idea that sociology is a study of evils, and look forward rather to a study of social life as a whole, good and evil existing together.

In this respect sociology does not differ from any other science that deals with a department of life. Sociology has as much to do with poverty, vice, and crime as botany has to do with parasitism and the diseases of plants, and it also has as much to do with the normal life of society as botany has to do with the normal life of plants. The illustration may be made still more accurate by saying that slavery, war, and parts of that which, at our stage of civilization, is called vice, are as natural, and *in that sense* as normal, as honest industry. Weeds are at least as natural as wheat, and the sociologist as well as the botanist or any other scientist must study the realities as they are naturally produced before he is prepared to exercise a selective control over their production. He must study the activities that go on in society as they are, and they are in part good and in part bad, according to our standards; it may be as important both for science and for those practical activities which may be guided by science that we understand the one as the other.

3

The Point of View.—Whatever else sociology may mean, it stands for the adoption of a distinct and consistent attitude, or point of view, in the discussion of intellectual problems the solution of which practically affects the life of man.

1.   It means, first, that social problems are to be discussed with primary reference not to the gains of the wealthy, nor to the stability and strength of states, but to the welfare of all the people. From this it results that a set of problems, once largely neglected, comes into the center of attention, namely, the problems of the distribution of wealth, opportunity, education, health, and the joys and worth of life. Machiavelli could teach that even the conscience of the individual should be sacrificed to the welfare of the state. Not long ago the liaison of a prince made history, but in the same year ten thousand subjects might starve and the fact be omitted by historians. Then an economic writer could declare that "high wages are the great obstacle to British trade"; but we regard high wages as the best evidence of the success of business, for we see wages not as an expense to be kept down but, by a reversal in point of view, as a product to be increased, as shares in the distribution of the proceeds received by participants in industry. Business and the state we regard as existing for the general good, and good or evil experienced by each individual counts at par.

Economics may be quite justified in insisting that it is a science of wealth rather than of welfare, or comprehensive ethical aims; and political science may be equally justified in regarding itself as the study of methods by which policies may be carried out, rather than as a study of social policies. If so, it is clear that each of these, though immensely important in itself, deals with a limited aspect of the field of social reality.

Sociology aims at nothing less than the transfer of ethics from the domain of speculative philosophy to the domain of objective science. It regards human welfare, which can be realized only in society, as a distinct kind of reality, the causation of which calls for scientific investigation. It has been common to say: "Science deals with what is, and only philosophy can deal with what ought to be." Sociology replies that good and evil are parts of what is, that human experience is as real as any other reality, and that the promotion of good and the limitation of evil must rest upon scientific comprehension as truly as the control of any other results.

The thorough-going adoption by sociology of the ethical point of view involves not only a distinct set of special practical problems, but also a distinct set of general fundamental problems such as: (a) what, as a matter of fact, are the ultimate values involved in social life; (b) what are the existing conscience codes and social policies of different peoples; (c) how have these widely varying codes arisen; (d) what justification in facts is there for the demands of these codes or of any codes of conduct; (e) what change in existing codes does this matter of fact criterion require? Sociology proposes to be a general science of values and of valuations; of *valuations* as they arise and become intrenched in social sentiments and dominate the contrasting life of different societies, and of *values* as they exist for human experience with special reference to the modes of causation by which these values are promoted or destroyed. First then, the sociological point of view is ethical.

2. The sociological point of view is causal. Sociology regards the character and welfare of mankind, individually and collectively, not as a matter of fate, predestination, or class heritage, nor even of free will, considered as an exception to the universal reign of law, and requiring only exhortation to transform men and society; but rather man's character and welfare are regarded as resulting from causal conditions, which up to the limits of the power of human intelligence must be understood. It is knowledge of causation which gives to man power over results. This has been proved in the realm of material phenomena. The knowledge that consequences issue in accordance with an orderly method of causation prompts man to conduct, which so conditions those consequences that they will turn out in accordance with his interests; for man is himself a part of the causal process of nature—in all his actions caused, and also a cause of his

own ruin or fulfillment, according to his ignorance or his knowledge of the method by which this ruin or this fulfillment issues from those conditions of which his own activity forms a part. Holding this view, sociology is bound to seek the general principles of causal explanation that show, not only how values are realized or destroyed, and how conscience codes arise and become a social heritage, but also how all social sentiments, beliefs, and practices, customs, institutions, and correlated systems of social activity evolve.

3. The sociological point of view is functional. It requires the transfer of chief attention from the external forms and incidents of social life to the inner essence of it, finding that the ultimate facts to be explained are built out of prevalent ideas, sentiments, and practices, that the ultimate values to be promoted are in human experience, and that progress and reform fundamentally consist in development of wants, interests, judgments and ideas, and that the passage of laws, or the production or distribution of wealth, or anything else whatever, has little significance for progress save as it expresses or promotes such inner changes in the life of society. The meaning of this will not be clear to the reader until he has made considerable progress in the study of sociology, but he will come to see that its importance is as great as that of either of the other elements in the sociological point of view.

4. The sociological point of view is synthetic. It implies belief that the time for synthesis has come; not that analysis has yielded all its fruits, but that instead of perpetuating the practice by which every social science exaggerates, and almost inevitably to some degree distorts, one set of factors by viewing it with too little regard for its interrelationship with other factors, one social science shall busy itself explicitly with the task of correlation, and with those generalizations which are based upon data, parts of which are furnished by each special social science, generalizations which find application in every subdivision of social reality, and which serve as safeguards against the dangers of narrow specialization, and as lamps to deeper insight.

As general biology is the science of physical life, so general sociology is the science of social life. As biology has generalizations which are based on data, furnished by every subdivision of biological facts, generalizations which also find application in every subdivision of biological reality, to mollusks and to vertebrate mammals, to the facts of cryptogamic botany and to the facts of physical anthropology, to all organic life from the toadstool to man, so general sociology has its generalizations based on data gathered from every subdivision of social life and applying to every subdivision of social life.

Former abuses of the supposed analogy between societies and biological organisms need not deter us from carrying out the comparison between general biology and general sociology as follows: (a) The principles of biological evolution are based on investigation which extends to all divisions of physical life, and they apply to the production of all types of physical life, so that the investigator of Mendel's law experiments, now with peas or other vegetables, and now with rabbits or other animals, and applies his generalizations to man. The data and the investigations involved and the applications of the laws of physical evolution cover the entire fields of both botany and zoölogy in all their subdivisions. Likewise the data, investigation, and application of the principles of social evolution relate equally to the entire field of politics, religion, ethics, and all other social activities. (b) The same comparison as that between biological and social evolution may be drawn between biological ecology and the sociological study which traces the relations of social activities (ethical, religious, economic, political, and of every kind) to their material environment. (c) A similar comparison may be drawn between physiological chemistry and social psychology. Physiological chemistry sets forth processes of life, animal and vegetable, in all their subdivisions, much as social psychology investigates the intermental relations which afford the only fundamental explanation of customs and institutions of every kind. (d) Cellular histology resembles the analysis of institutions and customs into their repetitious elements.

This comparison to general biology does not exhaust the definition of general sociology, especially because there is nothing in general biology that can be compared to sociological ethics.

5. Adoption of the sociological point of view means that all prejudices and settled questions shall be subject to reëxamination, in the light of adequate investigation and of the adopted conclusions of all previous sciences. We are to study, not as Republicans or Democrats, Northerners or Southerners, employers or employed, Americans or Europeans, but unprejudiced as if seated in a star and looking down upon earthly sects and parties—a hard requirement, to be approached, not easily to be fulfilled. All the social sciences aim to share in this fifth characteristic, but sociology, besides making this a conscious aim is peculiarly adapted to promote this intellectual achievement since it studies the method by which prejudices, sentiments, and beliefs arise and spread.

Sociology, then, is (1) ethical, regarding the weal and woe of all men as facts to be accounted for. (2) It views the facts of human experience as caused, and belonging to the orderly course of nature. (3) Though caused in part by material facts, the essence of the life of society is seen to be made up of a functional process of conscious activities. (4) Sociology sets itself to the task of synthesis, and searches out those principles which operate throughout the realm of social realities. (5) In the study of these facts, it aims to dissolve all bonds of party, sect, and prejudice.

Art and Science.—Sociology does not begin by telling how to usher in the millennium. Hundreds have set themselves to answer the question, how shall we mend society? for every one who has set himself to understand society. At present the most practical of all social tasks is the task of comprehension. Sociology would be a respectable pursuit if it were nothing but the art of wise social action, correlating the light shed by all the sciences upon practical problems of amelioration and progress, for which no single science affords the necessary guidance, just as the art, or science, of medicine correlates the practical knowledge of surgical mechanics,

Röntgen rays, electricity, chemistry, physiology, bacteriology, psychology and whatever else can serve the ends of healing and preventing bodily suffering. But sociology proposes to be not only a practical art, but also a science. Comte and his followers go further, and say that sociology will prove to be not only a science, but one of the more fundamental sciences. This, they say, is because social causation proceeds according to distinct fundamental principles not discovered by any other science. We commonly speak of the esthetic arts and the practical arts, and art in both of these senses we distinguish from science. This distinction between art and science must not be too strictly drawn; nevertheless, it has its usefulness. There is a clear difference between the art of dyeing cloth in fast colors, and the science of chemistry which discovered the aniline dyes and the methods of their use; or between the art of medicine, and the sciences of physiology and bacteriology and the other sciences which underlie the practice of medicine. Art aims directly to do, while science aims primarily to understand. In this sense sociology is primarily science and not art, although it well may hope, like other sciences, to afford the basis upon which art may be established.

Science is doubly worth while. It is an end in itself and a means to all other ends. As an end in itself, knowledge satisfies one of the elemental human desires. Purely scientific pursuits have frequently seemed trivial to "practical" men. Those who first learned to send an electric current across a laboratory table were said to be playing with the "toys of science," but the intellectual problems with which they dealt were not trivial. And it must not be forgotten that it is their activities, and not those of the "practical" men, that have made possible our great inventions and our control over nature. It was not the effort to send messages that made possible the discovery of the telegraph and telephone and of wireless telegraphy, but the effort to understand electricity. Trying to cure diseases yielded some crude knowledge of the effects produced by certain roots and herbs, but it is the bacteriologist with his cultures, the biologist with his bell jars of earthworms and sea-urchins, who give us the knowledge of the secrets of life and disease upon which the arts of scientific medicine are founded. The scientists themselves with their electric toys and all their curious researches have as a rule been unable to see that they were making possible any important practical results. They were busy in answering intellectual needs, in finding answers to hard questions. Yet there is but little knowledge about human life and its immediate conditions which has not been utilized as a means to other good. The order of progress has been, first, the crude arts developed by blundering empiricism, the method of trial and failure and occasional success, which takes man only a little way and at painful cost toward the mastery of life's problems; then science and comprehension; and at last the scientific arts leading to fuller satisfactions. Incomparably, the most important fact of recent history has been the expansion of the sciences. It is the scientists and not captains of industry nor generals nor statesmen who have contributed chiefly to our mastery over the material world, to say nothing of the reorganization of our intellectual life. Therefore, science, while of value as an enlargement of life, is of value also as the mightiest of all our tools.

Practical Application of Sociology.—But is it reasonable to suppose that the science of sociology can ever lead to developed social arts which will make it possible to control social situations and mold them in the interest of human welfare, as we have learned to control and manipulate material realities?

If we do not modify the social realities it will not be because we have no need of doing so. We have measurably solved the problems involved in utilizing our material surroundings. Although we shall still welcome improvements in the methods of agriculture, manufacture, and transportation, yet, speaking relatively, we may say that those problems have been solved. But has human welfare been attained? Approximately a tenth of our population has not even its physical necessities adequately supplied. Hundreds of thousands in our country annually die needless deaths, are needlessly maimed or undermined in health, grow into vicious, shiftless, worthless, hopeless beings. Good human possibilities, are born into the world never to be fulfilled. If we could look with seeing eyes beyond the youthful and the fortunate, to see the wreckage and ruin and woe, we might agree that Huxley spoke with justification when he suggested that should the experiment of human life go no further, we should have reason to hail the advent of some friendly comet that would sweep the whole phantasmagoria out of existence. Even if we had solved the special problems of the defective, dependent, and delinquent presented by the lowest tenth of our population, there would remain a problem even greater, which is presented by the medium five to eight-tenths, made up of steady laboring folk and of those who, in respect to culture and character, compose the mass. Agricultural scientists affirm that the corn lands of a state so rich in soil and so well tilled as Illinois might, by scientific methods, be made to double their production. It is probably quite as true that the values realized in the lives of these masses of our population might be doubled. They have not even discovered their own possibilities. The progress that we now need is progress toward securing the prevalence of desirable activities correlated into a social situation in which we shall utilize the material resources now under our control, and the human resources still so unmanageable, in such a way that the unmistakable possibilities of good, that now go unrealized, shall not be allowed to incur by wholesale the failure of their fulfillment.

But granting the tremendous desirability of modifying prevalent social activities, the ideas, moral standards, ambitions, and practices of men, the question remains: are they subject to modification by the application of sociological knowledge? Our present inability to control social situations is great, but is it greater than the abject helplessness in which men once stood in the presence of the physical environment? No science, while in its earlier stages, reveals what its practical applications are to be. The achievements of the physical sciences were once not only incredible but also unimaginable. There are already inspiring glimpses of possible applications of sociological principles. Comparative sociology, as we shall see later, at least has demonstrated that no other phenomena in nature are more variable than the activities, sentiments, and ideas of men. At this stage of our study familiar facts must serve to illustrate this variability. A ruffian is converted and becomes a minister of salvation. Japan, who had shut her gates to foreigners and clung to hoary traditions, becomes the eager seeker of occidental knowledge and methods, and brings her army, her government, her manufactures "up to the minute." We may know what we are, but no people knows what it might become in two generations. The most inveterate sentiments, enthusiasms, and detestations may in time be reversed. The course of life seems fixed by a kind of fate only because we have not understood the causes by which it is directed. In proportion to our knowledge of causes and our power to manipulate them is our power over results. We are sometimes told that the last forty years of the nineteenth century witnessed a greater progress in the utilization of the earth's material resources than all the centuries that had gone before. This was due to the tremendous development of the physical sciences during that period, which gave us knowledge of the causation by which material results are molded. What we now supremely need is scientific comprehension of social conditions, for in this field as in that of material realities comprehension alone can be the basis of any adequate control. The achievement of such comprehension is the supreme intellectual task, and the supreme practical task of the twentieth century.

The Need of a New World View.—There is an additional practical result which may be hoped for as a consequence of the intellectual movement of which sociology is the most characteristic expression: we need a new world view.

By a world view, I mean a set of dominant ideas in the light of which we form our opinions and shape our life policies, and from which we derive motives; ideas of the sort to which Comte referred when he said, "Ideas rule the world or throw it into chaos," ideas of the sort for which a wise man prayed when he said, "Give me a great thought that I may warm my soul withal." Among our ideas there are some that stand out like a general among an army of privates. Such is the idea of gravitation among our notions of physical realities. The presence of a few such ruling ideas concerning life may organize all our ideas about life into a "world view." Their absence reduces our ideas about life to a chaos or a fog.

To have an ennobling world view in the sense just defined might even be said to be the prime need of men, for without that, conscious lives cannot be well lived. It is one of the deepest tragedies when an individual loses his world view and therewith his sense of values and his motives. And it is possible for a whole society to have its ennobling motives run low, so that it stands like a mill upon the bank of a stream that has dried away until it can no longer turn the wheels.

Even barbarians have sometimes held a world view which gave them zest and power and a certain nobility. Great errors have sometimes proved inspiring and far better than universal vagueness and doubt. Radical changes in the intellectual outlook imply modifications in the world view. And never have there been changes so rapid and so radical as those which have taken place in recent years. Our forefathers had a definite world view by which, according to a kind of Divine fatalism, each saw his life as an element in a providential course of events. But the details of that world view which served our fathers so well were formulated in a pre-scientific past. The new and inspiring world view which we now deeply need will not result from study of material nature. It must be derived from a study of the facts of human life. Such study can yield us a world view in accordance with which each will see his life as a factor in a natural order, in which inestimable values are at stake, to be forfeited or achieved through an intelligible process of causation, in which, for good or evil, all men coöperate.

Sociology as an Intellectual Pursuit.—It was pointed out above that science has two kinds of value: value as an end in itself, as part of an elevated, satisfying, and truly human life; and also value for practical application in seeking other ends. Sociology proffers values of both these kinds. We have just seen that the practical applications of sociology are to be sought in the promotion of welfare through the modification and organization of prevalent activities, and also in the development of a world view at once inspiring and scientific. What shall we now say of sociology as an end in itself, as a part of life? What shall we say of the intellectual interest inherent in the pursuit of investigations that deal with those realities which are of the most intimate concern to men, and the causation of which present the most intricate of problems?

When Herbert Spencer set himself to write a synthetic philosophy which should focus the light which had been shed by all the sciences, he found that one great area of facts, namely the facts of social life, had not yet been subjected to scientific analysis, and that a synthetic philosophy could not be written until this gap in the explorations of science had been filled. So he undertook some contribution to this neglected field, and, as a consequence, at least one-third of all his writing was devoted to sociology. Auguste Comte also applied himself to the task of writing a philosophy which should be a synthesis of science, a *"Philosophie Positive."* Like Spencer, he perceived that the positive or synthetic philosophy could not be written until the methods of science had been applied to the study of social facts and, as a result, about one-half of his positive philosophy is a contribution to sociology. Thus it was that Comte whose writings shortly preceded those of Spencer came to invent the word "sociology" and is now spoken of as the first sociologist. Recently some of the most preëminent representatives of physical science and of psychological science, speaking independently each from his separate point of view, have agreed in the opinion that as the nineteenth century was the blossoming time of material sciences, so the twentieth century should be the blossoming time of the sciences which deal with man's conscious life. The study of society acquires special interest not only from the character of the subject matter but also from the fact that it is the chapter now opening in the world's intellectual life.

Comte's Hierarchy of the Sciences.—Both Comte and Spencer set themselves to explain why it was that this most interesting field of research had waited so long for scientific treatment. They found two causes. Spencer points out that it is in part because the intense interest of man in the problems here involved makes him cling to his prejudices. He fears to disturb the world view that in a prescientific age had satisfied him and to unsettle cherished opinions and sentiments. This renders him unwilling, and even unable, to assume the unbiased and disinterested attitude of scientific investigation. The second reason was emphasized chiefly by Comte. He said it lay in the fact that social realities are of all phenomena the most complex in their causation, and therefore the most difficult of scientific explanation.

In this connection Comte proposed his famous hierarchy of the sciences, saying, that as a matter of necessity those sciences which deal with the simpler phenomena preceded those which attack the phenomena which are more complex, not merely because the former are easier of explanation, but also because their explanation is a necessary step in preparation for the explanation of the more complex realities. Thus it was indispensable to have a knowledge of the movements of liquids and gases which is afforded by physics, and also the further knowledge of chemistry, before we could have our present science of physiology; and it was necessary to have physiology before we could have the present psychology; and it is necessary to have both physiology and psychology[1] before the explanations of sociology can be sought with success.

Comte's conception of the hierarchy of the sciences may be paraphrased as follows: Those sciences come first that are broadest in application but thinnest in content. Thus mathematics applies to all phenomena but tells us very little about any single phenomenon, and in mathematics the ancients made great progress. Next came astronomy which applies to the whole solar system and more but adds comparatively little to

---

[1] With reference to psychology this does not exactly follow Comte's statement. He omits psychology from the hierarchy of fundamental sciences, as is explained below.

our knowledge of details. Then, by the same rule, follow in order physics and chemistry; after them biology which tells us so much but applies only to living beings, and last of all sociology applying only to the interrelated lives of the highest organisms but dealing with the phenomena which are of all the richest in content.

It would have indicated still more clearly the reasons for such an order to say that scientific progress depends upon the observation of facts. Mathematics came first because it needs only such concrete facts as are observable anywhere by any student. Many of the movements of the heavenly bodies all men must see. Not till later do those sciences come which almost from the beginning require elaborate technique of observation and experiment, journeys of exploration and patient comparison of facts widely scattered in space and time. While, however, those sciences come first that deal with facts of widest range, those most accessible to common observation, this does not mean that within a given field of science the broadest generalizations are the first truths to be discovered. On the contrary the broadest generalizations within a given science wait upon an extensive knowledge of particulars; and this is a reason why general sociology came later than the specific social sciences.

According to Comte mathematics, astronomy, physics, chemistry, biology and sociology are the only "abstract" or fundamental sciences, and such disciplines as geology and psychology are "concrete" sciences, which apply the teachings of abstract sciences to special problems, but furnish no fundamental principles of explanation. Geology is mainly an application of physics; and psychology, according to Comte, is an application of biology (neurology and cerebral physiology) and of sociology. Comte and his followers, including such writers as Roberty and Caullet, agree with Baldwin in saying that the development of mind depends upon association, and they go beyond Baldwin in teaching that sociology and physiology supply all the fundamental principles necessary for the explanation of psychic phenomena. American sociologists prefer to regard psychology as having a place in the hierarchy of fundamental sciences, sociology resting on psychology, psychology on biology, biology on chemistry, etc.

Sociology, then, as both Comte and Spencer pointed out, is necessarily the latest born of all, because, first, it is the most intricate and therefore requires as instruments in its researches or as data for its explanations the results achieved by the antecedent sciences, just as every added physical science has in turn been built upon the foundation reared by its predecessors [1]; and second, because it is of all sciences the most fraught with human interests and so the last to be removed from the dominion of passion and prejudice and to be included in the gradually extending realm of calm, disinterested research and reflection. These great writers who have attempted to bring all science into one perspective do not hesitate to say that sociology is the supreme science.[2]

This, however, has reference rather to her tasks and opportunity than to her achievements already made. Sociology as yet has comparatively little conquered territory, and is upon the outmost firing line of the world's intellectual advance.

---

[1] This does not mean that all progress must be made in the simpler science before any progress can be made in the more complex, but that considerable progress must be made in the simpler before any considerable progress can be made in the more complex, and that additional progress in the simpler opens the way for additional progress in the more complex.

[2] Such a judgment from such writers as Comte and Spencer is at least interesting, particularly since they were distinguished for their grasp upon the whole field of science. This breadth of grasp is illustrated in that while we think of Spencer primarily as a Sociologist, many think of him primarily as a biologist, and an eminent German psychologist has called Spencer the greatest psychologist that has ever used the English language.

CHAPTER II

WHAT IS INVOLVED IN SOCIOLOGICAL EXPLANATION

Causation.—The goal of science is causal explanation. It is therefore of fundamental importance for us to have clearly in mind what we mean by "causes" and by "explanation."

The word cause is used in three senses, namely, with reference to the "first cause," "second causes," and "final causes."

The first cause is that which is conceived of as being antecedent to all phenomena. It may be called God, or it may be referred to in the language used by Spencer when he said that nothing is more certain than that we are always in the presence of an infinite and eternal energy from which all things proceed. It is the "one power" of the monistic modern philosopher. It is conceived to be measureless, immanent, omnipresent, operative wherever any phenomenon appears, in every atom of matter beneath our feet and in the remotest star, in every pulsation of light, in every chemical change or functional process. It continuously causes everything that appears, and without its action every phenomenon would cease. The first cause is absolutely beyond our observation. We know it only by inference from its manifestations. We conceive it to be the very substance of every phenomenon, but it is not itself phenomenal. It is as present and pervasive as the atmosphere or the ether,[1] but accessible to no human sense. It is beneath and beyond all science and with it science, as such, has nothing to do.

By a final cause is meant a *terminus ad quem,* an aim, an end, a finis. If one should ask what is the cause of a large

---

[1] Physicists are now considering whether the idea of the ether must not be replaced by some doctrine still more recondite.

number of students entering a certain house at about the same hour daily, the answer might be, "Dinner," or, "The thought of dinner; it is their boarding-house." Final causes or ends of action can be used only in explaining the conduct of intelligent beings. It may be conceived that there is a final cause for the existence and maintenance of the universe. If so, it has its abode only in the infinite intelligence.

Two sorts of phenomena are sometimes denoted by the term "final cause," it being used in the one case to denote a thought and desire existing within the actor's mind, in the other case to denote an external reality toward which he presses. If final causes play any part at all in scientific explanation it is because they are also second causes; that is, conditioning phenomena antecedent to resultant phenomena which are to be explained. Except as they may be regarded as second causes, science has no more to do with final causes than it has to do with the first cause.

Second causes are those phenomena which are necessary [1] antecedent conditions of some other phenomenon which has been taken as an object for explanation. Of all these three kinds of causes, it is with second causes alone that science deals.

It is conceived that the first manifestations of the One Power were simple but that they combined to form the conditions of additional manifestations; that these new manifestations combined with each other and those which had preceded them to form the conditions of yet other phenomena; that these in turn, when added to all that had gone before, afforded the conditions of still other phenomena [2]; that this was repeated until there was accomplished the evolution of systems of inorganic matter and the ascending forms of vegetable and animal life, culminating in man and the activities of man. Every observable phenomenon is thus condi-

[1] "Necessary" in the language of science and common-sense. Science, as distinguished from metaphysics, does not discuss the question of absolute necessity.

[2] The word "phenomena" does not mean "things" alone, but also qualities, movements, relations, etc.

tioned upon the preëxistence of antecedent phenomena, and upon certain necessary relations in which the antecedent phenomena are assembled, these relations themselves being in fact phenomena, that is, observable realities, as truly as the things which stand in these relations to each other.

Every fact in nature, every thought or act of man, every breath of a living thing, the path of every snowflake in January, is linked with other facts which we term its "causes," or "conditions," in the absence of which it could not appear, and each of these conditioning facts, in turn, is linked with yet others by which it is conditioned, so that the whole of nature is knit up in a unity of mutual causation. The task of science is to set forth the mutual conditioning of phenomena, by which they exist together in a system of antecedents and consequences. The antecedent phenomena which condition the rise of resultant phenomena are called second causes in contrast with the universal first cause.

Second causes are the conditions, *sine qua non,* of any result which is to be explained. Soil, seed, sunshine and the farmer's labor are such causes or conditions of the autumn crop. Every phenomenon which is capable of scientific explanation is in this sense caused, and it is to discover this causation which is the goal of science. It is a knowledge of this causation which renders possible the practical applications of science, for it is by controlling the conditions upon which results depend that desired results are obtained and the undesired are avoided.

Explanation and Scientific Law.—A clear conception of what is meant by causation carries with it our idea of explanation. An explanation is a statement of the antecedent conditions, including conditioning relations, which make possible the resultant phenomenon which was to be explained. Thus the explanation of a chemical reaction and a resulting compound includes a statement of all the substances which enter into the reaction, their quantities, their states of mass, mixture, and temperature, and whatever must be brought into conjunction in order to secure by experiment the same reaction and the same resulting compound. A scientific law in the most perfect form is a generalized explanation; that is, an explanation which applies not merely to a single fact but also to a whole class of facts.

There can be no law for the appearance of a unique phenomenon; it may be explained but its explanation cannot be generalized. A causal law of science is a statement of the conditions out of which a recurrent phenomenon regularly emerges. Explanation of a single occurrence may be thus symbolized, x representing the phenomenon to be explained and $a\ b\ c$ its necessary antecedent or accompanying conditions:

$$\frac{x}{a\ b\ c}$$

A causal law may be thus symbolized:

$$\frac{x}{a\ b\ c}\quad\frac{x}{a\ b\ c}\quad\frac{x}{a\ b\ c}\quad\frac{x}{a\ b\ c}\quad\frac{x}{a\ b\ c}\quad\frac{x}{a\ b\ c}\quad\frac{x}{a\ b\ c}\quad\frac{x}{a\ b\ c}\quad\frac{x}{a\ b\ c}\text{—etc.}$$

According to Wilhelm Wundt a scientific law has the three following characteristics [1]:

1. It is a statement in which subject and predicate are logically independent ideas; that is, the predicate is not implied in the subject. For example, the statement that every normal man has four limbs, or twenty-four ribs, is not a scientific law, because the possession of four limbs and twenty-four ribs is included in the idea of a normal man.

2. A scientific law either states or implies a causal relationship. "A causal law," which is the highest form of scientific law, is the explicit statement of a generalized causal explanation. The name "empirical law" may be given to the statement of any regular relationship between independent concepts which implies the existence of some causal relationship underlying this observed regularity, whether that cause is already known or still an undiscovered object for future scientific search.

3. A scientific law is a general truth which may serve as a guide leading to further discoveries; thus the law that man must eat or die, though it is a true empirical law and

---

[1] "Methoden Lehre." Stuttgart, 1895. Part II, p. 129 *seq.*

rests upon well understood causation, yet does not open a pathway into the unknown in such a way as to be esteemed a scientific law.

Problem Phenomena, Their Constituent Elements, and Their Environing Conditions.—Each of the higher sciences in the hierarchy has to deal with three sets of phenomena. First are those which it undertakes to explain, which may be called its problem phenomena and which are symbolized by x in the preceding illustration. Second are the conditioning phenomena, which are the terms in its explanations, and are symbolized by $a\,b\,c$ in the same illustration. Third are the elements into which the problem phenomena must be analyzed, which may be symbolized by $m\,n\,o$ in the expression, $x = m\,n\,o$.

It is of importance to observe that the problem phenomena of a distinct science all belong to one distinct class, while the conditioning phenomena may belong to all classes. Thus, the problem phenomena of botany are of one distinct class, but the conditioning phenomena by which they are explained include peculiarities of soil, variations in climate, etc., which are not botanical facts at all. Moreover, the botanical facts themselves when analyzed into their elements are found to be composed of a number of minute physical and chemical facts.

The failure to observe the contrast between conditioning phenomena and problem phenomena, as well as between the problem phenomena and the elemental phenomena of which they are composed and which, uniting, form a new and complex reality quite different from the particular elements entering into the combination, has caused a great deal of confusion of thought among those who have attempted to define sociology or to prove or disprove its importance as an independent science.

Failure to distinguish between the problem phenomena and the elements of which they are composed confuses sociology with psychology, for as we shall see more clearly hereafter, customs and institutions are composed of accepted ideas, sentiments of approval and disapproval, and common practices; that is to say, the massive and complex social realities are composed of minute psychic elements. Failure to distinguish between problem phenomena and conditioning phenomena confuses sociology with geography, physical anthropology, hygiene, engineering as applied to housing and sanitation, and whatever plays a part in conditioning social realities.

Sociology must deal with massed and correlated psychic elements, and with environmental factors of every kind by which social customs and institutions are effectively conditioned. Some people think that dealing with such a wide range of facts makes of sociology a hodge-podge, an attempted science, without boundaries and incapable of definition. But in this respect sociology is in exactly the same kind of position as biology, which, in order to deal successfully with its task, must recognize that all living beings and all physiological processes are massed and correlated physical and chemical facts, and in its ecology must explain variations in animal and vegetable species by reference to land elevation, quantity of rainfall, amount of light, etc., thus doing for biological forms exactly what sociology does for social types. The chemist, physicist, meteorologist, and geographer do not complain of the biologist because he employs chemical, physical, meteorological and geographic facts in the solution of his problems. If they did, the biologist would answer: "Can you as a chemist, or physicist, or meteorologist, or geographer, solve the problems of biology?" The reply of the sociologist is the same. This kind of objection is removed by an understanding of the proper mode of outlining the field of a science, which clearly differentiates problem phenomena from their constituent elements and especially from their conditions, and their consequences. The problem phenomena of sociology are of one clear and distinct class, as much so as those of the best established sciences. But neither they nor any other complex phenomena can be understood except by being seen and described with reference to their elements and their conditions and their consequences. The relation of sociology to psychology and to the physical sciences is freed from all vagueness or difficulty if these considerations are once clearly apprehended.

The Kinds of Conditioning Phenomena.—The conditioning phenomena which determine prevalent social activities are of four kinds: geographic, technic, psychophysical, and social.

1. Geographic conditions are the natural physical environment presented by the country inhabited and include: (1) aspect, (2) climate, (3) soil, (4) water supply, (5) other mineral resources, (6) flora, (7) fauna, (8) topography.

2. Technic conditions are the material products of human work, which, having once been produced, are conditions of further activities; geographic conditions are the natural physical environment and technic conditions are the artificial physical environment. Rivers are part of the geographic environment, but canals and bridges are part of the technic environment; caves are geographic, houses are technic; mountain passes are geographic, roads and railroads are technic; bays are geographic, but harbors, dredged and fitted with docks, are technic; herds of buffalo are geographic, but herds of domesticated and man-bred cattle are technic. Geographic and technic conditions alike are physical conditions of social activity, yet it is of great practical and theoretical importance to distinguish clearly between them, because geographic conditions are little subject to human control, while technic conditions are so highly subject to human control that their modification is one of the chief methods of progress; and also because geographic conditions have their major significance in explaining the earlier and indigenous stages of social evolution, while the relative importance of technic conditions increases as social progress becomes more advanced and more cosmopolitan.

Technic conditions are of two main sorts: (1) wealth, (2) grouping of population. Migration is a technic achievement as truly as the transportation of goods; so is the assembling and maintenance of city groups; so indeed is all increase of population beyond the tiny primitive hordes which were the only population units produced by unaided nature. The important variations in wealth as a technic condition of social activities are: (a) its forms, including nomadic herds, cultivated fields, and villages of settled abodes, steam-driven factories, railroads, etc.; (b) its amount, and (c) the distribution of its ownership or use among the individuals and classes of the population. The important variations in population groups are (a) in numbers, and (b) in distribution in space.

3. Psychophysical conditions are either (1) congenital or (2) acquired. Congenital psychophysical conditions include: (a) age, (b) sex, (c) race, (d) psychic predisposition, temperament, natural endowment, (e) hereditary disease and defect. Acquired psychophysical conditions include: (a) acquired diseases and defects, (b) developed strength and skill, (c) psychic dispositions, such as habits, second nature, and subconscious set.

In this connection it is necessary to have clearly in mind that no idea, belief, or sentiment, nor any part of the content of consciousness is ever inherited, but only the capacity for them. No one ever inherits in the literal biological sense, either his politics or his religion, or his conscience or his trade. The business of sociology is to bring together into one explanation all of the numerous and diverse conditions that determine the content of the life of society and of the individuals of whom society is composed.

4. Social conditions. Most important of all in determining what shall be approved and what condemned by the conscience of the Southerner, the Northerner, the Israelite, or the Turk, what creeds, crafts, prejudices and ambitions shall prevail in a given society, are the social conditions; that is, the already prevalent ideas and sentiments by which each individual and each generation is surrounded. In the study of social conditions it will be necessary to observe (1) the kinds of activity which prevail in a given social environment, and (2) the forms of relationship in which these activities stand to each other. What is meant by forms of relationship will be made clear later on.[1]

---

[1] With the foregoing discussion compare articles by the present writer on "The Social Forces Error." *American Journal of Sociology,* xvi, 613, 642.

PART I

THE CAUSES WHICH AFFECT THE LIFE OF SOCIETY

I. GEOGRAPHIC CAUSES WHICH AFFECT THE LIFE OF SOCIETY

CHAPTER III

GEOGRAPHIC CAUSES AND THEIR SOCIAL EFFECTS

The Less Conspicuous Geographic Differences Socially Important.—We are all familiar in a superficial way with the obvious fact that the activities of a people are largely determined by their geographic environment. Life cannot be the same in arctic regions as in the tropics, nor upon deserts of drifting sand as upon the grassy steppes which afford the natural home for wandering shepherds and their herds, nor upon the seacoast with its fisheries and commerce as among the mountains with their forests and mines. But it is not alone the extreme and unusual manifestations of nature which affect the life of man. On the contrary the very absence of extremes has helped to make Europe the seat of the richest civilization. So relatively inconspicuous a fact as the absence of a creature adapted to be domesticated and milked might cause one incipient social type to be crushed out in the struggle for existence, or the presence of a creature adapted to become a beast of burden might enable one people to grow into a triumphant race, contributors to a dominant civilization, and the absence of such a creature might condemn another race to backwardness and final extinction. The following effects of geographic conditions deserve particular mention:

1. Geographic Conditions Determine the Size of Populations.—Thronging cities are found at points of geographic advantage. And in the original development of civilization populations first assembled in considerable density where na-

ture was especially lavish of food. Thus the valleys of the
Nile, Euphrates, Ganges, and Piho became cradles of civilization. The familiar differences between city and country life
illustrate the importance of different degrees of density of
population in determining the character of society. Far more
in the earlier stages of development, when social activities were
mainly indigenous, any great advancement was conditioned
upon considerable density and number of population. Division of occupations could not go far save in considerably
numerous groups. Where the numbers were large the chances
of invention were proportionally increased, and where population was dense there was similar increase in the chances
that such inventions as occurred would not be lost but would
spread, and enter into fertile combination with other elements
of progress. Moreover, the permanence and accumulation of
a strain of social development has been largely conditioned
upon the military strength which enabled a group to maintain
itself and to absorb other groups, and this in turn depended
largely upon numbers.

2. **The Economic Occupations of a People Are Determined
by Their Geographic Environment.**—Geographic situation determines both demand and supply. For example, the economic
products demanded in a cold country are not the same as
those demanded in a hot country. Supply and the occupations
of production are determined also by the raw materials and
natural advantages available. In one region the men will be
farmers; in another, herdsmen; in another, fishers and sailors;
in another, hunters, trappers, woodsmen; in another, miners.
The business of one locality is determined by the presence
of deposits of coal and iron; of another, by the presence of
waterpower, and of another by the presence of lumber or
quarries or clay for the making of pottery and bricks. Thus,
we have steel mills at Pittsburgh, and textile factories where
the rivers that pass the Appalachians to empty into the Atlantic
afford abundant power. The correspondence between the
economic occupations of a people and the geographic character of the region in which they live is very complete during
all the earlier stages of development and until the railroad

makes it possible to redistribute raw materials, fuel, and finished products.

Moreover, whatever determines the way in which a people get their living, largely determines the way in which they live, so that the geographic conditions which prescribe their economic activities thereby indirectly determine to a very large extent all the other departments of their social life. It affects their form of government as will presently be explained. It influences the domestic organization—polyandry in Tibet arises from poverty of soil; woman has rights and influence among fisher folk of the seashore, where men are much away from home and leave its management to their spouses; the pastoral life of the steppes has for its correlate the patriarchate and as a rule polygyny. The occupations of a people give direction to their intellectual interests and to their esthetic and recreational tastes, and to their original religious creeds.

3. **Stagnation and Progressiveness Are Conditioned Largely by Geographic Surroundings.**—Mountain barriers, swamps, forests and deserts hinder the intercommunication which is the first condition of social progress, while rivers which are "highways that carry you," good harbors inviting a people to put to sea, mountain passes and other natural routes of travel, promote rapid social progress in favored regions. However, under some circumstances a certain degree of remoteness may aid progress. Thus Egypt early acquired a large enough population for fertile intercommunication through the lavish gifts of the Nile, and the wealth and progress there accumulated was, during the earlier stages of civilization, more easily defended from marauders by reason of the distance of other centers of population, which was caused by the surrounding desert. Egypt, however, was successively visited and peopled by various wandering folk. Isolation tends everywhere to stagnation, which, in the case of primitive peoples, occurs as soon as the most urgent natural wants have found a customary mode of satisfaction. On the other hand, the crust of custom is broken up where contact with other groups brings the indigenous modes of thought

and practice into frequent competition with those of other people, allowing not only a survival of the fittest, but also a fertile combination of diverse inventions.

4. Lawlessness Is the Natural Consequence of Geographic Inaccessibility. and Poverty of Natural Resources.—This is true for two reasons: first, because the people of a poor and inaccessible region feel little need of protection from invaders, and so do not desire and will not tolerate a strong guard over them; and second, because offenders in an inaccessible region are not easily caught and punished. Banditti and feuds and other forms of violence survive longest in mountain fastnesses where the arm of the law can with difficulty reach the offender, while in the open plain order is established with comparative ease, not only because all men are within the reach of the law, but also because all men desire that the law shall be strong, since their accessibility renders them open to the attacks of marauders. If a fertile plain exists in the neighborhood of mountain wilds the inhabitants of the plain tend to develop a government strong enough to hold at bay their poor and envious neighbors of the mountainsides and also to repress the disorders of their own unruly members. Geographic conditions indirectly affect the rapidity with which order is developed in that a region which is favorable to the accumulation of wealth calls for strong government to protect its treasures. Thus, in the case just supposed, the poverty of the mountaineers combines with their inaccessibility to postpone order, while the wealth of the plainsmen combines with their accessibility to hasten it.

5. The Form of Government Is Affected by Geographic Conditions.—Exclusively agricultural regions are nearly always aristocratic because land is a natural monopoly, and where agriculture is the only or chief source of wealth power goes with the possession of the land. Immigrant agriculturists, taking possession of a new territory, may remain democratic or become increasingly so as long as free land is obtainable. But as soon as the population increases so that land is costly then those who possess land may readily obtain more, but the landless laborer can rarely obtain land enough to support him; and such persons tend to become tenants or hired laborers if not serfs. In an old agricultural community the rich and powerful, by gradually increasing their holdings, widen the gulf between them and the landless.

There are two forms of agrarian aristocracy. First is that which gradually replaces common ownership of land among a long established agricultural people; and second, that in which land is seized by the chiefs of an invading people.

Commerce, on the other hand, tends to democracy. If people are settled about a favorable harbor or route of trade, and if they develop any industry the products of which can be exchanged and that depends upon skill and industry and not upon the utilization of a raw material that is liable to monopoly, then they tend to become democratic, as did the maritime cities of Greece and Italy, and the halting places of the caravans that connected Europe with the Orient. These did not become democratic in the modern sense of the word. That consummation waited for the development of popular ideals concerning the universal rights of man, and could not be brought about directly by mere geographic influences. But they were democracies in the sense that many were well-to-do, and the well-to-do were free. Commerce breaks down aristocracy not only because a larger number become prosperous, but also because social classes are no longer separated by an impassable line of stratification. Where commerce exists the poor peddler may become the rich merchant, and the son of the bankrupt, once wealthy, sinks into poverty. On the other hand, landed estates are less easily dissipated, as well as less easily acquired, and descend from generation to generation, so that the stratification of society becomes permanent, and the illusions of caste grow up. Not only does the noble claim to be of different clay from the peasant, but also the peasant, who was born in a hut, is attired in hodden gray, speaks the dialect of the furrow and not of the hall, and plods through a life of toil in the habit of obedience, admits that he is of inferior stuff and does not aspire to equality with those who sit in state or ride in armor.

and are taught from childhood to feel themselves born to command. Further, the early democracies are limited to dense populations collected within a small area among whom communication and coöperation are easy, for without facility of communication the many cannot combine to form and express a common will.

6. Tastes and Social and Domestic Customs Are Influenced by Geographic Conditions.—Football is out of place in the tropics, and ice-skating is impossible. Athletic sports are indigenous to cool climates, and are sometimes the objects of amazement to inhabitants of torrid regions. The long evenings of the northern winter call into being suitable pastimes. The working hours of torrid regions are interrupted at midday and the siesta is an established custom. Hours for calling and for social reunions and for work differ from place to place. Still more marked are the differences in dress, in houses, and in household furnishings and conveniences. These practical differences occasion differences in the fancies of fashion in dress and in architecture and in the art crafts which furnish the esthetic elements in household goods and articles of personal use. So great are these differences that the arts and fashions of one people seem to another strange and fantastic. The materials available in a given locality for making articles of use and beauty also affect the development of tastes. Clay makes possible ceramic arts, and marble was necessary to the Grecian taste for temples and statues. The art of Greece is due in part to the quarries of Mount Pentelicus.

7. Ethical Differences Are Largely Influenced by Geographic Environment.—The study of comparative sociology reveals the fact that the conscience codes of various peoples differ amazingly, and these ethical differences are largely influenced by geographic environment.

We are all familiar with the fact that the commercial and manufacturing North with relatively little use for the clumsy labor of the slave found it comparatively easy to see the moral objections to slavery, while in the agricultural South refined, gentle, and Christian people were long able to regard

slavery as a divine institution. Certain environments tend to
pastoral industry and patriarchal society. There filial duty
is the supreme obligation; child-bearing is the wife's ambition; sexual irregularities are seriously condemned, but the
increase of the family of the great by polygynous marriages
is thoroughly approved. Such was the family of Abraham.
Under the feudalism naturally resulting from predominant
agriculture, obedience and loyalty form the central pillar of
the ethical structure; each prays that he may do his duty in
his lot and station in becoming obedience to his betters. But
in commercial democracy independence and individual pride
are the motives of honor, and the test of honor is not a
loyalty to one's own patriarchal or feudal superiors which
may sanction treachery and pillage to all outsiders save the
accepted guest, but an honesty that extends even to the
merchant from overseas.

In northern latitudes the sharp alternation of the seasons
demanding that each season's work must be done at its proper
time necessitates promptness and energy that does not wait
for impulse. There nature, which enriches man by accumulated margins of saving but is never lavish, enforces thrift
and economy, and these become customs of society, habits
of the individual, and prized virtues. But the thrift of the
Northerner often looks to his Southern brother like niggardli-
ness, and the ease and lavishness of the Southerner to the
Northerner may seem like laziness, disregard of obligation,
and prodigality.

8. **Mythologies and Religions Are Influenced by Geographic Environment.**—What the nature-myths of a people
shall be depends in part upon what aspects of nature in
their neighborhoods are most impressive, whether they live
by the sea, upon the banks of a great river, among the mountains, in the depths of the forest, or on a plain where the
overarching sky with sun and stars chiefly command the gaze.
Moreover, geographic environments affect religions indirectly
through the other social forms to which they give rise. The
existing form of earthly power and authority tends to shape
man's notion of divine rule. Cruel despotisms are wont to

have bloodthirsty gods, and the patriarchal, as compared with other equally early forms of government, seems the most favorable to belief in a god interested in the welfare of his people. Indeed the patriarchate through the development of reverence and worship for the spirits of departed ancestors opens wide the way to belief in a father-god.

9. Geographic Conditions Affect the Moods and Psychic Tendencies of a People.—It is a fact familiar to us all that in humid weather the vital flame seems to burn with little draft, while in a crisp atmosphere it leaps up brightly. The rapidity or slowness of evaporation seems to affect directly the chemistry of the vital processes. Not only are the general vital processes, upon which the action of the brain and nervous system depends, affected by conditions of heat, light, and moisture, but the nerves themselves are directly stimulated or depressed. To this cause it has been ascribed that the cradles of civilization have been found in dry regions like the Egyptian oasis in the desert and the plains of Iran and of Central America.

The original seats of civilization have been in climates that were warm as well as dry. In the earth's warm belt only occasional spots have sufficient dryness and rapidity of evaporation, and these are said to have been the original seed plots or nurseries from which the germs of civilization have spread. Though food was abundant yet it was probably quite impossible that indigenous civilization like that of Egypt should arise in the dank heat that prevails in certain other portions of Africa. The wine of America's "translucent, transcendent, transplendent" atmosphere quickens the life of her people.

Not only does climate affect the permanent tendencies of races, but passing changes of the seasons [1] affect the moods of men. Alternations of the seasons give variety to life and stimulation to the imagination. Further, the experienced teacher or prison warden knows that there are muggy days

---

[1] Albert Leffingwell: Influence of the Seasons upon Conduct. Swan, Sonnenschein & Co., London, 1892.
E. G. Dexter: Weather Influences. Macmillan, N. Y., 1904.

when his wards are restless and capable of more erratic mischief than concentrated endeavor. The lashing of a dry wind increases nervous instability and crime. The curve of the statistics of crime shows a regular alternation of rise and fall corresponding to the change of the seasons, crimes against the person increasing in summer and crimes against property in winter. Even suicide, the causes for which would seem perhaps more peculiarly personal than the causes of any other human act or experience, fluctuates regularly with climatic changes. The frequency of suicide is much less in the despairing season of winter, with its scarcity of work and pinch of hunger and cold, than it is in the irritating and enervating heat of summer. And the darkness of night everywhere gives to crime its chief opportunity.

10. **The Routes Followed by Migration, War, and Commerce Have Been Marked Out by Geographic Highways.**— These routes have been the great distributors of human populations, customs, and commodities. The other determinant of the distribution and present location of societies has been the presence of natural resources. Furs lured the Russians, though not a migratory people, around the world through trackless frozen wastes of northern Canada, Alaska, and Siberia. Africa was little visited by Europeans until the supply of ivory drew them, and that mainly to furnish the means of playing the games of chess and billiards. The demand for billiard balls had much to do with the addition of Africa to the practically known world. The discovery of gold in Australia and California suddenly peopled those hitherto neglected regions. These are exceptionally striking illustrations of the general rule that natural resources, as well as natural pathways, determine social distribution.

The Sociological Importance of Geographic Conditions.— The importance of studying the geographic conditions of social activities is due largely to two considerations: First, they afford a part of the demonstration that social activities are not to be explained merely by reference to subjective motives or to the arbitrary decrees of man's will, but that the specific desires and volitions of men are themselves to be explained by reference to conditioning environment, so that, like other realities, human activities belong to that network of cause and effect which is the order of nature. Second, the geographic conditions afford a very considerable part of the general explanation of the course of social evolution, especially in its earlier stages and in the rise of indigenous cultures.

What great historic movement or epoch can be accounted for adequately without reference to geographic conditions? If for example, we seek an explanation of the efflorescence of Greece in the age of Pericles, must we not take account of the third, fifth, sixth, eighth and ninth of the principles of geographic causation above enumerated? We must observe how the Ionian Islands stretched out like eager fingers for contact with other peoples, how the ships of Phœnicia, and later of Athens, brought strange goods and strange ideas, till there arose one of those rare eras in which the crust of custom was thinned and broken, and men instead of hating and dreading change or innovation were eager to hear "some new thing"; how the commerce resulting from the peninsular and insular position did away with agrarian monopoly of place and power and aided in establishing an oligarchy of the well-to-do which though more or less allied with ancient rank, and more or less perpetuating its form by a fiction of identity between the rich and the well-born was nevertheless a type of democracy, and how the mythology, the esthetic tastes, and the inspiration of Greek life had all a geographic background.

A knowledge of the influence of geographic environment on social activities has a bearing not only upon the explanation of present situations and historic movements, but also upon the judgment of proposed plans for the future. Such knowledge is suggestive of lines of profitable enterprise in opening canals, dredging harbors, and otherwise providing conditions similar to those which nature has in places bestowed. And this knowledge has special application to projects of migration and colonization.

Limitations on the Importance of Geographic Conditions.—
Three considerations, however, set limits to the importance
of geographic conditions of social phenomena:

1. This is, after all, only one out of four sets of determining conditions. The geographic conditions set negative
limits to the possible forms of social activity and play an
important part in positively occasioning their rise and character, yet they no more suffice for their complete explanation
than one substance, which the chemist mixes with others in a
retort to secure a complex reaction, explains the total effect.

Various writers have been disposed to seize upon some
one factor in sociological explanation and to treat it as if by
itself it afforded complete solution. Thus some, of whom
Buckle is the most famous, have exaggerated the relative
importance of geographic conditions. Buckle writes as if he
came near to thinking that they afford the complete explanation of the life of societies. Others, of whom Karl Marx is
the most famous, teach that the economic activities by which
people get a living determine their moral standards, their
forms of government, their scientific progress, and their entire
life. Tarde would find well nigh the whole explanation in
social relations, especially in imitation. An activity becomes
a social phenomenon, he says, when it has spread by means
of imitation till many participate in it. Spreading waves of
imitation meet and modify each other, and combine into customs and institutions, and to understand how they do so is,
according to him, to comprehend the life and development
of society. De Greef finds the essential social reality, and
the chief factor in sociological explanation in the motives
which associates furnish each other, by which their association becomes a sort of exchange, or implicit contractualism.
Giddings bases his explanations primarily upon the fact of
social and psychophysical similarities, which lead certain
groups to similarity of response to stimulus, "consciousness of
kind," and sympathetic and practical likemindedness. Simmel
finds the universal social reality and the essential clue to explanation in the fact of leadership and of superiority and
subordination. Ross gives chief emphasis not to the leader-

ship of the dominant individual, but to the molding of individuals by the gradually developed activities of the mass. Ward finds the "social forces" in the inborn traits of human nature. Gumplowicz shows how largely social organization results from the conflicts between groups. Such writers are correct in emphasizing the factors in explanation to which they have given particular study, but wrong in so far as they slight other truths, and these examples show the complexity of complete sociological explanation which must include them all. Though Greece has kept her geography she has lost her Periclean grandeur; for geographic causes are far from being the only ones that affect society.

2. It is in the earlier stages of evolution that geographic conditions are most dominant, and after the conquest of nature has been carried far, especially when transportation, intercommunication, and migration have played their part, activities are practiced in regions where for geographic reasons they would never have originated, as the plants that fill our fields and gardens are carried and fostered far from their natural habitats. Thus the relative importance of geographic causes diminishes as civilization advances, while the technic and social factors steadily increase in importance. Modifications of this truth are found in the facts: (1) that advancing arts create new uses for geographic resources, for coal, petroleum, waterfalls and harbors; (2) that as the relative importance of geographic factors diminishes their absolute importance increases, because they condition an ever richer and more complex life of society; and (3) that not all the consequences of man's dependence upon external physical nature are felt until population has passed "the point of diminishing returns," later to be explained. But the very fact that man has reached the limits of nature's generosity increases his dependence upon the productivity of the arts.

3. Geographic conditions are laid down by nature, and there is no practical problem for man in determining what they shall be, except as he determines his geographic environment by travel, migration, and colonization. On the other hand the remaining conditions of social life are largely prod-

ucts of man's own activities. Indeed the social and technic conditions are activities of man and the direct result of man's activities and, being shaped by man, present to man the practical problem of so shaping them that they will result in securing the prevalence of desirable and not of undesirable social consequences. The *negative* importance of geographic conditions as setting limits to possible social activity is increased by the fact that they are so little subject to human control, but their *positive* importance as conditions of the ever differentiating and evolving activity of society is greatly diminished by this rigidity. Stupendous practical importance attaches to the study of those conditions of social realities which are not laid down by nature, but are subject to human control.

II. TECHNIC CAUSES THAT AFFECT THE LIFE OF SOCIETY

CHAPTER IV

RURAL CONDITIONS

We now pass to the second class of conditions affecting society, namely, the technic. It was stated in the introduction that the two main forms of technic conditions are: (1) the numbers and spatial distribution of population, and (2) the amount, forms, and distribution of wealth.

The effects of the numbers and distribution of population have not yet been adequately studied by sociologists. However a few points are reasonably clear.

Formation of Population.—The lowest savages live in small huddles or hordes. Those bands cannot attain great numbers because they have not the means of obtaining sufficient food. The necessity of seeking food compels a band to divide and separate if it increases beyond the number who can share the supplies of food that they come upon in their wanderings. At a later stage, when the same people have become expert hunters or herdsmen and so can live in larger companies, the groups tend to recombine, partly through the conquest and absorption of weaker groups by stronger ones, and partly through the sense of blood kinship uniting clans that have separated from one original stock. Thus, separate bands become unified more or less closely by conquest into a compound group, or by kinship into a "tribe" or "nation" composed of clans. Two compound groups may be united into a doubly compound unit when one conquers the other or two tribes may unite to repel a common foe. Thus several pastoral tribes of plainsmen may unite to repel the hunters from the mountains, or agriculturists may forget their rivalries and unite to repel the pastoral nomads; or pastoral nomads like the Israelites or the Huns may unite to conquer agriculturists. The population of every great nation is supposed to be thus doubly and trebly and manifoldly compounded.

Populations are formed by three processes: (1) compounding, as just described; (2) natural increase, i. e., excess of births over deaths; (3) immigration, which differs from compounding in that it is not the union of whole peoples but the addition of individuals and small parties to a population.

A population area is any inhabited portion of the earth's surface which for some reason it is convenient to treat as a unit and to describe with reference to its population. Thus, we may describe as a population area any geographic region, as a continent, a mountain valley, or a river basin. We do, in fact, most frequently take for description population areas that correspond with political boundaries.

Population may increase in numbers too rapidly.—The economic law of diminishing returns is this: An area may have too few inhabitants to utilize its natural resources, so that an increase of population, by adding to the labor force, increases production not merely enough to enable the larger population to live as well, but enough to enable the increased population to live even better than the smaller one had been able to do. This, however, cannot continue indefinitely. There comes a time when added inhabitants, though they add to the labor force, and to some degree increase the amounts of products, yet cannot wrest from the resources of the area owned enough to increase the amount of goods produced to such a point that when divided among the increased population each will have as large a share as was upon the average enjoyed by each of those who inhabited the same area before the last increment of population was received. The point at which that increment of population was received was the point of diminishing returns for the given area. If the population is to increase further, without falling off in its standard of living, it must either take up more land, or else adopt new methods of production.

It has this alternative, for not only does a given area have a point of diminishing returns, but so also does a given stage of industrial progress. A population of hunters may reach the point of diminishing returns at one individual to the square mile, where agriculturists may live as well at ten to the square mile or a people with diversified trades at twenty to one square mile; and the introduction of a new piece of agricultural or manufacturing machinery may still further push forward the point of diminishing returns. Therefore the point of diminishing returns, that is, the point at which further increase of population means a lowered standard of living, may be postponed either (1) by taking up new land or discovering new resources within the land already occupied, or (2) by using more or better capital, such as improved tools, machinery, and livestock, or improved methods of production.

For an increasing population to maintain its standard of living unimpaired means not only that each shall have as much to eat as formerly, but also that houses shall be as sanitary, spacious, and dignified, fittings as convenient and beautiful, the sick as well cared for, the aged as comfortable, books and music and travel as fully enjoyed, and sons and daughters as well educated.

A given territory at a given stage of industrial progress can maintain at a given level a given number of people. Its population may be less than the number who could be thus maintained, but when that number has been reached then further increase of population must be accompanied by a proportional increase of skill in producing, or of wisdom in consuming economic goods, or else by a decline in the popular standard of living. A few rich may go on living more and more expensively, but the living of the ordinary family must decline.

The wise ambition for a people is to maintain its life at a higher physical and psychic level rather than to increase the number of its members at the expense of degrading their life below an accepted standard. The fact that a people increases but slowly in numbers may be an evidence not of degeneracy but of enlightenment and prudence.[1]

Since the recent great improvement and cheapening of means of transportation, and the opening to Europeans of the great areas of North and South America and Africa, emigra- tion has offered a way of escape from the law of diminishing returns, but this way of escape cannot remain open forever.

It must not be thought that when population increases be- yond the point of diminishing returns agriculturalists are the only ones affected. When multiplication of the agricultural population has carried it far past the point of diminishing returns it ceases to buy enough manufactured goods to profit- ably employ similarly increasing numbers engaged in non- agricultural pursuits. Practically all other industries must use at least a little land. They must use increasing amounts of land if they are to employ increasing numbers of laborers with undiminished productivity, and the cost of this land is in- creased by population pressure. All manufacture depends upon extractive industry for the quantity and price of its raw materials. And all classes must be fed from the land, and scarcity of the agricultural products relative to the number of mouths to be fed, results in scanty (or costly) rations, not only for farmers, but for all. For such reasons, the law of diminishing returns affects all branches of productive in- dustry.

This law, coupled with the tendency of population to in- crease by reproduction "beyond any assignable limits" has given ground for baleful prophecies of inevitable progressive degradation for man. The point of diminishing returns can- not be indefinitely pushed forward, either by emigration or by

---

[1] Professor Alfred Marshall in his "Principles of Economics," Macmillan, 1898 (Fifth ed.: Vol. I, page 182), says: "There are many parts of Europe even now in which custom, exercising the force of law, prevents more than one son in each family from marrying; he is generally the oldest, but in some places, the youngest; if any other son marries he must leave the village. When great material prosperity and the absence of all extreme poverty are found in old-fashioned corners of the Old World, the explanation generally lies in some such custom as this with all its evils and hardships."

progress in the arts. To the most favored spot must come a time when the only remaining way of escape from progressive poverty and degradation will be the limitation of the natural increase of population.

It used to be believed that the power of the reproductive instinct was such that any discovery of new lands, or any improvement in the arts of production would simply lead to an increased birth rate, so that the only progress possible would be an increase of numbers, and that although a few, by taking more than their share, might live in luxury, the masses could by no means be raised above the level of mere subsistence. If we take the reproductive instinct and the law of diminishing returns as the only factors it is impossible to escape from this conclusion. This conclusion is mainly responsible for the name which Carlyle and many since have given to political economy—"the dismal science." But these two are not the only factors. The standard of living is a third factor. A standard of living is a set of desires strong enough to induce men to postpone or forego marriage, or to limit the number of children after marriage. It induces men before they marry to spend a considerable part of their most fertile years in prolonged training and competitive struggle in order to attain a degree of economic independence that will enable them to maintain a family in comfort and culture.[1] The beasts have no standard of living. It is a social product. It is a psychic reality. But it is strong enough to override imperious instinct. If we study only the effects of material conditions—geographic, technic, and psychophysical—upon social life, we shall be led, unless we blink the implications of the facts, to a pessimistic conclusion. It is only when we study also the control that may be exercised by elements of the fourth class—the psychic—that we have reasonable ground for hopeful courage. It is a part of the business of general sociology, as sup-

---

[1] If M and all his descendants marry at 22, while N and all his descendants marry at 33, in 300 years the proportion of Mature M's to N's will be as 26 to 1, according to the calculation of Francis Galton in Hereditary Genius, Appleton, 1871, pages 353-356; referred to by A. G. Keller: Societal Evolution. Macmillan, 1915, page 185.

piemental (or fundamental) to the special social sciences, to bring all the elements in the social situation into one perspective. Prevalent ambitions, personal ideals, and standards of social morality are as real determinants of social phenomena as the limitations of natural resources or the physiological instincts.

Agrarian Aristocracy and Population Pressure.—The agricultural sections of America have in general by no means reached that balance between population and resources which tends ultimately to establish itself. They are in a period of transition. The coming changes will offer opportunity for great improvements, but they will bring with them one great danger, namely, that of too rigid social stratification.

At first sight such stratification seems inevitable. Omitting qualifications, this tendency may be thus stated: When land becomes worth hundreds of dollars per acre, as it already has in certain sections, the landless youth can seldom, if ever, succeed in buying a farm, and if he remains in the country, must be a tenant or a hired laborer. On the other hand those who own land will be in a position to buy more.[1] Thus the ownership of land may be expected to concentrate and the number of landless dwellers in the country to increase. This tendency will be strongest where land is most productive and most valuable, and therefore hardest for the landless to purchase, and at the same time requiring the employment of a large number of hands to tend its heavy crops. The application of scientific methods to agriculture which will be necessary to make the best lands pay a return for their cost requires capital, and this will put an additional obstacle in the way of the landless youth and add to the tendency created by the high cost of the land to develop a small body of wealthy agrarian

---

[1] The tendency is at present increased by the purchase of lands by city investors. Agricultural land is an attractive investment where the rent equals the interest on bonds plus a margin sufficient to pay for the supervision necessary to secure the occupancy and cultivation of the land. It is especially attractive investment even at a lower rental than this so long as there is a rapid rise in value incident to population growth. The farm land of central Illinois has fully doubled in value during the decade 1900-1910.

aristocrats with a large body of tenants or paid farm laborers.

There are, however, three counteracting tendencies referred to above as omitted qualifications. First, the more intensive the agriculture, the smaller the number of acres which the landless youth must buy in order to become independent and to support a family. The increased price of good land and the demand for fine fruits, vegetables, and meats may be expected to force a more intensive cultivation, which makes fewer acres suffice for the maintenance of a household. So long as wasteful, extensive modes of cultivation prevail the growth of cities clamoring for food and raw materials powerfully tends to increase both "the cost of living" and the monopoly of land. But intensive agriculture tends both to reduce the cost of living and to combat monopoly of land. It is true that intensive agriculture by increasing the productivity of land tends to increase its price. But in intensive agriculture the proportional part played by labor is greater and the proportional part played by land is less, so that land values do not increase as rapidly as does product, and there is a gain in position to those who contribute the labor required for production.[1]

Whether the rural population is made up of independent farmers or of tenants and hired laborers, increase in the number of those who can dwell in the country and maintain a high standard of living there, is dependent upon the increase of manufacturing cities, either of the same nation or abroad, to

---

[1] Suppose land worth $200.00 per acre now rents at $8.00 per acre and with the expenditure of $6.00 worth of labor and $4.50 for machinery, teams and seed, yields on the average $18.00 per acre.

If by trebling the labor and doubling the other costs of production the yield per acre should be doubled the result would be:

	Land value	Crop	Rent	Capital	Labor
Extensive	$200	18	$8.00	$4.50	$6.00
Intensive	225	36	9.00	9.00	18.00

If this could be realized, labor could have more money and only about half as much land need be bought, the price per acre being but 12½ per cent. greater than now. Besides, the greater amount of labor means greater cost of superintendence to a landlord and consequent further reduction of the tendency to concentration.

absorb their product of food and raw materials. Thus the high rate of urban increase is favorable to intensive agriculture, and to the increase of rural population in numbers and prosperity.

A second and more important qualification of the tendency to form an agrarian aristocracy and proletariat is found in the absence of laws of primogeniture and the wish of parents, as testators, to divide their holdings among their children.

A third counteracting tendency is in the fact that in the long run farming land is worth more to the man who cultivates it than to anyone else, because it gives him a steady job, independent of the will of any employer. The price of farming land contains at least three elements: first, a sum which if invested at interest would yield annually an amount equal to the rental of the land; second, a price paid for the expected unearned increment; third, a sum paid by the purchaser for the opportunity of independent self-employment. In time the second element will dwindle, for there will no longer be so great an expectation of unearned increment, indeed that expectation might be largely extinguished by taxation, as the next paragraph will show. Then, unless land be valued as a basis of social prestige, or for some other extraneous consideration, the third element will tend to become the decisive factor in its ownership, for it will raise the price of the land above the capitalized value of its rental, and only he who values it as an opportunity for independent self-employment can afford to pay this third element in the price of land.

An artificial barrier to the concentration of land in large holdings would be the heavy taxing of unearned increments. The motive for land purchases by the wealthy who do not farm is largely the hope of enjoying the unearned increment which is resulting from population increase, improvements in transportation and general progress. Deeds might be required to state the true price paid, and proof of fraud in the statement of the price might invalidate the deed. The purchasers would then have two strong motives for having the price correctly recorded, first, in order to get a valid title, and second, because whenever in the future the purchaser became a seller, it would be advantageous to him to have had the full price recorded, since it would be the only amount which he could receive untaxed. On the other hand, he would not overstate the price lest he invalidate his title, and the seller would not allow it to be overstated, if there had been an increment since the previous transfer, because the seller is taxed on that increment. If the actual price at successive sales were recorded the unearned increment could readily be taxed.

To cheapen land by taxing the unearned increment, and rendering it unattractive to speculators would tend to make it more valuable to the man who would labor on it than to anyone else, and so to distribute it among independent farmers in holdings no larger than they could properly cultivate.

Density and Communication.—Density as directly affecting social life is practically equivalent to facility of transportation and communication. An improvement in the character of roads and means of transportation and communication may improve society as much and in much the same way as would doubling the number of inhabitants without such mechanical improvements. If railroads are the arteries of society, highways are the capillaries, and unless the capillary circulation is good both business and social life may be expected to languish. Trolley, telephone, rural free delivery of mail, the parcels post, the automobile, the school omnibus, horses, the bicycle, and, above all, because essential to the effectiveness of most of the others, good roads are a technic equipment which can go far to redeem rural solitude and render it feasible to maintain such a social life as to make the country the home, by choice and not by hard necessity, of a due proportion of those who are well-to-do and competent. At the same time the density of the city, in so far as it brings with it social as distinguished from bodily effects, is a technic condition created in part by great numbers in small area, and in part by excellent streets, rapid street transportation, telephones, and the railroad and telegraph, which makes the city a throbbing ganglion of world life. From this it follows that degrees of density cannot be properly defined by reference to the number of inhabitants alone. We may roughly distinguish several degrees of number and density, and may observe that each has its own social effects, and calls for appropriate adjustments.

1. Rural Solitude.—Most people would say that rural solitude exists wherever the country is a degree more lonesome than they are accustomed to. In fact, the condition which I propose to designate as rural solitude exists not only in the vast areas of the far western United States, but also in a large part of the Middle West, and is not unknown in New England. Most of our richest prairie soil is now yielding far less per acre than some of our comparatively poor land, because the prairie is devoted to crops that are adapted to an extensive mode of cultivation, that is, one requiring the expenditure of but little labor per acre. Two men spending all their labor on eighty acres of prairie soil might make it yield more than is now secured on the average from one hundred and sixty acres. The effects of rural solitude are mainly negative. The ministrations of nature may be glorious, but those of man are comparatively lacking. With reference to density, it is a state of lack and disadvantage.

2. Rural Community.—The line between rural solitude and what we will call "rural community" is passed when it becomes possible to maintain a satisfactory standard of school, church, and neighborhood life. The transition from the first to the second degree of density usually depends on increasing the number of inhabitants, preferably at the same time diminishing the size of land holdings, but it may be greatly hastened by improving the roads and means of communication, or both.

3. Hamlet.—The hamlet can be better described than defined and is too familiar to require detailed description. It often forfeits many of the advantages of the open country without securing those of the village or city, being a spot where man has deposited upon the landscape an accumulation of ugliness, the rival of the city slum.

It is a merciful provision of nature that we can get used to almost anything, but it is an anesthetic. Not in the hamlet only, but in societies of every sort, we become chloroformed to familiar evils. The dreadful hideousness of many a hamlet, bearable only because human beings can get used to almost anything, could be redeemed by a well kept highway, well kept dooryards, paint or vines over houses and out-houses, and properly placed shrubbery and flowers. Trees come more slowly but are a glory to hamlet and village.

The hamlet may not only surpass the city slum in ugliness; it may also rival it in its insanitary condition, due largely to shallow wells,[1] open vaults, lack of proper refuse disposal and swarming flies that breed in offal and then enter the houses laden with germs—conditions which modern and inexpensive scientific devices have made unnecessary even for the country. It may rival the slum also in tendencies to vice, drunkenness, and demoralizing as well as petty pleasures, because of lack of the dignity and elevation that go with beauty and fitness of surroundings, and dearth of elevating pleasures, a dearth often most pitiful and degrading, which may readily be removed by the traveling or local library and the periodical press, the literary circle, debating club, musical society, association for scientific farming, arts and crafts guild, and reconstructed school and church.

If community life throughout the countryside surrounding the hamlet were properly developed, then among the residents of the hamlet would normally be included a teacher and also a minister, each living with his family and each of such character and intelligence as could reasonably be expected only on condition that the income of each fully equaled that of a prosperous farmer, including the value of all that is consumed upon the farm. By their example and leadership, the minister, the teacher, and the physician, with other progressive and intelligent citizens, each sensible of responsibility for the community life, could insure to the rural community and the hamlet a life of beauty, joy and worth, the

---

[1] Dug wells are in general a fit source of water for human consumption only when surrounded by a water-tight curb high enough to keep out surface water, and continuing downward as a lining to the well for a number of feet, so that water which passes under it from the surface in wet times will be adequately filtered. How many feet this will be depends on the character of the soil and the sources of pollution to which the soil is exposed.

description of which would enrich our literature as the living of it would enrich themselves.

The fulfillment of social possibilities in city or country depends upon the somewhat general realization that a profession or trade and the influence it brings constitute a public function. No legitimate calling, from the pastorate to managing a moving picture show, or shoeing horses, can properly be carried on merely as a means of making money, but rather also as a man's work in creating a social situation. This it is which gives dignity and zest to work and this is the truest single test of morality. There are young men in America who are preparing to engage in professional work in rural as well as in urban communities in full consciousness of this principle of social responsibility and opportunity, the ignoring of which is the main reason for non-realization of social possibilities.

Another reason why teachers, ministers and others have not more usually afforded the necessary social leadership is that they themselves have not been ripe representatives of modern civilization and culture, and this is because we have not in our country a sufficient number of thoroughly educated men, the products of cultured homes and of liberal schooling, to fill the positions for which thorough training should be an essential qualification. For this reason the standards of educational requirements for schoolteachers, which are enforced in some parts of the old world, are as yet impracticable here. The American school system is exceedingly admirable as an organization. We have the best elementary-school textbooks in the world, which is both fortunate and necessary in view of the limited preparation of many rural teachers. But the supreme element in the success of a school system is still largely lacking, namely, adequate qualifications of the teachers themselves.

Yet another reason for the comparative poverty of life in rural districts is the subdivision of schools and churches which occasions a lack of dignity and power to inspire and lead on the part of these great social institutions. Where people are few the necessity of concentration is most urgent.

In the case of the school this need is being met in many places by "consolidation." By this plan numerous tiny and often disreputable schoolhouses are replaced by one central building of good architecture, attended by pupils numerous enough to be properly graded and classified and to have zest and interstimulation in work and in play. Since funds are conserved, instead of scattered, apparatus and libraries can be afforded. A few competent teachers replace a larger number of less competent ones. Group solidarity and democracy among the people of all sections of the region are promoted by the early friendship of the rising generation. Consolidated schools imply fairly good roads, and a bus and driver for each of the routes converging at the school center. Since a bus and driver cost less than a school and teacher the consolidated school may cost less than the numerous district schools which it replaces. But the great argument for the consolidated school is not that it requires less money, but that it makes people willing to spend more money on their schools and secures better education.

Corresponding advantages are to some degree secured to the church by the movement for church federation, or by "interdenominational commissions." In several states such commissions have already shown that it is possible to establish comity by which each important Protestant sect will refrain from establishing new churches, missions or Sunday-schools without the approval of a central council composed of representatives from each of the coöperating denominations, and by which tiny struggling congregations leave it to the council to decide which can best survive in a given community and then allow that one to absorb the rest in a single united organization. This is possible where one sect has more members, and a stronger hold upon the community than the others, and what a denomination yields in one locality it is likely to gain in another where it has strength to be the rallying center. In other cases a federated church is formed, each sect electing a clerk and treasurer preserving the continuity of its records and forwarding missionary and benevolent contributions to its own denominational board but all acting as one body in local matters. These valuable expedients should be utilized until Protestantism adopts a yet more rational mode of organization.

All rural progress, like progress everywhere, depends upon awakening popular desire for the objects that are of real importance and value, a desire strong enough to lead to the expenditure of such money as is available. Every thoroughly enlightened farmer will escape from that form of insanity which regards it as the object of labor "to raise more corn, to feed more hogs, to buy more land to raise more corn, to feed more hogs, and so on"—and will realize that life is no mere toilsome game with a score reckoned in acres or dollars or hogs or corn, but that life is conscious experience, that money is only a means to life, and that life is wasted if the means are obtained but the ends not reached. Such a farmer regards money as something to be obtained in order that it may be used in maintaining the agencies of life, and these for the farmer are almost summed up in the home, the school, the church, supposing the home to include all the private agencies of happiness and culture, and the church and the school to perform the functions appropriate to them. Not money in a stocking or in a bank, but the home, the school, the church, should represent the goal of his labor. The parsimoniousness of the farmer is not to be blamed when it is due to unescapable poverty. Many a farmer is overburdened with rentals or mortgages.

4. **Village.**—Any settlement which in size is between the mere hamlet of a dozen or a score of dwellings and the city is popularly called a village. Between the village that is scarcely more than a hamlet and the village that is scarcely less than a city there are many gradations in numbers each of which would doubtless be found by adequate study to have characteristic effects upon the life of the group. In the United States many communities that in numbers are as yet no more than villages are allowed to take the name and political organization of a city.

A good village improves with time. By the time it is shaded with full-grown, high-arching trees that never have been "topped" a village should have acquired a sort of ripe collective personality, rich in sentiment. For good or ill, the character of a village depends largely upon the example and activity of its leaders. Fortunate is that village in which the standard of ambition, taste, sentiment, and custom are early set by intelligent and highminded founders who leave behind a heritage of tradition that molds the lives of their successors for many a generation and causes the sons and daughters of the village to seek education and careers of service.

Young villages should plan for the future. Streets newly laid out should be wide enough to serve the purposes of a city if time so determines. Permanent trees should at once be set out at such distances as not to overcrowd each other generations later, while between each pair of permanent and slow-growing trees, may be set a tree of rapid growth, to be removed in time. The village council should at once see to it that grade lines are established, not only for streets but also for building lots, with reference both to beauty and drainage. And they should prescribe a building line, requiring that houses should be set at a uniform distance from the street, and also for a form of curved embankment or slope (not an angular terrace) wherever lots are above the level of the street. A standard cornice line should be established for buildings on the business street.

The architecture of the church and other public buildings of a village and also of the homes is a matter of no slight importance. It may determine whether people of taste make the village a summering place or permanent home. People like this place or that often without knowing why. The cause is frequently in that which appeals to the eye. Beauty is a silent and often unrecognized, but potent, element in the worth of life. Children growing up and men and women tend insensibly to live up or down to their surroundings. Beauty alone will seldom redeem men as it is said to have redeemed Goethe, but it is one agency of redemption. And it is of value not only as a means of moral uplift, but for its own sake. Beauty is like cheerful weather. The architect and the artist do man's work in the world and deserve the appreciation, honor, and fame which are accorded them by the folk-sense of old communities that have long enjoyed the experience of beauty. When the designs are once drawn, it is no more expensive to build in beautiful lines than in ugly ones. No community should allow a hideous work of man to be needlessly thrust upon its gaze, to stand like an affront to the eyes for decades or generations. They would not allow every man who would to establish a perpetual bad smell. Should they refuse to protect the higher sense of sight? Every moderately large community should employ the services of a consulting architect who need not be a resident, or of a commission which would pass upon the design for every permanent building erected upon a public thoroughfare. Whenever a plan was refused reasons should be given and suggestions for the removal of unsatisfactory features would be in order. How large a community must be, before availing itself of such services, each village or city must decide for itself. It is far easier to prevent ugly, and otherwise objectionable, architecture than to remove it after it has been built.

The small population was at a disadvantage in the earlier stages of social evolution in that the chance that progressive ideas would be originated was less under these conditions than where many minds were congregated. This was a serious matter in the old times of little communication between different communities, but that disadvantage has largely disappeared in our time of efficient communication through travel, post, conventions, and institutes for farmers and teachers and clergy, and, above all, through the press. In a small village group there is also less stimulation from very eminent representatives of the arts and professions. This disadvantage might be largely offset if doctors, lawyers, teachers, and ministers were trained to feel the responsibility and practice the arts of social leadership. Leadership consists largely in putting the proper ideas into the minds of the individuals who are in a position to give them effect and still more in supplying the necessary courage. Most things really worth doing have at first looked impracticable to the average person. But when there appears an individual having not only sufficient imagination and enlightenment to see what should be done, but also sufficient courage to believe that it can be done, the probability of the achievement has begun. The question of possibility or impossibility with reference to social improvements is largely one of psychic attitude of the people. The question with respect to most desirable social changes is not, could people bring them about if they would, but will they will to do so? Such changes are thought impossible and for the time being are so, because men do not believe that their neighbors will do their duty. The man who first says, "I for one will, and we together can," who breaks down the hypnotism of the present reality, who exhibits confidence in his fellows, who makes individuals begin to think "my neighbors will do their duty and therefore it is worth while for me to do mine," thereby creates new social possibilities. A village population, dense but small, derives particular advantages from these two technic characteristics, in the comparative ease with which its best members can influence the situation. One of the attractions of the small community for the rightminded citizen is that he may reasonably expect to make his influence count, to be a significant factor in constructive community life, while he could hardly hope to produce any very definite and recognizable influence upon the vast and complex situation presented by a great city.

The pressure of public opinion upon the individual is likely to be strongest, other things being equal, in a small, dense community like a village. Personal conduct is not easily concealed; the social reaction of increased or diminished cordiality and respect is powerfully and promptly felt. For the average individual personal relations tend to constitute a larger part of life's interest and value than in the city, and these relations are permanent, and not to be shaken off by changing one's boarding-place. This may be carried to an irksome excess and may be an evil if social standards are low, but it is a tremendous power and on the whole a power for good, and that increasingly, provided social standards are progressively wise and social intercourse instinct with sympathy and courtesy. In the village individuality is not obliterated by a steam roller of social pressure. Quite the contrary. This pressure is heavy upon indecencies, improprieties, and such breaches of the group conscience code as licentiousness, thriftlessness, dishonesty, or cruelty. On the other hand, interesting diversification of the social current of thought, speech, and action are encouraged. It is in country or village that we hear the phrases, "As Tom says," and "As Aunt Mary would say." Piquancies are appreciated in a group where individuals are thoroughly known and furnish to each other permanent sources of human interest. Local reputation is easily achieved and small talents that in the city would be lost to view are called out and often are discovered to be real accessions to the stock of social wealth.

Sympathetic bonds unite the population of the village far more than that of the city. Sympathy, being an emotion, depends on vividness of perception. Hence the poor and unfortunate of a village can generally depend upon a personal and friendly aid, while those of a city known to the more fortunate indirectly, by the medium of print, may receive only a remote and general interest on the part of those able to assist. Individual cases of suffering of every kind may go unheard of by any who could render aid, and if discovered it will be by the police or by the professional agent of a charitable organization who administers, it may be wisely and kindly, the funds supplied by benefactors who never see the suffering that they alleviate.

CHAPTER V

THE CITY[1]

Nine Characteristics of the City.—The city when considered sociologically instead of politically is seen as a large aggregation of population having a high degree of density and facility of intercommunication. How citified a group becomes does not depend exclusively upon its numbers. Many small groups in this country are organized politically as cities, so also there are not a few communities (in Massachusetts alone there are thirty-eight such communities), having over eight thousand population, that decline so to organize, that are not called cities and that conduct their political affairs by "town meeting," that is, by annual general assembly of all legal voters and by a standing executive commission of "selectmen." Following, in general, the practice of the United States census, we may speak of any incorporated place having 2,500 to 4,000 inhabitants as semiurban, one with 4,000 to 8,000 as a city of the fourth class, one with 8,000 to 25,000 as a city of the third class, one with 25,000 to 100,000 as a city of the second class, and one with 100,000 or more as a city of the first class. Among the characteristics of urban groups the following may be mentioned:

1. The city is the home of industries in which labor and capital, and not land, are the predominant factors.

2. A great many young people who have just completed their schooling or have just reached maturity go from country and village homes to seek employment in cities. Hence the population of cities contains a larger proportion of youth and of persons in the most vigorous years than do other groups. This helps to increase the atmosphere of hope, enterprise, pro-

---

[1] Housing, city planning and municipal conveniences are treated on p. 87 and following.

gressiveness and radicalism, to quicken the pace and intensify the energy and the passion of city life.

3. In these crowded groups there is a comparative lack of domesticity. Home ties have been left behind by many of those who go to live in cities, and new ones are not so likely to be formed as among those who move into villages or rural communities. Multitudes live in boarding-houses, at clubs, or at hotels. Space, indoors and out, immunity from contaminating influences and opportunity for developing home occupations are not easily provided for children. Agriculture makes the home its center. The men are too few and scattered to make boarding-houses profitable, and there is little opportunity for women to find employment except about homes. In the city, women as well as men can readily find other work and betake themselves to boarding-house existence. And even girls living with their parents do not find their interests centering so predominantly in home activities, but all the members of the household may scatter after breakfast to work with other groups in quarters of the city remote from each other.

Neither are the homes so predominant as in country or village as the centers of life's pleasures and values. The theater, the park, the gay and brilliant street, the saloon, the club, contend with the homes of the people for their money and affections. And it is harder and more costly to make the home a place of individuality and beauty when it is a set of pigeon-holes in an apartment house, than when it has its own trees and flowers and yard and is uninvaded by the dirt and noise, not to say the smells, of the crowded city. The city-dweller moves from one tenement to another while the farm-dweller strikes deep roots in a homestead.

4. In the city the artificial predominates over nature. The brooks are in the sewers; the forests are felled; the only trees were set out by hand of man; many a boy never had a stick that had not been through a saw-mill; the factory laborer is mostly engaged in making artificial products more artificial still, and he works not with nature but with a great building full of machinery and an army of his fellowmen.

Man tends to feel himself a match for nature; only sickness, death, and the weather defy his powers. The multitude of men seems the mightiest agency within his observation, and the crowd tends to become his god.

5. The city is a place of tremendous stimulation. Sights, sounds and the activities of thousands bombard the senses and the mind. No other class of realities is so stimulating to man as the activities of his fellowmen. The city street with its show windows and its throngs is a perpetual world's fair.

6. The city is a place of extremes and of the most glaring contrasts in human life. Here are the heaped Andes of plutocratic fortune, and here are the morasses of sodden poverty; here are the men of genius, great preachers, great lawyers, great scientists, great artists, great musicians, great captains of industry; and here are the incompetent who need a boss over them if they are to work and who can hardly hold a job; here are prophets and leaders of philanthropy, benevolence and reform, and here are the professionals of crime. It is often said that the brightest and best trained youths go to the city. It is equally true that the incompetent who cannot work except under a boss, the degenerate and depraved, and those who are ashamed before their neighbors, go to the city. The city seems to draw all extremes, the freaks and sports of nature, and it is the typical who are the breeding strength of a race.

From the overstimulation and the extremes of city life there follows a tendency, but not a necessity, for the common individual to live on the surface of his mind, distracted first by one stimulation and then by another, never reflecting deeply upon anything, and being far less intelligent for all his knowledge of the latest song, the latest style, and the latest newspaper sensation, than the better type of villager or farmer. From the same causes there follows a second closely related tendency for the common person to be overwhelmed by the massiveness of his social environment so that he never acquires a well developed personality of his own, being unable to assert himself against the pressure of that mass of influence and example by which he is surrounded.

These two tendencies, reënforced and played upon by the tremendous facility of superficial communication with great numbers of persons, operate toward giving to urban population a degree of "mobmindedness." Surface notions, catchwords and passing sentiments easily spread; each knows that thousands of others are reading the same headlines and moved by the same ideas and emotions. To-morrow or next week this sensation will have been replaced by another. The mob is fickle, now generous, now mean, now audacious, now panicky, to-day overpraising and to-morrow stoning with epithets the same man or measure. On the other hand the diversities and contrasts of economic station and interest of religion, race, and even of language tend to stem this tide of mob influence.

Furthermore, the extremes and glaring contrasts of the city make the difference between good and evil impressive to the discerning mind while the shamelessness of evil ensnares many. To be sure, familiarity with evil may obscure its character to the careless and youthful, and where the Devil walks at large with his hoofs and horns concealed, as far as he can conceal them, he captures many; yet sturdy souls are brought to clear moral choices. Again the extremes in every direction of human achievement enable the gifted and aspiring to find models, aids, opportunities, and stimulating example and fellowship. Thus in the city the rare man is likely to come to the completest fulfillment of his possibilities. A great university may create similarly favorable conditions for the exceptional individual in a comparatively rural community.

7. In the great city there is so much of a given variety of humanity, and given varieties so tend to aggregate and integrate that we have the phenomenon of "quarters"—the quarter of the rich and of the poor, the Ghetto, Chinatown, little Italy, the red-light district, the wholesale district, and the financial district with its banks and brokers' offices, and others more. This facilitates certain activities, intensifies certain traits, and hinders the spread of common sympathy, understanding, and social assimilation.

8. City life is characterized by an anonymity. In the city

next-door neighbors may not know each other by name. Not one in a thousand that meets John Doe in public places may know him by name, especially if he is out of his own "quarter." Families may reside in the same apartment house and ride up and down in the same elevator but never speak. The offices of successful men practicing the same profession are sometimes opposite each other, across the street, when the men may never even have heard of each other. Thus are lacking the repression of tendencies toward personal vices, as well as the elicitation of personal excellencies and values which depend upon the more personal group life implied by the word "neighborhood."

A highly developed police system may attempt to keep track of individual citizens and record the birth, schooling, occupation, dwelling-place, arrests, sicknesses and death of each. Old-world cities have gone much further than we in gathering such data. Records of such important facts would in the aggregate furnish a mass of statistical data, that would be exceedingly valuable for social guidance. However they are not a substitute for personal acquaintance.

It is to be hoped that a degree of neighborhood organization in the city may some time be achieved by developing recreational, cultural and religious activities in a parochial or district system. It may be that the neighborhood should rank next after the family as a means of developing personal and social values.

9. Urban life is characterized by a heightened dependence of each individual and household upon communal activities. In the country the farmer's own lamp in the house and lantern on the road furnish light; his own well or cistern supplies water; his own care defends him and his family against fire, tramp, and microbes, and his own conveyance transports them. But in the city rapid intramural transportation, light, water, sewerage, garbage disposal, fire and police protection, suppression of contagious diseases, inspection of food and milk, even clean air and a space in which the children may gather and play, all depend upon communal action. The individual is dependent for daily necessaries, conveniences, comfort, and

health upon activities which he alone cannot maintain, and which rest upon the general intelligence, fidelity and public spirit, or in an autocratic community, upon the presence of these qualities in the officials set over him.

Many thousands of deaths might be saved annually in American cities, and a vast number of illnesses prevented, if the best sanitary administration anywhere practised should be made universal. In New York City the death rate has declined in six successive ten-year periods from 27.17 per thousand to 25.27 to 23.26 to 19.17 to 15.51 to 14.13 to 13.0, a total decline of 52 per cent. In Chicago eight successive decades have seen progressive decline in the death rate from 37.06 to 12.8, a total decline of 65 per cent. A decline of 14 per thousand in the death rate of New York City means that 78,680 persons now live through each year who at the old rate would have died. In 1920 for the registration area of the United States the urban death rate was 14.1, the rural death rate 11.9. But conditions are in general better in the registration area than elsewhere, and the death rate for registration cities in the non-registration area was 17.0. A change in a city government may be followed by a fluctuation in the death rate. With intelligent and honest administration an efficient health department can be maintained by a moderate per capita expenditure.

The study of vital statistics throws a faint reflected light upon that which might be revealed if other phases of welfare which depend upon social activity could be statistically measured. In the city not health alone, but also convenience, prosperity, pleasures, and character itself, are largely dependent on communal coöperation. This last statement is so important that it would justify a volume to expand it.[1]

Urbanization.—The word "urbanization" is used to denote, not merely an increase in the absolute numbers living in cities, but increase in the relative proportion of the whole population living in cities. The progress of urbanization has been enor-

---

[1] There are a number of volumes that do expand it. See, for example, F. C. Howe: The Modern City and Its Problems. Scribners, 1915.

mous. In the judgment of some observers it is "the most remarkable social phenomenon" of our time. At the beginning of the last century New York had a population of only 60,489. The site of Chicago was a windswept swamp. Philadelphia, New York, Baltimore, Boston, Charleston, and Salem, these six, were the only cities in this country having as many as 8,000 inhabitants. In 1920 there were 924 such cities. During the nineteenth century "the urban population of the United States multiplied 87-fold, while that of the country as a whole, including the cities, increased only 12-fold." [1] In 1790 only 3.35 per cent of the people of the United States lived in cities. In 1920 this proportion had risen to 43.8. Adopting the new census classification, which counts as urban all incorporated places with a population of 2,500 or over, 51.4 per cent of the population of the United States was urban in 1920, 79.2 per cent of the population of New England, and 74.9 per cent of the population of the Middle Atlantic States. In 1920 the United States had 287 cities of over 25,000 inhabitants, 68 cities of over 100,000, 25 cities of over a quarter of a million, 12 cities of over half a million, 3 cities of over a million, and New York numbered 5,620,048. At that date over 37,770,114 people in the United States were living in cities of 25,000 or more. In the first twenty years of the twentieth century the cities of the first class in this country, that is, those having 100,000 inhabitants or more, grew in aggregate population from 14,208,347 to 27,429,326, and the 219 cities of between 25,000 and 100,000 showed approximately the same percentage of increase. The number living in cities of 25,000 or more had increased more than 90 per cent in these twenty years. There is no reason to doubt that the cities of this country will continue for a time to grow in some such tremendous proportion as hitherto.

The recent growth of cities, and especially the more rapid growth of cities than of rural population, is not a phenomenon peculiar to the United States. "London is probably two thousand years old, and yet four-fifths of its growth was added during the past century. From 1850 to 1890 Berlin grew

---

[1] A. F. Weber: Growth of Cities. Columbia University, 1898, p. 23.

more rapidly than New York. Paris is now five times as large as it was in 1800. Rome has increased 50 per cent. since 1890. St. Petersburg has increased fivefold in a hundred years. Odessa is a thousand years old, but nineteen-twentieths of its population were added during the nineteenth century. Bombay grew from 150,000 to 821,000 from 1800 to 1890. Tokio increased nearly 800,000 during the last twenty years of the century; while Osaka was nearly four times as large in 1903 as 1872, and Cairo has more than doubled since 1850. Thus in Europe, Asia, and Africa, we find that a redistribution of population is taking place. The movement from country to city is a world phenomenon." [1]

The Causes of Increasing Urbanization.—The more rapid growth of urban than of rural population is mainly attributable to two great causes which are of worldwide operation.

1. Recent technic achievements have made it more practicable for people to live together in large numbers, and people being sociable, gregarious, stimulated and pleased by the presence and activities of numerous associates, take advantage of the newly developed practicability of congregating in cities.

Only great achievements in transportation make it possible to gather for city-dwellers daily supplies of fresh food, sweet milk from a radius of half a thousand miles, fresh fish from across the continent, and delicious fruits from alien zones. Only great advancement in sanitary engineering makes it possible for the massed millions of a metropolis to live together upon a tiny area that remains sweet and clean. Until recent times no city could maintain itself without the influx of population from the healthier rural areas, but we now know how to make the city almost as wholesome as the country. We know how, though we have not yet generally accomplished it. If it is still true, as some good authorities think, that the great city cannot maintain itself without the influx of fresh blood from the country, it is not for lack of technic control, but for lack of social control, for lack of the

---

[1] Josiah Strong: The Challenge of the City. New York, 1907, p. 18.

citizenship that would secure adequate administration of our technic resources, and because of sterilizing vices, postponement of marriage, limitation of offspring, and other social causes of an excess of deaths over births.

2. The second cause of the excess of urban over rural growth has lain in the fact that men must live where they can find employment, and the recent developments of manufacture and commerce have occasioned an immense expansion in the demand for workers in the industries that are mostly carried on in cities, but no such expansion in the demand for agricultural workers. In fact, the application of the new machinery to agriculture and of scientific methods to crop production greatly diminishes the number of men that otherwise would be required in agriculture. It has been estimated that four men can now produce the food that formerly required the labor of fourteen. The other ten with their families must go to the city to find employment unless some other change takes place. It is true that scientific methods of production in manufacture also increase the amount of goods produced by each laborer, but there is this difference—the amount of food men can consume is limited, but the quantity of manufactured articles that they can consume is almost limitless, and the variety of manufactured goods that they can use is as little limited. The demand for agricultural products is therefore far less expansive than the demand for manufactured goods. With our improved agriculture we can feed an increasing population, and with our improved manufacture and commerce we can find employment for the added numbers in cities.

For the present and the near future it is useless to try to stem the disproportionate growth of cities. It is possible however to diminish it somewhat, especially in so far as it is due to the fact that since it has become technically possible for them to do so, men prefer to live in cities. The city has improved faster than the country; there is much room for improvement in rural life and good prospect that it will improve. We may believe on this account that in so far as the selection of urban or rural residence is a matter of choice and not of economic necessity, a larger number will prefer the peace, independence, nearness to nature, and personal ties of the country to the excitements of city crowds and sights. Moreover, the attractions of the city and yet more the ignorance of throngs of immigrants who are deposited at our ports and terminals, concerning the opportunities of the country has carried the excess of urbanization somewhat beyond the point of greatest economic advantage. The production of food has increased far less rapidly than the number to be fed, and the high prices of agricultural products and demand for agricultural labor and oversupply of labor in cities call for a slight increase of the proportion of country-dwellers. But most of the disproportionate growth of cities is due to the present character of the demand for labor and in so far as this disproportionate growth is due to the fact that men must go where they can find employment, it is useless to cry out, "Back to the land." A more general demand for a varied table, for fruits, poultry, and vegetables, will call for a larger amount of intensive and diversified agriculture, raising valuable crops on a small acreage. This will somewhat increase the number who find employment on the land.

An important modification of the tendency to concentrate opportunities for employment in the great centers lies in the more and more frequent location of manufacturing industries in villages and small towns. The Interstate Commerce Commission has interfered with the discrimination in freight rates which once almost forced business to gather about the great terminals, and allows it to spread to towns included in districts of equal tariffs. Distribution of power by electricity should have some influence in scattering industrial plants. Labor troubles are less in the smaller localities where workmen and overseers are not separated into different urban quarters, but live as neighbors, attend the same church, and send their children to the same schools. Some of the most intelligent and cultured among the manufacturers prefer to live and to rear their families in the village or small city rather than in the metropolitan center. For a long time, however, these things will only modify, and not end, the present trend toward increasing urbanization.

The disproportionately rapid growth of cities in this country is not so largely due, as many think, to removals from the country regions of our own states. It is true that in some of the older states the descendants of the native stock have, to a considerable extent, moved to town and their places in the country are being taken by immigrants. It must, however, be remembered that a large portion of those who have left the rural districts of our older states have gone not to cities but to Western farms. There is a world movement from country to city, and the movement to our cities is largely from the country districts of the old world. It has been roughly estimated that between 35 and 40 per cent. of the increase in urban population is drawn from the rural districts of our own country; that 35 to 40 per cent. of it is made up of immigrants from other countries, the great majority of whom settle in cities, and that over 20 per cent. of it is due to natural increase, for notwithstanding the diminished domesticity and small families of the descendants of native Americans who live in cities and the somewhat higher death rate in cities, the families of immigrants who live in cities are large enough to bring the increase by excess of births over deaths to about that figure.[1]

What Makes Americans Out of Europeans?—Before turning from the national distribution of population to the study of smaller and more temporary groups we must observe that the character of American social life, and the distinctive traits of the American people have resulted very largely from the fact that the population has been small relatively to the expanse of available territory.

If an English or German farmer of eighty years ago had four sons and the oldest son inherited the ancestral acres, the second was apprenticed to a trade in Sheffield or Erfurt

---

[1] The balance is from incorporation of suburban areas. Compare J. M. Gillette, Constructive Rural Sociology, Sturgis and Walton (Revised), 1916, page 85; also Quarterly Publications of American Statistical Association, Vol. XIV, page 649 and page 671.

but the two youngest emigrated to the United States, then after forty years [1] the two emigrants had probably become quite different men from their two brothers who remained in their native land. The oldest brother used a hoe, scythe, and cart which were heavy and awkward, while the tools of the American farmer were light and nicely balanced, and among them were some implements that the elder brother had never possessed, for example, a gang plow, and a reaper and binder. The emigrant to America who engaged in mechanical industry was required to learn time-saving devices which in some cases fully doubled efficiency as compared with that of men engaged in corresponding labor in the old world. The old-world brothers were custom- and tradition-bound while the Americans were eagerly looking for innovations, and confidently expecting them to be worthy of adoption. The American mechanic, if employed by a great industrial concern, did not, like his European brother mechanic, confine his interest and attention to the faithful discharge of petty details committed to him, but took an interest in the business as a whole in its various processes and its commercial relationships. The two Americans, unlike the elder brothers, did not assume a servile manner and mode of address in the presence of boss, or owner, nor of clergyman or mayor, but looked on all faces with level glances. The American mechanic was far less strictly dependent upon instructions than his old-world brother; instead he did what seemed requisite to make the process of work go forward, if necessary, without instructions, and sometimes in disregard of instructions which had not met the requirements of new conditions. The American not only felt himself equal to the demands of his daily work, though unguided by a foreman's directions, and even equal to comprehending the business as a whole, but also felt himself equal to serving as representative to the legislature, and believed that after a little experience in the state

---

[1] I date this description forty years back because the differences noted were greater then than now, as the peculiarity of American conditions to which "American" traits are due has already considerably diminished.

assembly he would be quite capable to take a hand in making laws for the nation. He had even a greater confidence than this, the faith, namely, that in spite of the blundering and the rascality of men inferior to himself, who had gone into politics, everything would come out well enough in the end and nothing could stay the march of the nation's progress.

These American traits were due to the rich natural resources, the sparseness of population, and the comparative lack of opportunity for special training in America. These are not the only causes peculiarly affecting American society; the social past and inborn traits of our early settlers, and the great diversity of our later immigration have also been powerful and peculiar determinants. But the traits just discussed are practically due to the geographic and technic conditions just named, and to the social lack of opportunities for special training.

Our new agricultural machinery and swift industrial methods have not been due to a mysterious genius for invention but to prairies to be tilled, and cities to be built, with but few hands for the work. There is no reason for thinking that the mechanic who emigrated to America had different inventive talents from that of his brother who remained in Europe. But in this new and sparsely settled land labor must be economized by machinery and technique because it was scarce and if ill paid would desert wage-paid industry and "take up" free land. And where necessity and opportunity pressed on millions, among those millions some were found to respond with the necessary inventions. Moreover, the rapid invention and the swift changes invited or compelled by new and untried but bountiful conditions broke the bonds of custom and tradition and substituted the confident expectation of successful innovation. Furthermore, in the old world special training was largely the privilege of the fortunate, but where nearly all men lacked special training a natural equality was established; and since there were not enough trained men for positions where older civilizations demanded training, untrained but able and forceful men rose from the ranks to every sort of position of command. Since it was the rule that men rose from the ranks to every level, therefore men of all ranks felt themselves potentially and essentially equals. Men who did not feel themselves condemned to eternal drudgery at a petty task, but regarded themselves as candidates for positions of management, lifted their eyes from their benches and understood the plant and the industry, and on occasion acted as their own foremen. And if they had little respect for authorities and much admiration for smartness, it was partly because untrained natural ability and bluffing and blind assumption actually succeeded. And if they succeeded it was because most of the problems to be met were simple and because with few people in a vast rich land with new forests, new mines, new oil wells, new prairie lands, there was elbow-room for enormous blundering, and the blundering brought no disaster so long as "Uncle Sam was rich enough to give us all a farm." And the daring and optimism of the hopeful appropriators of this wealth knew no bounds.

The free land is now almost gone. There are few mines, forests, oil lands, water rights, and railroad prospects to be seized upon. Special privilege is compactly organized. The keenness of competition, where competition is not stifled by such organization, and the complexity and evident difficulty of public problems and the higher level of intelligent public demands call for training as well as ability in positions of command. We have by no means forgotten the lessons of our past nor lost the triumphant audacity of our first easy successes, but if we keep them we must combine the teachings of our past with other lessons.

CHAPTER VI

PERSONAL GROUPS AND CROWDS

Personal Groups.—Not only large groups but also small ones, like the family and the circle of intimates, have in the aggregate an incalculably great and important effect in conditioning the character, activities, and happiness of individuals and of the societies into which individuals unite. Even temporary groups, such as are constantly forming and dissolving in parlors and saloons, on playgrounds and street corners, keep up a constant shifting of causal impacts like the stirring in of materials in a process of chemical manufacture.

In this chapter we are postponing consideration of the effects which depend on the quality of the speech and conduct of those who associate, and are recognizing the causal significance of mere juxtaposition in space and time of a given number of individuals, for in this grouping in space and time we see one of the technic conditions by which the life of society is to be explained.

When a group is so small that the personality and personal experience of each is known to all, we have a personal group, quite in contrast with the impersonality and anonymity of the city and the larger public of state and nation. Personal grouping has two marked effects upon the activities of those so associated. The first is an effect upon the individuality of the members of such a group, which has already been noted in contrasting the effects of the great groups of cities with those of the small groups of villages and rural communities. This individual effect was shown to be itself twofold. (a) It results in powerfully repressing conduct which is disapproved by the personal group. In a great population the individual who is disposed to commit acts of vice and crime can find and join personal groups that show no disapproval and may even applaud his evil deeds, while to the social whole which would disapprove, the individual is lost to view; but if the social whole is a personal group there is no such escape from its contempt and retribution. (b) It results in eliciting those achievements and attainments which the personal group approves, and applauds or demands.

The second effect of groupings small enough to be personal in the sense defined, is not upon the individuality of those associated but upon their social conduct in so far as individuality and social conduct are distinguishable from each other. That such a distinction may properly be drawn is proved by the fact that very frequently the same person exhibits one kind of conduct in a personal group and an opposite kind of conduct in impersonal relations. The social instincts operate most effectively only in personal groups. Thus sympathy can largely be depended upon to restrain evil conduct among those who personally know each other. The swindler is often honest and generous in dealing with personal acquaintances. The plundering, corrupt, and corrupting political boss may be a loyal good fellow to his gang. Society suffers from the vast mischief wrought at long range by good-hearted sinners. Instinctive goodness, precious as it is in personal groups, does not meet the requirements of a developed civilization. Even cruel and murderous savages live in kindly and sociable good nature among themselves. But in groups so large as to be impersonal we cannot depend upon the social instincts to secure conduct which is social, and to repress that which is anti-social, and we must rely either upon control, through law or other agency, or else upon a developed rational righteousness, which mere instinctive good nature does not supply.[1]

It is well to introduce a caution at this point against confusing the effect of the sentiment of blood-kinship, especially of a social tradition of the sacredness of kinship and clannishness, with the effect purely attributable to smallness of num-

---

[1] E. A. Ross: Sin and Society. Houghton Mifflin & Co., 1907; and Social Control, part 1. Macmillan, 1901.

bers; and to avoid confusing the effects of heterogeneity of interests and character with those purely attributable to largeness of numbers. The opportunity to Jekyll and Hyde between the respectable and vicious classes of a community and the difficulties that divergent interests and diversities of station place in the way of communism or of proportioned justice depend partly upon other factors than the mere number of associates. But after making all due allowance for complications, the mere technic fact of difference in the size of groups has the causal significance just attributed to it.

While instinctive cohesion is stronger in small groups, so also is personal friction greater, and the members of a small group much in spatial proximity, must have more in common in order to render their union permanent and strong, than is required to bind together larger populations. It is true that small dense groups are almost sure to have much in common, and if, as in the case of a savage horde in a howling wilderness, no other associates are available, the sociable instinct as well as practical necessity will keep them united; but such a group in the midst of a larger society will very soon either develop a strong and probably many-stranded bond of common sentiment or interest, or else fly apart. A great group can hardly have so multifold a bond of union, and it does not require it in order to endure for a long period.

Custom, which plays so tremendous a rôle in society and social evolution, is largely a matter of personal pressure and influence. Certain customs radiate afar in a democratic country, and an age in which the technique of transportation and communication produce the results that earlier depend on spatial proximity. Yet the characteristic range of custom is narrow, not the great nation, but the province or the canton and the social rank or class. Even when a custom has spread afar it is mainly the personal group that enforces it upon the individual.

The Group of Two.—The group of two takes on a peculiar character, a character which is changed if more associates are added. The addition of only one more impairs or destroys that peculiar character. Says Simmel: "How differently a common lot, an undertaking, an agreement, a shared secret, binds each of two sharers, from the case when even only three participate!"[1] As the difference between solitude and the presence of a companion is immeasurably great, so the next greatest social change is the difference between relation with a single individual and relation with a collectivity. In the former case the subtler communion of moods is possible. In that case, also, for one to leave is to destroy the group, for one to fail the other is to ruin the relationship—to the cost of both—and loyalty and the sense of responsibility are enlisted to the utmost, and the sense of reliance of each upon the other is strong.

The Federal Character of Large Groups.—If we admit to our discussion the heterogeneity which great numbers almost always imply and which they partly cause, then we must observe that great aggregates which have any social unity at all are almost sure to have a federal character; that is, they are a union of smaller groups which are comparatively dissimilar from each other and each of which is integrated by the very traits that differentiate it from other parts of the same great whole. And the bond which unites each part may be comparatively solid while the bond which unites the federal whole may be comparatively tenuous. Such great aggregates contain the possibility of secession, disintegration and recombination. Herein lies a clue to national politics with its shifting of majorities as interest groups change allegiance from one party to another, and with its succession of platform issues, as each party seeks to rally to itself those who, often unconsciously, are united by the different interests to which platforms appeal. Herein also lies the main obstacle to the various social Utopias, which require a subordination not only of individual interests, but also of class interests, to common principles to which the instinctive morality developed by

---

[1] On the present subject compare Georg Simmel: Soziologie, Chapter II. Dunker & Humboldt, Leipzig, 1908; and the same author in the *American Journal of Sociology*, viii, 1.

personal groups is not only inadequate, but to which it is often antagonistic. Progress in morality consists chiefly in the due subordination of particularistic interests to interests affecting larger social circles. The instinctive morality native to personal groups may suffice to establish and maintain the tradition of communism in a little horde of savages or in a Russian mir, but it does not suffice to establish any form of social justice among the great federations of interest groups which are characteristic of civilized society.

Crowds.—The mere assembling of a large number of people at the same time and place creates a situation comparable to the heaping up of materials that invite spontaneous combustion.

1. Crowds are characterized by great facility of communication, with respect to all ideas and emotions that can be communicated by gestures, glances, cries, bodily tensions, brief utterances, but with no corresponding facility of communication with reference to thoughts that would balance or inhibit those superficial feelings and notions. Explanation, argument, reasoning, with their ponderous tread, cannot overtake the swift suggestion that runs through the crowd like the wind over a field of wheat, bending every head. Moreover, even if they could be expressed in the signal code of crowd intercourse, the deepest thoughts are often hidden. Especially among the young, sacred ideals and cherished purposes shrink from such disclosure, even in the presence of a few boon companions, while the vagrant impulse is freely uttered and bandied from tongue to tongue. The fundamental social characteristic of the crowd is great facility of communication with reference to percepts and emotions, without corresponding facility in communication of ideals, and arguments.

2. The suggestion which emanates from the member of the crowd who is demonstrative enough to catch the general eye or ear, caught up by others, is presently reflected by many faces or many voices or many gestures, and so beats upon the consciousness of every member of the crowd from many sources, like echoes in a whispering gallery that converts

the lightest sound into a clamor, or like the sound of the circulating of blood in the ear which the sea shell converts into
the roar of the sea. When one is aware that what he feels
is felt by all those around him, then he feels it ten times
more. A single person has more or less power to make a
second person think the thoughts and feel the impulses which
the first expresses; two who agree have a still greater power
to influence a third, and the response which one or two could
but faintly arouse, a crowd echoing from one to another and
from all to each can multiply. The crowd not only communicates the lighter elements in consciousness with great
facility, but also tremendously emphasizes and intensifies
them.

3. This intensification of certain elements in consciousness tends to create a partial dissociation of personality, a
partial or complete absentmindedness concerning all else. If
certain ideas or feelings entirely absorb the attention then
they determine speech and conduct, even though they are
diametrically opposed to the intentions or principles of conduct which have been adopted in our balanced moments and
which usually govern us, but which for the moment are
forgotten.

4. The crowd is fickle, partly because crowd excitement is exhausting and short-lived, partly because of the
dissociative character of crowd action just explained. That
is, crowd excitement stimulates now one, now another, of the
instincts, acts now upon this idea, now upon that, incongruous
with the former, while the personality as a whole of each
member of the crowd, including those deposits left by past
experience and reflection by which in saner moments he judges
his thoughts and actions and correlates them into a consistent unity, is as if it were not, because the single thought
or sentiment that is intensified by crowd excitement for the
time so nearly absorbs his whole attention. Hence, the crowd
now displays frenzied courage and now is panic-stricken; is
now capable of heroic sacrifice and now of hideous cruelty.
To-day it raises its idol to the skies and to-morrow rolls him
in the gutter, as chance may determine.

5. The individual in the crowd tends to lose his sense of responsibility and to accept the way of the crowd as sufficiently authorized by the numbers who back it, when it may be that the sober judgment, the total personality of no single member of the crowd, approves of the crowd action. Thus the crowd commits crimes abhorrent to the conscience of the individual members of the crowd. Corporations, it is said, can sometimes act as if the whole group had not among its members materials enough to make a single soul. And partly for the same reason the morality of a nation in war and diplomacy lags far behind the morality of individuals.

Not only does increase of the number included in a group diminish both the sense of responsibility of the members of the group toward each other, and still more their sense of responsibility and obligation toward outsiders, but quite obviously it makes it difficult to fix responsibility and inflict penalty or assign rewards for the conduct of the group. The ruthless visiting of the whole penalty upon each individual of the group, which characterizes savage vengeance, is probably the only effective method, but civilized society does not tolerate that. Hence in our world, the famous saying of Napoleon has much truth: "Collective crimes involve nobody."[1]

Where deeds are required, a single person should, if possible, be made responsible; and one functionary can be in a high degree responsible for activities that transcend the power of a single actor, provided he is given the right to select his own coadjutors and to dismiss those who do not satisfy him.

Yet there remains truth in the Scriptural proverb: "In the multitude of counsellors there is safety." There is a difference in this respect between counsel and action, between plans and their execution, and this difference is the ground of our political distinction between executive and legislative functions. The numbers in a legislative assembly should be sufficient to represent adequately the different interests that may be affected by the actions decided upon.

---

[1] Cf. Scipio Sighele: La Foule Criminelle. Felix Alcan, 1901, pages 120 seq.

Councils are of at least two sorts: First, those adapted to decide what end shall be sought in action; these councils must be representative wherever the probability of conflicting interests is involved. Second, those adapted to decide the method by which the desired ends shall be sought; these councils must have adequate knowledge about the conditions of success in the particular field in which the action will apply. The latter is the function of the commission of experts, an agency which with the increase of public intelligence will be increasingly employed. These considerations apply not only to political councils and executives, but, like all that is here said, to homogeneous groups engaged in activity of every sort.

6. The fraction of the personalities of its members which the excitement of the crowd cuts loose must be one that they have in common, as well as one that can be expressed by the signal-code of crowd interstimulation. Hence the instincts and instinctive emotions that are common to all men, such as fear, anger, vengefulness, and pity, or else ideas that are ingrained in the minds of the mass, such as the notions upon which fanaticism plays, or party watchwords, or group ideals, are the subjects of crowd action.

Hence, also, it follows that a homogeneous population is more susceptible to crowd fury and "mobmindedness" than one whose members have different shibboleths and fixed ideas. This is one of the penalties of that form of social strength. In their heterogeneity cities have a safeguard against this peril, a peril to which they are otherwise specially exposed.

Safeguards against Crowd Perils.—In this day when there is so powerful and increasing a tendency to put faith in the multitude, it behooves us to study the sociological characteristics of crowds. We are told that we are witnessing the birth of new dogmas [1] which "will soon have the force of old dogmas; that is to say, the tyrannical sovereign force of being above discussion. The divine right of the masses is about to replace the divine right of kings." We are told that "civilizations as yet have only been created and directed

---

[1] Gustave LeBon: The Crowd. Unwin, 1903, pp. 6, 17, 19.

by a small intellectual aristocracy, never by crowds. Their rule is always tantamount to a barbarous phase." We are assured of "the extreme mental inferiority of crowds, picked assemblies included," and that this assurance, if somewhat too strong and unqualified, is still by no means without reason, the foregoing analysis plainly shows.

Moreover, the characteristics of crowds are not entirely confined to masses in actual physical proximity, but appear wherever there exists among large numbers great facility of communication (such as that now afforded by the press), provided that communication, necessarily or in fact, disseminates superficial, fragmentary, emotional states of mind more readily than sober, balanced, and reasoned views.

But the public in which modern democracy puts its trust is after all not the same as a crowd. In the first place [1] "in the throng the means of expressing feeling are much more effective than the facilities for expressing thought, but in the dispersed group both are confined to the same vehicle—the printed word (and picture)—and so ideas and opinions may run as rapidly through the public as emotions." In the second place different newspapers, each with its own public, secure simultaneous hearing for opposing views, among portions of the population, and it is even possible for the same individual to see both sides of a question in an impartial journal or in the pages of several publications. In the third place, access to the printed page depends upon the assent of the editor or owner, who, if known, is a more or less responsible person. In fact, the rôle of crowds is to-day even less proportionately than formerly being repl-aced by the power of "publics."

However, in spite of all this, it still remains true that our business, our politics and our international relationships are subject to constant peril from booms, panics, fads and crazes, all of which are exhibitions of the mobmindedness that is likely to appear when among great numbers there is great facility of communication, in which there is exhibited a degree of intelligence and deliberate reason far inferior to that of the leaders of society, and often inferior to that of the average

[1] E. A. Ross: Social Psychology. Macmillan, Chaps. IV. and V.

of society, because of the crowd reverberation of ideas and emotions which are easily communicated and the relative failure to communicate the solider elements of thought.

It is a wise law which requires the ownership of a periodical to be plainly indicated upon every issue. It would be well for our people to depend more upon the statement of fact and comment provided by the best class of weeklies and less upon the necessarily hurried and frequently distorted representations of dailies. The custom of presenting opposite views from the pens of able men representative of opposing factions in the same issue of the same journal should grow in response to a public demand. Above all, journalism should be a profession animated by the highest ethical standards and the utmost sense of public responsibility. The press is not merely a private business run for profit. It is the public utility above all other public utilities.

A great protection against mobmindedness on the part of the public is the presence of a few clear maxims or principles, fruit of both experience and reflection, established in the common-sense of the mass. Another is the presence of one or more leaders, thoroughly loyal to the general welfare, highly intelligent, able to make themselves heard, and loved and trusted by the mass. Finally, intelligence and moral principle on the part of the individual citizens is a great safeguard. Yet the intelligence of the individuals who compose a mob does not make the mob intelligent if once they become a mob, but such intelligence is the greatest safeguard against their being converted into a mob.

CHAPTER VII

SOCIAL EFFECTS OF THE AMOUNT, FORMS, AND DISTRIBUTION OF WEALTH

Effects of the Forms of Wealth.—Natural resources have already been considered in the chapter on Geographic Causes and Their Social Effects. Here we are discussing technic conditions and have reference only to those material conditions which are the results of human activity.

The material environment into which we are born is very different from that which nature supplied to primitive man. Where once stood the dark forest trodden by prowling beasts or quaking miasmic bogs traversed by winding streams, homes for the duck and bittern, now the city stands. The forest has been felled, the marsh drained, the landscape obliterated. Paved thoroughfares, towering structures, temples of commerce, of religion, and of art, subways, conduits for streams and sewers and for gas and steam and electric wires, tramways and radiating lines of rails and wires that unite this center with the homes of well nigh all mankind have replaced the isolated wilderness which nature placed here. Nature gave us no great speed of foot or wing. Yet we sweep across lands and seas, surpassing the deer in speed; nature gave us no vast strength, yet we bear burdens as we fly that a hundred elephants could not stir. In the service of every civilized man strength equal to that of many horses is employed through harnessed waterfall, steam, and electricity. We have separated continents and joined the oceans. We have denuded the mountainsides of forests, shrunken the streams, made deserts here, and there by irrigation have made the desert garden. By our houses, our fires, and our woolens we have made the temperate zone, which half the year is

84

frozen, the most habitable of all, so that civilization, starting in the favored spots that were dry of atmosphere and fertile and warm, has tended northward to regions where it could not have originated. We have brought into being new varieties of cereals and fruits and animals to serve our purposes.

The first great American economist and sociologist, who had seen the process of reducing a virgin continent to the uses of man, the making of roads and fields in trackless forests, went so far as to say that "land as we are concerned with it in industrial life, is really an instrument of production which has been formed as such by man, and that its value is due to the labor expended upon it in the past." [1]

So great is the significance of the forms of wealth that the stages of social evolution have most commonly been designated by reference to them, as the stone age, the bronze age, and the iron age, or, as the primitive age of hunting, the pastoral age of domesticated animals, the agricultural age of cultivated crops, and the age of manufacture. Again and again a newly invented commodity has proved to be the condition making possible whole reaches of further social advance. For example, the dish makes possible housekeeping, home-making, saving, thrift, economy, bathing in private, journeys requiring supplies of food and water. The wheel is so essential that we cannot conceive a high advancement of social evolution without it. Gunpowder did away with walled cities, iron-clad soldiers, and the tyranny of brute force, equalized serf and noble in personal combat, and opened the way to the new democracy. As gunpowder democratized the force of arms, the printing-press democratized the power of knowledge, enabled millions to have one organized public mind, so making possible the great modern democracies, and further rendered it possible for great masses of men not only to guide and govern their common life, but also to enter into a common heritage as heirs of the intellectual treasures of the race. Textile machinery gathered men into factories and

---

[1] J. K. Ingram: History of Political Economy, Macmillan, 1901, page 173, writing of the Principles of Social Science by H. C. Carey, who lived 1793-1879 and published the work referred to in 1859.

factory towns, changed the independent hand worker into the factory operative and brought on the Industrial Revolution. It has been said that in a geographic environment that afforded no domesticable beasts of burden, mankind could not rise above barbarism: the steam-engine is a technic condition quite as essential to yet further advance. If the present age were to be distinguished, as each preceding period has been, by a technic symbol, it should be named the age of power machinery.

The practical importance of understanding the social effects of technic conditions is indefinitely increased by the fact that those conditions are subject to human control and can be adapted to secure the results desired.

Transportation.—Of all the forms of wealth there are two upon which social progress appears now to depend more than upon any others: (a) means of transportation and communication and (b) housing. Among the technic means of transportation the steam and electric railway and the steamship are at present supreme. Nearly all industry is dependent upon them. By them the farmer in North Dakota markets his crops which find their way to Minneapolis, Chicago, Liverpool, Odessa. By them the manufacturer assembles his raw materials, machinery, and fuel, and by them he distributes his products.

The material of which a rubber button is made was imported to New York, then transported by train to the button factory. To the button factory other trains brought coal and oil. In constructing the button factory, building materials were used in the assembling of which many railroads participated, and in the production of those materials very many other trains took part and still other trains had brought to the button factory machinery of various kinds. Each machine used in making the buttons was itself made in a factory to which many trains had brought building materials, fuel, raw materials, and machinery. Each bar of brass or steel that was brought to one of the factories in which button-making machinery was made or in which materials for any of the numerous factories involved were made, had a history in which the railroad many times participated. The raw ore of which each of hundreds of bars of brass and steel were made, had been brought to the smelters, to which also fuel and machinery had been brought; pigs of metal had been taken from the smelters to the rolling mills at each of which other sets of machinery had been assembled. So simple a thing as this rubber button could not have been made as it was without the running of hundreds and probably not without thousands of trips by trains of cars. A rise in freight rates all around might easily wipe out the profits of the manufacturer. Discrimination in freight rates between different localities can make one of them a great city, while leaving the other, possessing equal natural resources and equally enterprising inhabitants, to decline. Private convenience is as truly dependent upon public means of transportation as is manufacture. Not one of us could have had the breakfast he had this day without the aid of the railroad. The oranges came from California or Florida, the corn for the muffins was grown in Illinois, the steak was from a steer bred in Texas, fattened in Kansas, and slaughtered in Chicago. The table, dishes, linen, glass, and silverware were assembled from far and near. The common conveniences of every home are rendered possible to us by modern transportation. The railroads are the arteries of economic life; they are to the nation what streets are to the city. It is as indefensible for one to be subject to uncontrolled private ownership as for the other. A modified private ownership may be allowed, but only under distinct provisions for adequate public regulation.

Housing.—Housing provides conditions favorable or unfavorable to health, morality, domestic content, and the dignity and joy of life. The most successful rival to the saloon and vicious resorts and pleasures is the home; but where home is barren, cheerless, repulsive, the glittering street, the "hangout," and the "dive," claim old and young. None can reasonably be expected to spend evenings, holidays or Sundays in such habitations as those which multitudes of Americans call home. Only the presence of the good can exclude the bad; and the home is the natural center of life's values and life's virtues. It should be the most joyous of all places to children and youth, the most satisfying to middle age, and the most peaceful to declining years. But dignity, self-respect, and the normal gladness which is the natural antidote for moral contagion are effectively fostered or as effectually prevented by material surroundings. They do not gain by extravagance and ostentation, but by comfort and comeliness.

In many a tenement sleep in hot summer weather is impossible till late at night, and little children roam the sidewalks or doze in parks. Thousands of rooms are ventilated only from other rooms, from hallways or from narrow airshafts, and are never reached by the rays of the sun. Here the seeds of contagion long survive and the air itself is a poison. Whole families live in two small rooms and there wash, cook, sleep, bathe, and accommodate lodgers and boarders. An investigation made some time ago covering six blocks in the city of Chicago found that 43 per cent. of the inhabitants of that area were living with an average of three persons to the room. A study of 1,600 families comprising 6,800 persons, or 4.5 to the family, found that the average floor space occupied per family was less than 12 by 24 feet. Investigations in several cities indicate that, as a rule, families that live in a single room have a death rate eight times as great as that of the population in general, those in two rooms four times as great and those in three rooms twice as great. The murderous death rate among the poor is not due exclusively to bad housing, but to that and its natural accompaniments.

The tenements that surround the suburban factory or mine are likely to be ugly, unshaded, set in patches of weeds and bare ground, without proper sanitation or conveniences. Laborers in an industrial suburb which is near to a city and connected to it by street cars are likely to live in the city tenements, while on the other hand the well-to-do who are engaged in business in the city reside in the suburbs. This is because with money and taste the suburban home becomes charming within and without but the suburban tenement is likely to be more cheerless than the city slum, because however dismal the lodgings, the brightness and entertainment of

the city street are free. Even in the country there is a housing problem. In the newer parts of America farmers live
mainly in cheap buildings that were erected before the land
was paid for. Our rural communities are mainly new. We
can hardly be said to have developed an acceptable type of
rural architecture, still less the level of taste that is ultimately
to go far toward making country life attractive to the well-
to-do and the country the permanent breeding-ground for
well endowed and well reared citizens. Instead we have half-
forgotten the simple and dignified colonial farm house, which
with widened verandas and modern conveniences and few
expensive moldings should be revived.

In multitudes of cases the wretchedly housed pay enough
to entitle them to better quarters. It is often said that the
worst tenements are the most profitable. Left to unregulated competition the homes of laborers are bound in many
cases to be unfit for human habitation.

There are two remedies for this: First, the spirit of
human brotherhood leads some investors to be content with
a profit of from four to six per cent., when all the rent that
their tenants can afford to pay might be collected from inferior property, representing one-third of the amount which
they have invested in providing fit human habitations. In fact
less benevolent landlords collect nearly equal rentals from
property upon which little actual outlay has been made for
many years, unless for inserting partitions to divide larger
rooms into smaller ones. By holding for rental old rookeries
instead of constructing new sanitary and cheerful tenements
they secure from the amount of their investment double or
triple the rate of return with which a few better-minded
landlords prefer to be content.

It may almost be set down as a general principle that
experiments in social amelioration must be made by private
agencies. After the method has been worked out and its
practicability and usefulness demonstrated by voluntary activity, then state or city may take up the work. This has been
the history of nearly all advance movements in social science
that have ultimately received governmental support. It is

too much to hope that an adequate supply of fit abodes will, in the near future, be supplied by such voluntary activity of real-estate owners. We are therefore forced to the second remedy, government action. Competent and reliable building inspectors enforcing intelligent legislation must condemn hopelessly unsanitary buildings and enforce their improvement or demolition. As much depends on the training, trustworthiness and social spirit of the inspectors as upon the laws; indeed without the proper officials the laws will be of little avail. New buildings must be required to conform to regulations more exacting than can now be enforced upon structures already reared, so that as the old are gradually replaced the standard will be raised. The ordinances of great cities relating to health and decency must create building zones such as are already created by the law relating to fire protection, so that conditions that must inevitably be permitted in the most congested areas will not be introduced in newer and more fortunate districts. Smaller villages and cities must not borrow their standards from cities where real-estate values are exorbitant, but instead must defend the advantages made possible by greater spaciousness.

Another form of government action with reference to the housing problem, or of coöperation between governmental and private action, is the loaning of public funds, for example, to associations that build for rental tenements which meet stipulated requirements, and the rental of which shall not exceed a specified figure, while the dividends of the association are never to exceed a certain percentage.[1] Coöperative societies independent of governmental assistance have in some instances purchased suburban tracts and converted them into "garden cities" of ideal homes, for their members.

Educating the Public on the Subject of Housing.—Voluntary and compulsory improvement of housing conditions may reënforce each other. Housing or city-planning societies founded by those proprietors who take a proper view of their

---

[1] The plan of making government loans has been in operation for years in Great Britain and Germany, and is at present advocated for the city of Washington, D. C.

obligations can affect the character of housing laws and, through their example and the proof which they afford of the practicability of better things, may arouse and enlighten public opinion which brings a useful pressure to bear upon other landlords.

One of the serious abuses that depress the home conditions of the poor, is the tendency of city governments to tolerate inferior paving, grading, walks, lighting and street-cleaning in neighborhoods inhabited by those who can provide least for themselves. This need not be attributed to heartlessness but rather to heedlessness. It is psychologically natural, just as it is natural to beautify the parlor and tolerate ugly things in the garret and cellar, but it is indefensible. An attempt may be made to defend it on the ground that the poor pay little in taxes and that those who pay most should receive most from the public treasury. But a mile of vile tenements may pay more taxes, and owing to the great rental they yield, may be more valuable than a mile of good residences. And the huddled poor pay these taxes every cent, not directly indeed, but the final incidence is upon their shoulders. Moreover, they receive something less than their due share in the proceeds of industry, and the business of government is not to render worse the inequalities of distribution by taking from the poor to give to the rich, but instead it should do something toward restoring the just balance in its application of that portion of the social income which it exacts in taxes. The expediency of equal public education is accepted, and the example of good "municipal housekeeping," of clean and well paved and well lighted streets and alleys, and of proper parks and breathing spaces in those sections inhabited by people having the lowest standard of living, who are mainly immigrants, is an important educational agency. And good sanitation in those sections of the city from which disease is most likely to emanate is demanded by common-sense.

Bad housing conditions are not wholly to be attributed to the negligence or greed of the landlord; there is also fault to be found with the tenant. Many are accustomed to a low standard of living, and if placed in a model tenement would soon make it unsightly, unsanitary, and dilapidated. Good housing requires the active coöperation of the occupants. This can be secured only as a result of education. Some builders of "model tenements" have offered prizes for good housekeeping, for example, the stipulation that every apartment maintained at a given standard should be redecorated throughout at stated intervals. Some have organized their tenants into a society which has officers and regulations, and made proper housekeeping a matter of group interest and group pride. Certain employers have sought to raise the technic standard of their industrial settlement by offering prizes for the best backyard, or the finest flowers, have secured seeds for those who entered the contest, and even provided lectures by a landscape gardener, and this has in some cases had gratifying results. In such undertakings the independence of the laborers should be respected and preserved. It is far better to work through the leading members of their number so that they appoint a committee to secure seeds, raise funds, conduct their competition, and all the rest, rather than to have the employer or his representative do any good thing that the men can be stimulated to do themselves.

Education in home-making is eminently a matter of neighborhood influence. The household that has a good standard can perpetuate it by its own traditions, but to communicate good standards to those who lack them, including masses of immigrants who are for the first time becoming financially able to maintain them, we depend mainly upon the formative power of the neighborhood. Landlords and employers are not the only leaders who have endeavored to develop within the neighborhood a sentiment for better home-making. Mothers' clubs associated with public schools have, in some instances, proved effective in this direction. And the social settlement is a home of cultivated people, who choose to live in a neglected neighborhood in order, by their example, and by the development of various neighborhood activities, to afford suggestion, encouragement, and helpful influences, cal-

culated to foster tastes, ideals and ambitions of the sort that
lead toward the attainment of life's values.

Great as are the existing evils of bad housing, Albert
Shaw declares that with the knowledge and experience now
acquired, it is as possible to wipe out the slum with its deplorable physical and moral effects, as to drain the swamp and
be rid of its miasmas. It would be still less difficult to "head
off the slum" for the benefit of the city-dwellers who soon
will double our present urban population.

City Planning.—With the urban population of this country
doubling in a generation the problem of city planning becomes one of intense practical interest. Shall the evils of
bad housing, inconvenience and ugliness go on doubling, or
shall we "head off the slum"? (1) The location of factory
sites, railroad terminals and sidings, zones of costlier and less
costly dwellings, public parks and playgrounds, public buildings, and lines of intramural transportation, can be made to
follow a well laid plan for the promotion of prosperity, convenience, and social welfare, rather than the temporary private interests of promoters who wish to affect the values of
their holdings of real estate, or the more or less accidental
selections of private industry. (2) Some of the suburban
areas soon to be built up might be purchased by the municipalities, as is done in Germany, provided the municipality
has sufficient public spirit and social intelligence to secure
by democratic methods such good administration as is more
easily obtained under oligarchical control. Then the sale of
land by the municipality would socialize the unearned increment, diminish tax rates, and furnish a fund for municipal
improvements in the newly urbanized additions.

Even if the German method of city planning and municipal
ownership of real estate is not followed, the city plans can
be developed and owners who open suburban tracts can be
compelled to conform to intelligent requirements before their
streets will be accepted or connected with the municipal sewer,
water and lighting system, or even before the deeds they give
will be legally recorded and defended.

The application of city planning to areas already built

up is more costly and necessarily limited in results, yet it is by no means to be neglected. The essential matters are, first, that the designs be expert, both in the practical and the esthetic features, and second, that public opinion be sufficiently enlisted in their realization. Ever so good a blueprint is only the smaller part of the undertaking; the social problem of instructing opinion, arousing sentiment, and organizing activity is the greater factor in the enterprise of improving a village or city.

Municipal Conveniences.—Streets, sewers, waterworks and lighting systems are forms of wealth which affect social welfare so vitally that they are usually provided by public agency. There are numerous other material conveniences which are highly important to the general welfare, and likely to be inadequately supplied or subject to special abuses it left to private enterprise, which have been successfully furnished by municipalities.

Municipal laundries are established in many European cities, and help to relieve the bad housing conditions of the poor. In a tiny cramped tenement the washings are serious obstacles to home life. A public laundry, where for a few cents scientific machinery for washing, drying, and ironing can be used, is a boon to the tenement-dwellers.

Public bathhouses promote health, comfort and decency. Municipal markets promote convenience, economy and health. Municipal slaughterhouses benefit the farmer and the consumer, reduce the needless freighting and storing of cattle and of meats with their cruelties and losses, and prevent the control of prices by a central trust.

Various forms of municipalized wealth are implied in the discharge of municipal services. Some cities provide municipal crematories and even municipal undertaking, which are designed to economize land, promote sanitation, and prevent exploitation; also municipal pawnshops as a cure for the loan-shark evil; also municipal employment agencies; and municipal theaters as part of the educational as well as recreational system. Municipal dance-halls have been successfully introduced in this country.

In order that the municipal corporation may fulfill its possibilities of usefulness it is necessary to divorce municipal affairs from state and party politics. Municipal elections separate from state elections, "citizens tickets," "the short ballot" in city elections, the "commission form of government" and "the municipal business manager" are measures intended to secure this separation, and to concentrate responsibility.

In Germany when a city wants a mayor, it advertises far and wide for the best man obtainable who has passed the necessary state examination for mayors.[1]

Relation of the Distribution of Wealth to Sociological Problems.—The causes that affect the distribution of wealth are studied by economics. But the social effects that flow from the distribution of wealth it is a task of sociology to trace. Moreover, as we shall later see, "economic laws" only partly state the causes of distribution. Not only are "value, wages and interest essentially social phenomena,"[2] but such social realities as custom and law supplement and modify the operation of economic causes in determining the distribution of wealth.

---

[1] The training school for municipal service at Cologne during the winter semester of 1912-13 offered the following courses:

1. Civics	17. Fire Insurance
2. Law	18. Hygiene
3. Administrative Law	19. City Planning
4. Local Ordinances	20. Schools (2 Courses)
5. Civil Processes	21. Ecology and Topography
6. Political Economy	22. Chemical Industries
7. Credit Exchange	23. Iron Machine Industry
8. Taxation	24. Coal and Mining
9. Finance	25. Electro-Technique
10. Statistics	26. Agricultural Management
11. Inspection Methods	27. Rhenish and Westphalian Economic Development
12. Labor Legislation	
13. Labor Unions and Societies	28. Art and History of the Rhine-Land
14. Social Insurance	
15. Welfare Work	29. Paris and Her Romance
16. Social Questions	

[2] J. B. Clark: The Distribution of Wealth. Macmillan, 1899, p. 40

We have seen that material "goods" are only relative or secondary goods, that is, means by which to secure or promote human experiences, which are the only real and ultimate goods. But since material means are employed in the service of every kind of human aim therefore the distribution of wealth affects the distribution of the real goods of life of whatever kind. It does not follow that the more wealth one has the more of good experiences one will have, for good experience does not depend on wealth alone, but on other conditions also, such as health, morality, culture, and friends, in the absence of which wealth may increase without the increase of life's real values. Moreover, the amount of wealth required for the highest realization of life's values is limited, and it may be increased to the point of being a cause of evil and not a means of good. Yet a certain amount of material means is necessary to life itself and to every kind of good in life, so that within the limits suggested the distribution of wealth directly affects the distribution of life's real values among the people composing a society. This we must observe in some detail.

Effects of Distribution of Wealth upon the Health of the People.—Health, or desirable physical experience, which is both an end in itself and also a necessary means of all other good ends, depends upon the possession of a certain moderate amount of wealth.[1]

(1) The poor usually live in sunless, or ill ventilated or overcrowded, or otherwise unsanitary tenements and neighborhoods. (2) They use the less digestible and less nutritious foods, including impure and ill-kept milk for their babies. (3) They often lack waterproof shoes and clothing for wet weather, and warm clothing for cold weather; they suffer excessively from colds. (4) They do not, promptly upon the appearance of need, employ first-rate medical attendance.

---

[1] Here as everywhere else we are using the word wealth not in its popular sense, to denote great possessions, but in its scientific sense to denote any salable material commodities adapted to human uses in whatever amount.

(5) They are employed in monotonous indoor occupations before they have attained their growth. (6) They are deprived of adequate mothering, because mothers can employ no household help, and the mothers themselves are very frequently employed, both immediately before the birth of their children, to the injury of the latter, and afterwards. (7) By reason of impaired vitality, monotonous and uninteresting labor, and dreary abodes, they lack natural cheer, and crave the artificial counterfeit of cheer afforded by stimulants. (8) For the same reasons and because wholesome joys are but little within their reach, while from childhood they live where they are forced to become acquainted with every form of vice, and are continually exposed to the solicitations of commercialized vicious pleasures, they are subject to the ravages of vice, though they are far from having any monopoly of its evils. (9) They frequently labor amid chemical fumes or in air laden with dust or under conditions otherwise exceedingly unsanitary. Nature as a rule does not indefinitely continue a futile protest, and so men can "get used" to conditions so bad that those who labor under such conditions are foredoomed to physical deterioration. (10) They are maimed and killed by accidents in mines, on railroads, and among the machinery of factories. Industrial accidents in this country are said to reach half a million annually, a number exceeding the annual number of casualties in both armies of the great war between North and South, added to those of the Russo-Japanese War. These accidents are largely preventable. As insurance rates and losses by fire can be diminished one half by proper precautions against fire, so also might be diminished the number of industrial accidents, and the poverty and physical and moral ruin of laborers' families consequent upon such accidents.[1]

---

[1] J. T. Arlidge: Diseases of Occupations. Percival, London, 1892.
Thomas Oliver: Diseases of Occupations. Methuen, London, 1908.
Massachusetts State Board of Health Reports—1905, 1907.
A. G. Warner: American Charities. Revised edition, Crowell, 1908, chap. iv.

From such causes as these it results that the death rate among the poor is approximately doubled as compared with that among the well-to-do, and the death rate among the children of the poor under five years of age more than doubled.[1]

The death rate among adult unskilled laborers is about double that among the professional classes. Perhaps worse yet is the fact that the number of days of sickness in proportion to the number of days of health is between fifty and one hundred per cent. greater among the laboring than among the professional class. It is estimated that there are at all times about 3,000,000 persons seriously ill in the United

---

Robert Hunter: Poverty. Macmillan, 1904, chap. iv.

Scott Nearing: Social Adjustment. Macmillan, 1911, chaps. iv and x-xiv.

Irving Fisher: National Vitality—Its Wastes and Conservation. U. S. Govt. Printing Office, 1910.

[1] This subject calls for governmental investigation. Our knowledge is inexact, but is sufficient to show the presence of an unthinkable waste of human life. Emma Duke, in a report on Infant Mortality in Johnstown, Pa., published for the United States Children's Bureau by the Government Printing Office, page 45, makes statements based upon a study of 1,463 babies, of whom 196 died within the first year, to the effect that of all live babies born in wedlock there die within the first year a proportion equal 130.7 to every thousand; of live babies born to fathers showing no evidence of actual poverty the proportion dying in the first year is equal only to 84 per thousand; while of live babies born to fathers earning less than $520 per year, or $10 per week for 52 weeks, the proportion dying within the first year is equal to 255.7 per thousand. See also W. B. Bailey: Modern Social Conditions, Century Co., 1906, pp. 246-254; and John Spargo: The Bitter Cry of the Children. Macmillan, 1906, p. 7 *seq.* He says: "As we ascend the social scale the span of life lengthens and the death rate gradually diminishes, the death rate of the poorest class of workers being three and one-half times [I have said approximately double] as great as that of the well-to-do. Arthur Newsholme (Vital Statistics. Swan Sonnershein, 1899, p. 163, quoted by Irving Fisher: National Vitality. Government Printing Office, 1910, p. 644) states that in Glasgow in 1885 the death rate of occupants of one- and two-room cottages was 27.7, and among occupants of houses having five or more rooms it was 11.2 per thousand. Lavasseur is quoted by Fisher as giving a death rate of 13.4 to 16.2 for the rich quarters of Paris and 31.3

States. At the same time sickness for the poor is even more dreadful than for the well-to-do. Daily great numbers of the sick poor drag themselves to tasks beyond their strength, preventing the chance of recovery. They often labor till within a few days of death, for they have no resources upon which to retire from work, and in the last extremity they and theirs in great numbers become dependent upon charity. And sickness in the tenements is not like sickness in a quiet, sunny, flower-cheered room, with skillful attendance, and with dainties to sustain the strength and to coax the capricious appetite. The enhancing of distress in all the junctures of greatest physical pain that befall men or women or children among the poor is pathetic and horrible.

Charity beds in hospitals, free dispensaries, visiting nurses and fresh air charities for children, relieve this distress only to a degree.

Not only does poverty cause sickness, but sickness causes poverty. The livelihood of the poor is pitifully dependent upon the precarious health of their breadwinners. The occur-

---

for the quarter of Menilmontant. See additional figures in Fisher: *loc. cit.* Richmond Mayo-Smith: Sociology and Statistics, Macmillan, 1896, pp. 164-165; and Amos G. Warner (American Charities, revised, Crowell, 1908, p. 127) reproduce the figures of Dr. Ogle, showing that the death rates for different occupations vary from a rate represented by 100 for clergymen to 308 for street sellers, 331 for Cornish miners, 397 for inn servants. B. S. Rowntree (Poverty, a Study in Town Life, Macmillan, 1902, p. 198 *seq.*) states that in the poorest section of the city of York, England, having a population of 6,803, of whom 69.3 per cent. were in poverty, the death rate was 27.78 per thousand, the death rate of children under five years of age was 13.96 per thousand of total population, and the mortality of children under one year amounted to 247 out of every thousand children born. In the section inhabited by middle-class laborers, having a population of 9,945, in which 37 per cent. of the residents were in poverty, the death rate was 20.71. The death rate among children under five years of age 10.50, and the proportion born who died within the first twelve months 184. In the section inhabited by the best class of laborers the general death rate was 13.49, the death rate of the children under five years 6, and the proportion of children dying within the first twelve months 173, while among the servant-keeping class in York the proportion of infants dying in their first year was 94 per thousand.

rence of sickness or of maiming accident plunges them into economic distress. Loss of health is the most constant of all the causes of extreme poverty and is directly responsible for something like a fifth or a quarter of that miserable poverty which becomes dependent upon charity and which suffers the distress that follows when the customary standard of living, however low, can no longer be maintained. The physical disability of old age is probably the only direct cause of poverty which exceeds it.

Poverty Is Effective in Preventing the Attainment of the Ethical and Cultural Values of Life.—The child whose mother answers the factory whistle at dawn, whose frontyard is the street, whose backyard is the alley, and whose home is two or three crowded rooms up the stairway of a tenement inhabited by honest laborers, striving for decency, and by debauchees and prostitutes, is in a poor way to attain the finest traits or realize the most elevating joys of life. The ambition and energy of such a boy may be the measure of his misconduct and of the swiftness of his destruction. As one has wisely and wittily expressed it, the very same motives that cause the son of more fortunate birth to imitate his father and George Washington cause this child to imitate *his* father and Blinkey Morgan. It has been said that many a boy in America grows up where he has no more chance of developing a normal conscience than he has of learning the Chinese language. At a tender age the child has learned the language of his environment whether it be the refined instrument of culture, or rude, coarse, and unclean, the vehicle of degradation. And by the time he has learned his language he has largely acquired the approvals, admirations, and detestations that will shape his conduct, and has failed to acquire those that in another environment might have shaped it. The swaggering tough, the sybarite, the safe-blower, the ward boss, can be as genuinely admired and ardently emulated as other types of success.

It is by no means the very poor alone nor the denizens of the city slums, but also the moderately poor and the residents of village and hamlet who commonly lack a thorɔughly civilizing environment. Fathers and mothers are likely to be too busy and hard worked; they themselves have not learned from their own parents the ideals of child-rearing and of home atmosphere which are the truest tests of civilization; their fireside is not attractive enough to compete successfully with the street, the livery stable, the rendezvous. Boys and girls who are properly provided with juvenile literature, and who live in an atmosphere of courtesy and of home pleasures, where work and conversation alike objectify generous ideals, these have a heritage of moral and cultural health, while many grow up in an atmosphere of moral and cultural miasma. The poor man has not money enough to properly equip and maintain home life, but hands on to his offspring the lack of culture and the low ethical standards which the poverty of his own parents bequeathed to him.

This must not be taken to mean that every poor man is coarse or bad. On the contrary, personal excellence is often maintained under unfavorable conditions. But it does mean that the moral and cultural handicap of poverty is heavy and thousands cannot bear up against it. The poor cannot freely choose their home surroundings. It is true that vice often sinks into poverty, and from this it results that those who are poor for other causes are compelled to associate with those made poor by vice; and the children of the poor, whatever the cause of the poverty of their parents, are early familiarized with moral degradation.

It may be said that the school must furnish the elements of personal education. But the school cannot replace the home, nor adequately offset demoralizing influences surrounding the hours of play. Moreover the children of the very poor go to school but too little.

According to the last report of the Commissioner of Education [1] the number of pupils receiving education in the first eight grades during the year 1914 was 19,057,948, and the number in the second eight grades, that is, in the high schools, colleges and professional schools during the same year was only 1,718,876. In 1910, 20,000 permits to quit school for labor

---

[1] Report of the U. S. Commissioner of Education for 1914, pp. 2-8.

were issued to children in Chicago. Of these 2,918 are known to have joined the ranks of labor on the first day after attaining the legal age of fourteen, and 2,413 had not reached the fifth grade. Labor laws that prescribe any educational standard to be met by children before they can leave school for work generally require only that they be able to read simple printed matter, and write, though incorrectly, simple sentences. A large proportion of the very poor do not go beyond the fourth or fifth grade. This is not necessarily due to lack of natural ability. It is largely due to lack of the backing which the family, by its influence, can give to the schools and which many poor families do give. And it is largely due to the fact that the children of the very poor are frequently in no physical condition to profit fully by the meager schooling received. Hundreds of them go to school either with no breakfast, or a breakfast of baker's bread and coffee. For lack of proper medical attention, eyes, teeth, hearing and breathing apparatus are often so defective as to handicap their work.

In one school in Chicago 55 per cent. of the pupils in the fifth grade are already working and earn an average weekly wage of $1.18; 35 per cent. of those in the fourth grade are working, and earn an average weekly wage of 85 cents. Fifteen per cent. of those in the second grade are working for an average weekly wage of 43 cents, and 12 per cent. of those in the first grade are devoting a portion of their leisure to industry from which they derive an average weekly income of 36 cents. Besides spending the regular twenty-five hours a week in school one of those boys works over fifty hours a week, four over forty hours a week, seven over thirty hours a week, and eighteen over twenty hours a week.[1] These children are frequently employed in demoralizing as well as health-destroying occupations. The street trades are a curse of the childhood of the poor. Little girls peddle gum on the streets until midnight. Boys serving as messengers are sometimes sent to the most abhorrent resorts of vice and become

---

[1] Chicago Child Welfare Exhibit of 1911.

familiarized with the post-graduate degrees of debauchery and degradation.

The poor are obliged largely to forego life's normal pleasures. These cannot be provided by the average laborer who attempts to support a family upon his wages. The pleasures accessible and attractive to the uneducated laborer, young or old, are not only meager but likely to be demoralizing. There are no statistics that reveal the death rate of the souls of the poor, but there is no doubt that thousands upon thousands go down in blight and ruin who in another environment would have come to blossoming and worth. Not that any human soul is without some spark of nobleness, not that the most disinherited life is without gleams of cheer, not but that there can be found many who amid adverse conditions have come in contact with some ennobling influence or responded with native inspiration to life's hard demands, but that among the tens of thousands who become debased or who live lives of wretchedness and misery, among the sixty or a hundred thousand tramps who roam our land, and the women and children they have deserted, and among the three hundred thousand more or less who are in prisons, jails, and lockups in the United States, among the four million who it is estimated apply for some form of charity each year, many of whom are so thriftless, devitalized, broken in body, and unformed in character that we are tempted to brand them "the unworthy poor," and among that multitude who frequent the tawdry and dirty haunts of vice or lie in crowded, uncheered sickrooms, there are a vast number, who, so far as hereditary capacity is concerned, are just as good as we. Neither is it true at the other extreme that all the rich are cultured and virtuous.

Actual Distribution of Wealth in the United States.—No one knows exactly how the wealth of any nation is distributed. On this subject only estimates are available and they must be regarded with great caution. One of the most intelligent estimates that has been made for the United States was published by Dr. Charles B. Spahr in 1896. According to that estimate "seven-eighths of the families hold but one-eighth of the national wealth. while one per cent. of the families hold more than the remaining ninety-nine." [1] And while "the general distribution of incomes in the United States is wider and better than in most of the countries of western Europe . . . one-eighth of the families in America receive more than half of the aggregate income, and the richest one per cent. receives a larger income than the poorest fifty per cent. In fact, this small class of wealthy property owners receives from property alone as large an income as half our people receive from property and labor." [2] Mulhall in England watched for a series of years the transfer of estates through probating of wills, and concluded that four-fifths of the property of England was held by one-sixty-seventh of the adult population of England. The most recent estimate on this subject is that of Dr. W. I. King. He states [3] that 65 per cent. of the people of the United States are poor, in the sense that they possess no property beyond a little furniture, clothing and personal effects; fifteen per cent. belong to the lower middle class having a little property, perhaps on the average a thousand dollars' worth; eighteen per cent. compose the upper middle class, or well-to-do, having property worth from $2,000 to $40,000; while two per cent. are rich. These two per cent. own about three-fifths of the property.

It appears that in 1900 there was no marked difference in the distribution of wealth in France, Prussia, Massachusetts and Wisconsin. But in England, under the law of primogeniture, the concentration of wealth is exaggerated. This, Dr. King regards as an illustration of the fact that differences in laws result in differences in the distribution of wealth, and that "a modification of the laws of a nation might bring into being a division of riches of a radically different nature." [4]

The distribution of income is always less unequal than the distribution of accumulated wealth. The laborer may be

---

[1] C. B. Spahr: The Present Distribution of Wealth in the United States. Crowell & Co., 1896, p. 69.

[2] Ibid., p. 129.

[3] The Wealth and Income of the People of the United States, Macmillan, 1915, pp. 78 to 82.

[4] Ibid., p. 92.

without property, but his wages are an income. The most recent estimate on this subject was published in 1921 by the National Bureau of Economic Research. This report finds the inequalities less extreme, and states that the effect of the war "was to diminish, at least temporarily, the inequalities in the distribution of wealth." [1] According to this report, as nearly as can be ascertained, about one in 5,000 *of those who receive incomes* belong to the class of the extremely rich, who receive from $100,000 to over $5,000,000 each per year, about eight in 5,000 receive $25,000 or more per year, about 34 in 5,000 receive $10,000 or more per year, and somewhat over 50 in 5,000 (or 1 per cent) of the income receivers have $8,000 or more [2] per year, the most prosperous one per cent having nearly 14 per cent of the national income,[3] while 86 per cent of those gainfully employed receive less than 2,000 per year,[4] and the average earnings of all employees, including hand and clerical workers and salaried officials, in 1913 was $723 and in 1918 was $1,078. However, in purchasing power this was equal to only $682 in 1913, so that "real" wages and salaries had somewhat declined since the war began.[5]

It is difficult to comprehend the rate at which fortunes have been acquired by those who occupy the central positions of control in American industry. The pyramid of Cheops is popularly said to have been built about twenty-five hundred years before Christ. If a man had earned ten thousand dollars a year from that time until the birth of Christ, and continued to do so every year of the briefer period that has elapsed since the beginning of the Christian era, and had saved every cent of it, his earnings, without interest, would now amount to forty-five millions of dollars. Andrew Carnegie is said to have retired with three hundred and seventy-five millions, or more than eight times that amount. According to statements brought out

---

[1] Income in the United States by the Staff of the National Bureau of Economic Research, Harcourt, Brace & Co., p. 146.

[2] Ibid., p. 135.

[3] Ibid., p. 147.

[4] Ibid., p. 146.

[5] Ibid., pp. 98-103.

in the course of a legal trial, the fortune of Mr. Rockefeller amounted to $900,000,000 in 1912. He began his career a poor man but acquired a large measure of control over a great industry and a great natural resource. To accumulate such a sum at the rate of $10,000 a year would require 90,000 years or 20 times the ages that have elapsed since 2500 B. C. In 1924, ten persons in the United States reported for taxation annual incomes the smallest of which was equal to the accumulations of four centuries at $10,000 a year. On the other hand, because of poverty, hundreds of thousands of families are suffering in physical health and stamina, largely missing life's normal joys, bearing an undue proportion of suffering in every form, and unable properly to rear their children. Their poverty is especially deplorable at two periods, viz., while the children are too small to contribute much to the family income, and when the mother can go to labor only at the greatest cost to herself and to them; and again when the children have grown to have families of their own to support, and the parents must face old age with early diminished earning power and great difficulty in securing employment. There is one period when the unskilled laborer is comparatively flush with money, namely, when he has just come into his full earning power and no longer contributes to the support of his father's family, and as yet has no children of his own, the very time when he is in greatest danger of sowing wild oats.

The statistics of wages of American laborers in a measure prepare us to realize not only that a very considerable proportion of American families normally and in good times live in poverty too great to permit full physical and moral efficiency, but also that in bad times, in sickness and old age and in the cases of physical or moral inefficiency, a multitude become dependent upon charity. Charles Booth, in the first great scientific investigation of its kind, found that 30.7 per cent of the people of London were in poverty too great to allow the maintenance of full physical efficiency. Rowntree found that the proportion similarly poor in the city of York was 27.84. Jacob Riis estimated that during the eight years previous to 1890 the actual recipients of charity in New York

City had equaled in number about one-third of the population of that city. Robert Hunter, whose estimate has been
somewhat exclaimed against but not invalidated, believes that
18 or 19 per cent of the people of the whole rich state of
New York were in distress at the time of his study. A map
of a part of New York City prepared for the Tenement House
Commission in 1900 shows a dot wherever, during the five
years preceding the preparation of the map, five families from
one house have applied for charity, either to the Charity
Organization Society or the United Hebrew Charities. "There
was hardly one tenement house in the entire city that did not
contain a number of these dots, and many contained as many
as fifteen of them," representing fifteen times five, or seventy-
five, families. As a result of his investigations and his experience as settlement worker and charity worker, Robert
Hunter would not be surprised if the number in poverty [1]
in our large cities and industrial centers rarely fell below
25 per cent of all the people. For our country at large both
urban and rural, the estimate indicated in the popular phrase
"the submerged tenth" is probably no exaggeration; and when
we consider how many millions are included in a tenth of
the population of our nation, and how many individual cases
of misery, blight, and ruin are included in a million of the
economically submerged we have a sufficient contrast with
the aggregated millions of our rich.[2]

---

[1] Mr. Hunter explains that by the number in poverty he means the
number of those who "are not able to obtain those necessaries which
will permit them to maintain a state of physical efficiency." (Page 5.)
They subsist, but their efficiency is gradually impaired by lack of such
things as sanitary abodes, adequate food, and suitable clothing.

[2] A Charity organization was formed in a university community of
about 20,000 in Illinois. It was an unusually prosperous and wealthy
community, having little manufacture, almost no immigrant population, and, as some said, no poverty. In the last twelve months this
organization, after careful investigation of each case, ministered to 354
resident families said to include 1,272 persons, besides receiving applications from 1,078 transients. The well-to-do do not frequent the un-
paved streets and the outskirts of our towns, and when they pass that
way they little realize the struggle that goes on when the breadwinner
falls by the way or a man earning $1.50 per day has five or six children
and a sick wife.

The extreme poverty of the submerged tenth is usually due, at least in part, to unavoidable or avoidable personal causes, like sickness, old age, large families, or vice, shiftlessness and incompetence. But the comparative poverty of the mass of normal laborers is due largely to industrial and social conditions. Thousands of normal laborers and their families live always too anxiously near the line of submergence. And although so much of the cost, waste, suffering, vice and crime that afflict society are due to the presence of a submerged tenth, yet their elevation might not add so much to the net worth of human life as would the securing of social justice to the far larger number who are not submerged, but who lack the means to fulfil their possibilities of happiness, service and personal development, and who by sickness or other misfortune may at any moment be forced below the line of economic independence.

CHAPTER VIII

THE INADEQUACY OF ECONOMIC LAW TO EXPLAIN OR CONTROL JUSTLY THE DISTRIBUTION OF WEALTH AND THE NECESSITY OF SOCIAL CONTROL

Why Do We Have So Much Poverty in Our Rich Land?— Our wealth is increasing as wealth has increased at no other time and place in the history of the world. A distinguished economist declares, nevertheless, that only one-fourth of our population is benefited by this vast increase.[1] Adam Smith, and other economists, have taught that the rate of wages depends upon "dispute," "contract," "custom," in one phrase, social adjustment. On the other hand, in the theory that "labor is the residual claimant," advanced by Francis A. Walker, but set aside by more recent economists, and in the theory of "specific productivity" now generally held, an effort has been made to show that economic law does determine wages as completely as rent or interest.[2] To the question, why does not the increase of wealth correspondingly diminish poverty, we reply: because there is nothing in the operation of economic laws to secure a just, reasonable, or tolerable distribution of wealth.

To begin with, labor is not a commodity; it is a man working. We refer to labor as a commodity only by a figure of speech. It is a convenient figure of speech to which we are so accustomed that we tend to think of labor as being literally a commodity, which it is far from being. A saleable commodity is a material thing that can be alienated from its possessor and become the property of another. Not so work;

---

[1] This is a serious exaggeration. Even factory workers and other semi-skilled and unskilled laborers have benefited somewhat, though less than justly, by our increase in wealth.

[2] The latter theory is referred to on pages 122 *seq.*

that cannot be separated from the worker. When a commodity, say a pig of iron, has been sold, it makes no difference to its former owner how or where it is used; it may be used in making sewer-pipe or watch-springs without injury or advantage to the man who sold it. Not so labor; it makes a difference to the laborer whether he is employed in a sewer or not. As labor is the laborer at work, the laborer is directly interested in the conditions of his work. But there is nothing in economic laws or forces to insure to him tolerable conditions of labor; that depends upon social adjustments through public opinion, custom, morality, and law.

Labor Bought at Forced Sale.—And now as to the price of his labor. Labor resembles a commodity in only one respect, namely, that it commands a price. But the price, or more accurately the wage, of labor is not fixed by the operation of the causes that fix normal prices for commodities. The first peculiarity of labor, in this respect, is one that it shares with some commodities, namely, those that must be disposed of at forced sale. In the case of such a commodity there is not time for the economic laws to operate and secure a "normal price." A man obliged to sell his house within a week would very often fail to find a buyer who would give its real value, and he would be obliged to sell to someone who took it just because it could be had for less than its worth. Half an hour before the stores close on Saturday night strawberries often sell for half or a third of their real value, because they must be sold at once or be lost entirely. Similarly each day's labor must be sold that very day, for when night falls it is gone forever; its owner cannot store it in bins, as the farmer stores his grain, to wait for the price. Even if the laborer at the cost of sacrificing his labor should refuse to work till a fair price was offered, hoping to gain in the remaining days enough to make up for the loss of waiting, then as a rule he and those dependent on him would be plunged in suffering by the sacrifice. Moreover, it would prove an unavailing sacrifice, for in practice there would almost always be another laborer ready to take the place at the price which the first had declined, unless indeed a general agreement among laborers had been reached by which all declined it together, and that would be a strike. That last expedient might succeed. Labor, as before remarked, resembles a commodity in just one thing, that it is paid for; the employer must have it to continue industry. The strike takes advantage of this one point of analogy between labor and a commodity, but only in a more or less abnormal way, namely, by creating a monopoly, for a strike is the demand of a monopoly. To the employer labor is like a commodity for which he has an economic demand, and he objects if he must buy it at a monopoly price. To the laborer it is not a commodity; it is his participation in industry, the basis of a claim in equity with the other participants, the employer and the investor, to a share in the proceeds of industry. This difference in point of view is the ground of endless misunderstanding.

Labor Not Protected by Cost of Production.—The second peculiarity of labor which excludes it from the operation of the economic laws that fix normal prices for commodities is that its production is not similarly regulated by cost. It is the cost of production that prevents the prices of commodities from falling permanently below the normal level. If for a time the price offered for any commodity is too low to pay for producing it, then its production is curtailed or the product is withheld from market, equally limiting supply until the very scarcity, if nothing else, restores the price. If the demand permanently declines, as it may in the case of a puzzle or fashion, so that the price does not rise again to a point covering the cost of production, then production of that commodity ceases permanently. A normal price level for commodities, especially staple commodities, is thus maintained because the supply offered for sale falls off and scarcity sets in if prices go below the cost of production. For labor there is no such thing as a normal price fixed by this law, since in the case of labor the law does not operate, for the supply of labor offered for sale is not reduced when prices fall. Labor cannot be stored to wait for a better price, nor can its production be suddenly curtailed; the supply is renewed with each returning day, and there is nothing that its "seller" could do to limit the production but to commit suicide. In fact when the demand for labor is poor, the supply, seeking a market instead of diminishing, as would be the case with any commodity, actually increases. The laborers discharged at such a time become applicants for jobs and thus the amount of labor put on the market is not less but greater, when the demand for labor is least.

It is true that when times are slack some laborers emigrate, some men retire to their little farms, and some women to their homes and when such adjustments have done all they can, the birth rate may decrease, and so the supply of labor diminish. But that is too remote a result to secure for us a normal rate of wages, nor will it ultimately secure it, for if suffering continues long enough the standard of living declines. It is those with an exacting and hopeful standard of living who rationally limit the number of their offspring and those who are miserable still propagate, not at the most rapid rate, but at a rate quite sufficient to maintain their numbers and keep up the supply of labor. It is therefore the quality and not the quantity of labor that will fall off. And while by that means skilled labor might ultimately become scarce and expensive, the number of applicants for the worst paid jobs, and the mass of misery at the bottom of society would be increased if the unfolding of events were left to the operation of economic laws alone. We are in fact at present experiencing this result. We are having more of the undervitalized, nerveless, stimulant-craving, untrained, incompetent laborers and a smaller proportion of capable and efficient ones than we should have reason to expect if the laborers could maintain a proper standard of living.[1]

The Differential.—Labor as we have seen is not a commodity, nor is any normal price for labor fixed by economic laws. Labor is instead man's exertion, and the basis of a

---

[1] America may have more than her share of such incompetents, in part because although a high standard of living is "the fulcrum of progress," yet the constant spectacle of an inaccessible "pleasure economy" drives some away from the patient grind to dissipation and the hobo's life.

claim to share with managers and investors in the proceeds of industry upon some equitable basis. The investor is sure of his return if the industry prospers and no fraud is perpetrated upon him. Some people think that interest is wrong and call it usury, but if there were no interest on capital a large part of it would be withdrawn and consumed.[1] It is necessary not only to induce owners to refrain from withdrawing and consuming their capital, but also to draw into productive investment enough new capital to cover losses and to provide for the extension of business, and the employment of the added population. The larger the amount of well-invested capital the more openings for labor and the greater the productivity of labor. The withdrawal of capital would paralyze industry. Industry cannot go on without the use of land and capital, and their owners can command a return for their use at a normal rate, which is approximately fixed by economic causes, as the studies of the economist in rent and interest have shown. Hence in cutting the cake of proceeds from an industry, off comes inevitably a pretty definite slice for the investor. There is also a necessary return to the manager without which adequate ability, application, and care could not be secured for the discharge

[1] According to Professor J. B. Clark, the existing stock of capital, unless lost by misfortune or bad management, or withdrawn and consumed, renews itself perpetually out of its own earnings. Its earnings include the renewal fund plus interest. The investor, unless he withdraws his capital, never gets it back for purposes of consumption, but gets only a permanent flow of interest. "To everyone who has a larger income than is necessary to sustain life, is presented the option of taking, as part of his income, something that will give pleasure for a time and then utterly perish or, on the other hand, of taking something that will never in itself give any pleasure, but that to the end of time will create, every year, a quantity of other things that will do so." (Clark: The Distribution of Wealth, p. 135.) But capital "produces" only when associated with labor, and its permanence depends on good management and social order. If, as Professor Clark believes, capital in general renews itself perpetually, then the Socialists have ground for the claim that if once society, and not individuals, owned the great bodies of capital, interest might become obsolete, re-investment of surplus earnings, aided by the enforced "abstinence" of taxation being depended on for extension of capital.

of his important task, and as sufficient training, steadiness of effort, and ability are more or less exceptional, their scarcity may secure for him a just reward, though the paid manager who is not an owner depends largely upon the necessity of continuity in the business, his knowledge of the particular industry and its secrets, personal relationship with owners,

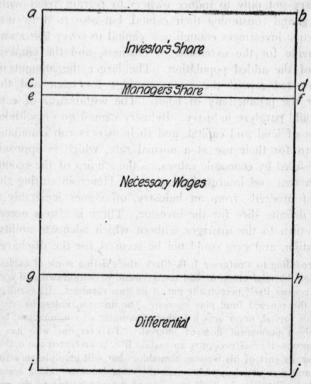

and custom, to secure for him a liberal share in the proceeds. There is also a necessary cost of labor, for without some wage labor is not to be had, though there is no guarantee that necessary wages will constitute a normal or equitable return for the laborer's participation in production. Now after cutting off from the cake that was to be sliced the various portions demanded by economic requirements, namely, the necessary share of investors and the necessary cost of management and necessary wages, in the case of the most prosperous industries a differential will remain.

This differential is the bone of contention. Who is to be its possessor? It may be consumed by inefficient methods or by wasteful competition. But when those establishments that produce at a disadvantage have been mostly eliminated by competition, and competition itself has been limited by consolidation of industry, most business carried on in a prosperous country, may show in all good years a differential.[1] And if the economists are correct in teaching that the normal return for land and capital invested in the industry is determined by economic causes, then the differential properly remains[2] to be divided among the people who coöperate in producing the output: that is, between managers and laborers.

No Share in Primary Distribution.—Here the laborer is at a tremendous disadvantage because the whole of the differential goes first into the hands of the management, and the laborers have the problem of getting their share of it out of his hands.[3] Herein lies the third obstacle to the just determination of wages. When the output of an industry, say a shoe factory, is sold it is all sold by the management. No laborer can sell a single shoe. The entire returns of all the country's industries are thus first distributed among the managers of the industries. This is called primary distribution. Then the managers pay what they must to the investors and laborers who have coöperated with them. This is called secondary distribution. We have seen that the normal return to labor is not secured by the operation of economic causes, for the laborer is not the seller or renter or lender of a com-

---

[1] On the necessity and justice of retention by employers, in good years, of an offset for the losses of bad years, see page 126.

[2] Economists do not teach that interest, rent, wages and profits are each determined by economic laws, independently of each other, for changes in one of them may affect the amounts of all the others. But after all these effects have worked themselves out, the "differential" remains as above stated.

[3] On the proposition that the differential is created by managers and remains inevitably in their possession, as a quasi-rent upon managerial ability, see pages 122, 127, 128, and especially 137.

modity for which a normal price is automatically maintained. Instead he is a man coöperating with other men, each of whom bases upon the fact of his coöperation a claim in equity to a share in the common product. A portion of the laborer's claim must be paid him as "necessary wages," but the balance of it is adjudicated, not by a disinterested outsider, but by one of the claimants who has the whole proceeds of the industry in his possession.

Organization.—Additional reason why equity can be defeated and enormous concentration of wealth take place, lies in the extent to which industrial and financial organization has been carried. A high degree of organization is essential to efficiency. But wherever there is centralized power there is peril and if the power is great the social control must be adequate. As organization proceeds and thousands are concentrated in one industry and different industries unite into systems it becomes possible and in the present condition of custom, morality, and law, it is natural for the men who stand at the nucleus of the system to take toll upon the labor of an army of their fellows. This occurs not only in the relation between laborer and employer but also at the financial end. In great industries the entrepreneurs often contribute little to the technical management which secures productivity, and devote themselves largely to financiering. Great portions of the social income are deducted in the form of profit on stock-gambling and on the sale of watered stock, and "bonuses" for promotion and underwriting. Corrupt dealing in worthless mining and industrial stocks and in fraudulent land speculations also abstract vast sums from the incomes of the common people. Of the abuses of financiering more can best be said later in connection with the discussion of remedies.

Finally, as consumers we are all exploited enormously, and that in part by organization and in part by the disorganization of wasteful competition in merchandizing.

The aspects of the present situation which have now been described are the main causes of the inequity in the distribution of wealth. The interests of managers and laborers are identical in this, that both desire the differential dividend to be as large as possible. Their interests are opposite when it comes to dividing it. It would be foolish to minimize the work of the manager. The effectiveness of all the labor employed depends upon the efficiency of management, and the necessary cost of management, high as it may be, must be paid out of the proceeds of industry. Likewise the necessary inducement in the form of rent, interest, or dividends, must be held out to the investors of the indispensable capital and land.

But the differential still remaining whenever there is such a differential will not be justly divided by force of economic causes. Its division is not an economic problem but a social one, for it depends upon public opinion which may be misguided and supine, custom which may be all wrong, morality which may be only embryonic at any given point, contract and law which obey custom and public opinion.

Though Present Distribution Is Indefensible, Equality of Incomes Is Neither Expedient, Just, nor Feasible.—In forming our ideal of what constitutes a just and proper distribution of wealth we must be careful to admit that there are great differences in the powers of men in the direction of any given kind of achievement; that it is important to have men of great organizing power in the positions of business control; and that such men may properly receive incomes far greater than those of the average laborer. They should receive as much as men of equal powers and equally arduous labors in any other walk of life. But when they receive ten or a hundred times as much as their equals in other walks of life, justice has no sanction for such inequality. The differences of income are carried to an absurd extreme when the business organizer is given too much power in deciding the amount of his own share, and when he is led to measure his success by the amount of the social income which he appropriates to himself. The stupendous difference in the rewards of labor is not proportioned to the differences between the qualities of men, great as these doubtless sometimes are. And as to the latter it would be absurd to think that the man who acquires wealth is always superior to those who do not acquire it. Abilities that can be equaled by one man in every twenty normal men, coupled with intense concentration upon the desire for wealth, may suffice for the acquisition of vast possessions. Concentration upon a purpose is one evidence of ability, but it is also true that concentration upon the pursuit of wealth may evince poverty of nature or of breeding. Many of the ablest men devote themselves to pursuits in which there is little or no opportunity to acquire great wealth. No one is likely to deny that in many instances the comparatively poor man has far greater ability of intellect, will, and sensibility than his rich fellow-citizen. And among laborers there appear to be some who surpass in these respects some of those who acquire great fortunes. The books drawn from public library stations in the poorer quarters of cities, the conversation, and even the writings of laborers, the devotion and the determination shown in pursuit of fixed aims under baffling conditions that try the courage and the will more severely than any progress along the pathway of success, demonstrate the frequency of high-class normality in the human breed in spite of poverty.

Caste is mainly a social illusion fostered by the differences of appearance permitted by wealth, including the differences of speech, manner, and culture due to differences of nurture. Since the "wish is father to the thought," and "belief the offspring of desire," the fortunate often believe in the native superiority of their class. This class creed has in it just enough of truth to make it a dangerous falsehood. It is especially groundless in this country where most of the poor have not enjoyed the opportunities of a free country long enough to prove their capacity, and where we have so often seen the children of European peasants rise to places of wealth and influence.

What of the Rank and File?—The way of escape from injustice is not in exhorting the laborer to rise from his class. If all men were capable of becoming captains of industry not all men could be such. The army of industry must have an enormous rank and file. All but a small minority must by the necessity of the case march all their lives in the ranks.

Democracy is a failure unless it can make the values of life accessible to the normal men in the ranks, instead of concentrating the proceeds of industry in the possession of a few. From each pair of industrious hands there flows a little rill of plenty to water their owner's garden, but these rills flow through the race-way of primary distribution, and the gardens of the many are left arid while these rills are gathered into Amazons to inundate the few. The captain of an industry is only a man "for a' that," and the laborer is also a man. And even if the manager be one man in a thousand, yet is he not a thousand times a man. If he receives a thousand times as much as certain other normal men engaged in regular work in the same industry, it is because equity is defeated through the power given the employer by his position in the economic organization.

Do We Need Plutocrats?—It is sometimes objected that unless we have a very rich class, life will be robbed of beauty, and great benefactions to education and philanthropy will be impossible. But the palaces of art can better be provided by public funds and devoted to general use. And education and social progress can be systematically promoted by public agencies, rather than by the donations of the rich. They should be enjoyed as of right by a self-respecting citizenship, and not accepted as charity. And sweet charity should issue in the gifts gathered from the prosperous many rather than from the largess of the overwealthy. The truth of all this may be recognized without forgetting that for the present many useful purposes depend for realization upon the liberal coöperation of the rich, and human nature at its best partly overcomes the evils of a bad system when great wealth is held as a trust by its possessors.

Wealth as Success.—Another objection to the more equitable distribution of wealth is that we must allow great fortunes if we are to attract great men and spur them on to the efforts necessary for the efficient leadership of industry. But is it true that if great men are to do their utmost they must be offered millions on millions? Has the best work of the greatest men been done for money? Is money the only motive that appeals to the great? Far from it. They strive even more for the respect and admiration of their fellowmen, for the sense of power and worth. Those who have powers find their joy in the exercise of those powers. And even when money is the chief motive must millions be offered, or will one who is working for fifteen hundred a year do his utmost to earn fifteen thousand? Do the greatest business men ever work harder than when they are seeking their first hundred thousand and uncertain whether they will attain it? It is true that the captains of industry must be allowed to receive large incomes. They may be double or treble or tenfold the income of the ordinary man but when they rise to a hundred times the income of the mass of normal men, it is absurdity. There are many grades of business success popularly measured by wealth. The business man struggles to reach the highest grade attainable. If that were measured by an income of fifty thousand a year, and only the rarest success attained that sum and no one had more he would struggle for that. After all it is the distinction, the success, the achievement, that great business men strive for. They do not need the millions save as the evidence and measure of their success and power.

Such vast financial rewards are not only unnecessary as motives; they are perversive. To make the differences in money so conspicuous obscures the difference in real achievement, makes men think themselves successful, and causes them to be regarded by others as successful, when they have achieved nothing worthy, rendered no service in the leadership of industry, but only managed through deals in margins or manipulation of stocks or otherwise to appropriate a large amount from the social income. By the glitter of mountains of gold men are hindered from perceiving that captains of industry are social functionaries; and so men now run mills to make money rather than to make shoes or machinery. They have too little ambition to organize the factors of industry so as to yield the most effective production, too little pride and satisfaction in doing so. And they may forget altogether that they have undertaken to captain the industrial lives of the men whom they employ, and that the efficiency of their leadership may be measured by the prosperity of the men they employ, of the whole detachment of the industrial army which they lead, as well as by the size of their own fortunes. Moreover, society as a whole forgets these things and admires the money-getter rather than the man of social achievement. As soon as society revises its perverted judgment on this point men of ambition will revise the direction of their endeavor. The desire for success is a motive entirely distinguishable from the desire for material possessions; and success is defined by social judgment. If at a given time and place success as such coincides with material wealth it is because society at that time and place so defines success. The obsession extends beyond business life, and other forms of achievement in science, art, literature, and social leadership, that evince the highest human powers and yield the greatest social benefits but do not make much money, are undervalued. This is important not so much because it is unjust to those who achieve as because fewer do achieve on this account, for the powers with which the people of a society are endowed go out in those directions which the popular judgment affirms to be most admirable. Incorruptible statesmen, great administrators managing the affairs of cities, creators in the arts, discoverers in the sciences, master minds engaged in leading social coöperation, can be had by the society that adequately appreciates and respects these forms of achievement. A perversion of the popular judgment of success is the most radical form of social degeneracy or crudity. No society has yet properly adjusted its appreciations and detestations, and a shifting of emphasis in the judgment of success is the most fundamental of all reforms.

Finally, it is objected that because the distribution of wealth has always been inequitable, it always must be glaringly so. This deserves the same amount of consideration as did the arguments by which men once proved that slavery was rendered inevitable by the traits of human nature, or those by which they once disproved the feasibility of railroads.

Competition as a Cure-All.—To all the foregoing consideration some reply that the only thing necessary in order to secure to labor all that it produces and to abolish abnormal profits of employers is to restore free competition. They say that when there is free competition there is no such differential as we have described, because under free competition an industry which yielded such a differential would attract so many entrepreneurs that the product would become so plentiful as to lower prices and wipe out these differential profits. There would indeed be a difference between the income of the abler and the less competent managers, but they say that this differential being created by the good manager, we can no more take it from him than we can refuse to pay the rental which economic law inevitably assigns to a superior piece of land. They add that the increased production by many employers would mean the employment of more laborers; that in fact each employer in a profit-yielding industry would continue to employ more laborers till the point was reached where another laborer would produce nothing above the wages paid; that this last laborer would therefore get all that he produced except just enough margin to induce an employer to engage him, and that when this becomes true of the last laborer it would be true of all similar laborers, for the laborers who have been employed on equal terms are interchangeable units. Thus it is claimed that if we only had free competition in any industry there could be no abnormal prices in that industry, since abnormal prices would attract new competitors and stimulate more plentiful production till the public had as much of the product of that industry as it would buy at a normal price, till all the labor needed to produce such an abundant supply was employed at a rate practically equal to the value of labor's product, and no differential profits would remain to employers save the "rent" of superior management.[1]

If all this is true, the fact remains that the operation of "economic forces" does not secure the free competition on

[1] For an elaborate presentation of this position see Professor Clark's work on The Distribution of Wealth, Macmillan, 1908, particularly pp. 4, 9, 83, 94, 105, 106, 116, 180, 321, 332, 400, 411, 418, 419.

which this economic millenium is founded, and if free competition is secured and maintained it must be done by the
exercise of social control. The economic interest of the most
forceful managers of industry drives them toward combination and the utilization of all the "elements of monopoly"
which they find available. "The prime importance of monopoly privileges in the distribution of wealth is shown by Professor Commons in his work on "The Distribution of Wealth,"
of which page 252 is quoted in Ely's "Principles of Economics," page 342. According to those authorities about 78 per
cent. of the 4,047 millionaire fortunes referred to as having
been investigated "were derived from permanent monopoly
privileges." And "there can be no question" that if the remaining 21.4 per cent. "were fully analyzed, it would appear
that they were not due solely to personal abilities unaided by
these permanent monopoly privileges." "It will be found that
perhaps 95 per cent. of the total values represented by these
millionaire fortunes is due to those investments classed as land
values and natural monopolies and to competitive industries
aided by such monopolies." In fact the economic tendency in
the direction of monopoly is so strong that all the efforts at
social control by which we have thus far striven to combat
it have proved largely futile. If those who are on the inside
of the management of a great industry have a powerful common interest in combining, how are we to prevent them from
doing so? We may forbid this or that legal form, we may
punish the grosser methods of intimidating possible competitors or exterminating those who have actually commenced
competition. In such ways we shall do what we may to keep
alive free competition. But unless we succeed in doing so,
we must also invoke other methods of securing the distribution of at least a part of the present differential. In some
of the greatest and most important industries unlimited competition will never be restored; in some the attempt to restore
it would inevitably be wasteful as well as futile. Chief among
these are the railways and other public utilities that are natural
monopolies. In these and in all the other great industries in
which free competition cannot be or has not been secured,

we must control the combinations that we do not succeed in preventing.

Even where free competition exists or might exist, it does not suffice to secure economic justice to the laborer. The argument of Professor Clark and others, by which they attempt to show that under free competition each factor in industry tends, without the exercise of social control, to receive practically what it produces, is fallacious. They tell us that because any manager will hire another laborer whenever another laborer would produce any more than the wages paid him, therefore every manager will be led by his own interest to continue adding to his labor force until the last laborer employed produces only barely enough more than his wages to make an inducement to engage him; and that in so far as laborers are interchangeable units, what is true in this respect of the last laborer is true of every laborer working in the same labor market, namely, each receives practically what he produces.

The fallacy lies in assuming that the last laborer employed produces only barely more than his wages. One engineer on a railway train may be paid five dollars a day but render a service for which the company would pay a hundred dollars a day if they could not get it for less. At the same time another engineer would only be in the way. The number of laborers employed is not limited by the productivity of the "marginal" laborer in their sense of that expression, but by the necessities of organization. As many will be engaged as fit into the organization, and the number that fit in is fixed, not by the productivity of the last laborer, but by the amount and kind of land, capital, and managerial ability. The manager with highly specialized machinery can employ only as many laborers as his machinery calls for, although those employed may produce far more than their wages.

It may be truly said that under free competition the amount of machinery and of every factor in production will tend to be as great as is justified by the demand for the product of the industry. Even then the last laborer employed may produce far more than his wages. And after as many laborers are employed in the industry as are required to complete the organization of that industry, if there remain other laborers who would gladly do the work but are left unemployed, then they will underbid the laborers who are receiving a just wage.

If the time ever came when there were no surplus laborers, economic conditions would tend to secure to every man at least a marginal wage. But since laborers must work or starve, and entrepreneurs receive the whole product of primary distribution, economic conditions, even then, would not insure that any laborer received the whole, or approximately the whole, product of his labor, if there were any man engaged in less productive labor who was a satisfactory candidate for the more productive job. In other words, wages for any given task would tend to sink toward the point where they barely surpassed the wages of the least profitably employed laborer who *could* perform the given task. And unless social control intervene, the point at which the reduction of wages will stop would still depend, as now, on the relative bargaining power of laborers and employers.

Should the Manager Retain All That His Activity at Present Conditions?—The conception of profits under free competition as "rent" of superior managerial ability leads many to conclude that there would be no justice in taking any part of his gains from the manager because he has "created" all the value that he now retains. Perhaps we could very well afford to let managers retain all that they could as pure rent of the abilities productively applied under free competition. But as the question has been raised in the assumption that they could still retain large differentials, and in the name of pure justice, let us consider it on that basis.[1] It must always be borne in mind that we approve and advocate a large income for the entrepreneur. The only question is whether justice requires that all the gains conditioned by his activity should remain in his possession in case such gains prove to be enormous.

---

[1] The question whether any part of the present differential can be taken from the entrepreneur, or whether such part of it as he cannot retain will cease to be produced, is treated on p. 137 *seq.*

Gains from Chance and from Foresight.—The differential remaining in the hands of the employer may be said to contain three elements: (1) the gains of foresight and risk-taking; (2) the gains of organization; (3) the gains of bargaining.

Capital "tied up" in an industry is paid back by the industry only after the lapse of considerable time during which there may be reduction in demand for the product which the investment helps to make, perhaps by the discovery of a better substitute for that product. And there may be invented better machinery for making the product before the machinery in which the investment has been sunk has been worn out or has paid for itself. Raw material must be selected and paid for and wages must be paid some time before it is possible to know exactly the price for which the product can be sold. Goods must be produced and put into stock in anticipation of the fashion and demand of the coming season. For such reasons as these, the entrepreneur must exercise foresight and must take some chances against which no foresight can guard him. As a result some employers are ruined, while those who remain in business in general and in the long run receive some gains which are due in part to foresight exercised in specific instances, and in part to the general caution which leads those who invest large sums in the hope of a mere margin of profit to allow for unforeseen contingencies.

It is well for the entrepreneur to take these risks, for such risks cannot be avoided, and the entrepreneur, more than any other, has the knowledge of all the conditions involved that is necessary to the exercise of the required foresight. Since he takes these risks investors and wage-earners are in part relieved of them, and their incomes are rendered steadier; besides society is thus assured of a steady flow of goods ready in anticipation of need. We may, therefore, grant that a part of the large income of the entrepreneur which justice and expediency require and which we have approved, should be regarded as reward for risk-taking or insurance against the unavoidable chances of business. While some grow rich others lose all. It seems just as well as expedient that the entrepreneur be allowed to profit by chance gains since he is obliged to bear chance losses. Both rates of profit and rates of interest include an element of insurance.

Gains of Organization.—Land, labor, and capital must be brought together; the various forms of capital goods and the various types of labor must be correlated; buying and selling relations must be established. This organizing is the characteristic function of the employer. The productiveness of labor is as truly dependent upon organization as upon tools and machinery. If, all other conditions being equal, given amounts of investment and of labor under one manager produce $100,000 while under another manager equal amounts of investment and labor produce $200,000, the better manager may be said to "produce or create" the extra $100,000 by his superior ability and exertion. This $100,000 may all be regarded as wages of management. It must be so regarded if it is necessary to allow the manager to retain the whole of it in order to induce him to exercise those abilities without which it would not have been produced. But if we have been right in holding that it is possible to secure the best exertions of the best managers without paying them so much more than is paid for equal exertion and equal ability in other callings, it remains for us to consider whether it is just to advocate ethical ideals or to pass laws that will make it impossible for managers to retain the whole of that wealth, the production of which is dependent upon the exercise of their abilities.

Before we admit that the labor of the manager "creates or produces" all of the additional $100,000 we ought to notice that there is a difference between producing and conditioning. An express train stopped because a nut had been lost from the machinery of its engine. Yet that nut did not produce the motion of the train. A great factory stops because a bar of steel has broken in the wheel pit. Does that imply that before it broke that bar of steel was creating all the values that ceased to be produced when the bar broke? No. Those values were produced by five thousand men using a million dollars' worth of capital goods of which the bar of steel was a minute part. Every necessary part of a producing organization derives importance and productivity from all the other parts. It cannot be said to "create" or "produce" all the values which it may condition. If the broken bar of steel be replaced by another which is of better shape, not only than the one that broke, but better than the corresponding part in the machinery of a rival factory, it may add greatly to the former productiveness of the five thousand laborers and the million dollars' worth of machinery that work together with that bar of steel. But we cannot say that the whole of the added output of the five thousand laborers and of the other machinery is produced by the improvement in the bar of steel. We should say instead that the added productivity of this factory and of these laborers is conditioned by the improved bar of steel. There is no reasonableness in the claim that we should pay for each element in an organization all that would cease to be produced if that element in the organization were removed. That would often require the payment of amounts equal to several times the total output. The very nature of efficient organization is that each factor not only produces but also conditions added productivity in all the other factors. Therefore there is no justice in the claim that all the "gains of organization" should go to any one factor in the organization, even though the factor selected be the organizer. The present power of the entrepreneur to retain the "gains of organization" is due to his bargaining power.

Gains of Bargaining Power.—The third element in employers' profits is gained from bargaining power. When no social control limits the operation of purely economic causes, it is chiefly bargaining power, and not justice, that determines how much of the product of industry shall be retained by the employer in his capacity as the agent of secondary distribution.

The relative value assigned by economic causes to the part played in organized industry by management and other labor depends largely upon their relative scarcity. Bargaining power is with the seller of that which is scarce and the buyer of that which is plentiful. The services of the man-

ager who made a factory and its laborers (himself included)
produce $200,000 instead of $100,000 are rare, while those
of laborers are plentiful. If laborers were few enough so
that this manager had been obliged to bid against other managers in the same and other industries in order to get workmen, he might have been unable to keep all of the extra
$100,000, for he might have been compelled to pay more
to laborers or else go without the labor necessary to the
production of the extra $100,000. Thus we see that the
manager's ability to retain this great sum is due to the fact
that common labor is plentiful, while his services are a
scarce commodity. Economic value depends as much on
scarcity as upon utility.[1] To define utility, as is sometimes
done, in such a way as to make it inseparable from scarcity,[2]
and especially to define the utility of a man's service in
such a way as to confuse utility with market value which
depends upon scarcity is to beg the whole question at issue.
By such a definition of utility the total utility of the heat
and light of the sun is less than that of tallow candles, and
the total utility of the atmosphere is less than that of smell-
ing salts. The air has no economic value though its utility is
boundless, while a diamond as big as the end of a man's
thumb is worth a great fortune; for air is even more plentiful
than the labor of common men, while such diamonds are
scarcer than good managers.

We may heartily grant that the work of the manager
should be paid for in proportion to its utility and still deny
that justice requires that it be paid for in proportion to its
scarcity. We may go further, for it may turn out that if the

---

[1] "Limitation upon the supply of goods relatively to the need gives
value." H. J. Davenport: Value and Distribution. University of Chicago Press, 1908, p. 569; and economists in general.

[2] If that definition of the word "utility" answers the purpose of
economic discussion it is only because economic discussion deliberately
excludes the ethical considerations, which are our chief concern. We
have the word "value" to designate the utility which depends on
scarcity, and we do not need the word "utility" also to convey that
meaning half so much as we need it to convey its full and original
significance.

work of managers is paid for according to its scarcity the work
of laborers cannot be paid for according to its utility.

The scarcity of his services, which gives the employer
power to retain so large a share of the increase in production which results from organization, is far from being entirely a difference between his natural endowment and that
of other men. In the first place other interests than those
of industry and money-making draw to themselves a large
proportion of the finest ability; this is socially desirable and
likely to be increasingly the case in our country. In the second
place, although men of first-class business ability often make
or discover opportunity where others would find none, yet
in a large proportion of the commoner cases the question
who shall be employer and who shall be employed is settled
by education, business openings due to fortunate connections, credit acquired by virtue of social connections or by
success in filling positions that were inaccessible to others,
or the inheritance of capital. As American society grows
older these artificial differences tend increasingly to be determining factors. However many have the native powers
and however widely we distribute opportunity to develop
inborn powers, relatively few can exercise them in independent economic management. Even in the freest country
the advantages possessed by tolerably large-scale industry
set a natural limit upon the number of managerial positions.
Managers of established industries have often added to this
natural limitation upon managerial opportunities an artificial
and sometimes dastardly opposition to incipient competition.
But in the nature of things the "scarcity" which gives to
management the power to retain so great a differential
is not wholly a scarcity of ability nor even of ability accompanied by training, credit, and capital; it is partly a scarcity
of positions, which bears a more or less definite ratio to the
degree to which organization has been perfected.

Moreover, we could not admit the automatic justice of
the claims of bargaining power based on scarcity even if it
were purely scarcity of natural ability. To admit that would
be to admit that might is right, and to adopt as our maxim

of justice, "Let him keep who can." We must recognize that when the Fates give to one man a special privilege which they deny to others, that special privilege is accompanied by a special responsibility, a responsibility which the operation of economic law does not enforce, which may occasionally be enforced by conscience but which generally must be enforced by social control.

To summarize, then: (1) The natural operation of economic tendency is not to maintain but to destroy freedom of competition. In those industries where it is practicable and desirable to restore or maintain free competition we must depend for this not on the operation of economic tendency, but upon the exercise of social control.

(2) It is erroneous to assume that even in those industries in which it is desirable and practicable to maintain free competition, such competition will secure justice to the laborer. The laborer's share, if left to the operation of economic causes, depends upon bargaining power which has no necessary relation to utility of the service rendered or to any other standard of justice.

(3) The excessive bargaining power of the employer is based upon (a) the scarcity of managerial positions or, in other words, the plentifulness of common labor and the concentration of management in few hands, the number and identity of the managers being largely determined by the necessities of large-scale organization, and by adventitious advantages. This power, whatever the ground on which it is held, is never divorced from corresponding responsibility. (b) This bargaining power is further based upon the facts that labor must be disposed of at forced sale; (c) that its price is not upheld by price of production, and slack demand does not lessen the supply; and (d) that the laborer receives his share only through secondary distribution out of the hands of the employer who first receives the whole proceeds of industry.

Conclusion.—In conclusion, the problem of distribution will never be settled by the operation of economic laws. The chief thing that the study of economics has accomplished in this connection is to demonstrate that impossibility and so to clear the grounds for the activities of social control. We are already more or less familiar with the fact that tenure of land, water rights, and the rights of widows and children as heirs,[1] and the application of the taxing power are not defined or secured by anything in nature, but are regulated in this way or that according to some adopted standard and by some adopted method of social procedure. Distribution as such is a problem in social equity and social organization. The necessary judgments of equity in their main outlines must be formed in public opinion and enforced by custom, morality, and law. The social sciences and the public opinion which they have molded are hitherto chrematistic[2] and not humanistic. Economics as such has often frankly declared itself to be non-ethical; it need not continue to be so. Sociology cannot be non-ethical without being unscientific. Private property has been sacred but general welfare has not. This must be reversed. Not indeed that we should have less respect for law, including the laws that define property rights, as laws must always do, but rather that laws should be made more respectable. Law itself is sacred and when changed it must be changed by legal methods—but particular laws are fallible and changeable, and law is not greater than society that makes it, or than the good or evil for the sake of which it exists.

A chrematistic system of law may possibly have been justifiable during the period in which the greatest problem was that of developing methods of production, but it has become intolerable and indefensible, now that the problem of discovering a system of distribution has surpassed in importance that of further promoting methods of production. The problem now pressing can be successfully approached only from the ethical or humanistic point of view. Society must develop for itself a new system of legislation wrought out with an eye single to the values realized in human experience.

---

[1] The law of primogeniture is an exceedingly glaring instance of distribution by social convention.

[2] That is, money-making, materialistic.

CHAPTER IX

HOW MAY SOCIETY REGULATE THE DISTRIBUTION OF WEALTH?

Public Opinion and Law.—If we adopt the view that it will be necessary to depend upon some form of social control in order to modify our intolerable state of economic injustice, which the natural operation of "economic laws" is powerless to correct, the momentous question before us is: What kind of social control will accomplish this end? Two kinds of social control can be considered. First, is the gradual development of a public opinion and sentiment which will both mold the character of our citizens so that their own ambitions and consciences will secure from many the conduct that is adapted to the requirements of modern industrial and social conditions, and which also, with or without enactment into law, will exert a tremendous social pressure upon those who might otherwise continue to transgress those requirements. We must not forget that this molding of individuality into fitness for membership in an advanced social régime, together with the pressure exercised by public opinion and sentiment, constitute the most fundamental form of social control and are more important even for this task of economic transformation than legislation can be. It is more important than legislation by virtue of its own direct results together with the fact that it alone will insure the passage and enforcement of the necessary legislation. No one need expect legislation to accomplish wonders in promoting democratic justice unless legislative progress is part and parcel in a moral progress of the people, a progress, that is, in judgments and sentiments in reference to their own conduct as well as the conduct of others.[1] Such progress is to be wrought by all the

---

[1] The following passage from President Hadley makes him seem to undervalue the function of pure self-defense, and of the righteous-

agencies of investigation and enlightenment, by methods that will grow more intelligible as we proceed with the study of the evolution of morality and social control. At the same time we must experiment cautiously and courageously in the framing of laws in order that legislation may advance as steadily as public opinion justifies, remembering also that the relation between public opinion and legislation is in a measure reciprocal, for while effective legislation must be an expres-

---

ness of the untempted. Nevertheless, the establishment of social justice does depend upon the presence of a group whose disinterested justice can shame the Devil, and who can wield the balance of power between selfish contestants.

"Most people object to trusts. Why? Largely because they do not own them. If a man really believes that a trust is a bad thing and would refuse to countenance its pursuits if he were given a majority interest in its stock, he can fairly dignify his spirit of opposition to trusts by the title of public sentiment. And it may be added that if things are done by trusts or by any other forms of economic organization which arouse this sort of disinterested opposition, they speedily work their own cure. If a considerable number of influential men [not all the culprits, of course] see the pernicious effects of a business practice sufficiently to condemn it in themselves as well as in others, they can speedily restrict, if they cannot wholly prevent, its continuance. Most of the effective control of combinations of capital has been, in fact, brought about by intelligent public opinion slowly acting in this way. If, however, the critic is doing on a small scale what the trust is practising on a large scale; if, in short, he simply complains of the practices of the trusts because he is at the wrong end of certain important transactions, and becomes their victim instead of their beneficiary, then his words count for nothing. No matter how many thousands of men there may be in his position, their aggregate work is not likely to reach farther than the passage of a certain amount of ill-considered and inoperative legislation. It cannot be too often repeated that those opinions which a man is prepared to maintain at another's cost, but not at his own, count for little in forming the general sentiment of a community, or in producing any effective public movement. They are manifestations of boastfulness, or envy, or selfishness, rather than of that public spirit which is an essential constituent in all true public opinion.

"There are some moralists who would deny the possibility of any such public opinion which should be independent of selfishness, and which should rise above personal interests. But they have the facts of history against them." President A. I. Hadley: Education of the American Citizen, Yale University Press, 1913, p. 25.

sion of public opinion, it is also one of the agencies, though only one, in the formation of public opinion.

"Trust-Busting."—It would be an empty pretense to claim that our distorted distribution of wealth conforms to any principle of merit or justice. Its right is might. Its might is due to the differences necessitated by organization. Should we attempt to destroy this might, or can we compel it to be just?

The talk about "busting the trusts" of which so much has been heard is probably folly. The unscrupulous among the magnates may even have fostered such discussion as a means of throwing dust in people's eyes and obscuring real issues. What we want first of all is efficient production, then just distribution of the product. We have secured the efficiency of production by means of a high degree of organization. What we now need is not to destroy the efficient producer because he keeps an undue share of the product, but to retain the efficiency and add to efficiency in production justice in distribution. We should not desire to go back to the wasteful war of universal competition. The elimination of the small producer in so far as it means getting the whole supply of any staple from the factories that are most favorably located with reference to raw materials and markets, most effectively correlated with the whole system of allied industries, most efficiently managed and most completely rid of the wastes of small-scale production and possessing the advantages of large-scale production and comprehensive organization, is to that degree a survival of the fittest, a saving of the national resources, and an increase of the product to be divided. The trusts have often lowered prices and raised wages notwithstanding they have kept for themselves vast profits; and the very fact of the vast profits is the ground for hope that more may ultimately be secured for labor.

Let m, n, o, p, q, r, s, t, u, v, w designate eleven factories engaged in the manufacture of the same product. Suppose the first five to possess the advantages of favorable location, abundant capital, comprehensive business relations,

valuable patent rights and highly efficient management, the
next three, designated r, s, t, to be prosperous in a more
modest way, and u, v, w to be marginal producers. In the
figure below let the verticals terminating in the irregular line
cd represent the necessary cost of producing a given amount
of output in each of these factories, and these verticals prolonged to ab represent the price for which that product
will sell. Then the dotted lines between cd and ab will represent the differentials between cost of production and price
for these factories. It is plain that if the price level should
permanently fall but very slightly factories u, v, w must cease
business, for their cost of production, including necessary
wages of superintendence, almost exactly equals price, so

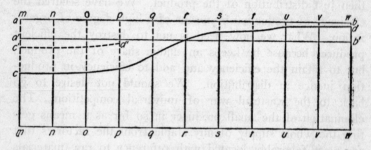

that these factories produce no appreciable differential. If
the price level should fall to a'b', factories r, s, t must also
go out of business, and the industry would then be monopo-
lized by factories m, n, o, p, q which probably would combine their management to avoid a war of extermination among
giants. They may shut down q, the plant that has least
advantages. The remaining factories still have a differential,
represented by the dotted lines below a'b' which might be
used in increasing wages. These great concerns may now
put up the price again, but not too much lest they should
invite new and powerful competitors into the field, or cause
the demand for their output to fall off too much. The public
should desire, not to break up these great concerns but, first,
to prevent them from raising prices and, second, to compel
them to share the differential with their laborers.

Will the Amount That Now Forms the Differential Be Produced if Part of It Is Diverted to Labor?—Is it possible to compel the captains of industry to share the differential with the laborers?

We are at once confronted with the objection that if the differential is to be turned over to the laborers it will not be produced. This objection is met if the increased share of labor can be added to the necessary cost of production so that it

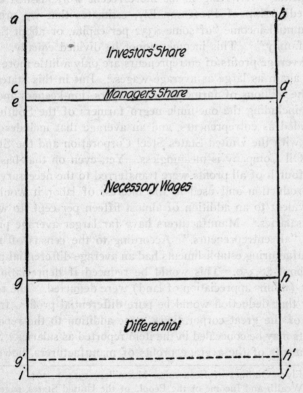

must be paid before any differential can be retained by the employer. In that case the line cd (page 136) would be raised to c'd' and that part of the former differential which lies between cd and c'd' would go to labor, and in our former diagram gh would be forced down to g'h' giving labor a thicker slice and diminishing the amount of that differential which escapes from secondary distribution. This can be accomplished by a combination of measures.

We must avoid overestimating the change in the condition of laborers that would result from a fair division of the differential. According to Professor Ely,[1] "we do not know whether, if the national income were equally distributed, a family of five persons would have $800 or $1,600 to spend." Dr. King in his more recent work, issued under the editorship of Professor Ely, estimates that we produce an annual income "of some $332 per capita, or about $1,500 per family."[2] This income cannot be divided equally.

Average profits of entrepreneurs are only a little more than half again as large as average wages.[3] But in this statement all the millions of farmers, shop-keepers, inn-keepers and the like, including the one-mule negro farmers of the South, are included as entrepreneurs, and an average that includes such men with the United States Steel Corporation and the Standard Oil Company is meaningless. Yet, even on that basis, if one-fourth of all profits were transferred to the necessary cost of production and used in the interest of labor it would be equivalent to an addition of almost fifteen per cent. to wages and salaries.[4] Manufacturers have far larger average profits than "all entrepreneurs." According to the census of 1910, manufacturing establishments had an average differential profit of about $8,350. This would be reduced if depreciation of plant (minus appreciation of land) were deducted. The result after that deduction would be pure differential profit. In the case of the great corporations, some addition to the reported profits may be concealed in the item reported as salaries. Such statements of the average profits of manufacturers, however,

---

[1] Ely: Outlines of Economics, Macmillan, 1914, p. 104.

[2] Wealth and Income of the People of the United States, page 248.

[3] Average wages according to King are $507, average profits $899.

[4] It would add a considerably larger per cent. to the income of labor if the highly salaried managers did not share in the benefit. According to King, 46.9 per cent. of the national income goes to wages and salaries, 27.5 per cent. to profits. One-fourth of the latter is almost fifteen per cent. of the former.

have only a little more significance than the statement of average profits for all entrepreneurs, for it places in one class the hugest establishments together with great numbers of tiny shops where, for example, a cigar maker works beside his one employee. Such an average conceals the amount of profits in great establishments. We do not know the size of the differential that ought to be shared with labor. But we know that there are great sums that ought to be divided, and that a moderate percentage of present wages added to the income of a family as a margin of increase makes a comparatively great difference in their status; and that many families and individuals sink below the poverty line, and many others miss opportunities of life they might have entered, for lack of the margin of income.

1. Factory Legislation.—This should require reasonable hours of labor for men [1] and should especially limit the labor of women and children. It should require the safeguarding of machinery and dangerous processes, and in certain places the provision of first aid for the injured. It should require sanitary conditions in places of labor, preventing so far as practicable dangerous degrees of temperature and humidity and providing for removal of dust and fumes by suction pipes, etc.

Such legislation does not directly put money into the laborer's pocket, but it does compel the employer to expend money for the benefit of the laborer and to forego a part of the excessive income derived from labor, and secures highly needful results which could not be attained by paying the money directly to the workmen. In the past such legislation has been opposed by employers, and at some points is still resisted. But it is a justice to the best employers, for it forces competitors who are less well disposed, to live up to a standard to which the best of employers now willingly conform.[2]

---

[1] What is constitutional, in the end, will be what public opinion holds to be required by the general welfare.

[2] Miss Tarbell regards the new model factory as the most interesting architectural development in this country. "Welfare arrange-

2. Tenement Laws and City Planning.—These diminish the gains of real-estate holders but secure far more than compensating advantages to tenants, and to society as a whole.[1]

3. Employers' Liability, Compensation and Industrial Insurance Laws.—According to the common law an employer was excused from legal requirement to compensate an employee or the surviving family of an employee injured in his works, on either of the following grounds, the application of which has been limited by statutory enactment in some states and should be in all.

1. *The Fellow Servant Doctrine.* If the injury were due to the fact that a fellow employee did something which caused the accident, or neglected to do something which would have prevented it, the employer was excused from making compensation. This was reasonable when a few men worked in a little shop where all were under the superintendence of each, but it is absurd now that thousands are employed by the same factory or railroad, and the lives of men are hourly dependent upon the faithfulness of fellow employees whom they cannot see and may never have seen. Effective superintendence can now be maintained only by the management and for such superintendence the management must be held responsible.

2. *The Doctrine of Assumption of Risk.* The employer was excused from responsibility if it could be shown that

---

ments of all kinds," she says, "are becoming as much a concern of architects and builders of industrial establishments as foundations and lights." She could give personal stories of great numbers, "who by their changed conditions of work have been transformed; of girls transfigured from slatterns to clean and tidy decency; of women whose bitter revolt at work performed in ugly and filthy disorder has been changed to cheerful interest; of men who have given up the saloon.

"It is hardly too much to say that these new industrial ideas are producing an entirely new type of employer; one who is almost as much of an educator as he is a maker of things; almost as much a friend of men as he is a 'boss.' He has discovered that no man or woman can reach and keep the point of efficiency which scientific business requires unless he is healthy, content, and growing. How to keep men and women well and happy is part of his business."

[1] Compare sections on pp. 87 and 93.

the injured man was aware of the particular risk he ran. The more glaring the neglect to provide for safety, the more obvious the defect in machinery, the clearer the defense of the employer against the responsibility for injuries. The theory was that the workman is free to accept or reject the employment with all its dangers, and if he accepts or continues in such employment when knowing its danger to himself then he alone is responsible for his injury. This theory is contrary to the facts. There is other compulsion than legal compulsion, enforced by other penalties than fine and imprisonment. The laborer is compelled to accept such employment as he can get and is powerless to remove dangers which he may see and deplore.

3. *The Doctrine of Implied Risk.* The employer was not responsible for injuries that resulted from the nature of the industry. Here the doctrine of the assumption of risks applied not to an occasional danger but to an ever-present peril.

The Modern View.[1]—The modern view is that if maiming and death are a part of the cost of carrying on an industry, then out of the proceeds of that industry some recompense must be made to the injured laborer or to his survivors. Experience and statistics show that the prosecution of certain industries requires not only the constant effort of laborers—that is, work—but also the actual destruction of a percentage of the working power by accident and untoward conditions. Unless such an industry by means of pensions or indemnities can restore the income-yielding capacity which it thus destroys, its output is not paying for the cost of production. In so far as it yields an income to the employer at the cost of terminating income to the laborers there is no net gain, but only transference of income from the injured to another, which is somewhat like robbing the murdered or the maimed and is socially intolerable. A part of the raw material required by industry is human flesh and it must be paid for if the proceeds of the industry are to cover the cost of their production, not indeed paid for as a living

---

[1] Compare statutes of Massachusetts and New York.

substance the destruction of which costs pain and bereavement, but paid for merely as an income yielding asset.

This payment is not made by the employer out of his personal income as a participant in the industry, but it is a disbursement made by him as the agent of secondary distribution, and it is difficult to see how he has any more ethical right to withhold it than he has to withhold payment of the price of raw material or the interest on capital. If he cannot make his industry yield these sums his industry is failing to pay for what it consumes. It may be objected that if this were granted then a great accident might at any moment bring a ruinous unforeseen expense upon any small employer. The reply to this is that such a requirement could not be made upon the occasional employer of labor, but only upon the regular employer of labor, and if it were enforced upon every considerable regular employer of labor, then it would become a part of the normal cost of production to carry insurance against the losses of working power as well as against losses by fire.

It may also be objected that dangerous labor is highly paid, and ought to insure itself against accidents, for by the high wages the employer has discharged his responsibility. Here a question of fact is involved; in so far as wages are advanced for this cause there is justice in the objection. Implied risks of a tragic and startling character often raise wages to some degree; those of an insidious character that gradually undermine the health as a rule do not raise wages. In fact compulsory industrial insurance was applied to the breaking of health before it was extended to accident.[1]

An important incidental result of adequate compensation and insurance laws is diminution in the number of accidents among laborers. When employers must insure against the

---

[1] The benefits of insurance against illness are even greater than those of insurance against accident.

No good thing invented by man is free from all dangers or abuses; under compulsory insurance a certain amount of malingering may be practiced, and carelessness as to very minor accidents may be somewhat increased.

loss of earning power due to these causes they take measures
to prevent such loss quite as effective as those which they
adopt to diminish danger from fire. Experience has shown
that this means of enforcing proper labor conditions in these
respects is often more effective than the system of direct
legislation and inspection devised for that end.

An effective compensation law must specify the conditions of payment so definitely that there will ordinarily be
no more occasion for an injured laborer or his family to
sue for indemnity than there is for the beneficiary of an
insurance company to do so. The payment must become
mandatory without suit upon establishment of the specified
facts. Otherwise the insurance taken out by employers is
largely used up in fighting against the payment of compensation, and while great sums are expended, little goes to the
injured, especially where statutes do not limit or abolish
the application of the old common law defenses against
employers' liability. The net result is largely litigation or
acceptance of pittances by the injured to avoid undertaking
the expense of litigation which the injured laborer or his
widow is ill prepared to bear, and embitterment of relations
between the laboring and employing classes.

A compensation law adequate in its provisions and resulting in practically universal insurance of large employers
against losses by destruction of labor power through industrial accident is a near approach to "compulsory labor insurance," though the statute may make no mention of "insurance." Insurance of all laborers employed in industries mentioned by statute is directly required by law in most of the
advanced industrial nations except the United States.[1] Compensation laws [2] refer only to losses by accident. While this

---

[1] See W. F. Willoughby: Workingmen's Insurance, New York,
1898; C. R. Henderson: Industrial Insurance in the United States,
Chicago, 1909; and American Labor Legislation Review, Vol. III,
No. 2, New York, 1913.

[2] Several states have recently passed laws of this kind; that of
Illinois may be studied as one of the best examples. Claims under the
Illinois laws are settled by a state industrial accident board. Any
employer in the class to which the law applies may relieve himself of,

cause of loss is so sensational as first to draw public attention, yet the losses and suffering from this cause are far less than those from sickness, and there is greater need of labor insurance against sickness, unemployment and old age.

The principle of compulsory insurance of workingmen was adopted by Germany in 1883. It first provided for sick benefits including free medical attendance, which insures a skillful effort to restore the earning power and prevent prolongation or permanence of disability, together with a weekly cash allowance, and a special addition in case death supervenes. A little later two laws were passed providing for accident insurance, the income of which commences after the period during which sick benefits are allowed has expired, and which provides, in case of death, besides the regular funeral allowance, a pension to dependent relatives up to 60 per cent. of the daily wages of the deceased. In 1889 pensions for old age and permanent disability were added to the German system of laborers' insurance.

The premiums for the support of these various forms of compulsory insurance should be exacted from three sources. A part, especially for sick benefits, should be collected from the laborers in the form of a slight percentage deducted before the wages are paid; a part, especially for accident insurance, should be collected from the employers; and a part, especially for pensions, may properly be contributed by the state. This is just, since the public, the employers, and all the laborers benefit by the maintenance of the industry, while the heaviest physical cost of the industry falls at any given

---

its operation by sending the board written notice of his decision not to abide by it, but he is then debarred from defending himself against suit for damages on the ground of assumed risk, contributory negligence, or negligence of a fellow servant. Although the awards of the board to injured laborers and their families have been liberal, only about one-eighth of the employers in dangerous trades have withdrawn from the operation of the law, while an equal number of employers whose works do not fall in the class to which the law applies, including the largest employers in the state, have availed themselves of the privilege of placing their industry voluntarily under its provisions.

time upon a few of the laborers who with their families are crushed by the burden unless it is in a measure distributed over a larger number of those for whom the industry exists and who benefit by having the risks of the industry incurred. The advantage to the laborers resulting from compulsory insurance is far greater than would result from adding the amount of the premiums to current wages. It is "compulsory," as Professor Henderson remarks, only in the sense in which our common schools are "compulsory"; it is an act of social coöperation on the part of the entire community.

At the outset there was antagonism in Germany against compulsory industrial insurance, but after nearly a generation of experience all political parties favor it. It has diminished poverty, largely substituted justice for "charity," and contributed to the great prosperity which the empire has experienced during recent years. Following Germany, the principle of legally required insurance has now been adopted by Austria Hungary, Italy, Belgium, France, Norway, Denmark, Finland, Holland, Luxemburg and Great Britain.

4. The Socialization of Wealth by Taxation.—The people through their governmental agencies have the power to take possession of the wealth of individual citizens and expend it in the interest of the many. This is the most essential function of sovereignty. It may be abused; the majority may become the greatest of robbers; they may exercise the taxing power in such a way as to discourage industry and so dry up the sources from which wealth is derived, reducing the whole land to poverty. Taxation is a great agency in the distribution of wealth, and when the distribution resulting from the natural play of primary and secondary distribution is unsatisfactory an extensive redistribution of wealth by taxation would be entirely possible. The masses of the people have never understood the subject of taxation and taxation has generally operated in such a way as to make the injustice in the distribution of wealth greater instead of making it less as it readily might do.

There are two chief questions in respect to the taxing policy of a nation: first, how much shall be raised; second, from whom shall it be collected? In the United States very much more might be taken by taxation and applied to public uses, such as schools, libraries, museums, art galleries, concerts, lectures, the drama, parks, playgrounds and recreation centers, city planning and housing, hospitals, convalescent homes, rural roads, scientific research, etc. The successful expenditure of vaster sums of public money would depend upon the development of sufficiently honest and able administration.

The other pressing question is who shall pay the money secured by taxation. It is a great mistake to think that the poor upon whom no assessor calls pays no taxes. Most of our taxes are now indirect, that is, they are finally paid not by the person upon whom they are assessed but by someone else to whom the nominal payer shifts the burden. Thus the tenant pays the taxes on his tenement, and the price paid by the consumer for every commodity on which there has been an import duty or an internal revenue tax includes the tax; and large quantities of goods have their prices raised as if they had paid an import tax and the extra price goes to a producer in this country, and this results from the character of our existing tax laws. Duties and internal revenue taxes go to the treasury of the national government; the income of state and local governments is mainly derivable from real estate and "personal property." Real estate cannot evade taxation. Personal property can. Under existing laws the owner of a home in village or city cannot escape the payment of an unjust proportion of the public revenues, while the owner of personal property can escape. Personal property consists (1) of consumption goods (or goods that yield no money income, but only the satisfaction derived from their use, such as furniture, pianos, jewelry and the like); (2) similar goods held for sale or rental; (3) buildings, machinery, tools or animals employed in industry; (4) money, and (5) securities, that is, stocks, bonds, notes and mortgages. The vast accumulations of the rich which escape taxation are mainly in the form of securities, especially the stocks and bonds of corporations. As a rule no one can know how many stocks and bonds another private individual has in his safety-deposit box unless the information is voluntarily given. For this reason a just tax on such property cannot be forced; a tax is essentially a forced payment; therefore such property in the hands of the private individual is not taxable and the attempt to tax it is a farce. It is worse than a farce. The owner of securities is forced to choose between a lie and an injustice. If he makes the statement required by the assessor a true one he does himself an injustice, for justice in taxation is proportionate uniformity, and if he discloses his possessions he pays disproportionately so long as the majority of similar possessions escape taxation. As a rule he prefers the lie and receives the premium which the law places upon falsehood. Thereafter he has in his sub-consciousness the admission that there are times when a lie is excusable, and in the pinch of occasion the weakness thus produced in his veracity is likely to show itself. This law is a robbery and a blow at the fundamental honesty of the American people.

Taxes upon all corporations should be levied against the corporation as such and paid by the corporation treasurer; and no attempt should be made to tax their securities in the hands of their individual purchasers. In fact the corporation treasuries are taxed in various ways, so that the levy on their securities is merely an abortive attempt at double taxation and a deterrent to the honest investor. Corporations might be so taxed as to socialize the excessive income derived from monopolistic power or to discourage the use of such power in extorting excessive income. A tax on the amount of business, however, or what amounts to the same thing, a tax on each unit of business, often would tend to raise prices and to encourage the supply of a reduced output at an advanced figure, so that the tax should be on net income, if that is ascertainable, not on each passenger or ton-mile or unit of product; and in some respects better still is a fixed charge upon the property of the company, or on its outstanding securities, to be met before any differential can be accumulated.

A tax on great inheritances would afford a particularly favorable method of socializing a portion of massed wealth. Wealth shows itself when it comes to probate in the transfer from testator to legatee. Its new possessor has a slender ethical claim upon it; his claim is a legal one and can properly be limited by law. Unless close of kin to the testator he is not yet accustomed to a standard of living dependent on the new wealth, and a proper tax upon great inheritances would cause little or no hardship except to the mind of the greedy. A tax on inheritances has all the qualities of a good tax; it is easy and inexpensive to collect, causes little hardship, is just, and is highly productive of revenue. Such a tax should be progressive; that is, the rate of taxation should be higher the greater the inheritance. Small estates might bear no tax. If industrial organization makes it easy for the managers of business to accumulate an unreasonable share of the proceeds there is no moral reason why this pernicious congestion of wealth should be allowed to remain undisturbed for succeeding generations. An attempt would be made to evade an inheritance tax by deeding away property and accepting in return a contract for a life annuity. Such deeds might probably be made illegal.

The Unearned Increment.—The followers of Henry George argue that no man made the land and no man has any but a merely legal claim to it, which society is at liberty to alter and regulate for the general good. They add that the present rental value of land, especially of the enormously valuable city land, has mostly been produced neither by the owner nor even by nature, but by society, and that society alone is entitled to collect such rental; that this rental value is largely due to the expenditure of money raised by taxation, in building and maintaining streets, waterworks, parks, schools, fire and police systems; that in other words the people tax themselves to create rental values which they donate to the holders of the land; that whatever society does by taxation, by building churches, developing industries, and by its other activities, to make it desirable to live and do business in a given locality creates a privilege for the enjoyment of which private individuals collect the annual rental. They tell us that by actual computation for specific localities, some of which may be more or less typical, a tax on rental values of land alone would yield as much as is now raised for state and local purposes, and that while the taxes of some individuals would be raised, the taxes of an equal number of persons would be lowered. They point out that under their system men could no longer afford to hold the most convenient land idle for speculative purposes and that building would increase and rents fall, both because the best lots could not be profitably kept unoccupied and because buildings would be untaxed.

Objectors to the single tax reply that to make the tax on land equal to its rental value is to confiscate all that its present owner paid for it. The single-taxers answer that ownership of vast quantities of American soil was acquired by free gift of the government or by inheritance at no cost to the possessor, or even, especially in the case of railroads, by the bribery of legislators, and that the legislatures having given away the patrimony of the people, the people have a right to claim its rental value. But it remains true that multitudes of owners have paid for their land in honest, hard-earned cash, and it is hard to see how the rental value of such land can be confiscated with any sort of decency.

However, the principle of heavily taxing unearned increments in land value is now established in several states and nations. The unearned, socially created increments in land value will in the future be enormous in this country; expenditure of the people's money in public works, growth of industry, and the increasing needs of a multiplying population will create incalculable rental values; and society ought to adopt and announce the policy of keeping for its own uses the values that *will be so created in the future*, instead of allowing them to accumulate as a terrific taxing power in the hands of those who will chance to inherit our lands. The ancient Jewish law which provided that at the end of every fifty years all land should revert to the heirs of its original owners, suggests the possibility of a law providing that fifty years after the passage of the law all land shall permanently revert to the state, except that land which at the expiration of that period is in the possession of the person who owned it at the time the law was passed, shall not revert to the state until the death of the owner. The person in possession of a parcel of land at the expiration of fifty years should have the right to retain its use by payment of rental and the right to sell that privilege to another. The selling value of land would diminish throughout the fifty years till at the end it was no greater than the right of tenancy which remained. Every landholder would enjoy till his death the full title to his property unless he chose to sell it. Landed property and inherited property are held more by a merely legal, or conventional, title than property which the owner may have produced, or for which he has given an equivalent. Neither one of these peculiarities by itself might justify confiscation, but both together might justify the social confiscation of property that is at the same time, in land, and inherited, especially if long notice were given for the adjustment of plans and expectations.[1]

----

[1] Nothing short of an amendment to the constitution could inaugurate such a policy. If public opinion were educated up to the point of adopting such an amendment there is little doubt that the policy would be persisted in.

CHAPTER X

FURTHER PROPOSALS FOR THE SOCIAL REGULATION OF THE DISTRIBUTION OF WEALTH

5. Minimum Wage Boards.—It would be unwise to pass a law that no man shall be employed at less than a specified wage, for unless the wage specified were so low as to render the law of little or no use, it would exclude from all employment the lowest class of laborers who are far better off to earn what they now can, than to be condemned to idle pauperism, and whom no one could afford to employ at the wages proper for competent, normal men. Minimum wages can properly be fixed only for particular industries, and then subject to change with changing conditions. Thus a minimum wage for teachers of a certain grade within a certain area can be fixed with perfect propriety. So also can minimum rates for each of the labor processes involved in a given manufacture. But to do this with justice and without danger of crippling the industry and so injuring all engaged in it as managers or investors or laborers, would require an authority possessed of first-rate business judgment and having access to all the pertinent facts relating to the industry affected. This would require hearings open to both sides and the power to subpœna witnesses. The minimum fixed should be subject at proper intervals to petition for reconsideration from either employers or laborers. This involves the establishment of minimum wage boards, an experiment now being tried by certain states, and which may find far-reaching and beneficent application.[1]

---

[1] Nine of the states of this republic now have minimum wage laws (1914). Australia has extended the application of such laws from six trades in 1896 to 141 trades in 1915. England passed a Minimum Wage Board Act in 1909, covering four industries. The industries most

Minimum wage legislation may do more harm than good unless its provisions apply to minors or unless it is accompanied by such child labor legislation as will prevent the discharge of those whose wages it would affect in order to replace them with children. A favorite way of circumventing minimum wage laws, if permitted, will be apprenticeship laws that will allow the employer to get his cheap work done by a continuous succession of rather long-term apprentices who are exempted from the decisions of the minimum wage board.

6. Collective Bargaining.—The instrumentality which has thus far done most toward securing for labor a share in the differential returns of industry is collective bargaining. "It is usually a matter of small importance to the employer whether or not he secures a particular laborer, while the securing of a particular employment is often a matter of the very greatest importance to the laborer. Under these conditions wages are apt to be fixed much closer to the minimum which the laborer will take than to the maximum which the employer will pay." [1] One laborer out of the hundreds employed in a factory is in no position to bargain with the employer, especially when other applicants for work are waiting at the gates. But the whole body of laborers in the factory, if united, are in a position to bargain with the employer on terms of equality and justice. "The laws of supply and demand, even where they operate far more perfectly than they do with reference to labor, do not give to sellers

---

needing such treatment in the United States are retail stores, tenement industries, and cotton manufacture.

Whatever the people in general sufficiently want will become constitutional. All who believe in seriously attempting to make government an agency of democracy in an age of machine industry will help to liberalize the constitution. Modern means of transportation and communication and large-scale industry make the nation an industrial unit. All who resist economic justice and wish to perpetuate existing abuses, as well as many others among the naturally conservative will take refuge behind the written constitution.

[1] R. T. Ely: Outlines of Economics. Revised Ed. Macmillan Co., 1914, p. 382.

normal prices, but only create a situation in which the sellers can successfully demand a normal price if they are sufficiently awake to their opportunity to refuse to sell for less."

Collective bargaining has special advantages in that it is in harmony with the spirit of our free institutions; by it the laborers help themselves without relying unnecessarily upon the intervention of government, and it develops among them economic intelligence, devotion, and leadership. It is true, however, that the labor unions have at times been foolishly and even wickedly led, or misled, and have then developed a spirit of hatred and of tolerance for violent and illegal measures. Bargaining implies a certain fairness and readiness to abide by reasonable conclusions, and each side has too often lacked this spirit and has been inclined to rely upon its power to compel the other party to yield to its demands, rather than upon justice, which as a rule requires mutual concessions from opposing interests. Nevertheless there is no room for doubt that collective bargaining has come to stay probably as long as the wage system lasts, and the sooner all parties accept it as a normal and necessary basis for relations between hired labor and employers the better for all concerned. In fact many of the most successful and intelligent employers in this country and abroad have so accepted it, and regard it as for their own interest to have fixed agreements for specified periods with the whole body of their employees. It is a shortsighted error for employers to oppose the organization of labor. Especially employers are inviting the worst disorders and abuses when, in order to make organization difficult, they prefer ignorant laborers unable, because of differences of language, race, and religion, to understand each other.[1] The best labor force is intelligent, well organized and responsible.[2] Collective bargaining implies that the labor

---

[1] This has been illustrated by the recent social and industrial dis, turbances in Colorado.

[2] "There can be no doubt that in the struggle among nations, which, at least in the immediate future, is likely to become more intense than formerly, the people that first brings its social organization into har-

union as well as the present corporation is, in some sense at least, a social person with rights and responsibilities. To say that the unions should have powers is equivalent to saying that they should also have responsibilities, for the two cannot be divorced. The great difficulty in this connection has been in enforcing responsibility by any legal means against hundreds or thousands of nearly propertyless individuals even though organized. They ought to be incorporated and to have valuable charter rights. The best way to make them legally responsible is to give them something valuable that can be forfeited by misconduct. As soon as legal privileges, like those of appearing before boards of conciliation and arbitration and wage boards, are granted, and as soon as good standing before the bar of public opinion is justly valued by the unions, there is some means of enforcing responsibility upon them by denying legal privileges as a penalty for violating legal obligations and by public approval and disapproval. Moreover, since the unions now handle large funds there is some opportunity for legal control by pecuniary sanctions. The difficulty of enforcing obligation upon the unions has been the serious obstacle to the success of compulsory arbitration. A board of conciliation may have practically all the good results of compulsory arbitration if law requires adequate notice of a proposed strike or lockout, and enables and requires the board to ascertain and publish the facts which reveal the merits of the dispute before the strike can legally be called.

A single body of officials might combine the duties of board of conciliation and minimum wage board.

7. **Profit-sharing and Coöperation.**—These are not compulsory but voluntary measures, the former depending on

---

mony with the new conditions will have an immense advantage. The country that can first raise its working population to an intelligent and enthusiastic solidarity of feeling and interest, a compact nation of free, instructed men, would in the scientific (industrial) warfare of to-day have an exceptionally strong position against a government of capitalists dragging after them an unwilling, demoralized, and ignorant host of proletarians." Thomas Kirkup.

the initiative of the employers, the latter on that of the laborers.

In profit-sharing, because he regards it as good business to bind the laborer to him by such means, or because he admits the justice of the laborer's claim to a share in the differential, or for both reasons, the employer pays the laborers a dividend in addition to wages. The amount of the dividend in the case of each individual laborer is usually based upon the amount of regular wages paid him, that is, upon the value of the laborer's investment of work. Sometimes it is based in part on the length of the laborer's service. This is objected to because it puts a penalty on striking; and the right to quit and seek a new employer or better terms is the cardinal difference between the free laborer and the slave. Profit-sharing is not general but sporadic and promises no general relief unless in response to a far more pressing demand of public opinion.

In coöperative industry the workers are themselves the stockholders in the company and elect their own managers. Coöperative stores, coöperative building and loan companies and other coöperative credit associations, coöperative elevator companies and fruitgrowers associations, and coöperative "garden cities" have proved successful. But in these (unless in an exceptional case), the majority of the stockholders are not employed by the company. On the other hand, coöperative industry, in which the coöperators have been their own employees, has rarely proved successful. There is great danger that the coöperators will not be willing to pay wages of superintendence enough greater than the wages of ordinary labor to retain competent management, that they will not refrain from jealousy and cross purposes as a result of questions of preferment, and that they will not submit to proper discipline in the works.

One of the main principles of coöperation is "one man, one vote." In an ordinary corporation a man who owns more than half the stock can outvote all the other stockholders. The principle of "one-man vote" is probably safer even in non-coöperative corporations than the principle of "voting the shares," for normally the stockholders all are interested in the prosperity of the business, and it is not so certain that the holders of a majority of the stock will be just to a scattered multitude who may own the minority of the stock. The interests of a business may be sacrificed by a few wealthy stockholders who are interested, for example, not in the legitimate productivity of the stock, but in causing the value of the stock to fluctuate so that they may profit on the stock exchange by their foreknowledge of its fluctuations. The objection to the one-man, one-vote plan is that a competitor may cheaply buy a share in the management. Coöperative companies survive this danger.

8. Bipartite Coöperation.—The articles of agreement under which business is done by a concern might provide that the company should be composed of two classes of members: (a) those who invest capital; (b) those who invest labor. Just as anyone may now become a member of a company by purchasing stock, so anyone might become a member of Class B by being accepted as a laborer. The members of each class would elect a board of directors. The directors of Class A would have charge of matters in which there is no conflict of interest between the two classes of members, including all buying, selling, general promotion of productivity and profit, including all handling of capital. The directors of Class B would devise methods for promoting the welfare of their class so far as there was no conflict with the interests of Class A. Whenever it was necessary to secure the consent of Class A to any plan for the benefit of the laborers, or whenever there was a question involving a conflict of interests between Class A and Class B, the matter would be referred to a council composed of four, including two representatives chosen by each board of directors. If the council failed to reach a majority decision the question would be referred to a joint meeting of the boards of directors. This body would have at its command all the facts of the case, would fully represent all interests, and should be able to promote good understanding. In case the joint meeting of the two boards could not reach a majority decision (a majority of nine to five might be required if the joint directorate numbered fourteen), the question should be referred to three arbitrators, one representing each class of members, and the third a disinterested outsider. The third arbitrator should be named at the time of organization and not after some difference has occurred. All members of both classes should bind themselves to abide by the decisions of the council of four, the joint directorate, or the arbitrators, and not to interrupt the continuance of the business under existing conditions because of any pending difference.[1]

The principle must be accepted that those who invest labor as well as those who invest capital are entitled to a share in the management of industry, and that it is intolerable for the former to be without voice or representation in deciding questions in which there is a clear division of interest between the laborers and the managers.

9. Prevent Stock-Watering and Limit Stock Gambling.— Stock-watering is the issuance of securities having a par value greater than the actual property of the company. Ostensibly a stock certificate is an evidence of ownership of property, but evidences of ownership of five million dollars' worth of property may be issued and sold, where only one million dollars' worth of property exists. Suppose a promoter sees opportunity to consolidate the four chief concerns engaged in a given industry and so establish a monopoly. These concerns having plants worth, say, a million dollars each ($4,000,-000 in all) agree to turn them over to the new company for stock having a par value of three million dollars each ($12,-000,000 in all). The underwriter who floats this stock, that is, buys the whole lot and sells it out as he can, receives a bonus of stock having a par value of, say, two millions, and the promoter who devised the plan and secured the coöperation of the four original companies and of the underwriting bank or syndicate, receives an equal bonus. This brings the

---

[1] The strike of the Hart Schaffner and Marx workers in 1914 was terminated by an agreement resembling that here outlined, as was also the previous strike of the New York Garment Workers.

total issue of stock up to $16,000,000 on a material basis of $4,000,000. The excessive issuance of stock by great corporations is the rule and not the exception, and a disproportion of four to one as in our illustration is sometimes much exceeded. The buyers of such stock are cheated. A vast supply of stocks and bonds is provided to be speculatively bought and sold, not seldom at "manipulated" values. In order to keep these securities afloat in the market, the industry must be made to pay dividends not only upon the capital actually invested in it, but also upon the money paid by purchasers of the securities and pocketed by the promoters of the organization. To make an industry pay dividends upon several times the capital really invested in it, managers are forced to depress wages and to employ every monopolistic expedient to exalt prices.

The change in the method of taxing corporations above proposed would itself tend to discourage stock-watering if the amount of the stock issued were made the basis of the amount of the tax; but a more direct method of preventing the watering of stock is available. The actual property of each corporation should be subject to government inspection and a statement of the amount of its property should be open to all investors and such a statement should accompany every public announcement of stock offered for sale by the company together with a statement of the bonded indebtedness of the company. The experience of Germany, Austria, and France taken together shows that with proper legislation, stock-watering is an unnecessary evil.

An additional abuse has frequently arisen when two or more corporations of this sort have united through the agency of a "holding company." A holding company could establish its control by buying half of the stock of the corporations so united. An individual or group of individuals could control the holding company and so the concerns which it had united, by owning half of the stock of the holding company, equal in par value to one-fourth of the stock of the companies consolidated and controlled. Indeed they need not own as much as one-fourth, for besides issuing bonds, which carry no right to vote, such corporations usually have more than one class of stock, only one of which may have the voting right, and to control the whole mass of "securities" it is only necessary to own half of the voting stock.[1]

Dealing in futures on margin is buying and selling commodities or securities, through a broker, at an unknown future price, without paying the price for what is purchased, but only depositing a "margin" with the broker sufficient to protect the latter from loss on account of fluctuations in the prices of that which he is ordered to buy or sell, the person commissioning the broker thereby standing to lose the margin deposited, and standing to gain if the future prices prove to be higher when selling orders go into effect than when buying orders go into effect. This is very largely a type of gambling and is responsible, like other gambling, for much fleecing of lambs; and like other gambling it is likely to be played as a "sure thing game" by the insiders. Much wealth amassed and shifted from hand to hand by this agency is wrongfully taken from its possessors. It is difficult to see why anyone should be allowed to buy stocks "on credit." This can hardly be regarded as investment. It is an absurdity to claim that we need in this way to swell the volume of speculation "in order to determine the true value of securities." And it seems probable that dealing in futures on

[1] *Congressional Record,* June 20, 1914, p. 10762. Senator Owen said: "Three groups of men having their headquarters in New York have been shown, through interlocking directorates and interlocking control, to have the direction of approximately $22,000,000,000 of property, and practically to have the control over nearly every railroad in the country, and every one of the great industrials. Those men can forbid the railroads to buy rails, to buy steel cars, to buy railroad frogs and switches, to buy lumber and to buy cross ties; those men can put out of employment thousands and tens of thousands of men; those men can constrict credits in the districts of representatives who are to be elected in the fall, and in the states of senators who are to be elected in the fall; they can by their power make hard times in districts where they want to have a change, and where they want to defeat those in sympathy with a correction of those conditions, whether these candidates be Democrats or Progressive Republicans."

margin will in time be regarded as an abuse,[1] no longer to be tolerated by public opinion or by law.

10. A Commission for Corporations.—The great concerns may be expected to employ the monopolistic power, which they naturally tend to acquire, in raising prices to the point at which the differential remaining in their possession will be as great as possible. Their effort to do this will not be decreased by encroaching upon the differential in the ways above outlined, which increase the cost of production in order to thicken the slice of labor. On the contrary their motive for raising prices will be increased by these measures. It is possible that the prices now paid by bargain-hunting consumers for certain products is not sufficient to allow the payment of proper wages to laborers. If so, adoption of these reforms will imply a rise of prices. Great manufacturing concerns have in general raised prices to the point at which they are checked by natural causes. The natural checks on monopolistic prices are the fear of calling into competition in any specially profitable industry new and powerful combinations of capital, and—more effectual still—the fact that with excessive rise of price the demand for any given commodity falls off, so that there is a point at which further rise of prices would diminish income instead of increasing it. It is not true that a monopoly can get for its output any price it chooses to ask. It is one thing to ask a price and quite another to get it. A monopoly aims to ask the highest price that people will pay for a sufficient quantity of its output to make the net returns greater than they would be if a larger quantity were sold at a lower price. Raising prices and limiting output are correlative. But the consumer is not contented with the limitation upon prices that is set by the causes just stated. If by producing and selling a given quantity of goods at a given price the monopoly secures the same net income that would result from producing double the quantity of goods and selling them at a price so reduced that the public would buy the doubled output, it might be a matter of indifference to the monopoly whether the larger

---

[1] This refers to securities, not to commodities.

or the smaller quantity were produced. But it could not be a matter of indifference to the public, for not to mention the increased opportunity afforded to labor in case of the larger production, the placing of a larger quantity of goods within the reach of the public purchasing power, the greater abundance of desirable commodities, and lowered price, are exactly the results most to be desired from the point of view of the consumers. The problem is: how are we to prevent monopolies and near-monopolies from limiting their output to the quantities saleable at high prices which yield them the largest possible net returns? If they could not arbitrarily raise the price then the chief way for them to increase their income would be to increase the quantity of the output of a given kind and quality up to the point where the public demand was satisfied; that is, the point at which the public ceased to buy at a price covering the cost of production, including, of course, the wages of superintendence.

Now if in any important industry monopoly has the power arbitrarily to raise the prices and to limit output, it is desirable that it be confronted by a power that can arbitrarily limit the rise of prices. There is no power adequate to accomplish this but the power of government. But that power must be exercised with great circumspection. Changing the price on each article by a small percentage may suffice to wipe out a great profit and substitute a deficit. To cripple industry by limiting the price of its product would be like the folly of the woman who killed the goose that laid the golden eggs. Arbitrary power to limit prices may be necessary to confront the arbitrary power to raise them, but if so it must be exercised by carefully chosen men of character, training, and intelligence, who have access to the facts relating to each industry over which they have power, and their decisions should be subject to appeal for modification at reasonable intervals. To attempt to regulate prices by general legislation rather than by specific action case by case, would be impracticable. This calls for the institution of a special court or commission for this purpose. To secure the necessary promptness and flexibility and authority, the commission must be able to make rules within the limits of its legally defined authority and to apply those rules to specific cases without the intervention of any other court. Legislation of this sort, if undertaken, should proceed tentatively at first to a few fundamental industries. We have already learned some lessons of experience by price regulation through a commission in an exceedingly difficult field, that of interstate transportation. The question of constitutionality need not be raised.

The existence of such a commission having power to ascertain the necessary facts and in the light of those facts to regulate prices, might very possibly render it unnecessary to exercise power over prices, save in rare instances and as a last resort. Such an agency with power to make public facts concerning the management of corporations in respect to certain topics including the issuance of stock, payment of wages, the cost of production, and the fixing of prices, would bring to bear the force of public opinion in such a way as to accomplish important results without resort to any legal compulsion beyond that necessary to ascertain these facts. The topics with reference to which the commission could publish information should be limited by law so as to guard legitimate trade secrets. But no corporation, creature as it is of the public will, has any right to refuse to the public information that is necessary for guidance of the public or its agents in protecting the general interests. Otherwise the corporation may become an afrit, a Frankenstein, able to defy and rule and rob its maker.

Before going so far as to empower a commission to regulate prices by decree it is well to try the effect of publicity alone. The Federal Trade Commission, which has been established by Congress since the foregoing paragraph was written, has power to secure all necessary information concerning great corporations and, at its discretion, to publish such information. On discovery of unlawful practices, it is authorized to recommend to the courts the steps by which to terminate such practices, by the application of existing laws, and to report to Congress any facts which may call for additional legislation. The commission may serve as a master in equity in case of suits brought under anti-trust acts. It is to report the manner in which decrees of courts against corporations are observed. Orders of the commission for termination of "unfair methods of competition" are enforced by the circuit court of appeals, before which the findings of the commission are conclusive as to facts.

The most mischievous of the unfair methods by which a monopoly can stifle incipient competition is to sell at a loss in the field of its competitors and recoup itself out of gains secured by higher prices in other districts, or to sell below cost the one grade or style made by the competitor. It is probable that in most cases competition or the dread of competition will force great corporations to keep prices down to an approximately normal level if they are prevented from stifling competition by unfair methods. It is at length recognized that penal laws against corporations should carry penalties enforceable against their officers as individuals. Fines amount to little in such cases; imprisonment amounts to a great deal.

Among other laws which have been recommended is the prohibition of holding corporations and even of the leasing of corporate property by corporations. We may advocate the prohibition of all unfair actions designed to injure competitors without advocating any war against fair combination designed to diminish competition by bigger and better organizations. It is possible to go too far in treating competition as a good in itself and in treating comprehensive and efficient organization as an evil. Comprehensive organization may go to any length, provided the power of individuals to control the organization is at the same time limited. To limit the power of individuals it has been proposed that we forbid interlocking directorates, and adopt some application of the principle which prevails in "coöperative" corporations by which the voting power of an individual does not increase in proportion to the size of his holdings. The trade commission may promote the confidence and prosperity of well disposed managers by answering questions as to whether proposed action would be treated as illegal or in violation of public policy.

11. Government Ownership.—This differs from "coöperation," already discussed, mainly in that in the former the co-operating owners are limited to a particular body of persons incorporated under the laws of the state and having no political or governmental authority, while under the present head we consider the legal voters of an entire governmental unit, a city or a state, as the coöperative partners. A highly important practical result proceeding from this distinction between the two, is that under government ownership funds derived from taxation may be used to make up a deficit incurred by an industry. This has its advantages, but also its perils; for it makes it possible for government industry to drift into lax and inefficient ways relying on the taxing power to sustain it, while "coöperative" industry, if inefficient, must fail and involve the coöperators in loss which cannot be hidden.

A still graver danger to success in the governmental ownership of industries is the likelihood that appointments will be made for political or personal reasons, and not with strict regard for qualification to do the work of the position held.[1]

12. Socialism.—In algebra we were taught to let x equal any unknown thing that it was convenient so to designate. Similarly the word socialism is a symbol which some people use to designate any proposal of reform that is too radical and destructive to deserve approval. Others use it to designate any proposal that is sufficiently courageous and constructive to deserve support. Others still use it to designate a definitely elaborated program of reform.

The central element in the socialism of avowed socialists is advocacy of the organization of industry in the interest, and under the control of all the active participants in industry. Some content themselves with advocating this principle broadly, proposing to utilize to this end whatever form

---

[1] It is true that advancement in privately managed business is very largely influenced by family and social relationships.

of organization proves best adapted to each given case. Thus their plan includes such voluntary coöperation as that now practiced by the great coöperative stores of England and by coöperative insurance, building and loan, fruitgrowers' and farmers' grain elevator associations. Others (the state socialists) concentrate their argument upon the extension of government ownership. These cite the public schools, the postal system, and municipal waterworks and gas and electric lighting plants as instances of the type of socialistic action in which they believe. Some industries they would assign to the municipality, others to the state, and others to the national administration. International carrying trade the majority of such socialists might assign to an international organization. They ardently believe that socialism would provide conditions under which the better elements in human nature would come naturally into predominance in the relations between individuals and under which war between nations would be practically done away.

State socialism is the opposite of anarchism; it is reform by the extension of government activity, while anarchism is reform by the diminution of government activity. Anarchism is the product of tyranny which breeds revulsion against all government; its natural home is a land like Russia. Socialism is the product of democracy which invites faith in the omnipotent beneficence of government. Anarchism is individualism relieved from all constraint; its motto is "more freedom is the cure for freedom's ills," and "that government is best which governs least"; its peril is chaos. Socialism is the curbing of individualism in the interest of the many and its peril is stagnation. Socialism and anarchism are somewhat difficult to define, except in their extreme forms, or else as tendencies. Using the terms as names for tendencies, Professor W. G. Sumner has said that every man is either an anarchist or a socialist, that is, he looks for progress chiefly from the exploits of untrammeled individualism, or from the increase of coöperation through organization.

Socialists differ from communists in their emphasis of the difference between "capital" and "consumption goods."

The most characteristic item in the program of socialism is collective ownership and management of all business requiring the use of large aggregations of capital, such as railroads, factories, and mines. They say that possession of such masses of capital by individuals creates an artificial distinction between men, makes competition on equal terms impossible, and renders the mass of workers slaves who depend on the consent of their masters for the opportunity to toil. The socialists, however, are not communists, for they would allow private property in consumption goods, such as homes and their furnishings, and most of them approve private possession of such production goods as the mechanic's kit of tools. Their primary aim is not equalization of wealth but equalization of opportunity; and they argue that concentration of the chief means of production in private hands destroys equality of opportunity and reduces society to a kind of caste system.

Socialists would make agricultural land public property, but the wisest of them would assign it to individual cultivators, and not attempt collective farm management.

One of the arguments of the socialists relates to the great savings which might be effected by comprehensive organization of industry, as against the wastes of competition in the manufacture of goods, and in the delivery of goods by a system which involves the passage of several milk-wagons down the same streets and the conveyance of parcels of every sort from many sellers to individual purchasers instead of allowing the districting of cities and states with one distributing point for each district, and of competitive salesmanship which requires a large part of the energy of the nation to be devoted merely to inducing purchasers to buy of one seller rather than another, and which sometimes causes the charges of middlemen to double the price of a commodity.

Socialists commonly divide themselves into two denominations: the "orthodox" or Marxian socialists, who advocate immediate government ownership and management of all extensive bodies of the means of production; and the "revisionists," who avow the tendency above described as socialistic and call themselves socialists, and yet in some instances do not propose any more radical reforms or any more impatient methods than those which are believed in by many persons who would be shocked at being called socialists.

Socialism has appealed both to some of the solidest thinkers, like J. S. Mill, and also to many of the type who are eager for something new and strange. The latter have mixed with their socialism numerous vagaries concerning the modification of other than economic institutions, but these have nothing to do with the essence of socialism. The most intelligent advocates of socialism do not propose any complete and detailed plan for immediate adoption, but content themselves with advocating the principle of ownership and management of each great body of capital, by and for "the people," or "the participants in the industry," and with promoting such steps in that direction as seem to be already justified. They believe that by a tentative and experimental approach toward the fulfillment of their aim the method of that fulfillment will gradually be discovered.

Although a complete socialistic system is not likely soon to be tried in this country, yet we may continue to extend government activity, now here, now there, now wisely and again unwisely, until we tentatively reach the limits beyond which we cannot go without making the machinery of life too cumbersome and oppressive, and the opportunities and motives for individual endeavor too limited. Aside from the two dangers already mentioned in discussing the extension of government ownership the evil most dreaded as a result of overorganization is that governmental industry will settle down into a jogging routine, and that men engaged in such industry will find no adequate motives to invention, improvement, and notable achievement.

Reform by Violence.—Sabotage (or the wrecking of machinery or damaging of work), murder by bomb-throwing and other "direct" methods, are far more associated with anarchism than with socialism and are no essential part of either.

Syndicalism of the I. W. W. (Industrial Workers of the World) stands for the widest employment of the sympathetic strike and a creed of violence. Some may honestly believe that no war was ever better justified than that for labor's rights, and no soldiers truer heroes than those who brave the perils involved in such acts. Perhaps this would be true if such methods would secure social justice and no other methods would. But since neither of those conditions is found, such acts are both follies and crimes. Vast reforms do not come in a day, but never in the world were they coming so fast as now and never before did labor have in its hands such effective agencies for securing its rights, as the ballot, freedom of discussion in press and speech, and freedom of organization. It is treachery to labor's cause to imperil these rights; and society as a whole, rich and poor, which has granted these rights, is justified in stamping out the abuse of them and the violence that is the subversion of all social order.

Necessity for Development in Industrial Legislation.— Nothing is more practically certain than that modern industrial conditions call for the development of a new body of laws, and that statutes and rules of common law which come down to us from before the industrial revolution, must be scrutinized and new ones must be developed. Certain principles of justice are eternal, but their application is frustrated if, when conditions change, legal methods are not adapted to the new requirements. The principles of the wheel, pulley, screw, and lever are the same as in the sixteenth century, but machinery has evolved. We have a highly developed system of laws to regulate the conduct of natural persons. There must be laws to regulate the conduct of artificial, legally created persons, that is, corporations, for the latter now play an increasing rôle in society, and even threaten to assume the sovereignty and rule us in their own interest, if indeed they do not already do so, in part through control of the agencies of government, in part through control of the organs of public opinion, in part through their mastery over the earners of wages, in part through the power to fix prices and lay us all under tribute. The new conditions call for new laws not chiefly upon the subject of prices, but chiefly upon the relations between the employers and laborers, as above pointed out. Next to the relations between husband and wife and parents and children, those between employers and employed are probably the most fundamental to social welfare. The marriage relation is automatically protected, for it involves companionship, the parent of sympathy, and rupture of good personal relations forfeits the ends for which marriage exists. Nevertheless, marriage requires the protection of law. How much more the relation between employer and laborer which has no such natural defenses!

Already considerable progress has been made toward the development of a system of law adapted to modern exigencies. But law is necessarily conservative and slow moving, and of necessity the situation arrives before the laws that are adapted to it. The situation is here, and without undue hurry or radicalism, but with courage and constructiveness, a corresponding system of law must be evolved.

Law No Cure-all.—After all has been said and done in reference to the direct attack upon injustice in distribution of wealth it remains to be added that the problem of poverty must be attacked in the flank as well as in the front. All the work of legislatures, courts, and labor unions directed against the evils of poverty will not remove those evils so long as there are thousands upon thousands who lack the physical and moral ability to earn a living. Poverty as we have seen is largely responsible for the lack of physical stamina and the lack of steadiness and thrift, but it is also true that these defects are largely responsible for the poverty. We cannot safely rely upon more just control of distribution alone. We must have fewer citizens who lack physical soundness, moral steadiness, competence, and intelligence, before we can approach the abolition of poverty. The campaigns for better public health and for better education of the mass of the people and for placing within their reach more wholesome joys, which are outlined in other connections, must also be carried out before we shall have done what must be done toward overcoming the evils of poverty. Evils of all these kinds reënforce and perpetuate each other and a blow at any one of them is a blow at them all, and progress to be surely successful anywhere, must be an advance "all along the line."

CHAPTER XI

TYPES OF POVERTY

Meanwhile what shall society do for those of its members who under existing conditions are unable to maintain themselves?

The dependent may be classified into four groups, each of which requires treatment different from that which is appropriate to either of the others: (1) the normally dependent; (2) the physically dependent; (3) the morally dependent; (4) the unemployed but employable.

The first class comprises children and the aged. It is normal for them to be physically unable to maintain themselves. It is the function of the family to care for them. The burden which they place upon those in the prime of life is heavy. Historically it has been a chief means of developing human sympathy and the crowning virtue of helpfulness. Through the death of breadwinners or otherwise, many families become unable to care for their young and their aged.

The Care of Dependent Children.—This presents a problem of great importance because it requires not only provision for present comfort but also for education and the development of personality. Unwise charity may condemn the child to life-long pauperism and make him or her the progenitor of a strain of miserables extending through generations, involving society in long-continued and heavy expense and adding needlessly to the world's misery.

No child ought ever to grow up in a poorhouse. As a rule with very few exceptions, if any, the orphanage is not a good place for a child. We cannot expect children to be properly brought up by wholesale; they require individual mothering. Budding individuality is in the way where many children must be cared for by a few attendants. The personality of the orphanage inmate is exceedingly likely to be deficient in independence, initiative, adaptability, alertness, competence, and self-control. Yet the orphanage is one of the most popular forms of charity. The dependent child appeals to sympathy and churches like to congregate children under the influence of their own sect. Many large endowments are devoted to the support of orphanages.

When the orphanage is unavoidable it should take the form of a number of small houses, each with its house mother and house father, rather than a large institutional building. The children should not be dressed in uniform and should be sent to the public schools with children from normal homes. Such an orphanage should preferably be in the country and the children should have opportunities for helpfulness about the homes and gardens.

It would be better still if the same funds could be devoted to securing homes for the children in real families carefully selected, where they should be adopted or received as boarders; and in maintaining a system of visitation among the homes where the children were placed, so as to see to it that they were receiving proper physical, mental and moral nurture. It is a source of surprise to one unacquainted with the facts to learn how readily adoption can be secured for homeless children. The parental instinct is strong in many hearts, and with reasonable care directed to this end the orphanage may be transformed into a "placing-out home," where children are retained only for a brief period till suitable homes can be found, and the children can be nursed into health and fitness for such homes.

The orphan does not present the most perplexing problem in the case of dependent children, but rather the child of the depraved home. Sometimes affection for their children seems the one bright gleam in parents whose character is flickering toward total darkness. Whenever it is possible to rehabilitate the home so that it can care for its own children, this should be done. Mere poverty, uncomplicated with other unfitness, should not be a cause for taking children from their parents or from their sole surviving parent, but in such cases steps should be taken for the relief of the poverty.

Widows with children are pensioned by the county under a law recently passed in the state of Illinois.[1] This legislation is the subject of warm debate. Its advocates claim that it is practicable before any system of compulsory industrial insurance can be introduced; that it is essential to the rearing of the children in a manner compatible with the interests of society, and that it removes from voluntary charity an insupportable burden.

The opponents argue that it cannot be administered without abuses. It must be conceded that the administration of charitable funds by public authorities has hitherto generally been a failure in this country. But it is not so everywhere and need not always be so here. The beginning of proper administration of non-institutional charity by public agency may well be in connection with mothers' pensions. To make these pension laws a success the court which allows them must either act in close conjunction with an intelligent charity worker of the local charity organization, or else there must be such a worker as an attaché of the court. The former is entirely practicable in smaller places, and the latter is now being attempted in Chicago.

Great as is the reluctance with which the representative of society steps in to break the natural tie between parents and children, and great as is the caution that should be exercised in resorting to this form of social surgery, it must be recognized that parental rights can be forfeited. The laws do recognize this fact and, with greater or less wisdom in their specific provisions, authorize the removal of children from delinquent parents. The absolute necessity of this course for the sake of the child and for the sake of society in which the child is to have his career, is in some instances

---

[1] The Illinois law was passed in 1911. Since then similar laws have been passed by 16 states. The Illinois law applies not to widows only but to any parent or parents who, being in other respects fitted to rear their children properly, are prevented from doing so by poverty only.

perfectly obvious, for example, when great cruelty is practiced or when parents are habitually or even professionally vicious.

The child of the prisoner has a special claim upon the state, since the state has forcibly removed its natural support. Probably the time will come when instead of keeping thousands of fathers in idleness in county jails we shall have workhouses where these prisoners will be required to earn something toward the support of their families.[1]

Since the child is a normal dependent and since his proper rearing is of so great consequence to society, many things may properly be undertaken for him by the public. Here, as elsewhere, it is often the case that a function is first performed by voluntary action on the part of persons who realize its importance, to be assumed later by the city or the state after its usefulness has been demonstrated and its method ascertained by the private agency. It is, however, possible for government to go too far and infringe upon the integrity and sense of responsibility of the family. School lunches, even in districts where a considerable proportion of the pupils are too ill breakfasted to study well and too anemic to develop properly in body or in mind, are frequently objected to on this ground. It may be argued that it is better for children to be taken to a day nursery or kindergarten that is maintained by the city than to one maintained by private charity, because of the pauperizing effects of the latter, the hurt to their self-respect and that of their parents, and the danger of accustoming them to receive charitable aid. For this reason it is usually wiser to charge some fee, though it be very small, for the services of a day nursery or a kindergarten privately maintained, or for school lunches even when provided by the city. School lunches furnished at the cost of the food can be made very nutritious and very inexpensive and perhaps a means of teaching household arts to the children who assist in their preparation. Day nurseries, wherever mothers in large numbers are obliged to leave their little children through the working hours to pasture in the tene-

[1] Compare p. 624.

ments and alleys of the slums, are demanded by every consideration of humanity and prudence. So also are the kindergartens and the supervised playgrounds for older children.

The care of the children is the greatest of all the problems of charity, not only because of the great numbers of its little beneficiaries, but because it is preventive of future miseries and constructive of future good. In the vast majority of instances the child can be formed for normal life, but it is from the ranks of unfortunate children that now come the majority of those who darken the world with misery and burden it with their care. Moreover, each single child saved to a life of usefulness might otherwise not only grow up to a life of misery and crime but, as already noted, might also become the parent of increasingly numerous generations of paupers and criminals.

Care of the Aged.—Society should conspire to cheer old age by its manners and its spirit of kindness and deference. The dependence of old age is not normal in precisely the same sense as that of childhood, for the aged have had a past in which under favorable conditions provisions for declining years could have been made. Under present economic conditions, however, for thousands of laborers the saving of an adequate provision for old age would mean the denial of really human existence to themselves and their wives and of a decent rearing to their children. For an aged laborer worn out by a life of honest toil in the service of society to be forced to spend his last years in the poorhouse, classed with those pauperized by physical and moral abnormality, in companionship with the abjectly incompetent and the depraved and diseased wrecks of debauch, is abhorrent to justice and humanity. Aged men and women who have led upright and honorable lives of ceaseless industry in some cases would rather die of starvation than accept the undeserved stigma and be exposed to the repulsive association of the poorhouse. Yet a high percentage of aged laborers are obliged to accept relief in some form. It is a shame to call it charity, when as a rule these laborers have contributed to the abundance of the well-to-do over and above the amount returned to them in wages. There should be in force in our country, as abroad, a system of old-age pensions like that described in a former section, adapted to secure them justice. Till that comes to pass there might be municipal or county "old people's homes" like that in Boston, where the self-respecting aged are cared for apart from all other classes of dependents. In some of our larger counties there should be, in connection with the county home, a separate cottage for aged couples, and possibly also aged individuals, who have behind them a good working record. As a first temporary step separate bedrooms and separate sitting-rooms might be provided in poorhouses for men and for women who meet certain requirements.

Care of the Physically Defective.—The second general class of dependents is made up of those whose inability to support themselves is due to some physical defect. These defects are of various kinds.

1. *Insanity* is the name given to a class of bodily diseases which manifest themselves in disturbance of the processes of consciousness. Insanity has been interpreted as the intrusion of a foreign soul, a demon, in the body and therefore as a supernatural visitation or a sign that the individual was no longer truly human; and these notions have caused and still cause unreasonable cruelty and lack of sympathy in the treatment of these dreadful diseases. Another important popular notion is that insanity is a disgrace. It may be in fact the result of heroic endurance. It is true that it is often due to venereal disease or to alcoholism, and that some families have a precariously balanced nervous organization that is liable to become deranged; but it is also true that insanity is no more a certain indication of hereditary taint or of vice than death from pneumonia is of alcoholism.

These diseases are in many instances curable, but the probability of cure diminishes with great rapidity if the early symptoms are allowed to continue without expert treatment; and it is unfortunately true that, because of superstitious dread or sense of disgrace or the existing legal barrier to voluntary application for treatment at public institutions, the necessary expert care is frequently not received until the possibility of cure is past. This is one abuse in the care of the insane and of the mentally disturbed who may perhaps be threatened with insanity. There should be psychopathic clinics open to such persons without legal formality. To such a clinic parents should go unhesitatingly on the first appearance of neurotic symptoms in a child. In this way many cures would be effected in cases that under the present conditions are allowed to develop into confirmed insanity.[1]

Another abuse is the retention of insane persons, especially the so-called harmless insane, in places where there is not only no possibility of remedial treatment but also no provision for humane treatment. Girls are chained to bedposts and sick old men shut in grated cages. Most poorhouses have harbored insane persons, frequently in grated cells, sometimes in chains. The most progressive legislation positively prohibits their retention in any institutions but those designed for insane patients. These institutions are best if not housed in great barracks but arranged on the cottage system where adequate classification is possible and separation of patients from other patients that interfere with their comfort and their recovery. The patients should be provided with abundant occupation of such a sort as they are able to perform, "re-educated" to the performance of light handicrafts, and should have as much of their occupation as possible in the open air. Occupation is a curative agency and even when all agencies

---

[1] In 1913 the state of New York initiated the experiment of treating the mentally diseased in their homes, as "out-patients," during the incipient stages or when provisionally discharged from hospital. Nearly one-third of the 5,000 new patients admitted to New York state hospitals for the insane during 1911 had been mentally diseased for at least a year. Thus the state began the annual expenditure of millions of dollars in the treatment of patients who had already passed the period when every dollar expended could have done as much as ten expended later on. It may be hoped that this movement will lead to the maintenance of psychopathic clinics in various parts of the state where the mother who has a child that is "different" from others, and the adult who is sensible of neural change or disturbance in himself or a relative may find council that will lead to the prevention of catastrophy.

must fail to produce a cure, still occupation may make life tolerable and even cheerful to those who, if herded in idleness in a crowd of the insane, would sink into hopeless and unutterable misery. Continuous life as an inmate of one of the wards of an old-fashioned insane asylum, daily and hourly witnessing the pitiful exhibitions of the insane, would seem enough to make a sane person crazy. We are still pitifully ignorant upon the subject of insanity and ill supplied with therapeutic measures. The states should provide liberally for research in this field.

2. Closely allied with insanity is *epilepsy,* a malady peculiarly pitiful because its victims in the intervals between their seizures may be endowed with admirable attractions and powers, which in most cases are prevented from bearing their normal fruit of joy and usefulness, and these unfortunates are overshadowed by the dread of their horrible attacks. Epilepsy usually involves the decay of powers, and is linked with various forms of physical degeneracy. It is even said that all born criminals are epileptic. While the American states make expensive provision for the custody of their insane, the public care of epileptics is in its infancy. Several states maintain colonies for epileptics where normal occupation and enjoyable society can be provided, but where marriage is prevented. About half the offspring born of epileptic parents are epileptic and practically all of the other half show some serious abnormality. Such facts make the prevention of marriage a social duty. The epileptic colony should be a large area where the life of the inmates is as much as possible like that of a normal village, with shops, fields and places of entertainment, where the intervals between seizures can be spent in work and pleasures. The work of inmates should go far toward maintaining the colony. And adequate provisions should be made for safety in time of seizure, for improvement of the improvable, and for the entire prevention of propagation.

3. The *feeble-minded* and their treatment will be discussed on page 249. They are prolific if allowed to be at large and pass on their defect to offspring that burden society with

cost and infest it with perils. Their own happiness, and the protection of society, require that they be isolated in homes or colonies.

4. *Sickness* is the most constant of all the causes of poverty, and is responsible for at least one-fifth of the cases requiring charity. The thing most to be desired is to reduce the vast amount of preventable sickness which exists among the poor. The sick but curable require temporary aid with avoidance of pauperization and permanent dependence. The requirement of the family impoverished by the curable sickness of its breadwinner is his complete cure. This should be studiously promoted, if only from motives of economy, lest permanent dependence ensue. The sick are cared for by institutions of three classes. The first are dispensaries and hospitals. The second are convalescent homes where patients may be taken when they no longer require the more expensive treatment of the hospital. It is often better as well as far more economical to found a convalescent home than to enlarge the hospitals. The convalescent home can be in the edge of the city away from smoke and noise. Its atmosphere is one of hope. Many a patient is discharged from the hospital in order to make room for sicker patients as soon as sufficiently recovered to expect reëstablishment of health under favorable conditions, and in the absence of a convalescent home is returned to the crowded tenement and the factory while still weak, an easy prey to new diseases and unable to reestablish sound and permanent health in that unfavorable environment. Third, are the homes for the incurables designed to provide for persons who even in the well-to-do home cannot be properly cared for or who would be too heavy a burden upon a home of poverty. A special class of the sick are the victims of alcohol and other drugs. Though their first trouble may have been moral weakness, there is no doubt that they finally become sick and that in their latter condition they are unable to shake off the habit that destroys them, while after a course of proper physical and moral treatment they may be saved to themselves and to society. The usefulness of special sanitaria for this class

of cases with compulsory detention, has been proved by experience.

The non-institutional care of the sick includes the work of visiting nurses' associations, which provide necessary attendance in the homes of the poor, and give instruction to the families they visit as to the proper feeding and care of invalids and babies as well as in the general preservation of the health.

The principle of substituting justice wherever possible for so-called charity would dictate the system of insurance, previously mentioned, against sickness and permanent invalidity of laborers.

5. The *crippled* for the most part should be beneficiaries of industrial accident insurance. In a few instances they are proper inmates for homes for incurables. Often they may become self-supporting. For instance, a legless man may be an expert cigar-maker, stenographer, or telegrapher. Very frequently they become mere beggars, or venders of pencils, court-plaster, shoestrings, and the like, selling poor goods at high prices and expecting to "keep the change." If they peddle they should be licensed as other peddlers are and upon the same terms. It is a demoralizing thing for men to trade upon their misfortunes. Frequently their injuries are faked, skin scalded by chemicals is carefully unbandaged and exhibited as evidence of suffering in a boiler accident, and the like. All beggars should be referred to the charity agent of the locality. No beggars should be allowed upon the street. They should be cared for in ways that are better for them and for all concerned.

6. The *deaf, dumb* and *blind* are properly provided for in institutions which may bear the double name of "School and Home." This name corresponds to the two requirements which this class of persons present, namely: first, special education that will give their lives cheer and worth and render them completely or partially self-supporting; and, second, an abode for those who would fall into poverty and misery without custodial care, and for some whose malady is transmissible and who must therefore be permanently isolated

from society. Many of the deaf and dumb and blind can leave the special school and take their places in society as self-supporting citizens. The blind beggar should disappear from the streets of every well regulated community; indeed, the demoralizing occupation of beggary should be wholly abolished.

Dependency Due to Moral Abnormality.—According to the enumeration with which this chapter opened the third class of dependents is composed of those whose poverty is due to moral defect.

Moral defect is closely related to physical defect. Often, though by no means always, laziness is undervitalization and neurasthenia. Shiftlessness and incompetence are characteristic of the feeble-minded of the highest class, the morons, some of whom in certain gifts may even excel the average person.

Quarrelsomeness, insubordination, and general inability to "get along" with superintendents and fellow workmen; drunkenness, licentiousness, idleness, wanderlust, absence of self-respect and ambition, and in general the lack of the disciplined habits which are described by the good old-fashioned designation of "steadiness," unfit men for retaining any desirable place in the industrial organization.

The typical hobo is the child of impulse. Mere impulse, though it be sociable and generous as often as it is sensual and heartless, does not make man fit to occupy a place in society. The habit of choosing between impulses and even of suppressing present impulse in obedience to the far-reaching purposes of reason must be formed if one is to be fit to live a human life. Obedience is the parent of mastery. Moral impotence may be partly due to an inborn crotchet, or to a dilution of the powers by hard conditions of life, but they are the characteristic products of bad rearing, due to illegitimacy, orphaning, break up of homes by divorce or desertion, parental absorption in business or pleasure, quick change that makes the rearing of one generation unsuited to the next, or mere lack of wholesome family traditions. Obviously these faults tend to perpetuate themselves from generation to generation. The trained charity worker who gains a helpful intimacy with the children, the friendly visitor, the probation officer, the Sunday School or day teacher, the settlement worker, the example of thrifty neighbors and associates, and sometimes marriage into a better trained family, may break the chain of moral incompetence.

To the bad qualities enumerated must be added the moral disease of pauperism. Pauperism as a term of social and ethical description corresponds to parasitism as a biological term. The moral disease of pauperism consists in willingness to get all one can from society while indifferent to playing any productive part in society. Moral paupers are mainly of two classes: first, the idle rich who make great economic demands upon society which they are able to satisfy by control of "unearned increments" or by taking toll directly or indirectly upon the labor of others; and, second, those who confine themselves to such small economic demands as are supplied by the good nature of society. Society has not always recognized its rich paupers as morally diseased, but now at length the gilded youth who is a mere idler and spender, whether vicious in his pleasures or a mere dilettante, begins to suffer a little in social standing and self-respect. To be sure, as there is a "criminal milieu" in which men boast of cracking safes and eluding detectives and stand high in proportion to the magnitude of their crimes, so also there is a "smart set" in which people advertise their bad taste and lack of sane standards of ambition by vying with each other in ostentation and stand high in proportion as they display wealth by extravagant expenditures. And both of these classes by the startling contrast they exhibit to the ordinary course of life excite attention and "make copy" for the newspapers; yet neither the one nor the other sets the standard of judgment for normal men. It is true that as yet the rich young man may escape the odium which is beginning to attach to the mere idler and spender by simply going into business and striving to concentrate on himself a still larger share of the social income. If such a man goes into business too little discrimination is made as to whether he merely becomes a dealer in stocks, discounting the future and betting on inside information in a sort of grand gambling with loaded dice, sharing in manipulations that are large-scale "sure-thing" robbery, or engages in other forms of exploitations; or, on the other hand, whether he sets about developing the productivity of great enterprises. It is true also that careers of artistic, literary, scientific, philanthropic and political achievement attract as yet comparatively few of the very rich; yet there are to be ages of progress, a century is a short span in the course of social evolution, and the development of moral standards, though slow, when once begun is likely to be sure.

At this point, however, it is only for consistency of definition that we need refer to the rich pauper; our attention must here be given to the poor pauper, the recipient of alms. Legally all who receive charity at the expense of a political body are paupers, and colloquially the term is sometimes applied to all the needy, but by no means all of the very poor, any more than all of the very rich, are moral paupers, willing parasites. On the contrary some of the very poor make heroic struggles against the acceptance of alms and if compelled by misfortune or cruel conditions to seek relief, cease to receive it as soon as self-support becomes possible and sometimes even regard it as a loan to be repaid to the giver or to other needy folk, when times mend. The moral paupers here to be discussed are those who, finding the struggle for honest maintenance hard and finding the satisfaction of their standard of living by beggary and usually by some fraud to be easy, throw themselves flat upon the good nature of the public. Unless some plan of prevention is resorted to, every city has its quota of resident town bums and dead-beats; and the army of tramps, or vagrant beggars, in the United States constantly numbers, according to different estimates, from sixty to one hundred thousand. Of these, five-eighths are said to be native-born Americans; next in number come the Irish, and then the Germans. Only about one-tenth of them are entirely illiterate. These people are deserters from life's responsibilities; often the men have wives toiling somewhere over washtubs to support the children whom they have begotten. They have been tolled away by careless almsgiving. Society can have about as many beggars as it chooses to feed. Indiscriminate giving to strangers in all cities and large towns should cease entirely. In every such community there should be one central agency to which these applicants are sent by all to whom they apply. By this central agency the deserving applicant would often be given far better help than the meal at the back door which only enables him to continue in beggary. As far as possible he would be given aid in securing employment or whatever his necessity demanded. At the same time even the professional tramp need not be turned away hungry. There would, however, be no place in that community where the tramp could beg a meal except the central agency, and to such a community few tramps want to come. This implies, however, a very difficult condition, namely, that promiscuous begging and almsgiving has been entirely suppressed, by the intelligence of householders, and the activity of the police. In every large town some agency should provide a chance to work half a day in return for lodging and a simple supper and breakfast. The habitual vagrant parasite when convicted, by aid of telegraphic or telephonic messages to other towns from which he had come or from which he professed to have come, or by other evidence, should be confined in the workhouse, as a deterrent against this form of desertion and parasitism, as a protection against the moral contagion and the easily concealed crimes of irresponsible vagrants, as well as against the petty blackmail which they levy upon housekeepers, and as an opportunity for enforced industrial education. At present we have almost no workhouses adapted to this purpose.

It is not so easy to maintain a central agency for administering charity and dealing with tramps in sparsely settled regions but even here the same principles apply, and "selectmen" or "supervisors" or a clergyman may properly discharge this function if enlightened as to proper methods. In some sections of Germany stations are maintained at intervals on the main thoroughfares where the wayfarer may secure supper, lodging and breakfast in return for labor, and the necessity for the honest man and the temptation for the tramp to beg from door to door are thus abolished. Of course even such an agency depends for success upon the co-operation of the public, who refer all strangers applying for alms to its ministrations.

The Unemployed but Employable.—The Charity Organization Society of New York has reported that from 43 per cent. to 52 per cent. of all applicants need work rather than material aid. The unemployed and their families must in general be tided over either by industrial insurance,[1] by labor union benefits, or by charity. The problem of the unemployed cannot be solved by charity, but only by insurance and reorganization of industry.

There is a permanent surplus of labor of the very lowest grade, largely corresponding in its membership with the classes of "physically" and "morally" impoverished. But there is also unemployment among the normal and employable who want to work. And it is with these that the present section deals. At the time of the census of 1900, 2,634,336 or 11.1 per cent. of all males over 10 years of age engaged in gainful occupations in the United States were unemployed three months or more during the year.[2]

Alternations of rush seasons with dull seasons, when many laborers are thrown out of work, are a source of trouble in many industries, especially when the wages are not high even in the rush periods. Some supplementary occupation during the slack periods and the collocation of alternating industries are desirable. The location of certain industries in the agricultural regions, providing alternation between factory work and the seasons of planting and harvest, would be ideal, an ideal which rural coöperation in some places may possibly

---

[1] "The Danes have demonstrated two economic truths: first, that unemployment is the most frequent cause of pauperism, and second, that insurance is the most effective remedy for unemployment." Prof. K. Coman. *Survey,* xxxi, 742. Denmark is not alone in this.

[2] F. H. Streightoff: The Standard of Living. Houghton Mifflin Co., 1911, p. 35.

promote. A beginning has been made in certain fruit-growing sections by the manufacture of baskets and crates. An industry to be best adapted to this alternation with agriculture must not require too much capital. In the case of most seasonal trades, aside from agriculture, there is no inherent necessity that they should be so seasonal, and they ought not to be permitted to be so.

The evil of unemployment of the employable is likely to be great when times are hard, building operations suspended, and factories closed or running half time. At such times aid might be found in pushing forward public works, and even in having certain state enterprises so organized that they would expand their labor force when times were slack and wages low, thus affording relief to the unemployed and economy to the state with no tendency to pauperization. In enterprises of the latter sort the wages paid would be small enough so that men would not be attracted away from normal industry, but would turn to other occupations when times were good, laboring for the state when no other opportunity to labor was open. A system of state road improvement would afford such elastic employment, where weather conditions permit such labor at the seasons of slackest employment. It would seem that it ought not to be necessary for a man to become a felon or even a misdemeanant in order to be sure of work. It is possible that in connection with the disciplinary labor colonies for vagrants and other misdemeanants there might be a separate department for voluntary workers. Here, at broom-making or some other industry requiring little skill, little capital to lie idle when regular industry called the workers, and having a sure market, the unemployed willing workers would then be sure of minimum wages. They should be piece wages. It is good economy for private employers to push on repairs and extensions in slack times. And some employers have begun to regard it as wise and right to retain all their workers on part time rather than to run on full time with diminished labor force. Better organization of private industry has great advantages over public intervention.

There may be openings for laborers in one locality and elsewhere laborers suffering for work. In hard times laborers out of work tramp many weary miles on the strength of a rumor that employment is to be had at a given point, often only to find that these great distances have been traversed in vain. There ought to be government employment agencies with announcement of openings displayed in every post office. In certain sections of Germany the government railroads have furnished transportation to laborers applying to such agencies, the fare to be deducted from their first wages. There should be interstate coöperation among public employment agencies; indeed this is a proper sphere for federal action under the Department of Commerce and Labor. The federal activity already includes the beginnings of an agency to properly locate immigrants, who now huddle in exploited masses in cities and about great industrial plants, by furnishing them information as to the places where they will be most socially useful and individually successful. Private employment agencies have been guilty of many abominable practices, robbing their clients, and also promoting commercialized vice. They require strict supervision and their proprietors should be required to take out licenses that would be forfeited for malpractices.

Unemployment of the willing and employable not only causes distress to them and to their families but also decreases general wealth in three ways. First, it is waste of an economic resource to allow idleness to replace willing labor. Second, the unemployed and their families must be supported out of the proceeds of the industry of the community. Third, idleness tends directly and in various ways to physical and moral deterioration of the laborers who are compelled to "loaf." The tramping or train riding of the honest seeker for work leads not seldom to family desertion, and the easy degenerate life of the hobo. The pathetic and tragic search for work thus ends in moral and economic defeat and surrender. "Modern life," says John Hobson, "has no more tragical figure than the gaunt, hungry laborer, wandering about the crowded centers of industry and wealth, begging in vain for permission to share in that industry and to contribute to that wealth; asking in return, not the comforts and luxuries of civilized life, but the rough food and shelter for himself and family, which would be practically assured him in the rudest form of savage society." Mercy, justice, and the defense of society against the multiplication of degenerates demand the adoption of a more efficient policy with reference to "the problem of the unemployed." It is beyond the sphere of charity. It is one of the most serious defects in our industrial organization. If it affected the powerful as it does the weak it would command the most earnest efforts at amelioration.

For an excellent basis for discussion presented in small compass, see John B. Andrews: A Practical Program for the Prevention of Unemployment. Published by the American Association on Unemployment, 131 E. 23d St., N. Y., 1915.

See also Frances A. Kellor: Out of Work, Putnam's, 1904.

CHAPTER XII

CHARITY ORGANIZATION

Underlying Principles.—To abate the causes which contin‐ ually recruit the standing army of the miserable is the first duty of society. But since that army exists there is an obli‐ gation, which every civilized nation admits, to meet by charity the necessities of those who under existing conditions are unable to maintain themselves. Upon this subject experi‐ ence has rendered clear certain principles:

1. Charity must be guided by a particular knowledge of cases. Society, as we have seen, can have about as many beggars as it chooses to feed. The indiscriminate distribution of dimes and quarters on the street and of food at the back door makes pauperism instead of curing it, and should be stopped. Distribution of groceries, coal and clothing by public or private agencies not seldom causes more evil than it cures.

2. Mere almsgiving when it does no positive harm is usually a miserable substitute for the higher charity of per‐ sonal service. Temporary material relief is frequently neces‐ sary, but often more necessary still is the coöperation of some wise and experienced individual who will assist the distressed to form a practical plan for permanent support and for restoration to economic independence. This may be accomplished by seeing that the earning power of the partially incapacitated is restored, by securing the formation or restora‐ tion of social relationships between the impoverished and relatives, employers, church, and school; by preventing the physical or moral ruin of children, and by other constructive measures. Well-meant almsgiving often perpetuates pauper‐ ism where highly competent personal philanthropy would cure it. Such service requires that someone be ready to give much time. And it must be the time of a person gifted with

first-rate abilities. No one who is unable to make his or her own life successful need expect to do this work, for here success must be wrested from the hardest conditions. The probability of success is greatly increased if the charity worker has had special training and opportunity to observe the methods by which many cases of baffling poverty have been successfully met.

3. There is more need of justice than of charity. Indiscriminate public charity has sometimes helped to depress wages, acting as a partial offset to injustice between employer and employed. There is at present little or no imminent danger that charity will slacken the struggle for justice on the part of the poor. The struggle of organized labor to raise wages is intense and there is no reason to think that it is at present made less so by properly administered private charity. The only danger in this respect is that interest in charity will satisfy the consciences of the well-disposed and well-to-do and direct their attention from the more fundamental problem of justice. On the other hand the study of the problem of poverty by the various agents of charity has been one of the chief means of securing for the laborers the interest, understanding, and sympathetic coöperation of the well-to-do, which appear to be indispensable to the success of the necessary reforms.

4. The cessation of charity would invite untold needless suffering, would outrage or deaden the generous sentiments of man, and set at naught the principle of Christianity: "Bear ye one another's burdens and so fulfill the law of Christ." The refusal of charity may result from ignorance of the conditions of the unfortunate poor, such that their suffering has no chance to make its appeal to sympathy; or it may result from caste folly which refuses to acknowledge our common humanity; or it may result from pure selfishness. In multitudes of cases charity has been pitifully inadequate and misdirected when it might have wrought great benefits. It is not enough, however, for charity to be abundant and well meaning. It must also be wise.

Institutional and Non-institutional Relief.—The expressions "outdoor relief" and "indoor relief" have become technical terms among students of charity. Originally they were English legal terms denoting charity supplied by public funds inside and outside the poorhouse. In that usage outdoor relief included that afforded by hospitals and asylums. This confusing use of words has been further confused by the fact that different writers have assigned to these expressions meanings at variance with their original legal significance. Their simplest and most intelligible use is to make "indoor" mean institutional and "outdoor" mean non-institutional relief. Even then some obscurity remains, for the care of the poor in their homes is still classed as "outdoor relief." This incongruity is avoided and perfect definition secured if we cast aside these old terms and speak instead of institutional and non-institutional charity.

Institutional charity is generally a function of governmental agencies. Even private institutions should be subject to governmental inspection. It is easy for the public to put its unfortunates into institutions and forget them, and even under well-intentioned management the situation invites abuses unless the laws provide for visitation by persons selected and authorized by high, responsible authority, at least some of whom are known to be conversant with the principles of scientific charity.

On the other hand in the United States non-institutional relief has hitherto been properly the function of private charity. In countries where bureaucratic efficiency is highly developed and is divorced from party politics, outdoor relief can be administered successfully by governmental agencies and may even be so extended as nearly or quite to render the almshouse unnecessary. But experience has clearly shown that in this country ministration by public agents to temporary and unclassified want in non-institutional relief, especially in large places, tends to degenerate into indiscriminate and pauperizing distribution of free groceries and coal, more particularly to those that vote with the party in power. In some instances an intolerable burden of public outdoor charity has been suddenly dropped by announcing that recipients of public charity must find it by entering the almshouse, and "there is no well-authenticated instance where public non-institutional relief has been stopped and any considerable increase has resulted either in demands upon private charity or in the number of inmates in institutions." In the city of Buffalo during the year preceding the organization in that city of the first charity organization society in America, more than ten per cent. of the population were receiving outdoor city aid. At the same time in Brooklyn one person in every sixteen of the population was receiving outdoor relief. "One woman received help under nine different names. Many sold what they received. Men came from the country every autumn to live at the expense of the city during the winter." [1] "As administered in the United States, it is found, apparently, that public outdoor relief educates more people for the almshouse than it keeps out of it, and therefore it is neither economical nor kindly." [2] In some small cities public non-institutional relief is tolerably managed. There such public relief is most successful and least injurious, this is because of close coöperation between the public authority and a voluntary private agency that supplies the necessary personal acquaintance with the recipients and their needs before the grant is allowed and which continues acquaintance with each case after the grant has been made and so long as aid is required. In rare instances an admirable arrangement has been put in operation by which a non-political official trained for charity work is supported partly by a charity organization society and partly by the county or city, and acts under appointment as the municipal or court supervisor of the poor, with responsibility over the expenditure of public relief.

The time may come when gradual transfer of non-institutional relief to public officials may be wise economy of time and effort. If so, this will be due not only to improvement in methods of public administration and deliverance from the spoils system, but also to the fact that private charity will have developed a class of workers having the necessary train-

---

[1] Warner: American Charities, p. 231.
[2] Ibid., p. 235.

ing and will have made the necessity of such special training clear to the public mind.

The Elberfeld System.—This system of charity, so named from the German city in which it developed, is based upon the unpaid personal service of citizens acting in systematic coöperation with each other and with the paid professional superintendent. "The fundamental principle of the Elberfeld system might also be expressed thus: thorough examination of each individual dependent, continued careful guardianship during the period of dependence, and constant effort to help him regain economic independence. But these requirements can be fulfilled only through the assistance and coöperation of a sufficient number of well-qualified persons."

The persons chosen for this service are citizens of character and ability, and they not merely examine, report, and act as friendly visitors, but also coöperate in deciding the plans of rehabilitation adopted in each case referred to them. They are selected and appointed by the city government and are required to serve as an honorable patriotic duty. If they decline, a percentage may be added to their taxes and they may be deprived of their vote at municipal elections. This service is regarded as the first step in official preferment, and is often essential to further advancement. The section of the city assigned to any individual is small so that usually only one or two cases and never more than four will be under the care of a single visitor. The visitor is to become thoroughly acquainted with his section and interest himself in the general improvement of its conditions.

The sections are grouped into districts and the visitors of a district hold regular and frequent meetings. The appointments are so made that persons of diverse social classes, bankers, lawyers, tradesmen, mechanics, gather in these district meetings to consult upon the problem of poverty. And the wisdom and experience of all the visitors in the district is brought to bear upon the plans to be formed for each case. The chairmen of all the districts also hold regular meetings with the representatives of the city government who are assigned to this duty. This central board includes a specially trained paid administrator and paid assistants. It prepares general instructions for visitors, advises the district leaders, and may review the action of the district boards. It divides the city into sections and districts, appoints visitors, supervises hospitals and other charitable institutions, keeps the central records, gathers statistics, investigates causes of poverty, and initiates legislation and other measures of amelioration.

Judged by its results and by the number of cities, particularly in Germany and Austria, that have adopted and still maintain the Elberfeld plan, it must be regarded as the best system of local charity in Europe and probably the best in the world.

The main features of the Elberfeld system might be widely adopted, but success would depend upon wise adaptation to local conditions. In most American cities, instead of assigning sections of the city it might be necessary to assign to each visitor specific cases.

Charity Organization Societies.—Proper administration of voluntary and unofficial charity in any large community in the United States practically requires the activities of a charity organization society, though the society may operate under any one of various names. Its ministrations are to charity like what first aid to the injured is to surgery and what diagnosis and prescription are to medicine. It may mean quick recovery and, if unwise, it may mean permanent, crippling pauperism. Such an organization should not be formed until every effort has been put forth to secure the coöperation in its formation of all the charitable agencies in the community. The importance of this coöperation will appear as the purposes of the organization are described. The charity organization society serves the following purposes.

1. Prevention of Overlapping and Imposture.—In any city, previous to the advent of the charity organization society, numerous useful charities spring up. A city of twenty-five thousand will probably have ten or more churches and a score of benevolent societies, lodges, and labor unions, all of which dispense some charity, besides numerous benevolent individuals who do so. In a given family one child may attend one

Sunday-school and receive aid from one church, while another does the same at another church, and father and mother may secure aid from several societies and individuals. If a reporter makes a "story" about some needy family at Thanksgiving time, it may have ten turkeys and have no coal to cook them, while equally needy families receive nothing. In a community so small that overlapping of charity seemed not only needless but to some almost incredible, a lady found a family in need and appealed for aid to three benevolent individuals in succession, each of whom declined on the ground of doing already what he or she could for another case; it turned out that each of the three was "doing" for one and the same case which, moreover, had ceased to require aid. In a great city with hundreds of charities and a great number of benevolent individuals, the charity "rounder" finds easy prey, unless there is a central organization.

One duty of the charity organization society is to keep a central record of all applications for charity to any of the coöperating agencies, showing the nature of the need and the treatment provided. If all the charities of the city report to the central agency each application they can always learn whether the applicant is already receiving assistance from another source.

The charity organization society is one agency for handling the tramp problem, a problem which results from the overlapping of charity given by many to one man until he becomes a charity rounder. The treatment of vagrants which was recommended in a preceding paragraph requires the existence of an agency to which beggars can be referred by every citizen with the assurance that each will receive the treatment appropriate to his case; and with the added insurance that by such coöperation between all householders and one central agency, no parasites are begging from door to door. The proper treatment of these wanderers often requires communication, perhaps by telephone, with the cities from which they profess to come, or to which they say they wish to go. To some of these men it is possible to give important help and to these it would have been a shame to give merely a "handout" at the door. But it is ordinarily quite impossible for the householder to distinguish these cases from the smooth impostors. To deal properly with the tramps requires painstaking and trained intelligence. The principles already set down with reference to moral delinquents must not be forgotten. Labor must be offered them.

Practically every community is visited from time to time by solicitors purporting to represent out-of-town benevolent enterprises. Some of them are frauds. The genuine should receive the indorsement they deserve, and the frauds would be suppressed, if all such solicitors were required by those to whom they appeal to present a recommendation from the local charity organization society.

Even within the city itself, if it be a large one, unwise and sometimes fraudulent so-called charities may be started, and all new charitable enterprises may reasonably be expected to secure approval of the Charity Organization Society before appealing to the generosity of the public for funds.

2. Properly Conducted Investigation.—The investigation of applications alone can prevent imposture. But the main object of investigation is not to prevent imposture but to discover the real needs and opportunities for help. Thorough acquaintance with the case is the prime condition of wise and thoroughly helpful treatment. For the private individual to investigate cases of poverty is usually impossible; it requires time as well as experience and training. It is a waste and a mischief when investigation of the same cases is needlessly repeated by several charitable agencies to which appeal is made. Every society and every individual that discovers a case of need in the community can report it to the Charity Organization Society with the assurance that it will be properly looked into, and the conditions and the needs of the case will be made known to the agencies that should assist in its relief; and that if the case has already been investigated that fact will be known and no repetitious investigations will take place.

3. Communication Between Need and Source of Supply.— The Charities Directory of the City of New York is a volume of 835 pages, that of Chicago of 350 pages, and that of Boston, of 500 pages, describing 1,424 charitable agencies.

In a large city there are charitable agencies designed to meet practically every form of want, and devoted to the service of the needy of particular nationalities, and of particular creeds. Yet individuals may starve, not knowing where to turn. It is impossible for the needy to be conversant with all the sources of beneficence, but there should be one thoroughly advertised charity, whose business it is to put each applicant in touch with the resources of the city which should be called upon to meet his needs. This is a function of a charity organization society. That society is to all the agencies of the community that deal with the needy what "Central" is to a telephone system. To care properly for a single needy family, it may be necessary to invoke many different agencies, for example, to call upon the police and the court to put a shirking breadwinner on parole, under sentence, suspended so long as he works and brings in his wages; and to call upon the dispensary and the visiting nurses' association to cure illness that drains the family resources, or disables a wage-earner; to look up the building inspector and the landlord in order to remove the unsanitary conditions that undermine the health of the family, and the society for rendering legal aid to the poor [1] in order to secure back wages due, or to relax the grip of a loan shark; to find a job for the father, or for son or daughter (for the charity organization society must be in touch with sources of employment throughout the city); and to furnish temporary relief in the form of coal and groceries. In the small town there may be a score, and in the great city, hundreds of agencies which may thus multiply their efficiency by coöperation through the central organization.

4. **To Restore the Impoverished to Economic Independence.**—It is an error to imagine that the charity organization society exists chiefly to defend the weak against the easy

---

[1] The public ought to maintain free courts, without privately retained lawyers, for adjudicating small claims. The expense of litigation places the justice of the courts beyond the reach of the poor.

pauperism and parasitism into which many sink as a result of a promiscuous almsgiving, and to protect society against an army of demoralized beggars. These things the charity organization society does, but its yet more distinctive aim is to furnish to the poor the patient, skillful, and adequate aid that will set them once more upon their feet. Mere almsgiving will seldom do that; it will render the poor more comfortable in their poverty, but the charity organization society aims to help them out of their poverty. For a man in real trouble the dole at the door for which he asks is a pitiful substitute for the befriending that he needs. For this fourth aim, the true aim of charity, the gift of coal and groceries in the case just supposed, would have been totally insufficient; it would have served only to help "tide the family over into next week's misery." The economically broken individual or family may need alms, but the chief need is "not alms but a friend." It must be a friend who has knowledge of opportunities for employment and of all the resources of the city that may be called upon to minister to the various specific necessities of the unfortunate. It must be a friend who by special training and by observation of many rescues from engulfing poverty knows how to solve the problem of regaining economic independence, a problem often baffling for ordinary ingenuity and knowledge. It must be a friend who can give the time for correspondence and for interviews with various parties. All this means, as a rule, that it must be the paid, trained agent of the charity organization society. To restore people to economic health requires special training and clinical observation. Though the training required may be less expensive, it is as truly necessary as the training which is required to restore people to physical health. To provide such a wise and skillful friend to the poor in a community is the greatest charity. Some charity organization societies give no material relief, but for that rely entirely upon coöperating agencies and devote all their time and funds to personal work among the poor and to the function of an investigating, recording, and communicating agency for all the organizations and individuals in the city that do give material aid.

It must be admitted that with the best of training and of coöperation the task of "family rehabilitation" is a discouraging one. Prevention is more promising than cure. Yet by such measures as restoring health of breadwinners who would otherwise sink into chronic incapacity, finding suitable employment for those with unsuitable employment or none, forcing deserting breadwinners to do their duty, finding relatives and reëstablishing family coöperation, cures are wrought. And when cure is out of the question it is by no means an insignificant service to supply the palliatives of "relief" in a way to do the most good and with the least of waste and harm.

Examples.—An illustration or two will render more distinct some of the four points just made. The accumulated case records of a charity organization society are a mass of such illustrations. Let us choose instances in which we can contrast skillful and unskillful procedure.

By an accident a man was rendered unfit for his accustomed labor. He had a wife and three children. Many gave sympathy but all intrusted the giving of material aid to the charity organization society. The society loaned the man the price of a pushcart and stock for peddling. The family did not become paupers, but lived in thrift and comfort. The children were reputed to promise becoming good citizens. Another man in a city with no charity organization society was similarly injured. At first many sympathetic persons contributed money, food, and clothing which were soon used up. The man could not return to his labor and the wife was not able to do washing regularly. Their needs continued to be more or less spasmodically contributed to by money, food, old clothes, and fuel. Husband and wife became confirmed paupers. The children have suffered in their self-respect and when thrown upon their own resources are likely at the first touch of hardship to become charges upon the community. The experience of this family has been repeated with variations in thousands of instances.

A man of good connection in England was sent to this country on an allowance because of his gross intemperance. He always claimed that his allowance was behind time and that he was without money. People gave him fifty cents or five dollars or nothing. What he obtained in this way went mostly for drink and dragged him further into the mire. At length a charity organization society was formed in the city. The secretary of the new society communicated with his relatives and found that the allowance always came on time and that he squandered it in drink. It was arranged with the relatives to have the allowance sent to the society and to have the society pay his board in an institution for inebriates where he received both physical and moral treatment. He is now working steadily in a position which the charity organization society secured for him.

The breadwinner of a small family fell ill. The family was supported by charity for a series of years. Meanwhile the invalid's suffering was relieved by morphine, and she became a regular "morphine fiend," and the family sunk into chronic pauperism. A trained charity worker was brought to the town. She immediately found that the breadwinner might have been restored to her work by a slight surgical operation and that relatives who witnessed the pauperization of this family with regret and shame would have rendered outside charity unnecessary if they had been appealed to and the pauperizing relief had been withheld.

Compare the money cost of wise charity with that of careless giving. The charity to the small family was far worse than wasted. In the case of the drunken Englishman, a few letters and a few calls saved him; all the money he had been collecting before was ruining him. In the case of the crippled laborer, there were years of giving to him and his wife and children and the likelihood of more paupers when the children grew up; indeed the effects of pauperizing a family may last for generations. The other crippled laborer cost only a little time and wise planning, and he and his family were saved to themselves and society.

Yet organized charity is by no means a device primarily intended for saving money for the community. Though in the long run, it does have that result, its chief aim is to render to the needy aid which is adequate and so intelligently planned as to be so far as possible curative and not merely palliative. In some cases it is much more expensive than thoughtless charity; it may give to a sick mother, milk, eggs, and nursing instead of beans and cast-off clothing. It may give medical treatment and surgical appliances to a broken breadwinner, when they alone can remove the cause of a family's distress and poverty. It is a saving in so far as it is curative and preventive. It does away with the rearing of children to lives of pauperism. It builds backbones instead of dissolving them. It is far more welcome to the better class of the poor than the unintelligent charity that often thinks itself more sympathetic, because it respects the self-respect of those it aids as well as because it offers adequate and curative aid, instead of the mere succession of tantalizing doles soon consumed.

The appeal of the needy to human sympathy secures the entrance into this service of people whose gifts of head and heart could not be commanded by the salaries which they receive. It is better that the salaries be low than that anyone engage in this work for mere money's sake. Low as they are, the maintenance of the workers adapted in character and training to this difficult task is the chief expense of the charity organization society, but it is indispensable and its chief means of usefulness. Scientific charity discovers a practical interpretation of the line, "The gift without the giver is bare." The charity worker may well cost more than the relief, somewhat as the doctor costs more than the medicine. Alms are like a sedative that relieves painful symptoms; the charity worker is like the physician or the trained nurse. Where every sympathetic person administered the sedative but there was no doctor or nurse, disease would abound and increase; so poverty and pauperism abound and increase in absence of the time-consuming labor of the trained minister of charity.

5. An Agency of Research and Public Instruction.—The fifth purpose served by the charity organization society is that of an agency of research and of public instruction. Through its reports and the addresses and conversations of its officials and frequent newspaper paragraphs, it renders the good will of the community intelligent, directs it away from the

well-meant blundering that in most places has become common, and toward effective and general coöperation in the methods which wide and long experience has shown to contribute most toward promoting the welfare of the poor. This public discussion not only guides but also arouses and increases the sympathy of the community for its poor.

Moreover, in addition to their paid workers most charity organization societies have a corps of volunteer "friendly visitors," each of whom agrees to become acquainted with from one to three poor families. These visitors may aid materially in the rehabilitation of the families that they befriend. Usually it is wise for them to agree to leave all giving of material aid to the paid superintendent. The societies usually have also advisory committees in addition to their board of directors, with whom the needs and proper treatment of cases are discussed. All this serves to enable the well-to-do to realize the problems of the "submerged tenth," and promotes mutual understanding and sympathy between classes that are too often and too easily estranged.

The investigation of concrete cases of distress with a view to discovering and removing the occasion of the trouble is a continuous research into the causes of social and economic failures, and is sure to yield knowledge of great value for the guidance of the particular community, in which the charity organization society exists, in its efforts toward removing its standing evils and fulfilling its good possibilities. This is one of the most important functions of such an organization. A community like an individual can get used to almost anything. As a rule the comfortable and well-to-do little realize the causes of evil from which the less fortunate fringe of the population continually suffer. Generally speaking, no theoretical discussion or agitation by eloquent specialists from abroad can move a community so powerfully in the direction of needed reform and progress as the definite local knowledge yielded by the daily investigations of the charity organization society.

The charity worker needs the guidance of theoretical instruction in order to perceive the significance of what he sees; leaders of progress need wide knowledge of the experience of other communities in righting their wrongs; and systematic investigation of whole problems must supplement the fragmentary clinical experience of the charity worker. Still it remains true that the discoveries of such workers are, as a rule, the most effective means which a community possesses for learning its urgent needs and possibilities and arousing itself to the required action. The directors of the charity organization society naturally furnish guidance and leadership for constructive social work in various lines. They may not always live up to their opportunity, but the opportunity is theirs.

The charity organizations of the whole country ought to coöperate in keeping a uniform record of certain results of their investigations, so that the totals of this information would be available.

The Almshouse.—The almshouse deserves a few special comments even in so brief a treatment of the subject of charities as this. Almshouses are well-nigh everywhere in the United States.

Historically the almshouse has been the catch-all for nearly every form of social breakdown.

It often contains children; it never should retain a child as an inmate.

It often contains the insane, the epileptic, the feebleminded, the blind, the deaf, the crippled, and the incurable. As a rule persons belonging to any of these classes should be removed from the poorfarm to institutions adapted to their peculiar needs.

It often admits and dismisses inmates practically at their option on the theory that one who is so hard up as to desire admission to the poorhouse ought to be received, and anyone who is willing to withdraw from being a charge upon the town or county ought not to be retained. Thus the bum has a winter home, which he may enter after the fall work of the farm is over, and may leave before the spring work begins. The debauchee has a retreat to which he may retire to recover from the effects of his excesses and from which he may depart when prompted by the return of appetite. Here the feeble-

minded woman may bear her almost annual progeny of inca-
pables, leaving at will to mingle in society. Sometimes even
within the institution there is no adequate separation of the
sexes.

It was formerly common and is sometimes the case still,
that the superintendent of the poorfarm receives as his only
pay that which he can save from the proceeds of the farm and
from an allowance, which is the lowest any bidder will accept,
and is either a lump sum or a specific sum for each inmate.
Whatever balance he can save from these resources after
feeding the inmates, remains in his own pocket, so that every
cent of expenditure that he can withhold from the inmates
and every item of milk, butter, eggs, vegetables, and other
produce that he can sell instead of feeding it to the inmates,
increases his profits. This abominable system invites abuses.
The proper rule is for the superintendent to receive a fixed
salary and an appropriation for expenses and to be required
to render an account of everything sold from the farm.

It is seldom that a poorfarm has a trained nurse or other
adequate provision for caring for its sick folk. Often the care
of the sick is intrusted to inmates and is not only ignorant
but careless and even cruel, being forced upon the reluctant inmate who hates to have his idleness disturbed by a
duty.

In many cases the opprobrious names "poorfarm" and
"almshouse" are replaced by the word "infirmary" and the
name "county home" is now preferred.

In the larger counties there should somewhere be decent
hospital facilities for the poor, acceptable to the medical profession and pervaded by no sense of disgrace on the part of
patients. In the poorhouse there might be a sitting-room and
sleeping quarters to which those only were admitted who met
certain requirements. The mingling of worn-out mothers or
of laborers, broken down by old age and long years of honest
toil, with repulsive idiots and the diseased wrecks of debauchery is often carried to perilous and cruel lengths.

In the case of every institution for the care of the unfortunate definite provision should be made for visitation by

chosen representatives of the public. Inspectors of an almshouse, whether voluntary or official, may properly inquire:

A *As to the inmates*	*As to management and plant* B
1. Total number	1. What classification of inmates with respect to apartments or treatment? On what basis? Sex, morals, health, race?
2. Number of each sex	
3. Numbers by races	
4. Numbers by age groups	
5. Able-bodied	
6. Feeble-minded	
7. Insane (Cells? Restraint?)	2. Financial system
	3. Work by inmates
8. Epileptics	4. Reading, recreation and religious privileges
9. Blind (Educable age?)	
10. Deaf	5. Manner of admission and discharge
11. Paralytic	
12. Other diseases	6. Character of building
	7. Amount and value of land
	8. Character of farming
	9. Cleanliness and sanitation
	10. Nursing and care of the sick
	11. Provisions for visitation

Government Supervision.—We have already observed the necessity of intelligent and authoritative inspection of public charitable institutions. Private institutions which appeal to society for funds, or which assume responsibility for the lives of inmates, ought to be subject to similar inspection. The best device for state supervision is a commission, composed of responsible persons of special acquaintance with the problems of charity, appointed by the governor, to serve without pay, but provided with a fund sufficient to enable the commission to employ a permanent, highly trained executive secretary, and the necessary inspectors, and to publish adequate reports. The commission need have no other powers than to get the facts and place them, with proper recommendations, before the public, the governor, and the law-making bodies of the state.

A separate, salaried board, charged with the centralized business administration of all the asylums, colonies, and other charities supported by the state itself, proves a means of economy and efficiency.

Both the supervising commission and the administrative board should have powers extending equally to the penal, as well as the charitable, institutions of the state.

The state of Indiana has led the way in a set of wise laws which require that upon petition of fifteen reputable citizens of any county the circuit court shall appoint six persons to act as a county board of charities. This board is required to visit all charitable and correctional institutions receiving public funds within the county, and to report the result of their inspection quarterly to the county commissioners and annually to the court, and to furnish copies of their report to the newspapers and to the state board of charities. Township trustees are required to file with the commissioners of their county, and with the state board of charities, statements giving certain definite information concerning every family receiving aid from the township. Each township is required to provide for its own poor by a special tax. In administering public charities officials are required to observe the cardinal rules which have been proved essential by the experience of private charity organization societies. This series of laws has resulted in a reduction of the proportion of the population of Indiana receiving public aid to much less than half what it was in 1897, before the first of these laws was passed, in reducing the annual cost of public relief by more than $100,000, and in affording more adequate and intelligent assistance to the poor.

In the management of local charities the example of Kansas City, Missouri, has been more or less completely followed by certain other cities, and may profitably be studied by many more. It provides that the mayor shall appoint three persons as a Board of Municipal Welfare. This board selects a general superintendent. and under him there is an extensive staff of paid workers. The board, through its officials, (1) administers the public charities of the city, closely coöperating with private agencies, and itself maintaining ten trained social workers for the service of investigating and rehabilitating families that have applied for help to the various private charities of the city, and operates as a registration bureau and clearing house of information between all these institutions. (2) It maintains a free legal aid bureau, and handles 6,000 to 7,000 cases per year, at a cost of less than one dollar per case. The board collects $14,000 to $15,000 per year from men who had been neglecting their families. (3) It operates a welfare loan agency; (4) a department of factory and housing inspection; (5) a free employment bureau, which supplied 31,600 jobs in 1914, a municipal quarry employing several hundred men per day, paying them in meals and lodgings, if homeless, in grocery orders if they have families, also a sewing room for unemployed women. (6) The board administers a reformatory for women, and a penal farm for the male prisoners of the city. The products of the industries of these institutions cover most of the costs of operation. It maintains a parole department, selects those who should be paroled from these institutions, and gives them supervision. Several hundred people are always on parole. (7) It exercises thorough supervision over public dance halls, skating rinks and moving picture shows. (8) It maintains a research department, which studies the city and its needs and possibilities with reference to such topics as unemployment, wage-earning women, the social evil, industrial accidents, what becomes of the children who leave school before reaching high school, etc.

Conclusion.—In conclusion, with reference to the problem of poverty, there are four aims which society ought to seek.

1. A situation in which none who are willing and competent to do work productive enough to yield their support shall be suffering poverty. Failure to attain that aim is due either to an imperfect organization of industry, or a population so excessive as to overtax the resources of nature and of art.

2. A situation in which all those who can do useful work but will not, if supported by relatives or by inherited wealth, forfeit social approval, and if supported by the public, are subjected to sympathetic but firm discipline, and prevented from distributing physical and moral contagion.

3. A situation in which the number of those unable to do productive work or useful service equal in value to their own maintenance will be reduced to the minimum.

4. That those unable to care for themselves be cared for with tenderness.

Finally charity for the most part is only a palliative, not a cure. Social justice and individual health and character constitute the foundation which must be laid for welfare— social justice which is yet to be attained; health which requires a birth not too abnormal, and youth spent in wholesome surroundings; character which requires a childhood passed under the influence of ideals of decency, thrift, and service, and of a tolerably regular discipline.

III. PSYCHOPHYSICAL CAUSES WHICH AFFECT THE LIFE OF SOCIETY

CHAPTER XIII

THE HEREDITARY CHARACTERISTICS OF THE POPULATION

The word "psychophysical" in this heading is intended to designate traits and conditions of the physical organism, including those of the brain and nervous system. The latter manifest themselves in the capacities and dispositions for psychic activity.

Data Which Physiology Furnishes to Sociology.[1]—In order to understand the place of social facts in the ordered unity of nature we must relate them not only to geographic but also to biological phenomena. Theoretical sociology must have one of its feet planted upon the facts of physical anthropology.

Since biological facts are less familiar than those of geography it may be necessary to insert a brief description of their character.

Complex aggregations of matter move or change when acted upon by other moving matter; a pile of jackstraws stirs and shifts when touched. This general fact of the instability of complex combinations of matter may be called "irritability." Life is specialized irritabilities. The molecule of protoplasm is an extremely complex and unstable compound made up of minute parts. It is the most complex and unstable of all molecules. Moreover, the arrangements into which the molecules enter are highly variable,

---

[1] H. S. Jennings: Behavior of Lower Organisms. Columbia University Press, 1906.

Jacques Loeb: Comparative Physiology of the Brain. Putnam, 1900, chaps. i and xii.

Maurice Parmelee: Science of Human Behavior. Macmillan, 1913.

and variations in their arrangement may be quite as significant as changes in the molecules themselves. The external cause acting upon a complex and unstable combination of matter may be called the "irritant" or "stimulus." It may be friction moving the minute parts or molecules; it may be heat setting the molecules into vibration; it may be an electric shock; it may be light with the effects of which on unstable compounds we are familiar in photography.

Molecules of protoplasm originally form in water, and apparently these molecules aggregate or integrate into masses as other molecules of a given kind do when suspended in a fluid. Some molecules when thus aggregated in a fluid medium form crystals. Protoplasm aggregating in water does not form crystals but it may be that it tends toward a more or less symmetrical arrangement.

The most striking characteristic of protoplasm is its power to contract and expand, or pucker and stretch. When a simple organism consisting of a single protoplasmic cell, let us say the ameba, is swimming in the water, if a drop of something soluble falls into that water, particles of the dissolving substance reach the swimming organism. If the effect is to pucker the side of the ameba on which these particles strike; then the ameba turns toward the source from which the dissolving particles come until they strike equally on both sides of it. Then it is headed straight for the source of the stimulus. Thus if a drop of beef juice is dropped into water where the amebæ are, they turn toward the beef juice and congregate about it as if eagerly answering the call to dinner. A drop of acid has an opposite effect and they flee from it as if scared.

There is no more reason to suppose that the ameba is conscious of what it is doing than to suppose that the potato sprout is conscious of what it is doing when it crawls along the cellar wall toward the window, the source of light, or that the rootlets of the potato are conscious of what they are doing when they turn away from the light, or that the vine is conscious of what it is doing when it grows more rapidly on the sunny side than on the side that is shaded and so coils around the object that shades it on one side.

Only those combinations of protoplasm can survive that turn toward what is good for them and away from what would destroy them. When you jostle the jackstraws they may fall toward the west, but next time you throw them down they may be ready to fall toward the east. Some combinations of protoplasm react in one way and other combinations of protoplasm react in exactly the opposite way to the same stimulus. Only those aggregations of protoplasm survive which are attracted to objects some part of which can be chemically assimilated to and integrated with the protoplasmic molecules and structures of molecules and which are repelled from or repel those objects that would disintegrate and destroy them. The behavior of irritable matter which results in doing the right things to secure preservation of that particular aggregation of matter and others like it, is called "functioning" and the aggregate of all functioning is life. When we speak of life as irritability we refer to the fact that a living thing is so complex and unstable an arrangement of matter that it will do more than dead matter when acted upon. When we speak of life as specialized irritability we refer to the fact that living matter will not only do more but that it will do the right things to secure continuance or survival.

Functioning aggregations or matter or living organisms not only behave so as to secure their own survival but also so as to give rise to new organisms counterparts of themselves, that is, to perpetuate their species by reproduction. The simplest organisms reproduce by merely breaking in two when they get too big for successful functioning; so that there are two smaller organisms where there had been one larger one. Higher organs set apart a portion of their cells for purposes of reproduction.

No man can completely trace out the physics and chemistry of the behavior of matter in its most complex forms. If we could we should know the method of growth, functioning, and evolution. We can trace enough of this intricate and microscopic chemistry and physics to be sure of the fact of growth, functioning, and evolution, but we have as yet discovered only some of the main features of the method.

The combination of differentiated cells into functioning structures in the higher organisms results in chemicophysical mechanisms which surpass in intricacy any machines that have been devised by man, as terrestrial distances are exceeded by those of astronomy.

Relations of Biological Traits to Social Life.—Two classes of factors furnish the preëxisting conditions out of which society arises: a group of biological organisms capable of affecting each other's activities; and an environing habitat in which these organisms are placed and by which their activities are both stimulated and limited. Given a number of psycho-physical organisms belonging to the genus Homo set down in a particular situation, forthwith stimulated by their environ-ment and prompted by inborn tendencies, these sensitive organisms will begin to function. Presently they will create technic and social conditions which will begin to affect their further activities, but the only preëxisting conditions of social activity are the geographical and biological. By referring to the outline of the theory of evolution on page 19, one will be led to put it thus: The combination of conditions necessary to the appearance of the new order of phenomena which we term "social" included the geographic phenomena plus the congregated organisms of a species adequately evolved. Given these conditions, social phenomena necessarily fol-low.

The effects of geographic habitats in conditioning social realities we have discussed in a preceding chapter and now we are ready to consider the part played by the qualities of biological organisms. Important as are the social effects of geographic conditions, the organic traits of the population are the higher and more specialized set of determining condi-tions.

Two Classes of Socially Important Psychophysical Condi-tions.—The biological traits of a population are of two sorts: hereditary and acquired. Even the lowest human beings of whom we have any knowledge are distinguished by acquired as well as by inborn physical traits.

Hereditary psychophysical traits are those which are sup-posed to be due to the character of the germ cells derived from parent organisms and which are not due to postnatal functioning or environment or even to any prenatal malnutri-tion, poisoning, or contagion which has taken place subse-quent to the union of the two parent cells. Prenatal contagion may transmit diseases with which the mother was affected, but no germ disease is hereditary in the strict sense. And extreme malnutrition of the mother during pregnancy can limit the development of the offspring and prevent the proper development of some of the organs. None of the defects so caused are hereditary in the strictest sense, for they are not due to inherent imperfections of the germ cells of the parent stock, but rather to injuries to the developing fetus.

Hereditary traits that affect social life include: (1) external characteristics such as height, weight and figure, complexion, character of hair, color of eyes, cast of features and muscular development; (2) predispositions; (3) general neural traits, that is, inborn powers and limitations of those talents which may function in the service of more than one predisposition; (4) temperament, a word to which I shall assign a somewhat peculiar meaning, namely, those traits of circulatory, secretive and other non-neural organs which have a recognizable effect upon the conscious activities; (5) race, a bundle of traits of all of those sorts just mentioned supposed to distinguish one of the varieties of the human species; (6) age; (7) sex; (8) hereditary abnormalities and subnormalities.

Under acquired biological conditions having important social consequences must be noted: (1) stunted youth; (2) alcoholism and other drug habits; (3) occupational diseases; (4) contagious diseases, of which tuberculosis and venereal diseases are the most important; (5) "second nature," habits, and subconscious set.

The external characteristics, although they form so large a part of the description given by the physical anthropologist, we must pass over with mere mention.

Instinct.—"An instinct is an inherited or an innate psychophysical disposition which determines its possessor to perceive and pay attention to objects of a certain class, to experience an emotional excitement of a peculiar quality upon perceiving such an object, and to act in regard to it in a particular manner, or at least, to experience an impulse to such action." [1] This special response is an important part

---

[1] McDougal: Social Psychology. Luce & Co., 1909, pp. 19 *seq.* He recognizes that the "relatively unchanging tendencies which form the basis of human character" include not only "specific tendencies

of the functioning upon which the survival of the individual and of the species depends, although, even in man, and still more in the animals, there may be no foreknowledge of the purpose which the instinctive act is to serve. The instinctive response is due to the possession of a special neuromuscular apparatus which is an hereditary characteristic of the entire species to which the individual belongs. Instinctive action is a special response to a special stimulus by a special hereditary apparatus for a special biological purpose. Thus each insect is prompted to lay its eggs only where its larvæ can find food. The yucca moth is provided with a needle-pointed tube with which to deposit her eggs in the seed pod of the yucca flower, and with nerves that make her place them there and that make her stuff the hole with pollen. Unless she put the pollen there the seeds which are to supply her young with food would not mature. She cannot know this any more than the mating animal foresees that its instinctive act will result in progeny. The turtle when attacked withdraws its head and legs into the shell, and the nervous coördination that causes him to do so is one part of a mechanism of which the muscles that pull, and the shell into which he is pulled, are the other parts. Either part without the others would be useless and each is as purely a prearranged biological adaptation to survival as is the other. Indeed the nervous

---

or instincts" but also "general or non-specific tendencies." As the principal human instincts he enumerates: (Intro. p. xii)

The instinct of flight and the emotion of fear;
The instinct of repulsion and the emotion of disgust;
The instinct of curiosity and the emotion of wonder;
The instinct of pugnacity and the emotion of anger;
The instinct of self-abasement and the emotion of subjection;
The instinct of self-assertion and the emotion of elation;
The parental instinct and the tender emotion;
The instinct of reproduction;
The gregarious instinct;
The instinct of acquisition;
The instinct of construction.

For another discussion of instinct, see Parmelee: Science of Human Behavior, chap. xi, Definition on page 26. Also Graham Wallas, The Great Society. Macmillan, 1914, chap. iii.

apparatus that prompts the conduct of the yucca moth or that secures the withdrawal of the turtle's head and legs is as purely a biological adjustment to survival as is the nervous apparatus that secures the secretion of gastric juice upon stimulation of the swallowed food.

The word reflex is used to describe simpler acts that serve the purposes of survival and are the functions of a less complex inherited neuromuscular coördination. Familiar examples are winking the eye to shut out an injurious body or putting forth the hands as one begins to fall. Between reflexes and instincts there is no sharp line of distinction but a gradation in degree of complexity. A reflex is a functional unit built up of minute tropismatic, chemicophysical changes in nature like those in the swimming ameba or the creeping potato sprout. An instinct on the physical side is a bigger functional unit, built up of the same kind of tropismatic elements. As we are employing the words, it would not be far wrong to say that those tropismatic elements are to reactions as reactions are to instincts.

Predisposition.—As yet there is no complete agreement in the enumeration of human instincts. The instinctive activities of man are not so cut and dried, so simple and definitely predetermined as those of lower animals. In fact the difference is so great that formerly writers anxious to exalt man above the rest of animal creation were accustomed to say that man had few instincts or even that he had none, and that while animals acted by instinct man acted by reason. There are three reasons why the instincts of man are vague and not easy to identify.

1. Upon the warp of instincts man weaves a woof of habits. Habits gradually come to resemble instincts in almost everything save that they are acquired and never inborn, and that they are by no means certain to serve the purposes of survival. Thus we say that to certain individuals certain conduct has become instinctive. But this is a figurative expression, for in literal accuracy only that can be instinctive which is so by virtue of an inborn adaptation common to all our race. Habits result from the organic modifications in

our structure which are due to our own individual activities. Habits belong to the individual, instincts to the species. But habits mingle with and modify our instincts. The great extent to which habit can go in overlaying and obscuring instinct results largely from the fact that man is born so immature, and requires years of adolescence before reaching the maturity of his organism. This is necessary to allow for adaptation to his social environment; to the special forms of activity prevalent in the particular society into which he is born and to which he must become adjusted. This high degree of flexibility and adaptability is evidence of his high organization. In general the higher an organism in the biological scale the more immature and plastic it is at birth. Low organisms have a nervous system that is comparatively fixed and finished as soon as hatched or born. The chicken just out of the shell is a "going concern" and commences at once "to scratch for a living." Not so the baby. Still lower organisms like the insects are yet more fixed and finished at the start. They do amazing things but they can adapt themselves to special situations by special training only in a very limited degree. What they do they do almost as automatically as a trap springs or as a potato sprout in a dark cellar crawls toward the window, or as the "touch-me-not" sows its seeds. Upon presentation of the proper stimulus they function as they are by heredity adapted to do, and so they live their simple life, but they can adapt themselves but little to change and therefore they are incapable of social progress. And out of their numerous and often myriad offspring relatively few survive to maturity.

2. In man the instincts "contaminate" each other more than is the case with animals; that is, several instinctive promptings may simultaneously inhibit or modify the conduct that any one of them alone would have produced.

3. Man is possessed of a rich variety of free powers. The hand is not restricted to a single instinctive act,[1] like the ovipositor of an insect nor are the eyes or the ears the

---

[1] Of course the difference in this respect between man and other animals is not absolute but only relative.

servant of any single instinct, nor, above all, is the complex apparatus of the brain. These free powers are like the servants in a hotel who do not obey one master alone, but respond to the call of any guest. By calling into its service these free powers a human instinct secures a rich variety of expression which enables it to appear in many rôles and under various disguises. An angry cat will practically always start the bristle-spit-scratch-bite response. An angry man will not always smite; he can think of a great many other hateful things to do. Moreover, his wrath may be aroused by a greater variety of objects than arouse anger or any other instinct in a cat. And similarly his other instincts secure a wide extension of their eliciting causes, and of the flexibility and resourcefulness of their adapted response.

All these things being so, it seems best for the sociologist to leave to the physiological psychologists the unfinished task of identifying instincts and to adopt the word predisposition [1] as a name for those inborn tendencies of the race which

---

¹ Life Biologically Considered

1. Tropism, simple chemico-physical changes like those in the amœba or the potato sprout, and their combinations in the functioning of higher organisms.

2. Reaction.

3. Instinct
   a Congenitally predetermined
   b Called into action by specific stimuli
   c Issuing in specific emotion and behavior which
   d Serve a purpose not necessarily foreseen, but essential to survival of individual or species.

4. Predispositions of man broader and vaguer than instincts of animals because
   a Habits mingle more largely in shaping the behavior.
   b Correlation between instincts or "contamination" of instincts by each other is greater.
   c The free apparatus just described vastly diversifies the occasions and the responses of instinctive action.

shape the course of social action, some of which can be recognized as true instincts, some of which certainly are not true instincts, and concerning some of which he need not trouble himself to inquire whether they are true instincts or not. In the wording of our list of predispositions it is not necessary to distinguish between these tendencies as they are felt by the subject and as they are manifested to others in overt conduct, but only to name and describe them sufficiently so that they may be clearly identified by every observer. These propensities are characteristic of the whole human species and they define types of activity with which mankind can respond to the stimulations afforded by environment. Their significance is so tremendous that they have sometimes been referred to as the social forces.[1]

The predispositions may be divided into three groups: those which are evoked by man's associates, which we will call the social predispositions; those which are evoked by the non-human environment, which we will call the economic predispositions; and those which may be evoked by either, which we will call the general predispositions.

I. General Predispositions.—1. The predisposition to *fear*, flee and hide.

2. The predisposition to become angry and *fight*, that is to destroy whoever or whatever opposes our will.

3. The *enterprising* predisposition, the propensity to risk and dare, and hope and undertake and prosecute with endurance, and determination in the face of uncertainty.

Probably every predisposition has both virtuous and vicious manifestations. The manifestations are vicious when they are out of harmony with the proper exercise of the other propensities. The vicious exercise of the enterprising propensity appears in dare-deviltry and gambling.

4. The impulse to self-expression, the so-called *"instinct of workmanship"*—namely, the propensity to take satisfaction in accomplishing something which is the overt realization of one's own will. In the case of children and the evil-minded or

---

[1] Compare Author's article on "The Social Forces Error." *American Journal of Sociology*, Vol. xvi, pp. 613 and 642.

antisocial, this predisposition finds satisfaction in mischief or destructive activity as truly as in constructive work. If the exercise of this propensity is on the whole constructive, it is because the will of man is on the whole reasonable and socially directed. There seems to be no propriety in calling this general predisposition to workmanship a specific instinct.[1]

The "instinct of workmanship" and the enterprising propensity are often confused and they may both be active in the same experience. But they differ both in their inner feel or subjective aspect and in their overt manifestations. The enterprising predisposition is daring, it persists and even rejoices in the face of uncertainty, and tugs men toward whatever course of action has the spice of a problematic project, even though the solid result promised is sometimes as futile as a track through drifting arctic snows. The "instinct of workmanship," on the other hand, can find its satisfaction in following the beaten track with patience, persistence, and grit, even in the absence of stimulating uncertainty, and it demands to issue in some objective accomplishment, for its inner essence is desire to see and gladness in seeing one's own thought and will realized in actual results. Most writers treat the "instinct of workmanship" as an economic motive, but I shall treat the propensity exhibited by the carpenter who enjoys making a good joint or by the architect absorbed in a design as essentially the same human trait as that exhibited by the teacher who enjoys making the classwork go or by the statesman absorbed in drawing a bill and securing its passage into law.

5. *Esthetic discrimination,* the predisposition to feel disgust and repugnance or admiration and desire and creative impulse toward both material and personal objects of contemplation is characteristic of man as man, and esthetic discrimination and idealism is as truly instinctive (in the sense of expressing an innate propensity) in respect to personal traits of conduct as in respect to material things. In both fields men everywhere have their likes and dislikes. But in respect to both, man is capable of great variation and progress

---

[1] Cf. Author in *American Journal of Sociology,* xviii, p. 493.

in standards of taste. Music has progressed from the tom-tom to the symphony, painting and sculpture from the sketches of the cavemen on their cavern walls, and drawings scratched in the ivory of the mammoth's tusks to Raphael and Michael Angelo. Ethical ideals have made similar advance. Ethical ideals, however, are not purely matters of taste and sentiment, for taste and sentiment tend to reënforce practical judgments as to the consequences of human traits or conduct, so that more and more as progress goes on beauty is seen in that conduct and character which practical reason, measuring the effects produced upon all the values which men have learned to prize, unites with instinct to approve.

6. The predisposition to *reason* and to rational conduct, the propensity to examine, experiment, explain, forecast, and act upon conclusions. The cerebral apparatus of reason would not have been developed, through natural selection, if it had not secured actual adaptations to environment. Reason is not merely receptive but also propulsive. The disposition to reason and, what is more, to act upon the conclusions of reason is an inborn trait of man. True enough, it may be inhibited and overcome by other propensities. But it is always there asserting its claims. And the more men know the stronger the claims of reason become.

The so-called play instinct has not been included in this enumeration because, far from being a specific instinct, it is rather the sum of all the predispositions which find expression in free and zestful activity. It is the propensity of living organisms to function.

II. Economic Predispositions.—1. Predisposition to *eat* whatever can be eaten.

2. A *hunting* (and fishing) propensity is usually thought to be definitely inherited from our remote ancestors.

3. *Acquisitive predisposition,* the tendency to seek and value things as an extension of the self, to collect and hoard.

Orderliness is apparently an expression of acquisitiveness, plus the instinct of workmanship.

The other predispositions that find expression in economic life are, I think, either general predispositions or social proclivities, like the desire for recognition and distinction and others of those next to be enumerated.

III. Social Predispositions.—1. The *mating* instinct.

2. The *parental* instinct, characterized by tenderness, provision and protection.

3. *Sociability.*

Professor Giddings, especially in his earlier writings, treats "the consciousness of kind" as the central sociological fact. The recognition by the subject of similarity between himself and his associates may be regarded as the stimulant of the instinct of sociability. It accounts for the way birds of a feather flock together. It lays the foundation for association which increases the similarities, and develops practical coöperation. (See the references to Giddings, on the following page.)

4. *Predisposition to communicate and to receive communication,* through all the agencies of social suggestion. Communication takes place wherever B gets an idea by observing the conduct by which A gives overt expression to that idea, whether A intended his conduct as a means of communication with B or not. All intelligible conduct is thus a means of communication between associates. Symbols are acts or objects devised for the purpose of communication. The propensity to communicate is so strong that all societies invent symbols. In the brain the convolutions of Broca and Wernicke appear to be devoted to the formation and interpretation of speech. And the conduct of children seems to show that any normal group of human beings in permanent association would begin the formation of a language.

5. *Predisposition to imitate,* "sheep-through-the-gap-ishness." It has been usual to speak of an imitative instinct, but there is no such instinct. Imitation is not the functioning of a special hereditary apparatus, but of any of our motor powers. It is not a particular motor response, but is any act "from saying, 'Mamma' to building a battleship."[1] We imitate not because we have a specific instinct

---

[1] Compare author's article in the *American Journal of Sociology,* Vol. xi, p. 31, and xvii, p. 387; also Wallas: The Great Society, p. 124.

prompting us to do so, but because we are alive and ready and eager to act; because we act upon "ideomotor" prompting, that is, every idea of an action prompts the action if there is nothing to inhibit the prompting; because we get ideas of action from observing the acts of our associates, and their acts are such as we, too, can perform. Moreover, the acts by which they serve their purposes will often serve ours; besides, to act as they do gratifies our sympathetic sociability, or "consciousness of kind," [1] to say nothing of our desire for recognition and our emulative self-assertion. We imitate most readily the actions by which members of our own species gratify and express any one of the predispositions that are common to our species. The fact of imitation is more general than a single instinct. Indeed the word imitation has been so broadly used as to include, not only the copying of overt acts, but also all passing of ideas and sentiments from one associate to another by communication and by sympathy. We shall use the word imitation to refer only to copying of overt acts.

6. *Sympathy.* Pain, like that of a cut finger or any irritation of the "pain spots" in the skin or other tissues, is probably never directly shared by sympathy. The sight of pain stimulates tender emotion and desire to help; this is not sympathy but altruism. Sadness and cheer, however, are directly communicable by sympathy, and the instinctive emotions, like anger and fear, are thus communicable (especially when exhibited by one of our own partisans), and when two or more persons have the same emotion aroused by the same excitant, the knowledge by each that the others have the emotion can greatly heighten the experience, especially when instinctive manifestations of the emotion are directly observed. Finally and above all, sentiments, like ambitions, tastes and distastes, and moral approvals and disapprovals are powerfully radiated by sympathy.

7. *Gratitude and resentment* or vengefulness.

---

[1] See Giddings: Principles of Sociology, p. 17 and *passim;* Descriptive and Historical Sociology, p. 275 *seq.,* and *passim:* Inductive Sociology, pp. 63, 99 and *passim.*

8. *Sensitiveness to social approval and disapproval,* the desire for recognition, distinction, approval, love and pained avoidance of disapproval, dislike, and slights. This perhaps is the chief of all the springs of endeavor beyond that required to meet the requirements of a low standard of bodily comfort, the chief fulcrum by which society controls its members and brings order and coöperation out of what would otherwise be chaos, and the chief basis of human happiness and misery.

9. *Dominance,* the predisposition to boss and domineer over all who will submit, self-assertion, self-aggrandizement, tendency to feel big and masterful, and to act accordingly. This may be thought by some to be a special manifestation of the foregoing. In that case it is so special as to require separate enumeration if our thinking is to be at all analytic. As a matter of fact dominance is relatively weak in many in whom sensitiveness to social approval and disapproval is strong, and instinctive dominance often appears to be stronger in those whose sensitiveness to approval and disapproval is weaker; that is, the two traits apparently tend, other things being equal, to vary inversely in strength.

10. *Self-subordination* is nowadays regarded as a distinct predisposition and even an instinct. Possibly, however, it is a combination of fear, sensitiveness to social approval and disapproval, imitativeness, and partisanship.

Each person has both the tendency to dominance and the tendency to self-subordination, and responds with one or the other according to the nature of the situation in which he finds himself. The person who most often responds with dominance is not at all certain to be the wisest or the bravest. A new suit of clothes will greatly increase the tendency to dominance; so will a robust figure or a deep voice, and so will the consciousness of acknowledged wealth, position, or prestige in any of its forms. One who, like Grant, is modest and even shrinking may have the necessary courage, determination, and wisdom to prove the greatest leader when the detection of his qualities by others causes leadership to be offered him. But it is the assertive, self-confident, instinctively domineering person to whom leadership at first gravitates. And one who lacks a due measure of these qualities is likely to shun responsibility unless it is definite and obvious and to be too much influenced by others to exercise cardinal functions with the greatest success. The domineering propensity and bigness of self-sense may be accompanied by a high degree of altruism as appears to have been the case with Washington.

11. *Partisanship,* we-feeling, or sense of collective identity, self-consciousness that includes group consciousness. This is illustrated by the boy who may bully his little brother, but will not stand by and see the boy from across the street do so; by the boys who go to school along the same street and snowball the boys from another street; by the pupils of one school as against those of other schools; by operatives in the same factory as against those of another factory, and workers on one floor of a factory as against those on another floor of the same factory; by neighborhoods, sects, cliques, clans, nationalities, and by all groups of individuals who share a common relation, as against all outsiders. On one side partisanship is group-loyalty, devotion, and tendency to extol and aggrandize; on the other side it is bigotry and unacknowledged prejudice, misunderstanding, depreciation, and tendency toward hate and active hostility. It is corporate self-consciousness and self-assertion. It is the circle of selfishness drawn larger. And while it swallows up the narrowest forms of selfishness, it creates the same need as does other selfishness for the struggle to be just. It limits the range of successful coöperation and mutual helpfulness. It is a universal predisposition of great strength and enormous social consequences. Intercommunication, enlightenment, and the habit of reasoned life tend toward the brotherhood of man.

12. *Altruism,* or "the impulse to help" or "the spirit of coöperation." Altruism is by no means the same thing as sympathy. Sympathy may be present in relatively high degree and altruism in relatively low degree. As we saw above sympathy provides for the radiation of emotions and sentiments and but little if at all for the radiation of specific

pleasure-pain values. Altruism is guided by reason and by remembrance of our own pleasures and pains, rather than by direct radiation of the pains and pleasures of others. Altruism or the impulse to help is by itself a specific propensity.

Many extend their conception of the parental instinct so as to include all altruism.[1] It may be quite true that the necessity of parental tenderness and care to secure the survival of species among mammals was the chief cause of the evolution of the propensity to altruism,[2] and possibly it is true that the emotion and the activities of altruism everywhere resemble those of parenthood. But group-helpfulness outside of the parental relation had a distinct survival value[3] among the gregarious creatures. And the propensity to group coöperation outside the circle of the family is of such measureless social importance as to require it to be emphasized here. It is not absolutely essential here to decide whether all altruism is or is not in origin an extension of a propensity originally evolved for the care of offspring.

13. *Justice.* Justice or fair play may be regarded as a distinct propensity inasmuch as it has a specific excitant, namely, the conflicting interests of associates, and characteristic manifestations. Justice,[4] however, is simply reason and altruism called into action by conflicting interests of conscious beings. It is the propensity to reason and to act upon reason in the presence of recognized conflicting interests of different individuals.

We are obliged to recognize that the propensities and interests often conflict. What is to act as umpire when they thus conflict? Reason alone is fitted to be the chief and ruler among the propensities of man, because reason is the freest of them all from bondage to any single aspect of the

---

[1] For a good statement of this view see Thornstein Veblen: The Instinct of Workmanship, Macmillan, 1914, pp. 25, 26, 27.

[2] See Drummond: The Ascent of Man, Jas. Pott & Co., 1894, chaps. vii and viii.

[3] Kropotkin: Mutual Aid a Factor in Evolution, McClure, Phillips & Co., 1903.

[4] What is called retributive justice is simply anger more or less modified by justice.

situation. It is remotest from the simple type of instinct that like the springing of a trap responds automatically to one form of external stimulus. It is affected by all the facts of the case and all the recognized consequences of conduct, both immediate and remote. Will is most truthfully conceived, not as a separate power, but as the whole being going into action. And will is most worthy of its name when man goes into action with total and not fractional response, all the propensities summoned by the occasion and by the memories pertaining to it functioning duly under the presidency of reason.

14. *Conscience.* No man is born with a conscience any more than one is born with a language. But just as we are born with the predisposition to communicate and so to learn a language if one is spoken by our associates, otherwise to begin to make one, so also we are born with the predisposition to acquire from society a conscience or to begin the making of one. Just how this making of conscience proceeds we shall have occasion to observe in a later connection. The making and acquisition of conscience is a function in which propensities already mentioned coöperate, namely, esthetic idealism, practical reason which estimates conduct by its consequences, amenability to social approval and disapproval and to sympathetic radiation that absorbs the moral sentiments already prevalent, and justice which applies to oneself the standards of judgment which we pass upon others. Conscience is not a single faculty but the combined resultant of individual and social reactions that ultimately shape the mental state which the individual has toward his own conduct.

The possession of all these predispositions does not make man civilized. Only a long process of social evolution can do that. The possession of all the predispositions in their highest development would not supply a society, still less an isolated individual, with a developed language, conscience, religion, government, or industrial arts. Only a prolonged process of social evolution has brought such realities into existence. Biological evolution even at its highest level leaves man naked of soul as well as body. Even the lowest savages already possess a rich heritage of social as well as of biological evolution. The differences between our life and theirs result mainly from the differences between their social evolution and ours. They also have all the propensities.[1]

Only Minor Variations in Instincts and Predispositions of Normal Individuals.—Those instincts that characterize one portion of humanity characterize normal humanity as a whole. It is a mistake to think that the nature peoples are "savages" in their dealings with the people of their own class. They are not brought up under the softening influence of the most advanced moral ideals; the conditions of their life occasion many customs that seem to us cruel; and ungoverned impulse impels the same men now toward tenderness, fair play, and

---

[1] In its tentative stage sociology, instead of explaining social realities by the scientific method, that is by an analysis and synthesis of all the conditions by which they are molded, has referred them to "social forces." This expression has meant human "desires" or "purposes," a mixture of the predispositions vaguely conceived, with the emotional outgo in activity. The same author will discuss the desires, or "social forces," now as if he meant the inborn predispositions, and again as if he meant the emotional aspect of activity. These two ought to be distinguished. The predispositions ought to be identified with a reasonable degree of analytic accuracy. When so recognized they are seen to be a part of the biological or psychophysical conditions of human conduct. The psychophysical conditions are only one of four sets of causal conditions, certainly no more significant for sociology than the *social* conditions, and far enough from being *the* social causes, far enough from giving complete or adequate sociological explanation, and far enough from defining the field of sociology—all of which has been claimed for the "social forces." And the emotional outgo in social activity is still further from being the cause, and adequate sociological explanation of such activity. The "purpose," the "desire" thus conceived, *is the social activity which is to be explained* and not the "force" explaining it. To say that the purpose or desire to migrate is the sociological explanation of the overt fact of migration is amazingly superficial. The purpose and desire to migrate is the social fact, on its subjective side (see p. 357). Until that purpose and desire is explained there is no explanation of the migration that has a particle of scientific validity or significance. For a summary of some of the attempts to enumerate "the social forces" see Ross: Foundations of Sociology, chapter vii, especially pages 165 ff. Compare the reference on page 218.

loyalty, and again toward treachery and violence. They usually regard warlike hostility toward outsiders as meritorious, vengeance for wrongs as a solemn duty, and the man who fails to exact revenge for an injury to himself or to any fellow-tribesman as a craven. But they also frequently regard the man who forgets a kindness as despicable and are often impulsively altruistic and highly sociable among themselves. Among a hundred peoples, savage and civilized, chosen at random, the Anglo-Saxon race would probably be by nature not more sociable and not less violent and vengeful than the average.

Although all the human instincts are supposed to be universal among normal individuals of our genus, yet they vary in their urgency more or less between races, between the sexes, and most of all between individuals; and these variations in sociability, in sympathy, in parental tenderness, in clannishness, in loyalty, in justice, in dominance, in acquisitiveness, in caution and timidity, in hardihood and hopeful confidence play an important part in the destiny of social groups.

Abnormal deficiency first in altruism and second in sensitiveness to social approval and disapproval characterize the born criminal. What we call natural conscientiousness is largely the manifestation of sensitiveness to social judgments together with the imagination and esthetic sensibility to cherish ideals. The conscientious child cannot bear to do what parent or teacher disapproves or would disapprove if knowing the action. Such a child judges himself by the standard used by his parents and teachers and is elevated or depressed by these self-judgments. The normal gamin will bear and do to win the admiration of the gang. The hero "seeks glory e'en at the cannon's mouth." The utmost development and exertion of every power that human beings possess can be elicited by these motives. Society can have from its members whatever it sufficiently admires and appreciates in them.

Altruism, sociability, and sensitiveness to social approval and disapproval, as well as vengefulness, are sometimes thought to be more strongly developed in women than in men, and in the races of southern Europe than in those of northern Europe.

Emphasis has been given by some sociologists to supposed differences in the urgency of the reproductive instinct, and in fertility. The fact appears to be that all races are sufficiently fertile, at least potentially, but they differ widely in the physiological and pathological costs of maternity and so in actual fertility. In this respect, civilized woman is at a great disadvantage as compared with savage woman, and physicians say that a difference in this respect can be observed among different social classes of the same population. Among possible causes may be named the elimination by death, among races and classes that do not have expert medical service, of individuals and strains that are incapable of normal maternity, also the deleterious effects of meddling with natural processes, of indoor life, of lack of free muscular movement, and of excessive nervous activity. Races and individuals differ materially in respect to the age at which the reproductive organs mature, a warm climate favoring early maturity. The promptings of the reproductive instinct are, generally speaking, distinctly more urgent in the male and retain this quality later in life. They are said to be specially so in the negro race, and this is spoken of as a biological adjustment to life in a region having a high death rate and requiring a high birth rate. The morality of numerous individuals of this race suggests that the laxity of others is due more to lack of inhibiting ideals and strength and lack of inhibiting motives furnished by the social environment than to excessive instinctive tendency. The instinct is probably developed to something like a biological extreme in normal and vigorous males of most races. It is excited or allayed by psychological as well as physical causes, so that its excitation is largely a matter of attention and suggestion. It should, therefore, be a point of good breeding not to call attention to it except for some important reason; not because any element in nature is despicable, but because life is a problem in proportion, and only by design can the proportion be maintained which duly subordinates the most excitable of all animal impulses, which was already evolved in paleolithic time, to the newer attainments of civilization and ethical idealism upon which our hold as yet is comparatively precarious.

General Neural Traits.—Having discussed the predispositions, that is, those complex coördinations which predispose mankind to certain more or less definite forms of activity and experience we should now observe certain inborn variations in the free powers of sensation, of perception, of memory, of associative intelligence and reason, and of attention and will, viewed broadly and not merely in particular combinations into which they enter. With reference to these native powers of the human mind there are variations which are of great significance in conditioning variations in social activity. We are speaking here of inborn variations, but it must not be forgotten that these traits of man are subject also to postnatal modification, repression and development. Among the inborn variations in these normal traits the following may be particularly mentioned:

1. *Keenness of the five senses, and pain.* Some savages under mutilation exhibit not only stoicism but also a marvelous insensibility to pain as well as an equally marvelous power to heal and recuperate from wounds. In the keenness of the five senses there are great differences between individuals and smaller differences between races. The wonderful superiority of the savage as an observer of nature is, however, for the most part not a superiority of sensation but a superiority of perception; that is, of the mental process that lies behind the sensation and gives it meaning. He has been educated to read nature's signs and we wonder at him as he wonders at us when we read a book, or as a child in the copybook stage wonders at the reader of a badly written manuscript or at his father's rapid turning of closely printed pages.

2. *Type of mental imagery.* The person who can draw well may not have better eyes than the person who can never draw; and he may not have better perception, but only a different kind of perception. His attention naturally occupies itself with spatial images, while that of the other person may occupy itself predominantly with auditory images. The mem-

ory stores of the one will consist more of visual elements, and those of the other of auditory elements. One will spell "by the looks," the other "by the sound." One may be a painter, the other a poet or a musician. The difference extends to the thinking of each. Most of our thinking is figurative and the figures of thought are predominantly visual or auditory. Even abstract words like dignity or meanness to many, if not to most of us, carry with them a vague, fragmentary, and dreamlike picture or tone.

3. *Esthetic sensibility*. Probably all races, including the lowest savages, have native esthetic sensibility. Esthetic sensibility may be: (1) sensuous, that is, excited by pure sensation; (2) idealistic or humanistic, that is, excited by ideas of personality or personal traits or conduct; (3) intellectual, that is, excited by the logical fitness, harmony and completeness of that which they perceive or imagine. It is sometimes thought that the races of southern Europe have more sensuous estheticism than those of the north, but it may be that the difference is rather that they like somewhat different color tones and objects. It is said that the races of the north have more esthetic idealism, but this would be hard to prove. There are some reasons for thinking that the southern races possess a higher degree of intellectual estheticism. Certainly the English-speaking race seems inclined often to ignore logical consistency and to be influenced only by practical considerations that are thrust upon men by present exigencies. Logical consistency is one guide to truth, but the esthetic enthusiasm for logical consistency may lead men to spin out their systems too far beyond their fragmentary knowledge. Individuals of the same race vary in their sensitiveness to the beauty perceptible to eye and ear, and also in respect to what particular sights or sounds will move them; the latter, however, as comparative sociology proves, is not so much a difference of inborn tendency as of education. We differ also both in responsiveness to ideal beauty and, as a result of social rather than psychophysical causes, we differ widely in respect to the particular manifestation of character which we admire.

4. *Retentiveness of memory* is in part a matter of con-

genital tendency but, generally speaking, varies far more from youth to old age in the same individual than it does from individual to individual. Hence, youth is the time for the collection of general memory stores, the acquisitions of maturity being mainly confined to fields of specialization. Quality of memory depends in part upon natural retentiveness, in part upon type of imagery, some having an enormous retentiveness for auditory and others for visual impressions. But it depends far more upon awakened interest and attention bent in particular directions, and upon mental organization.

5. *Degree of mental organization.* The most important difference between the intellects of men is in the way in which elements of consciousness relate themselves to each other. In one mind objects of perception and thought hardly relate themselves in any way except that in which they are presented to the mind by sense perception. In another mind any element in the mental content of one moment is likely to free itself from the other elements that were presented in connection with it, and relate itself to anything that the memory contains for which it has an essential kinship. The latter mind perceives the special significance of particular ideas, builds up about them new inventions and structures of thought. Such a mind finds intellectual activity interesting and is capable of prolonged concentration of attention, and is not sterile but fertile. Minds of a relatively low order can be stimulated to some constructiveness by the presence of practical necessity requiring the solution of a problem. Minds of high order find constructive thought a delight.

6. *Type of motor response.* Quite as important as intellectual quality is the promptness, force, and persistence of the set of attention and of conation that results from the presence of an idea in the mind. This, in fact, is the culminating distinction between human beings. Promptness and persistence may vary together or inversely. It is especially needful to distinguish between fractional and total response resulting in peripheral or central control. Each idea coming from the external world tends to elicit a response. I hear you speak and I answer, see an open magazine and pause to read, ob-

serve the brilliant lights at the entrance to a place of entertainment, am invited by a friend to enter and turn with him to go in. In each case there are in my memory other ideas related to the incoming idea. Do they remain latent and for the time being more than half forgotten? Do I act as if the idea coming from the external world were the only idea to be had on the subject? If I do, my response is fractional; but if the incoming idea which calls my attention to a given subject arouses the other ideas that I have on the subject so that my action expresses the resultant of all my thoughts about it and not merely of the one that is being externally emphasized, then my response is total. In the latter case my answer to you will not be suggested by the form of your question, but by my reflection; I shall not read the magazine if I ought to be doing something else; I shall not enter the place of entertainment if I had wisely resolved to go home to study. In the one case the control under which I act is peripheral, comes from without, and stirs up a fraction of my nature which goes off into action as if that were all there were of me. In the other case the control under which I act is central and I do not act save as that which is within me consents. The man of fractional response and peripheral control has frequently to say, "What a fool I was!" He says it truly, for he has acted as if the results of his past experience, deliberate reflection, and intention did not exist; for the time being they did not exist for him because they had no place in his attention. This is what Spinoza meant by saying that the passionate man is a passive man. The man as a whole, enriched by experience, reflection, and judgment is passive, inactive, while some mere fragment of his nature stimulated from without goes into action.

The man of fractional response and peripheral control is prompt in his responses, appears lively like a bouncing object, is often merry company, but he is light. The man of weight whom others respect and follow is often more silent and slow; though silence and slowness are no virtue in themselves, and in a man of the highest organization total response is rapid upon occasion and may be usually so.

The man of total response is the only one who can rely upon himself to carry out an intention. The man of fractional response is continually being called aside from the way he had chosen. This is the deepest meaning of the words, "straight and narrow path"; it is the path of the man who is going somewhere, who does not wander hither and yon, turned aside by every momentary allurement and suggestion, but keeps to the track and will arrive at his predetermined destination. It is the path "that leadeth unto life." It is often said that the people of southern Europe are more fractional in their responses than those of northern Europe. But when we contemplate their achievements we are led to wonder if it can be true. They seem to be quicker and more volatile, less deliberate, balanced, and so to speak ballasted, more gregarious and with stronger primary social emotions, more amenable to social suggestion and less independent. If they are somewhat less characterized by central control, they may be guided toward achievement by somewhat greater ardor for their aims and somewhat greater thirst for glory.

Temperament.—Besides the specific instincts and the general neural powers, human beings are characterized by inborn differences not in the special apparatus of conscious activity but in the other organs of the body, which, however, by their functioning or by the products of their functioning, act upon the brain and nerves and so indirectly affect the conscious activities. To this class of inborn traits I am appropriating the name temperament. Our physiological knowledge is not sufficient to enable us to determine just how much of the character of a man's conscious activity is due to traits of his brain and nerves, and how much to traits of his stomach, glands, and other organs. But we know that differences of both kinds play a part. After a strong cup of coffee a man may feel, think, and act very differently from the manner which he exhibited before the drink. A glass of whiskey will produce a still greater change. These beverages directly produce purely physical results, but these results manifest themselves in the thought, emotion, speech, and acts of the drinkers. The effects of temperamental differences are somewhat similar. Diminished activity of the thyroid gland causes lassitude and laziness; its removal causes idiocy. Dyspepsia and diabetes tend to produce sourness and depression of spirits. Pulmonary consumption promotes sweetness and hopefulness. The toxins of fever induce ravings and visions. Chemical action goes on in every organ of the body. Many organs thus contribute to the circulating blood elements which affect the other organs to which the blood flows. And it is probable that each of them "exerts in this indirect way some influence on our mental life."[1] In addition, many of the bodily organs directly affect the different nerves and so contribute something to "the way we feel," the big dim background of our consciousness. Thus, a well-developed and well-toned muscular system probably tends to pervade consciousness with courage. Though the difference in the influence of temperament between two given individuals be slight at any one time "it operates as a constant bias in one direction during mental development and the formation of habits"[2] and is thus responsible for much in the disposition, views and conduct of the adult.

One of the most pronounced hereditary contrasts is that between those persons who dwell upon dark thoughts, exaggerate caution into anxiety and dread, and seem to have their attention fascinated by ideas of the horrible, and those whose minds shy away from unpleasant thoughts, substitute for hard realities pleasant dreams and who may exhibit a lightminded cheerfulness or a dare-devil spirit. There is a normal balance between these two tendencies, and there are also two well-known forms of insanity in which one or the other of these tendencies is carried to an extreme.

The attempt is often made to enumerate the temperaments. The commonest enumeration is: nervous, phlegmatic, choleric, sanguine. The nervous temperament is supposed to favor mental activity; the phlegmatic temperament to incline toward heaviness of body and slowness both of thought and of muscular movement; the choleric temperament to exhibit itself in

---

[1] McDougal: Social Psychology, p. 118.
[2] Ibid., p. 116.

restless energy; the sanguine temperament to produce muscular strength and athleticism and instinctive impulsiveness of behavior. These titles are not without some rude correspondence to certain facts. But there are more than four or five or six respects in which temperaments differ, and with respect to each they may differ in all degrees, and the points of difference may appear in many combinations, each manifesting itself as a distinct temperament. And since six simple elements can unite in 720 different combinations and ten simple elements can unite in 3,628,800 different combinations, it seems of doubtful profit to try to name the temperaments.

Metabolism.—Differences of temperament, fundamentally considered, are mainly differences in metabolism, that is, in vital chemistry. Metabolism is the combination of anabolism and katabolism. Anabolism is the conversion of the materials derived from food into living tissue, in general the activity of the so-called unconscious or vegetative functions. The Esquimaux, for example, appears to be highly endowed in this respect, and woman seems to be more anabolic than man. The characteristic physical manifestation of anabolism preponderating over katabolism is plumpness, and this preponderance is thought to be both a cause and an effect of the psychic traits of serenity, placidity and comfortable quietism.

Katabolism is the tearing down and using up of living tissue, as in nervous and muscular functioning. It is explosiveness, while anabolism is charging. It manifests itself in boys as muscular activity, in men as laboriousness, enterprise, exploration, pushing out of the organism after active contacts. The European races are highly katabolic; the lean Yankee exhibits a katabolic type, and man as a whole is relatively more katabolic than woman.

Metabolism is the combination of anabolism and katabolism and the biological ideal is a high degree of each, so balanced that neither shall appear excessive. The appearance that woman is more anabolic than man may really be due simply to the fact that she is less katabolic. The two are complementary and each must be kept up in order for the other to be stimulated to proper activity, especially during youth when the habits of the organism are being formed. Endurance on the one hand and strength and agility as well as enterprise and mental activity on the other are functions of metabolism.

This is not meant to imply that differences in temperament are mere questions of balance between two tendencies, which are called anabolism and katabolism. On the contrary, the factors which enter into temperamental differences as above indicated are numerous and obscure; it may be that they are as numerous as the bodily organs, having each its specific function, and its own specific chemical product. And just as the botanist believes that the arrival of a chemical determinant causes what would have been only a bunch of leaves to grow into flower and fruit, so the determinants supplied by the various organs of the body appear to transform the feelings, thoughts and actions of men. Differences in temperament appear as differences in the urgency of instincts and in mental and emotional or motor tendency.[1]

One trait that might have been mentioned in the foregoing enumeration of inborn characteristics has been omitted, and that is "independence of character." The reason for omitting it is that it is compounded of elements that have already been mentioned; and what we recognize as independence varies in all degrees between baseness and nobility according to the elements of which it is composed and the proportions in which they unite. Thus the born criminal is independent of the judgments of society through social insensibility. The domineering tendency, the obverse side of which is hatred of being bossed, when uncoupled with intelligence and social sensibility, leads to mere obstinacy and contrariness. Strong katabolism increases the dangerousness of social insensibility and the domineering rebellious tendency, but also

---

[1] Certain sociologists have sought to identify social types characterized by a combination of traits, instinctive, cerebroneural, and temperamental, complicated further by the results of postnatal influences. The most interesting of these attempts are those of Ratzenhofer: Die sociologische Erkenntnis. Brockhaus, Leipzig, 1898, p. 260; and of Giddings: Inductive Sociology. Macmillan, 1901, pp. 74-90; and Descriptive and Historical Sociology. Macmillan, 1906, pp. 195, 209, 214, 236.

increases the usefulness of independence of character in its nobler forms. A courageous temperament reënforces independence. Great social sensitiveness may make the independent person suffer, yet even this and all the nobler qualities may unite with the domineering tendency and glorify it. And it is also true that without particular strength of the domineering tendency, altruism, humanistic estheticism, high mental organization, and central control may produce independence of character; for the man who clearly sees the ideal that ought to be realized in conduct and adequately appreciates it and who is guided and impelled by his own inward light and fire, will show great independence of character when the occasion demands it.

CHAPTER XIV

OTHER HEREDITARY CHARACTERISTICS OF POPULATION.
RACE. EUGENICS

Race.—Race is not a new kind of variable, but a particular combination of the variables already enumerated. There are many varieties of the human species, marked by striking differences in external appearance. Mere blackness of skin may be an excellence, a biological adaptation, in the inhabitants of a torrid super-lighted region. And each race tends to find beauty in its own type and to prefer it over other types. The more complex a reality is, the more it can vary and tends to vary, and as the brain and nervous system are enormously more complex than the features, it would be natural to expect the psychic traits of races to be at least as diverse as their faces. But while there are racial differences in organization of brain and nerves yet these differences are by no means so great as the complexity of these structures might lead us to expect, because cerebro-neural organization is the biological specialty of the genus homo, in all of its species or varieties, and the requirements of survival eliminate mental defects more certainly than they do mere external peculiarities. It is sometimes said that while races differ in mental and emotional characteristics these differences are compensatory, so that for every disadvantage that a race has it has also a superiority, and for every superiority it has also a disadvantage with the result that on the whole all races of man are equal. It may be quite true that each race has points both of superiority and of inferiority, but that all these differences should be arranged in a nice compensatory system is, according to the law of probabilities, incredible. We must admit that there are superior and inferior varieties of the human genus, although the differences between the races are by no means so wide as is usually imagined.

If a perpendicular line mn be drawn to represent the number of individuals in any race who have the degree of capacity that is oftenest found among that people, and other lines to the right of it to represent the number of persons of superior capacity, these lines growing shorter and shorter to represent the numbers possessing rarer degrees of endowment until at last a point is reached to represent the supreme example of that race, and if similar lines were drawn to the left of mn to represent the numbers possessed of decreasing degrees of endowment down to the zero of idiocy, and the upper

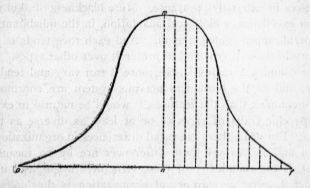

end of all these lines were joined, a curve like that in the accompanying figure would result.

If the curve so constructed to represent the endowment of a million members of one of the highest races were superimposed upon the curve constructed to represent the endowment of the same number of one of the lower races—taking, say, 1,000,000 Anglo-Saxons and 1,000,000 Congo Negroes, so that the perpendiculars representing individuals of equal capacity in both races would rise from the same point in the line af— something more or less accurately resembling the second figure would result. Our knowledge is by no means sufficient to enable us to draw the figure with entire accuracy, but such knowledge as we have may be expressed by such a comparison. The chief inaccuracy would follow from the fact that the qualities of the two races would not be exactly commensurable and men treated as on the whole equal would not have exactly the same qualities.

An idiot would be an idiot in either case; idiots are in the triangle abc. Only those members of the superior race represented by the triangle def would be biologically superior to all of the members of the inferior race. Those commonplace individuals who are represented by the line gh would find exactly the same number of their biological equals in either race. The great mass of the two races represented by the area B are biologically equal. The difference between the two is represented by the figure C, an extra mass of inferiority

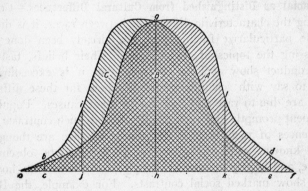

in the lower race, and A, an extra body of the superior in the higher race. The superior race contains members of every degree of inferiority, but it has not so large a proportion of the inferior. Thus of the low-grade individuals represented by the perpendicular erected at j the lower race has more than twice as many as the higher. And the lower race is by no means without superior individuals. Thus of the talented represented by the perpendicular erected at k the lower race has a goodly number, although there are fewer than are found in the other race; and it has none of the supreme geniuses represented by the area def. Notwithstanding that the great masses of the two races represented by the area B are biologically equal, the possession by the superior race of the extra mass of talented members represented by A and especially its

monopoly of the geniuses will result in great cultural differences, for the advancement of a people is originated by a small
but talented minority. A common man may be a good Christian, but only if there have been prophets. A common man
may be a patriot, but there must have been political geniuses,
a common man may wear good clothes, but it was not he that
invented the power loom and the spinning Jenny. A race that
lacks this upper one per cent. must borrow many of the
higher elements of culture. It must be borne in mind
that the quality of a race, as of an individual, is not to be
measured in terms of intellect alone, but also of will and sensibility.

Racial as Distinguished from Cultural Differences.—Concerning the characteristic differences between races, it is difficult to particularize further than has already been done in
discussing the topics of this chapter. Their beliefs, tastes,
and conduct show striking contrasts, but it is exceedingly
hard to say with scientific probability how far these differences are due to race and how far to other causes. Popular
judgment promptly and superficially ascribes such contrasts to
differences of race, because differences of race are thought
to be known, while the other causes are remote, obscure,
elusive, and largely unknown. People of the same race, however, show marked social contrasts. For example, the Bo-
hemian Czechs, the Hungarian Slovaks, and the Poles who
come to this country in great numbers, are all Slavs and all
belong, moreover, to the western subdivision of the Slavs.[1]
Yet, their esthetic, mental, and moral traits appear to be in
wide and marked contrast. The differences between their activities are due to social and not to biological causes and show
that in response to differing conditions the same race is capable of varying its social life within wide limits. The same
racial group may also show similar contrasts at different
stages of its history. The Catos and those members of the
Roman mob that in the time of the civil war when Marius
threw open the houses of the defeated faction, refused to
pillage, and the roman matrons of the earlier time, were the

---

[1] Deniker: Races of Men. Scribners, 1904, p. 344.

parents of the thieving and licentious Romans of the later empire.

Every race tends to claim that whatever cultural superiority it may possess is due to racial excellence. But science must distinguish clearly between cultural advancement and racial excellence. Racial ability is only one of the causes, and never the sole cause, of cultural progress. The fact probably is that each of the races that is, or has been, the bearer of a high civilization is developed up to or near the limit of possible advantageous variation, each differing from the other slightly in the direction which its development has taken, but each having carried its particular type of development to the limit beyond which lies insanity and various forms of nervous breakdown. The Chaldeans and the Egyptians were civilized when our own ancestors were wild and ignorant savages. The change in relative position is probably due, in very slight degree, if at all, to essential changes in the inborn characteristics of healthy and normal members of the races, but rather to causes of other kinds which the sociologist must learn to recognize. We may to-day boast our superiority over the Egyptians and even the Greeks, but we can by no means prove that it is a superiority of race. And as Chaldeans, Egyptians, and Greeks erred in assuming that they were by race superior to the savages of their day among whom our own ancestors were included, so we also may err if we take it for granted that we are biologically above every existing savage tribe. Every savage people, when sympathetically understood, reveals great powers. Among the causes that produce an elevated conscious life complex biological capacities are fundamental and essential, but they are only one in a combination of causes required to explain the different degrees of social advancement.

The descendants of Europeans and Africans living side by side in the United States are separated by social differences wider than the differences in natural endowment. This is because the motives, encouragements, and deterrents held out to the two races are not equal. The prizes of life are not offered to the Negro in the same degree and on the same terms as to the white man. Neither is the penalty of disgrace so heavy; moreover, the cultural advantages by which they are surrounded are by no means equal.

There are true racial distinctions even between European peoples, some items of which have been noted in earlier paragraphs. Yet, it must be held in mind that differences between individuals of the same race are far greater than the differences between races considered as wholes, and furthermore, that acquired differences and resemblances due to inheritance from ancient streams of social evolution, and lifelong response to social environments which press upon individuals from infancy onward, may greatly obscure inborn differences and resemblances, and may produce between individuals and between social groups, including nations, differences and resemblances which are by no means due to determiners in the germ cells. Patriotic pride and partisanship tend to exaggerate enormously supposed racial differences, both by imagining superiorities that do not exist, and by attributing real superiorities of group character to racial disparity alone when they are in fact largely or wholly due to other causes.

Ages.—Among the biological differences determined at birth which have important social consequences must be reckoned differences in age. A newly immigrated population contains a larger proportion of persons in active middle life, and fewer children and aged persons. We have already seen that a city contains a larger proportion of persons in these years of life than does the country. In a population where these age conditions prevail, activities will show greater energy and power as well as a higher rate of vice and crime. The supposed high percentage of criminals among the immigrants to this country is due to this cause. Doubtless criminals do immigrate, and pains should be taken to exclude them. Yet the fact that there are more criminals among 100,000 immigrants than among the same number of the native-born does not prove the greater criminality of the newcomers, since there are comparatively few children and old people among them, and a larger number of persons in the ages at which crime is most likely to occur. And if we compare 100,000 immigrant men between the years of 17 and 45 with the same number of native-born men of the same ages, it will be found that the latter include a larger number of criminals than do the men who have just come to our shores. The habits of immigrants were formed in an ancient civilization where the agencies of social control were strong. It is the children of the immigrants and not the immigrants themselves that swell our percentage of criminality more than any other class, except the Negroes. The children of immigrants, tempted to render too little obedience and respect to parents who are less proficient in the language and manners of their new environment than are the children themselves, largely freed from the social influences that molded the lives of their parents, and exposed to the worst aspects of American civilization in the slums of great cities, show a high percentage of criminality.

Sex.—Men are more aggressive or katabolic than women and bolder except when women act under a personal motive, particularly the maternal instinct. Accordingly men are far more prone to crime; in fact, about five times as many men as women become criminals. Women under similar circumstances become prostitutes.

A newly immigrated population usually has a much higher percentage of men, especially so long as pioneer conditions continue, while under settled conditions women tend to be slightly more numerous than men,[1] though as many male infants as female are born.

In the discussion of temperaments and of instincts attention has already been called to several of the differences between the inborn traits of men and women. Beyond doubt

---

[1] In Massachusetts females slightly outnumber males, while in Montana males constitute nearly two-thirds of the population. On the other hand, in the total population of the United States there are to every 100 females 106 males; among the native whites, 102.7 males; among the foreign-born, 129.2 males. In most European countries, females outnumber males, the ratio in England being 93.7 males to 100 females. The excess of males over females in the United States is considerably greater in the country than in the cities, notwithstanding the accumulation of immigrant men in cities. This is thought to be due to the opportunities for employment of women in cities, in factories, offices, etc.

the most fundamental biological differentiation and the one that is most profoundly significant as a condition affecting social life is the difference between the sexes. The difference is far more thoroughgoing than a mere physical division of labor in continuing the race. I believe that no observant person who has had much experience with little children is likely to think that the psychological differences between the sexes are due merely to social suggestion. Although the direction and degree of contrasting personal development is largely affected by the latter influences, there are also deep-seated differences in psychoneural tendency. Man and woman, of course, have very much in common, but they are complementary rather than identical. They are adapted to play different rôles. It is unprofitable to discuss the question, which is superior to the other; each is superior to what it would be if it were more like the other, for each is superior to the other for its own mission. Differentiation is the prime essential of organic progress, stages of evolution are measured by degrees of progress away from homogeneity through progressive differentiation. In general the obliteration of functional differentiation would not be progress but degeneracy; and the attempt to bring about homogeneity of the sexes and their life may be judged in the light of these facts. Every new movement is likely to imitate an earlier one that has already succeeded, until it has time to evolve an ideal of its own. This has been true of the feminist movement in its tendency to imitate masculine successes.

Woman should share all intellectual and esthetic interests. That implies liberal education. She requires less than man the spur of severely competitive rank to make her do her utmost in school work. Certainly the effect upon her of these forms of stimulation is different from its effect upon men. Not that this difference or others between the life of the sexes is by any means absolute; it is more like the differences between races. This difference in sensitiveness to marks and competition is an exhibition of the difference in sensitiveness to social approval and disapproval which was referred to in discussing the social instincts.

Chivalry.—Chivalry is not an insult to woman, nor an assumption of superiority on the part of man; it is the expression of reason and right feeling. A young woman in perfect bloom of health may be permanently injured by straphanging on street cars. Not so her brother. Work in the house lacks the variety and freedom and stimulus of wider contacts. It would be an immolation if it were not prompted by love of those for whom it is performed, that love should elicit appreciation and answering love. Chivalry is the right of woman and it is good for man. He cannot be a proper man without it. Woman because she is a woman and man because he is a man should stand in an ideal relation to each other.

By an ideal relation I do not mean a fantastic one, but simply one that gives outward expression to a rational judgment and an esthetic approval. With reference to a subject so all-pervasive and so fundamental to human happiness no society and no individual should be without a chosen concept, a standard, a deliberately approved ideal in the sense just defined. Every specimen of the genus Homo is an animal, but cannot be a man or a woman without such ideals. Though the libertine may find it hard to believe, yet it is true that the pleasure of association between the sexes is immeasurably heightened when it is conducted on the ideal plane, when caresses have measureless meaning and so can never be used save when those measureless meanings are to be expressed which unite lives in the most permanent and precious relationships. The full value of life is only for the strong. A large proportion of the negative failure to realize the best in friendship and in marriage and also of the positive wretchedness and woe that blacken the world are due to weakness here. The woman who, though never immoral, yet by a freedom which she regards as innocent, teaches men to hold the marks of woman's favor cheap is a traitor to her sex and a peril to man. Engagement is the sacredest vow that ever passes human lips. In rare cases it may honestly be unsaid; nevertheless, it is more sacred than marriage itself, for the latter, though it brings new possibilities and new duties, is after all the formal and public avowal of that covenant which has already been made in secret.

Hereditary Defects.—Up to this point in the present chapter we have been discussing the inborn differences between normal human beings, but there are human beings, and their aggregate number is great, who are born with serious abnormalities, and these abnormalities are responsible for a large fraction of the most lamentable social failures, including much of the poverty, vice, and crime. According to responsible figures published in 1910, which are probably within the mark, we have in this country 300,000 insane and feeble-minded, 160,000 blind and deaf, 2,000,000 that are annually cared for in hospitals and homes. Our annual public expenditures for the care of defectives reaches nearly $100,000,000. There are besides at least 80,000 felons in prisons, a larger number of misdemeanants in jails and lockups, and a still larger number of these classes at large in society, while in ordinary times about 4,000,000 a year are recipients of charity. By no means all of the defectives and still less of the criminals and paupers are defective by heredity, yet a great proportion of them are so.

Hereditary defects are of two kinds: first, those rare freaks of nature which can no more be predicted or accounted for than the appearance of genius, yet some types of which when once they have appeared have power to recur for generations; second, hereditary defects which are due to assignable causes. Of these known causes of hereditary defect by far the most productive of evils are alcoholism and venereal disease. These two poisons so pervade the organism as to impair the germ cells that reside in the body of one who may later become a parent, so as to inhibit the normal development of offspring. Similar results are probably occasionally, though much more rarely, caused by saturating the body with other poisons, such as nicotin, hydrocyanic acid, lead, and others which are used in factories where men spend their working days.

The forms of congenital abnormality which are of greatest social importance include the tendency to various types of insanity, certain defects of the eyes, deaf-mutism, epilepsy, inability of one or another of the vital organs to resist disease, and feeble-mindedness.

Certain defects of the eyes are properly included in this list, but most of those supposed to be born blind are in reality victims of ophthalmia neonatorum. This is held responsible for from 20 to 30 per cent. of all the blindness in the world and is not hereditary but is due to infection of the eyes at birth from gonorrhea. It is preventable by the application at birth of a 2 per cent. solution of nitrate of silver directly to the cornea of the eyes. The majority of physicians have been neglectful of this preventive.

We have seen that germ diseases are not inherited in the strict sense of that word, but an inability to resist the attacks of disease upon one or another of the organs is truly heritable. Thus, for example, tuberculosis of the lungs, which is the cause of more than 10 per cent. of the deaths in the United States, is not inheritable; but Professor Davenport declares, "It would not be difficult to pick out of my collection ten families comprising about one hundred deceased persons among whom, instead of the expected ten, not one dies of consumption. Similarly there are many families in which no nervous disease has occurred in three generations, others without kidney diseases and so on. On the other hand, in other families 40 to 50 per cent. or even 80 per cent. are attacked by lung and throat troubles, or nervous defects. These differences cannot be attributed chiefly to environment, because they occur in families of which the members are widely dispersed and have varied occupations. They indicate fundamental differences in the protoplasm." (Eugenics, page 20.)

Feeble-mindedness.—Feeble-mindedness is the commonest form of blighting hereditary abnormality. One highly reputable authority avers that "upon the most conservative estimates 25 per cent. of alcoholism, of pauperism, and of prostitution, is due to feeble-mindedness," and adds the opinion that this percentage is much too low to represent the fact. Feeble-mindedness may be caused after birth by illness or otherwise, but probably fully two-thirds of the cases are due to specific hereditary defect.

Investigations in the United States and in England, Scotland, and Ireland, indicate that it is conservative to estimate one feeble-minded individual to each 300 of the population.

By application of the Binet tests it is possible to recognize the feeble-minded child before, in meeting the rude practical tests of life, he has been made to suffer severely or has become a cause of injury to others.

The application of psychological tests to 1,547 children of one school system in the United States showed 78 per cent. to be either normal or not more than one year above or below the normal development for their age. Three per cent. were ranked as more than three years behind the normal development and were considered feeble-minded, 15 per cent. were retarded two or three years, and the remaining 4 per cent. were precocious. Similarly Binet found in France that of 203 children, 103 graded at age, 44 one year below, 42 one year above, 12 two years below, and 2 two years above. These tests apply not to the attainments of the child in school work, which may be dependent on attention and other elements than natural endowment, but relate to natural endowment exclusively, and are intended to test all the intellectual faculties of the child and to give an idea of his intelligence as a whole. A child of ten may have the mental development proper to a child of three, and be able to profit only by methods of instruction adapted to the ordinary child of three. These investigations seem to show that the vast majority of individuals are born with a medium or normal natural development. But of 600 children appearing before the Chicago Juvenile Court more than 26 per cent. were feeble-minded. Of 36,710 prisoners in Scotland, 2,500 were weak-minded or mentally unstable. Of 800 admitted to Elmira Reformatory, New York, 43 per cent. were mentally diseased and 37 per cent. mentally deficient. There is much more evidence to the same effect.

The feeble-minded are persons mentally deficient from birth or from early infancy to any degree that prevents them from competing on equal terms with normal individuals and from managing their own affairs with ordinary prudence. They are divisible into three classes:

1. Idiots never reach mentality equal to that of the normal three-year-old child. They have no use or understanding of language. Perhaps 10 per cent. of feeble-minded persons are idiots.

2. Imbeciles can talk, play and do some kinds of useful work, but do not advance mentally beyond a child of seven years, and rarely learn to read or write.

3. Morons learn to read and write and work sufficiently to earn a good living in an institution, but are not capable of doing so without the supervision and protection afforded by the institution. They are very suggestible, easily led, incapable of resisting temptation.

The feeble-minded are children, whatever their age. They have, as a rule, large families and propagate their kind. Isolation of all feeble-minded persons would be costly but would greatly reduce the amount required for prisons and alms-houses. Moreover, the morons, or working class of inmates, would make up the chief addition to the institutional population and they would nearly support themselves under institutional supervision, so that the cost of their care would be comparatively slight and the service to society from their segregation would be incalculably great. They themselves would be happy, for they are easily made so, instead of miserable and abused. And the burden of society in the next generation, in criminals and paupers, would be diminished. At present society is giving proper care to only a small fraction of its feeble-minded children. A very considerable proportion are confined as criminals and delinquents in reformatories and prisons which with proper care they would have escaped. A great number are at large, at peril to themselves and a menace to society. So long as our colonies for the feeble-minded are inadequate for the proper accommodation of all, it is important that preference should be given to the admission of females, especially to the morons and high-grade imbeciles, who are otherwise subject to vicious abuse and who will otherwise multiply and perpetuate their kind.

Retarded Children.—The retarded children in our public schools, great boys and girls of thirteen and fourteen, who are in grades with children of half or two-thirds their years, may be feeble-minded. This, however, is by no means always the case. They may be the victims of defective vision or hearing or of adenoids disturbing their breathing or of other non-neural defects, frequently removable. Their backwardness may be due to bad home conditions resulting in irregular attendance, to lack of proper nutrition, to lack of sleep, or to overwork out of school. Of course, the cause of their backwardness should be removed if possible. If actually feeble-minded they should be removed to special institutions. There will still be a remainder of permanently or temporarily retarded pupils in the large communities, who require a special school or room with an able teacher and adapted occupational training. If they remain with the regular grades they are likely to lose social standing and, with it, self-respect, and to abandon themselves to the careers of outcasts and pariahs, finding their way into haunts of vice and penal institutions. But they can often excel at some particular occupation, and if brought into competition with their equals under a wise teacher, may develop into self-respecting citizens.

Backward children illustrate the fact that dullness in one kind of work does not necessarily imply incompetence in all kinds of work. And at the other extreme great ability in one direction is not sure to be accompanied by great ability in other directions.

General excellence seems often to be due largely to encouraging home environment and to the habit of expecting well of oneself, which induces a psychological attitude in which good results, otherwise impossible, come within the compass of one's powers.

Biology and Caste.—The facts of biology throw a strong light upon the social ideas and sentiments that establish caste.

1. Who is thoroughbred? In the most carefully guarded strains some admixture creeps in; and this is likely to be their salvation from degeneracy. "Each individual is descended from two parents, four grandparents, and eight great-grandparents; and continuing this geometric progression for thirty

generations, it has been calculated [1] that if there had been no recrossing of strains to make the same ancestors count more than once, a child of to-day would have had in the time of William the Conqueror, 8,598,094,592 living ancestors. With all the recrossing to diminish that number there is still chance enough to have had a king and also a dozen idiots or criminals from whom some of the many interlaced strains have sprung. How many generations of ancestors make significant contributions to each germ cell we do not know, but experience sufficiently shows that the complexity of inheritance and the chances of variation are great.

2. Probably no two living organisms are quite alike, even though they spring from the same parentage. Puppies of the same litter differ greatly, not only in size and color, but as greatly in disposition and ability.

3. Some of the causes that produce congenital blight operate more commonly among the poor than among the rich, and degenerates tend to sink in the social scale.

4. Yet, in any given population of any given race the vast majority of individuals of whatever social class are, in respect to natural endowment, normal.

5. Moreover, every social class produces its share of variants both up and down. The upper classes have their idiots and the lower classes have geniuses. The main contention of Professor Ward's "Applied Sociology" is that only a small fraction of the genius and high ability born into society renders to society any notable service, all but a small percentage being lost by reason of lack of proper education and opportunity. We may discount his statement largely, if we think proper, and even then leave it impressively significant. In the words of Professor Thomas: "The world's intelligence largely comes up out of the lower through the middle classes. The intelligence is there and of the finest sort. Like opportunity, and that from the cradle, alone will show who is naturally superior."

6. In discussing the agrarian aristocracy and peasantry that form as a result of geographic conditions, it was pointed

---

[1] Walter: Genetics, p. 239.

out that differences of appearance, speech, manner, disposition, moral traits, and intellectual attainment, which characterize different families through successive generations, are
largely not inborn but due to differences of family culture
and mode of life perpetuated generation after generation. In
the words of President David Starr Jordan,[1] "We often mistake the bringing up of a child for characters 'bred in the
bone.' The kingly bearing of a king, still more the regal bearing of a queen, may be the result of habit, not at all of any
innate quality. To be called a king from childhood on makes
a boy hold up his head, if he has a head to hold. To be
despised by men leads the average man, or the average dog,
to the habit of dodging and skulking." Differences of speech,
manner, bearing, thoughts, occupations, ideals and hopes that
result from differences in daily surroundings, education, and
opportunity and in the attitudes of associates, where conditions remain unchanged for generations, may seem, even to
the victims of unfortunate station, to be family traits of blood.

The Method of Inheritance.—A unit character is a trait or
group of traits of the developed organism which is supposed
to result from the presence of a specific determiner, a special
molecule or group of molecules[2] in one of the germ cells
from which the organism has developed.

If a child has dark eyes it is because in the germ cell contributed by one or the other of his parents toward his origin
there was a specific determiner[3] for that unit character. We
cannot identify all of the unit characters of a highly complex

---

[1] Heredity of Richard Roe, p. 26.

[2] A visible character in the developed organism may require a
combination of determiners in the germ cells, and a trait may be
latent for generations in a given family, till by crossing there is
added the determiner necessary to bring it out. Such occasional reappearance of the latent quality we usually call a "reversion." According to the law of chance a few determiners are capable of a vast
number of combinations, each of which may appear in a distinctive
trait of the developed organism. Our purposes require a statement
of only the simpler aspects of the Mendelian law of inheritance.

[3] There are determiners both for eye pigment and for the pattern
of its distribution.

organism, but hypothetically all that is transmitted by heredity, external traits of stature and form, instincts, predispositions, and temperament, is due to particular determiners or particular combinations of determiners in the germ cells.

If one parent cell has the determiner for dark eyes, and the other parent cell lacks it, the eyes of the offspring will have dark pigment. Of two contrasting hereditary qualities one which whenever present in either parent triumphs and appears in the offspring is called a dominant unit character and a contrasting one a recessive character. Some dominant characters come out just as strongly in the developed organism when "simplex," that is, when the determiner is supplied by only one of the parent germ cells, as when "duplex" or contained by both germ cells, and some do not, as ink mixed with water looks black as ink, but wine and water does not look red as wine. The dark tendency triumphs over the blue tendency because darkness of eyes is due to the presence of a positive determiner while blueness of eyes is a negative quality due simply to the absence of the pigment determiner.

If the determiner for a trait is present in all the germ cells of both parents that trait must reappear in all the offspring; if absent from the germ cells of both parents the trait cannot be inherited by the offspring. If contrasting tendencies are present in the parents the dominant tendency will assert itself in the bodies of the offspring but of the germ cells developed in the bodies of these offspring one-half will carry the dominant while the other will carry the recessive tendency.

Among the offspring of this mixed stock three-fourths will show the dominant trait and one-fourth will show the recessive trait. The reason for this is as follows: Let + represent the determiner for the dominant trait and let — represent the absence of that determinant.[1] Since each parent belonging to the mixed stock has both + and — germ cells the

---

[1] Whether the recessive tendency is represented in the germ cell by mere absence of the positive determiner or by another determiner over which the positive triumphs makes no difference in this connection.

combination of two cells from two such parents may be + +
or + — or — + or — —. In three out of the four possibilities the dominant is present and will assert itself in the bodies
of the offspring; that is, while we saw that all of the first
generation of mixed stock exhibit the dominant trait, three-
fourths of the second generation of mixed stock may be expected to show that trait.

In the third generation of mixed stock a different result
will appear. Those whose parents of the second generation
developed from the combination + + will breed true thereafter, all of their descendants showing the dominant trait just
as if there had been no mixture in their ancestry. Those
whose parents developed from the combination — — will also
breed true as if they were of pure recessive stock. But
those whose parents developed from the combination + — or
— +, though exhibiting the dominant characteristics, will
breed exactly like the first generation of crossbreeds.

From these facts it follows that to be sure of securing
the appearance of a dominant trait, though not always in a
high degree, it is only necessary that one of the parents be
pure bred with reference to that trait, even though the
other parent lacks it. But the offspring of such mixed stock
though themselves exhibiting the dominant trait cannot be
counted upon to transmit it to their descendants. For though
both parents exhibit the trait by virtue of its dominance, if
they derive it from mixed inheritance, part of the offspring
may be expected to lack it, and only a fraction of those offspring that do exhibit the trait can be expected to transmit it
to their offspring as they would if pure bred with respect to
this trait. Furthermore, it may be quite impossible to foretell
which among the offspring that exhibit the trait can thus transmit it.

Of course the transmission of undesirable dominants follows the same law; all of the offspring exhibit the trait if it
comes by unmixed inheritance through one parent, even
though the other parent be normal, and if both parents have
the evil trait, even by half inheritance, three-fourths of the
children may be expected to have it, one-fourth of the children

to transmit it as a thoroughbred trait, and two-fourths of the children to transmit it as a halfbred trait. But it is important to observe that those of the third generation who do not show the evil trait, having developed from two recessive germs (— —) cannot transmit it. Thus an individual whose ancestry has an abnormality but in whom that abnormality does not appear, may safely mate with a normal person provided it be known that the abnormality is a dominant. An evil inheritance by this very brief process of selection can be entirely bred out, provided it is a dominant.

Recessive traits behave quite differently in inheritance. A recessive being overcome or at least partially overcome by the presence of the dominant determiner from either parent, does not appear, or appears only in a modified form, unless it was present in the germ cells of both parents. But though the recessive trait does not appear, yet recessive germ cells develop in persons a part of whose ancestry was recessive stock, and as soon as two persons mate, both of whom are descended in part from recessive stock, even though neither of them shows the recessive trait, there is a possibility of a combination of recessive germ cells (— —) and in this entire absence of the dominant determiner the trait which was hidden in the parents breaks forth in what we call atavism, or if the recessive trait has not manifested itself for many generations we call its reappearance a case of reversion. Recessive traits are thus more insidious than dominants. And most hereditary defects (though not all) are thought to be recessive and due to lack of a dominant determiner which is normally present.

When two strains of a distinct ancestry unite the probability of the absence or inadequacy of the same necessary determiner in both is greatly diminished and if a determiner for a given trait is present in either strain, that usually suffices to produce offspring who are normal with respect to that trait. But when closely related strains mate the probability that deficiencies in the determiners will coincide so that the necessary determiners for certain traits will be received from neither parent is greatly increased. Herein lies the peril of consanguineous matings.[1] One biological reason for the fact of sex appears to be to prevent the intense inbreeding of a single unsound line that would perpetuate and exaggerate defects, instead of allowing them to be rectified by crossing with another strain which, even if equally defective would probably have erred from the normal in other ways. In consanguineous marriages, the probability is greatly increased that the particular germ cells which unite in a given conception will be deficient with respect to the same necessary determinant, even though the presence of a contrasting determiner from some strain of the ancestry may have prevented any defect from appearing in the developed bodies of the consanguineous parents. On the other hand, in outbreeding the probability is that any defect in the germ cell derived from one parent will be offset by a determinant from the other. The union of similar excellencies is to be sought, without consanguinity which risks the union of similar recessive and hidden deficiencies.

Eugenics.—The problem of eugenics, as it concerns us, is not the discovery of biological laws, but the equally essential task of applying such laws by the diffusion of knowledge, popularization of ideals, and the employment of other agencies of social control. There is little doubt of the biological possibility of ridding society of a great mass of its congenital defectives and incompetents, and there is hope of raising the level of health, ability, and predisposition to morality, much as a mixed herd of grade cattle in a few generations can be rid of scrubs, brought near to a standard of form and color and greatly improved as to its production of milk and cream. The aim of eugenics does not imply the evolution of a new type of humanity, higher than has ever existed before, but more general conformity to the existing standard of human excellence. Biological knowledge of the complex problem of heredity as

[1] Let AA represent a trait normal in both parents, and Bb and Nn represent traits normal in only one parent, and AA ... to ZZ represent the whole hereditary outfit. Then let two persons mate; one may have Bb and the other may have Nn and the offspring develop normally, but if the two who mated are of the same stock there is danger that they both will have Bb or Nn, which when mated may give bb or nn, there being no normal determiner for the trait represented by B or N.

it relates to mental and moral qualities in man is as yet far from complete. As yet we can identify but few of the unit characters, and have not learned in respect to all of those we think we can identify whether they are dominant or recessive. But we have sufficient knowledge to show that certain things should, and certain other things should not, be done, and increase of knowledge is to be hoped for. Musical, artistic, literary, mathematical or inventive ability, a high degree of mental organization, cheerfulness, courage, caution, sympathy, sensitiveness to social approval and disapproval, and a high degree of central control are all transmissible by heredity either as unit traits or as combinations of traits.

But more is biologically possible than may prove to be socially possible. We cannot control the mating of men and women as we do that of beasts. Nevertheless, something immensely worth while may be accomplished.

To begin with, we can control those who are so defective that by reason of their defects they become wards of the state in prisons and asylums. We may also insist that those who belong to certain classes of defectives shall become wards of the state. In the words of Darwin, "Except in the case of man himself, hardly anyone is so ignorant as to allow the worst animals to breed." The mass of heredity insanity, epilepsy, feeble-mindedness, deafness and blindness, and the worst forms of special susceptibility to disease, are borne along upon a widening stream of germ plasm which for a generation society must at all needed cost prevent from propagation. Thus we may "dry up the streams that feed the torrent of defective and degenerate protoplasm."

Vasectomy, applied to defective males allowed to be at large, is advocated by some and is already legalized in eight states. The operation is slight and a corresponding operation upon women, though more severe, is free from any great danger. These operations when properly and effectively performed prevent parenthood. There is, however, difference of opinion as to the moral consequences of turning loose a body of defectives who may be physically attractive and who are entirely capable of sexual immorality, but insured against the possibility of parenthood. The chief moral danger is not to them, for they are little restrained in any case, but to others whom they may corrupt. Moreover, the harm to this and to succeeding generations caused by the spread of venereal disease through such persons might easily far more than offset the physical gains resulting from their sterilization. Furthermore, many of those to whom the operation would apply, indeed probably almost all of those to whom we can be sure that it might otherwise properly apply, require custodial care and can be restrained from parenthood without surgery.

Something may be accomplished by marriage laws. But a large proportion of the worst births are illegitimate. Forbidding marriage to any large class of persons who are not subject to custodial care increases immorality with its train of evil consequences.

If medical inspection is required as a prerequisite to legal marriage, there must be medical inspectors, both male and female, paid by the state, who engage in no private practice. This will be possible when, with the advancing socialization of the medical art and the relative increase of preventive as compared with curative medicine, every considerable community will have a public health official of high professional standing, receiving his whole compensation from the government.

It has been proposed that a public register be maintained, showing the heredity and heritable traits of all who voluntarily offer themselves for registry. It is thought that those with excellent ancestry might gladly avail themselves of the opportunity to have their quality thus certified and that eugenic excellence would be as real a matrimonial attraction as wealth or social station. "Health, beauty, and vitality are natural objects of admiration and love. Titles, wealth, and other extraneous attractions are not." There is no reason why eugenic fitness may not be included in love's ideal. Ex-President Roosevelt would have such fitness in marriage a matter of patriotism. "Some persons would even make it a matter of religion." A general social judgment affirming its importance will go far toward making it a part of the ideal of the individual members of society.

According to Professor Hobhouse: "Where the conditions of life are hard, where there is little regard for justice and mercy, and in a word for all the higher ethical qualities, those who possess these qualities have less chance of prospering and leaving descendants behind them. . . . From this point of view political and civil liberty and economic justice are the most important of eugenic agencies. . . . The actual progress of humanity depends far more on the survival of the best than on the elimination of the worst. . . . Eugenically considered then, the broad duty of society is so to arrange its institutions that success is to the socially fit. And this is possible only in proportion as the social order is based on principles of a just and equitable organization." [1]

The chief social agency for the promotion of eugenics is education and the development of a eugenic morality. Upon this depends the passage and effectiveness of laws upon this subject. And upon it depends the intelligent self-control of those who are a law unto themselves. The control of wards of the state may do much to diminish the prevalence of unfit births, but education resulting in morality is the chief means for increasing the proportion of the fittest births. Among well-instructed and high-minded persons who can transmit good blood, and who are so situated that they can afford to give their children good nurture, the realization should be made to prevail that parenthood is the highest and most sacred of all duties and of all privileges, the greatest of all opportunities for social service. Not, however, that we want an increase in the number of children born, but rather that we want an increase of the number of children born in families where they are both well born and properly nurtured.

Unplanned Selective Agencies.—1. Many unplanned selective agencies have operated to modify purely natural selection in determining the reproduction of society. Of these one of the most baleful has been war, slaughtering thousands of

---

[1] Hobhouse: Social Evolution and Political Theory, p. 53.

the fittest youth and leaving the less fit to live and perpetuate the race.

2. The extermination and expulsion of men who have the honesty and devotion to adhere to unpopular opinions deflowers a race, and it is thought by some to have had much to do with the decline of Spain from the first to almost the lowest rank among the nations of Christendom.

3. It must be admitted that charity and the arts of medicine and hygiene keep alive to become parents some whom nature would otherwise eliminate. This by no means offsets the good done by charity, but this interference with natural selection must be offset by some conscious limitation, voluntary or enforced, upon the propagation of the unfit.

4. The prolongation of the period of education, by postponing marriage during some of the most fertile years, diminishes the relative proportion of our people who are born of the class of parents who attain liberal education. Such parents not only give evidence of powers that may be transmitted by heredity, but they also are the ones able to give their children the best nurture. The fact that it takes two years longer to acquire a liberal education in American schools than in Germany constitutes a national handicap.

5. Too low a standard of living among the laboring classes increases the proportion which they contribute to each succeeding generation. Too expensive a standard of living among the more prosperous and ambitious classes diminishes the proportion which they contribute to each succeeding generation. Too wide a difference between the standard of living of the laboring classes and the successful middle classes, causes population to be recruited more from the former and less from the latter. The "business" standard of success which measures social position, not by services rendered nor by personal culture and character, but by scale of expenditure, is a genetic curse. A reasonable recognition of life's values (which are not economic) and a standard of expenditure neither too low among the laborers nor too high among the business and professional classes is to be desired from the genetic, as well as from every other, point of view. An ex-

cessively high economic standard not only postpones the time when the self-supporting man of good social standing feels that he can marry, or even prevents marriage altogether, but also limits the number of children that are welcomed after marriage has taken place. An exacting economic standard is one reason why native-born Americans have smaller families than newly-arrived immigrants. Another is the greater influence of the Catholic religion among the immigrants. Still another cause of the larger families of immigrants may be found in the general tendency for birth rates to rise when the prosperity of a class of parents increases so suddenly that the increased income is not eaten up by an equal advance in the standard of living. This third cause is to be taken into account only in the case of immigrant groups that show a higher birth rate than in the country from which they came. The progressive change in the racial character of the American population is due less to the volume of immigration than to the disproportion between the standards of living and consequently between the birth rates of native-born and newly-immigrated parents.

6. A chief cause for declining birth rates in general is the extensive employment of methods for preventing conception, and the employment of these methods is more extensive among the wealthier and more instructed classes.

7. Another selective agency exists in the difference between urban and rural life. The conditions of life in the country tend to make children more welcome, marriage is earlier, and sterility caused by venereal disease is less frequent. These factors tend to increase the proportion of the population derived from rural ancestry. At present the high birth rate of immigrants, most of whom settle in cities, causes our urban population to show a relatively high birth rate. Indeed this high birth rate among our immigrants causes the slums to swarm with children and to furnish a higher relative quota to our population than comes from any other source. But among the successful classes in the cities the birth rate is exceedingly low. According to Professor von Luschan, it is unusual for a family to continue to exist in the city for more

than four generations. Postponed marriages, voluntary limitation of offspring, and, worst of all, venereal disease tend to wipe out urban families. It is perfectly possible for a family to survive through many generations as city-dwellers, provided the temptations of the city do not overcome their morality and their family ideals. This is shown by the history of certain families of Huguenot refugees, who have succeeded as city-dwellers ever since France deprived herself of them hundreds of years ago. The city continually draws to itself a large proportion of our most highly endowed individuals and there their stock becomes extinct.

8. Finally, social ideals concerning womanhood are effective agencies of reproductive selection. A social class in which any other ideal for woman seems higher than that of motherhood, not the mere physical but also the spiritual mothering of children, will not contribute its quota to the life of the succeeding generations.

If the more intelligent and well-to-do half of a population exactly maintains its balance between births and deaths while among the lower half the births are to the deaths as three to two, in the fifth generation the progeny of the poorer and more ignorant parents will outnumber the descendants of the upper half of the population as five to one. If the generations of the lower half succeed each other as two to three, while those of the upper half succeed each other as three to two, then in the fifth generation the progeny of the lower half will predominate by twenty-five to one. After we make all allowance for the popular exaggeration of the difference of endowment between the members of different social classes we must still recognize the social significance of the differences between better endowed and the less endowed strains as well as the incalculable advantage of rearing in a home of education and refinement. There is no doubt of the tendency of the class that has not proved capacity by success and that has a low economic and cultural standard of life to contribute cumulatively its disproportionate share, and those of proved capacity and high standards to contribute a dwindling share to the population. Why have great races lost their preëminence

In most things the movement of history has been toward progress and not toward decline. Is there an inveterate tendency toward the decline of successful stocks? We answer most questions as we like to answer them, and we do not like to think that we are a deteriorating stock. The intelligent have a duty.

Tremendous as is the importance of reducing the number of degenerates, it is still more important to secure the presence of a large number of the well-born and well-reared. Family stock that shows a high level of talent and fitness for participation in civilized life is inestimably precious and should not allow itself to become extinct. Genius is unpredictable and non-hereditary, but talent runs in families, unless it is crossed out by improper mating. The loss of a few score from the hundreds of thousands who dwelt in Greece would have impoverished that nation, and the whole world would have been immeasurably poorer. Progress still depends much upon genius and very much upon talent, and talent in many citizens. So also does the maintenance of a high level once attained in government, in industry, and in culture.

The chief eugenic agencies are spiritual, or psychic: a standard of living high enough to limit excess of population among the poorer classes, as it has done in France, and most important of all a high morality, a noble family tradition, and a patriotic or even religious sense of the duty of those who are able to give to society well-born, well-reared sons and daughters. The experience of Rome, of France, and in less degree of other nations, exhibits the fact that society may be in even greater peril of race suicide through lack of a genetic conscience in the "upper classes" than of Malthusian degeneracy through lack of an adequate standard of living in the "lower classes." History shows no nation that has long remained great under a "pleasure economy." A pain economy knows the hard and shriveled virtues of necessity; a "pleasure economy" dissolves in gross vices or in an equally selfish dilettantism. Only a duty economy, in which men who stand in the light and are ruled by "the law of liberty" choose loyalty to the whole, of which the individual and his brief day are but a part, can know the worth of life or bring its possibilities to fulfillment.

The bane of social agitation is particularism, which sees the importance of one factor in human welfare to the partial exclusion of the others. In sociology nothing is all-important because many things are all-important; that is, here as in every organic correlation of realities, the ruin of one may ruin all, and by the same token the presence of all is essential to the worth of any. Eugenics, the securing of well-born citizens, is one of the many all-important factors in the fulfillment of social aims.

CHAPTER XV

IMMIGRATION

Immigration as affecting the density of population is a technic problem.[1] But immigration affects not only the density but also the psychophysical quality of population, and in that aspect calls for attention in the present connection. It would be folly to give great heed to eugenics while neglecting effectually to regulate immigration.

Immigration to the United States has so increased that by 1900 38.7 per cent. of the white population of this country had been born abroad or were the children of parents one or both of whom had been born abroad. According to Josiah Strong, the ferry *John G. Carlisle,* in her hourly trips from Ellis Island to the Battery, carried more immigrants in a year than came over in all the fleets of the nations in the two centuries after John Smith landed at Jamestown.

Never has any other nation had such an opportunity as the United States to raise its population quality by selection of those admitted to its shores. Nor has any had such occasion to consider the possibility of allowing its population quality to be lowered by immigration. We must not exclude any in a spirit of selfishness, for we hold this vast and rich domain as a sacred trust for humanity and for the ages. But we must exercise care to distinguish between idealism and sentimentality.

Effect of Immigration on Native Birth Rate.—When a country receives great numbers of immigrants with a lower standard of living than that of the previous inhabitants, the latter are forced to limit their offspring much more than they otherwise would do. The result is the substitution of immigrants and their children for the unborn children of the orig-

---

[1] Compare p. 43 and following.

inal population. It is erroneous to suppose that the immigrants
to the United States form a net addition to the population of
the country. They are largely substituted for native-born
sons and daughters. It is the opinion of numerous expert
students of the subject that our population is little if at all
greater to-day than it would be if we had received no immigrants during the last century. It is certain that the birth
rate has fallen off enormously in the families of the original
settlers. The birth rate in this country would have fallen
off gradually on account of increasing population pressure
whether that population pressure were due to immigration or
to natural increase. But if the population pressure were due
to natural increase, the birth rate obviously would not have
fallen off till it had done its work. In fact the birth rate of
native stock has fallen off not only on account of an artificial
increase of population pressure through immigration, but also
because of further artificial difficulty in maintaining the native
standard of living among the masses, due to the low standard
of living among the imported competitors. During the first
four inter-census periods the population of this country gained
227 per cent. with very little immigration. An estimate made
in 1815 based on the first three censuses, reckoned the probable
population of the United States in 1900 at 100,235,985. It was
instead only 76,303,387, in spite of the incoming of 19,115,221
immigrants since 1820, so tremendously did the birth rate of
the native stock decline. The native birth rate has most declined at just the periods and in just the regions that have
been marked by the great immigrant influx. At present in
sections of New England the native stock, once so prolific,
is not even maintaining itself. This is what the so-called
"laws of population" would have led one to expect. An established population will sacrifice its increase to maintain its
standard of living. From the influx of foreigners having a
low standard it results that the level of wages in the easily
accessible occupations is so low and the social standing so
inferior, that native parents shudder at the thought of having
children enter those forms of work which they would share
with the newcomers. Some of these occupations are almost

caste callings. And the natives will not rear children to break caste by entering them. There are not enough places in the upper caste work to call into being a large population.[1]

Immigration and the Standard of Living.—Socialists dream of a time when manual labor will be performed under sanitary conditions by men of developed intelligence and character. There seemed a near prospect of this when excavations were dug and cotton machinery tended by the sons and daughters of New England farmers. These have been displaced from such labor by successive waves of immigrants who would accept lower wages; and the stock from which they sprung has enormously diminished its rate of reproduction, limiting their offspring to the number that could find employment in occupations better paid. It is true the immigrants tend to acquire a higher standard and to insist upon better wages than they had at home, but our better wage acts as a magnet to ever new invasions of low-standard labor, and if immigration is unchecked will continue to do so until no very considerable difference between American and European wages remains. At the same time, the removal of laborers from old-world countries tends to increase the birth rate there, and to relieve congestion only locally and temporarily. In 1885 it was written: "Europe is able to send us nearly nine times as many immigrants during the next 30 years as during the 30 years past without any diminution of her population."

If we should grant that the immigrants are of a stock that is quite as good as ours and that they worthily represent the stock from which they spring, still it remains unquestionable that their standard of living is lower than ours. And by unrestricted admission of immigrants having such a standard of living we more or less substitute them and their offspring for our own unborn children, we invite the gradual but inevitable approach of old-world standards of living, and sacrifice the opportunity to establish a higher level of general welfare which ought to prevail in this country, and we do so without any assurance whatever that, save very temporarily,

---

[1] Fairchild: Immigration, pp. 215 *seq.*

the number of those who enjoy the advantages of the new world is materially greater, or the number of those who struggle against old-world conditions is materially less than if we enforced a policy of restriction.

The maintenance of a progressive standard of living among the laboring classes is a eugenic agency irrespective of racial differences. Without it each succeeding generation witnesses a progressive replacement of the stock that had risen in the economic scale by a larger and larger proportion born from those who have given no such proof of their ability. Besides, the high and progressive standard of living is inestimably to be desired on its own account. It means the juster distribution of wealth, opportunity, and all the values of life.

Immigration and National Development.—It is no wonder that the rise in wages and in the standard of living in this country has failed to keep pace with the increase of wealth when we consider that it is the period of prosperity that affords the opportunity for laborers to secure advancements in wages, but that every period of prosperity brings to this country a great influx of immigrants willing to accept lower wages and to content themselves with a low standard of living. This turns to sand the stepping stones by which labor should rise.[1]

To have maintained the high and progressive native standard of living among our laborers, instead of inviting these low standard workers, would have meant not only higher wages and a more equitable distribution of wealth. Incidentally it would have meant a greater demand for the products of industry and a stronger home market. And it would also have meant a more intelligent population, better governed cities, and a general higher level of national life. All this is entirely aside from the effect upon population quality and does not necessarily imply that the native stock was any better endowed than that which has more recently immigrated. It means that the increase in the numbers of the population

---

[1] King: Wealth and Income of the People of the United States, pp. 173-207 and pp. 235 to 255.

cannot go faster than it should without preventing the advance which would otherwise take place in the standard of living and the general level of society. And matters are made far worse when the individuals who compose the excessive increase in numbers are not reared by previous inhabitants, but have an established standard of living lower than that of the previous inhabitants. The desire to limit immigration does not necessarily imply any assumption of race superiority over the people to be excluded. It does not even depend upon the natural desire of a people to rear their own sons and daughters instead of deriving the population of their country from an outside source. It rests upon the desire to maintain a high standard of living, not merely in the economic sense of that phrase, but in all the aspects of national life.

America Aspires to World Leadership.—America aspires to world leadership not through war and conquest, but through ideas and ideals, through developed wisdom, rectified valuations and democratic institutions. Every great nation may have a share in this world leadership. For the United States as a nation to become the very best society that it can be may well enable it to render to all the world and to the centuries to come a far greater service than it can by affording an asylum now to a larger number of peasants than is consistent with progressive maintenance of the highest national life.

It is argued that we could not have built our railroads and developed our manufactures without the cheap immigrant labor. No one can prove whether or no we might have pushed forward our industrial development quite so rapidly by the labor of the native-born working for wages that would have secured a more equable distribution of the country's wealth. We did make the difficult beginning of our infant industries while paying wages that were relatively very high, high enough to draw men from the vast and fertile expanses of our free lands.

The immigration which we are now receiving in such vast numbers does little to bring our waste areas under cultivation, but largely settles in the slums of cities and in manufacturing districts that are already among the most congested districts in the whole world.

In resisting selective restrictions of immigration, humanity and greed have formed a veritable alliance, for it must be confessed that our immigration policy has been influenced by a desire, justifiable within limits but not beyond them, to cheapen labor. It has also been influenced by fear of the votes of immigrants already here, and perhaps by the desire for a class of voters easily herded by party leaders.

The New Immigration.—To immigrate no longer requires unusual courage, initiative, and thrift. It is estimated that from 50 to 70 per cent. of the present immigrants have their passage money earned for them in America by friends who preceded them. Immigration to the United States has been actively and effectively promoted by irresponsible agents of steamship companies. "When one of the greatest motives back of immigration is the desire of the transportation companies to make money, the mere fact of immigration is no indication of any real need of the immigrant in this country, nor of his fitness to enter into its life." And it is a fact worth recording that the cost is only one-third as much to export a pauper across the Atlantic as to keep him a year.

Not only has immigration to the United States increased enormously in volume but it has changed in character. The immigrants of to-day probably come, on the average, from lower social standing in their home countries than was once the case. And there has been a radical change in the representation of racial stocks. Prior to 1882 practically the entire immigration to the United States came from Great Britain, Germany, and Scandinavia. This was "the old immigration." "The new immigration" is mostly from Austria-Hungary, Italy, Poland, Russia, the Balkan States, Spain, Turkey, Syria, and the neighboring regions. Till 1870 all but about one per cent. of our immigration came from the old sources. In 1880 those from the new sources were still only about one-tenth of the whole. But in 1902 the "new immigration" outnumbered the old three and a half to one, and in 1907 the "new immigration" outnumbered the old more than four to one. A considerable number of those who come from the newer stocks are "birds of passage" and return after a time to their old homes. The number returning as well as the number coming varies from year to year. The net increase of population from immigration, after deducting departures, during the same period was for the year ending June 30, 1913, 815,303. Of these 15 per cent. came from northern and western Europe, 75 per cent. from southern and eastern Europe and western Asia, and the remaining 10 per cent. from British North America, Mexico, South America, eastern Asia, Australia, and elsewhere.[1]

The fact that people who come to us from eastern and southern countries of the old world are so largely illiterate and unskilled and socially undeveloped may be due to either, or in some degree to both, of two causes: either that they are of inferior native ability and worth, "the beaten men of beaten races"; or that they have never had a fair chance. If it is wholly because they have never had a chance then their children's children may perhaps be expected on the average to be quite the equals of the descendants of the Pilgrims. But if the fact that they have never found or made a chance is due, even in large part, to native inferiority, then they may be expected to work a permanent deterioration in the life and destiny of this nation.

Even if they are equal in native ability to the average of the races which they represent and to our present population, still their present lack of education and general social under-development and strangeness to our customs and institutions makes it impossible to assimilate without change and disturbance in the current of American life so large a number as could be assimilated from a population already more like ourselves in sentiments, customs, standard of living and general advancement.

Immigration Laws.—Congress has recently passed and the

---

[1] *Report of the Commissioner General for Immigration,* Government Printing Office, 1914, pp. 8, 40, 41, 42.

President vetoed a bill to apply a literacy test to immigrants, requiring that those above fourteen years of age be able to read and write some language. The supporters of this measure held that such a test would exclude a considerable part of "the new immigration," but practically none of "the old immigration." This is desired by some on the ground that the southeastern Europeans are so different in race from the original inhabitants of this country that a very great immigration from that source is inadvisable. It is desired by others who hold that the racial differences constitute no ground for desiring to lessen "the new immigration," but who believe that the illiteracy, lack of skill, low standard of living, and even mere vastness of numbers are putting too great a strain upon the assimilating powers of this country. An illiteracy test would not violate the "most favored nation clause" in our treaties, and does not contain an affront to the dignity of any nation. Of the other proposed modifications of our immigration laws, the one that has in its favor the greatest weight of authority proposes that examination for admissibility to this country be made on the other side of the ocean. There more facts can be learned about the prospective immigrant, more time can be spent with each applicant at the several points of examination than at the crowded port of New York, and the waste of hard-earned savings,[1] the bitter disappointments and tragic family separations, that are incident to the deportation of the rejected after arrival at our ports, can be avoided. No one doubts that regulations should be strictly enforced for the exclusion of criminals, paupers, and those suffering from communicable diseases. To object to the literacy test on the ground that it does not exclude criminals and paupers is entirely beside the mark. It aims primarily to protect the standard of living; it would also reduce the volume of immigration to more assimilable dimensions; it would act selectively in favor of those whose customs and

---

[1] Steamships make a cursory examination of third-class passengers before shipment, and they are obliged to return, without charge, to port of embarkation, those refused admittance to our shores.

traditions are more like our own, and those who are in race more akin to the present population of America, and would reduce the substitution of new population elements for those already settled here. It would not impair the effectiveness of laws directly prohibiting the admission of criminals and paupers. It would operate to exclude a disproportionately large number who become paupers.

We should be glad to provide by law exceptional privileges in order to allow the entrance of persons who have suffered from special political or religious oppression.

Whatever regulations may hereafter be adopted, the number of our newly immigrated fellow citizens and their children is, and will continue to be, vast. Both interest and duty require us to treat with hospitality and helpfulness those whom our laws admit. Our opportunity in this to serve mankind is measureless and our response to it is a true test of our quality. The spirit that expresses itself in the epithets "Sheeny," "Dago," "Hunky" and "Mick" is not the one that promises fulfillment of the best possibilities of Americanism. There was reason for the utterance of Dr. Strong when he said: "I do not fear foreigners half so much as I fear Americans who impose on them and brutally abuse them. Such Americans are the worst enemies of our institutions." At present the immigrants come in relatively little contact with the best elements of our civilization. Their second generation is in important respects worse than the new arrivals. They settle for the most part in foreign colonies, in industrial centers, near mines, and in construction camps. If we could stir in these lumps they would be more rapidly dissolved and assimilated. There is need to increase federal activities directed toward disseminating among them information about agricultural and industrial opportunities and toward guiding them away from the congested masses in which they inevitably increase our poverty and our "problems," and to the opportunities for prosperity, usefulness, and social achievement. The public school, including the evening school, is our chief reliance for the Americanization of the immigrants. They are on the whole more eager to learn the true meaning and method of our institutions than we are to teach them. The institutional church with its classes and its helpful social contacts and the social settlement, can render an invaluable service. They call for the enterprising coöperation of Americans of culture and leisure.

CHAPTER XVI

ACQUIRED POPULATION-TRAITS AND PUBLIC HEALTH

Are Acquired Characteristics Inherited?—There are two other developments of biological theory which have important applications to sociology: the doctrine of the non-inheritability of acquired characteristics, which is associated with the name of Weissmann; and the doctrine of mutation, which is associated with the name of DeVries.

The hypothesis that acquired characteristics are not inherited at present prevails among biologists, and appears to be universally adopted by those biologists whose study is specifically in the field of heredity. The man who has lost a limb does not beget one-legged or one-armed children. Mutilations which some races have practiced for many generations leave no mark upon their offspring. If the germ cells of cats or mice lack the determinant that makes the tail grow we shall get tailless kittens or litters of tailless mice; but it is found that if we cut off the tails of twenty successive generations of mice having normal germ cells the twenty-first generation has tails as long as were possessed by their remote ancestors. The developing organism sets aside a part of its substance as germ cells for purposes of reproduction; the remainder, or somatic cells, multiply and differentiate into the developed body. Inheritance is from the germ cells alone. The son of the blacksmith will have a strong arm because his father would not have chosen the blacksmith's trade if he had not belonged to a strong stock, and the son will inherit the strength of the stock but he will inherit none of the strength that his father gained by beating the anvil. A child does not inherit his arms from his father's arms, and his brain from his father's brain, but inherits all from his father's germ cells, and only that which is in the germ cells can be handed on by inheritance. A part of the determiners which the father inherited were used up in the development of his own body; another part of them multiplied as germ cells, to unite with maternal germ plasm and form offspring. The body can be modified by exercise and accident, but the germ cells can hardly be affected. They are nature's citadel, guarded to the utmost against those effects which are produced upon the bodies of those who carry them. It is well that this is so, for if the changes that affect the body of a man during the vicissitudes of life were to reach the germ cells he bears and be handed on to all succeeding generations of his offspring, what abnormalities would the race accumulate! It is true that a few causes of modification may penetrate even the germ cells. If the body of a man or woman is habitually saturated with a poison, as alcohol or lead or the toxins of syphilis, the germ cells may be rendered incapable of developing into normal offspring. The taste for alcohol will not be specifically inherited on that account, though the neurasthenia that craves stimulants may be; and the germs of syphilis will not be inherited, though a variety of hideous abnormalities may result from the poisoning of the germ cells and prenatal infection with syphilis may take place.

The only variations that are hereditary are variations in the germ cells themselves. These variations are ever taking place. Pups of the same litter vary because there were variations between the fertilized ova from which they have developed. Two fertilized ova of the same parentage differ again because each fertilized ovum results from the union of two cells; one bundle of characteristics has been chosen out of double the amount of materials required, and in no two cases, even in the same litter, need the selection be the same. They vary also for other subtle reasons. As the breeder drowns the pups that do not conform to his standard and breeds from the rest, so natural selection eliminates those individuals that do not conform to the requirements for success in the struggle for survival. Thus the development and maintenance of the types which nature demands are secured without the necessity of any inheritance of traits acquired during the lifetime of the parents.

There are many who think that social progress will result from the hereditary accumulation of the effects of education but this is contrary to the doctrine just set forth. The boy whose ancestors for generations have learned Greek has as much trouble with the Greek alphabet as did his great-grand-father. Musical talent is hereditary, but the results of prac-ticing five-finger exercises are not. It is an incalculable advan-tage to grow up in a home of culture, but the parental culture is not transmitted by the germ cells. The negro does not inherit the effects of generations of slavery, but he is born into a social situation that is made worse by the fact that his ancestors were slaves. Generations of education will not cause the negro to be born other than his ancestors in Africa were. Natural selection in a new environment may somewhat modify his type. The fact that the Chinese have been a culture people for ages will not cause them to outrival the nations of western Europe when they adopt the methods of western civilization.

Does the Type of Humanity Advance?[1]—It was once thought that evolution proceeded by the accumulation of infinitesimal variations. But in order for natural selection to operate there must be a difference between the fitter and the less fit, which is not infinitesimal but great enough to be a decided advantage in the struggle for survival. Mr. Burbank does not produce a new variety by the accumulation through ages of infinitesimal variations, but by selecting for propagation the occasional freak of nature. The change, in order to be a contribution to evolution, must be not only a difference in the developed body such as might be caused by better nutri-tion or acquired by the practice of a new mode of life, but it must be a variation in the germ cells. Then it can be per-petuated by heredity. A significant change in the determiners contained in the germ cells, revealing itself in the developed bodies of successive generations, is called a "mutation." Muta-tions are more frequent in the lower organisms and some, if not all, species which persist through geologic ages appear

[1] See p. 243.

to have passed through a mutable period before becoming relatively fixed. But mutations are rare in a mature species. Moreover, variation, when it takes place in a species already highly developed, is far more likely to diminish fitness for survival than to increase it. Finally, each highly developed species has, so to speak, specialized upon certain peculiarities of structure which it may carry to an extreme beyond which they cannot be evolved without becoming a disadvantage instead of an advantage. It has been suggested that in man the sensitiveness and complexity of the nervous system, which is the biological specialty of the genus Homo, has been carried to a point beyond which it cannot go without excessive liability to break down.

According to these conceptions, a mature and highly developed species may remain through a geologic period as fixed as species were supposed to be in the days of Linnæus before the fact of evolution was discovered. The notion that species are continually accumulating infinitesimal improvements has allowed some to dream that the time will come when men will be born saints and angels. But there now appears to be no scientific basis for the idea that the present rich complexity of human endowment will ever be materially exceeded. Neither is there any reason for supposing that the Chinaman of to-day is materially better born than was Confucius, or the Greek of to-day better born than were Aristotle and Pericles, or the Hebrew of to-day better born than were Moses and Abraham, or the Egyptian of to-day better born than were the builders of the pyramids, or the Mesopotamian of to-day better born than were the architects of the hanging gardens of Babylon, or the Germans and Americans of to-day better born than Germanicus and Agricola and Caracticus or the general population of half-naked savages that at the dawn of European history roamed through the northern forests.[1]

---

[1] F. Ratzel: History of Mankind. Macmillan, 1896, i, 18. "We may declare in the most decided manner that the conception of 'natural' races includes nothing physiological but is purely one of civilization. Natural races are nations poor in culture. . . . The old Ger-

The savage who invented the hollow, bow-driven, fire drill may have been as highly endowed as the inventor of wireless telegraphy; only the latter has been preceded by the discoverer of Hertzian waves, and by a thousand other investigators of electricity.

Biological Evolution and Social Evolution.—We differ from our savage ancestors because a social evolution has taken place, an evolution of sciences, religions, moral judgments and sentiments, customs, institutions, practical arts—in one word, of activities, of which they were by birth as capable as we and of which we as individuals are totally incapable. Which of us, if he were born into a group of savages, would ever have a coat such as he is now wearing? Your coat implies a thousand inventions. It is a social product. Social evolution is built upon biological evolution, as a superstructure is built upon a foundation. It is as distinct from biological evolution as that is from the evolution studied by dynamic geology, of the earth's crust upon which both biological and social evolution are built. Social evolution presents a distinct object for investigation as truly as does geologic or biologic evolution.

The Methods of Progress.—The following may be spoken of as the five methods of progress:

1. Biological evolution of man. This may be said to have been exhausted, or at any rate, to offer no ground of expectation on which one is justified in building any hopes.

2. Eugenics. Evolution has produced new types, but eugenics merely seeks more general conformity to a type already established, as the breeder rids his herd of scrubs and grades up to an accepted standard.

3. Euthenics, or the provision of more favorable physical surroundings, such as a better distribution of wealth, better

mans and Gauls appeared no less uncivilized beside Roman civilization than do Kaffirs or Polynesians beside ours. The gap which differences of civilization create between two groups of human beings is in truth quite independent, whether in its depth or in its breadth, of the differences in their mental endowments."

housing, hygienic conditions of life and labor, and the suppression of destructive microbes.

4. Education. The development of the habits, interests, skills, sentiments and knowledge of the individuals so that they possess and embody the fruits of social evolution.

5. Social evolution. Social evolution is to education somewhat as biological evolution is to eugenics. Social evolution brings into existence new varieties of practical arts, of intellectual concepts, of moral judgments, of customs, and of institutions; education causes the products of social evolution to prevail among the population so that individuals conform to the social type which the race has attained. But social evolution is not over. Its movement is at its height and shows no likelihood of abatement.

Preventable Diseases.— Under the heading of acquired physical traits may be placed nearly all the diseases that affect mankind and the results of maiming accidents.

According to the Senate report on National Health prepared in 1910 by Professor Irving Fisher it is estimated that there are constantly in the United States half a million persons suffering from tuberculosis, of whom about half are totally incapacitated and the remainder are able to earn about half what they would otherwise produce and receive. More than a quarter of a million die annually from this cause. This "great white plague is, of all diseases common to man, the most widespread and the most deadly." It does not alarm us by an occasional epidemic, but is a constant epidemic to which we are accustomed. Its ravages are greatest among those who are in the prime of life and in the midst of its responsibilities and opportunities. Though no age is exempt, the death rate from tuberculosis is highest between the ages of twenty and thirty, next between the ages of thirty and forty, and next between the ages of forty and fifty. One-fourth of all the deaths of men in the United States between the ages of eighteen and thirty-five are due to this malady.[1]

---

[1] The latest available figures for Illinois, which is fairly typical, show that of the deaths between the ages of twenty and fifty during two years, 26.92 per cent. were due to tuberculosis of the lungs.

Tuberculosis is a preventable disease and in its earlier stages a curable one. Its prevalence is decreasing and it is believed by experts on the subject that through intelligent social co-operation it will ultimately become as rare as smallpox. It is declared by some students of the subject that nine-tenths of the tuberculosis is caught by living in homes that have been infected by the sputum and cough-spray of an infected member of the family, or of some family that has occupied the house. Proper disinfection of infected tenements before a new family moves in is unusual. A single infected home or tenement is sometimes the cause of half a score of deaths.[1] The person with chronic tuberculosis or slow consumption who walks at large, unless intelligent and right-minded enough to take proper precaution against communicating the disease is the other great source of danger.[2]

Pneumonia causes about the same number of deaths in this country as does tuberculosis, but not so many weeks, months, and years of illness. The germs of pneumonia prey upon those in whom the resistant power of the mucous membrane lining the air-passages has been reduced by exposure, by the debility resulting from overwork, and unsanitary conditions of life, by a drunk, or by the habitual use of small quantities of alcohol.

There are annually about forty thousand cases of typhoid fever in the United States, each entailing on the average seventy-five days of incapacity, of which one-eighth are fatal. There should be practically none. The germs of this disease are carried chiefly by water, milk and house-flies.[3] In Munich

---

[1] Fumigation is not enough; scrubbing with a weak solution of carbolic acid does the work.

[2] One tuberculous man has buried three wives and now has the fourth; and one tuberculous woman has buried three husbands and nineteen children with the disease.

[3] In Cleveland, Ohio, picked schoolboys were organized as a sanitary police and instructed to find all the breeding-places for flies and notify owners, and, if necessary, authorities. During March and April ten cents a hundred was offered for the flies found in attic windows and other out-of-the-way corners, the seed-bearers for the next summer's swarms. The result was that after two years thousands of

where the death rate from typhoid had been 291 per 100,000 of population, that rate was reduced 97 per cent. by replacing wretched lack of system by a good system of water-supply, and sewerage. Installation of a water filter in Lawrence, Massachusetts, reduced the deaths from this cause in a year from 105 to 22. Dug wells in cities or towns are usually dangerous.

Milk, unless it is sedulously guarded from contamination, unless instead of being allowed to stand on doorsteps after being bottled, it is kept at a temperature too low for bacterial reproduction, swarms with microbes. Impure milk is the worst cause of intestinal disorders among children. Only well-planned social coöperation can prevent a holocaust of babies in the cities every summer. The frightful mortality of children under five years of age has been reduced in recent years but it is still needlessly high. Of those who died in the registration area of the United States in the year 1910, 26.98 per cent. were under five years of age. Infant mortality can scarcely be regarded as the selection of the fittest, for the causes of infant mortality here discussed carry off the strongest of children, and permanently impair the vitality of many that survive. Even if the limitation of population were desirable, child mortality would be a shockingly wasteful means of procuring that result, wasteful of time, money, suffering, and sorrow.

Smallpox has been practically vanquished wherever vaccination is general. A different vaccine prevents typhoid.

Malaria, once a frightful scourge, virtually disappears before intelligent preventive measures, but is allowed to continue its ravages, especially in certain sections of the South. Besides the suffering it directly causes, malaria shortens life by predisposing to other causes of death, and it reduces working capacity by a large percentage. The number of persons suffering from it annually in the United States is believed to reach three millions. This is practically all preventable.

---

households have dispensed entirely with screens at doors and windows, and "a recent inspection of the city markets, where quantities of meat and provisions are exposed, found only two flies." *The Survey,* Aug. 23, 1913.

Yellow fever, though it long made the Panama Canal an impracticable project and still causes many deaths in our southern states, is almost entirely preventable, as proved by the results of rigorous government measures in Panama and Havana. In the latter city during the eight years, including 1891 to 1898, 4,420 persons died of yellow fever. In 1898 the United States intervened, and in the succeeding eight years there were but 465 deaths from yellow fever, and nearly all of these occurred during the first two years of occupation by the federal authorities. During the fifth, sixth, and seventh years of federal control the death rate from yellow fever was reported as zero.

Hookworm is another disease for the prevention and cure of which medical and sanitary science has armed us, so that its elimination has now become a problem of social action. The great prevalence of this ailment in the whole southern part of our country, the large mortality which it causes, and especially the incapacity for work and normal living which it entails, make it an important modifier of the quality of our population.

Over certain diseases we have as yet no adequate control. Such, for example, are diabetes, Bright's disease, cancer and certain diseases of the heart. But over such diseases as tuberculosis, typhoid fever, smallpox, malaria, yellow fever, and hookworm, we have acquired the means of control. The discovery of methods of preventing disease is wholly a matter for other sciences than sociology. But the practical application of these methods on a significant scale, after they have been discovered, is not a matter for the medical profession alone, but depends upon organized social coöperation, by the agency of government, school, press, and specially created organs.

Losses Due to Preventable Disease.—It is estimated that those who die needless, that is to say, preventable, deaths in one year in the United States, if they had fulfilled the ordinary expectation of life remaining to them, would have produced and earned $1,000,000,000. There are always 3,000,-000 persons on the sick list. If only one-fourth of them are workers of all grades, and if their average earnings are only $700, the annual loss of their earnings amounts to more than $500,000,000. The extra expenses entailed by sickness amount to $500,000,000 more. Assuming that at least half of this illness is preventable we must add an annual preventable loss by sickness of $500,000,000 to the annual preventable loss of one billion which is caused by needless death, and have "one and a half billions as the very lowest at which we can estimate the annual preventable loss from disease and death in this country. The true figures may well amount to several times this amount." [1] Possibly the loss to the country is diminished by the fact that part of the work that these dead and sick would have done is after all done by others. But there can be no doubt about the loss to the particular families in which the needless illness occurs.

Social coöperation for the conservation of health costs something. But experience in combating infant mortality, yellow fever, hookworm, and other enemies of life and health, has indicated that the return on the money so invested is often several thousand per cent. per annum. An actuary suggests that if insurance companies should combine to contribute for the purpose of improving the public health one-eighth of one per cent. of the premiums which they receive, it would be reasonable to expect a decrease in death claims of much more than one per cent. Even this one per cent. would make a profit of more than seven times the expense.

In the foregoing no account has been made of the $100,-000,000 or over that the public annually expends in the care of the insane, feeble-minded and other defectives as defectives, nor of the vast sums which are paid for their care as paupers and as criminals.

It would be absurd to stop with estimating the money cost of sickness and death. Neither is the account completed when we remember the suffering and sorrow which they directly cause. The loss or disabling of breadwinners through preventable sickness and death is one of the chief causes of the breakdown of families, of the pathetic struggle of widows,

---

[1] Irving Fisher: National Vitality. Senate Document No. 676.

of the street trades of children, of pauperization, of the failure properly to rear the boys and girls of such families, and of consequent ignorance, shiftlessness, poverty, vagrancy and crime. A large proportion of the wretchedness and perversion faced by the charity worker and the juvenile court is traceable to this cause, as well as of the riper ruin assembled in the almshouse and the penitentiary.

Occupation and Disease.—Mention has already been made of the half-million who are annually killed or maimed in the United States by industrial accidents, of which a large part are preventable. And in discussing the relation between poverty and health some comment was made upon the increased liability to disease among those who work in unsanitary surroundings. Probably the most serious occupational foes to health are vitiated air and excessive fatigue.

The dust from stone-cutting, metal-grinding and the like, and the lint of textile mills, unless precautions are observed, so fill the lungs as to destroy the health of many of the workers. High temperatures, involving sudden changes of temperature in leaving the works on winter nights, and the excessive dryness or excessive moisture accompanying certain processes of manufacture undermine the power to resist the attacks of omnipresent microbes. Poisonous gases and chemical fumes in dye houses, paint factories and other work places have injurious and in thousands of cases fatal results. We may not quarrel with the inevitable, but most of the loss of health and life thus occasioned is not inevitable but is preventable by the use of suction tubes to carry dust from the point where it rises, hoods with forced drafts and other devices.

Fatigue so great that the sleep of night does not remove it and which accumulates from day to day and month to month diminishes economic efficiency, as well as resistance to disease and to moral temptation. It increases liability to accident. Industrial accidents occur largely during the last hours of the day's work, when watchfulness and agility are diminished. Employers have found that, in some industries at least, an eight-hour day is as productive as a longer day, partly because of the increased swiftness and vigor with which the work goes on and partly because of the lessened losses of the last hours of the day through spoiled materials, broken tools and machinery, and injured laborers.

Seven-day labor, twelve-hour shifts, or ten hours with excessive speeding up of machinery which requires the constant repetition of swift movements by the operators, and piece-work at wages so low that only immoderate striving after speed will yield a livelihood, impair population quality. The Senate report by Professor Fisher which contained the estimate that one and a half billions annually is the minimum cost of preventable illness and death, contains also (p. 669) the statement that the economic waste from undue fatigue is probably much greater than the waste from serious illness. The number that suffer partial disability through undue fatigue certainly constitutes the great majority of the population. Yet if only 50 per cent. of the population are suffering an impairment equal to only 10 per cent. of its working powers, the result is equivalent to 5 per cent. of the population suffering total impairment.

Stunted Youth.—Mothers who work all day in factories almost up to the hour of birth of their children rob the coming generation. Excessive speed and long hours make the evil worse. Laws limiting the hours of labor for men are generally regarded as unconstitutional on the ground that a man's freedom must not be abridged and he must be allowed to work as many hours as he chooses. The excessive hours of labor on the part of men in factories are not in reality matters of freedom and choice, but of economic compulsion from which they might properly be defended by law. But thus far the eight-hour day for men, in so far as it prevails, has not been obtained by law but by the unions. Recently, however, the constitutionality of limiting the hours of labor for women has been upheld on the ground of the necessity of defending the population quality. Limitation of the hours of juvenile laborers is not open to the constitutional objection of abridging freedom, since children are not legally held to have attained freedom.

The neglect of children after their birth by mothers who are obliged to work for wages occasions even more serious injury than does the labor of expectant mothers, and the injury is moral as well as physical. Schools, kindergartens, and day nurseries palliate this evil, but the care of children by their mothers is the norm toward which society should work. There is no substitute for it which serves the purpose with regard either to the welfare of the child or to that of the mother.

There ought to be abundant and free opportunity for unmarried women to secure adequate profitable employment. Yet some query must arise in the mind at this point with reference to the present enthusiasm for extending the industrial sphere of women, or rather for substituting newer occupations for her traditional office.

Child labor is not yet adequately prevented. Where laws on the subject are best their enforcement is not complete. And those states where the child-employing industries are most prominent are the very ones where it is most difficult to pass such laws, as well as to enforce such laws.

Unsanitary conditions that affect the health of adults may affect still more unfavorably the health of children. Injury to those who have not attained their growth may prevent them from ever attaining what would have been their normal development. And as the corn-stock that grows by the roadside may mature no seed, so also, notwithstanding nature's vigilant guard of her citadel, the germ cells, generations of stunted youth may permanently impair the racial quality.

School Hygiene.[1]—The United States has remained behind the procession of advanced nations in the matter of school hygiene. We compel the children to attend school for years and often we require them to do so under conditions which expose them excessively to contagious diseases and to still greater injury through imperfect heating, lighting, ventilation, and sanitation. We ought, while we have practically the whole rising generation in hand, to help to lay the foundation for health and to remove the handicaps which as years pass will

---

[1] Irving Fisher: National Vitality, p. 694.

otherwise undermine their welfare and efficiency. Dr. Cronin has maintained that of the 650,000 schoolchildren of New York 30 per cent. were from one to two years behind their proper class, and that 95 per cent. of those retarded were so principally because of defects of eye, ear, throat, or nose, including adenoids and enlarged tonsils which could easily be detected and remedied. Dr. Osler calculated that in New York City an annual financial loss of $1,666,666 results from lack of medical supervision of schools on account of the lengthened time which retarded children require in passing a given number of grades and that "the loss which came from moral deviation due to defective physical functioning was of far greater importance." Besides the defects just named, imperfection of the teeth of schoolchildren, preventing proper mastication and laying the foundation for indigestion, malnutrition, and stunted development are so important that in the opinion of high authority their treatment through inspection of schools presents a national problem of the very first importance. A "committee on the physical welfare of schoolchildren reported that in New York City 66 per cent. of the schoolchildren needed medical or surgical attention or better nourishment." [1]

Truancy, incorrigibility, retardation, and final physical or moral breakdown result from the physical handicaps which might be removed during childhood. No school should be without efficient or specially instructed medical inspection.

Indoor occupation, with eyes focused upon small, near objects, such as print, with mental strain and the stimulus of rank and demerits, make a most unnatural life for the child. There is good evidence that our younger schoolchildren could accomplish quite as much if the hours of school confinement were materially shortened. Parents who want their children taken care of oppose this shortening of hours. It

---

[1] In 1914 Dr. Wade Macmillan, of Cincinnati, initiated a movement to induce members of mothers' clubs, connected with the public schools, to bring to free clinics their children below school age, in order to detect defects when cure is easiest and the preventive effect most complete.

would be far better to care for the children a portion of the time on supervised playgrounds. Social welfare will ultimately demand that there be space on a playground for every boy and girl.

Socialization of Medical Science.—The physical examination of employees in large establishments is being promoted mainly as a form of "welfare work." The laboring man is not likely to incur the expense of consulting a physician until he is sure of serious illness. In the case of some diseases, particularly tuberculosis, the special foe of the laboring man, he often does not suspect the presence of serious disease until the proper time for curative treatment has passed. Consequently he does not seek examination in time; the examiner must seek him at intervals.

Half the states of the Union now require children to pass a physical examination before receiving the certificate permitting them under the child labor law to seek employment. There is wide difference in the efficiency with which such laws are carried out, but they are designed to discover in time defects which should preclude certain dangerous occupations.

These industrial examinations, the necessity for the medical examination of schoolchildren, and especially the preventability of the various forms of disease and death above discussed, obviously suggest the extension of our idea of the work of municipal, state, and national boards of health. The inadequacy of public health activities is in many instances farcical. A community that supports fifty to one hundred physicians engaged in treating those who are already ailing has usually not one whose main business is prevention of disease. This is absurd. A local health officer, among other functions, should aim to secure truthful statistics of the causes of all deaths,[1] to identify when possible the particular sources of contagion whenever contagious diseases appear, and suppress them instead of allowing them to multiply victims, to guard against the familiar and recurrent sources of contagion, and to provide industrial and school inspection and examination

---

[1] One of our crying needs is for adequate and reliable statistics.

of applicants for marriage licenses. Medical science will not always be regarded chiefly as the means by which a learned profession obtains a livelihood and by which those already very ill seek for relief, but rather as the means by which society seeks to prevent unnecessary illness and deaths.

Drugging.—Alcohol has the power to produce a temporary feeling of exhilaration, followed by reaction. The exhilaration [1] may go to the extent of insanity, the reaction is felt in drowsiness culminating in stupor, or if the doses are large and frequent, in depression culminating in delirium. The reaction is wont to be accompanied by craving for restimulation, and habitual use of alcohol produces a disease characterized by persistent and often insatiable and uncontrollable craving for the drug.

Arctic explorers find that although alcohol produces a temporary glow of the skin, it is followed by diminution of vital heat and impaired ability to resist prolonged cold. Athletes and superintendents of gangs of laborers find that it lessens power to endure protracted exertion. Railroad companies and other large employers of labor have begun to insist upon sobriety as a condition of retaining workmen, as a means of increasing regularity and capacity in work, as well as of preventing accidents to passengers, machinery, materials, and to the employees themselves, for whose safety modern legislation makes the employer to some degree responsible. The habitual use of alcohol even in small quantities reduces the power to resist diseases, so that the most robust-appearing drinkers die when abstainers would recover. Insurance companies by an extended experience find that even among "good risks" the average expectation of life for the insured who

---

[1] Experiments seem to show that even during the period which precedes exhaustion or so-called "reaction" the feeling of exhilaration produced by alcohol is accompanied by actual diminution of muscular and mental efficiency. Apparently the visceral disturbance is felt as exhilaration, but the muscular and nervous disturbance is in fact an impairment of powers. There is, however, a secondary effect on the powers, in that to think oneself able tends to increase ability.

habitually drink alcohol even in small quantities is less by 25 per cent. or more than for total abstainers.[1]

The use of alcohol is one of the constant and unmistakable causes of both pauperism and crime. It is difficult to separate the part played by drink from that of other causes of these evils, for drink allies itself with all other causes of pauperism and of crime, but that it is one of the great factors in their causation no competent person doubts. Alcoholism is one of the prominent causes of insanity. It is also one of the chief recognizable causes of hereditary defect; not that the desire for liquor is specifically inheritable, but that the germ cells poisoned by extreme use of alcohol fail in various ways to produce normal offspring.

The absence of normal vigor and cheer increase the craving for artificial stimulation. This lack may be due to constitutional weakness or to the exhaustion caused by excessive toil or to insufficient and improper food or to lack of cheerful surroundings and normal joys. Thus poverty increases drunkenness, as it does most other evils. The strong, well-surrounded and well-employed have no excuse for drugging.

The reduction of alcoholism, like the other forms of population deterioration which have been discussed, is mainly a social problem. Fashion [2] is largely responsible for the use of

---

[1] This does not mean that one-fourth of the deaths among adult drinkers are caused by alcohol, but that alcohol combines with other causes to produce death which neither the alcohol nor the other cause would by itself have produced; it also means that drinkers are more likely than abstainers to lead irregular lives in other respects.

[2] Charles Booth, an author not inclined to exaggeration, writes (Pauperism, p. 141): "Drink must be accounted the most prolific of all the causes (of pauperism), and it is the least necessary. It is hardly too much to say that it is principally a matter of fashion. Among the upper classes the fashion of drinking has passed or is passing away [England]. Among the middle classes it is accepted rather as a social necessity than as a desirable personal indulgence. Men meet and adjourn for a drink to which one must treat the other, but which both would as soon, or perhaps rather, be without. The whole thing is so baseless that it is conceivable it might very rapidly come to an end." This is also the theme of Jack London's novel "John Barleycorn."

alcoholic drinks. Where strong drink is regarded as the natural accompaniment of a good time, where "What'll you
have?" is the hail of the "good fellow," where the traditions
of hospitality demand the offering of alcoholic drinks, and
"society" sanctions and almost requires their use, there lives
will be shortened, careers will be blasted, and children will be
born to defect and depravity on this account. And if the
more privileged classes thus support its use, they make it
harder for the less fortunate classes that suffer most from
its ravages, to break the tradition; whereas they might lend
powerful aid by their example. The older nations, where the
most susceptible have to some extent been eliminated by ages
of exposure to the evil, where national liquors are mild, where
the climate itself is not an exhausting stimulant, are nevertheless beginning to exert the powers of government and high
scientific and social influence to combat the ravages of alcoholism. Our younger nation which has suffered incalculably
from this cause and does so still, is fortunate in that there
is marked progress toward the removal of social sanction
from this insidious indulgence.

The most effective means for curing the diseases of alcoholism is the government hospital where the patient can be
compelled to remain long enough to allow hygienic and moral
treatment to be adequately applied.

Besides alcohol various other drugs, especially opium and
its derivatives, are used to the injury of population quality.
This calls for laws providing for careful supervision of the
sale of poisons, and strong social disapproval of these vices
and of those who promote them commercially. The sale of
patent medicines that depend for their stimulating and cheer-
ing effect upon the harmful drugs which they contain is one
of the means of spreading drug habits. Probably some good
medicines have been patented, but on the whole patent medicines deserve their name of the "Great American Humbug,"
and the harm they do to our population quality is not limited
to the spread of drug habits. The advertising of harmful
medicines, of deceitful quacks, and the publication of adver-
tisements calculated to promote sexual vice are heavy sins

chargeable to the press, not however without honorable exceptions.

Venereal Disease.—It is estimated by Dr. Price A. Morrow that there are two million syphilitics in the United States. Gonorrhea is far more prevalent still.

1. Syphilis, while mostly caused by cohabitation with an infected person, may also be communicated by a kiss, or by the medium of a towel, drinking glass, or other object that has been in contact with the saliva or other secretions. Many cases treated early show no serious immediate consequences, but retain the power to transmit the disease to others even after years have passed. Other cases are fatal in spite of treatment. In other cases still apoplexy, paralysis, softening of the brain, or locomotor ataxia result, perhaps not until after the man has acquired a family dependent on him for support. Softening of the brain from syphilis or paresis is a common cause of insanity. The poison of syphilis is one of the few that attack even the germ cells. Children of a syphilitic may die before birth or be born to a brief and wretched existence or grow to maturity only to succumb to insanity or some other form of degeneracy.

2. Gonorrhea is a disease from which few who accept any illicit sexual intercourse escape. It is often spoken of as "no worse than a bad cold," yet it is stated that it kills one in two hundred of those whom it attacks. It often produces urethral strictures that later may cause loss of life. It persists in the deeper parts long after being apparently cured and retains the power to communicate itself from a husband to an innocent wife. It causes also the so-called one-child sterility which is due to the fact that during the process of childbearing it finds access to deeper parts and prevents subsequent parenthood. Physicians give statistical evidence that 80 per cent. of deaths from the so-called diseases of women and about 90 per cent. of all the work done by specialists for diseases of women are due to gonorrhea. In the words of Professor Davenport:[1] "Marriage of persons with venereal diseases is not only unfit; it is a hideous and das-

---

[1] Davenport: Eugenics, p. 4.

tardly crime," and its frequency would justify a medical test of all males before marriage, innocent as well as guilty.

The venereal diseases and alcoholism, but probably the former even more than the latter, are largely responsible for the insanity (of which it has been estimated that there are a quarter of a million cases in the United States), the feeble-mindedness, and various other forms of congenital, as well as acquired, abnormity. Since they attack the germ cells, from which all organs develop, they may produce a variety of different forms of blight. Dr. Price A. Morrow, quoted by Professor Irving Fisher, estimates that the elimination of venereal diseases would probably mean the elimination of at least one-half of our institutions for defectives. If this estimate were cut down one-half it would still be appalling. "In the opinion of very competent judges, social diseases constitute the most powerful of all factors in the degeneration and depopulation of the world." They merit their title of the "great black plague."

It is hardly necessary to add that the venereal diseases are entirely preventable and that their prevention is a social problem.

The spread of venereal disease is largely due to prostitution. Prostitution is a business.[1] It is as old as history, but the former notion that it is necessary to man no longer has the sanction of medical science and is an insult to the continent portion of male humanity. As in other business the offer of a supply increases demand, and the demand for the service of prostitutes is promoted by various suggestive devices. At the same time the recruiting of female victims is prosecuted with diabolical ingenuity. The traffic is in close alliance with numerous saloons, dance-halls, immoral shows and real-estate interests, and is one of the most constant corruptors of the honesty and fidelity of the police.

---

[1] C. H. Parkhurst: Our fight with Tammany. Scribners, 1895.

Chicago Vice Commission Report, 1911.

G. J. Kneeland: Commercialized Vice in New York City, New York, 1913.

Abraham Flexner: Prostitution in Europe. Century Co., 1914.

The medical examination and licensing of prostitutes as a prevention of the spread of venereal disease is a farce. Sufficiently thorough examination is scarcely feasible, and even if a prostitute is actually free from disease at the time of her examination she is likely to become infected within a few hours afterward.

Laws directed against the promoters of the traffic, the posting of the owner's name in every place regularly used for immoral purposes, and a special body of police under the joint supervision of the city government and of an unpaid commission of citizens appointed by the mayor are among the remedial measures proposed.

Second Nature.—There is no such thing as an acquired instinct or an inborn habit. Yet habit when once acquired closely resembles instinct in being organic.

Habits and instincts alike are definite tendencies to action ingrained in the organism. The plastic motor mechanism by acting acquires the tendency to repeat similar action; such an acquired tendency is habit. The most important single fact about the physiological mechanism of man's conscious life is that it is highly modifiable, especially during a long period of immaturity. Even the instinctive tendencies in man are not fixed and immutable, but heredity leaves them more or less vague and half established, to be rendered definite and fixed by the addition of habitual elements, or to be modified or inhibited by postnatal activity.

Habit is most often thought of as a foe that binds man with cords which by the repetition of objectionable actions during thoughtless youth grow thread by thread to unbreakable cables which fetter the will. Habit is, however, still more a friend that, by the repetition of acts dictated by necessity or by reason or by the experience of our predecessors, builds for us facile tendencies and ready powers to do that which life requires of us. The relation of instinct and hereditary talent to habit is illustrated by manual dexterity. We may inherit an "instinct of workmanship," the delight in seeing something grow under our hands, but we must acquire as habits the skill of the craftsman or the flying fingers of the piece-worker. We may inherit musical talent, but we must acquire as habits by the laborious practice of exercises the technique to perform a concerto.

The word habit is usually restricted to neuromuscular co-ordinations, predisposing to particular overt activities. It is not, however, overt activities alone which are subject to the law that action prepares for similar action, but thoughts and sentiments as well. The impressions made by the external world upon the mind are like the spray from a hose which, falling on a bare, grassless yard, cuts tiny water courses here and there. Inborn traits are like the irregularities of surface, pebbles and lumps of earth that predetermine in part what the courses of the tiny rills shall be; environmental influence is like the water falling from the moving nozzle of the hose, now here, now there. Those tendencies of thought and sentiment which together with habits we include under the designation, second nature, are like the courses worn by the water after an hour of sprinkling which give to the tiny rills a definite pattern, not so fixed as to be beyond modification, yet within certain limits fixed. So every thought and emotion opens for itself a runway in the brain or deepens a preëxisting channel, and besides our more or less vague and half-formed inborn tendencies we have our developed tastes, propensities, esthetic likes and dislikes and, if well reared, our moral enthusiasms and detestations, our opinions fortified by corroborations readily brought to mind, as well as ranges of thought where the mind, if it entered at all, would have to push its way along an unbroken path. The character of a mature man, regarded as a bundle of traits ingrained in his physical organism, is only partly nature, it is also largely "second nature."

Thus it is that education and rearing as well as hygiene modify the physiological quality of a population.

Subconscious Set.—By the "set of the organism" I refer to the fact that the organic tendencies of a person do not seem to be the same at all times, but one may be one man on one day and quite a different man on another day. To-day one set of tendencies is active and another dormant; later this adjustment is reversed. On one day a man is courageous and hopeful and the struggle for his ideals seems eminently worth while; on another day he may be discouraged and misanthropic. The differences between black and white may be no longer vivid to him, and he may be either negative and indifferent, or propelled by quite another set of reactions. By moving a lever the tune played by a hand-organ is changed from "Molly Darling" to "Johnny Comes Marching Home" or "Where Is My Wandering Boy?" Man is an organism vastly more complex, and with a wider range of possibilities than the hand-organ, and may be set to play anything from "The Messiah" to "The Devil's Hornpipe." To change the figure, there are as many stories to his nature as to a skyscraper. He may sink to the subbasement without effort, but he requires an elevator if he wishes to live on the higher levels. That is to say, the tendencies that he shares with his prehistoric ancestors are sure to assert themselves, while upon the higher and later achievements of civilization he has at first a more precarious hold.

By speaking of the "subconscious" set I mean that the organic adjustment often persists after the experience that caused it has passed from conscious memory. A youth setting out for the city in the morning has a few moments' conversation on the station platform with the leading citizen of his suburb, and all day while busy with his occupations he is a different person because of that interview, with added self-respect and a new bent to his attention and impulses. On another day he may have ridden on the train with a cynic and a rake, listening to talk that gave him for the day a widely different bent. Or on the evening before he may have read a noble book, or in the morning he may have given a few moments to the thoughts that he could share with his Maker. And in either case for a time after the experience that determined the set of his being has retired below the threshold of conscious memory the effect persists, although conscious attention is wholly occupied with the succession of affairs. It persists for a time, but it is by no means permanent. It must be frequently renewed. To keep men adjusted to life on a truly human level is an essential ministration of association with developed personalities, or with the nobler expressions of human life in tradition, literature, art, and religion. The subject is here referred to because the fact noted is a psychophysical adjustment.

We Pass to the Inner Essence of Society.—We have now
discussed three of the four sets of conditions that determine
what the life of a society shall be. They were: (1) the geographic, or natural physical environment; (2) the technic or
artificial physical environment; (3) the psychophysical traits
of the people themselves, hereditary or acquired, their temperaments and habits, the capacities and tendencies ingrained
in the biological organism, that are the bearers of the social
life; and now we have come to the fourth. The geographic
conditions are altogether external to the social life as soil
and sunshine are external to the life of plants. The technic
conditions, though produced by social life, are still external
to it as trellises, fertilizers, and plowed fields are external to
the plants which the farmer raises. The psychophysical conditions are not external to man as an animal organism, but
they are external to the conscious life of man. Indeed the
arm is as external to the conscious act of driving a nail as is
the hammer; and we never become conscious of the neural
processes by which we think. When we write a man's biography we do not describe the processes of his digestion, and
respiration; peristalsis and osmosis and neural katabolism are
not mentioned. And when I say "my life," I am oblivious
to all these and mean instead a stream of conscious activities
and experiences—activities which are experiences and experiences which are activities. But these experience-activities of mine are not only my life, but also a part of the

life of society. They are in part caused by the activities of many associates and in turn they affect the activities of those who are about me. Thus my experience-activities are knit together with those of other members of the society to which I belong to form one web. When we study the way in which the conscious activities of associates condition each other we are not studying the effect upon society of conditions external to it as soil, climate, and agriculture are external to plants, but we are studying the life of society itself, the interrelation of its parts, as the student of plant physiology studies the interrelation of chemical and physical processes that make up the life of the plant.[1]

Association—the Inclusive Social Relation.—Reason is sometimes defined as the power to discern relationships. Explanation may be said to consist in showing how facts are related; and to show how the life of society is determined from within we must show how the activities that play a part in society are related to each other. Association has usually been spoken of by sociologists as a kind of activity, but this is an error. Association is not a kind of activity; but all the kinds of our activity may go on in the relation which is association. Still there cannot be association without activity for association is a relation between activities. All of the causally significant relations between the activities of associates are forms of association, so that association is the all-inclusive social relationship. Notice that we do not say relations between associates, but between the activities of associates; not I am a condition of you and you are a condition of me, but my activity is a condition of your activity and your activity is a condition of my activity, is the accurate description of the fact of association.

The tide of interrelated activities which we have called "the life of society" is made up of the lives of individuals somewhat as rills make rivers, only these rills are not lost in this river, but keep their identity as they flow on within the larger whole. The psychologist calls the life of an individual "a stream of consciousness," and it is made up of

---

[1] Let no one attempt to carry out this figure in detail.

the interrelated ideas, sentiments and practices that constitute the continuous system of the individual's experience. The sociologist calls the life of society "the social process." The social process is composed of all the activities that go on in association. It is a process in two senses: first, because it is alive, it is composed of activities—causally interwoven activities; second, it is always becoming something more and other than it was, always evolving, as a result of the causal interrelation of its parts. It includes ideas, sentiments, and practices which are not peculiar to any one individual but prevalent among many. Individual streams of consciousness flow on side by side within the social process, and between these individual streams of consciousness there is a continual osmosis. Indeed the content of the stream of consciousness of any one of us has been mainly derived from the infiltration of ideas and sentiments from the society in which, from our empty infancy, we have been continually immersed. But as in osmosis there is passage in both directions through the separating membrane, so in association, as soon as we acquire a definite individuality and content for our own stream of consciousness, we give out as well as receive.

Whenever two human beings come into communication this osmosis of ideas and sentiments is set up. By it one associate derives something of conscious experience and activity from the other. Tarde calls it imitation, thereby giving to that word a scientific technical meaning, broader and deeper than it has in common speech. And he says that imitation is the universal and essential social fact, that wherever there is society there is imitation and wherever there is imitation there is society. There seems to be good reason for declining to adopt Tarde's name for the universal social relation in that we need the word imitation to carry a more restricted meaning, and it does not naturally convey this wider signification.

As in physical osmosis there is passage of a liquid or gas in each direction through the separating membrane but usually with a more rapid passage of one substance in one direction than of the other substance in the other direction, so also in association, while each associate is usually to some degree both a contributor and a recipient, yet in any given social contact one is the chief giver and the other the chief recipient. This latter fact leads Simmel to call association *"Ueber und unterordnung,"* or superiority and subordination. He says whenever two men walk down the street together or sit together at the club or wherever two human beings are in communication, the one is dispenser and the other recipient of ideas and influences. The superiority may alternate from one to the other, as the communication changes from a subject in which one associate reveals in his speech or conduct the greater clearness of ideas or positiveness of intention or depth of feeling to a subject in respect to which the other associate has the preëminence. For these reasons Simmel says that the universal social fact is superiority and subordination, that wherever there is society such "superiority and subordination" exist. Though there is truth in this, it is far from being the whole truth and probably Simmel would not have selected this designation for the inclusive social relation if he had lived in a more democratic country where superiority and subordination is a less conspicuous reality than it is in Germany. There it seems to be more or less vividly present to consciousness in nearly all social contacts, while here it seems to be practically absent from consciousness in much if not in most social intercourse, and an interesting phase or incident of social relation rather than the essence of it. Accordingly we adopt the name association as the designation for the universal social relation, the relation of which we can say that it is always present wherever there is society; or we may describe that relation figuratively by the phrase social osmosis.

Association Depends on Communication and Is Always a Causal Relation.—Association or social osmosis exists only when one is aware of the activity of his associate; therefore if not absolutely identical with communication association at least implies communication, not necessarily, however, intentional or even conscious communication, but only the fact that knowledge of another's activity is received, as it may be received by an eavesdropper, or by an observer using a spy-glass. Two men who are aware of each other's activities are in communication and association whether they are conversing or sawing wood. Whether there be any intention to communicate or not, the fact that the activities of associates are known to each other establishes the relation of association. The clearest difference between the common use of the words "association" and "communication" is that we prefer to use the word "communication" when an associate intentionally imparts a knowledge of his activities to another, usually by speaking or writing, but we use the word "association" with complete indifference to whether the relation is intentional or not. Yet even the word "communicate" we do not always confine to intentional communication; for example, we say that a crowd owes its peculiar character largely to the readiness with which its members communicate their emotions, though they may have no intention so to communicate. Two deaf and dumb men sawing wood together are in communication, and likely to work far more happily and efficiently than if alone. Not only will their communication satisfy the instinct of sociability, they will get suggestions from each other, will encourage and stimulate each other, or depress each other, will desire to command each other's respect as sawyers, and are likely to engage in half or wholly conscious emulation. Either of the two words "association" and "communication" implies the probability of mutuality or reciprocity in the relation. Possibly the word "association" carries that suggestion more distinctly and somewhat more suggests the fact of far-reaching consequences.

Everyone who gives a place in his attention to the activity of another is practically sure to be in some way influenced by that fact. The highest is affected by the humblest and the wisest by the stupidest, if it be only to despise his humble colleague and to exalt his own pride, to avoid resemblances and to exaggerate the differences between the two. This tendency of human beings to be influenced by each other is a universal, social fact; it is for sociology what affinity is to chemistry. Like gravity, it can be resisted and the effects of one social influence may be offset by another external tug or internal propulsion, but it is always there, one of the moments entering into the resultant.

Social Suggestion.—This universal social relation which we have termed association, or social osmosis, appears in various forms, which may be distinguished according to the nature of the particular activities that issue from the causal contact. The elements that enter into the life of society and of the individuals who compose society are of three kinds, namely, ideas, sentiments, and overt practices; therefore, the causal relationships that exist between the activities of associates may be of at least three main sorts: (1) those relations in which the *idea* of one associate becomes known to another, which we call social suggestion; (2) that in which the *sentiment* of one associate is felt by another, which we shall call sympathetic radiation; and (3) that in which the *overt practice* of one associate is practiced by another, which we shall call imitation.

When B has an idea because A first had it the causal relation between the conditioning activity and the resultant activity we call suggestion.[1]

It is not at all necessary that A should tell B his idea. Instead B may infer it from the practices of A. Thus the apprentice gets his idea of trade processes mainly by watching the skilled workman. Thus children learn the ideas of their parents and youths learn the ideas of business men and politicians. Sometimes we say we "wonder what he means," referring not to his words but to his conduct; and in general we infer the ideas of our associates from their overt practices, as well as receive them directly in what they say. Whether the idea of A is told to B, or is inferred by B, it is a case of suggestion.

Two important statements may be added about suggestion. First: there is nothing logical about suggestion; that is to say, we get the ideas that our associates have, or seem to have, without regard to whether they are true ideas or false ones.

---

[1] We do not need to discuss the psychology of suggestion, but only to observe the causal relationship between ideas of associates.

We are not using the word "suggestion," as some writers do to mean adoption of an idea, so that it is believed and acted on, in the absence of logical grounds, but "suggestion" as we use the term has nothing to do with the presence or absence of logical grounds for the adoption of the idea. After we get ideas from our associates we may test them, but we get them, false and true alike. The relation between the ideas of our associates and the ideas that we get from them is a purely casual one up to that point. This has vast consequences in the building up and perpetuation of systems of social belief, firmly held, but often superstitious and every way erroneous. We cannot test suggested ideas unless we have some data by which to test them. A child who grows up among associates whose religious and political and moral ideas are superstitious and distorted gets those false ideas. Later he may test many of them and replace some of them with better ones, but unless better ones come from some other social source there is but little chance of his doing so.

Doubt and Thought.—This section is inserted as a parenthesis, and as a comment upon the statement just made that there is nothing logical about suggestion.

I invite you to doubt everything that you read in this book. Doubt is the thought you give to an idea before you accept it as true, or reject it as false. Doubting is thinking about an idea without either affirming or denying the idea. When one says, "I believe that," then he has ceased to doubt; and when he says, "I do not believe that," then also he has ceased to doubt, or more probably he has never doubted in either case. Many ideas are so clear and simple that as soon as stated they must be believed. Two and two are four— one cannot doubt about that. Of other ideas one can be sure just as easily and promptly that they are false. Two and two are five—one cannot doubt about that; you know at once that it is not so. The more intellectual power and experience in thinking or doubting one has had, the larger the number of ideas about which he can decide at once that they are either true or false. And it is equally true that the greater one's intellectual power and experience in thinking, the larger the number of questions he can comprehend as problems but cannot answer; the higher one climbs the wider the dim horizon of uncertainty. And the greater one's intellectual development, the more he will be able, whenever the question is too complex or deep to be answered offhand, to suspend judgment and continue thinking until he has a rational belief. If you find that you cannot solve a problem do not be distressed about it, but put it aside and let it lie upon the shelf. Go back to it later, after you have learned and grown more, and try your strength upon it. Sometimes you may find that a problem that once baffled you yields readily to solution; other problems will forever transcend our powers. The person with little power of thought and experience in thinking answers deep questions with mere snap judgments: "Oh, I do not believe that," or, "Yes, I believe that." He condemns the book that was not written from his own point of view and shuts himself up in his own limitations.

Most of what people believe, they believe just because the notion has been presented to them when they were not old enough or not instructed enough or not thoughtful enough to see any reason for doubting it. So we take on the ideas that are current in our family and neighborhood without ever having doubted them and acquire a stock of beliefs that have stuck to us as burrs stick to clothing in an autumn walk through the fields. They are really no part of us. And most of what people disbelieve they disbelieve without ever having doubted it. They simply rejected it. When an idea is presented, even to the mind of an older and more instructed person, it may be eagerly welcomed or instantly refused without one doubt. It may be welcomed because it harmonizes with the cherished beliefs which we have already adopted; or because it is creditable to ourselves or our friends or our party of whom we are glad to think well; or because it excuses us from doing disagreeable things; or because if true it is a reason for doing what we like to do, or because it is an idea that we like to have prevail because of its effect on the conduct of others. Or it may be rejected because it disagrees with the cherished beliefs which we have already adopted; or because it is not creditable to ourselves or our family or our party of whom we are unwilling to think ill; or because if true it summons us to do that which is disagreeable or forbids us to do that which is agreeable; or because we fear its effect on the conduct of others. Most of the ideas and beliefs upon debatable questions which furnish the minds of men are held for such causes as these, having been first adopted during childhood and youth. And after being once adopted, arguments for retaining these beliefs can be seen and appreciated far more easily than arguments for changing them.

Thus it is that many people have eyes for facts and considerations that are favorable to their own sect or party, but none for those favorable to opposing sects or parties. One element in the "point of view" which at the outset was said to be essential to the study of sociology was riddance, so far as this is possible, from sectarian, partisan, sectional, racial, and every other bias. The first thing to do, and the hardest, if we wish to see the world as it is, is to get rid of our colored spectacles and be just as ready to see truth that calls in question our established beliefs and prejudices and is out of harmony with our personal and party interests as we are to see truth that reënforces our cherished beliefs, established prejudices, and favored interests—to be impartial and disinterested judges of truth. This is "the supreme intellectual virtue." It is intellectual honesty and far harder than the honesty that will not lie to another. It is a virtue but rarely attained in its completeness and that is largely why progress is so slow. I do not say that this emancipation of mind must be possessed in order to be a tolerably good person; there are many good people who do not possess it. In fact the mass of those who preserve the established order may get along so well without it that Walter Bagehot has been able to write a famous passage on "The Virtues of Stupidity."[1]

But society must have progress as well as order. And for the sake of progress the leaders of the people must have not only intellectual brightness, but also intellectual honesty and

---

[1] "Letters on the French Coup d'État," quoted by Carver in *Sociology and Social Progress*, p. 501.

openmindedness. This is a virtue that must be striven for by those who hope to contribute to the world's progress toward knowledge and light and so to fullness of life.

A new view that takes away the system of cherished beliefs upon which we had built our life does us a great hurt in order that it may do us a great good. It takes away the foundation of sand in order that we may build upon the rock. Many cannot face the possibility of such an overturn. It often takes sublime courage to want to know the truth even when the truth is unwelcome and to follow the truth even when it requires us to abandon cherished prejudices and courses of action.[1]

Moreover, it is hard work to readjust our habits of thought. It is immeasurably easier, having become the adherent of a given party or creed, to remain so, than to become a part of the movement of progress toward the unity of truth that lies deeper than all partisanship. Perhaps it is only the intellectual leaders who are called to do this arduous work. If so, these leaders deserve the sympathy and appreciation of those who take the easier course and join the intellectually inert mass.

The mass hates to be disturbed in its comfortable consistency by views inconsistent with its adopted opinions, and so stones the prophets from age to age. But in a republic it would seem desirable that the mass should be less inert, less manacled by prejudice, less unable to appreciate its leaders, the free-minded, until after they are stoned or crucified, or after more modern manners, sneered out of attention, or even ignored, until the reasonableness of their reasons compels slow and reluctant assent after costly and often calamitous delay.

Do not be afraid to doubt if you aspire to participate in intellectual progress; that is, to think without affirming or denying, not thrown into a panic by uncertainty. Cease to affirm that which you have shouted loudest and ask: "Why am I shouting so? Is this true after all, or do I believe it

---

[1] See Froude: Biography of Thos. Carlyle, i, 81 *seq.*, or the avowedly autobiographical passage in "Sartor Resartus" on "The Everlasting No," p. 156 *seq.*

just because it has clung to me like a burr, or because others do, or because I like to believe it?"

On the other hand, there is no virtue in uncertainty when conclusions can be reached. Moreover, there are a few things concerning which there is no necessity nor pretext for uncertainty, but which lie open to perception. Especially no normal mind can doubt the difference between black and white; we cannot doubt that there is such a thing as suffering, heartache, blight and ruin; nor can we doubt that there are such things as gladness and peace, happy homes, love, health of body, mind, and heart, the joy and worth of life's possibilities fulfilled. As long as we do not become so blinded that we cannot see the difference between black and white we shall not become inactive, but even in our periods of greatest uncertainty we shall have light enough to walk and work by, and in our hours of clearer vision enough to summon us to an enthusiasm of devotion.

Social Suggestion Determines Conduct and the Desire for Conduct Determines Invention.—The second statement to be made about social suggestion is that it determines conduct. The social suggestion which provides society with prevalent ideas thereby controls the conduct and practices of society.

The human organism is a mechanism adapted to function under the stimulation of ideas. That is the key to the life history of man and society, in so far as that mystery can be unlocked with any one key. Let someone put his head in at the door of a crowded theater and say that the building is on fire, and if he is believed the whole audience is lifted and put in motion. Drop an idea in the slot and the wheels of human activity revolve. And it makes no difference whether the building really is on fire or the alarm is uttered by a madman; provided he is believed the audience is equally moved until undeceived. Man is as readily moved by a false idea as by a true one, provided only the idea is accepted. Since ideas directly determine conduct it follows that suggestion, by supplying a body of current ideas, controls socially prevalent conduct.

And this leads into a third statement not about suggestion,

but about invention, and it is one of the most profoundly important principles of sociological explanation: Since ideas determine conduct, the need of conduct prompts the invention of ideas that will evoke the conduct that is wanted. Man cannot carry his conduct beyond the original responses of instinct except by getting ideas that will move and guide action. A primitive mother has a sick child. She yearns to do something about it, and so she thinks of things that she might do. She cannot know but that any idea of action that occurs to her may be the right one. She tries it and has at least the comfort of doing something to meet the emergency. Or she asks a "wise man" to do something. A practice once started easily acquires an established authority as the way to meet the situation. Thus all peoples build up whole systems of practice to meet life's emergencies; to cure the sick, to make it rain, to cause the corn to grow, to make deer show themselves, to settle quarrels, to pacify the unseen powers. The necessity that is the mother of invention is necessity of ideas, and invention is invention of ideas. Invention is guided by knowledge provided there is pertinent knowledge, but it is by no means limited by the extent of knowledge. In some respects, the less knowledge the freer is invention. Thus to make corn grow and to lure deer and to serve a hundred other ends activities are prosecuted partly under the guidance of knowledge and partly under the guidance of other ideas that come in answer to the need of guidance. In some realms of action knowledge is far more readily accumulated than in others and in the latter, speculation continues to furnish man with the ideas by which he is guided. It is thus that the desire for conduct creates the need and desire for ideas, so that people invent and disseminate those ideas which evoke the sort of conduct which is wanted. Current beliefs have been the products not of unbiased logical probability but also, and in many instances far more, they have been the products of practical need. Man must have ideas or he cannot get in motion. When he does not know the true ideas he will guess and act on his guesses, until they are displaced; for ideas he must have. During the long eras while the world waited for the slow-grown fruits of science, men have supplied themselves with ideas born of their own speculation. Being practically free because of their ignorance to choose the ideas they preferred, they have chosen the ideas that stimulated them as they liked to be stimulated, or more often their leaders have taught the ideas that would stimulate the masses as the leaders desired to have the masses stimulated. Thus we have had no lack of ideas even where knowledge is least, of political and religious and ethical ideas, adapted to control the conduct of men. And both leaders and led have said and thought that ideas that worked well were vouched for by the fact that they met human needs, and that they were substantiated by the testimony of the human heart. Many "pragmatists," it seems, would have us ask no other test.

Error May Work for a Time.— A noble error that works well may be one of the most precious possessions of a society. The only thing better than an error that works well is a truth that works well. The great trouble with a useful but erroneous product of speculation is that it is likely sometime to come in contact with incongruous facts. It may survive the shock if such contact does not take place with too many or too impressive facts, or in too many minds, and often does survive such contacts, but there is always grave peril that if social order is founded upon noble errors, they will crumble to sand under the corrosion of exposure to newly discovered realities. Many a man has lost his religion and his philosophy of life when he found by sad experience that the comfortable doctrine he had held concerning the protection of special providence was an error. Many have had their world view clouded over or destroyed because there had been wrought into it some superfluous error to which they could not cling, and the abandonment of which destroyed their faith in the whole fabric. In a time of intellectual revelation like that in which we live it is assuming a terrible responsibility to teach the young good but weak speculations, speculations once implicitly believed, which worked well so long as they were believed but which cannot live in contact with the facts of life, of history, and of nature. The only safety for society lies in having the leaders of its thoughts dig boldly down through all speculation to the facts of life, through the sand to the rock. We have often been urged to hold on to our faith when that has meant build in the mind a hermetically sealed compartment, and stow our creed and our ideals in a safety vault where the facts of life and the current of thought cannot get at them. To return to our former figure, the faith to which men need to hold is faith that if we dig through the sand we shall find the rock; that under the best and holiest that men have dreamed is the holier and better reality that God has created, and that life consists in adjusting our ideas and our conduct to the actualities. Not all are bold enough to hold such a faith as that. Men have long sought to derive their comfort and their inspiration from the unknown. We must look for it more and more in the known. Within the circle of human concerns, and the range of human faculties, there are values at stake which are adapted to furnish inspiration and call forth man's utmost of endeavor and devotion.

Psychological Principle Underlying These Two Statements Concerning Social Suggestion.—The fact that socially suggested ideas need not be proved in order to be believed, nor approved in order to control conduct, is an application of the psychological principle that ideas function [1] unless inhibited by other ideas.

A critical attitude toward new ideas may be developed after one has been frequently deceived; but even then an idea once formed in the mind has the tendency to be believed and acted out, though its tendency to be believed may be negatived by the presence in the mind of contradictory ideas, and its tendency to go into action may be negatived by the presence in the mind of ideas with an opposite motor urge. We tend to hold and act upon not only those ideas which we have deliberately accepted or approved but also all that have entered the mind and have not been definitely cast out or rejected.

---

[1] Of course this means that they set up, or evoke, functioning of the psychophysical organism. Sociology has no need to meddle with the metaphysical question as to the relation between the psychic and the physical.

The nickel in the slot effect is produced and the wheels of activity are put in motion whenever the idea has a place in the attention, and just in proportion as it has a place in the attention. If several ideas have a place in the attention they may so offset each other as to produce suspense, deliberation, inaction, and it is painful to keep the attention trained long upon the subject of such contradicting ideas. As a rule the stimulation of one idea or set of ideas triumphs soon over its opponents and the course of thought and action are thus determined. Attention is, or at any rate involves, a physical adjustment. If the object of attention is external, attention may involve the direction of the eyes upon it; if internal, an idea and not an external object of perception, then attention involves the focusing of the neural organs of its contemplation. Attention to an idea involves a physiological fact and it has physical consequences, which may appear in the blushing of the cheek and the palpitation of the heart, and also in setting up the thought processes of the brain and stimulating the muscles to overt activity, as in the case of the cry of, "Fire!" Every idea dropped into the mind tends to set up its appropriate series of functions, cerebral and muscular.

The fact that an idea tends powerfully at once to become a belief, if it is uncontradicted and satisfies any intellectual or practical interest, accounts for the naïveté of children and savages. They may have excellent minds but they have so little in their minds that there is nothing to contradict or challenge the ideas that are suggested to them. Similarly an idea of action goes into muscular effect upon presentation of opportunity if it is uncontradicted and satisfies any interest. It tends to go into effect even though it satisfies no interest; thus one absent-mindedly drinks the glass of water before him simply because the glass suggests the usual action and an action need only be suggested to be carried out though there is no desire for the action or even a good forgotten reason for inhibiting the action. In fact the thought of doing a most undesirable thing, like casting oneself from a high bridge, tends to be carried out if because of its very horror it so rivets the attention as to drive out of mind all inhibiting ideas. The idea when we get it has a purely and directly causal effect. And suggestion by which we get so many of our ideas is as really a causal relationship as any in science.

Sympathetic Radiation.—Tremendous as is the significance of social suggestion in building up the massive social activities we shall now see that sympathetic radiation is scarcely less so. Sympathetic radiation is the relation between the activities of associates which exists when the manifestation of feeling by one evokes similar feeling in the other. This is the mode of causation by which tastes, sentiments, and moral approvals and abhorrences become characteristic of whole societies.

Most of the definite sentiments, which are popularly regarded as instinctive, are in reality caught by social radiation from the society by which we are surrounded from our infancy. The comparative study of social evolution will show us that societies differ as much with reference to their tastes, sentiments, and approvals as they do with reference to their ideas. There are people who think it beautiful to dye their fingernails red; in China it was long thought beautiful to let them grow two inches long, and to crush the feet into lumps; there are people of very considerable advancement in civilization whose women blacken the teeth and regard white teeth in the mouth of a married woman as unseemly, others among whom the men dye their beards sky-blue, and others who eat the body of dead parents as a mark of honor to the deceased. If we examine pictures of the styles of successive periods we are often amazed that any sane being should willingly appear in such fantastic array. Yet these gowns, hats, and hairdressings were felt to be beautiful in their time. The "hideous" old sofa of colonial pattern that formerly reposed in the attic and would have disgraced the parlor, has lately been brought down and set in the place of honor and is prized as much as a fine diamond. The diamond itself is treasured by each mainly because it is treasured by all; who on first seeing a great diamond would of himself conceive that it was worth a fortune, or so desire it as to part with its price? There was a time when a single tulip bulb brought the price of a diamond, not because tulips were rare but because certain particular colorings, by cumulative sympathetic radiation had acquired a fantastic value. Now, feathers on the legs of a rooster can multiply his value two hundred times. The appalling squawks, squeaks, and clangs of a Chinese orchestra can entrance the soul. Most of the "higher" artistic appreciations have to be cultivated, and the method of their cultivation is partly a process of sympathetic radiation from persons whose tastes are trusted. Styles, esthetic tastes, in so far as they belong to particular periods or localities and not to universal humanity, and economic wants result mainly from sympathetic radiations emanating from parents and teachers or from "everybody" or from the "four hundred" or from those who live next door.

The same is equally true of standards of ambition. They differ from place to place and are established and perpetuated by sympathetic radiation. The Malay head-hunter is ambitious to have a long row of skulls above his door. That desire is not common to mankind; neither is it original with him as an individual. He measures his own success and worth by this standard because it is the standard of his group and he has caught it by sympathetic radiation. As a group possession that standard has had a social evolution and a specific cause. Similarly the urchin on the streets of Florence may be ambitious to become a sculptor, and on the streets of Chicago such an urchin may be ambitious to become a professional ball player or a ward boss. For the same cause the same boy who measures his future success by the ward boss, measures his present greatness in spring by the number of marbles he can win, and in the fall by his prowess at football or the number of inedible horsechestnuts he can gather. Marbles are intrinsically as valuable in autumn as in spring but the boy does not desire them then, for the social valuation has deserted them for the season. And as the boy seeks marbles or inedible chestnuts so his elders, often oblivious to worthier aims, pursue with ardor the ostentatious display of wealth or other aims, base or noble, which derive their glamour largely from sympathetic radiation.

Not tastes, wants, and ambitions only, but quite as much moral standards differ from place to place, arise by a social evolution, and spread and perpetuate themselves by sympathetic radiation. A generation ago it was entirely possible for many of the most cultured, Christian, and refined to approve of slavery, because there was a great group of civilized and Christian people in which the approval of slavery still prevailed, and the approvals of the group by sympathetic radiation form the conscience code of the individuals who are born into the group. Abraham practiced polygamy with a clear conscience because he belonged to a society that felt no disapproval of polygamy. It is possible for a people to have strong feelings on the subject of sexual propriety and to punish adultery with death, and yet regard it as the part of hospitality to furnish a guest with a temporary wife. Many peoples, including the North American Indians, are brought up to feel that he who fails to avenge an injury either to himself or to one of his tribe is a craven. It is by no means necessary or justifiable to think that savages by nature find the practice of vengeance more congenial than it would be under like circumstances to our own race. There is nothing that may not be made by sympathetic radiation to seem right to the individual if as a result of previous social evolution it already seems right to the group into which he is born.

No one is born with a conscience, though all normal human beings are born with the capacity to develop one. Thousands even in civilized society never have the opportunity to acquire a normal conscience. A conscience code is a product of race experience in social evolution, and this product of race experience is imparted to each new generation by sympathetic radiation. By the hard lessons of experience each society that survives and progresses learns that certain types of conduct are essential and other types of conduct are destructive to the realization of its standard of social welfare. The little child, before it can speak, learns that some acts are smiled upon and some are frowned upon. When doing a forbidden thing it knows that the action would be disapproved "if mother knew," and usually believes that the act is known to a disapproving God. The child, like the man, passes very censorious judgments upon others who do the things that are regarded by the group as mean and despicable; and having passed such judgments on an act when performed by another, cannot straightway do the same without feeling that there is something wrong. The logical consistency of the mind turns the judgment which he has passed upon others in upon himself. Which of his actions shall be approved and which condemned depends upon the group code of the society into which he chances to be born. He acquires his equipment of moral sanctions so early that he cannot remember that he ever lacked them, and believes that they were born with him. Especially if all, or nearly all, of those to whom he looks up in his habitual social contacts have the same conscience code, he thinks that all properly constituted men are born, having within them that set of moral sanctions which he himself has felt from before his earliest recollection.

The conscience code is not imparted to the young merely or even mainly by precept. To state the idea that others approve or disapprove such and such actions does not insure that the child shall feel approval and disapproval for those acts. Rather he acquires by sympathetic radiation the feelings of approval and disapproval that are not merely stated but actually felt and manifested by those about him. Not moral precepts but the common table talk, the daily conduct, words spoken of neighbors behind their backs, the ordinary course of life, these manifest the standards of ambition and self-judgment that are actually felt and that are communicated to the young.

Sympathetic radiation secures the prevalence and permanence not only of tastes, ambitions and approvals but also of such sentiments as prejudices, hatreds, and loyalties—the sentiments which attach to the name Republican or Democrat, to Columbia, the flag, and the hymns we have sung in great congregations, enmities between Bulgarians and Turks lasting for centuries, and the like. Of these principal social realities some may be so grounded in nature and circumstances that, if by magic they could be wiped out, they would spring up anew in many breasts; yet even these spread by sympathetic radiation to thousands in whom they would not have taken independent rise, and they not only spread but are intensified by their radiation to each from many. Sentiments survive by sympathetic radiation long after they have ceased to be grounded in any justification, and have become a bar to progress.

Imitation.—Imitation is less fundamental than suggestion, indeed both imitation and radiation imply the presence of some degree of suggestion. But suggestion may exist without imitation, and in many instances the suggestion is inconspicuous while the imitation is impressive.

In the last chapter we treated suggestion and imitation as functions of the same predisposition and set aside as erroneous the teaching of Lloyd Morgan and others that there is an "instinct of imitation."

We do not need to suppose an instinct in order to account for the fact of imitation; we only need to remember that an idea suggested tends to realize itself in action. The acts of associates are constantly suggesting the ideas of actions. Action, not resistance, is pleasurable, and especially actions of members of our own species are congenial to us; besides to act as they do brings us into sociable relations with them.

There are two varieties of imitation, namely, ideomotor imitation and rational imitation. The simple and often unrecognized imitation which is due merely to the fact that an idea moves us to corresponding action is called ideomotor; but purposeful imitation, like that by which the apprentice copies his master, is rational.

Imitation as a factor in building up and perpetuating prevalent social activities may be illustrated by the fact that a Northerner going South or a Southerner going North to reside, in time and without any purpose to do so, assimilates his pronunciation to that of his neighbors. It was by the same method that those born into that society caught the pronunciation of their section with their earliest speech. An American who has resided for years in France is likely to accompany his French speech with French gestures. Perhaps all peoples raise the eyebrows and open the mouth when astonished. Esquimaux, Tlinkits, Andamanese and Brazilian Indians accompany this play of feature by a slap on the hips; the Ainus and the Shin-Wans give themselves a light tap on the nose or mouth, while the Thibetans pinch their cheek; the Bantus move the hand before the mouth, while the Australian and Western Negroes protrude the lips.[1] The modes of salutation with which students greet each other in the halls of German universities differ widely from those exchanged by the American students. While the salutations practiced by savage and barbarous peoples present curious variations between groups, and established uniformities within the groups, Polynesians, Malays, Burmese, Mongols, Esquimaux and others sniff each other or "rub noses," while the kiss is unknown over half the world. The gaits, manner of carrying the elbows, and postures of ladies change with the fashions. Table manners, as well as other forms of etiquette, are matters of imitation. Some of the peoples that do not use chairs sit crosslegged, others squat without crossing the legs. But each people is likely to have a way of sitting which for them is *the* way. Similarly games like baseball or tennis or boxing develop a "form" which for the time being is accepted and prevails, though any champion who has an idiosyncrasy may start a new wave of imitation. Fighting also has its "forms." The peoples of northern Europe are smashers, pounders, the swinging blow is their fighting form, and the hammer of Thor, the club, the mace and the battle-axe their characteristic weapons, and when they adopt the sword they make it a saber, falchion, or broad-sword, and swing it as if it were a club. With the peoples of southern Europe the piercing stab is the fighting form. The Romans conquered the world thrusting, and the characteristic sword of their descendants is not the saber or broad-sword, but the rapier. We wonder that the Japanese who can make so exquisite a blade give it so awkward a shape and hang and handle. It is awkward for a swinging blow but not so for a slicing push, which is the fighting form of the Japanese. Barbarous and savage peoples have each

---

[1] J. Deniker: The Races of Man. Scribners, 1904, p. 110.

their fighting form.   Fighting form may be somewhat influenced by build and temperament as well as by imitation. Peoples have also their characteristic working form.   The Chinese pull the saw and plane, while we push them.   The apprentice learning to plaster a wall, or the practitioner of any craft or art learns his style and method by imitation.

Imitation is a causal relation between an overt action and the antecedent action of an associate.

CHAPTER XVIII

PRESTIGE AND ACCOMMODATION

Prestige.—There is one point of verisimilitude in the myth which attributes the custom of creasing trousers to the example of an English lord, who being unable to get his trunks out of the custom-house in time to dress for the social engagements that waited upon his arrival in New York, purchased a pair of readymade trousers and wore them with the creases they had acquired from lying in a pile in the store. A million ordinary immigrants might have done the same without affecting the fashions of New York society. An opinion or a sentiment uttered by Mr. Gladstone or Mr. Roosevelt at the time of their greatest influence might become at once an important element in the life of the nation; it might initiate a reform or precipitate a war. Ten thousand common men might form and express the same opinion or sentiment with no greater effect than the momentary interest of the immediate hearers. As in the topography of a continent, a farm, or a dooryard there are high points from which the water flows to the lower lying portions, so in the surface of society, whether that society be a nation, a neighborhood, or a household, there are points of comparative elevation from which social influence flows out.

The comparison is not perfect because water will not flow uphill, and social influence does flow in some degree in both directions. Yet the comparison and the foregoing illustrations suffice to bring to mind a fact of social relationship of universal presence and immeasurable import to which we give the name of "prestige."[1] Every socius has some degree

---

[1] The social relation or association includes
{
1. Suggestion
2. Sympathetic radiation
3. Imitation
}
All of which depend for main effectiveness upon prestige.

of causal efficiency, as a modifier of the activities of his associates. Whatever heightens the causal efficiency of an individual or of a class so as to make that individual or class more effective as the source of social suggestion, radiation, and imitation is said to give prestige.

Kinds of Prestige.—Professor Ross classifies the forms of prestige thus:

1. The prestige of numbers
2. The prestige of age, or of the elders
3. The prestige of prowess, such as is enjoyed by athletes or military leaders
4. The prestige of sanctity, or of the priestly class
5. The prestige of inspiration, or of the prophets
6. The prestige of place, or of the official class
7. The prestige of money, or of the rich
8. The prestige of the ideas, or of the elite
9. The prestige of learning, or of the mandarins [1]

To these may be added (10) prestige of birth or of family, which in origin is a prolongation of other forms of prestige.

The comparative influence of these forms of prestige in society goes far to determine the character of that society. For example, preëminence of *the prestige of numbers* tends to make a society impulsive rather than reasonable, because feelings easily become the common property of the mass, while reasons for moderating impulse and for adopting well-considered plans are less easily popularized. It is by no means impossible for a mass of people to act reasonably; but if they do, it is because wise leaders enjoy prestige and have means of ready communication with the multitude. Mass prestige may be combated by other forms of prestige, but of itself it tends to produce an impulsive, as distinguished from a reasonable, people. Impulsiveness often displays itself as fickleness, but often too it displays itself as stubbornness and resistance to change, whatever the prevalent feeling prompts.

The *prestige of the elders* played a leading rôle among primitive men and still does so among savages. In civilized

[1] Social Control, p. 79.

society the prestige of elders has a tremendous significance in shaping each rising generation. Among the civilized it has its chief, but by no means its only, sphere of influence in the family. The prestige of elders tends to make society conservative, to resist new-fangled notions, and to maintain the venerable traditions. It is a bulwark of order and stability. It is possible for an advanced society to get its character from predominance of the prestige of elders. Prevalence of ancestor worship heightens this form of prestige. Regard for the venerable members of society and the conservative effect of this form of prestige as a basis of social organization has been made familiar by the rigidity of Chinese traditions which for centuries almost ossified that great society.

A manifestation of the *prestige of prowess* is seen in the athletic heroes who gratify the instinctive impulses of group combat as they are aroused by intercollegiate athletics.[1]

The *social dominance of the military* class enables that class to impose upon society, tastes, moral standards, customs, and social stratifications. The original discussion of the broad general contrast between a society formed by military prestige and one formed by industrial aims and ideals is that of Herbert Spencer.[2] This contrast largely explains the differences between the civilization of the sixteenth and that of the nineteenth century, and between the social life of nineteenth-century Prussia and of nineteenth-century America. One of the numerous characteristics of a society dominated by military prestige is the punctilious insistence upon rank and station. In Prussia to this day two gentlemen on the sidewalk are quite

---

[1] Athletic sports are among the priceless possessions of our society. In college we ought to convert a large proportion of the "rooters" into active participants in athletic games. Intercollegiate athletics, because they have advertising value, have been allowed to receive disproportionate emphasis as an element of college and university life, in some respects to the detriment of sport that enlists the participation of larger numbers and that develops other leadership than that of the hired coach, as well as to the detriment of intellectual competitions that appeal more to reason but less to instinct.

[2] Spencer: Principles of Sociology. Appleton, 1901. See index to volumes i and iii for many references under "Militancy" and "Industrialism."

aware of judging which is entitled to walk on the other's right, and in Austria even the wife of the chimney-sweep is vividly conscious who are her social inferiors and expects them to address her as "Mrs. Master Chimney-Sweep." It must be understood that the military class do not impose their manners, tastes, moral standards, or opinions upon society by the exercise of force, but that society voluntarily and as a matter of course adopts the ideas, sentiments, and practices of those of its members who have the greatest prestige.

The *prestige of sanctity,* or of the priests, powerful as it has been in the past, and still is in many places, has nearly faded away among American Protestants, among whom the "minister" must win his influence, as a man, and not as the official of a Heavenly Court.

In modern society the *prestige of the official class* is considerable and among us it tends to increase with the elevation of politics, and with the extension of governmental activities.

The *prestige of birth* has been most influential in molding societies and very often has so outranked the prestige of wealth that the chief of the clan though in rags commanded implicit imitation as well as obedience. Where the prestige of birth and of military prowess prevails, society is so stratified that it is in general hopeless for one to seem to belong to any other class than that to which he is assigned. Then the serving girl may wear her hood or a kerchief, declining, as absurd, to wear a bonnet like that of her mistress even if it were given her.

The *prestige of wealth* is the first and crudest of the democratizing standards. It is democratizing because wealth is not permanent; the rich may sink into poverty and the poor may rise to wealth, so that rank according to wealth is not like rank by birth—hopelessly fixed. Yet social estimation based on wealth is only one step above that based on prowess, and on birth from men of prowess, and in the ages to come ought to yield the chief place to prestige of the elite and prestige of achievement. In an intelligent democracy even prestige of place is a nobler standard than prestige of mere wealth. In an advancing democracy the prestige of wealth is as conservative as the prestige of the aged. It resists change, it "stands pat" and does what it can to make the advocacy of progressive change "bad form." This form of prestige is at its height with us and molds our manners, social customs, and our ambitions. How much it influences us we can learn only by comparing ourselves with a society less influenced by this form of prestige. We have so thoroughly adopted money standards that we find it difficult to imagine a state of society in which men do not commonly rate themselves and each other by their scale of income and in which people do not commonly try to appear to have spent more money than they can really afford. Yet such societies have existed and will exist again when other forms of prestige sufficiently outrank the prestige of wealth. The prestige of wealth is not the same as prestige of economic achievement. Economic achievement as an evidence of personal power and economic production as distinguished from mere acquisition is a socially admirable exercise of power.

The *élite* should not be defined exclusively in terms of intellect, but also in terms of morality. It is not enough that the élite have "ideas," they must also have the social spirit; those who follow them must be justified in believing that they think and act with sincere interest in the general good. With the increase of public intelligence, and of experience in democracy, the public does increasingly insist upon devotion to the general good as a characteristic of its leaders. Doubtless there is still great room for progress in the attitude of the public on this point. Yet we have learned to be suspicious of self-seeking in public places. And disinterested devotion to public aims, and honesty and courage in the pursuit of them, already powerfully command the following of the masses. That is a wise society in which the masses know how to pick their leaders. No society has ever been thoroughly wise in this respect, but there is progress.

The *prestige of the learned,* or of the "mandarins," tends to be conservative in a conservative age, and progressive in a progressive age. Mere learning, as distinguished from the intellectual quality ascribed to the élite, does not originate, but it represents acquaintance with the intricacies of authorized knowledge and opinion. It is the equipment of the specialist. The prestige of the specialists is rapidly increasing in American society. That is because science has an ever-accumulating treasure of knowledge applicable to practical themes, and still more because technic, industrial, political, and social problems are ever increasing in complexity; as the native resources of the continent are appropriated, congestion of population increases, heterogeneity of population grows more menacing, the disparities in the distribution of wealth and opportunity become more glaring, class antagonisms grow fiercer, and perhaps most of all because the partial or total failure of half-instructed experiments reveals the necessity of greater intelligence in the guidance of endeavor.

Nature and Grounds of Prestige.—The elements that enter into prestige and form the bases of its effectiveness may be classified as logical, quasi-logical and non-logical. These names refer to the attitude of those who are influenced and led: Do they or do they not have a logical ground for accepting the leadership which they follow?

Sometimes it is enough to set down a given individual leader or a group which exercises leadership as an instance of a particular form of prestige, but quite as often it will be necessary to make an analysis and observe that while the leadership of the group or individual rests primarily on some one ground it is also bolstered up by several other elements of prestige.

1. *Logical prestige* is based upon a rational judgment that the opinions, sentiments, or acts of an individual or class of individuals can be accepted as true, right, or beneficent. Such is the prestige of the family physician in matters of health, of the successful man in the concerns in which he has succeeded. Of this type are:

(a) The prestige of the specialist,

(b) The prestige of achievement and

(c) The prestige of the élite, that is those who have given convincing evidence of originality and social spirit.

After all that has been said of the non-logical character of social suggestion it would not be surprising if the reader had determined not to be influenced by any kind of prestige, but to lead an independent life. But that is as impracticable as it would be to live without eating. It is impossible for an individual to lead an independent life; by that process one would never become an individual in any significant sense. We should all be naked savages if we did not borrow from society. It is only by becoming "heirs of all the ages" that we develop a life that is worth while. Our only room for choice is in selecting which of all the models and teachers presented we will follow; it is as if we could choose our parents with a view to inheriting their qualities and their estates.

2. *Quasi-logical prestige* is apparently justified by a mental process which, while seemingly logical is fallacious, by a conscious or subconscious inference which is not justified by the facts. As illustration of quasi-logical prestige may be noted:

(a) *The prestige of antiquity.* This form of prestige is, no doubt, partly sentimental and non-logical. Yet it is largely based upon the conscious or subconscious reasoning that what has stood the test of time and long experience must be true, right, and beneficent. But as a matter of fact it is not unlikely that the ancient is the antiquated, the superseded.

(b) *The prestige of modernness.* In an age that has witnessed the discovery of many new truths and the introduction of many useful inventions, it is natural to infer that prestige belongs to whatever is most modern on the ground that it presumably embodies the results of all progress "up to date." But among the innovations there are not a few futile speculations, revivals of ancient errors, new superstitions, and untried experiments, destined for to-morrow's scrap-heap.

(c) *The prestige of numbers* is largely due to the more or less conscious inference that what "everybody" does or believes must be good or true. It would be at least as justifiable to say that despised and persecuted minorities are always right. The history of science and of religion has led some to say that heretics are always right. Those who differ from the mass and bear the cost of non-conformity are likely to have some reason for doing so. The new beliefs and practices which create progress necessarily start with minorities.

(d) *Transferred prestige* is that which is based upon reasoning like this: "He is a great man and therefore ought to be followed," when the facts only justify such reasoning as this: "He is competent in certain matters and therefore in respect to those, he may safely be followed." That is to say, the prestige which is justly ascribed to one in reference to certain matters is transferred to other matters also. Thus the specialist on bridge-building or etymology may have undue influence in matters of religion, and the football player may set the standard of neckties. The rich are thus allowed unduly to influence manners, morals, tastes, and opinions. And the "prestige of the metropolis" leads the young minister erroneously to imagine that a city congregation will certainly be more intelligent and responsive to his best efforts than a village parish and leads the small town to borrow from the great cities building ordinances which import evils that are unavoidable where congestion of population is greatest, but absurdly unjustified in the country.

3. *Non-logical prestige* includes the following elements:

(a) *Physical prestige.* This is the power to hold attention and charge suggestion with power, that comes to the man on the platform, the man on horseback, the man in uniform, the man with a loud voice, the tall man, the strikingly homely man, the man with long hair or a tall hat, or to the big headline. Physical prestige belongs also to the person who assumes the confident and expansive bearing expressive of an aroused instinct of dominance.

(b) *The prestige of contrast.* The mere fact of being unusual or "different" excites notice, quickens interest and to a degree gives prestige. This is the principle of notoriety. It is also the principle of "news." This accounts for the fact that the daily papers find it worth while to print anything, however insignificant or revolting, if it be only unusual, and for the fact that the news of the daily press gives a highly distorted view of the life of society, omitting the regular, normal, and usual, and seizing on the abnormal and unusual. The unusual is so likely to be inferior to the normal and regular that the prestige which is based upon it is more likely than other forms of prestige to be counteracted by an emotional or logical antidote.

(c) *Esthetic prestige.* Beauty of every kind attracts and holds willing attention and gives prestige.

(d) *Emotional prestige.* All other grounds of prestige are likely to awaken emotion so that emotion pervades and supports prestige in nearly all its forms. Whatever excites strong feeling rivets attention, and attention is the beginning of thought and action. This is true even of the emotion of fear. Men are like the birds fascinated by the snake; and what we fear we are likely also to admire. The same is true of envy. And it is preëminently true of liking and affection. Partisanship exalts the influence of leaders within the sect, party, or other "we-group." And there is, moreover, a specific predisposition toward eager and loyal subordination to leaders.

(e) *The prestige of desire.* Society must have leaders. This is one of the fundamental human needs, and when leaders are not great enough to satisfy the demand, men magnify their leaders by their own sentiment and imagination. The loyalty of masses to particular leaders is often to no small degree based upon a foundation of popular sentiment and imagination built by desire. Little boys choose one of their number to pitch on their ball team, and then attribute to him wonderful speed and mythical curves, till they are disillusioned by the facility with which their opponents hit the ball. A nation going to war needs a great general, and attributes greatness to the general it has. McClellan is a second Napoleon until his failure. Parties similarly magnify their candidates.

Moreover, one of the desires of society is for glory and this leads society to magnify to the utmost the glory of its conspicuous representatives. The glory of the dead heroes of a people waxes thus, unhindered by the jealousy of the living, and in a credulous age the results are marvelous. Even in a skeptical age and with respect to living heroes, the desire of the multitude heightens the prestige of representative citizens for the mere love of glory, as well as when the station occupied is one where men feel that for practical reasons they need a great man.

But the prestige of desire plays its chief rôle in the way indicated at the opening of this section; that is, when men comfort themselves with the belief that their leaders are equal to the practical demands upon them, and pay greatest heed to those for whose success they feel the greatest need. If riots break out in Paris, says Tarde, everybody knows the Prefect of Police, and his ideas and sentiments have publicity and influence, though before the riots nobody knew the name of that official or thought of his existence. Professor Tarde devotes one of his books [1] mainly to elaborating and illustrating the thesis that the seat of power in any society rests with the class which discharges the most desired function and shifts with changes in popular desire or conscious need, as for example to the military class when protection or glory is the dominant desire, to the priestly class when fear of the unseen gives rise to the most urgent sense of need, to the captain of industry when material wants are uppermost, to the specialist when the need of guidance is realized. And with the shifting of the chief seat of power in a society the general character of that society alters. [2] But many of the elements of prestige working together, go to determine the character of every society, and which of these elements is predominant may depend upon all of the types of causes which we have recognized as playing their rôle in the molding of social realities. Like everything else the alterations of prestige in a given society are both effects and causes.

---

[1] Les Transformations Du Pouvoir.

[2] An interesting study of the rise and fall of scholarship averages of fraternities at the University of Illinois culminates in the conclusion that "in most cases high or low averages are not dependent so much upon the presence in the chapter of a number of exceptionally high- or low-grade men as upon the presence or absence of a masterful leader. Transformations in the character of society at large accompany the shifting of prestige from one type of achievement and leadership to another.

Accommodation.[1]—When a pebble falls into a pool of still water, circles of wavelets begin to spread across the surface. Similarly whenever there is an innovation in society it tends to spread in widening circles of prevalence. New ideas spread by suggestion; new sentiments, tastes, wants, ambitions, approvals, and disapprovals spread by sympathetic radiation; new practices spread by imitation. If two pebbles are thrown into the pool the widening circles sooner or later meet and interfere. Similarly the circles of spreading social suggestion, sympathetic radiation and imitation meet and interfere, and they may either reënforce and heighten each other or impede and even obliterate each other. For example the idea that man was created by a very simple mechanical process on the last of six creative days of four-and-twenty hours each was passing in regular pulsations from generation to generation, when suddenly new rings of suggestion emanated from the laboratories of certain scientists, bearing ideas of a far diviner mode of creation, and these new emanations began to disturb and finally to break and smooth away the ideas borne by earlier suggestions. But socially suggested ideas corroborate each other quite as often as they conflict. Thus successive scientific discoveries, such as those relating to embryology and the finding of prehistoric human remains of far greater antiquity than had been ascribed to man, corroborated each other and raised higher and spread faster the widening circles of belief in evolution. Specific suggestions are often borne on upon the waves of some general belief already current. Thus the general belief in witchcraft or in miracles made it easy to credit many tales that to-day would make little headway in our society. Rumors about a man or an institution spread or die out according to their relation to existing opinion in relation to the man or institution concerned. Thus ideas corroborate or undermine other ideas. New scientific and historical ideas have corroborated each

---

[1] The discussion of this topic may be supplemented by reading Tarde: The Laws of Imitation, Tr. Henry Holt & Co., 1903, p. 23 ff.; and Cooley: Social Organization a Study of the Larger Mind, Scribners, 1909, chap. xii.

other till their common strength has become irresistible. At the same time these scientific ideas have obliterated many superstitions and erroneous pre-scientific views concerning the subjects to which they apply, and have even had power to recast traditional theology.

As ideas corroborate or contradict each other, so sentiments reënforce or weaken and even nullify other sentiments. For example, patriotic and partisan loyalty heightens admiration for the qualities of our own heroes. Practical selfish desires may deaden moral sentiments of which the classic example for Americans is the disappearance of anti-slavery sentiment in the South after the invention of the cotton gin. A large portion of private, business, and political life illustrates this principle.

Not only may ideas corroborate or undermine ideas, sentiments heighten or nullify sentiments and imitations combine into systems of conduct or replace each other, but also an element of any one of these three kinds may either heighten or diminish the strength and prevalence of elements of either of the other kinds. Thus an idea may heighten or impede the spread of overt activity or contract the prevalence of an activity already widespread. For example, ideas concerning the effects of alcohol and sentiments of disapproval in regard to it have greatly contracted its use in society. Ideas tend to heighten or suppress sentiments, and sentiments often have as much power as arguments to promote belief or disbelief in ideas. People find great difficulty in entertaining beliefs that are too radically opposed to their desires and other sentiments, but have great facility in adopting beliefs that coincide with their sentiments. Thus belief in the divine right of kings appealed to philosophers and common people alike when society was emerging from the disorders of the Middle Ages and the hope of peace and prosperity seemed to lie in developing an irresistible sovereignty: but when the power of central government had grown oppressive, then men no longer thought that the right of kings to rule was divine, but that it depended on "the consent of the governed"; they no longer thought that in a state of ungoverned nature "man is a wolf to man," but rather they believed that nature makes men free and happy so that the way to welfare is by removal of restraints and "return to nature." The people of silver-producing states were convinced by the free silver arguments; not so those of the commercial states. Because of the same principle different social classes hold different economic and political creeds.

The effects of ideas and sentiments upon each other within the individual mind the psychologist studies, but the sociologist takes this knowledge from psychology and from common experience as a datum. By "accommodation," the sociologist means that the partially conscious, but largely unconscious process by which individuals "change their minds," or correlate their ideas and sentiments into an established individuality, works on a grand scale in society, molded by suggestion, radiation, imitation and the conditioning material environment, so that the prevalent social activities change in character, or correlate into a solid social constitution.

By this process of accommodation the activities of a society, its practices, beliefs, and sentiments adapt themselves into a correlated and organic unity into which disturbing elements make way with difficulty. Yet they do make way, partly by their own power to move the minds and hearts of men, but partly also by virtue of changes in the conditions. And when a new idea, sentiment, or practice has made its way it tends to become part of a new establishment of a balance of power among social activities—a natural social order. [1]

We have now passed in review the four kinds of conditions which are the causal antecedents out of which social realities issue and by the modification of which social realities are modified, namely: (1) the natural physical environment; (2) the technic environment, including (a) population groups in varying degrees of density and (b) wealth in diverse amounts, forms, and states of ownership; (3) the psychophysical conditions, or tendencies and capacities of the human

---

[1] EXERCISE: Give an instance of accommodation. What is the nature of each of the elements involved—idea, sentiment, or practice, and what the effect of the collision on each?

organisms composing the population, both hereditary and ac quired; and finally (4) the social conditions, or causal relations between the activities, similar or diverse, which are included in the social process, or life of society.[1]

The relative importance of these different factors has been variously estimated. Indeed each student who has devoted his attention to tracing the consequences of any of these four seems to have been so impressed with the importance of that one as to be inclined to regard it as the most important of all. One of the services of sociology is to afford a standpoint from which the importance of all four can be perceived.

---

[1] The analysis of social conditioning, and its place in the general system of causes affecting society may now be thus presented in outline:

1. Geographic conditions

2. Technic conditions $\begin{cases} \text{Population grouping} \\ \text{Amount, forms and distribution of wealth} \end{cases}$

3. Psychophysical conditions $\begin{cases} \text{Hereditary} \\ \text{Acquired} \end{cases}$

Social conditions or association $\begin{cases} \text{Social suggestion} \\ \text{Social radiation} \\ \text{Imitation} \end{cases}$ Heightened by prestige $\begin{cases} \text{Logical} \\ \text{Quasi-logical} \\ \text{Non-logical} \end{cases}$ Complicated by Accommodation

PART II

NATURE AND ANALYSIS OF THE LIFE OF SOCIETY

CHAPTER XIX

THE NATURE OF THE LIFE OF SOCIETY

Life of Society.—We have now provided ourselves with the clues that must be used in explaining social realities, and it is time for us to fix attention upon those realities themselves which we wish to explain.

What kind of realities out there in the real world are the objects to be explained by this particular study? What is it that we see when we look across the world of social reality? We see people working and striving or amusing themselves; pursuing aims base and noble by methods well or ill devised; a number of scientists deployed over the face of the earth seeking to understand nature; politicians and statesmen striving for power and its prerequisites with greater or less regard for the interests of their fellowmen; business men competing for the success which they measure by wealth; laborers toiling for a modicum of the material means of comfort; mothers engaged mainly in domestic pursuits, and other women engaged mainly in the various pursuits of amusement, including the game of competitive ostentation; artists bodying forth their souls and catering to the tastes of pleasure-seekers; professional sportsmen also catering to pleasure-seekers, and professional sports seeking to amuse themselves and fleecing the lambs for the means thereto; criminals devising and executing the plots by which they prey upon their kind; church people endeavoring to maintain and extend their several zions, nourish their own souls, and save as many as they can reach; philanthropists within and without the church endeavoring, some as their chief occupation and others with such energies as the demands of other callings permit, to promote the welfare of their kind; many pursuing useful callings less usefully than they should, or even harmfully because so selfishly, and spreading moral contagion by their presence; others pursuing their callings with the aim to do their work as part of the coöperative fulfillment of good human possibilities, and by their presence keeping alive man's faith in men and in the worth of noble endeavor and its fruits. What we see is a vast streaming of diversified and mutually conditioning *activities*. Whatever else we see that is sociologically important are the changes, conditions, consequences and relations of these activities.

The In and Out of Conscious Life.—All these activities of society are of course carried on by the individuals who compose society, and as the activities of individuals are made up of psychological elements, so the activities of society as a whole must be made up of psychological elements. For an understanding of the minute parts of which the vast stream of social activity is composed, sociology must fall back upon psychology, much as physiology must rely upon chemistry for an understanding of those minute processes which are included in physical life. A custom or an institution is made up of psychic elements, as a tree or an animal is made up of chemical elements.

Consciousness grows out of the necessity of making one's conduct fit one's situation. We feel the pain of fire in order that we may escape it; we see the path in order that we may follow it. The acts that go forth from us must be guided by the impressions that come in upon us from the external world.

Speaking schematically,[1] therefore, we may say that the conscious life of man, whether regarded as an individual or as a member of society, is an in-and-out process. The ray of light from a red apple comes in through a child's eye, and out

---

[1] As only this short paragraph is devoted to recalling the teachings of psychology, its crass schematism will not be severely judged by any just critic. Especially there is no intention to minimize the "spontaneous" activities of the organism, which are as out of proportion to the momentary stimulus as the burning of Chicago to the overturning of a stable lantern, because memory and propensity are wakened and set to work, and each inner activity that is aroused arouses others still.

flashes the impulse that carries his hand to the apple. The incoming sensation of light combines with remembered sensations of touch, taste, weight, and smell to form a conception of an apple, for the previous income of the mind has been saved up in memory to be used in interpreting whatever may come in later. As new sensations combine with remembered sensations to form perceptions, so also new perceptions combine with memories of former perceptions to yield more complex ideas and inferences. All the perceptions, ideas, and inferences thus compounded out of incoming sensations, new and remembered, constitute the subject matter of intellectual life. This is the mind's income.

The outgo is of two sorts. Whenever an incoming sensation arrives and sets the interpreting ideas trouping out of memory into consciousness a twofold outgo also takes place.

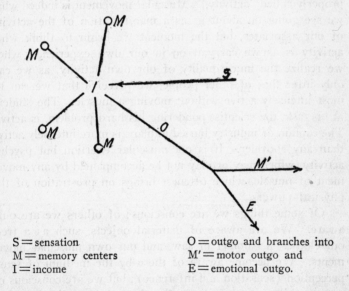

S = sensation
M = memory centers
I = income

O = outgo and branches into
M' = motor outgo and
E = emotional outgo.

First, out go the propulsions that incite the muscles to grasp the apple or to seize or repel or manipulate the object, whatever it is, or to speak, to write, to smile or to shout. This is the part of the process which can be observed by the bystander. We each observe this form of outgo in all those who surround us, and this is the part of the whole process which first gets the name of "activity," although it is no more intensely active than the income or the emotional outgo.

Besides this outgo to the muscles which are adapted to doing definite things and to affecting the external world, there is also an indefinite, vague, and diffused outgo to the whole body which may be strong enough to cause the sinking or bounding of the heart, the flushing or the blanching of the cheek, and which for consciousness is feeling or emotion. So our conscious life may be said to be composed of intellectual income and motor-emotional outgo.

Experience-Activity.—This brief discussion of the in-and-out of conscious life, it may be hoped, will help to rid us of the common feeling that only muscular movement can be properly called "activity." Muscular movement is indeed what we see going on about us as a manifestation of the activity of our associates, but the moment we begin to think what activity is as we carry it on in our own experience, when we realize the inner quality of our own activity, as we can only infer that of other people, we perceive that we can be most intensely active without moving a muscle. The student at his task, the scientist pondering his hard problem, is active. The captain of industry buried in plans is more intensely active than any shoveler. It is not muscular exertion but psychic activity, which may or may not be accompanied by any movement of muscle, which oftenest brings on prostration of the physical powers.

Of some things we are conscious; of others we are only aware. We are aware of material objects, such as a tree, our clothes, a hammer or saw, and our own muscular movements. We become aware of these by the medium of sense perception (sensation and inference); but we are conscious of our own ideas and feelings directly and immediately. Our own ideas and feelings are the only phenomena of which we can be conscious. A man may be aware of the movement of his muscles as he may be aware of the movements of his clothes or his tools but he is never conscious of such movements. He is conscious only of the psychic income; but the physiological outgo, both the outgo to the muscles, and that to the visceral system, is promptly reported back as sense of our own activity and as emotion; and these become part of the mind's income and help to determine the next outgo. These psychic elements are man's activities as they exist for his own consciousness.

For his own consciousness the activity of any worker, say a carpenter successfully engaged in building a table, is a set of ideas defining that which he will make and the methods he will use together with a liking for the design of the table, desire for its fulfillment, and the confident expectation of its gradual realization as a result of his own activity; then also a series of muscle and joint sensations reporting how the physiological outgo from these neuroses is being carried on, and as a result of these muscular movements, he also perceives the table taking shape and the outgo from this perception is felt as emotional approval, that is, satisfaction. Muscular movements of our associates reveal to us their psychic activities but the muscular movements are not psychic activities but physical, physiological, mechanical. The conscious life is made up of the in-and-out of ideas and feelings [1] which combine in each concrete state of consciousness, each "experience." Therefore, the compound word experience-activities is descriptive and helpful as a designation for the concrete psychic activities, the only activities which one owns in the sense that they are parts of his stream of consciousness, his conscious life, as distinguished from the vegetative and the muscular physical activities of which one is never conscious but only more or less aware by aid of sensation, as we are aware of our tools and our clothes. Social activities as well as individual activities for the consciousness of the actors are not visible muscular movements but inner movements of the mind. This fact gives rise to such expressions

---

[1] Some would add "volitions" but I agree with those who teach that what we call volition can be analyzed into feelings and ideas, and are not a separate kind of psychological element. Volition is the net resultant of our ideas and feelings.

as "public opinion," "public sentiment," and "the will of the majority." [1]

The Essential Social Phenomena Are Psychic.—The essential social phenomena are the spiritual heritage of a people. A Robinson Crusoe cast naked upon an uninhabited island would take with him his individual share of the social possessions of the group to which he belonged, religion, language, practical arts, and all. They never could have been developed by a man in isolation; some of them cannot be much used by a man in isolation, but in so far as a lone man can have them he needs no baggage to take them along, but takes his share in the social realities wherever he takes his conscious life. For example, he has taken the practical arts and will begin to make use of them so far as the raw materials of his island permits. It is often said that the Pilgrims in the *Mayflower* brought over to these shores their English institutions. They did; but where did they bring them? Were they packed in a cedar chest? Were they stored in the hold of the *Mayflower?* No, they were in the minds of the Pilgrims. Their religion and their institutions were their main freight, but these were wholly immaterial psychic or spiritual possessions.

If when visiting a strange town you point to a large building and ask, "What is that institution?" the true answer would be, "It is not an institution at all, it is no more an institution than a chest of tools is a carpenter, it is a piece of apparatus employed by an institution and so by metonomy may be called an institution." Suppose it is a courthouse. If that courthouse should burn down to-night, would the institution of the courts be destroyed from that community? No, it would be there ready to rebuild its apparatus. If the people

---

[1] EXERCISE: Has this university or community a life and character of its own which gives it unity and identity as a distinct society? If so, what are the elements included in the life of this society? In the list which you have made, in answer to the preceding question, which items are substantive and which are merely adjective? Are all the substantive elements activities that prevail in this society? Which of the adjective items in your description of this society name qualities of the prevalent activities? Which items in your list name conditions of those activities?

of the town should emigrate, as the Pilgrims did, they would not take with them their courthouse, but they would take with them their institution of the courts.

A church building may be changed into a factory or a skating-rink, and a bigger and better building be dedicated to the religious uses that the older structure had served. The beliefs, sentiments, and practices that combine to form the living institution which we call "the church" has then changed its shell. The building never was the institution; an institution is a particular system of activities, which we must later learn more accurately to define.

The Scientific and Practical Problems of Sociology.—The scientific problems of sociology are: (1) to describe and analyze the prevalent and socially conditioned experience-activities which constitute the social life of different peoples; (2) to classify these social activities according to their specific types or varieties; (3) to compare the different but homologous varieties of experience-activity characteristic of different peoples, different social classes, and different epochs (as comparative anatomy compares homologous but different biological structures) in order (4) to study their causation and evolution, by noting not only differences and resemblances between social activities, but also differences and resemblances between the internal and external conditions out of which they arise, so as to discover the correspondence which exists between changes in conditions and changes in the resulting social activities, and thus to identify those tendencies, or methods in causation, which if stated with sufficient precision are scientific laws; and also (5) to evaluate the social activities according to their quality as experiences, and according to the effects which they are observed to have upon further social activities. The phenomena to be described, evaluated and accounted for are, throughout, prevalent socially conditioned experience-activities.

The word "tendency" is preferable to the word "law." Simmel, author of "Philosophie des Geldes," says he knows of no economic law, and the claims for sociology must be at least as modest in this respect as those of economics. Even in biology there is hardly a law that can be stated with the mathematical definiteness of the laws of inorganic phenomena. But knowledge of a tendency may be of the greatest scientific and practical importance. For example, it is not necessary to know the number of typhoid bacilli in a given well, nor the mathematical relation between the number of ingested bacilli and of leucocytes that is the threshold between immunity and liability to disease; nor even to suppose that there is a fixed relation between them that can be so regarded; it is of incalculable value merely to have identified the microbe and the medium by which it is borne. Without that knowledge men rely upon nostrums and die; with it they close the well and live. The like is true of tendencies that result in the prevalence or decline of good and evil forms of social activity. Between that knowledge which is so complete that we can reduce it to mathematical expression, and metaphysics at the other end of the scale, lies the vast body of our knowledge, including nearly all of our knowledge about life, vegetable, animal or social, which largely guides our practical conduct and the extension of which, though we never reduce it to quantitative expression, is of immeasurable concern.

Similarly the practical problem of applied sociology is to secure the prevalence of the desired experience-activities. There is no other kind of realities in the direct causation of which the study of sociology can make men expert. There is no other kind of reality upon the improvement of which the progress of social welfare from this time on so directly and so preponderantly depends. As already observed, we have measurably solved the problems of production in agriculture, transportation, and manufacture; we have developed architecture and sanitary engineering, but in order that the millions may be sufficiently well fed and clothed and housed, to say nothing of their enjoyment of higher goods of life, it is necessary that we now proceed to secure the prevalence of right methods of coöperative endeavor, right standards of success and objects of ambition, right pressures of social condemnation and of social approval. We can manipulate material things, we must now learn, in so far as we can, to modify the facts of conscious life as they prevail in society. They are highly modifiable, no other realities more so. However, they are not dead and inert, but living; they cannot be shaped by force like wood and iron, but modified as the stock-breeder modifies his charges or as the husbandman transforms a field of weeds into a garden.

The Sociophysical Phenomena.—When one rises in the morning and looks out of the window he can see houses, streets, and passing vehicles, but he cannot see the admiration of wealth as a standard of success, the taste for ragtime music, or for automobiles, or the anti-trust movement, or the Bull Moose movement, or patriotism, or the jury system, or Methodism, yet they are out there, and they together with other realities equally invisible make up the social life of the American people. If one reads the newspapers, listens to the talk at the club and in the offices, attends the concert halls, examines the shop-windows and the attire and conduct of the throng in the street, and is present at political rallies, he will see and hear in the speech and writing and conduct of people and in the things they buy and use continual manifestations of their ideas and tastes and ambitions. These material acts and things manifest the invisible psychic activities that make up their life.

Physical manifestations of social activity are *the sociophysical phenomena.* The psychologist calls the speech and other overt actions of an individual "psychophysical phenomena"; now a muscular activity or material product which expresses some activity which is not peculiar to a single individual but which is a social activity, may be called a sociophysical phenomenon. This does not correspond exactly to the psychologist's use of the word psychophysical, for he uses that word to include the functioning of the nervous system which in a sense lies behind the conscious act, as well as to denote the muscular deed which expresses or manifests the conscious act, while our word sociophysical includes no reference to the functioning of the nervous system, which we leave to the psychologist, but only to the outward manifestation, that is, the muscular deeds, and the products of muscular deeds, which are the *overt expression of social activities.* The psychologist's word psychophysical may be symbolized by n c o, in which n = neurosis, c = the accompanying state of consciousness, and o = resulting overt act. To symbolize the sociologist's word sociophysical we strike out the n and the c and add t thus getting o t, in which o = the overt activity and t = the thing, if any, which that activity produces.

For example, roads and cities and libraries are sociophysical phenomena. In a great ethnological museum we can see here a section devoted to the weapons, tools, playthings, religious and ceremonial paraphernalia of the Zulus; there another section devoted to a similar exhibit from the Esquimaux. Passing from section to section we see material embodiments and manifestations of the social activities of one people after another. A total stranger to the activities of these people would need someone to interpret and would often say, "What does that object mean?" Perhaps the answer in one case would be, "That is a rattle used in the rain-making ceremony, and means that a people believed that their magicians could cause it to rain by rites and incantations." One must already be somewhat acquainted with the activities of people in their stage of development in order to understand the revelation made by their material products, just as one must know its language in order to read a book; but a book and an ethnological exhibit are equally material revelations of psychic activity. A World's Fair tells us more than many volumes of description about the activities of our fellowmen. If there could have been such a thing as a World's Fair held in the second century and its exhibits had been preserved to us how it would have enlightened us concerning the social activities of that age!

Social activities as we have seen are psychic phenomena. These psychic phenomena are the ultimate realities which sociology is to describe and explain. But the sociophysical phenomena are the immediate consequences of the social activities; they reveal the presence and the nature of those activities and render them accessible to scientific observation. The in-and-out of conscious life is revealed in the material results of its motor outgo. Furthermore, these material consequences are explained only by explaining the psychic activities which lie back of them, as the rattle was explained by explaining the rain-making belief, and as the Roman Coliseum is explained by explaining the amusement customs of the Romans.

Spoken and written language, pictures, mechanical products, houses, and railroads stand intermediate between mere material things like unopened mines, untrodden forests, rivers, and woods, on the one hand, and the psychic activities of men on the other, for they are material things as are the rivers and the woods but they give expression to the activities of men.

The material works of man have significance for sociology in two ways: first, in the same way and for the same reasons that the works of nature have significance for him, that is, as part of the physical environment which conditions the progress of human activities; second, since they have forms and characters imparted to them by the activities of man, they reveal the activities of man which sociology seeks to explain and are themselves explained by the explanation of these activities. The life of society is made up of prevalent and socially conditioned experience-activities, which are revealed and bodied forth in the sociophysical phenomena. The experience-activities could not become known to any observer if they were not thus bodied forth in speech, writing, tools, weapons, clothes, buildings, and the other material works that express the activities prevalent in society. DeGreef says that these material expressions of social activity are as much a part of society as the shell is part of the turtle. The psychologists say that the individual's thought of himself commonly includes the idea of his clothes and his work and that the lady feels herself assaulted when her dress is torn and the mechanic feels himself harmed when his work is damaged. The sociophysical phenomena are a part of the life of society only in the same sense that the product of the mechanic's skill is a part of his life.

We must not lose sight of the fact that in their essence

social phenomena are spiritual realities.   Streets of sky-scrapers, factories crowded with machinery, libraries of books, crowded city populations, legislative assemblies, might all be wiped out of existence but if there remained in the minds of the survivors all those ideas and sentiments of which these material realities are the expression, the life of society, hampered for lack of tools, but undestroyed, would soon replace them.   But should the spiritual wealth of the world developed through the age-long coöperation of many minds, be wiped out of existence and man be set back naked-souled at the starting-point of social evolution, he could not read a book, nor run a factory nor understand the wants to which all these things minister.   The social realities would then have been destroyed.

The social phenomena are psychic, but not all psychic phenomena are social phenomena.   Those psychic phenomena which are social are distinguished by three clear characteristics.

The First Characteristic of Social Activities.—The first characteristic of social activities is that they are prevalent. A social activity is not the unique possession of any single mind.   Methodism, for example, is not the peculiar property of any single Methodist but it is a definite set of activities (beliefs, sentiments and practices) which are common to many minds.   Or, the Republicanism of any one Republican is like the Republicanism of thousands more.   A belief in the desirability of free and unlimited coinage of silver dollars at the ratio of sixteen to one a few years ago became a significant social phenomenon widely prevalent, that is, common to multitudes of minds.   Long ago the belief in witchcraft and insistence upon the punishment of witches came over New England like a visitation of locusts.   Every fashion, custom, or institution, every prevalent sentiment, belief, or moral standard is a social reality partly by virtue of the fact that the same activity exists in many minds.

To this it may be objected that the activities of no two individuals are ever precisely alike, that the Methodism or the Republicanism of no two individuals is identical.   This is probably true.   It is also said that no two leaves in all June are quite alike. The botanist who collects different specimens of the same variety never finds two specimens that are identical. This, however, does not prevent the existence of botany nor the identification of botanical varieties; no more does the variation between specimens of a given social activity prevent them from being recognized as belonging to the same sociological species. Your Methodism, or other experience-activity, is one specimen of a prevalent variety of social phenomena, just as one daisy is a specimen of a prevalent botanical variety.

The Second Characteristic of Social Activities.—Social activities are manifested by sociophysical embodiment in speech, writing, conduct, or works. Logicians call any phenomena "public" which, although they may be observed by no one or by only a few, yet are of such a kind that they can be known by any competent observer who may pass that way. In this sense the "flower born to blush unseen" is public for it is a reality of such a kind that it can be observed. They add that only those objects which are public in this sense are open to scientific investigation. Social phenomena, being immaterial or psychic realities, are not open to direct observation. The consciousness of each individual is known directly to him alone. But psychic realities have physical consequences so direct and so manifold and so exquisitely adapted to disclose the character of the psychic realities themselves, that prevalent psychic realities manifest their presence, character, extent, and changes in a way that makes possible their description and explanation. This would not be true, in a degree that is adequate to the purposes of science, if each of us did not have in his own consciousness a fine collection of specimens of the very same kind of psychic realities. It is true not every specimen of a social reality is manifested. John may have a social idea or sentiment which he never reveals to anyone, although the social reality of which John's idea or sentiment is a specimen is well known. It is also true that many a botanical specimen is never seen by man though its species is known. Of course our knowledge might be completer if we could examine every specimen or at least knew their number. But we do not know the number of oaks or pine-trees, to say nothing of buttercups, or grass, or microbes, and need not observe or even know the existence of every instance of social activity. An activity which occurred in the experience of but one individual would lack the first characteristic of being a social reality; it would not be prevalent. An activity which though it recurred many times was so perfectly concealed that no one could suspect its existence in the experience of anyone besides himself would lack the second characteristic of a social reality. It would not be manifest.

There has been a little objection to regarding sociology as an objective science on the ground that social realities, being psychic in nature, are not observable, or "public" in the logician's sense. But this objection never received much heed and appears to have died out.[1] Our whole social life is built upon the fact that we do become aware of the activities, opinions, and sentiments of our associates. In this way social activities constitute our effective environment. The social activities which we observe about us mold our childhood and elicit and direct the endeavors of our mature life in general far more effectively than even the material realities by which we are surrounded. They constitute an ever-present, alluring, intimidating, and tremendous environment. Not only do our associates take pains to show many specimens of their social activity, but even when they try to conceal them they do not always succeed in doing so. And they testify continually, by accepting our replies and responses, that we have correctly apprehended their states of consciousness.

The Third Characteristic of Social Activities.—The third characteristic of social activities is that they are the result of antecedent social activities. They are socially caused. Let the reader pause to see whether he can think of one single activity of his which he performs, one belief which he holds, one definite desire, ambition, or judgment which he cherishes, aside from the mere functioning of his animal organism, which would have been his if he had been the first man or if he had

---

[1] See article by present writer in *American Journal of Sociology,* xi, 623.

lived in such isolation as to be unaware of the antecedent activity of any associate. He would have eaten but not with knife, fork, and spoon, not from dishes, and not the cooked viands of which he now partakes. He would have performed the physical functions; he would have slept and yawned and sneezed, but beyond the functioning of his physical organism scarcely one element in the current of activity which now constitutes his "life" would have been possible to him. He would have ideas but scarcely any idea that he now holds save merely the presentations of sense perception which he has in common with the animals. One's life is not his own, but is his share in the inheritance which comes down from a long social past, in turn to be transmitted, improved or degraded, to his successors. Each social activity is not only prevalent and public, but it is also made possible to each of those among whom it prevails by an antecedent social evolution; it is socially caused.

An apparent exception to the last statement is the original idea or sentiment, and if it were necessary we could afford to modify that statement so as to say that each prevalent activity is socially caused in the case of each individual who performs it except its originator. Even with that modification it would remain true that the activity does not begin to be a prevalent, that is, a social activity, except by the agency of social causation. But we scarcely need make even that modification, for in the mind of its originator the new idea or sentiment as a rule is simply the last step in the path of thought along which evolution has been moving, or a reaction upon a social situation, so that generally speaking the new activity is as truly socially caused in the mind in which it first arises as is its subsequent adoption in the minds of others. The inventor adds a new element to that which the social process brought him, but only by what the social process brought him was his new contribution made possible. The most primitive inventions of savages may have been purely individual reactions of one mind upon the natural physical environment, but such an invention at our stage of development would be of the utmost rarity. The very wants to which inventions minister are for the most part social realities. The third characteristic of social activities then, is that their prevalence is socially caused; that is, it requires the previous activities of associates to make a social activity possible to any of those among whom it prevails, except perhaps its originator, and even to him also, as a rule with negligible exceptions, it would have been impossible but for the previous activities of others.

Relation Between Sociology and Psychology.[1]—The foregoing recognition of the psychic character of the elements of which social realities are composed creates the necessity of stating what is the relation between sociology and psychology.

The relation between sociology and psychology may be compared to that between biology and chemistry. We have already seen that as all biological specimens are made up of chemical elements, and all biological life of chemicophysical action and reaction, so all social realities are made up of psychic elements, and the life of any society is composed of psychic activities. The difference between sociology and psychology can be brought out under two heads:

1. Notwithstanding what ultimate analysis would reveal as to the elements of which they are composed, we do not think of plants and animals as chemical phenomena or of social realities, like a language, a religion, or a political system as psychological phenomena. The truth is that the concrete compounds into which chemical or psychic elements combine differ enormously from the elements as such. Biology and sociology study not elements in their abstractness, but highly complex compounds in their concreteness. Psychology studies certain elemental abstractions from life, a knowledge of which is essential to the understanding of life, but which remain abstractions. Sociology studies life itself.

2. As the chemical elements of living tissue as well as the processes of physiological chemistry are everywhere practically the same, yet flora and fauna vary from place to place, so also psychic phenomena: perception, memory, feeling, atten-

---

[1] A fuller discussion of this topic by the present writer may be found in the *American Journal of Sociology,* xiv, 371.

tion, etc., the abstract elements of life, as well as the processes of neurocerebral functioning, are the same in the twentieth century as in the seventeenth, and the same in Boston as in Bombay, but social phenomena vary enormously from age to age and from place to place, as flora and fauna do. This gives to sociology problems of quite different sort from those of psychology, the problems of describing and explaining these different and changing realities. One way to state the scope of sociology would be to say that sociology aims to describe the differences between the activities of different groups and individuals, to discover the methods of causation by which these differences can be accounted for, to evaluate these differences, and to point out how those differences which, according to the adopted standard, are desirable, can be promoted, and how those which are undesirable can be diminished. This involves investigation which combines into a synthesis of explanation, effects upon human activity of the differing geographic conditions of different countries, of the differing psychophysical conditions, hereditary or acquired, pertaining to different populations and different social classes, and of the differing technic conditions of different peoples and ages, objects of investigation with which the researches of psychology have little or nothing to do. It involves also the ethical problems, which psychology does not handle. Finally it involves the problem of causal relationship between social activities, in which there is an overlapping between psychology and sociology analogous to that between chemistry and biology.

There are no gulfs nor even line fences between the sciences, because there are none in the order of nature which science investigates. The nearest approximation to such a line is between material phenomena and the facts of conscious experience. On each side of that more or less imaginary line lies a group of sciences. One of these groups of sciences contains physics, chemistry, biology, etc., which deal with material phenomena. These sciences are clearly different from each other and their centers of interest are quite wide apart, but at their boundaries they shade into each other so that there are, for example, certain problems that might with equal propriety be assigned either to chemistry or to physics, and others that might with equal propriety be assigned either to chemistry or to physiology. On the other side of that line are the sciences that deal with conscious life of which the fundamental ones are psychology and sociology. These also are clearly distinct and have their centers of interest apart, but like the sciences that deal with material phenomena they shade into each other at the boundaries. On the practical side sociology is related to economics, politics and education, but on the theoretical side the closest kinship of sociology is with psychology and philosophy; with psychology because it carries forward the application of psychological principles as an essential part of the completely synthesized explanation of human life; with philosophy because the best approach to the most inclusive inductive synthesis is the explanation of those phenomena which have the most complex causation, namely the social phenomena, and also because sociology includes the transfer of ethics from the realm of metaphysical speculation to inductive investigation of the rise and spread of valuations, and of the conditions which actually promote or destroy values.

CHAPTER XX

THE ANALYSIS AND CLASSIFICATION OF SOCIAL ACTIVITIES [1]

Tarde, Giddings, DeGreef and Small.—According to Tarde the social life is entirely made up of two kinds of elements; namely, beliefs and desires. He uses these two words in a somewhat peculiar sense. His word beliefs does not refer alone to religious tenets, political creeds, and the like, but to all of the ideas which are held in common by the members of a society. Thus according to Tarde's formula the vocabulary and grammar of a language are sets of beliefs as to the way in which to express one's self, and the methods of the carpenter in making joints and the cobbler in lasting shoes, are beliefs as to the way in which to accomplish the desired results.

To recall the mode of expression used in an earlier paragraph, by "beliefs" he means the entire psychological *income* of society while by "desires" he means the psychological *outgo,* as it is felt by the individual experiencing it. The phase of the psychological outgo which is witnessed by the bystanders is, of course, that which goes to move the muscles in speech and conduct but the phase of it which is felt by the actors is represented by desire. The psychic outgo is like a shield, one side of which is presented to the world—the other side of which rests against our hearts. Tarde names it from the inside and so calls it "desire."

According to Tarde simple social activities (beliefs and desires) unite to form compound social activities, such as customs and institutions. These massive social realities are of six kinds as follows:

[1] Compare an article by the present writer in the *American Journal of Sociology,* xvii, p. 90.

    I   Language
   II   Religion
  III   Government
  IV   Legislation
   V   Economic Usages and Wants
  VI   Morals and Arts [1]

Professor Giddings designates the simple social activities by the words "thought" and "action" instead of Tarde's words "belief" and "desire." "Thought" instead of "belief" is his designation of the *income* half of social activity; and as he names the social *outgo* from the external side of the shield he uses the word "action" instead of Tarde's word "desire." Professor Giddings' classification is as follows:

    I Cultural
        1. Cultural Thought (or "income," corresponding to Tarde's "beliefs")
           a. Linguistic
           b. Esthetic
           c. Religious
           d. Scientific
        2. Cultural Activity (or "outgo," corresponding to Tarde's "desire")
           a. Ceremonial: of manners, dress, and festivities
           b. Games and amusements
           c. Fine arts
           d. Religious exercises
           e. Exploration and research

   II Economic
        1. Economic thought
        2. Economic activity

  III Moral and juristic
        1. Moral and juristic thought, including ideas of private revenge, notions of rights of

---

[1] Exercise: Enumerate the "beliefs" and "desires" included in the composition of Methodism and Republicanism.

property and of marriage, belief in the sacredness and binding force of custom, ideas as to methods of trial, duties of judges, etc.

2. Moral and juristic activity, such as approbation and disapprobation, private revenge, lynching, and tribal trial and execution, and the work of formal courts.

IV Political
   1. Political thought upon matters of policy and method
   2. Political activity

According to DeGreef the classification of social activities, proceeding from the most fundamental and universal to the most ultimate and controlling, should be:

I Economic
II Genetic, relating to love, marriage and the family
III Artistic
IV Beliefs: religions, metaphysics and sciences
V Morals and manners
VI Juridical
VII Political

Professor Small offers a suggestive basis for classification in his doctrine of the six interests. The attempt may be made to classify social activities according to the interest they serve. The interests which Professor Small describes are:

I The *health* interest, meaning that which prompts all seeking of bodily gratifications
II The *wealth* interest
III The *knowledge* interest
IV The *beauty* interest
V The *sociability* interest, including all the desires which are met by relations with our fellows
VI The *rightness* interest

A Further Classification.—The foregoing sketch of the classifications of Tarde and Giddings, together with that which has been said concerning the "in-and-out" of conscious life, illustrates how different observers studying the same reality arrive at similar results, differing in terminology enough to show that they have worked independently, yet agreeing so far as to corroborate each other. It also illustrates how by combining the results of independent workers, nearer and nearer approach to a complete view of reality may be promoted. In dealing with the massive compound social realities, like customs and institutions, it will be convenient to use a fourfold or sixfold or even sevenfold classification, like those just quoted. At the same time, for purposes of scientific investigation, we must also come at the matter more analytically, from the side of the simpler social realities. The first half of scientific investigation, as Wundt teaches, is adequate analysis. The most fundamental division between those simpler and more elementary social activities which are revealed by ultimate analysis is between activities in which the elements of psychic income predominate and activities in which the elements of psychic outgo predominate. But since the outgo is of two sorts, motor and emotional, it is possible to introduce another division, and so to recognize all the facts that have influenced either Tarde or Giddings. Thus we have: (1) the social activities that are composed predominantly of elements of psychic income, the "thoughts" of Giddings and the "beliefs" of Tarde; (2) those in which emotional outgo predominates, the "desires" of Tarde; (3) those in which motor outgo predominates, the "activities" of Giddings. It is thus that we shall now attempt to classify the social activities as first, the *sciences and creeds,* the "thoughts" and "beliefs," the intellectual *income* of society; second, *social sentiments,* or more accurately the social activities in which feeling or emotional outgo predominates; and third, social practices, the arts of life, the objective outgo, the application of the first, that is, of the ideas included in the sciences and creeds to the satisfaction of the demands of the second, that is, of the desires. This form of statement brings out the fact that there

is a certain general correspondence between sociological classification and the psychological analysis, but the correspondence
is only rough and general, and not precise. Psychological
analysis and sociological analysis cannot be made precisely
to correspond, because even simple and elementary social activities are not psychological abstractions, but from the psychologist's point of view are concrete and composite, for they are
not composed exclusively of any one kind of psychic elements.
Thought, feeling, and volition are abstractions which can be
thought of apart but which hardly ever exist apart from
each other. Sociology studies concrete activities as they really
exist, and so more than one kind of psychological element is
pretty certain to be present in a single prevalent social activity
of the simplest kind, just as more than one chemical element
is present in a speck of protoplasm. Thus every "social sentiment" implies and includes the presence of an idea, and all
"social practices" imply and give expression to ideas and sentiments. It is the predominance of feeling or of overt action
over the other psychic elements contained in a social activity
that causes it to be classified as a sentiment or as a practice.

If there were coincidence between psychological and sociological elements then possibly instead of proposing a tripartite
classification we might adhere to the twofold division between,
first, the income of sensations, perceptions, memories of the
same, and their derivatives and combinations which compose
the intellectual life; and second, the outgo which is witnessed
by observers as muscular activity, but is experienced by the
actors as feeling, emotion, desire, and satisfaction. As it
is we see that even the simpler social activities are of three
classes: practical arts which are compounds of ideas and
their motor-emotional outgo; tastes, distastes, approvals, and
disapprovals which are compounds of desires and ideas, in
which the desires predominate; and sciences and creeds which
are the social activities that come nearest to being composed
of one variety of psychological elements.

When we take as units the very great and complex social
realities like Methodism, Republicanism, and the courts, it is
impossible to fit them into even a tripartite classification, for

each one of them is itself a whole bundle of social activities. For these massive social realities we employ a fourfold classification like that of Professor Giddings, or the more extensive ones of Tarde, DeGreef or Small. Only when we analyze them into the constituent activities which they include do we get units which will fit into either of the classifications last discussed.

I. Creeds and Sciences, or Social Ideas.[1]—No absolute division can be made between creeds and sciences. It is a difference of degree, the word "science" implying relatively adequate observation, or relatively clear and logical inference from observed facts, and the word "creed" implying less of observation and logical inference and a more subjective or conceptual origin. Every hypothesis is at first nothing more than a creed. And the most competent scientists hold their teachings in general as "working hypotheses" always subject to the test of further observation. Guessing and speculation give creeds which observation either dispels or else corroborates and so converts into science. On subjects that lie entirely beyond the range of observation only creeds are possible. On all other subjects men have creeds long before they have sciences. Therefore as here used the word "creed" does not refer to religious beliefs alone, but also to all of those ideas about things in general which serve the purpose of science before the advent of science.

An Australian black fellow on a journey, finding that night is approaching while he is still far from his destination, takes a stone or a clod and puts it up as high as he can reach in the fork of a tree to trig the sun. It is not a religious act, it is simply a piece of applied science, or rather manifestation of one of those ideas which precede science, and which serves the purpose of satisfying curiosity or guiding conduct before science comes. The theory that stars are the camp-

---

[1] The following notation is used in this classification:
I. II. III., main divisions;
1. 2. 3., subdivisions;
(a) (b) (c), sections of subdivisions;
(1) (2) (3), sections of sections.

fires of departed ancestors is a bit of prescientific astronomy. Even little children ask hosts of hard questions and if there is no one to answer them truly they invent answers to as many as they can. A population composed entirely of children would in this way gradually accumulate many ideas. All known peoples, including savages, have curiosity or a desire to know, and have also the need of ideas by which to guide and motivate their conduct and they formulate sets of ideas which satisfy these needs. These are what, for want of a better name, I am calling creeds. No people has achieved scientific answers to all of the hard questions about which it desires knowledge, but even the most civilized mingle creeds and sciences, though with respect to many subjects they are gradually replacing the creeds that served them as their first temporary working hypotheses, with more scientific ideas. Creeds, of course, differ in their degrees of rationality, and different objects of interest differ widely in their degrees of accessibility to scientific observation or inference; some must remain permanently in the fringe of inference. There are:

1. CREEDS AND SCIENCES RELATING TO MATERIAL PHENOMENA.

2. CREEDS AND SCIENCES RELATING TO PSYCHIC INCLUDING SOCIAL PHENOMENA.

3. CREEDS AND SCIENCES RELATING TO THAT WHICH IS BELIEVED TO EXIST BEYOND THE SPHERE OF OBSERVATION. "We live in a little island of sense and fact in the midst of an ocean of the unknown." Our finite faculties do not take in the whole of things, but enable us to see what we need to see, as one walking in a mist sees the next step, but not the distant landscape, or as one standing on the beach looks out to sea, and his gaze loses itself in the distance. It may do us good to gaze out to sea. Our knowledge extends a little beyond the sphere of observation by means of inference. We infer the existence of power and intelligence adequate to the origination and continuous causation of such a universe as this.

Among savages, and in all those stages of thought that remotely precede the scientific, the explanations of material things lie, in large part, beyond the limited range of observation, so that thought about material things quickly runs into thought about that which is believed to exist beyond the sphere of observation. This is what Comte called the religious stage of explanation, which he might perhaps better have called the mythological stage. At this stage the explanation of most material phenomena is largely beyond the sphere of the observations that have as yet been made. Hence, creeds of the first, second, and third class tend to coalesce. Thus, the idea of storms at sea as caused by an act of Neptune appears to fall under the head I-1; but the idea of Neptune as ruler of the waters appears to fall under the head I-3. Similar difficulty of classification is found in low stages of biological evolution, but differentiation becomes clearer as evolution advances.

II. **Social Sentiments. Prevalent Activities in Which Feeling Predominates.** 1. Tastes or Likes and Dislikes. The fact that tastes are social products is exhibited by their enormous variation from place to place and age to age, and by the swift changes of fashion.

(a) *Economic wants.* Social phenomena of this class are exemplified by the Esquimaux's demand for furs and sleds, and blubber, and by the American's demand for silks, automobiles and china table-service. The description of contrasting societies must include the enumeration of their diverse economic wants, and the economic progress of society consists largely in the rise and transformation of such wants.

(b) *Artistic tastes.* The artistic tastes of the Greeks were innovations which have become permanent possessions of the western civilization. They were grafted upon tastes that had been developed by antecedent cultures. The tastes of the Egyptians, the Arabs, the Japanese, the Parisians, and no less those of barbarians and savages which are gratified by objects which to us seem flaunting and grotesque, are essential elements in the description of those societies. Their contrariety illustrates the fact that tastes are social products and not instinctive to man as man.

(c) *Likings for plays and recreation.* Examples are the Chinese craze for gambling, the society woman's taste for bridge, and the small boy's springtime longing for marbles. Play may be defined as an activity which is enjoyable enough to be continued with no ulterior aim, and which, if it be mere play, has no ulterior aim beyond the satisfaction found in the activity itself. Many kinds of work may become play; thus hunting, fishing, gardening, carpentry and scientific research are often carried on by persons who are forced to them by no economic necessity, and frequently as a diversion from other employments. The play of children is often an imitation of work. The division between the activity of slaves and that of freemen once made work seem despicable and painful, a curse. For ages the free have shunned work as a sign of inferior social station. But free work is not a curse. Work that is play may be more enjoyable than long continuance in any mere play, because it is enjoyed both for the satisfaction found in the activity and for the hope of its result, as well as for the satisfaction which it yields to the demands of self-respect. On the other hand, work may be painful and not a pleasurable activity, and then it is mere drudgery and toil, unless redeemed by the hope of result either to the worker or to some other for whom he cares, or by the satisfaction of self-respect; these may redeem even toil and pain and make them zestful and joyous, as in the case of the soldier, the mother, the pioneer, and at times in the careers of nearly all who consistently follow a purpose to its accomplishment.

We must distinguish between mere play, work that is at the same time play, and mere work. Under the rigors of a "pain economy" and before the development of efficient technology, the majority of adults had less opportunity for play than they now enjoy, and play was peculiarly the affair of children. This still is true to a degree, especially of mere play, not because adults cannot play but because children cannot work as adults can. Adults also play. The play of children is simple but that of adults is the free play of developed powers. Every free activity that contains in itself a satisfaction sufficient to constitute a motive for its continuance is play. It seems impossible to draw any other valid distinction between play and mere work.

With the definition of play in mind, the enjoyment of art is seen to be a kind of play. Play is not any particular kind of activity, but it is the free play of any or all of our powers; it is by no means confined to muscular activity but includes the activity of emotion, imagination, intellect, and of all our being. The enjoyment of art, literature, science, or sociability, is an emotional or intellectual activity which is largely independent of any motor activity on the part of the person enjoying the pleasure.

There is a universal tendency among all men and the higher animals to find pleasure in the activity of their powers. This is usually but erroneously spoken of as "the play instinct." Far from being a particular, specific instinct, the tendency to play is simply the tendency for live things to act and to take pleasure in action. Stimulated by their environment they begin to function not in any specific way, but in any and all of the ways in which they are adapted to function, and when they begin and continue to act just for the pleasure of action, it is play, whether it be the frisking of lambs, the playing house and store and tag of children, or the golf, fishing, music or reading of grown men or women.

The liking for an art or play is a social element distinct from the technique or practice of it. The technique may easily become dissociated from the taste so as to become no longer play but mere work. Thus a professional player of a game, say baseball or billiards, may have a great mastery of its technique but have thoroughly tired of it, continuing only for the pay or the winnings. The game is then his work, and may be mere work. Again the taste for an art or a game may be dying out though the method of it is still well known, or conversely, the knowledge of an art may be introduced to people who regard it as a curiosity and perhaps an absurdity, having acquired no liking for it, as Americans know the Chinese theater with its frightful orchestral accompaniment, but the taste for it remains a social possession in which they have little or no share. The chief sociological importance of distinguishing between the liking for an art and the practice of it appears in the fact that the taste for an art may be made the common possession of masses of the people, even though its technique necessarily remains the possession of the artist class alone.

Each of these four sets of likes and dislikes is of immense importance in the description of the life of peoples.

(d) *Taste in etiquette and ceremony.*

2. STANDARDS OF SUCCESS AND APPROVAL, OR THE SOCIAL SENTIMENTS THAT ARE FELT TOWARD PERSONS, OR THE TRAITS AND CONDUCT OF PERSONS. Standards of success and approval are ideas defining those objects of desire by the attainment of which the individual measures his own worth and wins the admiration and respect of other members of his group.

In nothing do different societies show more characteristic contrasts than in their standards of success. One society acclaims the member who can drink the most beer, another the member who can write the best poetry, one the member who can boot a pigskin with greatest force and accuracy, another the member who can devise the most brilliant mathematical demonstration. Nations differ widely in the relative value which they attach to the various forms of success. A nation may measure success in skulls, like the head-hunting Malays, in scalps, like the Indians, in flocks like the pastoral nomads, or in dollars, like the more vulgar of Americans. A great society as well as a little one may be on the wrong track as to what constitutes the aim of life. Possibly no other basis of comparison between different peoples is so significant of their character and stage of advancement as a comparison of their standards of success and approval, and no other reform so fundamental as the shifting of the emphasis placed upon the different standards of success in the regard of a people.

In his heart of hearts each individual judges himself by standards derived from the groups large or small, in which he has been a member. He may be proud of his success as a safe-blower or as an incorruptible cashier. Each normal person is impelled by these inner promptings, and by a desire for the respect, esteem, and favor of his fellowmen. Each tends to turn the social judgments which he shares inward upon himself, so that they become his conscience as well as his ambition. For these reasons society can get men of the type that it really admires, in almost any number and almost any degree of development—mighty money grabbers and powerful bosses, or serviceable statesmen, and creative scientists. Progress, not only in the moral character of a people, but also in the direction in which their efforts are exerted, is progress in the prevalent approvals. And the approvals of a people are decidedly changeable. Seventy-five years ago a minister was obliged to resist the hospitality of his parishioners if he wished to return from a round of pastoral visits sober. Another century may witness a similar advance in the conversation and conduct of men in relation to sexual decency. Not only does progress have a main root, if not the tap-root, in changes with respect to social approvals, but so even more especially does degeneracy. Ideas and arts once discovered are not likely to be lost, but standards of approval more easily decay. Among the common standards of success are:

(a) *Physical prowess.* Social groups differ in the estimate which they place upon the manifestation of physical prowess. Among savages it may rank highest of all the forms of success, and it has never been, and one may prophesy that it never will be, lightly estimated by Anglo-Saxons. The approved forms of its manifestation vary from group to group, as our own prize-fighting and football, and as Spanish bull-fighting illustrate.

(b) *Gratification of Appetite and Taste.* The man who is able to gratify his appetites and tastes may have not only that gratification, but with it the gratification of being admired by his associates. In that case he is likely to partake of his gratification publicly and ostentatiously, whereas, if he were a member of a different society which refused to give its admiration upon this ground, or even turned an ascetic condemnation against such gratifications, he would be likely to conceal them and would not have the social satisfaction by which in the former case they were accompanied. New and unusual forms of pleasure are often sought not so much for their own sake as to excite the admiration of those to whom such pleasures are inaccessible, and some men are proud even of the marks of dissipation because they associate with a group which regards them as evidences of success.

(c) *Wealth.* Just as pleasure may be desired not alone for its own sake but also for the social approval which it secures, so too wealth is desired not alone that it may be used but also that it may be displayed. The multimillionaire who continues the eager pursuit of business as a rule does not do so in order that he may have more economic goods to enjoy but in order that he may have a greater success. The tally of life's success is counted by him in dollars, and he will run up as high a score as he can.

For this reason we spend a great deal of our money in order to show that we have it. New inventions spread first not alone because people desire to make use of them, for at first they may not feel the need for a commodity to which they are not yet habituated, but also because people desire to be classed among those who can afford them. This is one element in the immense demand for automobiles; men like to be classed among those who own them. Certain natives of Central Africa, having scarcely any other way of showing wealth save by a rude abundance of food, fatten their wives until they become such monsters of obesity that they can scarcely rise; thus they display their plenty. Next to lavish expenditure, or "conspicuous waste," [1] as a means of displaying wealth has been "conspicuous idleness." The slave, the serf, and the poor man must work, but the rich man in most mammon-worshiping societies has taken pains to make it plain that he did not have to work. With us, although we worship mammon no less, this second form of wealth display has largely gone out of vogue in the case of men, but not in the case of women. This is because of increasing respect for achievement, by men. However, the

---

[1] T. Veblen: Theory of the Leisure Class. Macmillan, 1899, chaps. ii and iii.

type of achievement most admired, is probably the specious one of economic acquisitiveness, admiration of which, as distinguished from economic productiveness, is only one step higher than admiration of sybaritic self-gratification, and as a chief standard of social approval marks a relatively low level of social judgment.

(d) *Power Over Men.* Power over men is acquired and exercised in many ways, and it is enjoyed as a proof of success apart from the results which it may achieve. The tendency for society to admire power over men is so great that it is with difficulty overcome even when the exercise of the power is injurious to society. Conquerors and tyrants are admired, and the exploited admire those by whom they are victimized in some instances more than they do those who attempt to offer them aid. One of the subtler forms of power is personal charm which is exercised by both men and women in every walk of life.

(e) *Sanctity.* This word is here used to designate conformity to religious as distinguished from moral requirements. In the higher manifestations of religion its requirements tend to coalesce with those of morality, but in many, if not most, human societies admiration, respect, and influence have been commanded by strict observance of mere ritualistic requirements. The Hindoo fakir and the medieval saint are examples.

(f) *Achievement.* Happily the forms of achievement are numerous; among others they include the following: (1) domestic efficiency, home-making and child-rearing, have been the form of achievement most open to half the members of the human race. (2) Economic productivity in general is a form of achievement deserving high esteem. There is a distinction between economic productivity, which increases the supply of utilities, and mere "business" which appropriates utilities to an individual owner. Most business, though not all, is more or less productive, but even in productive business success is popularly measured not by its productivity but by its appropriativeness. Admiration and respect for economic achievement in the true sense of productivity is a widely different thing from admiration of economic acquisitiveness or the accumulation of wealth. A society that pays little honor to the organizer or to the inventor as such may honor the successful exploiter of inventions and of the organizing ability of others as the exponent of its chosen form of success. Such a people will admire the man who accumulates wealth by such financial manipulations as could with difficulty be shown to have any productive value, and which expropriate producers of their earnings, while it may not occur to them that improvement in the quantity or quality of useful commodities placed upon the market is in itself an object for ambition or a form of success. This is an abominable social perversion. The true dignity of labor rests upon its value as achievement. It is a great loss for any productive laborer to value his work solely for the wages or profits that it brings. It is his part in the social team play, his work in the world. If horses should cease to be well shod agriculture and traffic would be hampered, and the whole system of civilized life largely disorganized. Carpenters and all those working at "the building trades" make a perfectly inestimable contribution to the maintenance of civilization. Each craftsman and even the machine-tending factory operative administers the product of an age-long evolution, and is an important social functionary. The world needs relatively few "distinguished servants," but it requires millions reliably discharging the vital functions of society. The fidelity and the joy with which work is performed, largely depends upon the worker's attitude toward his task. (3) Scientific and professional achievement. (4) Political achievement. (5) Achievement in literature and art. (6) Military achievement.

(g) *Goodness*. Standards of success are also negatively standards of failure, and standards of disapproval. Goodness is the standard by which moral approval and disapproval are applied. Goodness differs from other standards of success in that society allows the individual to choose between other forms of success, which he will aspire to and which he will neglect, but lays the claims of goodness upon all, and measures all by that standard. Goodness, like other forms of success, is in part a matter of natural endowment, but its achievement requires continuous and protracted endeavor. One is good, the whole outgo of whose life, both the overt outgo which may be called conduct and also the emotional outgo which may be inferred from conduct, corresponds to a personal ideal. A personal ideal is necessarily a complex concept. It is in reality a combination of numerous appreciated traits in their due proportion, none omitted, and each subordinated to the whole. The personal ideals, being social products, vary from one society to another exceedingly, and such group ideals develop gradually. They appear as sentiments of admiration of, and disgust at, personal traits and conduct. What conduct and disposition shall appeal to the sentiments of a group as admirable depends in part upon experience and reason, for the ethical leaders of a people select for approval such traits and such conduct as have been shown by experience to promote individual and social welfare, and mark for condemnation such traits and conduct as tend to undermine individual and social welfare. Individuals differ both in the rational perception of the consequences of conduct, and in the strength of their sentiments of admiration and repugnance for human qualities. The mass of men have a more or less vague sense of the dangerousness of the conduct which they recognize as evil and the promise of good in the conduct which they approve, and more or less strength of sentiment in admiration or detestation of moral qualities. The moral genius is one who is endowed with exceptional strength of these perceptions and sentiments, as the esthetic genius is endowed with exceptional discernment and enthusiasm for beauty, and repugnance for the hideous. The moral genius is endowed not only with strength of sentiment, but also with rational insight into the consequences of conduct which enables him to see what to approve and what to condemn. The growing moral ideal of a society is little by little revealed to it by the folk sense and by the leadership of its moral geniuses. It becomes effective in the social consciousness only as it is embodied in the personality of admired individuals. This embodiment is commonly fractional, not all elements in the ideal being embodied with equal clearness in any single individual.

Moral approvals are as truly social elements socially caused, as tastes, beliefs, or any other type of activity. This is illustrated by the fact that the moral approvals which grow up in the course of social evolution in different societies and which characterize different stages of evolution in the same society, vary so widely. Prevalent sentiment has approved slavery, polygamy, infanticide, human sacrifice, cannibalism, wife-lending as a duty of hospitality, and it would be hard to imagine any act of greater enormity than has been sanctioned by some relatively advanced society. As a rule the moral approvals of each individual are those that have been radiated by the social contacts to which he has been exposed. Of course, when one has been exposed to contradictory radiations an "accommodation" results (modification or displacement of some approvals by others). The approvals which one has as a member of society are those which he turns in upon himself and which become his conscience.

There never has been a society which did not tolerate or approve some conduct that was bad for it. Our own does, particularly in connection with certain amusements. There has been great progress in moral approvals and disapprovals, at the same time there probably is no other point at which change is so likely to be degeneration. This danger results from the fact that approvals, like tastes, are sentiments, and therefore are not bound to the path of progress, as ideas should be, by logical consistency; and though they have a basis in reason, this basis is the rational appeal of results which though great are largely diffused, obscure, and remote, as against the appeal of pleasures that are obvious and immediate.

III. The Arts of Life, Social Practices.—1. THE ARTS AND CRAFTS FOR THE ACQUISITION AND MANIPULATION OF MATERIAL THINGS.

(a) *Extraction*
(b) *Transformation*
(c) *Transportation*
(d) *Personal service*

(e) *Personal aggression.* Crimes and the arts of criminals must be included among socially prevalent activities.

(f) *Exchange*

(g) *Theft*

(h) *Exaction.* By exaction is meant the forcible taking of material goods or services when recognized as morally justified. The exactions of parents upon children, and all taxation of individuals by the state fall here.

(i) *Giving.* Bequests fall under this head, so that all durable property changes hands by this method once in every generation. Aside from bequests, the sums transferred by gifts in this country amount to hundreds of millions annually, mainly support the institutions of religion, largely those of charity, education, and scientific research, and powerfully affect the social welfare.

2. IN THE ACQUISITION AND MANIPULATION OF PSYCHIC POSSESSIONS:

(a) *Methods of Thought and Proof.*[1] (1) Mythology. This earliest stage of intellectual development characterizes all primitive peoples, and also the children of the most advanced peoples. The children of an advanced people are not allowed to remain in this stage because they are taught by adults who have passed beyond it. The principal characteristic of this stage is the inability to reject clear ideas. The tendency of the child is to believe every idea that is clearly formed in the mind. This is not because he is dull but because he knows no conflicting facts which disprove the clear idea. It is not due to stupidity but to lack of data. Heraclitus and Empedocles, with all their intellectual ability naïvely accepted ideas which to us seem absurd because they had not the necessary knowledge with which to test them. Previous knowledge is the touchstone for new ideas and their naïve acceptance is due to lack of the touchstone.

The second characteristic of the mythical method is that it proceeds by analogy. The savage and the child ask many

---

[1] For the sake of putting all the "practical arts" in one class, we must modify at this point our criterion of "predominance of the overt." Here the outgo is from brain-center to brain-center.

hard questions. For the savage there is no one to answer. He has not sufficient data for his problem to enable him to infer the answer from observations which pertain to the matter in hand, and so the mind, restless without some answer, frames one by analogy with those matters concerning which he does have some knowledge. Thus proceeding by analogy he says, for example, that the stars are the campfires of his departed ancestors, and having no knowledge about the actual nature of the stars which is incongruous with this idea and as the idea satisfies the hunger for a reply to the inquiry and is in harmony with the most analogous realities with which he is acquainted, it is not merely adopted by its inventor but also with still greater readiness and certainty by the less inventive minds of his associates.

The mythological method of thought is not an art. It is artlessness. At this stage there does not prevail a social conception and approval of the method employed. The method is not an additional social reality besides the employment of the method. There might, therefore, be question whether it ought to be included here. This primitive method of thought is, however, a distinct and definitely describable fact in the life of the peoples among whom it prevails.

(2) Authority. After a society has answered its hard questions by the mythological method and so has established a traditional body of doctrine, and after it has developed considerable skill in detecting logical inconsistency, it no longer naïvely welcomes new suggestions if they are at variance with the established creeds. Thus it is that the second stage in the development of human thought follows upon the first as a natural and undesigned consequence. This second stage of thought comes to be recognized, approved, and insisted upon and is therefore practiced as the adopted method of procedure. It is the method of deducing ideas from some previously accepted body of teachings which is chosen as the major premise of reasoning, and that not merely by a choice of the individual thinkers but by an established social judgment from which the individual can hardly escape. The prevalence of this method of thought and proof is illustrated by the He-

brews at the time of Christ with their law and tradition, their Torah and Talmud,[1] by Europe during its age of scholasticism, by early protestantism with its "proof-text method," and by China until the present time.

(3) System. The third stage in the development of the art of thinking arrives when the crust of authority has been broken up, but when there is not sufficient knowledge of the objective world to serve as data and tests of thought. The mind is, therefore, set free to speculate. It is equipped with ideas from previous stages of development and with the numerous suggestions of present speculation, and sets out to test which of all those ideas shall be retained and which rejected. The test applied is the demand that ideas shall be congruous with one another. This stage was exemplified by Greek philosophy. Among the Greeks logic became not merely a practical art but also a fascinating game. The defender of an idea was successful in argument provided he could avoid the admission of any idea incongruous with his thesis. By this method, elaborate systems of philosophy or, as Steinmetz says, "philosophic poems" have been built up. The process was to seize upon some fundamental doctrine as a main clue, one that was sufficiently vague to escape collision with known facts, and sufficiently ingenious so that it might conceivably serve as the explanation of problems; then to supplement this main doctrine, when necessary, with other concepts not inconsistent with it nor with each other, which if true would help out the explanation of the problems presented. In this way it was possible to piece together a structure of speculative philosophic explanations more systematic and complete than could be attained, at any rate in that day, by the patient and halting method of science.

(4) Science. The methods of science differ from the previous methods in their greater objectivity, in keeping closer to observable realities, in looking longer and more painstakingly before making a guess and then looking again and again

---

[1] The words "Mishna" and "Gemara," which are the names of the two parts of the Talmud, each mean "a deducing" and indicate the method of drawing out teachings from the previous sacred scriptures.

to test the guess. In this stage the search for descriptions and explanations which are transcripts of objective reality is carried on by the consciously adopted method of detailed observation, inference, and objective test; that is, by the painstaking accumulation of objective data, until they suffice to yield an inference which can be tested by reference to additional objective realities, of such a sort as to confirm the inference if true and to contradict or modify it if erroneous. Science in its earlier stages is unsystematic. It consists of beginnings made at many points of least resistance. But if all realities could be successfully subjected to the scientific method then all the apparent inconsistencies between our fragmentary beginnings of knowledge would be reconciled, for we should at last see all the realities together as they exist together, and they cannot contradict each other. Then all our sciences would have become one science, and that science would be philosophy; not the easy system constructed by speculation, but the positive synthetic philosophy sought by Comte and Spencer. They sought in vain, for the older sciences were far too incomplete, and the last science which investigates the most complex phenomena, the consummation of natural causation, was barely born with them, its phenomena but vaguely conceived by them and by most of their contemporaries even regarded as falling outside the realm of natural causation and so excluded from the system of science. The complete synthetic philosophy will probably always be a dream unrealized, for the circle within which we observe and infer and test our inferences does not bound the universe. But the social facts are within the circle of our observation and are as proper objects of scientific investigation as any facts.

Creeds give way to science first with reference to material things, next with reference to psychic and social realities, and in the realm that lies beyond observation never, save in so far as inference from facts can be built out cantilever-wise into the unknown. Since science is dependent upon observation to suggest and then to test our hypotheses, it naturally comes first where inference is easiest because observation is most facile and abundant, and where the testing of inferences is easiest because there is readiest resort to experiment or comparison. In all these particulars, material phenomena are more accessible to the method of science than are the social and psychic.

Social realities are indeed open to indirect observation, but there is comparatively great difficulty in testing theory by experiment. Instead of experiment social science must rely mainly upon comparison which requires acquaintance with long stretches of time, or with many widely different specimens of social evolutions. The latter, that is, comparison between contrasting social types, is by far the greatest aid to objectivity and the best antidote to bigotry and doctrinalism upon social problems. Social science as such must rely chiefly upon the comparative method.

The most advanced societies are scientific in their treatment of material phenomena, predominantly in the stage of authority and precedent in the social sciences, and systematizers in religion.

Sociology is an intellectual movement resulting from the insistence of the mind that the methods of science shall be carried out in the realm of human activities. Any of the social sciences may become sociological by applying the comparative method with sufficient breadth and thoroughness, in the effort to discover and to test general hypotheses as to the methods of causation which underlie all social life, just as botany or zoölogy or any division of them becomes biology by discovering, exemplifying and testing hypotheses concerning the general principles which underlie equally all forms of organic life.

(b) *Arts of Communication.* (1) Language. Language is a typical social activity, the invention of no individual but the product of social causation and the common possession of entire societies.

(2) Literary and rhetorical arts.

(3) The arts of secrecy and of deception.

The arts of secrecy and deception are not commonly—perhaps not elsewhere—included in such an enumeration as this, but they are social realities and these arts, and the practice of them, are not to be omitted from any complete and truthful analysis of the social situation.

(4)   Arts of communicating across distances; signaling, post, telegraph, telephone.

(5)   Arts for communicating to large numbers, or arts of publicity, the maintenance and utilization of convocations, pulpit, platform, press, exposition, museum, and library.

(6)   Pedagogic arts and practices, parental instruction, the school, arts of self-culture.

(c)   *Fine arts and play, the activities of:* (1) Music; (2) painting; (3) sculpture; (4) architecture; (5) art-crafts; (6) ceremony and etiquette; (7) theater and exhibitions; (8) amateur athletics; (9) games of mind, or mind and chance; (10) outdoor locomotion, as play; (11) primitive industries, as play; (12) gambling; (3) drinking and other drugging; (14) feasting; (15) dancing; (16) social reunion; (17) sex indulgence.

(d)   *Arts of organization and administration.* To elicit diverse activities adapted to specific ends and correlate them into effective systems in which the interrelation of the activities multiplies their effectiveness is among the finest of the practical arts.   There are five spheres of activity in which special arts of organization have been developed, adapted to the special requirements of each :

(1)   Domestic organization.

(2)   Political organization.

(3)   Economic organization. In times of feudalism, serfdom, and such slavery as that of Sparta, economic and political organization are largely identical. Subsequently, the differentiation between political and economic organization has gone far; now, however, there is a movement toward increasing their interrelationship. The enforcement of contracts, the collection of debts, the definition of hours and conditions of labor, and the enforcement of the liabilities of employers, illustrate the relation between economics and government, so also do the definition of weights and measures, the coinage of money, and the inspection of banking, insurance, and trans-

portation. Every corporation is to a considerable degree a public organization.

Organization as an art of manipulating human activities, plays nearly or quite as important a part in economic achievement as do the technic arts and crafts which manipulate material things. This is illustrated in manufacture, transportation, and nearly all modes of economic activity. It is only in the simplest forms of economic activity, particularly in the elementary forms of extractive industry, such as farming and trapping, that the organization of coöperating human activities occupies a place distinctly subordinate to the technic crafts.

The facts of nature almost defy logical classification; in this the facts of sociology do not differ from others. But if the results of classification are uncertain and a makeshift convenience, the process of classifying is one of the greatest aids to exact observation. It is not easy to determine whether convenience and understanding are best served by classifying exchange among the arts for manipulating material things or among the arts of economic organization. If one adopts, as we do, the purpose served as the basis of classification, the arrangement already given is correct. One who tried to base his classification on the nature of the technique of an art would put exchange among the arts of organization and could claim that exchange is an adjustment of psychic realities. The salesman, as truly as the teacher or preacher, is seeking to induce mental states. He wishes to have men make up their minds to accept what he has to offer and to relinquish what they have to give. Is not exchange then a correlation between activities of the parties, and is not promotion of exchanges an act of organization, a manipulation of psychic realities as the method of obtaining possession of material goods? The truth is that the practice of every art includes both psychic and material elements; even language involves the use of vocal organs and air waves, and the telephone employs poles, wires, and batteries. It would seem more scientific to classify with reference to the predominant character of the art itself, rather than with reference to the purpose which it serves, but that would require a classification far less obvious, and far less in accord with popular usage; it would put the telephone and other arts for communicating across distances among the arts with a technique of material manipulation and it would put exchange among the arts of organization.

(4)   Religious organization.

(5)   Organization of public opinion.

Professor Cooley, in his valuable book entitled "Social Organization, a Study of the Larger Mind," showed that what we call public opinion is a correlation or organization of the ideas and sentiments of great numbers of people. The organization of public opinion might be termed the art of organization par excellence. It is true, however, that the shaping of public opinion has been largely an artless and undesigned product of natural causes. But in all developed societies the artful manipulation of it is attempted on a considerable scale. And the art of organizing public opinion would be the consummate application of the science of sociology.[1]

The Fourth Kingdom of Realities.—This bare enumeration of the different kinds of social activities is enough to make us realize that their extent and variety are tremendous. They constitute a fourth great kingdom of natural phenomena which is neither animal, vegetable, nor mineral. A single concrete prevalent social activity, like a language, a science, a religion, slavery, or polygamy, is an objective phenomenon as real and imposing as a mountain range or as a biological species. A single feature in an institution, like trial by jury as a feature of court procedure, or a single item in the political policy of

---

[1] EXERCISE: Name a specimen of each variety of social activity mentioned in the preceding classification. When possible select specimens that are to be found in the community where you are, preferably such as differentiate that community from the surrounding society.

Go about it as a class in botany goes about gathering and classifying the botanical varieties to be found within walking distance of the University. The classification is largely based on quantitative marks; that is, the question of *predominance* of sentiment over the idea that evokes it, or overt practice over the sentiment or idea that guides it. This is unavoidable, since all the elements are usually present in a social activity, and it is concrete social activities and not psychological abstractions that we must classify.

a great people, like the separation of church and state, or the
protective system as it long existed in this country, is a reality
out there in the world with which we have to do, which has
had a long and interesting evolution; and to remove such a
reality is a feat like tunneling the Alps, although unlike the
Alps it is a living thing, a part of the life of the people, and
though it may endure for centuries, and while in full vigor
stubbornly resists change, yet it is not petrified but at the proper
conjunction of conditions will show that it possesses the capacity for change which is characteristic of life. Few have
formed the habit of thinking about these invisible but momentous realities, and for lack of the habit most persons find
some difficulty in the first attempt. Yet these realities are as
truly capable of description and explanation as are the different species of animals or of plants. The ideas that we
may form concerning them are perfectly definite and clear, if
not simple, and the difficulty of thinking clearly about them
rapidly diminishes with familiarity.

CHAPTER XXI

MODES OF VARIATION IN SOCIAL ACTIVITIES

The next step in describing the social realities is to distinguish the modes of variation to which they are subject. We are not speaking of variation from place to place and from one society to another, such as the contrasts between the social activities of Zulus and Esquimaux, but of variations in the activities of the same people or of their children and children's children, and of variations in the same activity of the same people at different stages of development, save as the activity ceases to be the same by the very fact of variation. We are using the word "variation" as the biologist uses that term, to mean, not differences between unrelated or remotely related species, but those filiated changes in a species by which a new variety of the species is formed and a new stage of evolution is reached.

A study of these modes of variation is of the highest scientific importance since these modes of variation may be called the terms in the evolution of social realities. It is of the highest practical importance, for the practical application of any science of life (biology, psychology, or sociology) consists mainly in securing desired and preventing undesired variations in realities the modification of which can be controlled only by understanding the natural tendencies that effect them.

The principal modes of variation in social phenomena are five, of which the fifth has several important subdivisions.

1. Social Phenomena Vary in Prevalence.—Expansions and contractions in the prevalence of social activities are perhaps the simplest form of their variation. The method of this expansion and contraction is the chief subject treated by Professor Tarde in his great book on the "Laws of Imitation." Generally speaking, each new element introduced into a social activity is originated by an individual, and from the originator the innovation spreads. It is indeed possible that a simple and obvious innovation, or one to which previous development had led up so that it is naturally the next step, may occur independently to several minds. In that case we have an instance of multiple origination. But even then the only departure from the ordinary is in the fact that social suggestion, radiation or imitation issues from several centers instead of from one. Multiple origin frequently accounts for the origination of similar activities in independent communities, but it seldom, if ever, suffices to account for any considerable prevalence of an activity in a community. In securing the prevalence of social activities the overwhelmingly predominant factors are social suggestion, sympathetic radiation and imitation. The conditions that limit expansion of prevalence or actually cause its contraction and even bring about the extinction of activities once widely prevalent, are found chiefly in the interference of prevalent activities with each other, which is one of the phases of "accommodation" already discussed, by help of comparison with the interference of spreading circles in the water where stones have fallen.

2. Social Phenomena Vary in Strength.—(a) An idea may be held merely as a fancy, or as a plausible conjecture, or as a working hypothesis, or as an unshaken conviction. Ideas that have been held as convictions may be questioned, fall into doubt, become weakened so as to lose their power to hold a prominent place in attention or to express themselves in overt deeds. An individual may either lose his power or be transformed from weakness into strength by the weakening or strengthening of his dominant convictions; and an age or a people may be full of power because of a general assurance of conviction, or their strength may be dissolved in doubt, or in some departments of their life they may be confident and strong and at the same time in other departments of life be in the uncertainty of transition. This does not depend upon the degree of truth in their ideas, but in the degree of strength with which the ideas are held. Erroneous ideas may be strongly held and may give power to a man or to a society, as religious and political history abundantly illustrate. Erroneous ideas are mischievous and destructive in the long run if they relate to matters of practical experience, but not necessarily so at first, because they may impel in the direction of needed progress and cannot be carried to their full logical expression. Society is prone to err in one direction and then to secure reform by advocating the opposite error or exaggeration. Thus under a despotism, society may profit by the doctrine of anarchism that human nature would blossom into every excellence if all restraints were removed, and in a time of violence and disorder, society may profit by the doctrine of the divine rights and unlimited prerogatives of rulers. Furthermore, ideas that afford consolation and inspiration may be speculatively held concerning matters that are beyond the sphere of observation and experience and have no direct practical consequences save in the minds of the believers. Thus men have been prone freely to draw inspiration from the unknown. But as the advancing boundary of knowledge compels the abandonment of one and another of the beliefs thus speculatively adopted, we are more and more compelled to seek our sustaining and guiding principles from the facts of life which we are at length trying to study with scientific care. If it turns out that we cannot live in the clouds we may build habitations upon the solid rock; if we cannot have the moon and the stars we may gather flowers and fruits and even discover diamonds in the dust.

(b)   A popular taste or sentiment may vary in all degrees from the zero of absolute indifference to the boiling-point of enthusiasm. For illustrations recall the rise and passing of the "bicycle craze" or the "tulip craze" that made a bulb as precious as a diamond, the increase of musical interest in certain American cities, the decay of the power of the ideals of chivalry or of the prestige of "noble" birth, and the immensely increased respect for business success in recent times, the occasional effervescences of patriotic fervor which mark the history of peoples and the alternating periods of widespread religious coldness and of revivalistic fervor which have characterized the religious history of our country.

It is important to distinguish clearly between the two forms of variation thus far mentioned. Variation in strength is by no means to be confused with variation in prevalence. It is true that when all our associates hold a given belief or feel a given sentiment, we tend to hold that belief with firmer conviction or to feel that sentiment with greater zeal. Nevertheless the first disciples of a new belief or sentiment may hold it with far greater strength than the thousands who later become converted to it. And it may hold its own in the number of adherents or even go on extending in prevalence after its strength has greatly declined. Consequently, to measure the social power of a belief or sentiment by the number of professed adherents may be utterly misleading; variations in strength must be recognized as distinct from variations in prevalence.

3. Compound Social Activities Vary in Uniformity.—Just as there is organic variation between the specimens of the same species of animals or plants, so that no two specimens are alike, similarly between prevalent activities of the same kind there is variation. Customs, institutions, and all the more massive prevalent social activities are compounded of various elements of belief, emotion, and expression.[1] Variation in

---

[1] Thus Republicanism has long included a strong sentiment of loyalty to the party name, pride in the names of great leaders from Lincoln to Blaine, and in historic traditions of the sixties, belief in nationalism as against state sovereignty, in the policy of protection versus free trade, in the gold standard for money, in the inviolability of the "rights of private property," in a strong navy and colonial expansion and in representative government as against direct legislation. Recently there has been much diminution of uniformity with reference to the last of these ten items. On the other hand, many other sentiments or ideas have, from time to time, entered into the make-up of Republicanism, either increasing its uniformity and solidity, or diminishing it; for example, belief in the Panama Canal Project, in the civil service merit system, in publicity of campaign funds, in reciprocity, in postal savings-banks, and parcels post; and in the conservation of natural resources, etc.

Methodism, when its uniformity was greatest, included emphasis of the "spirit" versus formalism, in theory, sentiment, and practice, belief in free will versus predestination, in the possibility of falling from grace versus the perseverance of the saints, in a supernatural

some of the included elements may take place without destroying the identity of the activity as a whole. The political ideas and sentiments of two men need not be identical in every respect, in order for the political activity of each, taken as a whole, to be truly identified as Republicanism. Thus the Republicanism of men in Maine, with its desire for a tariff on lumber, is not identical with the Republicanism of men in Missouri. Neither need the religious ideas and sentiments of two men be identical for both to be Methodists. A given kind of activity may at one time be comparatively free from variations and at another time it may vary quite widely and tend to break up into subvarieties. For example, Republicanism in the time of Grant, while by no means without variations, was comparatively uniform, mingled with various moral principles and private interests no doubt, yet the Republicanism itself not only a widely prevalent and strong, but also a highly regular and uniform social activity, as compared with the Republicanism of to-day. Democracy during the same interval has also lost in uniformity, though it has recently gained in prevalence and strength. Methodism, what with the introduction of radical changes in the interpretation of the Bible in the minds of some, while others refuse to accommodate the creed of their forefathers to the progress of knowledge, may have diminished in uniformity at least as much as either Republicanism or Democracy. At the same time we are witnessing the spread and solidification of certain political ideas not the possession of either great party, and of certain religious and moral ideas not the possession of any denomination, which may soon lead to a reorganization of parties with or without change of names and to a progressive amalgamation of religious sects.[1]

---

change of heart, in baptism by immersion or sprinkling according to the conscience of the candidate, the class meeting, the episcopacy, the probation of members, the ban upon "worldly amusements," hell fire, the personal devil, the Trinity, the physical second coming of Christ, the inerrancy of the Scriptures and pride in and loyalty to the sect.

[1] EXERCISE: 1. Analyze great social realities besides Methodism and Republicanism into their component activities. 2. Which components are social ideas, which social sentiments, and which social practices?

4. Compound Social Activities Vary in Content.—Variation in content is the disappearance of some element that has been included in a composite social activity, or the addition of some element not previously included. Each complex social activity is in reality a system of ideas, sentiments and practices, and therefore can suffer the loss of some of its elements or the addition of a new one without losing its identity as a whole. Sometimes the use of and attachment to a given name is the one element in an old system of activity which persists.

Variation in content ordinarily comes gradually and so involves a variation in uniformity till the loss of the disappearing element is complete or till the acceptance of the new element is unanimous. But while variation in content almost necessarily implies variation in degree of uniformity, variation in uniformity by no means implies variation in content. At the end of a period of great variation in uniformity analysis of a complex social reality may find it to include the same elements as at the beginning, there being only a variation in the strength and prevalence of the separate elements with no addition to or subtraction from their number.

Let each line represent a belief, sentiment, a practice included in a composite social activity; some lines break off to

indicate that certain elements in this composite activity do not prevail in all sections of the party, sect, or class that carries on the composite activity as a whole. Some of the lines are a part of the way heavy and a part of the way faint to indicate that certain elements in the composite activity vary in strength in different sections of the party or sect or class. These breaks and shadings indicate variations in uniformity. But the entire disappearance of an included activity indicated by one of these lines, or the addition of a new line would represent a variation in content. If the obliterated idea or sentiment had prevailed throughout the party, sect, or class or the new one came to prevail throughout the party, sect, or class, then the variation in content would bring with it no variation in uniformity.

In applying the statistical method it is highly important to take heed of variations in strength, uniformity, and content and not merely of variations in the prevalence of complex activities, for the units of complex activity tabulated by the statistician, while remaining the same in their general character, may vary so greatly in these subtler ways as to require significant modification or even a reversal of the conclusion based on statistical results.

5. Compound Social Activities Vary in Phase.—Social activities exist in several phases, and it is possible for the same activity to pass through all the principal phases. Thus a fashion may in time become a custom and a mere custom may become an institution. The principal phases of social activity are custom, fashion, rational acceptance, institution, and organization. Custom, fashion, rational acceptance, and institution are due to the addition of certain elements to the content of a compound social activity, which leave the dominant elements in the activity undestroyed but give it a new character, as overtones make the "do" of an organ and of a violin different in character from each other though each is "do." For example, the cremation of the dead in India is mingled with elements of sentiment which make it a custom; but the cremation of the dead for sanitary and economic reasons in an American city has not these overtones and therefore is not a custom and without them could not be a custom however prevalent it might become. Instead it has mingled with it other elements which make it a case of rational acceptance. It is essentially the same act, as middle C is "do" on the organ or on the violin, but it appears in quite different phases because of these different included elements.

(a) Custom. If we take human history as a whole and include in our view the life of savage and barbarous ages and of the savage and barbarous peoples of the present, we shall see that custom has been the overwhelmingly predominant phase of social activity. The word "custom" applies most obviously to overt practice, yet in a sense all beliefs and sentiments as well as practices may become customary. And there is no custom that does not contain ideas and sentiments.

The definition of custom includes at least three parts. The first is an idea, propagated by mass suggestion; the idea of what one has usually or always seen others do, think, and feel upon given occasions is powerfully thrust upon the mind upon the appearance of the appropriate occasion. The second is group expectation. The group has learned to expect that each member upon the appropriate occasion will respond in the customary way, and any other response causes a shock of surprise. The member shares this expectation, consciously or subconsciously, and would be surprised to find himself acting in any other way, and is quite aware that he would surprise his neighbors. The third is the emotional preference due to familiarity. The group, surprised by uncustomary behavior on the part of one of its members, and the member himself assailed by the mere thought of behavior which violates custom, feels a shock not only of surprise but also of displeasure or disgust. We become psychologically adapted to that with which we are familiar. One who leaves home for the first time suffers from homesickness, not because the new surroundings are inferior; they may be vastly superior and the homesickness be all the greater, for it is due not to the inferiority of the new, but to the mere fact of difference from that which is familiar. Likewise the unsophisticated traveler in a foreign country is likely to look with pity and contempt upon what is different from his own land, notwithstanding it may be superior.

This predilection for the customary modes of activity due to preference for the familiar and repugnance to the strange, is ordinarily reënforced by group pride, and by vague fear of the unknown and its possible consequences. The preference for the familiar says, "That is not the way—what a way that is!" Group pride says, "That is not our way, and our way is best, you would not find one of us doing so!" And fear of the unknown says, "Nobody can tell what may come of it."

Custom we see is capable of as precise definition as that of a biological order or class. A custom is the idea [1] of an activity, propagated by suggestion from the already established prevalence of the activity, together with group expectation that the given activity will be enacted upon every appropriate occasion, and emotional preference [2] for the customary activity rather than any substitute for it, due to familiarity, together with the activities which upon occasion give renewed expression to the idea.

Custom-bound epochs. The emotional preference for the familiar and the feeling of shock and disgust at the unfamiliar and unexpected have at most times and in most places had a degree of strength that we little conceive; for we live in an age of innovation and have become accustomed to change, as a tame moor hen can become accustomed to her master's dog from which it is her nature to fly in an agony of terror. The power of custom is by no means obsolete even with us in this most innovating time and country. Does the American man consciously decide whether he shall wear trousers or flowing oriental robes or a Roman toga? No; custom decides that for him; group expectation would be shocked, and established emotional preference outraged by "men in skirts." At most times and places custom has similarly decided nearly all practices, ideas, and sentiments. Established custom makes departure from the customary more or less preposterous. Among savage and barbarous peoples its weight has so com-

---

[1] We in this assembled class have our marriage customs, although there is no wedding in progress; that is to say we have the idea of how a wedding would be conducted if there were occasion to celebrate one.

[2] These are the "overtones." A figure may serve to visualize the idea. Let the heavy line represent the idea of an activity radiated by mass suggestion, and let the thin lines represent the overtones:

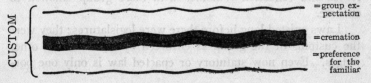

pletely held down individual choice or invention in the types of activity that individuals have had little more to do with deciding for themselves the character of their beliefs, preferences, ambitions, moral approvals, or practical arts, than a daisy or buttercup has in deciding the shape of its leaves or the color of its flowers. Some men among barbarous peoples wax mighty and dominant as some plants grow tall and strong, while others remain stunted, but all according to the customary mode of exercising power. Some men among them have innovated slightly as plants show universal organic variation and occasional sports. But in general the reign of natural causation, through mass suggestion, radiation, and imitation, in the case of savage and barbarous men, has been as little affected by the freedom of individuals as the reign of heredity in plant and animal life is interfered with by mutation. An explanation of the evolution of customary beliefs and activities is a problem of natural science.

The social protoplasm. It may excite some surprise that among the five phases in which social activities appear, custom is the first to be mentioned. Custom is a somewhat ripened phase of social activity. But all of the most primitive peoples that we know are already thoroughly imbedded in custom; and it is from this stage that the earliest visible social progress sets out. Custom has been termed the "social protoplasm," because from it morality, law, and religion have been differentiated. A passing remark must suffice us here, as the process of their differentiation will later be traced.

Morality is in origin that which the *mores* prescribe. It is that approved course of action, any departure from which is strange and abhorrent to the common feeling of the group and feared for its possible consequences. The portions of the requirements of mere custom which become differentiated as morality are those which group judgment based upon experience and reflection combines with mere group emotion to enforce.

Laws existed long before there were legislatures; they were the customs of the group as enforced by chieftains or other judges. Even now statutory or enacted law is only one portion of the law. The "common law" is simply the custom of courts which is treated as being as truly law as statutory enactments.

Religion begins as the customary etiquette and ceremony of dealing with the unseen powers who must be constantly propitiated. It is sometimes said that the whole life of the savage becomes a ritual, because he is always acting as in the presence of powers that must not be offended, but propitiated, and there is a proper way for doing everything so as to keep their favor and all other ways incur their wrath.

The latent power of custom. Custom is present and powerful even when no one is performing the customary act or exhibiting or consciously experiencing the customary thought or emotion. We have our marriage customs, not alone when there is a wedding in progress. Custom is always ready and waiting for the occasion to call it forth, into the foreground of consciousness. Thus all social activities can exist stored and latent in memory, as well as in active consciousness. Custom may even exist on the part of individuals who never in their lives actually fulfill the custom. It is not alone those who have themselves been married who possess, or are possessed, by our marriage customs. This illustrates the meaning of that part of our definition which states that custom is "the idea" of an action. The customs and institutions of a government or religion may exist unimpaired in the minds of the masses even though the functionaries of government or religion are active in violation of the customs; and at such a time custom is likely to be not merely latent in memory, but aroused and active, and that in the minds of those who never have occasion to carry the customary activity into execution, and it will condemn the violation of it and demand the return of obedience to it on the part of its proper executors. Yet custom could never have become custom unless conformity to it on the part of those to whom the occasion for such action was presented had been the rule, and departure from it the glaring exception.

These facts show how superficial and erroneous is the ordinary idea that custom is simply prevalent activity in the sense of overt muscular activity. There are a great many prevalent activities which are not customs, and a custom can exist in the entire absence of any overt manifestation of the customary activity. What is the nature of this tremendous thing that throughout ages has held mankind like living beings imprisoned in an atmosphere but slightly elastic, the power of which remains latent and ready during the intervals when there is no occasion for the customary act, and which when occasion for execution of the customary act presents itself to one member of society, springs into insistence in the minds of all the rest? It is an idea of a certain action, and the idea can exist in the absence of the action; it is an idea radiated by suggestion from the previous prevalence of the given action; it is expectation that the given action will be carried out when the occasion for it arises, and this expectation can exist in the absence of the action; it is an emotional preference for the familiar activity, and repugnance to any departure from it, and the repugnance felt when the custom is not fulfilled is even stronger than the feeling of fitness and satisfaction when it is fulfilled; and it includes as one element the overt activities which upon occasion give expression to the idea, gratify the preference, and meet the expectation.

Custom and habit. Custom is often called social habit, but this is only a figure of speech. The definitions of custom and of habit show them to be totally different things. The essential thing in habit is a modification of the physical organization of the individual due to the repetition of a given activity. Custom involves nothing of the sort. We have marriage customs but no one of us has a habit of being married in any particular way.

However, a custom may lead to the prevalence of a habit. Thus drinking habits are largely due to social customs. Moreover, if we may speak of habits of thought and feeling, then customs in general may establish corresponding habits, the customs of a society thus intrenching themselves in the physical organisms of its members as established cerebroneural tendencies that sometimes seem as strong as inborn instincts and may even be mistaken for instincts.

(b) FASHION. Fashion is in some particulars the opposite of custom. Like custom it is characterized by emotional attitudes (particular overtones) toward a more or less prevalent activity, but they are the opposite emotional attitudes. The central element in custom is preference for the familiar; the central element in fashion is preference for the novel. It is odd but true that opposites may excite similar emotions, and among the most far-reaching tendencies of human nature are the principle of familiarity and the principle of novelty as grounds of preference. Only old activities can be customary, only new or renewed activities can be fashionable. Custom requires that that which is already old shall continue. Fashion demands that each innovation shall soon be succeeded by another novelty. Customs continue long but do not spread afar. So long as custom reigns each province has its own costume, dialect, and modes of conduct. Fashion, on the other hand, continues only a brief time but diffuses itself abroad. The fashions of Paris and London are seen in North Dakota, and the latest song of Broadway is presently sung, and the latest slang of the Bowery talked in San Francisco. Thus customs are long and narrow but fashions short and wide. Or to change the figure: custom has long roots in the past, and, as custom, cannot be transplanted but endures long in its native place, while fashion has but shallow roots and can be transplanted with ease but very soon withers away.

It is not only the pleasure of novelty which prompts the rapid changes of fashion. With reference to a changeable fashion people of the same society at the same time will differ and such differences will afford a superficial mark of classification. Hence a class that desires easy distinction will adopt change for the sake of the distinction secured. And if this class actually has prestige and if other classes are not restrained from imitation, the change adopted will be imitated till the distinction is obliterated or obscured, and the same motive will then prompt the adoption of a new change. Hence fashions must rapidly succeed each other if the fashionable are to keep ahead of their imitators. Doubtless this succession is helped on by business people who profit by the resulting demand for new goods. While custom includes an "overtone" of expectation and desire of conformity, fashion with the originators and leaders of fashion contains an "overtone" of desire for distinction. The tardy followers of fashion would in time convert it into custom, if the fashion-leaders would leave it undisturbed.

Sumptuary laws which prescribe modes of dress and the like, were due to the desire of upper classes to preserve class distinction, and were peculiarly hateful to the spirit of democracy. The tendency to make fashions as expensive as possible is largely due to the desire to make it difficult for the masses to imitate them, and so to render them more serviceable as marks of distinction. That tendency is also due to the desire to display wealth. This is especially the case in an age and country like ours at the present period of its development, in which success is largely measured by wealth. Desire to have things look expensive may pervert esthetic taste.[1] Real beauty is most often found in simple lines. One redeeming feature of a society that is stratified into castes is the relief from pretense and from the struggle to seem to belong to a class above one's own. Struggle to rise is good provided the standard of success is reasonable, but evil if the standards of success are trivial or false.

There has been an immense decline in the extravagance of fashions in the dress of men since the era of ruff and puff and slashings and toes turned up towards the knees. It is not merely because of the abolition of sumptuary laws and the spread of the spirit of democracy. To what then is it due? It is due in part to the diffusion of wealth and the ability even of laborers to wear something better than a smock frock. When the butcher can dress in velvet the lord dresses in tweed and golfing-cap. After that why should the butcher continue to buy velvet? It is due much more to the fact that it has become the custom for men to work, and the business suit is a universal style, while formerly the aristocrat must every-

---

[1] Compare Veblen: Theory of the Leisure Class, chap. vi

where display by his attire the fact that he did not have to work.[1]

Why have not the extravagances of fashion in the dress of women similarly abated? Such extravagance is as natural to the cock as to the hen. Men were not always outdone by women in this form of folly. It seems to be largely because well-to-do women are still an idle class. Frequently they do not even care for their own children, if they have any. They are without any occupation that is worthy of them, and present a pathetic spectacle and a terrific waste of good human powers, their lives worn out with care of servants, social trifling, and hypochondria. And they set the fashions for poorer women. When women fully discover and apply themselves to the real interests and services to which life specially invites them we may see less, not of beauty, but of rapid change and fantastic extravagance, in their dress. There will be more of beauty because fashion is forced more or less to disregard both beauty and comfort in the effort to secure "distinction." It is driven to fantastic extremes in order to make the fact of being in fashion sufficiently noticeable. Another reason why less fashion would mean more beauty is that relative permanence of tastes in dress among a culture-people would allow time for the development and diffusion of real esthetic excellence. The economic wastes of fashion at present are enormous.

Fashion holds sway not only in matters of dress and speech and manners and amusements, that is, in externalities and matters of taste and whim, but also, though less characteristically, in matters of creed, opinion, and conduct. Whenever those who enjoy social prestige adopt any new belief or practice it is likely to be imitated as fashion in dress and speech are imitated, without any rational judgment of the intrinsic worth or reasonableness of the model. Such imitation directly contrasts with that to be discussed under the next head.

---

[1] Veblen: Theory of the Leisure Class, chap. iii.

CHAPTER XXII

MODES OF VARIATION IN SOCIAL ACTIVITIES—RATION-
ALIZED SOCIAL ACTIVITIES

Rational Acceptance.—Customs and fashions do not owe
their prevalence to reasoned approval by the individuals among
whom they prevail. On the other hand a prevalent activity has
entered upon the phase of rational acceptance when its prevalence is due not, as is the case with fashion, to liking for novelty or desire for class distinction nor, as is the case with
custom, to emotional preference for the familiar and to social
suggestion, which as we have seen operates without any regard to the logical quality of the ideas suggested, but when
its prevalence is due to recognition of intrinsic excellence of
the activity.

Certain activities that have prevailed as mere fashions or
customs may stand the test of experience and reflection and
pass into the phase of rational acceptance. Groups with injurious customs tend to die out or lose prestige, and those with
beneficial customs tend to survive, increase, and gain in prestige, so that there is a natural selection among customs which
secures for them a degree of fitness without necessarily involving any rationality in their acceptance by those among
whom they prevail. The fact that a custom is beneficial does
not prove that it has passed into the stage of rational acceptance any more than the harmful custom which survives
beside it.

Tarde called all acceptance of new activity "fashion-imitation," and wrote as if fashion and custom were the only phases
of social activity. In this respect the most famous discussion
of this theme is in error. The rational adoption of a new
activity because of its intrinsic excellence is quite a different
thing from "fashion-imitation." This first error led Tarde to

the second error of announcing it as "an extra-logical law of imitation" that "imitation proceeds from within outward." This means that doctrines are imitated before rites; ideas are imitated before words, phrases, or mannerisms; practical aims are imitated before the mere forms of conduct by which aims are sought and admiration precedes envy.[1]   That is to say, borrowers seize upon the solid inner worth of what can be borrowed, instead of copying external expressions and mannerisms.   This is exactly the reverse of the common idea that imitation is the monkeyish copying of externalities.   The fact is that neither the common idea nor that of Tarde is a whole truth; imitation may be either ideomotor and monkeyish, or rational.   Tarde's "law of imitation" is not true of all imitation.   It is true of rational acceptance.   Most of Tarde's illustrations of his principle that "imitation proceeds from within outward," are cases of inter-group borrowing, not of borrowing from leaders within the same group.   Some inter-group borrowing, like the styles that issue from Paris and London, are cases of mere fashion-imitation, but the more impressive cases of this sort are not fashion-imitation but rational acceptance.   The fact that elements of solid worth in the activities of a people have power to set up new currents of inter-group imitation is not an "extra-logical" or "non-logical" law, but the contrary.   Instead of a non-logical law of fashion-imitation we have here the fact of rational acceptance.   It is the recognition, however reluctant, of intrinsic superiority in the activities of another group that has power to crack the crust of custom and to let in models derived from another population. We must recognize both in inter-group imitation and in intra-group imitation, in addition to fashion and custom, a third phase, namely, logical or rational acceptance.

The facts adduced by Tarde are real, though the universality and extra-logical character of his "law" are unreal.   Rational acceptance of new models is followed by fashion-imitation of the same models, provided the first imitators enjoy such prestige in their own group that an innovation which they in-

---

[1] Gabriel Tarde: Laws of Imitation, translated by Parsons, Holt, 1903, pp. 199 *seq.*

troduce for that reason becomes the fashion. When the king and court or the rich and traveled rationally imitate a foreign model, that model may be expected to become the fashion. After leaders capable of recognizing real excellence have accepted the inner essence of foreign models, "in the spirit of admiration and not of envy," later the rabble may imitate the superficial externals of the same model in the spirit of mere fashion.

Affinity of Certain Kinds of Activity for Certain Phases.—Social activities may be divided into three classes, which in general contrast with each other in respect to the phase into which they most readily fall: (1) tastes and distastes or likes and dislikes are the characteristic field of fashion; (2) sciences and the practical arts for the manipulation of material things are most amenable to logical variation and rational acceptance, and (3) social arts, religious creeds, and standards of ambition and conduct with difficulty escape from the bonds of custom.

The non-logical innovations of fashion are easiest in those activities which we have denominated likes and dislikes including economic wants, artistic tastes, likings for play and recreation, and tastes for etiquette and ceremony because in these, feeling is the chief element, and they are regarded as less fundamentally important than the other division of activities in which feeling predominates, namely, the standards of success and approval. The latter, though they are largely matters of feeling, are not willingly allowed to be matters of caprice or easy alteration, because they are the springs of conduct and there is dread of the harm that might result from change. Even in matters of taste, however, the liking for novelty is not given free rein, though the age be an innovating one, but changes in ceremony, amusements, and dress are often dreaded and repressed. And in a custom-bound age there is little tolerance for innovation in any activities.

The activities which most readily find rational acceptance are the material arts and the sciences. Rational acceptance comes first of all in those practical arts which deal with material things, because those activities are subject to the direct test of success or failure. For this reason their choice is more a matter of judgment and less a matter of mere emotional preference either for the old or for the new. Even successful practical arts may for a time be refused by the power of custom, but new practical arts are more likely than any other form of activity to be the first to break down the power of custom, because their superiority to the old can be demonstrated by immediate results. If many new practical arts are rapidly introduced then a general preference for the new may be established as a competitor with the general preference for the customary. We then get an age of innovation in which men expect to find excellence in the "up to date," "the latest." But it must be borne in mind that an innovating age is a great rarity in human history. Western civilization by reason of the sudden triumphs of applied science has found itself in such an age.

Perhaps it is only in the modern Western world that the crust of custom has been broken up by innovations and discoveries rising from within a society. Custom as a rule has been able to hold down the initiative of a people. It is the inventions of foreigners demonstrating their superiority in war or commerce or literary intercourse that has usually wrought the change in those rare and temporary intervals of progress when custom has given way to innovation. And the progressiveness of our own civilization is due not alone to emancipated and emancipating sciences and their practical applications, but also in part to the universal travel and communication which tends to make all the world one society, brings all ideas into competition, and in the sweeping current of world life refuses to let the provincial stagnation of custom settle down. The awakening of the Orient illustrates the more usual method of the liberation of a people from the incrustation of custom; Japan and now China, convinced by the ships and tools and other products of the West, enter upon an innovating age. In the earlier stages of progress, before science was able by its wonders to convince stubborn custom of the superiority of the new, the periods of progress which alternated with far longer eras of relative stagnation resulted mainly from the collision of groups.

Science is to be classed with practical arts for the control of material things as constituting the characteristic area of logical innovation. This is because science is the exercise of the logical faculties and the fruits of their exercise, and especially because its teachings can usually be subjected to the test of experiment. Rational acceptance comes earlier in the material sciences than in the social sciences, because in the former, hypotheses can more often be tested by experiment (social science relies largely on comparison of instances to replace experiment), and because in the material sciences prejudice and interest are less opposed to progress than in the social sciences.

Last of all to advance to the stage of rational acceptance or rejection and so to yield to innovation are the other provinces of belief, the ethical sentiments and the arts of social organization and control, especially law and religion together with all the subsidiary beliefs, standards of judgment, and arts upon which they are thought most directly to rest. With activities of this class societies dare not experiment rashly, and with respect to them above all others, change is the most stubbornly resisted. By these society controls the conduct of its members; their power to control men rests largely upon the veneration with which they are regarded, and veneration is weakened by changeableness and increased by permanence. Moreover, the control of conduct is society's most vital and most difficult practical problem, with which rash experiment is therefore most dreaded. To tamper with the achieved order is like digging at the dikes. The resistance to change in these props of social order may be thought to be in a sense rational, but it takes the form of resistance to rational test and comparison and insistence that what is established shall be kept, however irrational it may be, merely because it is established. This resistance to change is in fact caution or fear dreading to take a step, and often resembles the child with shut eyes standing on a stone in the brook and refusing to look to see how near the shore is for dread of taking the stride.

We may note one apparent exception to the general rule just stated that practical arts and science are first to yield to rational change and prepare the way for a general acceptance of innovation. Sometimes it has been literature that first broke over the barriers of custom, either because there was great superiority of one people over another in literature at a time when there was no such great advancement in science or in economic arts as to command foreign imitation; or because literature appealed to a class that had prestige enough to introduce innovations while the higher strata of society took little heed of technic arts; or else because books are easily transported across the boundaries that separate peoples; or for a combination of these reasons. Such an instance occurred at the time of the renaissance in the fifteenth century when the poetry of Italy invaded other European lands, and again when in the sixteenth century the literature of Spain invaded France, and once more when in the seventeenth century, through the agency of Frederick the Great and his court, the literature of France opened the way for French fashions in Germany.[1] Literature gives guarantees of its own superiority which indeed are far less convincing to the minds of the masses than those which secure the acceptance of a successful practical irt, but which convince with sufficient certainty those who are prepared to appreciate the excellencies of literature. And when it is the king and the court who adopt foreign literature and foreign ways, their prestige suffices to secure the adoption of the same by humble folk. Thus aristocracies, though conservative in political, religious, and economic matters, have repeatedly served the cause of progress by the introduction of cultural reforms.

Culture Peoples and Nature Peoples.—A society, the activities of which as a whole have reached the phase of rational acceptance, may be designated a culture people.

According to Professor Vierkandt the distinction between "nature people" and "culture people" is more fundamental and important than the common division between the savage, the barbarous and the civilized. Nature peoples, says that writer, are those among whom the development and permanence of customs is a matter of natural causation very little compli-

---

[1] Tarde: Laws of Imitation, *loc. cit.*

cated by any element of design. Each rising generation adopts the prevailing beliefs, sentiments, and practices as a matter of course.

Even after the process of social evolution, by natural reactions between human organisms and their environment, has developed a complex civilization, it is possible for the individual to be a nature man in the sense defined, wearing such clothes, speaking such language, pursuing such a calling, holding such religious, political, and ethical ideas and sentiments as his social contacts have afforded him and as he has uncritically imbibed. The familiar figure who is a Republican because his father was, and a Presbyterian because his mother was, and whose whole equipment of prejudices has been acquired as a result of social causes and not of intelligent choice, Professor Vierkandt would call a nature man, that is, a product of natural causation.

Culture peoples, the same authority says, are those who, having become acquainted with a number of models, select their ideas, sentiments and practices as a result of the exercise of free, critical intelligence. Nature peoples adopt their ideas, sentiments and practices because of causes; culture peoples adopt theirs by reason of reasons. Being affected by causes is widely different from being influenced by reasons.

Among a culture people not only do individuals become individuals indeed by the emancipation of their activities from non-logical social domination, but also the general current of social progress is in some degree understood and guided by the general intelligence, and in this resembles more the growth of cultivated fields where civilized men reap harvests, and less the wilds in which savages gather roots and berries. The process is no less natural than before, but the individual factors have become so evolved that they as well as the mass factors are causally significant, the idea of individual freedom has been grasped and approved, and the social activities have become so differentiated that variety of combination in individual consciousness is invited and new structures of mass activity are no longer impracticable.

Peoples acquire their cultural freedom first with reference

to economic arts, and next with reference to material sciences in the order already discussed. The advanced nations of to-day Vierkandt describes as half-culture peoples, the great majority of their population being still nature men with reference to these activities in which rational acceptance is more tardily developed. They may have escaped entirely from the mythological method but on psychological, social, and religious subjects they still alternate between the authoritative, and the systematizing method.

Although there is as yet no great society in which the population as a whole and with reference to their activities as a whole can be said to have reached the stage of rational eclecticism and to have become a "culture people," yet there is an increasing number of individuals whose lives are thus guided.

Institutions.—An institution is the idea of a set of overt activities together with a twofold judgment lodged in the popular mind; namely, a judgment that the result which the institutionalized activities attain is necessary or greatly to be desired and that the given activities are so well adapted to securing that result that they should be prized, defended, perpetuated and, if need be, enforced. Of course the overt practice of the institutional activities upon proper occasions is implied in this definition; however, the institution does not cease to exist in the intervals between the occasions of its overt exercise. Briefly and with perhaps sufficient accuracy for most purposes, an institution is a set of activities which a society adopts as its deliberately accepted method of attaining a deliberately approved end. Often institutionalized activities require a special personnel for their execution, and most writers would include this in their definition. The inclusion or exclusion of this element in the definition may be left to the reader. We must call to mind such institutions as the institution of private property and of monogamous marriage which prescribe modes of activity in which any member of society may engage, only insisting that if he does engage in them he should follow the institutionalized methods. If there were any fear that not enough would engage in them of their own accord society might appoint a special personnel for the execution of any set of institutionalized activities.

Institutions are compound social activities which contain a rational element, as customs as such do not.[1] Yet a people may have institutions long before it reaches the stage of rational eclecticism; that is, it may have institutions without having rationally chosen its institutions from among a variety of conflicting suggestions. The "age of discussion" may not have dawned. Institutions have most often and most typically developed from customs. The customs were formed without rational judgment having been passed upon them by the mass of those who practiced them. But at length the mass had an intellectual reaction upon their customs which converted some of those customs into institutions.[2]

An institution shows its difference from a mere custom, in that variation from an institution is opposed not merely because of emotional preference for the familiar and resentment against the strange, but because of a practical judgment of the utility of the cherished practice. In fact while custom insists on conformity for the sake of conformity and resists

---

[1] Developing the figure that was used to illustrate custom we have:

AN INSTITUTION

Rational approval of the effects of the activities

Group expectation

Idea of specific activities radiated by mass suggestion

Preference for the familiar

Rational approval of the special fitness of the activities to secure the approved results

All these elements must exist, not merely in the minds of a few, but in the minds of the many.

[2] Professor Sumner calls mere customs "folkways," and customs upon which an intellectual reaction of the group has passed deliberate approval he calls "mores," a word which has the same root as "morals," "Folkways," page 30. However, page 59, foot, he quotes with approval another author in applying the word "mores" to mere customs, and offers this usage as a "more exact definition of the mores." On the relation between institutions and mores compare pages 53 and 56.

all change, an institution, valuing conformity for its usefulness, may welcome change which promises to enhance its
utility. Therefore, to institutionalize an activity which has
previously prevailed without being an institution may be to
open the door for its reconstruction. The formation in the
public mind of a rational judgment concerning the practical importance of a set of activities and their adaptation to
produce desirable results may prepare for the intelligent transformation of those activities. Thus such judgments as would
institutionalize the theater [1] in America, if they should become
prevalent in the public mind, would largely transform it.

A family, a school, or a business concern may have its
own institutions, but in practice the name institution refers to
the activities of a population, with the same implications of
extent which the word "population" carries. The definition
of a population as a number of people who occupy the same
area, or are together in time and space, applies to small as
well as to large groups. There is no precise rule by which to
determine how large a group must be before it can be called
a population, or its activities can be called institutions; but
usage practically confines the words population and institution
to large groups.

Institutions usually receive the sanction of law and sovereignty, and some great writers define an institution as a public
activity which is governmentally sanctioned and maintained.
But when we study the origin of institutions in the light of
the practices of savage and barbarous peoples, it does not appear that religion, the family, or the institution of property
owed their institutional character to governmental action;
certainly government itself did not. It appears rather that
the institutions had independent origin and were institutions
by virtue of judgments enacted by the public mind and not

---

[1] The theater is a taste and an art, but it has not universally and
distinctly the overtones of either fashion or custom. Adequate intelligence would make it an institution. That does not necessarily mean
that it would receive governmental support any more than the church
does in this country; it means that it would be prized and controlled
by public judgment and not merely by a taste, and that public taste
would be deliberately educated.

by legislators or rulers. The institutions of a conquered
people may survive without governmental support and even
in spite of governmental persecution; for example, the Protestantism of a people conquered by a Catholic invader, or the
domestic and religious institutions of an Asiatic dependency
of Great Britain. Apparently the institutions of a people have
their rise independently of government, and their power to
survive without the aid of government; the relation between
government and the other institutions of a people is merely
one of correlation such as must exist between the dominant
factors in one system of social order. It is just as true that
government is shaped by the other institutions of a people
as that the other institutions are shaped by the government.[1]
A public activity becomes an institution by virtue of psychic
elements, overtones contained within the institutional activity
itself, and not by virtue of any external power or influence
political or otherwise.

It is not necessary that all of the population having an
institution should engage in the sociophysical activities that
give it expression and effect; it is only necessary that the mass
have the idea of this overt activity together with a rational
judgment of its utility, as above described. This psychic
activity on the part of the people as a whole together with,
but even more than, the corresponding overt acts performed
when occasion demands, is the institution. Thus it is that the
Pilgrims in the *Mayflower* could bring with them institutions
which on the *Mayflower* were not in exercise, just as they
brought marriage customs which were not then in exercise.

Thus it is that political institutions are the possession of
all free citizens and not of the rulers alone, while the tyranny
of a conqueror is not an institution of the conquered and the
social constitution of a people is no mere written document
but a tough and gigantic reality existing in the minds of the

---

[1] DeGreef teaches that progress in the development of political
institutions rests causally upon progress of all other institutions, much
as the last science in the hierarchy depends upon those preceding. Introduction à la sociologie, Rivière et Cie, Paris, 1911, tome i, chapitre
vii.

people. Those pyschic realities which we call institutions are to society what sills and timbers are to a house, or what pillars, trusses, and girders of steel are to a towering office building. There is this difference, that they are alive, like the bones of a man, liable indeed to disease, decay, disintegration, but capable of growth and change without destruction, though not without pains, and only as they grow and change can they escape dry-rot and crumbling ruin.

Naturally those activities first become institutionalized which seem to the people concerned to have the greatest practical importance. The most conspicuous varieties of institutions are five: (1) domestic institutions; (2) religious institutions; (3) economic institutions; (4) governmental institutions; (5) institutions for the organization of public opinion and sentiment, especially the school and the press.

This is far from meaning that all political, religious, educational, domestic, or economic activity is institutional. There are for example, practices of ward heelers that are neither generally prized nor generally understood, and among economic, religious, domestic, and cultural activities there is much that does not rise to institutional dignity.

Organization.—Most institutional activities become organized, but by no means all organizations are institutions; on the contrary, non-institutional organizations are numberless. An organization is a set of differentiated activities serving a common purpose and so correlated that the effectiveness of each is increased by its relation to the rest.

It would be less accurate to say that an organization is a set of people carrying on such activities, for it is those activities that constitute the essence of the organization; the participation of each person in the activity of a given organization is ordinarily a small fraction of his activity as a whole, and a definition should specify just what is included in the concept defined, neither more nor less, and that in the present case is just the particular activities which are intentionally correlated in the service of a single aim. It is true the activities could not exist without the people, and for that very reason the thought of the activities sufficiently includes the thought of the people. It is these purposefully correlated activities of the people that constitute the fact of organization.

The concept of an organization includes three ideas. (1) The activities united must be different. The activities of a company of men all doing the same thing, rushing against a door, pulling a rope, or yelling without a leader, cannot be said to constitute an organization, but the moment one of them ceases merely to do as the rest do and begins to direct the efforts of the others, though the same people are present, there is such a change in their activities that organization begins. The change consists essentially in this, that differentiation and correlation of activities are introduced. (2) Correlation is the second element in organization, such correlation that the effectiveness of each kind of activity included in the organization is increased by its relation to the rest. (3) Third, this correlation and heightened efficiency of differentiated activities must be in the service of a common end. Perhaps the simplest illustration of organization is the work of two men lifting a weight, say, a stone or a box. Their work must be differentiated to the extent that they take hold so as to balance the stone and then one signals to the other what to do, if only by beginning the task in such a way as to show what must be done in order to coöperate. A higher exemplification of organization is shown by the work of a section gang and its boss on the railroad, who may be the men handling the stone, and a still higher one if we see the work of the section gang as correlated with that of the track inspector and all the officers of the division of "maintenance of way and structure" and the work of that division as correlated with that of the other divisions of the "operating department" and the latter with the "traffic department," the "auditing department," and all the differentiated and highly correlated activities which together constitute a railroad organization.[1]

---

[1] EXERCISE: Name other organizations and the differentiated and correlated activities of which they are composed.

CHAPTER XXIII

NATURAL SOCIAL ORDER

The differentiation and correlation of social activities which make them into one organization may be either intentional, and in that sense artificial, or they may be the undesigned result of natural evolution.[1] In general the different activities carried on by the same population become so correlated as to secure in some imperfect degree the ends which they may have in common, and this without the necessity of any plan of correlation, simply because activities that conflict with each other so as to refuse utterly to become correlated tend to inhibit and exterminate each other, and irreconcilable activities might even put an end to the life of the group.

This is an exemplification of a universal law of nature. All phenomena inorganic and organic which permanently exist together tend to become accommodated to each other, each yielding what it must to the rest, and establishing a more or less harmonious *status quo* or *modus vivendi*. This is inevitable, since concomitants affect or condition each other; some being affected to the extreme of extermination disappear, those which continue together being so modified as to allow the continuance of all that survive. This is the most universal generalization of science, continuation is secured by accommodation and correlation. From inorganic matter, through all the forms of life, including the social process, all phenomena by virtue of their mutual conditioning tend to a correlation which is the method of the continuance of such as survive or remain. Thus the activities of a permanent group tend to form into a natural system before they reach the institutional stage and without the presence of any "arts of organization."

---

[1] It is important at this point to call to mind the facts stated earlier, under the heading Accommodation, p. 333.

The distinction between artificial organization and natural social order is the main subject of discussion in Professor Tönnies' Book entitled "Gemeinschaft und Gesellschaft," [1] words quite imperfectly translated "Community and Society." The family, according to Tönnies, is the original and typical natural social unity, and next the expanded family or clan. The *Gemeinschaft,* or community, he says, is "real and organic"; the *Gesellschaft,* or society, is mechanical and optional: the former is exclusive, a person belonging to but one family or natural society of a given kind, while one may enter numerous schools or corporations or other artificial societies; the former is ancient, the latter are recent; the former permanent, the latter evanescent; the former natural and undesigned, the latter artificial.

As blind customs in a later phase of development change into self-conscious and judiciously progressive institutions, so natural social order tends to become purposeful organization, the differentiation of activities being no longer wholly due to the unplanned reactions of human organisms to their physical and social environment, nor the correlation of activities due to mere mutual inhibition and natural selection, but to intelligent design.

The products of human intention and of artificial selection are grafted on to the natural growth of undesigned social causation.   But even the members of the most advanced of great populations carry on their activities in a completeness of correlation that as a whole is undesigned and by most of the associates only dimly apprehended.

By the aid of the printing press, the post, and the telegraph it becomes possible to form into one self-conscious and purposeful organization the political activities of a population numbering millions and spread over thousands of miles of latitude and longitude.   The most statesman-like minds are able with some degree of adequacy to grasp as correlated elements in a single organization, not only the political activities but all of the institutionalized activities of such a population, economic, religious, cultural.   And the aim of science

---

[1] Leipzig, 1887.

is to see all those, together with the mass of other activities, not institutionalized but prevalent, which are interwoven in the streaming process of a people's life, in their interdependence, so that the direction and character of the effect produced by each upon the rest can be approximately known, and also the way in which each in its turn is modified by all the rest. How far this complex totality of social life can be shaped by design can be known only by first learning how it is shaped by nature and how far the conditions that determine its natural course are subject to intelligent control by man.

Static and Dynamic.—In the science of physics the word "static" is used to describe a situation in which there is no movement. Such a situation is maintained by a combination of stresses and forces which are in equilibrium. The word dynamic is used to describe a situation in which motion takes place. A static situation may be transformed into a dynamic situation by bringing to bear a new force, by increasing one of the forces which were in equilibrium so as to break down resistance, or by weakening one of the forces or stresses until it is overcome by one which it had previously held in equilibrium. Thus a static situation in which weight is sustained may become dynamic by the addition of an impetus from without, by increase of the weight, or by diminution of the stress which had upheld the weight. The earliest sociologists borrowed from physics the terms "static" and "dynamic" and carried the comparison between social and physical phenomena so far that by Comte and Quetelet the phrase "social physics" was used as a synonym for sociology. These sociologists employed the term "static" to describe a situation of established or stationary social order, and the problem of social statics was to point out the conditions which maintain such a state of order. The term "dynamic" they used to describe a social situation which was undergoing progress or transformation, and the problem of dynamic sociology was to point out the factors or conditions which caused these social changes.

These two sets of problems are not so different as they may at first appear, because the same kinds of conditions operate in both, although in different degrees and combinations.

Moreover, it is very especially to be noticed that even a social situation which is described as static is composed of nothing stationary, motionless, rigid, dead, but is a system of activities. This is contrary to the natural implication of the words "dynamic" and "static," especially when we remember that dynamic means revealing the presence of power. Social activities may go on with quite as much power when most unchanging, as when they are in a state of transition. In a static situation the activities of a people are regular and constant. They consist of firm beliefs, generally accepted judgments, inviolate customs, and established institutions; and the tide of the people's life may flow on with quite as much power as in an era of transition which would be described as dynamic. Indeed as in physics a static situation may become dynamic by weakening a support, so a dynamic era may be introduced in society by the weakening and undermining of settled beliefs, the breakdown of established customs, and the wavering of public sentiments, and the life of the people may not regain its full power until the changes have been for the most part accomplished and society is ready to enter again upon an era of established order. The life of society, both when changing and when most constant, is a dynamic phenomenon in the sense that its substance is power, it is activity, it is life.

The problem of change in social activities and in the orderly systems into which they unite is of the utmost importance both scientifically and practically, for it is the problem of past evolution and of future progress. And the modes of variation in social phenomena which have just been enumerated are terms in this process of social change. At the same time the "social order" above described, including within itself unplanned customs, institutions, and organizations, together with the engrafted products of design, is the biggest social reality that we can contemplate; and for welfare, order may be as important as progress. We may recall that the life of society is process, both in its being and in its becoming. The words "static" and "dynamic" somewhat obscure this truth; we shall not employ them, but define their use in sociology because it prevails with many writers and has done so from the time of Comte. The static and dynamic problems, when considered from the viewpoint of practical endeavor, may better be termed the problems of order and of progress.

The Radical and Conservative Principles.—In any given social situation the conditions which tend to strengthen and maintain the existing order and those which tend to induce change are set in contrast. Among the conditions which universally promote or hinder the modes of variation just enumerated, there are certain traits of temperament (psychophysical conditions) which are believed directly to promote change while others conserve stability. The bold and sanguine temperament is radical, while the cautious and still more the timid temperament is conservative. The active katabolic temperament is radical, while the ease-loving and phlegmatic temperament is conservative. Further, and still more important, the interests of those who in any given situation find themselves well fixed prompt them to exert themselves to keep the situation fixed as it is, while the discontented classes are prone to desire change sometimes for the mere sake of change; that is, without due regard to the question whether the change gives reasonable promise of improvement or is mere destruction. These differences of interest are at bottom mainly differences in the distribution of wealth or of honor and opportunity; that is, in the technic or social conditions, which society has itself produced and which society may change. These qualities of temperament and interest together constitute what are called the principles of radicalism and conservatism which are continually at war in society. They are, however, nothing more nor less than conditions of activity, physiological, technic, or social, which regularly tend in the one case to induce change, in the other to resist it.

The phases of social activity are to be contrasted in this connection. Fashion and rational acceptance are phases of activity which are favorable to change; while custom and institution are phases of activity which resist change and preserve order. Both social change and permanence have their logical and non-logical phases. Fashion is emotional or non-logical change and logical acceptance of innovation in reasoned change. Custom is emotional or non-logical stability and order, while institutions are logical stability and order. Social welfare implies less of the unreasoning rigidity of custom and more of the stable but not inflexible order of institutions and organizations, together with less of the wasteful and destructive variations of fashion and far more of logical acceptance of innovation.

Since the well-fixed—the rich and the powerful—tend to conservatism, conservatism has advantage over radicalism in power. The rich, the influential, those who mold opinion and enjoy prestige, who now own great newspapers and who once commanded armed retainers, are mostly conservative. "The respectable classes" have usually been conservative, and in general it has been decidedly "bad form" to be otherwise.

Persons affected by the contrasting conditions of temperament and interest which produce conservatism and progressiveness are as a rule more or less uncongenial to each other. But it should be remembered that radicalism and conservatism are in themselves equally mere natural consequences of causes, and one may be just as moral or non-moral as the other; and also that the conservative principle is as necessary to society as friction and gravity to a locomotive, which must indeed have steam or it will not run, but which without gravity will fly the track at the first curve, while without friction its wheels would fly around without moving the engine forward a foot. There is no advantage in change merely as change, and while "we can have order without progress we cannot have progress without order." There is, however, a vicarious radicalism which is worthy of honor and admiration; it is the interest of the well-to-do in bettering the condition of the less fortunate, the fidelity of the individual to his group, and the interest of those who live in the present in preparing a happier future for those who come after them; it is the public spirit that is loyal to the coöperative enterprise of progress.

Up to this point we have had a great deal to say about social activities, about the conditions by which they are molded, the elements into which they may be analyzed, the kinds into which they may be classified, the variations to which they are subject and the accommodations and correlations which are established among them, but as yet we have not asked and answered the question: What is a society? It would have been impracticable at the start to give to that question an answer that would have added much to our knowledge, but we are now ready to attack it.

The First Characteristic of a Society.—The first characteristic of a society is that its members have some important activity in common such as a common language, a common creed, or some common practical aim and common activities by which their common aim is pursued. It is sometimes said that among a company of savages the similarity of activities goes so far that there are practically no variations except those directly due to bodily differences. Some of the clan are men, some are women, some old, some in their prime, and some children, some more and some less endowed with cunning and strength; but save as these bodily differences cause divergences their activities are alike, they have the same superstitions, the same prejudices and enmities, the same desires, the same practices, their streams of consciousness are composed of similar elements; notwithstanding these elemental activities may be very different from those prevailing among any other race of savages. Each child born into the clan, as it grows up, inevitably acquires the beliefs, desires, and practices of the group. Thus Professor Fairbanks defined a society as "a group of persons sharing a common life."

In a highly developed nation there are different creeds seeking adherents and different sentiments radiating from old to young and from leaders to followers, and there is no complete uniformity of activities among its members, but the members of every society have some mode of activity in common; otherwise they would not be a society at all.

In an advanced civilization each individual may belong to many societies. And while a great population, like that of the United States, is unified into one society by some common interests or sentiments or ideas, it is also subdivided into many minor ones. Each individual member could probably find upon examination that those of his ideas, sentiments, or practices which he does not share with the entire population he does nevertheless share with a considerable number of other persons so that while he held certain sentiments and interests in common with all the citizens of this great republic with whom he forms one vast society, he also held other ideas and practices which he shared only with other Methodists or other Republicans, with whom he was united into other and smaller societies; that in fact he belonged to numerous societies each characterized by some common activities, down to the choral union, or Browning club, or Turnverein.

The Second Characteristic of a Society.—The second characteristic of a society is that the activities of its members causally condition each other. The similarity of their activities is not due merely to the inherent tendencies of human nature. A comparative study of different societies reveals the fact that despite the kinship of all mankind which makes "human nature much the same the world over," the beliefs, the tastes, sentiments, moral standards, and practical arts of different peoples vary as widely as different species of animals and plants. This is because the different tribes of man have had different social evolution and so have developed different languages, superstitions, creeds, tastes, wants, ambitions, and moral codes which each tribe confers upon its own members. Thus the similarities which prevail among people of the same group are mainly due to the effect produced by the members of the group upon each other. Each generation passes on its own type of social life to its successors, though modified by a gradual process of evolution. Not merely are we all molded during the "plastic" years of childhood, but throughout life our activities are repressed or elicited or directed by the past, present, and anticipated activities of our associates. A society is bound together not only by the relation of similarity but also by the causal relation. The unraveling of the social causation in which the activities of associates mutually condition each other is a main task of sociology.

The Third Characteristic of a Society.—The third characteristic of a society is intercommunication. It might have been called the first characteristic for upon it depends the mutual causation of social activities, and upon their mutual causation depends their similarity. Yet by itself communication reveals less than either of the others, the essential nature of society; it might perhaps even be omitted as having been already sufficiently implied in "mutual causation." The mention of a third item, however, enables us to see how the three characteristics of a society correspond to the three characteristics of social activity, thus:

The characteristics of social activity are:	The characteristics of society are:
Manifestation	Intercommunication
Social causation	Mutual causation
Prevalence	Similarity of Activities

By intercommunication the activities of one member of society are known to others, those of some prominent leaders are known to many, those of the obscure are known to a few, the activities of each are known to some, though perhaps those of none are known to all; acquaintance radiates from each to others, and from each of those to others still, making a network of intercommunication. In small societies the line of acquaintance may pass back and forth in both directions from each to each, each knowing and being known by all. In a larger society the prominent are known to many whom they do not know. By communication all the members of a society are wrought into a unity, notwithstanding that, as a rule, each communicates with but a small fraction of the rest, as a coat of chain mail is a unity though each link is locked with but few other links.

Population and Society.—The condition most favorable to communication or knowledge of another's activities exists when associates are together in time and space. Yet mere togetherness in time and space is not of itself enough to make the people who are together a society; it is only a condition favorable to the existence of society and not the essence of society. The essence of society is common, correlated, and mutually conditioning activity. A citizen of New York or Boston may be in closer association with the members of the same scientific or business circle who reside in Berlin, Paris or London than with his neighbors two blocks away in the Ghetto or little Italy. If a Turk, a Zulu, a Hindoo, a Negrito, a Parisian, and other previously unrelated people could suddenly be assembled in one place at a world's fair, or on an ocean liner, they would not at first be a society, although they might in time become one. If by the waving of a magic wand some existing society could suddenly be transformed like the people at Babel so that they should have no common language, no common ideas, beliefs, desires or practices, derived from a common social past, then mere togetherness in space and time would not make them a society, though if they remained together they might in time once more become one.

It is necessary to emphasize this because many writers have thought that grouping in space and time was the very essence of society, instead of being merely a condition favorable to the establishment and maintenance of society. People who are together in space and time constitute a population. We might perhaps as properly speak of the population of a room as of a country, though we commonly reserve the word to designate a large number who are permanently together in space and time. A permanent population will become a society, for togetherness in space and time is a condition as favorable to associative activity as milk is to the growth of bacteria. Milk and bacteria are not the same thing; it is conceivable that milk should remain without bacteria. In fact some milk in Paris, which was drawn and bottled under the direction of Pasteur, is said to be still sweet after the lapse of many years. But just as the conditions must be very unusual indeed to prevent milk from swarming with bacteria after a few hours, so must they be very unusual indeed to prevent people who are together from engaging in social activities and so becoming a society, for presence is the culture condition of society.

The fact that togetherness in space and time is only the condition favorable to society and not of the essence of society itself is clear enough after we get an adequate conception of what society really is; it is only by way of a help toward this adequate conception that we have pointed out the fact that such togetherness may conceivably exist for a time without generating a society. To this we may even add the fact that society may continue without such togetherness. The society of letters is more than a figure of speech, and it is not conditioned by space, and hardly by time. Professor Tarde says that a Frenchman at the antipodes is a Frenchman still. His daily thoughts are products of a French past, and if the mails bear him papers and letters and return his own messages he is still influenced by French life and may himself be a force in French society of which perhaps he is a consul or ambassador. Professor Cooley reminds us that the modern school boy is under the influence of Cæsar and Cicero. Apparently he would say that Aristotle and the apostles and Jesus of Nazareth are still members of society. And he teaches that so long as the idea of a man's activities, thoughts, and sentiments are present to the minds of others that man is still an associate. Since the dead influence us without being influenced in return, they present at most an extreme and imperfect instance of association; but the mails, the telegraph, and the telephone daily illustrate that intercommunication, not presence, is the essential condition of association. Before their invention society might indeed be practically limited to spatial presence, but by their aid a nation stretching three thousand miles across a continent can be one society.

After all, however, society does ordinarily imply population, which is as much as to say that communication is far more effective within comparatively close relations of space and time. Yet if dwellers of the same tenement always knew each other and peoples only a block away were never socially remote and presence in space and time always resulted in effective communication, still presence would not be the same thing as communication, still less would population be the same thing as society. Presence or spatial grouping is a visible and conspicuous accompaniment of society, while the social phenomena themselves are psychic realities in a measure hidden from direct observation. And in thinking we practice a kind of metonomy, seizing upon some conspicuous trait or accompaniment of the given reality, which we keep in mind as its symbol, and we conceive of the reality by this symbol. Thus it is that to common-sense society becomes practically a group of people who are together in time and space, a population; but science must perceive that this togetherness, though a usual accompaniment of society, is only the condition most favorable to communication; and it is intercommunication that is the primary, rudimentary characteristic of society, from which the others follow.

Nature of the Social Unity.—The essential unity of society consists in common, correlated, mutually conditioning activities.[1] The people who compose a society are the people who carry on such and such activities and affect each other's activity in such and such ways. Indeed we shall think of society most truly if we put the activities rather than the people foremost in our attention. For example, we shall form a truer notion of a Browning society maintained by four ladies if we think, not primarily of the four ladies in all the interesting multiplicity of their activities, but rather of the particular activities which those ladies carry on as a Browning society. To say Mrs. Smith plus Mrs. Brown plus Mrs. Jones plus Mrs. Clark equal the Browning society would be extremely inaccurate. There is vastly more to Mrs. Smith than her participation in the Browning society. A small fraction of the activity of Mrs. Smith and similar fractions of that of the other ladies by communication combine and also direct and elicit each other, and these particular fragments of activity thus uniting make the life of the Browning society. Correlated activities, sentiments, and beliefs are the essence of every society.

---

[1] We must not forget that "activities" include ideas and sentiments.

But can a society be a true unity? There is no phenomenon, that is, nothing that appears to human observation which is a unity without parts. Even an atom, we now are told, is a kind of miniature solar system. Unities are combinations that naturally hang together and are naturally distinct from the rest of the world. Relationship is the only bond of union anywhere observable in nature. Most relationships are limited, and where they stop the unities which they form terminate. The boundary which shuts off one unity from all others is the termination of the relation by which the unity is bound together. For a relation that binds parts together at the same time separates them from whatever does not share the relation. Relationships are real phenomena and are among the most important phenomena both scientifically and practically. And what seems to us to be physical contiguity is not the only, or necessarily the most important, kind of relation for the formation of a unity. The solar system is as true a unity as the agglomeration of molecules which we call a pebble. Failure to apprehend that the only kind of unity we know is unity of interrelationship has led some to object that the supposed unity of a society is only a creation of the sociologist's mind. Such objectors tell us that there can be no real objective psychic unity of society unless there is some single consciousness, a social mind or oversoul which thinks the common thoughts and entertains the common sentiments and puts forth the common efforts. This is as if a blind man standing on the curbstone and hearing others speak of the unity of a passing company of soldiers should say, "What you call the unity of that marching body is a figment of your imagination. There can be no such unity unless there is one colossal pair of legs to do the marching." "The social mind," although as a figure of speech it may stand for an objective reality, as a literal expression has no more meaning than the "colossal pair of legs," just mentioned. But without any such literal social mind, the unity of a society is as real a fact as the unity of the marching company. The psychic unity of many in a society integrated by community of thought, sentiment, and action, is incomparably richer in content than the unity of a marching body of soldiers, and it is bound together and separated from the rest of the world, not only by this rich interrelationship of similarity in its psychic activities, but also by relationships of mutual causation among its activities. Intercommunication, as we saw, creates a unity like that of a coat of chain mail, but unlike the coat of mail it is a living unity and it grows link by link; the links are interlocking sentiments, ideas, and activities which are made possible to each associate by the fact of association with the other members of society.

Kinds of Societies.—The kind of society corresponds to the kind of common activity by which its members are united. Probably no two species of social activity are participated in by exactly the same persons. The persons who speak the English language are not all Protestants nor all Catholics nor all Republicans in the American sense nor all Liberals in the English sense, still less are they all Anglicans or Presbyterians or Congregationalists or members of the consolidated mine-workers' union. Even the citizens of the United States who are united by certain common civic rights and political interests and sentiments are also subdivided into many societies, classes, sects, and parties. The wealthy, scientific, and artistic American cosmopolite does indeed belong to the same political society with the humblest dweller in the slums, but the humbler dweller in the tenements may belong to a trade union which is a society to which the cosmopolite does not belong, and to a political party which is a society to which the cosmopolite does not belong, and to a church which is a society to which the cosmopolite does not belong, while the cosmopolite may belong to numerous societies from which his fellow citizen of the tenements is excluded and of which some are made up of select individuals from many nations.

The citizens of a state, though composing one political society, are at the same time divided into many mutually exclusive societies great and small, some wholly within the membership of the state, others overlapping the boundaries of the state and drawing members from various states.[1] It is clear then that such societies are not political phenomena that can be included as functional groups within the state; on the contrary states are only one kind of societies, a vastly important and imposing kind, but no more the only kind than trees are the only plants. There can be as many kinds of societies as there are species of prevalent activity capable of uniting the body of people among whom they prevail, and differentiating them from others among whom they do not prevail, of uniting them not only by similarity into a class, but also by the mutual conditioning of their similar and communicating activities, into a society.

Societies then are differentiated according to the character of the common activities by which they are united. The most important societies are:

1. Families. The mere fact of blood kinship makes a family in the biological sense, but not in the sociological sense. It is the common and mutually conditioned ideas and activities that constitute the social life of a family, and an adopted person may be a true member of the family in the sociological sense and a blood brother may cease to be a member of the family society. Of course the word family has to carry both the biological and the sociological meanings. The family enlarges into the clan and the nationality.

2. Lingual societies. All English-speaking people are in this sense one society. If one of us while in a land of strange language should meet an English-speaking person we should recognize him at once as a fellow member of our own lingual society.

3. Economic societies.
4. Political societies.
5. Religious societies.
6. Other cultural groups.

---

[1] That a society may recruit its members from more than one nation is illustrated by numerous organizations represented in the magazine *La Vie International*, published in Brussels. Such internationalism in a society's life is a more familiar thought in Europe than in America. These nations are in some respects comparable to our "states."

Societies and the Social Process.—Societies, as we have now seen, get their identity and quality by virtue of mutually conditioning activities. The various species of social activity are the central concepts with which sociology has to deal. These species of activity taken together constitute the life of every society and are as we have seen an order of reality which might be added as a fourth to the familiar mineral, vegetable, and animal kingdoms. The vast totality of these interrelated human activities may be called social life just as the sum total of biological functioning is called physical life. Social life thus conceived is the field for our investigations. This fourth kingdom of reality, this total tide of prevalent interwoven, and interdependent activities is the social process.

It is a process in two senses. First, it is made up of activities. Even a "static" society, quite as truly as one that is undergoing change [1] is functional, alive, its very being is activity. Second, society evolves. In spite of relative pauses that have sometimes been long, social life has a current of change. Like a river with seemingly silent pools, which nevertheless moves on across vast areas, the life of society has reached its present state out of a far different past, and moves toward a future still unforeseen. Not only is its very being activity, but also its being is a becoming. Therefore "the social process" is perhaps the most adequate, and so the most scientific, brief designation for the reality which we are studying.

Society, social life, or the social process is unified not merely by the similarities that constitute it one kingdom of reality while differentiating it from all other kinds of reality, but also in vast areas by the mutual causation of the parts, each individual act, belief, or sentiment which is one of a million specimens of a social species of activity, being what it is by reason of its relation with the antecedent and accompanying activities which also are elements in the indissoluble unity of the social process. A society can be identified and picked out from the mass of social life whenever a par-

[1] Compare p. 414.

ticular mode of activity prevails among a number of people who by communication are made aware of each other and of their similarity with respect to this mode of activity, and each of whom engages in the unifying activity as a result of his knowledge of the past, present or potential activity of other members of the group.

Definitions.—Among the terms some of which we have already been obliged to use and by which it is important for us to denote accurate concepts are: society, population, class, sect, party, functional group and caste.

The definition of a society must include the three characteristics above set forth. [1]

(a) The very essence of a society is the *common life* of beliefs, sentiments, practical arts; some or all of these prevailing to such an extent among a number of persons as to constitute a real objective similarity and unity among them, and to mark off these people from others among whom the same activities do not prevail.

(b) A plurality of psychophysical organisms capable of such activities must be *in communication.*

(c) By virtue of their communications they mutually elicit, repress, and direct each other's activities, so that the prevalence among them of the unifying activity is due to the *causal interrelationship* of these activities. These three elements are included in the definition of society; the common unifying activities, continuously growing out of causal interrelationship, between the activities of communicating associates; or to put the obvious first and the essential last, a number of people in such communication, as to set up a relation of reciprocal causation and so to establish among them a union in common activity.

A population is a number of persons who at a given time inhabit a given area; it is any considerable number of persons who are together in space and time and distinct from those who are outside of the same temporal and spatial relations. Such a group presents the condition most favorable

[1] See p. 417.

to the development of a society, and is important in proportion as its numbers are great and their spatial relation permanent.

A class is a group of persons unified by any observable relation of similarity, as the scientific or literary or priestly or wealthy class. A class may be distinguished by a similar relation between its members and their associates outside their class, as the respected and the despised, or even by their similar material environment, as mountaineers and plainsmen. As these illustrations show, the members of a class need not be together in time and space or in communication, and their similarity need not be a similarity in activities, therefore they do not necessarily constitute a society. They may belong to different populations or ages; their similarity, however, must be real and if they are to be recognized as a class their similarity must be known to an observer.

A functional group is a class included within a larger society and united by similarity with respect to some activity which is regarded as a necessary part of the established social order of the larger society; as the carpenters or the printers, the medical profession or the official class.

When a class becomes "self-conscious," that is, aware of the similarity by which it is united and by which it is separated from outsiders, it may be a sect, a party, or a caste.

A sect is a self-conscious class whose bond of similarity consists in common beliefs or common tastes and sentiments or both.

A party is a self-conscious class whose bond of similarity consists not merely in common ideas and sentiments but in a common practical interest and aim and the activities prompted thereby. Of course a party, as much as a sect, must have some common idea and sentiment, but in the case of a party, idea and sentiment have practical objective reference and find expression in overt endeavor. An alternative name for a party is "interest group." The scientific explanation of political forms and of political movements is to be found in the study of parties in the sense just defined. The importers are a party who want the tariff reduced; consumers as such are a party; the manufacturers of a given commodity are a party; the "liquor interest" is a party.[1]

A caste is a self-conscious class, membership in which is determined by birth and not by activities of those included in the class and whose bond of similarity consists in judgments of superiority and inferiority held by others toward all the members of the caste and generally acquiesced in by the members of the caste themselves. Castes are groups that stand upon different levels before the bar of group judgment. Inequality before the courts is often a less serious matter and may be included or implied in the inequality of caste. Group judgment can dispense life's rewards and penalties, opportunities and disabilities more effectively and upon more subjects than the courts which are only one agency of group judgment. Members of a lower caste as a rule themselves accept the group judgment by which they are condemned to inferiority, and members of a higher caste are certain, except in the cases of rare individuals, to accept a group judgment by which they are assigned superiority.

A duke would cease to be a duke if men ceased to think him one. The essential reality in the case is an attitude of mind. There are no dukes where the public mind lacks that attitude. This once more illustrates the psychic character of social phenomena. There was a time when the obliteration of the social ideas and sentiments by virtue of which dukes were dukes would have been an exploit more momentous than digging a Panama Canal, and those ideas and sentiments, though purely psychic phenomena, were as real as the rocks at the Culebra cut.

The natural social order includes and produces not only societies, classes, castes, sects, parties, and functional groups,

---

[1] This conception was developed by Gustav Ratzenhofer: Wesen und Zweck der Politik. Brockhaus Leipzig, 1893, vol. i, chaps. 5, 7, 18, 19; vol. iii, chap. 71. Compare Albion W. Small: General Sociology. University of Chicago Press, 1905, part iv; and A. F. Bentley: The Process of Government: University of Chicago Press, 1908, chaps. xiv and following.

but also individuals. To this last statement a separate chapter must be devoted.

The Social Realities.—The phrase "social realities" refers primarily to social activities which constitute the social life, including both the compound social realities of which the most imposing are customs and institutions, and also the simpler social activities which were classified as social ideas, sentiments, and practices. The profitable study of sociology will conceive of society functionally,[1] that is, will center chief attention on the social activities. But the structural[1] aspect cannot be ignored and viewing the structural aspect we see that social realities include the social order with its societies, classes, castes, sects, parties, functional groups, and organizations. Of these, societies, sects, parties, and functional groups are bound together by common activities; castes are held together and distinguished from the rest of society by social judgments and sentiment of others as well as of the members of the caste; organizations get their character and unity from a particular correlation of activities; and classes, the loosest entity of all, are held together by any perceived objective resemblance. The "social realities" may be said to include also the social shell of sociophysical phenomena. The social order itself is primarily and essentially an inclusive correlation of social activities, but that statement implies that it includes, when structurally viewed, all of the realities just enumerated.

---

[1] Of course, these words do not have exactly the same meaning for us as for the biologist, but there are no better words by which to express the meaning here indicated.

CHAPTER XXIV

SOCIETY AND THE INDIVIDUAL

1. Identity of Individual and Social Activities.—Each individual's Methodism or Republicanism, as we now see, is a single item in the great social reality "Methodism" or "Republicanism." The individual activity is one instance of the prevalent activity and is itself known to associates and is socially caused. If we could take a great social reality [1] and pull it out, as one does a telescope, to show its parts, those parts would be seen to be individual activities. Or to use a better figure, as when we put a piece of animal or vegetable tissue under a powerful microscope we see that it is composed of individual cells, so when we look at a social reality closely enough, so to speak, microscopically, so as to discover its histology, we perceive that it is composed of individual activities. Each cell in a tissue is a living individual but it could not live except as a part of the tissue nor could the tissue live except in the life of the cells. So a social reality, however great, is made up of individual activities so interrelated as to compose it; at the same time the individual activities can exist only as social realities. As cells can be adequately understood only as belonging to tissue and tissue can be adequately understood only as composed of cells, so also the individual activities can be adequately understood only as items in social realities and social realities can be adequately understood only as composed of individual activities. Individual and social activities are identical in the same sense that cells and tissue are identical.

---

[1] We are referring to the essential social realities, or social activities, like Methodism and Republicanism, although the figures of the telescope and tissue would better correspond to static realities. A comparison cannot be expected to illustrate more than one point at a time.

2. Subjective Individual and Objective Social Reality.—
By a subjective reality we mean an activity which is a part
of the consciousness of some individual who is called the
subject. His name is the subject of the verb which expresses
the activity, as when we say John thinks, feels, or endeavors.
John can be conscious only of his own activities, the activities
of which he is the subject, or which are "subjective" to him.
John can be aware of another man's activity, but not conscious
of any but his own. John can be aware of the sun and the
stars, the trees and the house, but he cannot be conscious
of any of these things. Everything of which John can be

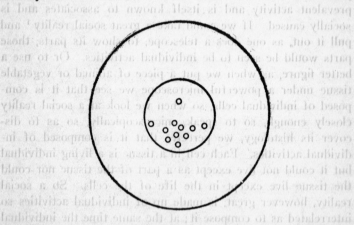

aware only is objective to him and can be the object in a
sentence of which "John" is the subject, as when we say
John sees the sun, or respects his neighbor's act.

Every atom of psychic reality is subjective to someone,
therefore the words subjective and psychic are sometimes
treated as synonymous, but that will not do here because in so
far as John or any other person becomes aware of the activities of his associates they are objective to him; they are objective, psychic realities.

In the diagram each of the tiny circles represents the
consciousness of one individual, a closed circle belonging peculiarly to the single person who is its "subject." The circle
surrounding these tiny circles represents the social world com-

posed of these tiny circles of individual consciousness like
cells in a living tissue. All the activity that is contained within
one of the minute circles is subjective to someone—call him
John—but all of the other tiny circles are objective to him,
that is all the rest that is contained within the circle of the
social world, in so far as it is known to John at all, is objective to him. The outer circle represents the boundary of
the observable world and includes within it, but outside of
the circle of social reality, such realities as sun and stars and
houses and material things in general. Thus every atom of
reality included in the social process is subjective to someone,
but only a very little of the social process is subjective to any
one. The social world as a whole is objective to any observer.
The material realities outside the social world within the largest
circle are subjective to no human consciousness; though the
idealistic philosophers believe that all phenomena of whatever kind are subjective to the all-inclusive consciousness.
That, however, is a question of metaphysics and not for us.
We need only observe that every atom of social activity is
subjective to someone, but only a small portion even of any
single social reality is subjective to any one. Thus the American patriotism is a very big and very real thing as an invader
would soon find, and every atom of it is subjective to someone, part of it to me and part of it to my reader; but it is
only a very tiny portion of the American patriotism that is
subjective to any one of us. The American patriotism as a
whole is an objective social reality out there.

Thus we see that while there is clear distinction between
what is individual to me and what is individual to you; namely,
that what is subjective to me is objective to you, and what
is subjective to you is objective to me, in so far as it is
anything to me at all, yet this is a distinction of mine and
thine, and not at all a difference in the kind of reality, but
rather in the way of knowing it. My own activity I know
directly, that is, consciously or subjectively and far more perfectly, while yours I know only objectively and less perfectly. But both yours and mine would be equally objective
to a third person, and my individual part of the social reality

and your individual part of it as observed by any other person are both in and of the social reality, as a little water of the sea is in and of the sea.

Individual Life Composite.—If every point in a line should be taken to stand for the Methodism of some one Methodist so that the entire line should represent the whole social reality of Methodism, and another line should similarly represent Republicanism and if John were both a Methodist and a Republican, he would stand at the intersection of these two lines.

Let another line represent carpentry. John is a carpenter.

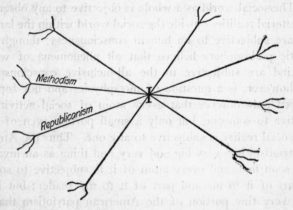

Let another represent lying. John is a liar.

Let the letter I be the first personal pronoun. John and every other individual stand each at the intersection of many lines, each line representing a social activity one point of which is subjective to him, his own activity and a part of his individuality.

The little sprangles at the ends of some of the lines indicate that most of the social activities that intersect are compound and could be raveled out by complete analysis into a number of included activities. This, however, is not the point which we are emphasizing here, but rather the point that many social activities intersect in every individual. Our diagram represents only a portion of the truth. To make it represent the whole truth the lines would curve and cross and recross. The essential facts for which it stands are these two: first, that each activity of one's life is a point in a line, a specimen in a prevalent species of activity; and second, that the life of any individual among us is a compound which may be different from the compound of activities included in the life of any other person, for it may well be that in no two persons do the same group of lines intersect.

To abandon our diagram and adopt a figure suggested by the fact that individual activities are specimens of species, we might compare the activities which are gathered into a single individuality with the flowers which are gathered into a bouquet. Every single flower belongs to a prevalent species but no two bouquets are alike. The lives of two savages of the same clan would resemble each other as would two bouquets gathered in the same meager garden, but the lives of two of us would each be like bouquets which had been gathered while roaming through many gardens and many fields. We have grown up in different homes, in different neighborhoods, attended different schools, spent our vacations at different resorts and have been members of scores of groups from each of which we have taken something of our individuality, and by the medium of the printed page we have associated with some or other of the impressive personalities of distant lands and ages. These are not the only reasons why our lives are compounded of different elements, but this suffices to make it clear that individual lives in their totality are both highly compounded and highly diverse from one another. We have now seen in what sense individual and social realities are identical, have pointed out the social significance of subjectivity and objectivity, and have shown that individual life is a peculiar compound of numerous social realities, no one of which, generally speaking, would have been possible to the individual as an individual in isolation. John would not have been a Methodist or a Republican or a carpenter, if he had been the first man. Either of these implies a long preceding social evolution.

The Unit of Investigation.—According to Wundt[1] all scientific investigation consists in one or both of two processes, analysis and synthesis. We approach the vast, baffling, and confused reality and analyze it into the smallest discoverable parts and then we observe the interrelationship of these parts so that we can think them together again into a unity which is no longer baffling cr unintelligible. In order to give a scientific account of a complicated field of reality it is necessary to analyze it as completely as possible into minute elements which recur in many instances.[2] It may be possible to explain a great and unique fact in its entirety, but there is little prospect of complete explanation without minute analysis; and there can be no law for the occurrence of unique phenomena, but only for the appearance of those which recur and recur. Superficial analysis merely divides society into individual persons or associates. Thus it has been common among sociologists including such a founder of the science as Spencer and such a modern promoter of it as Giddings, to look upon the socius as the unit of sociological investigation. But the socius is far too complex and far too unique to be the element yielded by ultimate analysis of social reality. To take the socius as our unit of investigation would be much as if botanists were to take bouquets as their units of investigation. As we saw above, any examination of society which is microscopic enough to reveal its histology shows that its elements are particular activities, beliefs, sentiments, and practical arts. Each social element in these activities is subjective to some individual, although belonging to a kind of activity which is prevalent among many individuals and in its prevalence constituting a sociological species. Methodism is not a social element, and John is not a social element, but John's Methodism, John's Republicanism, John's carpentry,

---

[1] Wundt: Methodenlehre, erste abtheilung, p. 1.

[2] Compare also Tarde: Laws of Imitation, p. 1, where it is set forth that whether "we can have a science or only a history, or at most, a philosophy of social phenomena," depends upon whether "they can be reduced, like other facts, to series of minute and homogeneous phenomena."

and John's lie are each elements in the social situation. Such elements are the ultimate units of sociological investigation; they are the units the prevalence and modifications of which must be accounted for if there is to be any sociological explanation. John's Methodism may be said to be a specimen and the prevalent Methodism as a whole a variety and religion a species, or perhaps a genus of social activity.

What Determines Individuality?—Various elements in the determination of personality have been separately discussed. An answer to the present question would require these separate elements to be brought together. Such recapitulation as is possible at this point will refer to the social, and certain of the psychophysical causes under four heads.

1. The crop that grows on any field depends upon two sets of factors: first, soil, dew, showers, and sunshine, the gifts of nature; and second, the seed and cultivation. Likewise the content of any life depends upon two sets of factors: *first, the gifts of nature, the hereditary capacities and tendencies;* and second, the seeds implanted by social suggestion, sympathetic radiation, and imitation, and the general euthenic and cultural conditions. One cannot raise oranges or pineapples in Maine nor can we make a poet or mathematician of every boy. We cannot raise any crop in the middle of the Sahara, nor can we make anything of an idiot. On the other hand, the seeming sand barrens of Florida and the shale lakeshores of central New York produce crops of fruit more valuable than the yield of the black acres of the prairies, and under proper treatment unpromising youths may yield a priceless fruitage of life. And aside from idiots and the possessors of special gifts the 99 per cent. of normal human beings resemble ordinary soil in that such soil will readily bear either of many crops or quite as readily run to weeds, and such lives will readily respond to social stimulation in equally various and contrasting ways.

During the last ten-year period for which figures are available the corn lands of Illinois yielded on the average thirty-six bushels to the acre, while the experimental plots of the College of Agriculture of the State University, yielded on the average eighty-six bushels to the acre. Agronomists declare that the average yield of the corn lands of the state might by scientific culture be doubled. It is probably much within the truth to say that the values of life realized by the people of the commonwealth might be doubled. This is the problem of education and of all the agencies of social control which should have it for their goal and guide to apply the conclusions of sociology.

The chief problem is not to upraise the paupers and criminals, the degraded and debased classes, imperative as that is, but to bring nearer to realization the possibilities of normal lives passed in ordinary conditions.

As a rule the importance of heredity is recognized by all intelligent persons, while the other factors in the determination of personality are neither understood nor appreciated.

Each individual must accept his heredity as it is, but within the limits set by his heredity his career will vary according to the variation in the other factors, and these are largely subject to his own control. Even society as a whole has for the present at least a very limited control over the hereditary endowment of its members, but might exercise a vastly important control over the other factors that determine their personality. The theoretical question, which most affects the careers of men and societies, heredity or environment, will probably never be answered. But the practical importance of understanding the operation of a set of causes is largely proportioned to their amenability to human control. This gives incalculable importance to the understanding of the non-hereditary factors in the life of men and of societies.

2. *The molding of the individual by society.* The adult member of society has a conscious life composed of hopes, ambitions, tastes, distastes, approvals, disapprovals, beliefs, plans, methods, and their expression in a round of conduct; and probably he would find the greatest difficulty in naming a single one of these activities aside from the mere functioning of his animal organism which he would have in its present form and content if he had grown up in isolation. He has developed from childhood in the presence of a thronging

multitude of activities which were in the world before his arrival. For every child the question is which of all these activities shall be adopted by him and become a part of his own stream of consciousness.

This depends largely upon the character of the social contacts to which he is exposed. Each of us has entered into hundreds of different social contacts, each of which has left some contribution, desirable or undesirable, to our content of life. Each of us might have been quite other than he is had his social contacts been radically different. There is no one of us who, introduced in infancy into Turkish society might not, as well as not, have talked only the Turkish language, believed in Mohammedanism, practiced polygamy, and adopted the arts and crafts, personal and social customs, sentiments and tastes of that people. It is a matter of common observation that opinions, for instance, in religion or politics, are firmly fixed in youth by the influence of parents, teachers, and neighbors. If they are modified later it is almost invariably as a result of suggestions received from other teachers, writers, and associates. Prejudices, sentiments, tastes, standards of ambition and morality are equally dependent upon sympathetic radiation and suggestion. Overt practices are likewise dependent upon imitation, suggestion, and radiation.

3. *The effects of social molding upon the permanent cerebroneural organization of the individual.* A human being, the organic development of whose brain and nervous system stopped at birth or soon after, could never become a man or woman, whatever the increase in stature. The organic changes that take place after birth may go far in determining what shall be one's character, ability, and disposition at maturity, what lines of thought, feeling, and activity have become congenial and easy, and what remain difficult or impossible.

We remember the vast mass of our experience, significant or trivial. Much of what we remember we may never recall but it remains stored away in the modifications of our cerebral structure, and every now and then, so to speak, something that we had thought forgotten falls off the dark shelves of memory and comes rolling into the bright light of consciousness. Constantly the mind reaches up to take down those items of the vast store which we are accustomed to make use of. Now as our intellectual life depends not upon the comparative vacancy of the baby's natural endowment, but is enriched by the stores of memory, so also our life of emotion, morality, speech, skill, self-control, and whatever else goes to constitute our personality depends not upon hereditary tendencies and impulses alone but upon developed interests and established dispositions. And as ideas, even the countless trivial ones, keep their place in the memory store by virtue of the modifications which they have made in the substance of our cerebroneural system, so likewise our feelings and acts imbed themselves in our structure as permanent tendencies to repetition. The book of remembrance in which our deeds and thoughts and emotions are recorded is our own living substance.

4. *The effect of social contact upon the temporary set of the organism.* The human organism is an immensely complicated mechanism having the capacity to respond to stimulation in many different ways. To-day one may be trifling and purposeless. Nothing seems to him to be worth a struggle. Life's opportunities and demands provoke a smile of cynicism. On another day he may be full of the joy of zestful endeavor. The struggle for righteousness and service engages his powers and there is steadiness and momentum in his activities. Except in so far as it is due to cruder physiological causes, this results from the law of attention. Attention is an adjustment of the whole organism. When the object of attention is external and visible we turn our faces toward it and focus our eyes upon it, but these external adjustments are simply the beginning of an adjustment of our inner apparatus of consciousness. All the association paths that converge toward this object are opened. Ideas consonant with the object of attention start up and begin to flock toward the foreground of consciousness. Any idea that is capable of fixing the attention and arousing the feelings produces an adjustment of the entire organism which continues for a time

even after the object of thought which occasioned the adjustment has been dismissed from consciousness. The individual who lives through a day in such an adjustment produced by contemplation of a thought or purpose to which his whole organism responds, passes through his environment as a magnet passes through a pile of sand and iron filings and selects those things congenial to itself, or to speak literally the organism thus adjusted by an act of attention responds to stimulation in ways that are consonant with its state of adjustment. This we called the "subconscious" set because the effects upon the organism and its disposition linger for a time after the object of attention which has established its dominance is no longer in consciousness and the mind has become occupied with external objects which elicit its active response.

But this effect is only temporary. It fades away like the after-image which vivid light leaves upon the retina. No man can live at his best who does not frequently renew his adaptation to his purpose by contemplating such ideas as he has found by experience are capable of producing the necessary adjustment any more than a watch that is not wound up will keep time. The human organism is simply a mechanism designed to be controlled by the process of attention. To expect to fulfill a high aim that is only occasionally in the mind is folly, while on the other hand it has been wisely said that only one rule of practice is essential to the attainment of such aims, namely, to live habitually in the presence of the best in the field where one's aspiration lies.

One can be as different on different days as if born of other parents, the whole tendency of the organism transposed. We often speak of our "better self." We have not several selves, but our one self is so complex and so rich in possibilities that it has material enough in it for several selves, for sound and balanced life and for fragmentary piecemeal life, for saint and demon.

Paradoxes.—We are now ready to understand the famous paradox: "Society existed before the individual." Before there could be individualities like our own there must first be evolved the various activities which we inherit from a long social past and which no isolated human being could have originated, and also the elaborate opportunities for communication through diverse social contacts.

Another terse embodiment of the same truth is the saying that "One man is no man"; it may have been originated by someone who had in mind the power of organization and the comparative impotence of isolated and unorganized endeavor, but it is literally true as a fact of social evolution. One man alone could never become a man corresponding to our conception of man, but such an isolated creature lacking all the activities that compose our lives would be nearer to the other animals than to us. Would he speak the English language? No, for even here and now those born deaf are also dumb since language is not a gift of nature but a social product. Would he have heard of Christ or have discovered for himself His message? No, he would be more destitute of religion than any known heathen. Would he despise deceit and indecency and theft? No, he would have no conscience for no one is born with a conscience and conscience is the product of social experience. Would he have clothing of cloth woven from spun yarn? No; these require the previous accumulation of many inventions which no one of us alone would have made. An isolated individual of the genus Homo would be a naked savage and a dumb brute. "The individual man," says Bastian, "is nothing, at best an idiot." [1]

Whether the first man was as gifted as Aristotle or possessed an intelligence scarcely superior to that of a chimpanzee would have made very little difference. In either case he would have had no language and very little to say if he had possessed one. His content of consciousness would have been mainly confined to the ideas directly presented by sense-perception. He would have been aware of external objects of sense-perception. He would have been conscious of hunger, pain, and instinctive promptings. But *self*-consciousness,

---

[1] Compare Ludwig Gumplowicz: Outlines of Sociology. (Tr. by Moore) *American Academy of Political and Social Science,* 1899, p. 45.

according to the elaborate study of Professor Baldwin,[1] is developed only in association. The possession of great capacities or small would mean but little to any descendant of Adam who was obliged to live in absolute isolation from his kind. Society, as Professor Ellwood and others have remarked, produces its individual personalities as truly as an organism produces its cells. It produces their tastes, sentiments, opinions, and arts. We do not inherit a single idea but only the capacities for ideas and activities. If these capacities should not be awakened by social contacts and enriched by the results of social evolution they would be like seeds in bottles.

With all our education not even the greatest man originates a contribution to the social heritage of ideas, sentiments, and practices that is large when compared to the whole vast store of that heritage to which the humble and common individual is an heir. And the rare contributions that are of greatest moment would be impossible without the previous possession of the common store. We originate a little because we inherit much; we inherit enough to make us men and women because the common store has been produced by ages of social evolution; that which a single life deprived from birth of all association would develop, is as nothing.

"The individual is an abstraction" is another paradoxical expression which has become common among sociologists. McDougal[2] writes: "The strictly individual human mind, with which the older introspective and descriptive psychology contented itself, is an abstraction merely, and has no real existence." An abstraction is that which can be thought of by itself but which cannot exist by itself. We can think of the individual apart from society but that which we know as individual life is in and of the larger life of society. When once produced it might for a time continue in isolation but it could never have been produced in isolation, and cannot be understood if thought of only by itself. Says Professor

---

[1] Baldwin: Social and Ethical Interpretations in Mental Development, chap. I.

[2] McDougal: Social Psychology, p. 16.

Cooley[1]: "Self and society are twin born, the notion of a separate and independent ego is an illusion." Possibly Professor Cooley's discussion in his "Human Nature and the Social Order" may seem a little extreme to some readers; for example, in his italicized statement: "Self and other do not exist as mutually exclusive social facts." But the thought of self includes thoughts of social relationship. John thinks of himself as Thomas' son, as Charles' partner and as Mary's husband; the content of John's consciousness, the very substance of his life, is socially derived and self-consciousness develops on a background of other consciousness. In the language of Professor Baldwin: "Both ego and alter are essentially social."[2]

Sociology the Study of Life.—It is clear that individual and social life cannot be separated, that society cannot be understood except as made up of the activities of individuals, nor individual lives except as made up of participation in prevalent social activities (tastes, judgments, beliefs, and practices), and as molded by social contacts. The real object of our study is life, the conscious life of man in its concrete richness and variety. Life is at once both individual and social; these are two aspects of the one reality.

When the biologist uses the word "life" he means a set of activities partly chemical, partly mechanical—digestion, secretion, osmosis, respiration, circulation, and whatever else is included in the functioning of the animal organism, a complex process which as yet he imperfectly understands but which furnishes the object of studies of exceeding interest and value. But when one of us says "my life" he is not thinking of nutrition, peristalsis and the circulation of the blood, nor are these what we read about in a biography, but of a succession of interrelated activities going on in consciousness and more or less imperfectly manifested by the muscular movements which are mediated by those states of consciousness, and which we call

---

[1] Social Organization, p. 5. Scribners, 1902, chaps. i-vi; see also Index under "Self."

[2] Social and Ethical Interpretations in Mental Development. Macmillan, 1897, p. 9.

psychophysical or sociophysical according as we have in mind the work of one or the common work of many. Life in this sense is precisely the object studied by sociology. The study in a scientific spirit and by scientific methods of this conscious life, which is both individual and social, is a new step in intellectual progress. It is a realm which has been given over to speculations, dictated by practical interests, largely didactic and ethical, of which many have become popularized and intrenched in prejudice but which fall far short of giving scientific comprehension or practical control of the realities which are of greatest interest and import to man.

psychophysical or sociophysical according as we have in mind the work of one or the common work of many. Life in this sense is precisely the object studied by sociology. The study is in scientific spirit and by scientific methods of this conscious life, which is both individual and social, is a new step in intellectual progress. It is a realm which has been given over to speculations, dictated by practical interest, largely didactic and ethical, of which many have become popularized and interpreted in prejudice but which fall far short of giving a lasting comprehension or practical control of the realities which are of greater interest and import to man.

PART III

SOCIAL EVOLUTION

CHAPTER XXV

THE PERSPECTIVE OF SOCIAL EVOLUTION

Comparative and Genetic Sociology.—Comparative anatomy, by observing the resemblances and differences between homologous organs in different species, discovered the first hints of the interrelationship of animal forms and of their evolution, and helped to reveal the orderly reign of natural law in the animal kingdom. Comparative philology, comparative religions, comparative jurisprudence, comparative folklore, the comparative study of the family and of moral systems, have shown that there are homologies in the forms of social activities, that they, too, have had an evolution, and that the orderly reign of natural law includes the social kingdom. The comparative method of investigation is characteristic of the sciences of life. In investigating inorganic phenomena we guess with such reason as we may at the conditions that give rise to a phenomenon that is to be explained, and then supply the conditions, and if the phenomenon emerges we regard our hypothesis as confirmed. And we vary the conditions and observe the corresponding changes in the resulting phenomenon. But in sociology we observe the phenomenon to be explained wherever we can find it, note the conditions in presence of which it appears, eliminate from the explanation those non-essentials which are not always present and observe the differences between the different instances of our problem phenomenon and the corresponding differences between the conditioning situations in which it emerges. The contrast between experimental and comparative science is that in experimental science we make our facts, while in comparative science we search for the facts as nature supplies them. In order to eliminate non-essentials and identify essentials in the explanation and to correlate changes in the resultant with changes in the causal conditions, we may need to observe many instances and to find these instances we may have to search through many ages and climes, especially among many different, contemporary societies, in as wide a variety of conditions as possible.

The comparative method develops into the genetic method, in which we see results being produced in nature's laboratory. This means that science now sees every problem of life against an evolutionary background. Not long ago our state of mind with reference to these problems resembled that of the California Indians with reference to the giant sequoias, which they thought had not grown like other trees but had been from the beginning as they are now. The vastest and most ancient realities, as well as the new and trivial, have grown, have issued out of non-being by an orderly process of causation. This gives us a clue for the comprehension of the present, and even throws some gleams upon the future.

In the development of every peculiar animal or vegetable form some special conditions are involved, but the general laws of organic evolution, the main principles of explanation, are the same for plants and animals, mammals and mollusks, phenogams, and cryptogams.[1] Likewise every peculiar social activity involves some special conditions, but the general principles of social evolution are the same for languages, religions, governments and laws, arts, plays, and ceremonies, sciences and philosophies, economic arts and moral codes.

Both in biology and sociology genetic investigation is especially fruitful when applied to lower forms. Possibly the brightest lights have been thrown upon the nature of human life itself not by the dissection of human bodies, but by the study of such creatures as rabbits, guinea-pigs, flies, sea-urchins, and earthworms, partly, it is true, because with such cheap material the experimental method can be applied, but largely also because there the structures and processes are simple enough to be intelligible, and because these simple early stages offer explanations of the final result which study of that result by itself could hardly furnish. We may not be

---

[1] Compare p. 7.

able to experiment extensively with the lower social forms, but their number and variety afford scope for the comparative method. Their greater simplicity as compared with later social forms offers the investigator an advantage like that which the neurologist finds in studying the elements of nervous organization in worms and mollusks, and their successive stages display the methods by which final results have been attained. A sociology which was confined to a study of the civilization of Europe and America would be like a biology confined to study of the mammalia.

We cannot assume identity between the life and conditions of surviving savages and those of our own remote forbears; it is only in a figure of speech that Professor Thomas refers to the savages as "a sort of contemporaneous ancestry." But archeological evidence indicates the close resemblance between the Stone Age of the present and of ten thousand years ago. The biological evolutionist is by no means better off than we in respect to the ability to see past forms in the lower orders of the present.

Caution is to be observed in the criticism of materials. By no means all the tales of travelers about strange peoples are to be received as data for comparative sociology. But we are supplied with a mass of evidence which has been accumulated by trained and reliable scientific observers. Another caution is not out of place: The best evidence, other things being equal, is that gathered by our own senses; and interest in more primitive social types must not make us undervalue the patient study and analysis of social facts as they appear about us, but rather should turn us to the first-hand observation of our own society with increased interest and competence. We seek afar in order to gain data not to be found at home, and especially to find scope for comparative and genetic study.

Anthropology, Ethnology and Sociology.—These three words have been used with vague and variable meanings. The word "anthropology," as it has been used by Professor Mason and others, is a blanket term for all study of man, including human anatomy, physiology, psychology, the description of races, and all other description of the traits of man, and also including history, folklore, archeology, the study of religions, languages, technic and fine arts, and investigation of all other branches of social activity. It is quite obvious that when the word "anthropology" is thus employed it covers a range far too vast to be the field of one science.

This vast and vague connotation for the word "anthropology" resulted naturally enough from the fact that when men visited and described strange peoples they reported all that they had learned about them, both about their stature, form, color, and other physical traits, and also about their social activities. Similarly exploration parties returning from a strange land bring back information about its flora, fauna, minerals, climate, and topography. These exploration parties commonly realize that they have been collecting materials for various sciences. Possibly the word "anthropology" may continue to be used as a general name for such collections of materials for all of the sciences dealing with man and the life of man. There is a tendency, however, to give the word a more definite and scientific meaning by narrowing its connotation to the study of the biological, including the cerebro-neural, traits of the genus Homo and of its racial varieties.

The word "ethnology" originally and etymologically meant that subdivision of physical anthropology which deals with racial characteristics. It has, however, almost completely lost that meaning. This is partly because we are less confident of our ability to differentiate men biologically according to racial types and groupings, and so feel less need of the word as a designation for this special study. Anthropology, in the old vague usage of that term, was divided into two parts: (1) the study of the biological traits of the genus Homo; (2) the study of social activities. The word "ethnology," according to Mason and others, designated one subdivision of part one. Now being no longer specially needed for that use it has slipped quietly across the line that once separated the two divisions of anthropology and is used as a designation for the whole of part two. It might now be defined as the study of social activities with special reference to the activities of primitive peoples. Thus we find Brinton saying: "Ethnology . . . contemplates man as a social creature. It is more concerned with the mental, the psychical part of man, than with his physical nature, and seeks to trace the intellectual development of communities by studying the growth of government, laws, arts, languages, religions, and society." [1] Accordingly ethnology is a collection of the materials for study of genetic sociology, and in so far as it includes the interpretation of these materials so as to make them reveal their explanation, it becomes identical with genetic sociology. It is somewhat common, especially among German writers, to distinguish between ethnography and ethnology as follows: The description of a people with reference to all their varied activities would be called ethnography, but the description of a particular division of social activity, like domestic organization, or magic, as it appears among various peoples, would be called ethnology.

The fluctuation and uncertainty in the meaning of the names which stand at the head of this paragraph has been due to the fact that the sciences that deal with man have been young and immature, and the special divisions of science in this field have only very recently become clear. The word "ethnology" might never have been coined if we had realized the limitations upon our knowledge of racial distinctions, if our notion of anthropology had been definite enough to serve a specific use and render needless another term for the study of human varieties, and if the idea of sociology had formed itself in the minds of men as it has since the work of Spencer has been supplemented by that of other scholars like Bastian, Letourneau, and Sumner.

Some persons continue to call the study of primitive social activities "anthropology," and some call the study of those activities "ethnology." But whatever it is called it is a contribution to the comparative and genetic phase of the investigation of that kingdom of phenomena which is composed of socially prevalent and socially evolved activities. The word "anthropology" should be used as meaning physical anthropology. The word "ethnology," in so far as it need be used

---

[1] D. G. Brinton: Anthropology, Philadelphia, 1892, p. 6.

at all, means comparative and genetic sociology, considered mainly in its descriptive phase and with chief reference to the less advanced societies.

Social Evolution and Cosmic Evolution.—As sociology is the youngest grand division of science, so also the kingdom of social phenomena, the fourth kingdom of reality, is the youngest of the four. As sociology rests upon the antecedent sciences, so also social evolution grows out of the previous stages of cosmic evolution.

Geologists declare that the earth's crust has been formed for a hundred million years, that the record of slow geologic processes indelibly written in the rocks is at least as old as that. Physicists used to say that the sun could not have shone so long; it would have burned out. But since the discovery of radio-activity the physicists withdraw their objection and say that for anything they know to the contrary the time may have been far longer even than the geologists declare it to have been. Life appeared and began to deposit its remains as soon as the waters of the sea became sufficiently cooled nearly a hundred million years ago. The oldest unmistakably human remains however are only between 200,000 and 500,000 years old. If we should let the width of a man's thumb represent the time that has elapsed since the oldest preserved records of Egypt and Mesopotamia were made, the length of a man's walking stick would proportionally represent the total age of the genus Homo, and a line representing the age of the earth's crust would have to be prolonged down the street for several blocks. As compared with the eons which were required to build this habitation of man, it is only a short time since he moved in, and he has only just now got the use of the conveniences of the establishment.[1]

"A few hundred years ago the parents of the English-speaking nations were as savage as the savagest, without temples to their Gods, in perpetual and bloody war, untamed

---

[1] It is often said that the last half of the nineteenth century witnessed more progress in subduing the resources of nature to the uses of man than all the preceding ages; allowing for all possible exaggeration in this estimate, the statement in the text is moderate.

cannibals; add a few thousand years to the perspective, and man over the whole globe was in the same condition." [1] As seen by an intelligence to which "a thousand years are as one day" the whole period of recorded history has been very brief in comparison with that which every reason leads us to anticipate during the ages through which our sun is likely to shine.

We may not look backward to find our ideals, but rather to gather confidence for further progress by contemplating the hole of the pit whence we were digged and out of which we have climbed. Bacon was right in saying: "We are the true antiquity, that which we call antiquity was the childhood of the race." Apparently ever since men began to grow old and lose the zest and glamour of youth, they have mistakenly lamented the "good old times." Memory and tradition dwell upon that which is picturesque and pleasing, but present experience feels existing evils in all their sharpness. Already in ancient Israel the rebuke was needed: "Say not thou, What is the cause that the former days were better than these? for thou dost not inquire wisely concerning this." [2] It is said that one of the clay cylinders dug up at Babylon among the oldest of all records of human thought contains a complaint on the decadence of the times.

The common-sense native to man reveals such reaches of time and space as concern his daily actions. He can see as far as he can walk in a day, and he discerns objects as small as he can handle. He can also remember and foresee a little. But the telescope reveals abysses of vastness previously inconceivable; and the microscope and the experiments of the physicists reveal abysses of minuteness as unfathomable; and the study of evolution opens similar vistas of past and coming time. As compared with other students of evolution the sociologist "deals with a fresh young world," rich in the prospects of future change.

Social Evolution Continuous with Biological Evolution.— Organization, in the sense of the adjustment of interrelated

---

[1] D. G. Brinton: Religions of Primitive People, Putnam, 1897, p. 12
[2] Ecclesiastes, 7: 10.

and interdependent parts so as to maintain a status quo whether of rest or motion, is perhaps the most universal fact of nature. Such organization pervades even the "inorganic" world. The solar system itself is such an organization and such also according to recent teaching are the atoms.

The behavior of the most complex and nicely adjusted organizations we call life. Such living organizations we name "organisms," and their organization is studied by the biologist. Many of the biological organisms feed, reproduce, and protect themselves by uniting into colonies, flocks, or herds. Some of these animals manifest special instincts or inborn tendencies, which promote the correlation of their activities, such as sociability, sympathy, partisanship, anger, dominance,[1] submission, imitation, and emulation. It is hard to draw any but imaginary lines across the continuum of nature, hard to say just how or where life begins or where society first appears. Says Espinas, "If an exact observer should succeed in showing in the relation of plants to each other or in the relations between parts of the same plant any traces of co-operation, we should see no difficulty in admitting these studies to the body of social science, and do not doubt that one would find that the general principles of the science applied to them." Then stamens and pistils are married and cells are associates. Espinas would not flinch from this logical conclusion. Doubtless the unity of nature is such that the simpler sciences that first came within the compass of the mind afford the light by which later and more complex investigations are made possible, and also that these later studies throw new illumination upon the earlier investigations; and so the study of organization throughout all nature is in a sense one. Yet

---

[1] To round up a herd of 12,000 to 15,000 cattle it was only necessary to make sure of the presence of the 15 to 50 leaders, for each leader was followed by a band of from 40 to 100 individuals. Alfred Espinas: Des Sociétés Animales. Baillière & Co., 1878, Paris, pp. 496, 497. The soko, a species of chimpanzee, lives in permanent communities composed of monogamous families, in which all, even the males, render obedience to one chief (Espinas, p. 502), and they aid each other actively and evince strong partisanship. This last is done by herds of wild pigs and other animals.

we must limit our task somewhere; and though we may be aided by the study of organization wherever found, especially the organized groups of lower animals, we will draw the line of definition for our undertaking at the point where *invention* begins to play a conspicuous part in originating the activities that become organized into a self-maintaining functional unity.

Merely tropic congregation and coöperation such as exists among infusoria, and probably such instinctive coöperation as exists among insects [1] result from purely biological evolution. But as soon as psychophysical organisms are sufficiently evolved so that they can do useful or otherwise interesting things that are not exactly prescribed by instinct, can remember and repeat those interesting actions, and can imitate each other in the doing of them, then all the materials are present for the beginning of distinctively social evolution as distinguished from merely biological evolution. As we have noted, all evolution, biological and inorganic, is social in the sense of organized, correlated, but with the above conditions fulfilled we get the correlation of a new kind of elements, and so a new type of evolution. Of course the instinctive activities, especially the social instincts (sociability, dominance, etc.) continue to play their part in the more complex and higher correlation of activities in which the new elements are involved, just as the higher unities of nature are in general differentiated from the lower, not by the absence of all that had preceded, but by organizing preceding elements with the new elements into a new type of entity. The life of all human societies is rich in invented elements. The maternal instinct is as biological as mammae, but every human society has an array of socially evolved and communicated practices which are included in the exercise of the maternal function. Many of the animals that hunt in packs or graze in flocks have leaders, but the governmental

---

[1] There may be no more intelligence in the wonders of coöperation among ants and bees than there is in the yucca moth's method of securing the fertilization of the seeds its larvæ are to eat, or in the amazing process by which the beetle Sitaris gets inside the honeycomb.

organization of men includes not only instinctive dominance and submission, but also elements of custom and institution which instinct does not supply.

If, though gathering hints from lower orders of facts whenever they have hints to give us, we limit the range of phenomena which we make it our business to describe and explain, to those social (that is, correlated and interdependent) activities in which invention plays a part, we shall even then be obliged to begin with prehuman conduct. Most, if not all, of the animals concerning which we can be sure that the social instincts are well developed not merely as modes of muscular behavior, but also as emotions, have begun to invent, although with them instinct and instinctive emotion are relatively far more highly developed than invention.

Animal Invention.—The first essential of invention is experimentation. A race of animals whose instincts are so fixed and whose capacities for random or non-instinctive activity are so limited that they never do anything interesting that is not strictly prescribed by instinct, cannot advance their life by social evolution beyond the point to which biological evolution has brought it.[1] The remaining essentials of invention are effective memory and discrimination between pleasure and pain. The animal that can do new things, find them pleasant, remember, desire, and so repeat them, can invent; and if his associates can imitate him the invention may become a social possession.

Where the Rio Grande flows through a wooded region of Texas with waters so cold from melting mountain snows as to afford no "food, the ducks have learned to feed on seeds and grain," and can alight on a stalk of growing corn with the ease of a blackbird, and are quite at home among lofty

---

[1] Bembex, the wasp that is said to keep fresh supplies of meat by stinging grasshoppers so deftly as to paralyze them and not kill them, is obliged to labor to provide great stores of food for its young, because grubs infest the nest and eat the food and may even cause the young wasps to starve. The wasp cannot step aside from the instinctive path enough to sting the intruders and be rid of them. The inert things do not stimulate the stinging instinct.

trees where they make their nests." Here, apparently, is not only invention but invention spread by imitation.

Of imitation, as well as invention, among animals there is no doubt. It is familiarly observed in the parrot, magpie, raven, jackdaw, starling, and other birds. One mocking-bird is reported to have imitated thirty-two species found in its locality. In Germany bullfinches are taught to sing, or whistle, tunes. The characteristic songs of birds are apparently in part matters of art and social traditions developed on a basis of instinct. Three young linnets placed one with a skylark, one with a woodlark, one with a titlark, learned each the song of its foster-parent, "nor did they abandon this for their true song when placed among songsters of their own species." [1] The elaborate courting and mating practices of some animals are apparently in part matters of social invention and convention. Speaking of certain practices of the prairie hen and the jacana, C. Lloyd Morgan says: "The young birds are born into a society in which certain habits of dance, song, or other modes of activity, are already organized. By that subconscious and half-aware imitation which seems to be a trait of animal life,[2] they fall into the habits of their elders, as their elders did before them when they too were young and plastic." If they did otherwise "they would probably die unmated." [3]

It seems probable that not only the impulse to build a nest but also the impulse to build according to a more or less definite method is instinctive with birds, but it also seems certain that the method of nest-building is at least modified by experience and conditions as to material, choice of location, and other particulars.[4] In the presence of men, beavers exchange their noticeable abodes in cities for isolated burrows like those of the otter.[5] The numerous animals that pasture in flocks or herds, or that place their abodes in groups, like

---

[1] Morgan: Habit and Instinct, p. 178.
[2] By precisely this method men acquire moral standards, tastes and customs.
[3] Morgan: Habit and Instinct, p. 227.
[4] Ibid., p. 235.
[5] Espinas: Des Sociétés Animales, p. 494

the prairie dog, and depend for safety upon the vigilance of sentinels, may have invented that practice. Buffalo form with the horns of the bulls presented to a foe, the cows inside the ring of bulls, and the calves in the center of the mass. The courage, pugnacity, and partisanship of the bulls, the maternal instinct of the cows and the fear of the calves might well suffice to produce this result entirely without the presence in advance of any thought of this geometric arrangement; but the arrangement once experienced, a memory of it might be added as a supplement to the instinctive equipment. Primitive invention as a rule is similarly built upon a foundation of instinct. And the instincts of the higher animals, instead of narrowly prescribing certain movements, considerably resemble the instincts of man in being vague enough to allow room for random experimentation and so for invention. Thus in the cunning of beavers, foxes, elephants, and apes instinctive and invented elements seem to be indistinguishably mingled. When this is true the imitation of the old by the young may well furnish a part of their equipment for life, and social tradition may be established.

Inventions resulting from random experimentation do not imply the exercise of reason; even chickens are capable of such accidental discoveries. Reason is analysis and hypothesis. It picks to pieces a situation and recognizes the relations between its parts, especially the causal relations that account for the practically interesting result. As Lloyd Morgan recounts, puppies whose master had crossed a wire fence threw themselves upon it experimenting in every way that their anatomy allowed. One chanced upon a sufficient opening higher up where the wires were farther apart, and passed through, thereupon another imitated him and also passed through. The first puppy did not examine the fence and so discover the wider opening. A terrier searching for a ball in the street never found it except in the gutter and presently ceased to look elsewhere. He did not first observe that the roadway was crowning to shed water and that the ball must roll into the gutter. The same dog learned to open the yard gate by lifting the latch. He did not first distinguish the gate from the rest of the fence and then distinguish the latch from the rest of the gate; but he frantically thrust his head between the pickets, here and there, until by accident he touched the latch. Thereafter he remembered where to thrust his head in order to get out, but he never lifted the latch with his nose, but merely thrust his head in at the right place. Reason would have put its finger on the latch. Thus do animals and men make primitive discoveries by random experiment.

Man and His Poor Relations.—Man is not thought to be descended from any living ape, though both man and the ape had probably a common ancestor. And the lowest savages would not too greatly despise the kinship; indeed the savages are often proud to claim relationship with the animals. During the nine months preceding birth the human organism apparently retraces the course of its evolution. The human embryo at its successive stages resembles first the unicellular protozoan and subsequently the embryos of vermes, fish, amphibian, reptile, and tailed quadruped. "The same processes of development which once took thousands of years for their consummation are here condensed, foreshortened, concentrated into the space of weeks." Thus does each man born into the world "climb his own genealogical tree." At birth the ascent is not quite complete, for the anatomy of the human infant is adapted to the quadrumanal and not to the erect posture. Even when full-grown, man still has scores of rudimentary organs, which as man he cannot use but which his ancestors have required, such as muscles for pricking up the ears, three to five tail vertebre, and bands of fibrous tissue which in the human embryo, and in the prehuman ancestor were the tail-wagging muscles. Man and all the anthropoids most closely allied to him have long since lost their external tails. In certain animals the "blind tube" is as long as the body and of great use in digestion; in the early human embryo it is equal in caliber to the rest of the bowel, but in the orang it is but slightly larger than in man with whom it persists as a shrunken rudiment, the useless and mischief-making vermiform appendix.

In the order of primates the genus Homo stands structurally nearer to the old-world apes than the latter do to the apes of South America. Not only is this true as a general statement but, according to Professor Huxley,[1] there is no series of organs in the structure of which man and the higher apes are not nearer to each other than are the higher and the lower apes. It is social evolution that raises man far above the brutes and gives him his human dignity, that clothes him and puts speech in his mouth, and conscience in his breast.

The important differences between man and the Catarrhine apes are correlates of one fact, namely, increased dependence for survival upon brain work. The use of the front limbs, not for supporting the body but for manipulation which is begun by the apes, is a correlate of increasing brain work and brain power. Improvements in the hands are selected for survival when the brain can use the hands. Adjustment to the upright posture, strengthening the lower limbs to bear the whole burden of locomotion, diminishing the relative weight of the fore limbs and shortening them so as to manipulate at the present focal distance of the eyes, and the degeneracy of the jaws, no longer selected for the purposes of prehension which the hands have assumed, together with increase of brain mass, are all parts of one correlated change. The excessive lengthening of the arms in apes is an adjustment to the period of transition during which there is frequent alternation between the quadrupedal and bipedal posture.

Social evolution begins among the higher animals, and social coöperation heightens the efficiency of brain work and renders more certain the selection for survival of advantageous brain qualities. Primitive man had not completed the complex change just described; association hastened that change. Each of the least developed human races retains one or more marks of resemblance to the other primates, such as color of skin, thinness of legs, excessive length of arms, bigness of paunch, shortness of stature, prehensile toes, big and protruding jaws, or slightly smaller brain mass.

Although the beginnings of social evolution afford condi-

---

[1] Huxley: Man's Place in Nature. Appleton, 1863, p. 144.

tions that help to completion the final stages of physical evolution, the two do not long continue to progress *pari passu,* but physical (including cerebral) evolution presently reaches its culmination while social evolution continues indefinitely,[1] that is, the systems of activity, socially prevalent and socially evolved continue to enrich and extend and complicate their correlated processes.

Stages of Social Evolution.—No thorough agreement has been reached as to the standards to be applied in determining the stage of advancement which has been reached in the social evolution of a given people. (1) Ethnologists, like Brinton, Ratzel, and Frobenius, depend upon the general impression left by a comprehensive description. (2) Liszt, Bücher, Peschel, and in general those writers who adopt the economic interpretation of history classify peoples according to the character and intensity of economic life. (3) Spencer, DeGreef, Giddings, and Durkheim would classify according to the degree to which invention has carried the differentiation of social activities. (4) Steinmetz, Vierkandt, and Comte classify according to the methods of thought and proof employed.

If the attempt is made to classify the many peoples that exist or that are known to have existed on the earth with reference to the level of social evolution which they have attained, it must be borne in mind that people who with reference to social evolution are but savages in the Stone Age, like our own savage ancestors, may be biologically of the highest development and entirely capable of reaching the highest levels of social life. It is true, however, that the lowest of the peoples who to-day are in the savage state are also biologically the lowest representatives of the genus Homo. The same is not true of the higher of existing savages. And when we are told that savages are incapable of prolonged attention and that thought quickly wearies them, we do well to bear in mind that savages can ponder their problems, if not ours, and that the power of attention is largely measured by interest, and that what they lack may

---

[1] Compare section beginning on p. 279.

be, in some races at least, not brain power, but developed interests. And the violent and transient passions of nature men are due, in part at least, to the absence of inhibiting ideals and of discipline from childhood. They sometimes show great control when they have ideals that demand it, and patient and persistent purpose when they have aims that can summon it. "Among the savage races of to-day we find great differences in endowments,"[1] but the classes or stages which we are about to enumerate have very little to do with levels of natural endowment, and peoples totally unrelated physically will be assigned to the same class or stage of social development.

The words "savage" and "barbarous" which are commonly employed as designations of the earlier stages of social progress express unjustified feelings of race partisanship, prejudice and bigotry, and if we use those words we must divest them of such connotations. Perhaps there is no better way to strip them of these false meanings than to put them to scientific use as terms of classification, and to put our own ancestors and the peoples from whom we have learned great lessons under these headings.

Sutherland[2] proposed the following classification:

"I. SAVAGES.—Deriving their food from wild products of nature; therefore always thinly scattered and in small societies; their lives engrossed in the constant struggle for sustenance.

"1. *Lower savages.* Dwarfs in stature; pot-bellied and spindle-legged; wooly-headed and flat-nosed; wandering in families of ten to forty; without dwellings and with only a trace of clothing; with the smallest cranial capacities of all mankind. Including[3]: Bushmen (South Africa), Akka (Guinea Forests), Negritos (Philippines, etc.), Andaman

---

[1] Friedrich Ratzel: History of Mankind. London, 1896, i, 23.

[2] Reproduced with slight changes from "Origin and Growth of the Moral Instinct," by Alexander Sutherland. Longmans, Green & Co., 1898, p. 103.

[3] In identifying "lower" and "middle" savages Sutherland takes account of both biological and social traits. With respect to *social* evolution alone some of his "middle" savages are far below the Bushmen.

Islanders, Semangs (Malay Peninsula), Veddahs (Ceylon), Kimos (Madagascar). Scanty aboriginal remnants of this dwarf negroid description are found on the west frontiers of China,[1] in Formosa and Hainan; in the innermost forest ranges of Borneo, Sumatra, Celebes, Flores and Ceram. The females of these races are often under four feet in height; Emin Pasha measured a full-grown female Akka under three feet ten inches, and Barrow, a Bushman woman, the mother of several children, who was under three feet nine inches. Prevailed throughout Europe thousands of years ago.

"2. *Middle savages.* Range up to average human height; of finer physical aspect; dwellings only screens against the wind; use of clothing known, but nudity common in both sexes; canoes are rudely fashioned; weapons well made of wood and stone; wander in tribes of fifty to two hundred; without ranks or social organizations, but tribal usages have the force of law. Including: Tasmanians, Australians, Ainus of Japan, Hottentots, Fuegians, Macas and other forest tribes of Brazil and Guiana.

"3. *Higher savages.* Dwellings are always made, though in general only tents of skin; clothing is always possessed, though nudity common enough in both sexes; notably better weapons of stone, bone or copper; wander in tribes of one hundred to five hundred; incipient signs of rank, chiefs have an ill-defined authority, but tribal usage relied on to maintain orderliness of life. Including: most of the North American Indians, such as Esquimaux, Koniagas, Aleuts, Tinnehs, Nootkas, Chinooks, Decotas, Mandans, Comanches, Chippeways, Haidahs, Shoshones, Californian tribes; South American natives: Patagonians, Abipones, Uaupes, Araucanians, Mundurucus, Arawaks, and other coastal or river tribes of Guiana and Brazil; African races: Damaras; Asiatic races: Nicobar Islanders, Kamtschadales, Samoyedes; Aboriginals of India: Todas, Kurumbas, Nagas, Dhimals, Kukis, Santals, Billahs, Karens, Mishmis, Juangs.

"II. Barbarians.—Obtain the larger part of their food by forethought in directing productive forces of nature; hence

---

[1] Lockhart: Ethno. Soc., i, 178.

agriculture and breeding of animals are notable features, but each family secures its own necessaries, there being little division of occupation; yet food being more abundant and more evenly divided through the year, arts and sciences become incipient.

"1. *Lower barbarians.* Dwellings generally fixed, forming villages; clothing regularly worn, except in hot climates; nudity of women rare; earthenware manufactures; good canoes built; characteristic implements of stone, wood or bone; cultivation of small plots round dwellings; trade incipient; ranks determinate but founded on individual prowess in war; government by chiefs with traditionary laws; living in tribes of one thousand to five thousand, but capable of forming larger confederacies. Including: In America: Iroquois, Thlinkeets, Guatemalans, Nicaraguans, Mosquitos; some in Australasia: Maoris of New Zealand, Biaras of New Britain, Tombaras of New Ireland, Obaos of New Caledonia, natives of New Hebrides, natives of Solomon Islands, natives of New Guinea; in Africa: Kaffirs, Bechuanas, Basutos, Wakamba Negroes; in Asia: Dyaks of Borneo, etc., Jakums of Malay Peninsula, Battaks of Sumatra, Tunguz, Yakuts, Kurghiz, Ostriaks; Indian aborigines: Hos, Mundas, Oraons, Paharias, Gonds, Khonds, Bheels.

"2. *Middle barbarians.* Good permanent dwellings, generally of wood or thatch; formed into towns of considerable size; always able to make clothing of moderate comeliness, but nudity not considered indecent; pottery, weaving, metal working carried on to some extent; commerce in its early stage; money used, regular markets held; consolidated into states running up to 100,000 persons under petty kings; traditionary codes of laws administered; ranks well defined, arising partly from individual, partly from family prowess in war. Including: in Africa: Negro races—Dahomeys, Ashantees, Fantees, Foolahs, Shillooks, Baris, Latookas, Wanyamo, Waganda, Wanyoro, Wanyamwezi, Bongos, Niam-niams, Dinkas, Yorubas, Monbuttus, Balondas, Ovampos, Foorians. In Polynesia: Figians, Tongans, Samoans, Marquesas Islanders. In Europe: Lapps of two centuries ago. In Asia: Kalmucks. Historically:

Greeks of Homeric ages; Romans anterior to Numa; German races of Cæsar's time, etc.

"3. *Higher barbarians*. Able to build with stones; clothing necessary in ordinary life; weaving a constant occupation of women; iron implements generally made; metal working greatly advanced; money coined; small ships made, but propelled with oars; law rudely administered in recognized courts; people welded into masses up to 500,000 under rule of a sovereign; writing in incipient stage; ranks hereditary; division of occupations advancing. Including: in Africa: Abyssinians, Zanzibar races, Somali, Malagasies. In Asia: Malays of Sumatra, Java, Celebes, Borneo, Malay Peninsula, Sooloo Archipelago, etc.; Nomad Tatars, Nomad Arabs, Baluchs, etc. In Polynesia: Tahitians, Hawaiians. Historically: Greeks of time of Solon; Romans of early Republic; Anglo-Saxons of the Heptarchy; Mexicans at time of Spanish Conquest; Peruvians at time of Spanish Conquest; Jews under the Judges.

"III. CIVILIZED.—Food and necessaries obtained with increased facility by the coöperation that arises from intricate subdivision of occupations. This leads to great efficiency through specialization, and in consequence the social organism becomes extremely varied in function but consolidated by interdependence. Steady growth of arts and sciences.

"1. *Lower civilized*. Cities formed and surrounded by stone walls; important buildings elaborately designed in stone; the plow used; war tends to become the business of a class; writing established; laws rudely written; formal courts of justice established; literature begins. Including: in Africa: Algerines, Tunisians, Moors, Kabyles, Touaregs, etc. In Asia: Turcomans, Thibetans, Bhutans, Nepalese, Laos, Cochinese, Anamese, Cambodians, Coreans, Manchoorians, settled Arabs. Historically: Jews of time of Solomon; Assyrians, Egyptians, Phœnicians, Babylonians, Carthaginians; Greeks after Marathon; Romans in time of Hannibal; English under Norman kings.

"2. *Middle civilized*. Temples and rich men's houses handsomely built in stone or brick; glass windows come into use; trades greatly multiply; ships propelled with sails; writing grows common, and manuscript books are spread abroad; the literary education of the young attended to; war becomes an entirely distinct profession; laws are framed into statutes and the class of lawyers arises. Including: in Asia: Persians, Siamese, Burmese, Afghans. In Europe: Finns, Magyars of last century; Greeks of Pericles' time; Romans of later Republic; Jews of the Macedonian Conquest; England under Plantagenets; France under early Capets.

"3. *Higher civilized.* Stone dwellings common; roads paved; canals, watermills, windmills, etc.; navigation becomes scientific; chimneys used; writing a common acquirement; manuscript books largely used; literature in high repute; strong central government extending over tens of millions; fixed codes of law reduced to writing and officially published; courts elaborate; government officers numerous and carefully graded. Including: Chinese, Japanese, Hindoos, Turks; Romans under the Empire; Italians, French, English, Germans of the fifteenth century."

IV. CULTURED.[1]—1. *Lower.* (a) Problem of *production* measurably solved. (b) Extensive substitution of natural forces for human muscle, and increasing efficiency of organization secures to the masses *leisure* to cultivate mental and esthetic faculties; universal education the only tolerated standard. (c) Warlike prowess and birth steadily losing preeminence as standards of personal excellence, and even in countries inheriting a military aristocracy, high if not equal social rank and reputation can be had on the ground of wealth and of achievement in science, art, literature, politics, etc. (d) General education and the press render possible the prompt formation and effective expression of intelligent public opinion by great populations, resulting in democracy; laws are made by the representatives of the people. (e) National efforts begin to be directed to other than military and economic ends, particularly the promotion and general propagation of sciences and arts.

---

[1] From this point on we offer a substitute for the descriptions of Sutherland.

This stage has been reached by the most advanced nations of the present.

2. *Middle.* (a) Problem of *distribution* measurably solved; all normal persons well fed, clothed and housed.

(b) Liberal education practically universal.

(c) War universally disapproved (as brawls between individuals now are), though of occasional occurrence. Limited armies and navies of all nations coöperate as a world police.

(d) Mere wealth no longer regarded as success but economic achievement in the form of invention or highly efficient organization and management is ranked with political and other achievement, business success being measured by productivity of goods or services rather than by profits retained by the manager.

(e) So much may be ventured as inferences based upon existing tendencies, but to complete the description would be to venture too far into the field of prophecy. Centuries may intervene before this stage is fully reached.

3. *Higher.* No prophecy is ventured—a thousand or two thousand years may pass before the aggregation of progress justifies an additional classification of the leading nations. It may be that the conquest of diseases and physical defects will have progressed so far through the advancement and popularization of science and the organization of public preventive activities, that lack of health will be the rare exception. And it may well be that all great advances will have become known to practically all the world, though differences of geographic environment will invite different adaptations of life. And the diversification of life may have become a world cult so that different populations will be consciously developing characteristic arts and activities by a world-wide division of labor in the practice of culture-life.

The Stages of Social Evolution According to Vierkandt, Steinmetz and Comte.—Vierkandt, taking as the most fundamental distinction that between nature peoples and culture peoples,[1] would make nature peoples include the savage and barbarous, would call the civilized and lower cultured "half-cul-

---

[1] Compare p. 403.

ture peoples" as having reached the phase of rational acceptance with reference to physical sciences and practical arts, but
not with reference to political, religious, ethical and other
activities, and would make the culture people coincide practically with the middle and higher culture people of Sutherland. Steinmetz accepts Vierkandt's fundamental division
between "nature" and "culture" peoples but classifies the leading nations of the present as culture peoples on the ground
that the dominating members of the most advanced societies
are in the phase of rational acceptance with reference to life's
activities as a whole, and that a people should be classified
with reference to its leaders rather than by the more democratic method of Vierkandt who would wait until the masses
attain that level before classifying a population as a culture
people.

Steinmetz[1] adds that other discriminations than that between nature peoples and culture peoples can be based upon
recognition of well-marked stages of intellectual method.

First are the primitive, men whose attention was occupied
almost exclusively with the objects of sense perception, who
had no ideas about the unknown but were materialists and
positivists such as exist nowhere else, without religion or
idea of the soul, spirits or fetishes—sensationalists we may
call them, whose method of thought did not differ much
from that of the chimpanzees. Though traces of this stage
may perhaps remain, it was in general prehistoric.

Second are the people who are characterized by the mythological method of thought with its naïveté and procedure by
analogy. Among such people fetishism, ancestor worship and
animism develop. There is no felt need of bringing conceptions into a system.

Third come the systematizing peoples. This term Steinmetz uses so broadly as to include the makers of the greater
mythologies with their hierarchies of supernatural beings; and
also those peoples whom we have spoken of as in the authoritative stage who do not invent mythologies but may believe
in them and who base their thinking upon the already accumu-

---

[1] Steinmetz: L'Année sociologique, 1898-1899, p. 71.

lated teachings of the past; and also the metaphysicians, or speculative reasoners, having but a slender basis in facts for their theories, though possessing "a kind of erudition," and insisting upon logical consistency in their doctrines, whom we have regarded as the systematizers proper.

Finally come the critical peoples, as Steinmetz calls them, in some respects a happier designation than that of Vierkandt, but meaning the same as the latter's "culture peoples." Steinmetz remarks that the Protestantism of the sixteenth and seventeenth centuries was one of the first manifestations of the essential spirit of this stage of social activity. Protestantism in that sense was, however, a rather temporary and sporadic phenomenon, and Protestant populations in general have till very recently not been "critical" in their acceptance of religious beliefs and activities, but, authoritative, have exercised their intelligence rather in defending traditional deductions from the Bible than in deciding what views should be held. The critical societies are increasingly characterized by humanitarian morality which recognizes the worth of men of every class, by methodical, not spasmodic, social reforms, and regular scientific progress in the various departments of life.

Of all the generalizations concerning the stages of progress perhaps the most famous is that of Comte. He teaches that human thought passes through three stages, which he calls the "theological," the "metaphysical" and the "positive." The facts which he represents by these designations are those above indicated as the mythological, the systematizing and the critical or scientific stages.[1]

Economic Stages or Types.—Mention should be given also to these familiar designations: (1) The rough stone or paleolithic age; (2) the smooth stone age. It would be better to say stage or type rather than age because peoples still surviving have reached only this stage. In fact this is the type of savagery with which we are most familiar. Among people in the neolithic stage may be found domestication of the

---

[1] Compare also p. 374 on the classification of methods of thought and proof. There an authoritative stage is recognized in addition to the three stages noted by the authors just cited.

horse, ox, pig, sheep, goat and dog; spinning, weaving and pottery, and even beginnings in the working of bronze and iron. Vast periods of slow beginnings were passed before these things were done. (3) The bronze age; (4) the iron age; (5) to this we must add the age of power machinery.

These as well as the "stages" described by Sutherland, Vierkandt, Steinmetz and Comte are believed to have succeeded each other. But if we attempt to classify the different types of cultures minutely we shall find it impossible to arrange our types in series in which the highest have passed through all the lower forms; for social evolution has branched at various points and the higher social types have not successively passed through all the lower forms.

As the biologist selects certain structures or characters, of which cephalization is the chief, as a basis for classifying animal forms, so Steinmetz proposes that we adopt the economic activities as the basis for classifying social types. And on this basis he proposes ten types or species, each of which may be subdivided into varieties.

1. Collectors of roots, berries, fruits, grubs, ant larvæ (Bushman's rice) and small slow animals; pasturers upon nature's gifts with only the very simplest weapons or tools; neither hunters nor fishers; "wanderers" making no better shelter than a windbreak of bushes. This type in its unmixed form is wholly prehistoric, but its activities survive, mingled with higher activities.

2. Hunters. The lowest class are also largely collectors; others are pure hunters; others still hunters and fishers; and yet others have various occupations as supplements to hunting.

3. Fishers. Including fishers who also collect and hunt, pure fishers, and fishers who are also ferrymen, sailors, pirates, or who mingle other occupations with their characteristic work of fishing.

4. Agricultural nomads. Pure agriculturists, nomadic agriculturists with whom hunting and fishing are almost as important as the raising of crops, and those who combine with their agriculture still other occupations.

5. Lower settled agriculturists.

6. Superior agriculturists. Industry and commerce represent no separate calling, save in the case of the smith, and possibly one or two others. Hunting has passed into entire subordination. Far more careful tillage is aided by somewhat important artificial means, sometimes including irrigation.

7. Nomadic herdsmen.

8. Societies characterized by division of occupations, but with little concentration of laborers into trade centers and occupational groups. Here would fall the Europeans till the last third of the Middle Ages.

9. Manufacturing societies. The "mercantilist" period.

10. Societies of our own type, business life based on the factory system, or what Ward calls "machinofacture" in what we have denominated the "age of power machinery." Extensive division, not only between occupations, but also of labor within occupations, all economic life included in a system of international commerce.

CHAPTER XXVI

ADDITIONAL ELEMENTS IN THE THEORY OF SOCIAL EVOLUTION

Social realities are so much alive, and so continually in process, that in describing their nature it has seemed necessary to include statements which go far toward explaining their evolution. These statements were included in part under the subjects of Social Suggestion, Sympathetic Radiation, Imitation, and all of the five Modes of Variation to Which Social Realities Are Subject. Now we must complete, so far as possible, the general concept of social evolution. At the outset let us again remind ourselves *what* it is the evolution of which we are attempting to understand. It is that fourth kingdom of reality which was described in the chapters entitled The Analysis and Classification of Social Activities, and The Social Order. To place ourselves in thought at the beginning of the process of social evolution we must conceive of the time when there was upon earth nothing that we should recognize as language, religion, conscience and conscience code, government, economic art, superstition, far less science, and when the lowest of the stages that have been referred to in the preceding chapter was barely beginning.

Application of General Principles of Evolution to Social Realities.—As we have seen, the general theory of evolution is that the simplest and most primitive realities unite to form a situation out of which a new kind of reality emerges which being added to the preceding realities creates a situation out of which yet other realities emerge which in turn are added to all that went before to create a situation out of which emerge other realities still, until at length there emerge organisms that include in their make-up social instincts of sociability, sympathy, partisanship, dominance and submission, as well

474

as power for action in ways not narrowly prescribed by instinct, for random experimentation, for memory, pleasure-pain, and for imitation. Such organisms being added to all that had gone before we have a situation out of which emerges the fourth kingdom of realities—massive systems of social activity. In the following figure each point in a horizontal line represents an activity. Each horizontal line represents a plane of social advancement, built out of correlated and prevalent social activities. Each perpendicular represents an invention, a new activity which, spreading through the social plane, raises it to a new level on which yet further inventions become possible.

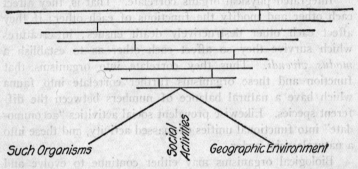

Such Organisms   Social Activities   Geographic Environment

An activity that is imitated throughout a group creates a situation in which additional invention becomes possible. A society that moves heavy weights on rollers is one in which the wheel may be invented and with the general use of the wheel come various further possibilities of invention. An invention that is imitated, from being a point (the activity of one) becomes a line, a new level (in which each point is the activity of one); from any point of the new level a further activity may shoot up to spread out into a higher level still with still higher possibilities of further invention.

Biological evolution begins in homogeneity, a mass of undifferentiated protoplasm with neither parts nor organs, a mass of jelly. Social evolution also begins with homogeneity with the dead level of custom, with groups in which all imitate the same activities, share the same wants, tastes, fears, superstitions, and practices, and almost the only differentiations are biological; some are men, some women, some young, some old, some weak, some strong, but all have the same homogeneous and protoplasmic lives.

Biological evolution escapes from structureless homogeneity by differentiation, and what differentiation is to biological evolution invention is to social evolution.

Cells bearing a similar differentiation integrate; sensitive cells stretch out toward each other and form the beginnings of a nervous system; secreting cells unite into glands. Likewise by the process of suggestion, sympathetic radiation, and imitation social activities integrate into masses.

Integrated physical organs correlate. That is, they affect each other and modify the functions of each other; if they affect each other destructively death ensues; in creatures which survive they so affect each other as to establish a *modus vivendi*. Thus they correlate into organisms that function and these organisms further correlate into fauna which have a natural balance of numbers between the different species. Likewise prevalent social activities "accommodate" into functional unities of massed activity, and these into a natural social order.

Biological organisms may either continue to evolve and to multiply or they may degenerate and become extinct. Likewise the functional unities of social activity may continue to evolve by further invention, social suggestion, radiation and imitation, and variations in strength, uniformity, content and phase, and may either extend in prevalence or decline and disappear.

Biological Evolution	*Social Evolution*
Homogeneity	Homogeneity
Differentiation or Mutation	Invention
Integration	Suggestion, Sympathetic Radiation and Imitation
Correlation	Accommodation
Structures and	Functional Unities of Social Action and

Biological Evolution	*Social Evolution*
Fauna	Natural Social Order
Structures survive and	Social Activities continue, gain in prevalence, strength
Evolve or	and prestige and
Degenerate and	Evolve or
Become extinct	Decline and
According to fitness to evolving environment.	Disappear
	According to logical and practical fitness under changing conditions.

Invention.—Now having gained some aid from comparisons, let us proceed again with perfect literalness. By invention we mean any activity that is interesting enough to be remembered and purposely repeated and imitated.

The first pithecanthropus semi-erectus who in excitement seized a stone and afterward remembered the increased efficiency that it gave to his blow so as to repeat the act upon the next occasion made a great invention.[1] And inventions are not always mechanical. We speak properly of rhetorical and artistic inventions, and we invent explanations. The idea of carrying a rabbit's foot to bring luck was an invention, so also was the nebular hypothesis and the doctrine of hell fire; these were inventions in the realm of creed and science; the tum, ta-ta, tum, tum of the characteristic tom-tom beat accompanying a particular dance was an invention that doubtless made gleeful its originator, so also was the dance itself, so also the hit-and-run play in baseball, these and thousands more in the realm of art and play; so also was the idea that poisoning war arrows was unfair and unworthy of a fighting man, the disapproval of cannibalism, and later of slavery, the idea of taking the skull or the scalplock as a trophy, and the golden rule—all in the realm of approvals; so also was trial by jury and election by ballot, in the realm of political organization.

There are three grades of invention:

---

[1] We do not know that any *ape* ever made this invention.

1. Most of the earliest inventions were of the random-experiment type, which even in modern times plays no unimportant part.

2. But another element was added by the imaginative recombination of elements furnished by experience, this reconstruction of elements being guided by reason. Men like other animals lie down to sleep on the lee side of a rock or thick clump of bushes; they often wake up cold because the wind has changed. They may in time stick bushes into the ground in a circle making a circular windbreak, thus affecting a rearrangement of familiar objects of experience. They often wake up wet by rains. Like other animals they have often crept under the branches of trees and shrubbery for protection from rain, and if now they draw together the tops of the bushes in their windbreak then, by this additional rearrangement of familiar objects, they have the beginnings of a hut of wattles. Of this sort of invention necessity is the mother. Reconstructive imagination is a great improver of previous inventions.

3. Every invention is itself an additional element that may enter into the constructive combinations of imagination; thus invention is cumulative like a snowball—or like other evolution. A later generation, though of no greater natural capacity than their ancestors, can make inventions that to their ancestors were impossible. For one with the knowledge of mechanics that was common property in Stephenson's day to invent the steam-engine may have required no greater natural ability than that which was displayed by the first maker of a wheel, a bow, or a friction device for fire-making.

Inventions before they can become group possessions must form themselves in individual minds, and the occasional appearance of exceptional minds is of great importance at every stage of social evolution. But "the individual mind cannot rise much above the level of the group mind. The extraordinary individual works on the material and psychic fund already present, and if the situation is not ripe neither is he ripe." Moreover, "when the state of science and the social need reach a certain point a number of individuals are likely to solve the same problem." [1]

Attention Foci.—The direction of progress in invention is determined by two sets of factors: wants and occasions, or predisposition and environment.

1. Under the spur of *wants* experimentation redoubles, constructive imagination makes its short leaps, and along the hot association paths old elements, or old and new, shoot together into new combinations. This temporary heating up of special areas of mental activity we call attention. Attention is the mother of invention, want is its grandmother. Wants may be spoken of as primary and secondary. (a) Hunger, mating instinct and fear are the most conspicuous of the primary wants, the strongest urgencies to primitive invention. Fear not only leads to warlike activity and organization, but also leads as much to religious ritualism. (b) The social instincts, curiosity, and the desires that find expression in art and play, may represent the secondary group of propensities. The social instincts prompt various modes of display and emulation, ornamentation, exploits and trophy-taking. Beliefs originate mainly in the practical necessity to have guides for action, but the richness of invention of new beliefs from early stages is increased by the desire to reach an understanding of conditions and events. Among the most ancient remains of the cave men are the drawings of animals long since extinct on bits of bone or ivory and the walls of caverns. The tom-tom and the dramatic dance foreshadow the opera.

2. *Crises.* To understand the foci of attention and the budding of invention we must take into account not only the above-mentioned wants, or propensities, with which man is endowed, but also the occasions that bring special stimulation to these propensities. These occasions Professor Thomas names "crises." Instinctive activities and after the beginning of social evolution the habits that are built up about instincts and supplement them with conduct almost as automatic as the functioning of instincts and involving only a minimum

---

[1] W. I. Thomas: Source Book for Social Origins. University of Chicago Press, 1909. Introduction, p. 20.

of attention, flow on unchanged until an occasion arises in which the instinctive and habitual conduct does not satisfy the wants, so that the propensities are unusually stimulated and attention unusually excited; then inventions may occur. Crises are of two sorts, recurrent and singular. (a) Recurrent crises. Besides the still more frequently returning occasions for the excitation of propensity (hunger, fear, etc.) there come now and again to every group birth, death, adolescence, marriage, sickness, psychic irregularities such as dreams, intoxication and swoon, and crimes and injuries between members. About these foci of excited attention man early builds up systems of characteristic conduct. (b) Singular crises. Invasion, defeat, pestilences, and failure of the customary food supply illustrate what is meant by singular crises. They may prove blessings in disguise, not to the individuals who suffer them, but to the social evolution of the group, because they break up the fixity of custom, compel new adjustments of activity, and so introduce periods of progress.

The Fixation of Social Species.—1. Invention that supplies a need tends to inhibit other inventions that might supply the same need differently. This is especially true of primitive peoples. For a people who build round huts of wattles the very idea of a shelter is the idea of just such a hut and nothing else.[1]

2. The psychological principle of familiarity and homesickness tends to make the usual comfortable and satisfactory and to make every departure from the familiar method of activity uncomfortable, repulsive and absurd.

3. Group pride reënforces this repugnance to the strange, renders any innovator within the group who attempts to modify the time-honored practices, the object of scorn and disapproval, and causes the suggestions which emanate from other groups to be treated with hostility and contempt.

---

[1] Some build round and some in parallelograms, each after their kind; and some set the huts of the encampment in a circle and some set them in rows, with a specific place for each hut according to the kinship of the occupants. The Russian "ring villages" and "row villages" may well be survivals of these customs.

4. With the acquisition of a considerable body of tradition, the ascendancy of the aged becomes pronounced. This ascendancy is surprisingly strong in undeveloped societies. They have no notion of social evolution by gradual improvement, but as a rule attribute every completed invention to some ancestor or half-mythical personage of a more heroic age. The declining generation forms the connection with this past, through which has been transmitted all its bequests, the social heritage of arts, customs, and beliefs. Moreover, through childhood and youth the habit of looking up to the members of the preceding generation has been formed and this habit holds men fast throughout their lives and assists in maintaining the prestige of the aging generation long after the departure of their power to enforce obedience. This ascendancy of the aged is an additional preventive of innovation. With the old the principles of familiarity and nostalgia operate with increased force, and so also does group pride in those traditions which were good enough for their forefathers whom they revered, which they themselves have followed all their lives, and upon respect for which their own prestige is founded.

5. The fear of innovation is both a natural dread of additional uncertainties in the life already sufficiently fraught with uncertainties and perils, and also a superstitious dread of offending the departed spirits of ancestors whose customs innovation would violate and of offending whatever other mysterious powers have assented to the usual course of living and might be angered by departure from it. A man of a round-hut building group would probably shrink in terror from lying down to sleep in a shelter which he had constructed according to an unauthorized design; a man would expect no crop if he planted without the usual ceremonies.

For such reasons as these the activities of relatively undeveloped societies are extremely fixed and rigid. Each group adheres to its own characteristic superstitions, sentiments, and practices, with almost as thorough conformity to type as that with which a given kind of plant retains the shape of its leaves and the color of its flowers. A representative of any one of scores of primitive peoples will resemble in all his activities any other member of the same group as closely as two specimens of the same botanical species resemble each other. The system of group activity becomes a fixed social species bound to continue generation after generation with but little change unless overtaken by some crisis that breaks up the traditional usages. There is evidence that certain groups have thus maintained their social type for many generations practically unchanged, and there is probability that some have done so since a bygone geologic age.

Cross-Fertilization of Cultures.—The one thing above all others that has had power to shatter the crust of custom and induce mutation and progress is contact with other groups. If one group, being thoroughly custom-bound, comes in contact with another group having different ways all in working order, the people of the first group are compelled to admit at least that other ways than their own will work, and usually also that some of the new ways work better than their own traditions.[1] Such contacts have three results: (1) There are two complete systems of activity to choose from, and the competing methods of activity adjust themselves according to the laws[2] of accommodation. (2) New inventions, which would have been impossible to either people in isolation, now arise, because of the access of materials for imaginative combination, according to the third principle of invention. (3) A progressive and hopeful frame of mind, in which new ideas and ways have good opportunity to gain acceptance, to spread, and to become incorporated into the common stock, temporarily replaces the repellant rigidity of custom.[3]

War, migration, and commerce have been the great agencies in the cross-fertilization of cultures.

The great significance of geographic environment in con-

---

[1] Compare discussion of amenability of different modes of activity to rational innovation, p. 400.

[2] Compare page 333. The word "laws" is here used in a broad sense.

[3] It would be profitable to compare and contrast the above with the main teaching of Ludwig Gumplowicz, in "Der Rassenkampf Innsbruck," 1909, especially pp. 179 *seq.*

demning some groups to isolation and long stagnation, and in placing other groups in the highways of intercommunication has already been discussed.[1]

Not only in the earlier stages of social evolution when the bondage of custom is most strict, but also in the development of historic nations, the great blossoming times and places have been the points of unusual inter-group contact, such as oft-conquered Egypt, Syria, Phœnicia the great gatherer and scatterer of culture seeds, Attica and the Ionian Islands, Rome when all roads led to her and her emissaries traveled all roads, the track of Rome's armies through Gaul, the seaports of medieval Italy, the Hanseatic trade route, the pathways of monks scattered from ancient seats of culture and of pilgrims and crusaders who brought Orient and Occident face to face; and now we see the Farther East, Japan and China, included in the current of cosmopolitan life. The dark ages and places have been those given over to provincialism.

Folkways and Mores.[2]—We live in one of those rare epochs when progress is believed in.[3] There has never before been such an era of hope as this. Cosmopolitanism forbids stagnation; the inventions of nearly all the world at once become the common property of many millions; science deliberately prosecutes advancement of knowledge; new ideas bring not dungeon and stake, but honor and fame, and the powers of government are employed not merely to terrorize the unruly and to repel or attempt spoliation, but also to promote progress toward a condition of general welfare. But we must not think on this account that the long process of social evolution has resulted from efforts to promote progress. That would

---

[1] Compare p. 31.

[2] Words adopted in their present sense by Professor W. G. Sumner: Folkways. Ginn and Co., 1907.

[3] Social life is so complex in its nature and causation that one may almost declare that nothing is true of man without qualification. Rare souls in dark and stagnant times have believed in progress and have inculcated a vague messianic hope. But it correctly represents the general tone of the picture and states a great fact to say that the creed of progress has been the possession of only rare epochs.

be fatal to our understanding of the facts. Men have not set themselves to invent new and higher wants. The masses of men have not believed in progress but as a rule each tribe has dreamed of a heroic age in the past when they were more gloriously successful than now in doing all that they now attempt. The first social ideas, sentiments, and practices simply appeared as a resultant of the combination of biological propensity with stimulating environment, as other products of natural causation arise. In primitive times individuals in whose minds there was no conception of social progress strove to satisfy their individual wants and to meet their exciting crises. And in so doing they occasionally made inventions which became social possessions. These inventions created a situation which was ripe for still further inventions, previously impossible. Ideas, sentiments, and practices that would not work or that would not work together with the previously existing set of ideas, sentiments, and practices could not spread and continue, though according to the principles of accommodation the old was somewhat adapted to the new, as well as new to old. Groups with an inefficient set of usages disappeared, and when group systems collided those elements tended to survive which were more effective in satisfying wants or in securing bodily survival. Indigenous culture elements and culture systems are not chosen but evolved. When contact takes place with another group having another system of social activities, a brief interlude of rational eclecticism may result. But in the absence of such contacts where there is no choice between usages and each act is compared not with rival ways of meeting the same want but with failure to do the only thing that there is to do in the case, there the existing usage that meets the want tends to be practiced by the mass of men as a matter of course like swallowing or walking, and not as a matter of rational approval.

Yet barbarians and savages are far from thoughtless. Moreover, they cannot be called pure individualists, even if they are pure egoists; for their ego is tribal. Even the desire for survival under certain circumstances is desire for group survival, and what we have called the instinct of partisanship makes the savage feel group injuries as injuries to himself and group aggrandizement as his own. Being neither thoughtless nor pure individualists they reflect upon their ways, and reflect upon them as group ways. And so activities which come into being by what is as purely a process of natural causation as the evolution of plants, later are cherished as objects of rational approval. Indeed the rational approvals which come to be mixed with such activities are themselves natural products of organic tendency and environment. Social activities may continue without any element of rational approval, or even in spite of an unwilling and therefore partly suppressed disapproval. But activities that have come to include an overtone of rational approval are what Professor Sumner calls mores. Reflection guided by group interest develops more or less clear generalizations as to what is good group policy, and the definite and consistent system of activities which are prized and insisted on by the group judgment as the accepted methods of attaining desired ends is the portion of social activity which may be spoken of as the institutions of the group.

Natural Selection.—Natural selection so pervades social evolution that its manifestations have necessarily come to the surface at many points in our discussion. (1) It appears in war between groups as a result of which the practices of the conquered perish with them or are suppressed or discredited, while the activities of the conquerors gain in confident strength and in prestige that is calculated to secure not only the continuance but also the wider spread of those activities. (2) It appears in economic competition between those who sell either commodities or services. Absence of demand kills the unsuccessful practices while strong demand multiplies the prevalence of successful practices. (3) It appears in the natural decline in numbers and prestige on the part of groups and classes whose activities are relatively ill adapted to actual conditions of physical survival which are laid down by the natural physical environment which applies the tests of hunger, cold, and disease. (4) It appears in the decline of activities within the group even when the group itself does not decline, owing to the practical test of pleasure and pain, and likewise in the spread not only of those material arts that yield food and warmth, but also of such social realities as promote mental peace and cheer, including pleasant play, fine arts, political routine that promotes instinctive justice, religious notions that allay anxiety and fear and minister consolation, for example, by supplying something to do on which the votary can repose in faith that protection has been secured, or that the future is not wholly without a clue. And those activities which in a given society promote reputation and elicit favor are pleasurable and tend to spread while those that evoke ridicule or contempt are painful and so are naturally repressed or exterminated. (5) A form of natural selection appears in the test of reason. Logical absurdity may exist unperceived, or if perceived it may be little attended to when interest urges the acceptance of the absurd belief. Yet on the whole there is a selective preference in human nature for the reasonable as truly as for the pleasant. In fact, to hold beliefs the unreasonableness of which cannot be overlooked is unpleasant as well as intellectually difficult and becomes impossible. The judgments of reason are most readily formed in the light of an objective material demonstration, such as the comparison between the earth turned up by a spade and that turned up by plow, or between the distance covered by a pedestrian and by a man mounted upon a camel, or between the camel rider and an express train. But it is necessary to observe what has usually been overlooked, that material advantage is not the only practical test, for pleasure and pain, as these terms must be used in this connection, include the psychic experiences referred to above in the statement numbered four, as truly as the agreeable or disagreeable stimulation of a nerve end situated in the skin. Moreover, reason does promote or resist ideas according to pure logical congruity with other accepted ideas in the absence of any immediate practical demonstration.[1]

---

[1] The fact that material arts and sciences are more promptly amenable to reason than the religious, political conceptions, tastes, or

In Professor Sumner's day and at least for the popular mind until this time, the prime necessity for sociology was to replace the erroneous notion that the social order is the product of the design of human reason, with the truth that the social order is a product of natural causation in which human reason has played but an humble rôle. So humble indeed has the rôle of reason been that the first discovery of the facts caused men in revulsion against the former absurd notion to adopt the doctrine of *laissez faire*. This was the attitude of practically all the great early sociologists, of Spencer, Gumplowicz, and Sumner. The chief positive characteristic of Ward was that he reasserted the social efficiency of reason; his chief negative characteristic was that he was too little objective in the defense of his position. We may do but little towards shaping social situations by direct methods, such as votes of mass meetings or even of legislatures backed by sovereign power. But that fact does not leave us hopeless. Our power over the results which are realized in the social order is exactly proportioned, not to our direct efforts, but to our understanding of the causes out of which those results must issue, and our power to control those causes.

The five forms of natural selection just mentioned are all instances of the adaptation of social activities to their conditions: (1) the geographical environment, which by cold and hunger and disease exterminates man and his activities, except on condition that his activities be adapted to the requirements of the natural physical environment; (2) the

---

codes of approval, was sufficiently noted in the discussion of the amenability of different classes of social activity to different "phases," especially the phase of "rational selection," page 400. Professor A. G. Keller in his "Societal Evolution" (Macmillan, 1915) instructively elaborates the proposition that rational selection, while it operates directly upon economic activities, operates in the main indirectly upon other social activities through the trend to bring those other activities into consistency with the economic practices which reason more directly controls. This indirect adaptation of the social activities to economic practices and to natural material limitations has been somewhat noted in our earlier discussion of the effects of geographic conditions, page 33. Professor Keller's work did not appear until the present book was about to go to press.

technic environment which when once produced is effective in the same ways as the geographic in compelling the adaptation of man's social activities on penalty either of death or of pain and discomfort sufficient to deter men from the ill-adapted practices; (3) the biological nature of man himself conditions his psychic life and makes man shrink from whatever is out of harmony with his predispositions; (4) the social environment which can select for extinction with the sword, or lack of patronage, or can blight with contempt and scorn.

But here a great contrast must be noted: the adaptations of natural selection in the biological realm are, so far as we can observe, merely negative, for nature appears to depend on chance, that is to say, upon unexplained causes, for her biological mutations; and they are as likely to impair fitness for survival as to promote it. And so to all appearances nature can secure progress only by selecting among those chance mutations the less fit for extermination and the more fit for survival. But social mutation, that is to say, invention, is not wholly blind. Its blind blundering is repressed or encouraged by pleasure and pain, as the mutations of germ cells can hardly be; moreover, pain and pleasure not only select between the random experiments of man's functional responses, they even prompt groping search. In biological nature necessity is not the mother of mutation but only the stepmother that destroys the ill-born; while in social evolution necessity is fertile, the mother of invention. It is true reason can see but a very little way down the path of social evolution, yet its function is to make conscious adaptations to the demands of environment. And that it succeeds in performing its function is shown by the very fact that reason has been selected for survival and development. The greatest and final biological adaptation to survival is the development of the faculty for non-biological, rational adaptation, which does not wait for the slow process of evolving new organs but makes tools, and conceives beliefs. Furthermore, it must not be thought that rational adaptation directly applies only to those activities that control material results. There are other things besides material goods that make a great difference to human happiness and so are subject to practical as well as abstractly theoretical tests of reason, and all the success which man has had in adapting material products to his uses encourages the strain of reason towards progress in science, morals and organization.

CHAPTER XXVII

EXAMPLES OF SOCIAL EVOLUTION[1]

The beginnings of social activity lie far beyond the dawn of history. The fact and the general method of social evolution are known; but if we try to make our description of social beginnings specific and detailed, after utilizing as fully as we can the data furnished by archeology and by study of existing savages, we still must present the description of details largely as a system of justified working hypotheses, not as a body of certain knowledge.

Implements.—The first economic stage of which we have evidence is that of the wandering collectors or pasturers who have been described, in which every individual that had been weaned foraged for himself, as the chickens do. The most primitive economic implement which survives is the digging stick carried by women and children in Australia, and once no doubt by the men, for grubbing roots and overturning stones under which larvæ[2] and lizards may be hid. Next may be placed the club and the throwing stick, including the flat curved stick that will scale somewhat in a circle—the boomerang—a curiously interesting discovery of random experimentation. A stick is more likely to hit, especially when sent whirling through a flock of birds, than is a stone. But stones excel for crushing marrow bones or nuts. And pounding with a stone upon a stone would sometimes chip or scale a stone and give a sharp cutting or scraping edge.

---

[1] For the facts used in this connection I am far more indebted to Professor W. I. Thomas than to any other source, and more to his instruction to which it is impossible to refer by pages, than to his published writings.

[2] The larvæ of ants are called "Bushman's rice"; grubs are apparently as edible as oysters.

The first three stages in getting implements are: first, to seize the object that is at hand; second, to keep an eye out for a stick, stone, bone, shell or other object that is fit for a given purpose; and, third, to shape a stick or stone or other material so as to fit it for the purpose. Bits of stone and bone bring within reach all the great principles of crushing, piercing, cutting, boring, scraping and grinding, each as important as the principles of wheel and axle, screw and lever which our later mechanics discuss.

In weapons there is great advantage if one can strike an enemy from a safe distance or hit the wary game before it takes flight. And so the knife blade lengthens into a sword, or earlier the handle lengthens till we have a spear, and the throwing stick, javelin, and bow further increase the range.

Play as Random Experimentation.—It can hardly be doubted that play, the activity in which healthy and rested beings engage just because they are alive and because activity is pleasant and too much inactivity an insufferable bore, contained much of the random experimentation that hit on acts that were repeated for a purpose; sticks and stones and thongs and shells and bones were handled and experimented with. Many of the properties and possibilities of these materials must have been stumbled upon. The elasticity of wood, the possibility of flipping a pebble with a bent stick, and the bow itself were probably among the discoveries of play. That some peoples never discovered the bow seems more wonderful than that so many did discover it. Other things being equal the chance of adding useful discoveries or inventions to the social stock is obviously directly proportionate to the number of communicating persons who are experimenting, and the time elapsing. War or the eager excitement of the chase, the stalking of an animal that barely escapes the hunter, afford the excitation of attention in which there may shoot into the mind the new association between the act which play discovered and the practical purpose to which it can be applied. And the excitement of war and the chase continues after the event into hours of brooding and dreaming. The bolo, lasso, snare, and spring gun might easily have had their origin in the horseplay of the camp and found their application to the exciting problems of the chase. Likewise spinning and weaving may well have had their birth from the play of female fingers. It is hardly thinkable that the purpose to spin or weave was formed without some hint derived from previous purposeless activity. If so, from the beginning progress was the offspring of leisure conditioned by economic well-being, for it sprung from the playful employment of the full-fed savage in the intervals of the food-quest. The discovery of methods of making fire must have been accidental, for no one could conceive in advance that such a result could come from clinking stones or rubbing wood. Striking sparks in the dusk from the right kind of stones would be easy, though the accident of a spark falling so as to kindle a flame would be rare. Man may have waited many centuries for that. Friction fire-making might first have come as an incident to some patient, laborious process, like the boring of a hole when the fine dry dust of the boring was heated to a flame. Man doubtless was acquainted with fire as a result of lightning and other natural causes long before he learned to make a fire.

Cooking.—The invention of fire-making methods made possible great advancement. In the first place materials previously too hard and tough or too indigestible were added to the food supply. In the second place fire afforded a reason for bringing food to camp. The campfire was a place to which to return and it became the germ of home. Men, women and children ceased to be mere pasturing wanderers, though the camp itself was nomadic, and woman became the fire-keeper. In the third place—to go no further—the door was opened to mastery of metals, though ages passed before that open door was entered.

Primitive man, accustomed to a raw diet, was indifferent as to whether his food was cooked or raw, provided it could be eaten. Livingstone found that his African followers accepted raw and cooked food apparently with equal relish. The Fuegians crunched their fish raw just as they came out of the water, killing them with a bite behind the gills and devouring from head to tail. The body of a stranded seal or whale, softened by incipient disintegration, furnished to Fuegians, Patagonians and Esquimaux a ready feast. The tenderer parts, the entrails, of a hippopotamus require no cooking for the Bushmen or Hottentots. The Polynesians though they can cook are so indifferent to cooking that they are said to eat their fish or meat raw "as often as not." They may be right who think that the cooking of vegetables originated in the burning away of hulls and husks, a practice that has been observed among various peoples, and that the cooking of meats began in accident or play. Having a fire would not of itself give knowledge of the advantage of cooking food.

The simplest form of cooking is just to put the food, be it bird, lizard, hog or dog, with all its hair and entrails, on the burning coals as do the Papuans of New Zealand. The next step is broiling on hot stones, or wrapping meat in large leaves pinned together before putting in or on the coals, as was done by the Tasmanians. Boiling is a step more difficult than broiling, and even boiling does not require a dish that can be set over the fire, for it is possible to boil, as the Polynesians do, by dropping hot stones into water contained in a hole in a ledge or in a wooden vessel. These people also roast with a fireless cooker. They dig a hole, putting into the hole stones that have been heated in fire; on these stones they put the animal to be roasted, wrapped in aromatic herbs; then they put in more hot stones, and cover the whole with earth. In three or four hours the meat is so cooked as to be highly approved by white guests. In New Guinea rice and sago were cooked by stuffing a cocoanut which was put into the fire. The cocoanut was mostly burned away, but doubtless flavored the pudding well.

All this has implied no possession of dishes except the cocoanut. Dishes are among the possessions that render possible a higher level of life. Among other advantages they furnish a place besides the stomach in which to put food and so invite people to save and provide, instead of merely devouring, and to have regular meals instead of merely eating what they have whenever and wherever they have it and then going hungry. Three meals a day are a highly advanced institution. Savages show an amazing power to stuff away food when they have it and to fast till more is obtained. Pottery is a great acquisition.[1] It depends on the presence of suitable clay. Any hole in the clay, as a sun-dried buffalo's track, is a rudimentary dish. Some peoples appear to have invented pottery by accidentally burning a basket that had been lined with clay to make it hold water, leaving the lining as a pot. This is still one of the primitive ways of pot-making. Another way is to coil long rolls of clay, that have been made by rubbing the clay between the hands, as all children do who have clay to play with.

Agriculture.—The boiling-pot is an invitation to agriculture, and woman was the original agriculturist, as indeed she was the first to develop nearly all the economic arts, except metal-working, boat-making, and others that are directly connected with hunting, fishing, war, or ceremonial. Into the pot she threw whatever promised to add to the stew— roots and herbs and the seeds rubbed from the fattest heads of the large grasses. When the clan moved from a camping-place where these grass heads abounded, she took some along. By accident or design some of the seeds fell on the ground at other camping-places. In time these grasses grew at many of the camping-places in the round of the tribe's migration. Ever she gathered the biggest heads and some she carried away, and by this process of selection, little by little, maize, wheat, and the other great grains were developed from different grasses of different continents. Hunting will sustain but a sparse population and while population increases game grows scarcer, but products of agriculture grow more varied and more desirable. In time man is forced to depend on woman's food and take a share in woman's work.

It is a hard transition for man, first because it requires the development of new aptitudes. There are other occupations which the boy of to-day prefers to hoeing corn, as much

---

[1] Australians, New Zealanders, and Polynesians were among the peoples that had no pottery.

as did his savage ancestor. Civilized life calls for a new set of aptitudes which the boy of to-day is made to acquire; including pleasure or at least steadiness in work, in monotonous work that lacks the stimulation that comes of uncertainty as to what will happen next, a stimulation which makes even fishing with the mere hope of a bite exciting. For this excitement men flee from work to gambling, even when they know the game is "fixed" against them. If the son of civilization does not acquire the aptitude for steady continuance in effort motived only by a foreseen remote result, he belongs to what Professor Thomas calls the "criminaloid" class. He may have many good qualities as a sport, but he lacks other good qualities that fit him for a place in an advanced society. But men as a mass have acquired the aptitudes for work. Aptitude is the child of interest. Ex-president Eliot, of Harvard, declared that a small boy whom the great man took to a ball game afterward repeated the plays of the nine innings with a completeness that would have been impossible to the president. The boy excelled in this aptitude because he excelled in interest in the game. A vital interest in the results of continuous and farsighted labor was essential to high social advance. This the necessities of agriculture forced upon man. At first he was not interested in scratching the ground with a forked stick—one fork cut short and sharpened, the other longer for a handle—and many savages are still spoken of as "incapable of agriculture."

Hunger alone is a master that can teach the lesson. Not only aptitude for work, but foresight, saving, and punctuality enforced by the seasons were developed by agriculture as a schoolmaster of the wayward child of impulse. It would not let him live and die a child; it made him a man.

The necessity of developing new aptitudes was not the only difficulty in the way of adopting agriculture as a mode of life. Droughts and other weather changes would sometimes blight the product of his long toil. Weeds in land half won from the jungle and insect pests and herds of beasts were unspeakable foes. But the worst foes of all were wilder men. Hunting and, to a somewhat smaller degree, pastoral life keep men in training for war but agriculture does not. Huntsmen prey upon herdsmen and both upon the inviting stores of the agriculturist. Thus Persia was overrun by men from Turkestan. Egypt was conquered by shepherd kings. The Toltecs were overpowered by the ruder Aztecs. The Arabs and the hordes of Genghis Khan thronged across great areas. Mongolians and again Manchus established themselves on the throne of China. And the cattle-driving Highlanders preyed upon the Lowlanders across the border. The same type of conquest and depredation has gone on among less advanced peoples whose history is unwritten.

Besides the education of man in new traits, agriculture brings with it a regular instead of a precarious food supply and conditions favorable to regularity in all the departments of life, including above all the settled habitation, in place of the old wandering food-quest. Man gathers social treasure faster after he ceases to be a rolling stone.

Agriculture also makes it possible for men to live together in large numbers. Large numbers living in such proximity that the invention of one becomes the property of all are essential conditions of rapid social advancement. Again, agriculture provides food enough so that some individuals can be supported who are not food-getters, but are devoted to mechanical and intellectual and esthetic pursuits.

Domestication of Animals.—Whether increase of population, thinning of game, and growth of intelligence lead men to agriculture or to pastoral life depends mainly on geographic conditions. In the case of most of the great nations, dependence on flocks and herds has preceded dependence on agriculture. The peoples that speak the great Indo-Germanic family of languages appear to have been herdsmen before they separated and scattered over most of Eurasia, for their languages, from Sanskrit to English, have in common the roots of words referring to the life and tending of cattle,[1] but not many of the words that apply to plant life and agri-

---

[1] For example, Daughter, Tochter, θυγάτηρ (Thugater) and Sanskrit Duhitar, said to mean milkmaid (duh—milk).

culture. The earliest history and traditions of nearly all the peoples of Europe and western Asia are pastoral.

Domestication of animals seems to have originated not in the desire for food but in the desire for entertainment. The cubs of slain animals are of interest to all hunters, and not seldom are brought into camp and domesticated. Chickens are domesticated in Africa for their beauty and their crowing. Dogs following the camp for the bones and refuse left by man, who is the mightiest of the carnivora, became regular parts of the wandering troupe and were frequently eaten. Calves often follow the body of a dead cow to the hunter's camp.

The Hottentots surround a herd, the wildest break away; of the remainder all are killed save the gentlest, which are kept and bred. The Mexicans at the time of the Spanish Conquest had a great annual animal round-up when they surrounded a large area, drove the included animals toward the center, slaughtered many, but kept alive many females and the finest males.

Reveling in flesh food, in fat, marrow and blood, is characteristic of the earliest remaining hero tales and folksongs of pastoral peoples.

Survivals of cannibalism are so widespread that many assert that it has been at some time a practice of every race. Cannibalism sometimes reasserts itself among the civilized under pressure of starvation. Horror and disgust, like tastes, admirations, and moral approvals, are largely regulated by the principle of familiarity and by social radiation. Africans of the Gold Coast having passed from hunting to agriculture have been known to get so hungry for meat as to cast lots in a friendly way to see which of their number should be eaten. Cannibalism is by no means confined to the lowest races, but appears to be much more characteristic of peoples more advanced, such as the Fijians, New Caledonians and ancient Mexicans. Cheap lives are the ones that have been observed to be most often sacrificed, women, children, especially deformed children, the aged, the sick and criminals. The Maori eat only adulterers. But cannibalistic feasts of religious sacrifice require the best, a youth. The desire for an easily accessible and desirable food that would otherwise go to waste is by no means the only motive for cannibalism; religion and superstition often furnish the motive. Eating the heart of a brave man, the brain of a crafty one, or some part of a witch whose qualities and powers are desired, illustrate this second class of motives as they are exhibited in regions scattered from the equator to the Arctics. Drinking the blood which the drinker himself or herself has lost is not unknown to-day among ignorant Europeans. And the dead, especially parents, may be eaten, as in Thibet, as a mark of honor, instead of consigning their bodies to the birds and beasts or to the worms—an extreme example of the variability of sentiment as molded by social radiation.

Pastoral life usually implies wandering from place to place to obtain food, grass, and water, in groups relatively small though much larger than could be sustained by the methods of the primitive "wanderers." To mark the contrast these peripatetic pastoral groups are called not "wanderers" but "nomads." This mode of life compels a close organization. The basis of this organization is the family, though the group may "adopt" any whom it will into its brotherhood. When the flocks become too numerous to find common feeding- and watering-places, the group separates and we have then two clans, or "gentes" of the same tribe. The flocks and herds are common property of the group but the patriarch, or ruling father,[1] has disposing and governing power over the property as well as over the labor and conduct of the members of the group. The spirits of heroic patriarchs glorified in tradition are usually worshiped as clan divinities. A tribe may also have one or more divinities, common to all its clans. Each clan expects the members of another clan to be loyal to the divinities of that other clan. And adoption from one tribe or clan to another means acceptance of this filial relation toward the divinities of the adopting clan. The ceremony of marriage is such an adoption if the two who are joined are not already of the same clan. Shepherds and fight-

---

[1] Abram means "great father" or patriarch.

ers are desired, recruits strengthen the group, children are a welcome blessing and polygamy is usually approved wherever men are sufficiently rich and powerful to practice it. Such were the early Greeks, Romans, Semites, and probably also the earliest Teutons.

Personal Adornment.—The motive that led to the wearing of clothes apparently was neither modesty nor desire for warmth, but the desire for adornment and distinction. Even now let the reader ask himself whether appearance is not the chief consideration in the selection of a suit or hat or even a pair of shoes. By nature human beings are not ashamed at being naked. This form of modesty is a result of wearing clothes, and is a socially developed and socially radiated sentiment. And like other social sentiments it varies among people who have developed it; thus the Japanese are shocked to see the nude in works of art, but not to see men and women bathing together in complete nakedness; for a Chinese woman no exposure could be more indecent than to show her foot; for a Mussulman woman, no other exposure so indecent as to show her face, and on the Orinoco both sexes feel shame unless painted; all of which we may better comprehend if we remember that for American women the costume of the bathing-beach or the ballroom would be disgraceful on the street.

People have desired not only that their appearance be beautiful, but still more that it be distinguished, or even imposing and terrible. The story of man's self-adornment may well begin with painting. Grease paints are no invention of the modern drama. The Australian gloriously stripes his face, breast, and legs with red, white, and yellow made by mixing grease chiefly with ashes and ochre. Fuegians and Patagonians paint red, white, and black images on their bodies. Hottentots and many other Africans are remarkable for such decorations, and some of them paint tribal designations on their bodies. Red is the usual favorite color of savage and barbarous peoples, but in some places where a good blue dye is available, blue is much the fashion. Men can be seen with magnificent azure beards, and women with hair stained blue, and a full toilette may include hair and eyebrows stained with indigo, lashes black with kohl, lips yellow and hands and feet red with henna.

Close akin to painting are the more permanent adornments of tattooing. The Esquimaux tattoo by drawing under the skin needles [1] and threads that have been soaked with oil and soot. The tattooing of Polynesians made by inserting pigments in skin-punctures shows great elaboration of design and nicety of workmanship.

Mutilations are a means of improving on common nature and securing distinction of appearance. Apparently the most primitive form of this method is making cuts, most often on the breast and arms, which are kept from healing until very conspicuous permanent results are assured. Australians and Tasmanians wore these scars parallel like stripes; Papuans made them criss-cross; the New Zealanders used both patterns. Australians knock out one or two upper front teeth as part of the ceremony of initiation into manhood. Others file the front teeth into striking shapes. Melanesians and many others [2] pierce the septum of the nose so that it will receive an ornament of wood or bone. Many tribes scattered from South America to Alaska, and central Africa, slit the underlip in order to insert ornaments some of which are exceedingly effective, if not to our eyes beautiful. The lobe of the ear is pierced for the same purpose, a practice which till recently was common among us and which may become so again. Circumcision is practiced by both black and white Mussulmans in both Asia and Africa, by Kafirs, by the Hovas of Madagascar, by Australians, Papuans, New Caledonians, and others. Deforming the heads of infants by bandages, by boards, and by baskets (as tight as the web of custom that shapes the inside of their heads) was practiced in ancient Peru, by the Chacta, Natchez, and Chinook Indians, in Tahiti and many of the Polynesian Islands, in Sumatra, and is still more or less in vogue in different localities in Europe, notably in the neighborhood of Toulouse. The

[1] Bone needles are part of the apparatus of savage life.
[2] The Papuans carry this to an extreme.

deforming of the feet by Chinese women is not confined, as often has been stated, to the upper classes who do not have to work, but the desire to imitate the classes that enjoy prestige has induced working-women to adopt the practice, and Chinese women with crippled feet may be seen hitching along on their hands in the fields or shuffling on their knees at their household tasks. The practice may have originated in a desire for daintiness, a motive that leads nearly all shoe-wearing peoples to cripple their feet more or less, reënforced by desire to differ from the common people whose broad feet were unconfined by shoes. It has been perpetuated as a badge of leisure. The long fingernails of the Chinese are a means of proclaiming membership in the class that devolves all manual tasks upon servants. The discussion of personal mutilations would not be complete without allusion to the corset, the abuses of which have been greatly modified in this generation.

The wonderfully elaborate and fantastic hair-dressing of human beings, from the Zulu and the Papuan to the English judge and the Parisian belle, is a part of the story upon which we are engaged. Among many nature peoples a pillow that enables one to sleep without disturbing the coiffure is one of the most treasured possessions. The Japanese still use such a pillow—a tiny stool supporting a piece of plank with a semi-circular notch in the edge of it in which to place the neck so that the head is sustained by the neck alone. This device is in the same class with the mustache trainer in which some German gentlemen sleep.

The Desire for Visible Distinction.—The motives which have been discussed under this topic are by no means peculiar to the "lower races." Our European ancestors were not free from tattooing and painting. Among the Thracians, nobles were once distinguished from commoners by their painted bodies. Celts and Illyrians tattooed in black and blue, Picts, Britons, and Germans painted their bodies, especially with blue. According to Pliny, in the early days of Rome conquerors painted their bodies red on the day of victory. And one who turns the pages of an illustrated history of the fashions of Europe and America, during the last century, will see exhibited the same propensities.

We must remember that in matters of personal adornment desire for distinction mingles with desire for beauty and helps to explain the extravagances. How strong these motives are is exhibited by the pain and long-continued discomfort which people have endured and which they have solicitously inflicted on their children, the discomforts of tight shoes and corsets, and the tortures of scar-making, tattooing, and foot-binding, and the inconvenience of women of Egypt and India laboring with fifty pounds of brass or iron on wrists and ankles, and the women of China hitching on their hands or shuffling on their knees through lives of toil. The strength of these motives is probably even more powerfully exhibited by the terrific economic cost at which they are gratified. A great part of human labor has been—and is no less to-day—expended for adventitious, physical prestige. It may be hoped that this terrific waste will some day be curbed by sumptuary laws formulated in the interest, not of exclusive privilege but of democracy, and enforced not by government, but by public opinion as other laws of etiquette are enforced. Then attire will be governed by regard for beauty, health and convenience, and its prostitution as a means of distinction will be outlawed among the well-bred. However, the desire for individual distinction will not die out, and if we refuse its silly and wasteful gratification we shall be obliged to find some better way of meeting its demand. If so one of the most powerful of all human motives will be turned in the directions sanctioned by public opinion.

Esthetic Conventionality.—But beauty as well as distinction has been sought in nearly all of this mutilation and arraying of the person, from the women of the miserable Tasmanians and Veddahs, with their necklaces of shells and flowers twined in their hair, on and up throughout the whole scale of societies. And most striking is it to observe what monstrosities have actually been beautiful to beholders. Prestige can awaken the sense of beauty as well as command belief; social radiation can communicate the feeling that objects are beautiful as well as suggestion can communicate ideas. Familiarity, the prestige of the great within the group, and the desire to admire their own type make each people tend to admire their own kind; blackness is admired among blacks, the blacker the more beautiful, and yellow skin and slanting eyes with a visible membrane among Mongolians, Moreover the strange colors applied with paint, the mutilations and septum ornaments and protruding labrets and horns of hair are regarded as beautiful, even as were the monstrosities of style that our grandmothers and great-great-grandmothers wore. Some of our most beautiful toilets may look just as absurd and hideous as the latter to our children's children The artistic conventionalities of China and Japan were looked upon by our grandfathers as curiosities and largely as absurdities; it has become a mark of culture to appreciate their conventionalities in addition to those which we have inherited from the Greeks.

Metaphysicians formerly spent a great deal of thought and writing in the attempt to reach an abstract definition of "the beautiful." Beauty is a subjective experience and what objects shall awaken that experience is determined largely by social influence. Even economic value is now recognized to be mainly a mental attitude toward commodities. Two dishes of pottage, though just alike, were not of equal value to Esau full and to Esau hungry. And a garment uninjured, but hung away till it is out of style may lose both its economic value and its beauty because the subjective attitude toward it has changed. Beauty, like value, has a subjective and an objective pole and the objective pole gets its charge of economic or esthetic value from the subjective pole at least as much as the subjective pole receives it from the objective.

This is not saying that the objective has no esthetic importance or that there is nothing in the nature of things to help in deciding what shall be regarded as beautiful, except social influence. On the contrary the natural elements which may help to arouse the experience of beauty are numerous, varied, and even contradictory.

The beauty of nature makes the most universal esthetic

appeal. This seems to be a case of adaptation to environment. Elevation and serenity of mood has a biological value, and it would be dreadful if the aspects of nature were to us harsh and disquieting. We have become at home in our terrestrial habitation. The principle of familiarity is at work to make us at home in any surroundings to which we are long exposed; in a strange environment we miss the result of its gentle ministry and grow homesick, and are deeply moved by one familiar sight. The principle of familiarity is perhaps the most fundamental element in beauty aside from conventionality to which it is not unrelated. But there is also a principle of novelty which helps to make objects beautiful.

The other objective principles of beauty fall likewise into contradictory pairs. Thus obvious adaptation to dear human uses is the first variant from familiarity as an element in beauty, but remoteness from possible use can also enhance beauty. Art vases are sometimes made solid so that they can contain nothing, in order to heighten their beauty and proclaim that their beauty is their sufficient cause for being. The "romantic" which plays so large a rôle in art is an effort to get away from life's common uses and its drudgery, as well as an effort to set the imagination free from the bonds of knowledge.

Symmetry is one of the most generally recognized elements in objective beauty, but asymmetry is also an element of beauty; a Japanese drawing of a flower owes half its charm to the asymmetry with which it is placed upon the card and would be almost valueless if the flower were primly placed in the middle. Subtle asymmetry is a chief, if not the chief, element in Japanese conventionality. Symmetry seems the most essential element in good architecture, yet baroque architecture gets its character largely from asymmetries.

Simplicity, according to Ruskin, is one of the prime qualities of beautiful art; Greek architecture was so simple in design that it made its glorious impression at a blow; but an arabesque is effective because of its intricacy; Wagnerian involution adds grandeur and lasting magic not possessed by the simple melody that catches the ear by revealing all it contains at the first hearing, and Gothic architecture owes its power largely to the fact that the mind loses itself in its mazes.

Harmony is of the essence of beauty; but so also is contrast. The restful and subdued, the neutral tint, the soft and soothing sound, the unjarring harmony we delight in, but also we want vivid experience, the thrilling and exciting, even though it be horrible—trumpet and fortissimo, and the touch of scarlet.

Finally we delight in the perfect, but there is also a place in art for the grotesque. Familiarity and novelty, fitness for use and remoteness from use and wont, symmetry and quaintness, simplicity and intricacy, harmony and contrast, the reposeful and the thrilling, the perfect and the grotesque, all play their part in furnishing the objective occasion for experiencing beauty.

Availing itself of all these possibilities of beauty, conventionality creates a social influence which evokes the experience of beauty. But because conventionality varies, societies vary widely as to the objects which evoke this experience in their members. Even our own most classic works of art owe their power largely to conventionality. How many of the tourists who stand uncovered and speak only in whispers in the little room where the Sistine Madonna hangs would be so stirred if they had never heard of Raphael's masterpiece, and saw it, robbed of the evidences of the approval of others, in a store window? Their experience is real, as real as the countless cures that have been wrought by therapeutic suggestion. We abandon ourselves to the experience of beauty when we are assured of the approval of the competent, and that experience is heightened by the sense of sympathy with generations of our kind. Some beauty experience is mere social hypnotism; some is original response to one or other of the causes enumerated above, but most is a combination of the two; it is due in part to objective causes and the nature of the soul of man, but it is heightened when we feel the group heart beating against our own. And so great is the influence of conventionality that many things which seem beautiful to one people to another appear indifferent, or grotesque and absurd, or even hideous.

A complete account of esthetic origins would require chapters on music, the dance and pantomime, art in ceremony, drawing, painting, and carving.

Clothing.—The previous statement that the wearing of clothes did not originate chiefly in modesty or in desire for warmth implies no denial that these two motives were soon developed. Custom is as insistent in respect to clothing as in other matters, and as we have seen men and women may be ashamed of appearing without their paint, much as a man of fashion would be ashamed to appear at a ball without evening clothes. And sex self-consciousness soon mingles with dress customs. Man almost certainly originated in a warm climate where clothing was not required for warmth; but to drape himself with skins, grasses, and strips of bark, as well as belts of beads, was an early means of distinction and adornment. The wearing of trophies was one of the most glorious modes of adornment. And the skins of formidable beasts are trophies. Skins are worn by people whom we usually think of as "naked savages," for occasional protection not so much against cold as against wet. Whether man first got the idea of wearing furs as a protection from the fact that the animals had worn them or from the comfort incidentally furnished by them when put on as trophies and adornments we are not sure.

In the relatively stable climate of the tropics man does not appear to develop a want for the constant use of clothes as a protection from the weather. And even in the bleakness of Tierra del Fuego the miserable savages meet the cold with a biological rather than a sociological adjustment. They become "all face," and allow the falling snow to melt upon their naked bodies, only a fraction of their persons being scantily protected by a piece of pelt. Yet wherever cold seasons alternate with warm, clothes worn for display and later for decency would clearly reveal their advantages as protection. Summer migrations toward the north followed by tarrying to face winters of unfamiliar severity, would cause a need to which men were not so accustomed as to be oblivious to it. And the gradual encroachments of glacial cold made early peoples live, even in central France, as companions of the reindeer.

A stick, thorn, or bit of bone used as a pin would hold the pelt in place, or it could be tied with a thong run through holes. Rows of holes gave lacing, which is a rudimentary seam, while a bit of bone fastened to the thong to make lacing easier, on the principle of the shoe-string, made a rudimentary needle and thread. The needle was used in the Ice Age.

Clothing and the ornaments that developed into clothing were chiefly hung about the neck and about the waist. The girdle becomes apron, loin-cloth, skirt or kilt, and in the north the skirt divided and its parts closed changes into trousers, while the girdle widened and supported by bands across the shoulders becomes the waistcoast. About the neck are worn the mantle, "poncho," tunic, shirt, and finally the coat. Lippert points out that clothing worn wholly or almost wholly for ornament, distinction, and "effect," remains flowing, but that in the north where clothing is largely worn for protection against cold, it becomes snug and is fitted to the limbs; thus he says tailoring (*Schneiderei*) is a product of the north. In the north, however, drapery long continues to be worn for effect by men on ceremonial occasions, by women, and even by caparisoned horses. The last is a good illustration of the relation between clothing and ornament. The simplest and probably the most primitive fitting is cutting through a pelt a hole through which to put the head, poncho-fashion. The skin then hangs down before and behind, and may be closed by a belt or by a lacing or seam.

Woven stuffs in time largely replaced pelts. The New Zealanders, having migrated from a land of fur-bearing animals to an island where such animals were not found, had already developed the want for garments, and were forced to meet it by plaiting the split leaves of an iris-like or yucca-like plant. Weaving as already suggested grew by degrees of refinement out of plaiting. This too is well illustrated by such fine-plaited garments as are found in New Zealand.

CHAPTER XXVIII

EXAMPLES OF SOCIAL EVOLUTION (*Continued*)

Language.—Language is a typical product of social evolution. It is not produced by biological evolution, though for this as for all other social evolution biological evolution furnished the prerequisite organic conditions. Even to-day language is in no sense an inborn gift. The deaf remain dumb, and no one has knowledge of any language that he has not learned from others. In this, language is like religion, morality, science, politics, art, special tastes, and the whole content of life which has been socially evolved.

There are four steps in the development of intercommunication:

1. Organic Reactions Are Intelligible to Others.—The chicken cheeping in the shell already can understand its mother's warning or reassuring note; not in the sense that the chicken gets an idea from the mother's note but that it receives a radiated feeling by that medium and stops or resumes its pecking and cheeping accordingly. The bleating of the lost calf and the snarl of rage carry a meaning for other animals and for man. So also do attitudes and actions. Flight proclaims terror, spreads panic, and invites pursuit. Slinking, fawning, love-making, and threatening convey their meanings within the group or between enemies. None of us knows just how extensively or how subtly beasts and birds thus communicate; doubtless more than we see though less than we can imagine. That their sociable hearts thus get some degree of comfort and guidance there is no doubt. These means of communication never cease to play a part in the intercourse of human beings; they are not readily made deceitful; they have much to do with liking and dislike and with degrees of influence and mastery among men. But mere organic reactions are products of biological evolution and are of significance for us in this connection only as they prepare for or mingle with higher elements of communication. However, they cease to be mere organic reactions as soon as they are done on purpose. If a dog barks not merely as a physiological result of a state of excitation but in order to let its master know the presence of an intruder we have at least a step toward speech. Some animals and the lowest men do discover that their spontaneous cries and movements are understood and thereafter they cease at times to be mere spontaneous reactions. And when some individuals begin the intentional use of these as media of communication and other individuals are stimulated by their example to similar intentional use of natural cries and gestures we have a true social phenomenon.

2. Mimicry.—What one can mimic he may thereby make known to another. The ideomotor tendency to imitate is strong in children, apes, monkeys, and in many birds. The imitator, like the parrot, may have no understanding of that which he imitates [1] and even when there is understanding, it is not communication in our meaning of the term, so long as the imitation is purely ideomotor, but only when it is intended for the purpose of being understood. "Bow-wow" and "choo-choo" are not language so long as they are mere ideomotor responses to external stimulation, but only when they are prompted by an inner desire to attract comprehending attention from an associate.

The mental activity of man is largely of the visualizing type. Auditory mentality must have been developed mainly through the selective agency of an environment which included talking associates; if so, primitive man was even more predominantly a visualizer than we are. Auditory mental skill is also heightened in the modern individual by the process of education through the medium of language. Mimicry, while partly vocal, is largely of bodily movements. The language of primitive man may well have been largely mimetic and in so far as it was mimetic comprised less of words than of

---

[1] This does not mean that the parrot never in any degree understands any of the words he utters.

other signs. As a matter of fact existing savages make very considerable use of signs as a means of communication. It is said that an ordinary Indian and a deaf mute could understand each other and that there is a world sign language differing among savages of the different continents only as dialects of one speech vary. But developed oral speech has such great advantages that gesture ultimately sinks into relative unimportance. Vocal mimicry undoubtedly played a part in forming the beginnings of vocabulary and in familiarizing men with the notion of speech so that they became able to develop its less obvious resources.

3. Association of Sounds with Experiences.—The simplest form of memory which recalls situations, that is to say, experiences *en bloc*, includes memory of sounds that were part of the experience. And the sound may serve to recall the experience, and so may be used to call to the mind of another, who shared the experience, not only the experience as a whole, but also any prominent element in the experience or any other act or thing of the same class. Thus Mr. Darwin's grandchild having been excited by a visit to a duck pond thereafter called all birds "quack," money on which there was an eagle "quack," and water "quack." To call ducks "quack" was mimetic, but to call other birds, and still more to call water or money quack, was association of sounds with ideas. It must be added that children, having the anatomical apparatus for articulation,[1] "da-da" and "a-goo" spontaneously as they wave their hands. Many, if not most, children make beginnings toward constructing a language. Their beginnings are usually soon brought to an end because a developed language is supplied them; but according to Romanes, "the spontaneous

---

[1] Romanes (Mental Evolution in Man, chap. vii) believes that some of the more intelligent animals would use articulate sounds as signs if they had as good organs for articulation as birds have, at least that they would certainly learn from man, when domesticated, to use simple words intelligently. Indeed even parrots do, in many instances, use words by associative intelligence as means to ends, for instance, "Polly is thirsty" as a means of getting water, etc. See pp. 127 *seq.*

and, to all appearances, arbitrary word-making, which is more or less observable in all children when first beginning to speak, may under favorable circumstances, proceed to an astonishing degree of fullness and accuracy," the words may become "sufficiently numerous and varied to constitute a not inefficient language" and "the syntax of the language presents obvious points of resemblance" to that of the most primitive languages in vogue among adult populations. Such extensive and "arbitrary" word-making suggests the fourth step in language-making, a step which implies a higher mental evolution than is necessary for the first three.

The three steps in the development of rudimentary languages thus far mentioned were possible to men who had not advanced in psychic capacity beyond the stage which our children reach at two years of age, to men, that is, whose intelligence did not differ greatly from that of the highest animals, and whose marked advantage consisted in the possession of better organs of articulation.[1] This rudimentary speech sufficed to give to such intelligence as they possessed, increased efficiency and gave to increments in intelligence great

---

[1] Compare the curious paper of Professor Garner on "Rudimentary Language in Apes," in the *New Review* (see *Spectator*, June 6, 1891). By means of the phonograph Professor Garner caught distinct sounds, uttered to express such meanings as desire for food, drink and even possibly for special kinds of food, which, when uttered by one ape, are readily understood by others of the same species. Professor Garner himself learned to speak these words so as to be readily and intelligently understood by the apes. Compare R. P. Gregg: Comparative Philology. London, 1893, p. viii. Compare also the statement of Ratzel that no race of human beings is too dull for language-making. (History of Mankind, i, 31.) "Hunting savages like the Bushmen speak a finely constructed and copious language, while we find among the race which has developed the highest and most permanent civilization of Asia what according to evolutionary views must be regarded as a most simple language, the uninflected Chinese with its four hundred and fifty root words, which may be put together like pieces in a puzzle and taken apart again, remaining all the time unaltered." The Bushman language may be much older than Chinese; compare the section "Fixation of Social Species," and Churchward's "Evolution of Primitive Man" on the antiquity of the Bushmen, pages 13 and 36.

survival value. To beings possessing good organs of articulation in addition to the intelligence and dexterity already developed by the apes, brain power was the predominant condition of survival and so with them the course of evolution took the direction of brain development.

Better brain power got its greatest usefulness as a means of survival by enabling men to communicate and so to coöperate with greater efficiency. Coöperating men could face the mammoth and the cave bear, could overcome hunger and cold, and also less coöperating human hordes, and could accumulate by tradition the growing store of working ideas which at length enabled them to live together by millions. And thus it was that by being social, from being something less than man, our remote ancestor became man. Man, even biologically, is a product of association. Association furnished the condition for the highest stages of organic or biological evolution and gave to man not only the social or so-called "moral" instincts but also his superior intelligence. Association then furnished the condition for superorganic or social evolution which developed the vast and rich content of modern life. Finally, association furnishes the condition of the education by which each biologically developed individual born into the world gets his share in the products of social evolution.

4. The Generalized Notion of Using Sounds as Symbols.— Many instances of symbolizing a mental content by a vocable having arisen spontaneously in the three ways already mentioned, as they still arise among little children, these specific instances in time led to perception of the general notion that ideas can be thus symbolized. And this idea once reached language grew apace in the constant comradeship of horde life. Indeed with this notion once established in the mind there is no limit to easy word-making save the limit of demand and convenience.

Philologists tell us that about five hundred roots with modifications and combinations suffice for building such a language as the English. Professor Müller presented a list of one hundred and twenty-one root concepts with which, as he maintained, every thought that ever passed through the mind of

India, so far as it is known to us in its literature, has been expressed.[1] To which Romanes adds that few of these original concepts rise much higher in the scale of ideation than the level attainable by a dumb animal or an infant. But the original concepts of language are greatly extended by figurative use; and words that in their literal meaning conveyed simply sensational ideas later carry psychic meanings. Thus we *understand* that *propositions support* the *obligation* to *discharge responsibilities* —to stand under and to tie down are ideas of the child or the primitive savage, but the roots that first conveyed such primitive ideas later embody the concepts of metaphysics. Compounding of roots and figurative extension of meaning multiply and enrich the vocabulary.

Grammar.—Primitive words stood for complete ideas while the words of developed languages are so specialized that each conveys only a fragment of an idea. Adverb, adjective, preposition, noun, and verb are differentiated organs of speech, while a primitive word is a protozoan of speech, without organs yet discharging all functions. Thus the child's "up" is noun-verb-adjective all in one, and means "I want to get up," "He has gone up," etc., or "By-by" (sleep) means cot, bed, pillow, blankets, asleep, sleepy, I want to go to bed, etc. Such words have to be helped out by pointing and gesture. There was probably an immensely long period during which men communicated by such comprehensive vocal signs while gesture and pantomime partly compensated for the poverty of grammatical differentiation and structure. However, every group of men, even the lowest now living upon the earth, has a somewhat highly developed language.

The first differentiated vocables for expressing relation seem to have been pronouns and adverbs of place that replaced pointing. These could enter into permanent composition with other words to enlarge their meaning, as in the Sanskrit "digging-he" = laborer; "digging-it" = spade; "digging-here" = labor; "digging-there" = hole, etc. The attachment of pronominal forms to verbal roots, as illustrated, takes

---

[1] Science of Thought, p. 549, quoted by G. J. Romanes. Mental Evolution in Man. Appleton and Co., 1884, p. 274.

the place of inflection, and ultimately becomes inflection proper.

When the vocabulary becomes rich enough to furnish more than one word that may be connected with the same thought, these words are simply uttered in succession; the same word being in one connection noun or verb, in another adjective or adverb. Thus "gold" is a noun but becomes an adjective, as "gold cup," and in the mouth of a child or a savage the expression "cup gold" means, "This cup is of gold," and such radical contraries as "Tom hit me" and "Me hit Tom" are expressed by a mere change in the order of words, while hit, the verb, is also the noun, blow; and eat, the verb, is also the noun, food.

The Sanskrit speech of the pastoral Aryans was far from being a primitive language. Grammar may long remain very simple, as is shown not only by many languages of savage and barbarous peoples but by the language of a people so highly civilized as the Chinese. "The Chinese Empire, Burmah, and Indo-China are ignorant of that which we call grammar. From the beginning of the world (sic!) these people have made use of isolated syllables to which a strict syntax (arrangement of words) assigns in turn the value of verb, substantive, adjective, adverb or preposition."

Language is said originally to have consisted mainly of only two elements; first, the names of objects and actions; second, demonstrative or pronominal sounds. "These two classes of roots are the only elements of language; there are no others [1] and all tongues are the result of their different combinations, either (1) by simple juxtaposition of unaltered syllables, as in Chinese; (2) by agglutination of several syllables round a central syllable as in the case of all the languages called agglutinative which the polysyllabic speech of the American Indian illustrates; or (3) fusing and contracting into a single whole the central and subordinate syllables, as in all the inflected languages." [2] In inflected languages instead

---

[1] Possibly this statement is somewhat exaggerated, and the verbal protozoan had adumbrations of other meanings also.

[2] Compare Le Fèvre: Race and Language. London, 1894, p. 49.

of heaping together verbs and substantives as in agglutinative speech, a single verbal or substantive root is modified and supplemented by originally pronominal elements. Inflected languages have shown a tendency to pass into (4) analytic languages, largely escaping the complexity of inflection by use of a few prepositions and auxiliaries, which "supply with greater subtlety and precision the vanished forms of declension and conjugation."

Agglutination can be carried to a bewildering and deforming complexity, as shown by the Basque and American Indian languages. The inflectional method may get well under way before the agglutinative is outgrown. "In Algonkin languages the verb is very rich in its inflections; more so even than Greek.[1]

Spoken languages are well described as "living." They are always developing. And when we remember the constant need of speech, the facility with which even little children coin words and originate sentence structure, and the fact that numberless groups have been talking for ages in relative isolation from each other, it is of great interest to notice that families of nations express themselves by the use of comparatively few word roots and that the grammatical structure of language conforms to so few types. Even here nature is not capricious but produces the results which are prescribed by the conditions. Moreover, the strong tendency for existing inventions to inhibit further inventions that might differently serve the same end, is strikingly illustrated by the development and combination of existing roots, instead of simple coining of new words.

The greatest simplicity consistent with accuracy and full-

The title of this book suggests the remark that it is extremely easy to carry too far the assumption that lingual group and biological race coincide. Some peoples have adopted the language of another race, while other peoples have been composed by mingling stocks that had previously spoken diverse tongues, one of which ultimately predominates.

[1] R. P. Gregg: Comparative Philology. London, 1893, p. x. The Algonquin, however, is still largely agglutinative and has no auxiliary verbs.

ness of expression is a test of excellence in language. Needless multiplication of technical terms and of rare and recondite words confuses and obscures speech; and excessive elaboration of inflection may encumber the mind of both speaker and listener. For example, the indication of gender in both the subject and the verb is flying too many flags for the same signal. Analytic languages lay aside most of the complexities of inflection. The ideal in language would seem to be the greatest possible reconciliation of simplicity with precision, and sufficient variety for the purposes of art.[1]

Inflection is a way of escape from the clumsiness and complexity of the agglutinative method, as auxiliaries and prepositions are an emancipation from the intricacies of inflection. Only Semitic and Indo-Germanic languages have passed the agglutinative stage. The Germanic and Romanic languages have progressed to the analytic stage, French and English being the best examples. French and English, however, are of all the European languages the most imperfectly represented by their present spelling. English is enriched with both Romanic and Germanic vocabularies and is the most analytic of all languages.

[1] There is little present likelihood that any artificial or "scientific" language will make great progress in popular use. It would be a tremendous advantage to science and literature and social progress in general if the advanced populations used a common vehicle of communication. French and English at present are the leading competitors for this service, with English gaining in the race. The fact that so many millions already speak English, and that it is already the medium of so great a literature gives it inestimable advantages over any "scientific" languages. It is the native tongue of more millions by far than any other European language, and even some of those who speak rival tongues admit that it also possesses the greatest literature. And it would be the easiest of all great natural languages to learn if it had phonetic spelling. The movement toward reforming the spelling of our language is not radical enough to do much good. It accomplishes so little that not many people care to bother with it. A consistent system of phonetic spelling should be worked out and then it should be adopted by publishers. It should follow as closely as possible the established continental use of the letters, and so be far less artificial than the system of phonetic spelling that has been proposed by Bell.

Writing, Measuring, and Counting.—(1) Primitive records are only reminders. They serve to recall ideas already known, but not to communicate ideas to those by whom the ideas had not already been known. Indians "talked into the wampum" by weaving in distinct marks commemorative of events. The Iroquois have intrusted to the officials of the state of New York at Albany such records of their tribal history. Hostile tribes have kept account of their losses and their revenge by preserving bundles of sticks to which one is added for each death of a tribesman at the hands of a given enemy. The amount of a future payment is indicated by a similar bundle. A South American Indian leaving his aged parents gave them a string in which he had tied a number of knots and took with him a string having the same number of knots. Parents and son agreed to untie one knot each day; when the parents reached the last knot they expected their son, and when he reached the last knot he knew that the time for his promised return had come.

(2) Picture writing is a kind of permanent and transmissible sign language. It is not writing proper for it represents ideas and not sounds. (3) In "ideographic" writing (like the Chinese) each picture or symbol represents a complete word. (4) In "phonetic" writing each symbol stands for only part of a word, either for a syllable ("syllabic" writing as that of the Japanese and various ancient peoples), or (5) for a still smaller vocal element ("alphabetic" writing which modern European nations have derived from the Greeks, and the Greeks derived from the Semitic Phœnicians). Picture writing becomes ideographic when usage settles upon given pictures as the signs of given words rather than of the objects which those words mean, so that a combination of these word symbols would no longer be interpreted as combining to form a picture, but as standing for a succession of words. Thus in picture writing a wavy line may stand for water, and a boat may be put upon it or fishes under it, but in ideographic writing the wavy line stands for the word "water" and is read in connection with the signs that precede and follow it to form a sentence. Such ideographic writing

becomes syllabic or alphabetic when the sign that had stood for a word comes to stand only for the first syllable or the first letter of that word. The advantage of this is that there are many more words than syllables, and vastly more words than elementary sounds. An ideographic language requires as many symbols as it has words (save as it lets the same symbol stand for either of several words) while a syllabic language can represent the same number of words by a much smaller number of signs, and an alphabetic language represents thousands of words by twenty-six letters. The forms of characters become greatly simplified as picture writing passes into ideographic, and finally into syllabic or alphabetic writing. Thus the wavy line that stood for water, and later for the initial letter of the word for water, becomes the letter *n*. Swiftness in writing reduced the sign to its simplest form, and usage and conventionality make the sign perfectly intelligible after it has been reduced to the merest vestige of the original picture; there is no longer any need that it should resemble the object for which it once stood, since now it stands only for a sound.

The primitive units of measurement are largely those found ready at hand. An inch was originally a thumb's width. The "hand" still survives among us as a measure of the height of horses. The span is practically obsolete among us save among boys. The foot, however, is our most usual standard. The ell was originally the same as the cubit and equal to the length of forearm and hand. The fathom is equal to the reach of the extended arms. The original meaning of the word yard is walking-stick or goad, and the similar origin of the rod is suggested by its name.

The general practice of counting on the fingers almost certainly gave us the decimal system. The universal method of counting large numbers is to repeat groups of ten or of some other denomination. That many peoples count by threes and not by tens is not a reason for saying that they have no conception of numbers above three, any more (as Bleek and Ratzel remark) than the fact that the French say "dix-sept" and "quatre vingts" is evidence that they cannot count beyond ten or twenty. However, it is true that skill in reckoning is not developed till people have interests that require it.

The simplest subdivisions are halves and quarters and eighths, and to this fact it is doubtless due that our week is of seven days, being one-fourth part of the lunar month. The practice of observing one rest day in each seven rose before the Hebrews became a distinct nation. It originated in Mesopotamia. As soon as gangs of men were kept regularly at severe toil it became manifest that to conserve their power and to secure the greatest amount of work the slaves must be given periodic rest.

Property and Commerce.—Counting, measuring, and writing are developed largely in connection with property and trade.

Primitive property is largely personal property in the strictest sense. A savage is recognized by his weapons and ornaments and not only by his stature or other bodily traits. He thinks of himself as the man who has and wears these things and would regard any disparagement or misuse of these belongings as an attack upon himself. So that it is often said that the savage at first does not distinguish clearly between himself and his belongings. Indeed we all include in our thoughts of ourselves a varied combination of ideas— Tom to Tom is the man who is, does, and has, a variety of things. It has been suggested that the idea of property first became clear in connection with the ownership of slaves, for slaves were property that was necessarily separate in thought from the personality of the owner.

At first man respects the belongings of another only as he respects the person of another, that is, out of personal regard for the owner or fear of his vengeance. The institution of private property does not appear until the idea is formed in the mind of the group and enforced by public opinion, that a person can have a claim to goods which others are bound to respect, not only when those goods are entirely detached from the owner's person, but even when no vengeance for trespass is to be feared. The first step toward the institution of private property is the fear of the owner; the second is fear of the group which has learned to acknowledge and support the claims of the owners, including fear of the ghosts and gods of the group who are believed to take part in enforcing group customs; the third step is the turning in upon himself, by the individual, of the condemnation which he has learned to feel toward others who violate group standards of regard for property rights, so that the individual's own self-judgment enforces upon himself the regard for property which as a member of the group he has learned to help enforce upon others. The institution of property is a typical moral institution.

Some of the earliest instances of institutionalized property rights which we can observe have been developed in connection with forms of property which must be let alone while they are maturing. If there were no social convention to protect a bunch of bananas or a bee tree, few fine bunches of bananas would be allowed to ripen on the tree in a populous neighborhood and few bee trees would be fully stored with honey, for every man would say a little honey and green bananas are better than none. The native of the Upper Nile Valley or the pygmy of the Congo finding a choice bunch of bananas shoots an arrow into it, and thereafter all comers know that it has been spoken for, and let it alone. Similarly a bee tree, or one of those trees that when broken off at the top become receptacles for a rich deposit of edible grubs, are marked by the finder and his rights are recognized. The Australian black fellow setting out upon a journey on which he does not wish to carry all his belongings, deposits those he will leave behind in a conspicuous place, makes a clear imprint of his foot beside them and expects them to be unmolested during his absence.

Communistic institutions of property have also a very early origin. Groups assert their common ownership of hunting grounds, of nesting beaches where eggs abound, and other natural sources of food supply, and of the stores which have been laid up for seasons of scarcity. It does not require the existence of an institution of communal property to make people assert such claims against alien groups, but the existence of such an institution appears in the assertion of these claims by public opinion not merely against aliens but also against the rapacity of individuals within the group. Group opinion among savages tends steadily to subordinate all individual claims to communal claims and this may be done in the case of property by an elaborate and precise system of institutionalized requirements. Such is the case, for example, among the Australians, where a hunter by no means regards the game he kills as belonging exclusively to himself, but knows exactly how it should be divided among the members of the encampment. Among the Esquimaux also and other savages whose institutions have not been mixed with those of civilized invaders, "life is based upon communism, and what is obtained by hunting and fishing belongs to the clan." Normally, in accordance either with fact or cherished fiction, every savage regards all clansfolk as his near kindred, and shares with them according to established customs. Savages of this stage of economic development are unable to understand how superabundance and pitiful want can exist side by side as they do in our cities. "I remember," says Kropotkin,[1] "how vainly I tried to make some of my Tungus friends understand our civilization of individualism; they could not, and they resorted to the most fantastical suggestions. The fact is that a savage, brought up in ideas of tribal solidarity in everything, is as incapable of understanding a 'moral' European, who knows nothing of that solidarity, as the average European is incapable of understanding the savage."

The exchange of presents is more primitive than trade. It is common for savages to express and cement friendship in this way, as David and Jonathan did. They also frequently exchange a little of their blood on similar occasions, and there is little or no more evidence of an institution of property in the one way of exchanging pledges than in the other. The practice of securing the favor and protection of powerful men by means of gifts has continued throughout barbarism, has survived in feudal benefits which were nominally the free

---

[1] P. Kropotkin: Mutual Aid a Factor of Evolution. New York, 1903, p. 105.

contributions of loyal impulse, and was a forerunner of "taxes" paid by the citizenship of a nation as distinguished from "tribute," which was paid by aliens for immunity from slaughter and spoliation. Exchange of gifts has often been a customary accompaniment of the exercise of hospitality and by this means distinctive products of savage industry have been known to pass from people to people, so as to be distributed in regions very remote from their places of origin. Foreign commerce appears to have been more primitive than domestic trade; that is to say, a people living where there is a supply of salt, or some other natural product which other peoples lack, or having developed some craft or skill the product of which other peoples want, exchange with each other the goods with which they are especially well supplied for other goods in which they are deficient. Those who bring these rare products are welcomed; and among Negroes, East Indians, and Polynesians, understandings have been reached by which, even among hostile tribes, persons may go back and forth as merchants with immunity from violence, or else certain places have been set aside as markets, where fighting was taboo and goods might be exchanged in inter-tribal barter; and among the Mosquitos of Honduras, "Aboriginal wars were continually waged . . . neighboring tribes, however, agreed to a truce at certain times, to allow the interchange of goods." Thus early does commerce demand peace.

The fiction that barter is a friendly exchange of gifts is considerably persistent even though in such exchange the formidable savage tends to get from the weaker what he wants for whatever he chooses to give. The principle of novelty which makes the proffered article more interesting and alluring than property that has been long possessed, and the possibilities of suggestion and of filling the purchaser's attention with advantages so that disadvantages are overlooked, make the savage an easy victim to practiced traders; indeed for his more sophisticated descendant the arts of salesmanship too easily lead to bargains that are followed by regret, and give trade a name that is allied to *Trug* (deceit).

In the exchange of gifts the thought of equivalence in

value has little or no place, and the idea of such equivalence develops rather slowly. It may be that this idea does not become clearly established as a principle of trade until after some one commodity has come to be customarily thought of as the standard of values.

Whenever there is a commodity that everybody wants, then whoever has more of that commodity than he cares to use can be sure of getting the things which others have to sell in exchange for his surplus of this universally desired commodity. This causes such a commodity to be desired not only for its original uses, but also as a means of getting other things; and when any group of people customarily regard any given commodity as their means of getting other things in exchange, then that commodity has become their money— certainly a medium of exchange, probably a standard by which to measure all other economic values, and possibly a means of storing accumulations, as well as ultimately a standard of deferred payment and a reserve basis for credit transactions. Where there is no medium of exchange each buyer, besides wanting what the seller chances to have, must also have what the seller chances to want, and trade takes place only now and then, by virtue of this double coincidence. But where there is a recognized medium of exchange—a money commodity—whoever has that commodity can buy whatever he wants of whoever has it to sell, and whoever can produce a saleable commodity is encouraged to do so since he can afford to dispose of it, not only to one who chances to have what the producer wants to use, but to anyone who has the money commodity. He can always afford to take the latter, though he does not want it save to give in exchange for whatever else he may desire. Under these conditions trade takes place on every hand, and production for purposes of trade is stimulated, so that instead of the poverty and hand to mouth existence of the earlier savages, we are on the way toward possessing the necessary economic basis for civilization.

General desirability and acceptability is the primary qualification for a money commodity. Various commodities have served as the medium of exchange: a standard food, as rice, maize, wheat, dried fish, cacao beans, dates, nuts; a condiment, as salt, olive oil, cocoanut oil; a pleasure drug, as tobacco, tea, coffee, betel nut; a clothing stuff, as furs, cotton, silk; cattle, sheep, and horses; a standard tool or weapon; above all a generally prized means of personal adornment as gold (even the placer dust put up in goose quills), other metals, cowry shells, teeth of whales, fine feathers; indeed "it would be difficult to say what has not been used as money at some time or place."

The early planters of Virginia and Maryland used tobacco as currency for a century or more. The settlers of New England adopted the wampum currency of the Indians in trading with each other as well as with the aborigines, and used beaver-skins among themselves and in trade with the mother country. To serve well as a medium of exchange and standard of values a commodity must be highly divisible, so as to fit either small or large transactions; to be convenient and to be suitable for a means of storing accumulations it must be durable and portable and have great value in small bulk. All of these qualifications, together with homogeneity and malleability by which to receive a recognizable stamp, are possessed by no other commodity in such degree as by the metals, especially for large values, the "precious" metals. It is significant that for both savage and civilized men the precious things par excellence, are the means of personal adornment—gold and beads. The diamond and ruby and pearl are our favorite beads.

CHAPTER XXIX

EXAMPLES OF SOCIAL EVOLUTION (*Continued*)

The Family.—Scholars may never agree in their inferences and conjectures as to the primitive relations between men and women and their offspring. Those primitive conditions passed away long before the dawn of history. Perhaps a little amusement is justified whenever we see the practices of savages in this respect seriously appealed to for light as to what should be the ideal of an advanced society. We might as well appeal to the wattle hut and the dugout for our architectural designs.

There are, however, no living savages among whom the relations between the sexes are entirely promiscuous and unregulated. Savages who tolerate or approve some practices that to us seem most shocking often enforce their own regulations for the conduct of men and women with tremendous severity. "Monogamy appears to be the prevailing form of family precisely among people the least advanced in general culture and particularly in the economic arts. Among some of the very lowest, as the Veddahs of Ceylon, there is free courtship, no divorce, no prostitution and no form of marriage but monogamous unions and these characterized by great fidelity and lasting until death." [1]

If we are to form inferences concerning the primitive state, in these respects, we may well remember: first, that not promiscuity but pairing as a rule is characteristic of the animals most closely related to man; second, that in a state of nature the jealousy of males tends to forbid any second male to have relations with a female to whom a first male asserts a claim; third, that the method of nature with the lower animals is to provide a multitude of offspring and

---

[1] G. E. Howard: History of Matrimonial Institutions. University of Chicago Press, 1904, i, 141.

leave their survival to chance, but with the higher animals the method of nature is to afford to a few offspring the utmost care, and in the case of the highest animals this includes the care of both parents, the father joining with the mother, not only in defending their offspring, but also in providing food, at first for the mother and later for the young as well. Pairing, which affords to the offspring the care of both parents, has great survival value, and is therefore selected as nature's method by the operation of her inviolable law. This is especially true of the highest of all mammals because the helplessness of human children is greatly prolonged, maturity not being reached until after the lapse of years, and it is far from being the case that the offspring of one birth is independent before another birth takes place, so that mating when it lasted through the dependency of the offspring would as a rule cover the whole period of the parents' fertility and be practically for life. Primitive pairing appears to be based upon instinct and biological necessity.

But after man begins to emancipate himself from the control of nature, after certain groups become strong enough and rich enough to secure survival in spite of biologically costly indulgences, there is invented every sort of aberration from nature's simple and biologically efficient plan. It is among the higher savages and especially among the barbarians and lower civilized people that pairing is set aside for group marriage, polygyny, and polyandry. It is useless to attempt to arrange the different marriage customs in a serial order of development. All that can be said is that under one set of conditions a corresponding set of customs grew up and under other conditions other customs. Among these customs we must note exogamy, the classificatory system of relationships, the matronymic family, wife-purchase, group marriages, polyandry, polygyny, and patriarchy.

Exogamy.—The practice of exogamy and the matronymic family have been so widespread that the statement is sometimes ventured that all peoples which rise high enough in social development pass into and finally out of a stage characterized by this usage. Hordes of savages that increase in number till the food supplies which they find do not suffice, are forced to separate into two hordes or "moieties." These two likewise tend to become four, and the four to become eight, and the eight, sixteen. This scheme of multiplication by division is not sure to be exactly carried out, any more than the characteristic phyllotaxy of its species can be traced in every botanical specimen; the growth of a given twig, or savage tribe, is subject to too many accidents, yet the general tendency is discernible. These subdivisions of the same tribe are called clans. Each clan is likely to be distinguished by its peculiar totem. Exogamy is the custom which requires a man to find his wife in another clan or totem-group than his own.

Why at a certain stage of social evolution men should have been so generally required to seek their mates outside their own group is somewhat difficult to understand.[1] It can hardly be due, as McLennan thought, to infanticide compelling man to seek his mate abroad, for on that hypothesis why should another exogamous group be better supplied with marriageable girls than the man's own; besides that theory gives no explanation of the fact that such girls as do grow up within the clan cannot be married by men of their own clan, moreover infanticide though somewhat common among peoples who have developed motives that override nature, is not a general practice of any primitive people, and when it occurs among the primitive is due to scarcity of food and ill health of the mother, which may cause the death of boys as well as of girls. A practice so widespread must probably be due to something inherent in human nature; though the fact that it passes away shows clearly that some transitory condition also plays a part in its causation. One such transitory condition was clan organization. The trait of human nature may have been the preference of out-wandering savages for women who had the charm of novelty and mystery, rather than for the women whom they had familiarly seen from

---

[1] For a summary of the theories of Bachofen, Morgan, Lubbock, Tylor, Kohler, McLennan and Spencer, on the causes of exogamy, see Howard: History of Matrimonial Institutions, especially vol. 1, chap. 2

girlhood about the drudgery of the camp and from whose company they had been formally promoted by the ceremonies
which at puberty transfer boys from association with the
women and girls of the clan to association with the men.
Lack of sex interest or even a feeling of repugnance to sex intimacy with respect to individuals with whom there had been
too great familiarity before puberty has been remarked, and
by some is thought to amount almost, or quite, to an instinctive aversion, to be indeed the real essence of the supposed
instinct against incest. The study of evolution in all fields
teaches that great results flow from seemingly small causes
provided the causes are sufficiently general and constant. Such
a preference for unfamiliar women even though slight, if it
were actually general, might be effective in causing the custom of exogamy. The futility of the numerous and ingenious
attempts to account for exogamy on any other theory than
that of general preference leaves that cause as the principal
one that has been discovered. Doubtless the prestige of
leaders had also a part in fixing the practice of exogamy as
an accepted custom. This implies that the most vigorous and
admired men were the ones at first most likely to break away
from the commonplace of the camp in finding their mates.
Spencer would have it that mating with a woman of one's
own group ultimately became disgraceful for all men because
great chiefs possessed captured wives.[1] And the custom of

---

[1] This suggestion of Spencer receives apparent corroboration from
the pantomime of wife-stealing which so often occurs in the marriage
ceremony of barbarous peoples. This piece of mimicry, however, is
not thought to indicate that wife-capture was once the usual mode of
obtaining a mate among all those peoples among whom exogamy has
prevailed, for the clan solidarity is such that to steal a woman would
make every man in the clan of the thief liable to vengeance from
every man in the clan from which the woman had been stolen, and
therefore would be likely to make the thief reprehensible to all the
men of both clans. Sufficient causes for the frequent pantomime of
wife-capture in wedding ceremonies may be found in the occasional
occurrence of the theft of a woman, especially in time of war, in the
romantic and dramatic interest of such an act, and in the fact that it
is a concession to the coyness of the maiden who is made to seem to
be forced to give her consent.

mating outside the clan once fixed, marriages within the clan were usually regarded as immoral, though some peoples have allowed exogamy and endogamy to exist together. Mendelism has reënforced our belief in the evils of inbreeding, and while it seems incredible that foresight of these evils should have originated the general practice of exogamy, as Morgan thought, still it may be that natural selection favored the survival and spread of those peoples who practiced it. But exogamous unions carried on for generations between the same clans do not preclude inbreeding, and while some of the rules for selecting wives seem to be aimed to prevent inbreeding, others of these rules actually require it. We may refuse to think as Tylor and Kohler propose, that exogamy arose from the desire to prevent inter-clan slaughter by a system of diplomatic marriages, yet exogamy once established would tend to keep the clans from exterminating one another and to secure survival, multiplication, unity, and strength to the peoples practicing it, and so help to account for its wide prevalence.

The Classificatory System of Relationships.—Among exogamous peoples it is not always every clan outside his own in which a man may choose his wife, nor every woman in a clan to which he may go a-wooing that he may select. On the contrary there exist various and sometimes amazing regulations as to which woman he should and which he should not, marry. These regulations often commend the marriage of a woman related to the man in blood, so that after the mating takes place the wife's relatives are related to the husband both by blood and by marriage. The intricacy of kinship and the punctiliousness with which it is traced and regarded among such peoples as the Australians and Melanesians are astounding. This is accompanied by the classificatory system of nomenclature, under which most and in some cases all, of the designations of kinship—father, mother, husband, etc.— do not refer to single individuals but to whole classes of persons. "The term 'father,' for instance, is applied to all those whom the father would call brother, and to all the husbands of those whom the mother calls sister, both brother and sister being used in a far wider sense than among ourselves. In some forms of the classificatory system the term 'father' is also used for all those whom the mother would call brother, and for all the husbands of those whom the father would call sister. . . . Similarly the term used for the wife may be applied to all those whom the wife would call sister and to the wives of all those whom the speaker calls brother, brother and sister again being used in a far wider sense than in our own language." [1] In fact our words "father" and "wife" do not serve as equivalents for these classificatory designations. Furthermore it is often though not always the case that this nomenclature carries with it clearly defined duties, privileges, and restrictions governing the conduct of the individual toward all those whom he calls by a given classificatory name. The individual is imbedded in a ramifying network of social relationships. We have by no means reached complete explanations of all these facts, but they seem to be bound up with the sense of the supreme importance of group solidarity, or perhaps it would be better to say, with an instinctive emotion of partisanship. "All the main features of the classificatory system become at once natural and intelligible if this system had its origin in a social structure in which the exogamous social groups, such as the clan or moiety, were even more completely and essentially the social units than we know them to be to-day" among the peoples referred to.[2] The unity of the clan is apparently a more vivid and important fact of consciousness than the individuality of any person, and when a man forms a union with a woman, the fact that one of his clan has married into her clan seems more important to both groups than the mere relation between the two individuals primarily concerned. Such a society has

---

[1] W. A. R. Rivers: Kinship and Social Organization, p. 2. Compare: History of Melanesian Society, Cambridge University Press; and Systems on Consanguinity and Affinity of the Human Family, Smithsonian Contributions to Knowledge, 1871, xvii; and A. W. Howitt: Native Tribes of Southeast Australia, Macmillan 1904, chaps. 3, 4, 5; and Spencer and Gillen: The Northern Tribes of Central Australia, Macmillan, 1904, chap. iii; and The Native Tribes of Central Australia, Macmillan, 1899, chap. 2.

[2] Op. cit., p. 71.

a set of organizing concepts utterly foreign to our way of thinking.

Classificatory use of the words that apply to wives and husbands may have arisen in connection with the practice of group marriages later to be described. But application of the word "sister" to wives' sisters and brothers' wives in some cases definitely excludes from sexual relation the very person who would be included in such relation under group marriage. "To a Melanesian, as to other people of rude culture, the use of the term otherwise applied to a sister carries with it such deeply seated associations as to put sexual relations absolutely out of the question."[1]

The Matronymic Family.—The matronymic family exists as long as the wife continues after marriage to be a member of her clan, and her children belong to her clan, inherit her name and totem and household gods, and if the children are male and there is rank and property to be inherited they inherit from their mother's family. Neither can the man nor his belongings be alienated from his clan, and if he leaves anything to be inherited it must go to his nearest relatives within his own clan, that is, to his sister's children and not to his own. That descent should at first be reckoned through the mother's and not through the father's line and that children should belong to their mother's clan is most natural, in view of the obvious connection between mother and offspring, in view of the fact that savage children follow their mothers for a long time, and frequently are suckled for a period of years, there being no other milk and little other proper food for infants, and wherever exogamy existed it was rendered almost inevitable by the powerful clan solidarity which would not allow children so long in the group to be separated from it, to become part of the father's clan.

Matronymic society is sometimes referred to as "matriarchal." It is true that population groups originally gathered about mothers by natural increase, though usually the number of children reared by a savage mother is not large; it is true that the camp and the first tilled patches were made and

---

[1] Rivers: *op. cit.,* p. 62.

occupied by the women with their children; and in these senses women were the living protoplasm and roaming men were the rind and spines of the primitive social organism. It is also true that in exogamous society woman has the power to reject unwelcome suitors, and that the power of divorce belongs to her, while man is obliged to make himself *persona grata* to her and to her group. Yet woman never ruled man, as the word "matriarchy" implies. But in very early society men and women have been more nearly on an equality than in barbarous and lower civilized societies.[1]

Transition to Patronymic Family.—The state of custom by which a man's wife and children belonged to one clan while he belonged to another was not very satisfactory to man. He was obliged to go away from his own people, and to make himself acceptable to a group of outsiders whenever he desired her company. His wife did not tan hides or prepare food for him. His children did not reënforce his own clan, and were not in any important sense his own.[2] Yet it was impossible to take his wife away from her own people. They claimed her labor and her children. To have stolen her would have made every man in the husband's clan an object of vengeance to every man in the clan of the wife. One expedient remained, and that was to purchase her.

But the desire to make such purchases arose before men had any accumulations of transferable property adequate to the purpose. This led to the exchange of women. A man would give a sister, or later in life a daughter, in exchange for a wife. Such has been, for example, the usual practice of

---

[1] Among the Iroquois we have perhaps the nearest approach to true matriarchy. The women who kept the "long house" elected one sachem who should join in council with four chosen women, and when this council of five went up to unite with similar quintets from the other long houses in tribal council the men were outnumbered by the women four to one. Yet the men, partly by virtue of their wider experience, are supposed to have been looked to for the chief guidance.

[2] The curious custom of the "couvade," in which the father took to his bed at the birth of a child, may have been a means of asserting the claim that he, too, was a parent of the child, as well as being an exercise of "sympathetic magic" in the interests of child and mother.

the Australians. Another method has been for the poor man, or any man in a society too primitive to have stores of transferable wealth, to give personal service in exchange for a wife.[1] This practice has prevailed widely in Africa, Asia, the island countries, and in America [2] in regions as widely separated as Alaska and Tierra del Fuego. Among a hunting people the aspirant to a maiden's hand brings game and fish to her parents, builds the hut, provides firewood, makes canoes, nets, and weapons. Under this custom the suitor has a protracted period of probation, implying acquaintance, friendship, and the acquiescence of the woman, and a high sense of her value on the part of the man.

But with the accumulation of wealth these practices give way to mere purchases in which wives become regular objects of barter, paid for in cattle, horses, camels or shell money, and the wishes of the woman are no more consulted than the wishes of the cattle offered in exchange. Under this system woman, of course, loses the power of divorce which she had formerly possessed with other rights and advantages. The rich and old men buy young wives and young men often must content themselves with wives that are old and cheap. Among the Zulu a woman whose lack of health and strength prevents her from being a good laborer, or who proves childless, can be returned and the purchase price demanded back. Sometimes a wife is pawned or mortgaged, sometimes paid for on installments.

Among every people that has risen to the patronymic organization of the family, of whom we have sufficient knowledge to justify any assertion, wife-purchase has been practiced. Such evidence as we possess indicates that it has existed in all branches of the Aryan and Semitic races.[3]

---

[1] Compare the twice seven years of service which Jacob rendered to Laban in return for Rachel and Leah. Genesis, 29.

[2] Compare H. H. Bancroft: Native Races of the Pacific State. Appleton, 1875, i, 134 *seq.*

[3] That the form of marriage among the Hebrews at the time of Ruth and Boaz, was calling witnesses to attest a bargain by which the wife had been purchased is indicated by Ruth 4:10. Compare Deut. 22:29.

Wife-purchase makes the man the center of the family and the children his children.

Group Marriage, Polyandry, and Polygamy.—Among the marital vagaries into which men entered after they had broken away from nature's stricter régime is the "punaluan" family.

In the punaluan [1] family a little group of men, usually brothers, married a little group of women, usually sisters, every woman in the group being a wife to every man in the group. This type of domestic organization is but ill adapted to develop the higher type of personal relationship which makes families the crystallizing centers of social stability and the foci of life's values. The punaluan family has existed within historic times, not only in Hawaii, but also in Europe, Asia, and America.

Polyandry is that type of domestic organization in which a little group of men, usually brothers, become the husbands of one woman. Westermark and Howard state that polyandry is usually connected with an excess of males over females in the population, due to natural causes, or to female infanticide, or both, and that the husbands ordinarily live with the wives by turns. Among the Thibetans all the husbands save one are commonly away with the flocks in distant pastures. Polyandry seems to have but one advantage, and that is its disadvantage, namely its lack of fertility. It persists only under hard conditions; where nature is most niggardly and not many mouths can be filled. Polyandry is the form of family best fitted to keep down population. It still survives in a few places, especially in Thibet, on the cold Himalayan plateaux ten thousand feet and more above the sea, and among the probably socially decadent Nairs and the Dravidian Todas of India. The so-called polyandry of the Todas, however, is rather an extreme liberty on the part of the women to divorce husbands and choose new ones. Not all the women among the Todas exercise this freedom but some permanently retain a single mate in monogamous union.

Polygyny is the custom which allows one man to have several wives at the same time. This practice has generally

[1] A Hawaiian word.

been permitted by higher savage and barbarous peoples, indeed it may be said to become universally approved when the custom of wife-purchase is established. However, among polygynous peoples, as a rule, only a small minority composed of the rich and powerful actually have plural wives, because the difficulty of maintaining so large a family and the approximate numerical equality of the sexes forbid it to the majority of common men. The numerical equality of the sexes is not exact and at times there is a very considerable departure from it. Indeed, when men lead lives of great exposure and much fighting the excess of females as well as the need of recruits are conditions highly favorable to polygyny; while among the impoverished but peaceable inhabitants of a land that no one cares to invade, the males survive while infanticide and harsh treatment diminish the number of females. Polygyny is not due to indulgence alone. Women are desired as workers. Numerous children are desired to bear the father's feud and make him formidable and in general to recruit the fighting and working strength of the group. Further, the more wives the more pretentious the social standing of the establishment. Even the women may welcome additions to their husbands' corps of wives both as increasing the ostentatiousness of the household and as dividing the labors which all the wives must share. A woman would naturally prefer to be her husband's only wife, but once given plural wives additions to their number have compensations. Finally, whatever the accepted leaders of society do and approve acquires the sanction of morality and religion. Polygyny is characteristic of the patriarchal pastoral ancestors of the Indo-European peoples whose characteristics in this respect have already been mentioned. Those who, like the learned Sir Henry Maine, describe the patriarchal organization as the original form of the family and the germ of the state, do not study the practices of peoples more primitive than the Aryans and Semites.

Polygyny has no practical justification after the point of diminishing returns has been reached. It abases woman, tramples upon her highest interests, and tends to embitter her life. It is inconsistent with the better type of personal relationship between the members of the family which are essential to the social value of that institution. Turkish gentlemen have sometimes drawn envious and even pitiable comparisons between their own state and that of the heads of English and American family life which they have observed.

Mankind has experimented on a great scale and through long periods with every possible form of domestic organization, and among all highly advanced peoples monogamy increasingly survives and prevails. Its predominance has been assisted by social and religious sanctions due to the approval of the influential, but this predominance has been essentially due to natural selection and the survival of the fittest. Nothing human is perfect, no domestic arrangement makes ideals automatically fulfill themselves; but it would seem that if anything can be said to have been demonstrated by experience, the incomparable superiority of monogamy over other forms of the family is removed beyond argument.

Slavery.—Slavery has been practiced by all peoples who have risen sufficiently high in the scale of social evolution. Like the fire drill or the hand loom, slavery would be a pitiful anachronism in a society of the highest development, but like them it has played a useful part in social evolution. Wide prevalence and long continuance of an institution are impressive if not conclusive evidence of its usefulness. The disappearance among the most advanced peoples of an institution which has prevailed so widely and so long, is equal evidence that it has been superseded and has become naturally obsolete.

It was a decided advantage when the conquered were enslaved instead of being devoured or tortured to death or even merely slaughtered. In all probability slavery began with the keeping alive of women of the conquered as spoils of war. The enslaving of men from an economic motive could not take place on any considerable scale until industry was somewhat advanced. In some instances conquered men were kept alive in that early stage of development when industry, except the chase and certain mechanic arts, was still almost exclusively the affair of women and a part of the degradation of the slave was that he was set at woman's work. This tended to lighten the labors and improve the status of woman among the conquerors. Industrial toil from having been the lot of women became the lot of the conquered, and slavery became a basis of social castes. When later conquests were made by a people who had already absorbed and enslaved one conquered people, those later subjugated were almost sure to constitute the lowest caste.[1]

Slavery, moreover, served the inestimably important purpose of disciplining men to work. Among the African porters employed by the explorer Van Götzen those who had been slaves expressed scorn for the comparatively worthless and untrained sons of the wild. American Indians have often been regarded as unfit for agriculture, and they are, if they grow to manhood untrained for it, as unfit as the son of a millionaire, unless some mighty motive spurs them on. A failure of the potato crop is said to have been regarded as a blessing by the manufacturers of a certain civilized region, since it made it possible to get regular labor in the mills, for regular labor is ordinarily not to be had when the requirements of the existing standard of living can be met without such labor. An efficient class of laboring men, is, not without reason, regarded as a product of slavery.

Slavery enabled the conquerors to have at the same time a considerably high standard of living and leisure. This condition was essential to high development of other than economic progress. The classic civilization of Greece rested on the backs of slaves and to the ancients such a foundation for civilization seemed indispensable, and probably was so.

Slavery, like everything else that becomes imbedded in custom, so long as it is thoroughly customary seems thoroughly natural, and the idea of doing away with it, if suggested, is likely to seem grotesque and absurd. So thoroughly accepted is slavery in Africa that Africans have long con-

---

[1] It is not necessary to hold, as some appear to do, that conquest in war was the sole origin of social stratification. Social stratification came sometimes through the exaltation of the rich and the sinking of the impoverished within the tribe into practical or even actual slavery chiefly through debt.

ducted extensive enslaving expeditions, in order to sell their captives to the Arabs or other traders. And in some sections of Africa it is said that three men could hardly be induced to go on a journey together for fear that two of them might combine to sell the third. The Africans have often been as eager to sell slaves as the traders to buy them. Adequate valuation of human life and happiness is a culture product, and when that valuation is low slavery is perfectly natural. With the cultural advance of social sentiments slavery passes through all degrees of diminishing brutality till in some instances it becomes a kindly tutelage and finally is no longer possible.

Slavery wherever established has a remarkable effect on the other customs of society. "When adopted into the folkways," says Sumner, "slavery has dominated and given tone and color to them all. . . . It has been a terrible afrit, a demon which promised service but which became a master."

It is commonly held that in slavery is to be found the origin of the state, that the state had its rise not in bodies of freemen uniting for self-government, but in bodies of conquerors organizing to hold the governed in subjection. There is no doubt that slavery in this way had much to do with the development of strong governments. However, this aspect of political development can be too exclusively emphasized.

Origin of the State.—Government has two distinct roots, one in foreign, and one in domestic relations.[1]

Effective warfare requires organization, whether the warfare be offensive or defensive and whether the vanquished are enslaved or merely slaughtered. The first war chiefs are not elected or appointed; they merely lead. The man who plans a raid and wins the coöperation of a band of followers, or the man who, when his clan is attacked, responds to the emergency in such a way as to win prominence and leader-

---

[1] I Samuel viii: 4, 5. "Then all the elders of Israel gathered themselves together, and came to Samuel unto Ramah, and said unto him, . . . Now make us a king *to judge us* like all the nations." 19. "And they said, Nay; but we will have a king over us; that we also may be like all the nations; and that our king may *judge us,* and go out before us, *and fight our battles.*"

ship is for the time being a *de facto* chieftain. When the fight is over such a man retains a certain glory, but has no definite authority. His chieftainship is temporary, lasting only as long as the emergency that evoked it.

Permanent chieftaincy involves the evolution of an institution, that is, of ideas, sentiments, and judgments common to the members of the society, which maintain the authority of rulers and which prescribe the selection of rulers to fill vacancies as they occur. The king of Dahomey does not have power to command his hordes of followers by mere virtue of any personal qualities that reside in him, any more than he has power to strike off the heads of any who disobey by virtue of the mere strength of his arm. No arm is strong enough to have such power for an hour over his thousands of followers, any of whom would enter his presence groveling on all fours with face to the ground. The development of such folk-ways and institutions involves: (1) the temporary supremacy over a few immediate followers due to response to emergency; (2) the more lasting prestige engendered by such prowess; (3) a sense of the necessity of military success as a matter of group policy; (4) the instinct of dominance expressed in conduct that suggests and evokes subservience; (5) the habit and custom of obedience; (6) partisanship and the prestige of desire [1] glorifying leaders; (7) mob reduplication of these sentiments in times of pageant and triumph; (8) specific inventions, due to incident and accident playing upon predispositions and ingenuity, which define the conduct proper to a king and the conduct proper in approaching him; (9) rational approval of the necessity of established group organization. All these together produce a constitution, unwritten of course, but imbedded in the minds of the participants in the social process.

The rapidity of political evolution on the warlike side, depends upon the frequency of warfare; and is especially promoted when a conquering group has the necessity of holding under continuous repression subjugated and tribute-paying or regularly enslaved peoples.

[1] Compare page 331.

The second strand in the evolution of government starts, not with the temporary chieftainship of bold fighters, but with the head men or elders who direct the primitive communism of savage hordes. The enforcement of group customs and taboos regulating food distribution and other matters, the carrying out of ceremonies, particularly the ceremonies of initiation, which with a little stretch of fancy may be regarded as the germ of a public school system,[1] the organization of coöperative hunts and game round-ups, the direction of the group wanderings, later the distribution of plots of ground, and the settling of disputes and quarrels, all these functions of the elders illustrate the fact that the early folk-ways are regulative of the internal affairs of the clan as well as of inter-clan hostilities.

The economic and inner social life of the group seems to have played the predominant rôle in the governmental evolution of some peoples, and the subordinate importance assigned to it in the usual accounts of the evolution of the state may be entirely due to the romantic interest of warfare which has held the attention and to the inadequate attention paid to the facts of peaceful life in savage and barbarous communities. Many facts could be adduced in support of the proposition that the predominance of militarism increases as we advance from the more primitive social forms to barbarism and early civilization, and tends relatively to decline as we approach the culture period. Yet even among some of the pastoral barbarians, a class especially prone to war and depredation, the regulation of economic, domestic, ceremonial [2]

---

[1] Compare Arthur J. Todd: The Primitive Family as an Educational Agency. Putnam, 1913, chaps. 6 and 7.

[2] Ceremony includes the beginnings of all the arts, notably the drama. It plays a great rôle in the interest, development, and happiness of savage and barbarous peoples. Ceremony itself is an agency of government of very great importance among savage and barbarous peoples, and is by no means insignificant in this respect even among us. Compare page 679. In an ethnographic collection everyone can understand the bows and clubs but not the masks and belts and tom-toms and rattles and magic bundles and sand pictures.

and other intrasocietal matters could probably be shown to have as great a part in governmental evolution as war and slavery.[1] It might even be shown that there are two types of feudalism: that which results from the distribution of conquered lands among the leaders of the conquerors with which Norman England has familiarized us, and that which gradually arises as the power of head men to regulate the distribution of the right to till patches of ground, which ground at first is regarded as common property, changes at length into practical ownership of the land by the descendants of these head men.

The separation of church and state is a very modern differentiation. The development of religious and political government in their early stages are thoroughly entangled and contribute essentially to each other. Divine rulers tend to be a magnified reflection of earthly rulers: despots if the earthly rulers are such, or patriarchs where earthly rulers are of that character. And earthly rulers derive a great part of their power from the supposed backing of invisible potentates; among whom mysteriously magnified spirits of the departed ancestors from whom the earthly rulers have descended are often the most imposing figures.

Morality.—1. *Conscience codes are exceedingly various.* Comparative study of the life of different societies reveals the fact that man is not born with a table of commandments "etched on the soul." On the contrary "the mores can make anything seem right." Cannibalism to one whose group approves it may be as proper as "a dinner of herbs"; it may even be a religious rite, or a mark of honor to a parent whose flesh is consumed. Murder of choice youths may be committed as a devout sacrifice to the gods, and slaying the aged as an office of affection. Though "love your enemies" may be the nobler injunction, yet the solemn duty of vengeance has been commanded by the consciences of most men. No people live without a code for the regulation of relations

---

[1] For an accessible example the book of Deuteronomy will serve, even though it describes the life of a nomadic pastoral people at the very time when they are engaged in a great invasion.

between the sexes, yet while punishing with utmost severity acts which they disapprove they approve polygamy, concubinage, wife-lending, and ceremonial license. Our own ethics of property rights which allow Dives to roll in wealth with an unruffled conscience, knowing that three blocks away Lazarus and his offspring exist in squalor and blight, are in the eyes of some savages as incomprehensible a violation of morality, as the practices of savages are to us.

2. How far conscience codes are from being a universal metaphysical imperative is shown by another set of facts to which the term *"ethical dualism"* has been applied. The consciences of savages, barbarians, and in some degree of all but the most ethically advanced persons, prescribe one code of conduct towards fellow clansmen or members of any we-group to which the actor belongs, and prescribes another code of conduct or allows immunity from ethical requirements toward outsiders. This results from two causes: (a) sympathy partly, and partisanship and justice wholly, depend upon "consciousness of kind," upon admission of the persons by whom benevolent propensities are evoked into the we-thought. The white settler does not fully thus admit the American Indian, the Australian Blackfellow, or the South African Bushman. He can shoot them like vermin. The Arab does not so admit the Zulu, the Zulu does not so admit the Hottentot, the Greek did not so admit the Barbarian, the Hebrew did not so admit the Samaritan. The white native American does not always so admit the negro, the "wop" or the "hunkie," and savage and barbarous peoples as a rule have a narrow and definitely limited we-thought. (b) The ethical dualism so characteristic of the less developed peoples is due also to the fact that the conscience code, like language, is a group product and a group possession. It is not the property of the individual as an individual or of the whole human race as a race. It prescribes the conduct which a given society demands from its members primarily in the interest of that particular society.

3. Nevertheless *predispositions common to humanity* lay the foundation for the evolution of consciences. Ethical valu-

ations take their rise in discriminations between pleasure and pain, not merely sensory pleasure and pain, but all the satisfying and distressing qualities of consciousness, and in practical reason which recognizes causal relations between conduct and its consequences, and so identifies the conduct that has hurt us or benefited us, or that may either hurt or benefit us. Altruism extends these rational judgments to conduct that will affect others in whom we are interested, our children, our family, our tribe, our nation, and finally humanity. Reason both identifies specific forms of conduct, like obedience to parents, as good, and others, like poisoning arrows or wife-beating, as bad, and also generalizes so as to recognize as good or bad, abstract qualities such as truthfulness, chastity, courage, benevolence, and their opposites. Esthetic discrimination reacts strongly upon ideas and ideals of conduct that have been defined by practical reason, and elevates the judgments of reason into enthusiasms and detestations. Thus wrong conduct becomes not only inexpedient but disgusting. It is this esthetic emotion which gives to ethical valuations a quality distinct from mere "counsels of prudence." Finally, anger is ready to be aroused by whatever thwarts a natural impulse, and the thwarting of the parental and altruistic impulse is no exception. Accordingly conduct that arouses moral disapproval is felt to be not only hideous but also an object of indignation.

Every capacity for pleasure or pain is an inborn biological tendency which we must regard as a part of man's adaptation for a survival. This seems obvious enough in connection with the pleasures and pains that are connected with the elementary physical instincts. On the theory of evolution it would seem that it must be equally true of esthetic discrimination, as an inherent capacity of the species, including that esthetic discrimination which applies to qualities of conduct. It would seem that this moral esthetic discrimination, as well as susceptibility to suggestion, imitation and radiation, desire for approval, and altruism, are parts of man's adaptation to survival, after survival has come to depend upon coöperation.

But here we must be careful not to go too far. Evidently inborn esthetic discrimination has not gone so far as to prevent the amazing variety in conscience codes that has been noted. Just as esthetic taste in general is based upon inborn adaptations, yet does not determine for us whether black skins or white, the fashions of 1861 or of 1915, a confused din of clash, blare and tom-tom beat or a symphony shall seem more beautiful, so matters of moral approval and disgust are left by nature vastly uncertain. Nature makes us love the familiar but she also makes us love the novel, she makes us love harmony but she also makes us love contrast, and she does not determine what shall be familiar or what shall seem novel to us, nor in what we shall perceive harmony. Likewise our moral approvals and disapprovals are left by nature full of contradictions and uncertainties. Probably no man needs to give himself a reason why he should see beauty in gratitude, generosity, fidelity, and courage, or why he should see ugliness in ingratitude, meanness, and treachery. But delight in courage and prowess and fidelity to a few may hide the presence of every hideous vice, so that treachery and cruelty are practiced with innocent glee. Biological evolution has gone only part way towards furnishing us with a conscience. Moreover, there seems to be little or no ground for hope that the inborn esthetic equipment for moral discrimination will ever become more complete, for we cannot see any effective natural selection weeding out those who are in this respect less fit. But the progress of rational moral judgments by social evolution gives a constantly increasing supplement to that which biological evolution has done in this direction; it corroborates the discriminations of esthetic sense, and it also completes them by bringing the various activities of man clearly within the compass of these esthetic discriminations. This combination of reason and esthetic sensibility in evaluating forms and qualities of human conduct is what we denominate the moral sentiments.

All that we have noted, however, does not complete the rôle of man's inborn endowment in the development of conscience. The judgments which form the substructure of the moral sentiments are communicated and built up as social possessions by social suggestion; the conduct required by the moral sentiments is disseminated by imitation, and above all, those definite moral sentiments which a society has evolved are spread abroad and imparted to each rising generation by social radiation. Thus the child that is born into a group in which certain moral sentiments already prevail catches them, and they become the expression of his own propensities, although he would never have originated them.[1] Moreover, the inborn desire for social approval molds his habits, and above all this, natural desire molds his self-thought, his conscious and subconscious aims, in conformity with the ethical standards of his group.

Thus we see that pleasure-pain, reason, altruism, esthetic discrimination, susceptibility to suggestion, imitation and radiation and desire for approval—all play a part in the development of conscience. And conscience, instead of being any single faculty, may be far more truly regarded as the net result of the individual and social reactions of all man's faculties upon the problem of conduct.

4. The gradual perception by society of what it is that harms and what promotes its interests, arises in two ways. First, the hard *lessons of age-long experience* rub into the folk-sense a perception of what hurts and what helps. Second, more adequate judgments are derived from *the insight of the élite,* the individuals who are keen enough to identify the causes of good and evil, and in whom the type of emotional response that enters into moral sentiments is sufficiently developed to react to the conduct which they thus identify with indignation and detestation or with enthusiasm.

In regard to ethical progress, especially that which takes place in the folk-sense, the following facts are to be noted: (a) Nice judgments as to the ultimate consequences of a given form of conduct are not likely to be formed by one who is urged toward that conduct by a prospect of some immediate gain or by the clamor of some excited propensity.

---

[1] Compare page 226 and page 318.

Bad conduct is not in the least likely to be first identified as such by one who is engaged in it. A child does innocently what he will later learn to condemn; a savage does innocently what a more evolved society abhors; even in an advanced society new sins, not yet branded by social sentiment, may be innocently committed. In a rapidly evolving society the opportunity for new sins, of wholesale destructiveness, may arise before there is any conscience against them. Of this our "spoils system," and the abuses of "high finance" are examples.[1] Indeed these acts are not sins until they are seen to be such. For a time conscientious Sunday-school teachers may commit such acts and the general public may admire them; later the public judges them mischievous but feels little sentiment of revulsion against them, but ultimately it may draw away from them as by pure instinct.

(b) Self-interest may contribute to ethical progress. If the tempted are in no favorable position to discover the evil of their way, that discovery must usually be made by the victim or by the bystanders. And the by-standers are seldom wholly disinterested, for a mode of conduct which injures one, if it is allowed to go uncondemned and unsuppressed, is likely sooner or later to injure the by-stander, and is sure to injure the group with the interests of which every member of the group is concerned. It makes very little difference whether the harmfulness of conduct is proclaimed by a disinterested prophet or by the victims or by the prudential self-interest of bystanders, provided that its harmfulness is an actual lesson of experience, and provided that by one means or another a perception of its harmfulness gets into the folk-sense.

(c) The tendency to "put the best foot forward," to conceal the worst promptings, to utter the sentiments which the group approves, makes social intercourse less mean than secret musings.[2] Besides, although men often conceal their

---

[1] E. A. Ross: Sin and Society. Macmillan, 1907.

[2] Ross: Social Control, p. 342 *seq.* "The conscience of the social group, as soon as it appears, is several points better than the private conscience, just because it is social." p. 347.

best sentiments from the crowd, yet there is also a tendency to utter and advocate the sentiments which they wish others to feel, which they think tend to make society good to live in, and which they regard as promotive of their own welfare and that of those for whom they care. Especially, parents speaking to children, teachers to pupils, in general those who are set in places of authority, and indeed most others who have occasion to address the public[1] utter the sentiments which they believe that the group approves and which they think it would be well for the group to feel. The members of society are in an unplanned natural conspiracy to keep each other straight. The very fact that the sentiments uttered and advocated are somewhat better than those acted upon, and somewhat stronger than those felt, keeps boosting the mores. This would not be true if it went so far as visible or conscious hypocrisy. If it does not go so far as that, it has the power of auto-suggestion and so reacts strongly upon the speakers. The fact of intercourse tends to repress at the fountainhead the meaner impulses, to elicit the social promptings, and to create a social atmosphere that is better than the individuals would be by themselves and even better than they yet are.

(d) Since those who have social prestige and caste superiority are likely to feel themselves entitled to the advantages which they enjoy and to invest the existing social order with a kind of sanctity, and since men are far less likely to discover their own duties and sins than those of other people, the rulers and teachers of the people are likely, with or without conscious unfairness, to shape the mores in their own interest. The members of an aristocracy radiate as proper attributes of the lower classes commendation for obedience, respect to superiors, loyalty, industry, and frugality, which they do not practice.[2]

Similarly every distinct and intercommunicating class, as the military, the firemen, the police, the labor unions,

---

[1] Even high school orators at graduation time.

[2] Thus the food and sex taboos of savages allow special privileges to the elders.

"society," and even college students, tends to develop its own adaptations in the conscience code. Prevalent sentiments in such a group may support its members in those violations of the general code to which they are particularly tempted, such as vice among "single men in barracks," grafting among the police, and cribbing among college students.

On the other hand these sub-group adaptations of the conscience code are likely to lay certain distinct exactions upon the members of the group in which they must excel the average outsider. One who cannot face death without flinching is "no soldier." The British civil-service official who falls below an exacting standard of punctilious efficiency is "a disgrace to the service." And the aristocracy, instead of warping the mores in their own interest as far as they might have done, develop the principle of *noblesse oblige*. This brings us back to the fact that altruism which prizes the group welfare; moral estheticism or moral idealism which makes sin, when once clearly identified, hideous and despicable, and duty beautiful; and logical consistency which relentlessly turns in upon the actor the judgments which he has passed upon others and thereby converts his idealism into self-respect or shame, are inborn traits of man.

(e) While the age-long lessons of experience, interpreting through the folk-sense the method of weal and woe, slowly contribute progressive variations toward a knowledge of the moral law, mutations in the conscience code are originated by the élite. Science, with its statistics of death rates and speculative losses and standards of living, helps to disclose the remote and diffused consequences of conduct. And the moral genius employs his powers in reasoning, not upon a method by which he may turn stones to gold or call the kingdoms of the world his own, but upon the causes that prevent and the causes that would promote the fulfillment of the good possibilities of mankind. The calculus of methods of welfare which one may help to force upon others but avoid himself, does not lead to the greatest moral advances. The prophets have not flinched from stoning or the stake or the cross, but have given guarantee of the social character of the aims they sought by renouncing common ambitions and paying the price of living by a standard for which the world was not ready. No great people and no great age has lacked such spirits.

(f) The conscience codes of different peoples vary for the same reasons that have caused their modes of agriculture to vary. The chief of these reasons is that they have progressed in various degrees toward a knowledge of the requirements of the laws of nature. Like agriculture, morality is a practical art, the supreme and inclusive practical art of the coöperative promotion of the values of human life. Moral law is not, as Kant and other moral philosophers have imagined, a metaphysical absolute apart from the laws of nature. Yet, in spite of the variability of conscience codes the moral law is as absolute as the laws of nature, for it is the laws of nature, the laws of cause and effect, as they operate in the production of results in human experience.

Moral invention or discovery proceeds by the insight of the élite and by the experience of the many in all the ways which have just been indicated. And natural selection among moral sentiments proceeds actively in all of the five ways mentioned under the discussion of natural selection in the theory of social evolution.[1] Especially is it to be noted that although they are sentiments, ethical elements are subject to the test of practical reason, because they are evoked by judgments concerning the consequences of conduct.

(g) While progress in discovering the content of moral law depends upon reason interpreting the causation of experience, these discoveries are distinguished by the fact that they awaken their characteristic response of sentiment; and the sentiments of moral repugnance or approval are more readily disseminated in society than the logical grounds upon which these moral discriminations rest. The moral sentiments of parents and teachers are radiated to the young, and those of the élite are radiated to the masses in the absence of any adequate perception of the remote and diffused consequences which justify the condemnations and

---

[1] Compare page 485.

demands of virtue. The child whose mother shakes her head and looks aghast and says, "That isn't pretty," knows no reason why "that isn't pretty," but feels it and condemns the act in another child. Unchastity is abhorred without a thought of the horrors of venereal disease and blighted offspring or of the still deeper causes for its disapproval in the fact that the home, about which the character and happiness of mankind center, is founded upon the virtue of unquestionable chastity. And falsehood is despised without reckoning that by falsehood the individual imperils his power to command belief and undermines the faith of man in man which is the foundation upon the solidity of which depends the height to which the social structure can be reared. The ordinary mind cannot be expected to comprehend the weight of the reasons for the requirements which the insight of the élite and the experience of the race have bound upon the consciences of man. Least of all can the tempted man be expected justly to balance those remote considerations against the urgency of his impulse. And the value of morality is that it stands firm at the very times when the attention is driven away from remote considerations and concentrated upon hot allurements, and when rational balancing of consequences is impossible, but inveterate sentiment still utters its deterring or commanding voice. The strength of moral sentiment is the measure of the degree in which the net result of the experience of the race and the insight of the élite is precipitated in the conduct of the individual. And so it is the measure of the social conservation and progressive realization of human interests.

CHAPTER XXX

EXAMPLES OF SOCIAL EVOLUTION (*Continued*)

The Evolution of Religion.—It is often said that no people entirely destitute of religion has ever been discovered. And it is true that no people, whose thoughts and practices we have learned to understand adequately, have been without social activities to which the name religion could be applied, provided that name be given a sufficiently wide definition.

The word "religion" has received many definitions. Historically the most characteristic substance of religion has been beliefs concerning relations with unseen powers or beings whether here or hereafter and the emotions and practices elicited by those beliefs. Religion might be defined as those ideas, contemplation of which is found in the experience of any individual or any people to raise life to the highest level, together with the emotions and practices prompted by the contemplation of those ideas. The latter definition, however, would express rather an ideal of the meaning which the word religion may sometime convey than a description of all the religions that have existed or that still exist; for religions have contained much that debased life, and omitted many of the most ennobling elements in the life of the peoples by whom they were believed.

Religion, far from being a matter of indifference to the "savage," in reality "absorbs nearly the whole of life." "His daily actions are governed by ceremonial laws of the severest, often of the most irksome and painful character."

The Dyaks of Borneo "when they lay out their fields, gather the harvest, go hunting or fishing, contract a marriage, start on a warlike expedition, propose a commercial journey, or anything of importance always consult the gods, offer sacrifices, celebrate feasts, study the omens, obtain talismans, and so on, often thus losing the best opportunity for the business itself." [1] "It was a severe shock to the Pueblo Indians to see the white settlers plant corn without any religious ceremony, and a much greater one to see that the corn grew, flourished, and bore abundant crops." Captain Clark, an officer of our army with the widest experience of Indian life, is thus quoted: "It seems a startling assertion, but it is I think true that there are no people who pray more than the Indians. Both superstition and custom keep always in their minds the necessity for placating the anger of the invisible and omnipotent power, and for supplicating the active exercise of his faculties in their behalf." And Brinton says of primitive people that the injunction to "pray always" is nowhere else so nearly carried out.

The beliefs and practices commonly spoken of as religion grow from four roots, each of which requires our attention.

I. Magic.—Magic may or may not contain any idea of relationship with unseen persons.

(a) Magic which does not depend upon ideas of relationship with unseen beings probably is not to be regarded as a part of religion, but it is too important and too closely related to religious notions to be omitted from our discussion. This magic which depends upon no ideas of unseen persons is the predecessor of applied natural science. Primitive man, not knowing what really causes the effects that interest him, that harm or benefit him, guesses what might have caused the evil or the good he has experienced and what may cause the good or evil that he anticipates with hope or dread and like the man of science he acts upon his hypothesis. In the development of magic there are certain steps which must be enumerated at the outset, since they are to be seen in the development both of impersonal and of personal or religious magic:

1. Desire suggests ideas. The desires are at first predominantly practical. Man wants to do something that will secure good or avert harm. His child is sick and he wants

---

[1] D. G. Brinton: Religions of Primitive Peoples. Putnam, 1897, p. 17.

to do something to cause recovery. He is going fishing and he wants to insure a catch. Because ignorant of what does affect the result he is free to imagine that anything *may* affect it, he feels that he must do something and so he thinks of something to do. The brighter, more imaginative he is the more he thinks of what may bring either good or harm.

2. Whatever arrests his attention in connection with the result, so far as he knows, may cause it: especially do suggestive *analogies* rivet attention and hint at causal relation; thus the father during the *couvade* must not eat what would disagree with the new-born babe, the pregnant woman must not eat any animal that was killed by a wound in the entrails; to eat the heart of a lion will make one brave, and to cause sand to patter on the hut is part of the ceremony of making rain.

3. In order to be believed an idea has only to be clear, of practical interest and free from inconsistency with previous knowledge or belief. The less one knows the less there is to contradict whatever ideas may occur to him so that to one who lacks established ideas by which to test new notions almost any fancy may be true.

4. Once the idea occurs to the mind that a given act or thing is favorable or unfavorable to a keenly desired result, no chances are taken, the lucky thing or act is not omitted and the unlucky one is avoided. This tendency we still witness in the reluctance of many to sit among thirteen at the table.

5. To act upon an idea strengthens it in the mind of the actor and also suggests it to others. When the idea that this or that will bring either good or evil is suggested to B by the action of A, the faith may be stronger in the mind of B than if it had first arisen in his own mind—it comes with authority; and after such an idea has become prevalent in a group of savages people do not dare take chances with it.

6. One instance in which the belief works, that is to say, one coincidence between the belief and the event, arrests attention, is told, exaggerated, and retold, and does more to con-

firm the belief than many instances of failure. Instances of the failure of an established belief to work are explained away on the ground that the rules of the magic were not exactly followed or that the expected result was otherwise prevented. By the process above outlined nature men develop elaborate systems of pseudo-science for the control of the results which they desire or fear.

The tendency to invent magic is still strong among children and the ignorant, and would go to great lengths if not corrected by knowledge of natural causation supplied to children by their elders and to the ignorant by the better educated. Physicians who attend the ignorant have opportunities to witness the spontaneous invention of new magic to meet emergencies, to insure strength and brightness to newborn infants, and recovery to the afflicted. Farmers who insist on doing certain work at "the right time of the moon" illustrate the persistence of the tendency to rely on magic. And the whole system of astrology which commanded belief among the intelligent during certain stages of our own civilization shows how hard it is to deny causal efficiency to whatever powerfully arrests the attention, even though as remote as the very stars, provided the nature of real causal connection is dimly apprehended.

(b) Magic that is based on supposed relation with invisible persons implies the development of belief in such persons which grows from the second root of religion, next to be discussed. Man seeks to influence unseen beings in three ways:

1. He may believe that by magic he obtains control over them, that if he knows how, he can command them and they must obey. The desire to control them suggests a method, as the desire for other results suggests methods by the mental process above described.

2. He bargains with the unseen beings and seeks their favor by gifts, sacrifices, and services.

3. He seeks to influence them by his words; by flattery and praises he conciliates, and by imploring he seeks to persuade them. Impersonal and personal magic differ in that

by the former, men seek to produce results directly, while by the latter they seek to cause invisible beings to produce the results.

II. Zoömorphism.—The word anthropomorphism denotes the practice of conceiving of unseen beings as having the form and attributes of men. Zoömorphism denotes the practice of conceiving them to have the form and attributes of either men or other animals, or of fantastic combinations of human and beastly shape and character.

Zoömorphism is based upon the idea that every effect implies an actor. In the early stages of mental life the idea of causation which is most familiar and intelligible is derived from the issuance of results from our own activity and that of other persons and animals resembling us in activity. Thus, as mentioned before, the child and the savage ask, "Who made the moon"; not "what caused" but "who made" is the natural form of inquiry. Of causation by reflection, refraction, chemical combination, evolutionary processes, etc., there are at first no ideas. And so they ask who makes the sun rise, traverse the heavens, and set; who makes the rivers flow, the tides surge, the thunder roll, the ice form, the trees put forth their leaves in spring. Wherever there is a deed there must be a doer; there must be great and mighty beings to produce the grand effects in nature, and there must also be a multitude of little beings to produce the countless small effects too trivial to occupy the dignitaries of the unseen world, to sour the milk, to cause a wart to come or disappear, to cause all the noises, incidents, strokes of luck, and bafflings that fill the hours. To the imaginative mind at this stage of education it appears that the unseen population of the world may well be far more numerous than the seen, and that there must be among them diverse beings, some friendly and some unfriendly to man, great gods and great devils and little sprites, nixies, fairies, gnomes, goblins, elves, brownies, nymphs, dryads and fauns.[1]

---

[1] A priest, it is said, went on Walpurgis night to count the devils, and being observed by one of them was asked what he was doing. When he confessed his intention he was told that if the Alps were

Primitive man feels himself surrounded by unseen beings who can mysteriously benefit or harm him much as the civilized man feels himself surrounded by the omnipresent microbes. And accordingly the one seeks for disinfectants and the other for spirit-scarers.

Here, just as in impersonal magic, the desire to do something about it, suggests something to do; and the wish that something might have protective power suggests that almost anything that sufficiently arrests attention in connection with the wish, may be the right thing.[1]

Among the objects[2] that are thought to be effective as protections against spirits one of the most universal is fire. Fire is highly arrestive to the attention, it is mysterious and has powers to harm or to bless, it comforts us with warmth, it cooks our food, it melts the hard iron, it dispels the terrifying darkness, it spreads a circle of safety from beasts—why not from spirits also? Peoples in all quarters of the globe have regarded a fire, a lamp, a candle, a sacred flame, that must on no account be allowed to go out, as the source of safety from unseen terrors. English farmers used to gather in the wheat fields and build one large fire and twelve smaller ones, representing Christ and the apostles by this means, together with a great shouting to drive away the spirits that might cause blight and mildew.

Next to fire as a spirit-scarer is water, a mysterious element that drives out the spirit of thirst and washes away many evil things. The sprinkling of infants to keep away bad influences, holy water and baptism in many forms represent ancient practices common to many peoples.

Hardly anything is easier than to give an old ceremony a new meaning; even among us baptism means the descent

---

broken into grains of sand and for each grain there were a devil, and he should count so many he would only have begun to number the devils.

[1] All the better if it is something that is almost sure to be handy at time of need. Thus we choose to "knock on wood" as a means of protection.

[2] Professor W. I. Thomas enumerates to his classes a longer list of spirit-scarers.

of the Holy Spirit or the washing away of sin or the death of an old life and the beginning of a new one. Ancient ceremonies survive with new interpretations. Of this baptism, the sprinkling of holy water, and the burning of candles in churches appear to be illustrations.

Metal that requires the magic of the smith to melt and fashion it, that makes weapons which let out the life, is thought to have mystic powers. So also is food that drives out not only the spirit of hunger but also other evil spirits as well, and brings us strength and cheer in place of despondency, moroseness, and weakness; hence, to scatter rice or other grain is protective and of good omen.

There are not only protective objects but also protective acts and protective words and speeches formulated by the mind in answer to the desire for safety from the unseen powers. Yelling and racket, bells and tom-toms, are thought to drive away evil spirits and assist in the cure of the sick, in the safe passage of the dying and in the guarding of infants. Threatening gestures, blows, and whipping serve the same purpose. It was thus that the soldiers of Xerxes scourged the Hellespont to drive away or subdue the spirits that disturbed the waters. Liquor is full of "spirits" as we still say, both good spirits that cheer and evil spirits that make men violent and wicked. Therefore, before broaching a cask whip it well with switches, and if you want to sell it hang the bundle of switches or bush over your door to show that you have plenty of new and well-chastened wine; but "good wine needs no bush" to advertise it. A whip becomes in itself a protective object and finally any piece of leather may be so regarded.

Thirteen centuries before Christ to draw a cross was already a way to make a spirit trap that would catch and hold the invisible beings of evil intent, and far and wide the drawing of a circle or curve is regarded as a way to make a trap to keep them in, or to erect a fortification to keep them out. Perhaps both the curve and the metal of the horseshoe made it seem to our forefathers protective.

In order adequately to understand the tendency to

zoömorphism it must be borne in mind that the savage does not look down upon the animals as we do. He cannot build an abode equal to that of the oven-bird or the beaver, he would gladly possess eyes like the hawk, strength like the bear or the ox, courage like the lion, cunning like the fox, the deadly power of the serpent, vigilance or skill in stalking game like that of the leopard. In most things to which he aspires the animals surpass him.

Moreover, the sense of mystery demands strange symbols and sets the imagination roaming, and often the fittest embodiment of the powers he fears or worships seems not to be a form like any that he sees but one in which there are combined the shapes of men and beasts, as in griffins, sphinxes, and other imaginary monsters. And when a people has once formed conceptions of the forms of the gods, these conceptions are likely to survive filled with an enriching symbolism, as ancient ceremonies survive with changed interpretations, and still to be retained when the people become as civilized as the Hindus or Egyptians.

Primitive people not only fear the unseen zoömorphic beings, but also seek their aid. This leads to fetishism. The savage, with the vague notions of causal relationship which alone are possible to men who have made little progress in explanation, thinks that to possess anything that has been in close relation with a person is to establish a mystic relation with that person. He does not carelessly throw aside the skin of the banana he has eaten, for if his enemy should pick it up would he not have power over the man in whose vitals the pulp of the banana was! The hair cut from his head or any cast-off article that he had made or long worn he carefully secretes or destroys. Now if this same savage finds a strangely gnarled stick or a bit of fossil or meteorite, which evidently has been shaped by some mysterious power, he hopes that by possessing it he may establish relations with the power that shaped it and perhaps still haunts it. And if while he keeps it he has good luck and his prayers are answered, he prizes it and will not willingly part with it unless for a valuable consideration. If, however, it seems to bring him no good luck he will throw it away. The value which the savage attaches to the fetish which he carries about with him seems to be of precisely the same sort as that which devout Catholics have attached to relics of the saints, objects that have had close relation with a supernal being and which aid the possessor in maintaining special relations with that being. Grottoes, strange bowlders, trees of unusual shape or size, men everywhere seem prone to call "devil's den," or "witches' seat," or the like. Such manifestations and abodes of strange powers also become fetishes. But it is not the great rock or tree that is worshiped. Probably men never anywhere have literally worshiped sticks or stones. As one savage in answer to inquiry declared, "Tree not fetish. Fetish spirit not seen; live in tree."[1]

III. Ancestor Worship.—Belief that man is surrounded by spirits arises not only from zoömorphic interpretation of natural processes and natural events, but also from belief in the survival of human spirits after the death of the body. Thus Codrington in his "Melanesians" says that that people have two words for spirit, one denoting zoömorphic nature spirits, and the other denoting the spirits of ancestors. Savages do not regard the death of the body as the termination of life; doubt of life after death arises later in men's minds. Belief that the spirit survives dissolution arises in perfectly natural, even inevitable ways. When a man awakens in the morning and declares that he has been in the forest, seen a foe, or encountered a lion and barely escaped with his life, or that he has been on a journey or had a successful hunt, and those that are with him in the hut know that his body has lain there all night, they conclude and he concludes that he can have experiences in which his body does not participate. It is hard to persuade the child who wakes up terrified that the cause of his fear was "only a dream." Savages have no one to correct their belief in the reality of dreams. Often to gather at dawn to recount the experiences of the past night is a regular and important part of the day's interest. Some tribes decamp and flee if one of their number dreams of

---

[1] Brinton: Religions of Primitive Peoples, p. 122.

seeing an enemy approaching. Some think that in their shadow and in their reflection they catch glimpses of their own "double." If one is struck in the head his spirit leaves the injured body, after a while he "comes to," or if the injury is too severe the separation is permanent and the body is not reanimated. Then where is the spirit that has withdrawn from the visible form? It must be near! You cannot see it. You can never know when it is seeing you and listening to your words. Therefore "speak no evil of the dead," for who can tell in what mysterious ways the invisible can affect us, or how much of our sickness and ill-luck are due to their ill-will. Nothing sets bounds to the fancy in its dreadful conjectures about the hovering ghosts. Moreover, ghosts have reason to be vengeful and ill-humored for have they not been driven out of the body and deprived of visible life? Death by blows gives ground for taking vengeance and death by sickness no less, for sickness is practically always attributed by savages to magic, exercised by an enemy. And savages are not prevented from taking vengeance by the fact that they do not know what individual caused the injury.

For such reasons as these savages sometimes try to prevent the escape of the ghosts of those about to die by strangling them and leaving a ligature about the neck, or by driving a stake through the breast. Some peoples who have no permanent abodes decamp and flee the haunted place whenever a death has occurred, exercising precautions that the ghost shall not follow them, for instance carrying their weapons pointed backwards and stacking them in that position when they stop to sleep. The precautions to be taken are suggested by desire and analogy, and faith in them is developed by the process already repeatedly referred to. More frequently people try to conciliate the ghost. They gather in the presence of the dying and praise him inordinately and exhibit signs of mourning at his departure. They are careful after his death to continue the forms of praise and mourning, even at times hiring men to keep up the demonstration of grief. No one dares to use anything that had belonged to the dead, for fear of exciting jealous vengeance. His standing crops are burned and his personal belongings are burned or cast into the sea or buried with the corpse. Thus there is no saving from generation to generation to promote economic progress, but each generation destroys the accumulations of its predecessors.

The burning of property with the body of the dead results not only from fear of using the belongings of a ghost but also sometimes from an intention to provide the departed with the spiritual essence, the double, of that which he has used here and will require hereafter; for if the man has a double, why should not a bow or a knife or a tree or a mountain have a double, as well as a shadow and a reflection? Belief that inanimate things as well as living beings have an unseeable counterpart or essence, a soul or "anima," is widespread. For example the Japanese housewife attributes a soul to her kitchen utensils, and the soldier to his sword. This belief is called "animism." The conception is difficult to us only because it is unfamiliar. We may not always distinguish from each other the manifestations of that fetishism described above, which is based upon the idea that a thing has been associated with a supernatural being, and those of animism which is based on the idea that a thing is, or has, a spiritual essence of which its observable qualities are a manifestation.

The propitiation of the spirits of the dead by praises, prayers, and sacrifices is carried on at the places of burial. Thus, said Spencer, graves become the first altars and tombs the first temples.

It is felt to be especially necessary to propitiate the spirit of a great and powerful chief whose mysterious powers the timorous imagination is free to exaggerate unchecked and uncomforted by any saving ray of knowledge. All peoples, as they progress, tend to gather glorifying traditions about some great characters in their history. Thus while each family or clan worships and propitiates the spirits of its own particular dead forbears, the families enter also into the common worship of the heroes of the whole tribe or people. This implies a considerable degree of advancement, and is especially characteristic of the patriarchal phase of social evolution. Any patriarch, under whom the tribe particularly prospers, contributes real incidents, and patriotic and religious imagination add more, all of which tend to gather about the name of a few or of one of those from whom the group believes itself descended. The spirits of these dead heroes become the tribal gods.

In the earlier stages of its development religion is chiefly a matter of fear and not of hope or love; but in the stage just described it is natural to think that the household or tribal divinities will exercise their powers in the interest of their own "chosen people." This is accompanied by the belief that other peoples have their gods who are favorable to them, so that in case of warfare the contest is thought to be between both the unseen and the visible representatives of each people.

A conquering people believes that its gods are conquering gods, lords of lords, and kings over both kings and gods. To regard their own god as superior in power and other attributes is not the same as to become philosophical monotheists. This belief is not monotheism but monarchy among divinities. Monotheism comes very late.

Visible rulers have been quick to avail themselves of the obvious addition to their power which resulted whenever people could be made to feel that the gods required that which the visible rulers commanded. The fact that the difference between gods and kings was not very wide in the minds of ancestor-worshiping peoples who as yet were far from the concept of monotheism, is shown by the practice of according divine honors to living potentates as was done by the Romans. To accord divine honors to a living man was to acknowledge that he was one of those whose mighty spirits, after disembodiment, have to be propitiated. Through all discussion of this subject the word "god" means unseen being, powerful enough greatly to harm or to help men. The Devil and all the saints are gods, in the sense in which we all use those words when speaking of the religions of non-Christian peoples. If we had discovered Milton's "Paradise Lost" written in a strange tongue and calling its supernatural beings by other names than ours, we should not have hesitated to pronounce it the expression of a highly polytheistic religion.

In the roots of its development religion has no essential connection with morality or righteousness. The gods were thought of as exhibiting the motives and passions which man would exercise if he feared no superior, and religious conduct was simply the etiquette or ceremony of the court of the unseen potentate. And as man was always in the presence of the unseen he was always living at court and must regulate his every action by the required ceremonial. It was natural and inevitable to think that the requirements of the unseen would resemble those enforced by visible rulers, and there was a general correspondence between the obeisances, adulation, and tribute rendered to both. Conversely, visible rulers have been quick to avail themselves of the obvious addition to their own power which resulted whenever peoples could be made to feel that the gods required that which the visible rulers commanded. Omitting for the present many qualifications, we may say that ethical requirements result from the lessons of experience concerning that which promotes or diminishes the common welfare. Rulers early recognize the teaching of experience as to what promotes the tribal strength and solidarity for purposes of war, and in the patriarchal phase they are not blind to that which promotes economic prosperity. As soon as rulers or leading men (prophets) become deeply interested in the tribal welfare they feel certain that what they are convinced the common good requires, is in accordance with the will of the unseen spirit-patriarchs and divinities of the tribe, and so they declare to the people that to secure divine favor and avert divine wrath, to secure prosperity in basket and store and victory over their adversaries, they must fulfill not only ceremonial but also ethical requirements. When to proffered rewards and threatened punishments in this life is added the thought that the same unseen potentates will rule over and continue their favor or disfavor in a life to come, religion becomes a yet more stupendous agency of social control.

Two distinct tendencies in the development of religions are recognized by scholars. The first may be called the priestly tendency and the second the prophetic; the first is based chiefly on fear, the second more on hope and love; the first inculcates ritual requirements, the ceremonies and observances by which to court the favor of the invisible potentate and all distinctively religious requirements while it looks down upon "mere" morality, insisting far less loudly upon righteousness than upon religious conformity, but the second inculcates chiefly ethical requirements, it may even say, "Incense is an abomination unto me.[1] Will the Lord be pleased with thousands of rams, or with ten thousand rivers of oil? . . . What doth the Lord require of thee but to do justly, and to love mercy, and to walk humbly with Thy God." The first approaches deity with supplication, praises and flattery, conciliation and atonement in order to secure favor and favors; the second trusts an ever-waiting love and does not seek special favors but finds the sufficient reward of communion in the sense of personal relation with the divine. The first is predominantly selfish, a means by which the worshiper may secure to himself the divine favor, avoid calamity, secure prosperity, and save his own soul; the second is benevolent and patriotic, prescribes the method by which to secure the common prosperity and triumph of the group, and at its highest aspires toward a universal kingdom of righteousness, the establishment of which is the supreme coöperative enterprise in which all good men combine with God, and what is "done to one of the least" of the great brotherhood is done unto the God of all. The first is conservative and reactionary, ever calling upon men to maintain "the religion of their fathers," and unwilling that any belief or practice regarded as religious should be abandoned or modified; the second is progressive, always adapting its requirements to existing exigencies and apt to say, "Ye have heard that it was said unto you by them of old time . . . but verily I say unto you"—that requirements once thought essential are unimportant and that only vision that distinguishes the ethically

[1] Isaiah 1:13-17; Micah 6:7, 8; Amos 5:21-24.

fundamental from matter of observance and opinion and applies universal principles to the present demands of society can fulfill the will of God.

IV. Inspiration.—The fourth root from which religious beliefs and practices have grown is found in inspiration and miracle. These are unusual psychic states and unusual events which are ascribed to supernatural agency.

By the words inspiration and miracle I here refer to realities. In a prescientific age with a people among whom religious beliefs are already established miracle tales spread and grow with great facility, but it is real events and experiences that play a part in the origination of such beliefs.

Between inspiration and miracle no absolute line need be drawn, but we will first give attention chiefly to inspiration. It is said that "by far the majority of the impressions on our senses leave no trace in conscious recollection, although they are stored in the records of the brain." According to this view the subconscious stores are our capital, our states of consciousness are the interest we collect, and all our past experience is on deposit. It is sufficiently impressive to think that even a major part of the sights and sounds and thoughts that ever were present to our vivid consciousness are stored as records in the recesses of memory and that from this vast half-hidden accumulation we draw the interpretations that give meaning to the perceptions and thoughts of each passing moment. We have not only this vast hidden store; we have also hidden processes of combination and recombination, of fermentation and growth among these hidden elements. It is even said that such subconscious action "is not only common but practically if not absolutely constant," and even if we are staggered at the thought of its continuity we may all admit that "the results of this unperceived labor of our minds are often far more valuable than those of our intelligent efforts." Now and then, under stimulating or otherwise favorable conditions, one may experience an upgush out of the stores of his mentality, so far beyond his ordinary powers and containing conceptions and conclusions that have been reached by a process of which he has been so unconscious, that he says, "This is not mine; it has been given me!" Thus the poets and the novelists often speak. Most of the great art work of the world has been of this character, it is everywhere spoken of as the product of inspiration. In this respect as in certain others religious revelation resembles art.

A state of concentration and eager expectancy is favorable to such experience, so that the earnest prayer of faith is likely to be answered by consolations and decisions. An experience that is eagerly desired and at the same time sought and expected is naturally produced by auto-suggestion, so that the "seeker" is likely soon to cry out, "I've got it, I've got it." The presence of an expectant surrounding group and similar experiences on the part of others effectively heighten the power of auto-suggestion.

Dreams also are upwellings out of the unconscious. They are likely to be closely related to recent or intense waking states. Thus, for example, those whose death has been recently witnessed are likely to be seen in dreams. This powerfully confirms belief in life after death, not necessarily in immortal life, for at least some savages have not formed that concept, but believe that those who are no longer seen in dreams or remembered by the living are spiritually and totally deceased. Because of the close relation between waking thoughts and dreams the latter frequently suggest answers to problems of the waking life, and even when this relation to any reality is least, still the thoughts that come with waking are likely to interpret the dream into some connection with themselves. Moreover, the elements contained in dreams, however fantastically they may be recombined, all are afforded by previous mental states and so they are likely to corroborate and powerfully confirm the beliefs already held.

The last is also true of visions seen in trances and other abnormal states. Especially death-bed visions are likely to confirm, as with ocular demonstration, faiths concerning the life to come. Visions and hallucinations are common in disease and often occur in the final disturbance of the brain that precedes dissolution, and at that time the mind is full of thoughts and hopes or fears concerning the hereafter and established beliefs are not unlikely to visualize themselves.

One of the widespread practices of early religions is to induce the physical states that are accompanied by hallucinations. Inhaling of gases, long abstinence from food, dances carried to the point of exhaustion, are among the familiar means of obtaining trances and visions.[1]

Quite commonly boys, at the time of initiation into manhood, are expected by aid of fasts and vigils, to secure some vision, revelation, or ecstatic state. The breaking down of normal nervous coördination is a cultivated art so that among certain peoples, as the African Zulus, it is said that "any adult can cast himself or herself into the hypnotic state." Those with especially unstable nervous systems are regarded generally as religiously gifted and likely to become medicine men, priests, or priestesses. The supernatural origin of the mental states thus obtained is confidently assumed and unintelligible babblings are regarded as mystic utterances in unknown tongues. Even in America and in present times a person who becomes cataleptic under great religious excitement is sometimes spoken of as "possessed by the Holy Ghost."

Miracles.—And now as to miracles: any strange and unexplained event is practically certain to be regarded, by people who are in a prescientific stage of development, as a miracle. The miracles which especially deserve our attention are the miracles of healing. The power of the mind over the body is now an established fact. The action of the mind not only constantly controls our voluntary muscles but also in common experience it causes the vital organs to alter their operations, so that the cheek flushes or blanches, the heart palpitates, the functions of the alimentary canal and of the liver, salivary, and other glands are stopped, quickened or perturbed. The great majority of diseases (it is said four-fifths) are caused by irregularities in the functioning of the organs rather than injuries to the organs themselves. This being so, how vast

---

[1] Davenport: Primitive Traits in Religious Experience; James: Varieties of Religious Experience.

a power over health and disease has the mind! As the mind through the nerves can absolutely control the voluntary muscles, so it seems that scarcely less absolutely can it control all the functions of the body. If one were to be as certain that his heart would double, or abate by half, its beating at a given hour as he can be that he will leave his office for his home at that hour, the effect upon his heart would apparently be little, if at all, less direct than that upon his muscles of locomotion. The facts in substantiation of such a view are exceedingly numerous.

"A Frenchman of rank was condemned to death for a crime, and his friends, willing to avoid the scandal of a public execution, allowed him to be made the subject of an experiment. He was told that he must be bled to death. His eyes were bandaged and his arm having been lightly pricked a stream of warm water was made to trickle down it and fall into a basin, while the assistants kept up a running commentary upon his supposed condition. 'He is getting faint, the heart's action is becoming feebler; his pulse is almost gone,' and other remarks of the sort. In a short time the miserable man died with the actual symptoms of cardiac syncope from hemorrhage, without having lost a drop of blood." [1] "Among savage tribes, in undoubted and repeated instances the curse kills as certainly as the knife. Among western Indians of our country, when a medicine man 'gathers his medicine,' that is, rises to the full height of inspired volition, and utters a withering curse upon his antagonist commanding him to die, the latter knows all hope is lost. Sometimes he drops dead on the spot, or at best lingers through a few days of misery." [2]

But the power of the mind over the body is not only for cursing and death, but also for blessing health and recovery. "A mind to live" and "the expectation of recovery" as well as "the welcoming of death" have their direct effect. Scientific books are now written concerning the part of suggestion in

---

[1] C. Lloyd Tuckey: Treatment by Hypnotism and Suggestion or Psycho-Therapeutics. London, 1907, 5th ed., p. 30.

[2] Brinton: Religions of Primitive Peoples, pp. 90-100.

therapeutics.[1] "In all ages wonderful cures, real amid a multitude of shams, have been wrought at holy places dedicated to various saints of various cults." Of the throngs who for centuries have sought and still seek healing at Mecca, at the sacred rivers and shrines of Hinduism, Buddhism, in the Grotto of Our Lady of Lourdes, before the holy coat of Treves, and at a hundred other holy places of the Catholic Church by no means all have been disappointed. "Touching for the king's evil did no doubt effect many cures." Great numbers of healers in all lands and ages, from the savage medicine man to Alexander Dowie, and of all degrees of sham and of sanctity from charlatans who inspired faith in doctrines that to them were pure pretense, to Martin Luther, Dorothea Trudel, and many a devout believer in divine intervention in behalf of the sick, have taken practical advantage of the mind's power over the bodily functions. They have inspired confident expectation of recovery by appeal to the most various beliefs, and the confident expectation has caused effects that have confirmed the belief whether it was belief in the power of Gunga or of Allah, and whether the prophet were Brigham Young or the reverent and saintly Charles Cullis.

Homologies in Religion.—Out of the "four roots" which we have now described there have grown masses of the most various belief and practice characteristic of peoples of every stage of ethical advancement. But quite as impressive as the variety of these beliefs are the resemblances between many of them. Similar beliefs about the zoömorphic cosmogony are widely diffused and were participated in by the early Semites whose traditions we inherit. Beliefs concerning the hereafter exhibit many interesting similarities. Various peoples possess a cycle of myths based upon the conflict of nature, of day with night, of light with darkness, of summer and warmth with winter, cold, and storm, of youth with age, health with disease, life with death, good with evil, and hold that victory will not always rest with the powers

[1] Georg Wetterstrand: Hypnotism and Its Applications to Practical Medicine. Tr. by Henrik G. Petersen. See Bibliography.

of darkness for, as they believe in great heroes, conquerors, and teachers of useful arts and virtues who have lived in the past, so also they have for the future a messianic hope.

The foregoing discussion has not raised the question whether the religious beliefs of the tribes of mankind correspond with any reality, but has only traced the method of the origins of these beliefs, considered as prevalent social phenomena. Human intelligence, developed in connection with fitting a tiny round of activities to certain superficial aspects of a very limited environment, is inadequate to comprehend in detail the whole and ultimate truth about the universe. Science has somewhat widened the narrow circumference of man's knowledge and replaced his earliest guesses, but has not illuminated the telescopic spaces of his ignorance. The more man's knowledge grows, the vaster his estimate of that which lies beyond the compass of his senses. At first he imagined nature spirits in the form of men or beasts; long he conceived the methods of creation on the analogy of human artifice. Later he has begun to get some hints of a method of creation far more divine than man's imagination could have invented, to see that the power at work in nature does not operate by the contraction of muscles, that a universal intelligence cannot be dependent upon the neuroses of a brain, that power and intelligence independent of organic mechanism may well be freed from boundaries of space or limitations of attention, that the words omnipotent and omnipresent may have real meaning, and that the power and the intelligence that are adequate to the continuous causation of all the phenomena of such a universe as this cannot be portrayed in human terms and under a bodily semblance.

All savages and all children are idolaters—in the sense that they tend to imagine visible embodiments of divinity. The God of childhood is likely to be "a benevolent old gentleman with a long white beard." We first shrink from chiseling or painting him not because we doubt that he has a limited and sensible shape, but because we think that we know his form and features imperfectly, as we do that of a relative whom we have never met, and because we think our art inadequate. In the Middle Ages, artists confident of their pictorial powers did not hesitate to paint portraits of Jehovah. There is no fundamental difference between the worship of a god whose features are portrayed in stone or upon a canvas and worshiping one whose eidolon is conceived in human form within the mind. As we have seen, probably no men were ever idolaters in the crude sense of worshiping images as more than the representation of an unseen being, and probably no people that has risen high has been free from the tendency to make of its god an eidolon in spatial form. When the beliefs of any people seem to us utterly absurd we may be almost if not quite certain that it is because we do not understand them or get at their point of view. Perhaps, for some purposes it does no harm for men to think of God in terms of human *personality,* as distinguished from spatial or corporeal form. But they should remember that He is more than can be comprehended in those terms. As one cannot drink the Amazon, but afloat upon its mighty bosom may dip up from those waters in a cup as much as he can drink, so we who live and move and have our being in the infinite, because we cannot conceive the infinite, may slake our soul's thirst with thoughts of God in terms of human personality judging that our thought is not then more than the truth but immeasureably less.

The Three Stages of Social Evolution.—There is one more generalization relating to the subject of social evolution, and one which may prove to be as important as the famous generalization of Comte concerning the theological, metaphysical and positive stages of thought. It was not stated at the outset in connection with the stages of social evolution partly because its apprehension requires a knowledge of facts such as have now been presented. The evolution of social activities tends to show three stages, in the first of which social activity is defined by instinct and biological necessity, in the second of which social activity breaks those definite bounds and enters upon a career of random vagaries, in the third of which the modes of social activity again become more definitely systematic, being defined by reason in the light of past experience; and there is a marked resemblance between the social activities of the first stage which are defined by instinct and biological necessity and those of the third stage which are defined by reason, the latter however being carried on with immensely developed resources, and upon a far higher plane. Thus the course of social evolution is like a spiral stairway of many broken steps, which traverses one complete circle to reach a landing directly above the starting-point, but on a far higher level.

1. The family, so far as evidence justifies an opinion, had originally a form that was forced upon it by instinct and biological necessity, namely, primitive pairing. The family passed through a second period of random experimentation with every conceivable vagary. Finally it settles again to a uniform and regular type which is the product of natural social selection and racial experience, as comprehended by reason. And this form, adopted by reason, is monogamy, bearing a close resemblance to the supposed primitive pairing.

2. The position of woman was at first equal to that of man. The family was matronymic, and the deities of primitive folk were quite as likely to be goddesses as gods. But with respect to the position of woman social usages passed into a long period of random vagaries in which under many forms appeared one general characteristic, namely, the subjection of woman. There is however a tendency for advanced societies to enter a third stage with respect to the general treatment of woman, a stage which does not arrive until some time after the monogamous family has been firmly established as the social norm. In this third stage there is a strong tendency for experience and reason to suppress the endless ingenuities of feminine subjection and restore her to the social equality which she originally enjoyed.

3. Politically the savage is the freest of men. But soon political development enters a second stage characterized by endless forms of conquest, slavery, serfdom, villenage and

finally more moderate forms of tryanny. Even in comparatively recent times the rank and file of English "freemen"
were not free to come and go, to choose and pursue their
callings, and to express in untrammeled action their beliefs;
and their participation in the affairs of the state of which
they were members was comparatively slight. Only of late,
and in the most advanced nations, has reason made civic
equality a matter to be granted without avowed opposition
and asserted a claim to a political equality like that which upon
a lower plain was enjoyed by savages.

4. Prestige, probably the most powerful factor in social
organization, which by its particular type gives color and
character to all the customs and institutions of a society, is
at first based upon personal qualities, those qualities which
most awaken instinctive admiration and self-subordination,
particularly prowess, and above all prowess displayed in the
defense or aggrandizement of the group. But presently the
prestige of personal prowess degenerates into caste, and later
wealth becomes the chief foundation for social eminence.
But there are already signs that here also reason will assert
itself and reëstablish personal qualities as the basis of prestige, not those qualities of personal prowess which most
strongly appeal to instinct, but those qualities of character
and achievement which appeal to reason. As Spencer was
the great spokesman of the transition from militarism to
industrialism so Professor Veblen may be regarded as a
spokesman of the transition from the social ideals of industrial individualism to those of social service.

5. The economic life of society at first was in a large
degree communistic and secured a fair distribution of food;
none could starve while others waxed fat. But the second
stage, that of random vagaries, allows great disparities in
wealth and poverty, and so organizes the control of society
as to render those disparities largely self-perpetuating and
self-intensifying. But there is some justification for the belief
that reason will so assert itself as to restore, not instinctive
communism and economic equality, but a rational distribution of wealth and of economic opportunity, and a universal

supply of the necessaries for a decent standard of living among all normal members of society.

6. The earliest economic organization is not individualistic but coöperative practically always where there is an enterprise large enough to call for coöperation. During the period of random vagaries the principal of coöperation in the interest of all the participants in industry is lost to view. Finally, if reason, which regards all the facts and interests involved, ever molds our industrial order, it may succeed in establishing an industrial system more democratic in its aims and even in the method of its direction and control.

7. Morality is originally instinctive, the expression of sympathy, altruism, and partisanship in personal relations within the group. But morality also has its period of random vagaries, in which relations are formed between individuals and classes in which the instinctive controls do not function; and exploitation, and cruelty are practiced with no protest from the social instincts. But moral evolution through the rational interpretation of experience, by the folk-sense, and the insight of the élite, defines and extends the application of ethical sentiments until morality establishes over the extended relationships of civilized society a control which is as definite and, in its applications if not in its strength, as adequate to the needs of the case as the instinctive good nature that prevails within a savage horde.

8. Peace within the primitive group is established by the social instincts. Savages are not savage to their own clansfolk. But during the second period, the period of evolution, through random experiment and natural selection, in this case very long, inter-group relations play a great rôle, and in these relations the social instincts provide no basis for order. The establishment of group expectations and inter-group conventions that shall serve for the maintenance of inter-group order is perhaps the most difficult social task of reason. But if reason ever has its way in this sphere of human action it will extend the application of ethical sentiments to international relations, as it has done and still is doing with reference to the wider and more impersonal relations within the

group; then group peace will extend so as to include the brotherhood of humanity.

9. Crime, or infraction of the group code of custom or of formal law, at first is treated with severity dictated by instinctive vengeance. Later sentimentality, the realization that the criminal is often the victim of unfortunate heredity and social environment, and a clutter of legal provisions intended to qualify the evil of ancient usages that society could not make up its mind entirely to abolish, largely replaced the prompt certainty of instinctive vengeance with weakness and delay and uncertainty. In the third stage of development reason will seek to restore the swiftness and certainty and necessary severity of the law, together with intelligent discrimination between the treatment demanded by the individual character of criminals. Thus the prompt efficiency of instinct, which in the second stage is bewildered by new conditions and groping reason, in the third stage would be replaced by a promptness and efficiency dictated by the definite conclusions of maturer knowledge.

10. The daily life of the savage "is a ritual." Among barbarians the details of conduct, the forms of everyday objects, and the character of dress and ornament are dictated by long-established custom. In the second or mutating period of social evolution the more superficial aspects of common things and ways are subject to a perfect riot and dissolution of successive fashions. But after the possibilities of invention have been somewhat exhausted, fashions have repeated themselves in cycles, rational eclecticism has identified the most practical, and developed canons of taste have recognized the most beautiful, we may replace the constant meaningless changes of fashion by a new custom era. It will not be rigid and bigoted custom, it will allow for variety according to personal convenience and taste, but will avoid the colossal wastes of fashion, and will preserve chosen forms, instead of an endless succession of forms that have no claim to superiority to justify their existence.

11. Simplicity characterizes the practical arts and the conduct of life among primitive peoples, a simplicity which

results partly from poverty of ideas and partly from practical directness of method dictated by necessity. After the period of extreme and ever-increasing complexity, it may be that there will be restored to life a simplicity which is rational and due to the choice of the best out of many offered modes of action; as the analytic languages largely escape from the intricacies of inflection, and as modern Roman type sloughing off the flourishes of medieval copyists and engravers returns to a form closely resembling the simplicity of the first Phœnician alphabet.

12. The intellectual life of early man is fixed and established in tradition and authority. The second stage of social development is full of intellectual uncertainty. Every thinker speculates for himself. Systems of philosophy clash and though many are convinced, they are convinced without general agreement. But as science removes one problem after another from the realm of speculation and adds its solution to the body of our knowledge, and education popularizes these results, although from the intellectual elevation reached we may see upon the wide horizon of our knowledge more unsettled problems than ever appeared before, yet we shall have a basis of relative certainty and general agreement, not the dogmatic certainty of ignorant tradition, but a substantial island of firm common standing ground in the ocean of the unknown.

13. That effect of biological necessity which is termed "natural selection" undoubtedly plays its part vigorously among the population of little developed societies. But later it is thwarted by scientific methods of prolonging the life of the feeble. A large proportion of civilized women would die in their first attempt at motherhood if under savage conditions. In a variety of ways civilization appears to be counter-selective. But here again reason is seeking to step in and to apply scientific knowledge in a eugenic program. And though natural selection no longer gives us a highly selective death rate, eugenics may do something toward giving us a selective birth rate. The very fact that the most intelligent and idealistic will be most affected by the agitation to establish

a genesic conscience may secure an increase in the proportion of births from such parents.

Such considerations will have interest rather than solid value, unless they are strictly confined to tracing a tendency which can be discerned in the facts of the present and the past.

PART IV

SOCIAL CONTROL

CHAPTER XXXI

THE PROBLEM AND PRINCIPLES OF SOCIAL CONTROL[1]

The Necessity of Social Control.—In our previous discussion we have treated social realities as natural phenomena molded by causal conditions like other products of nature and culminating in a "natural social order" which is a largely spontaneous correlation between prevalent sentiments, current ideas, customs, institutions, individuals, sects, parties, functional groups, and societies, each and all of which are natural products of social evolution. But although social realities are as really products of nature as plants or animals, yet we cannot tell the whole truth about them without recognizing how conscious intentions, themselves products of natural social evolution, become united with the other elements in social evolution, so that social activities came to be like domesticated animals and the social situation to resemble not a jungle but a garden.

Men might live together in a simple and barbarous social order produced entirely without design. Sociability or pleasure in the presence of our kind, and the "we" feeling or partisanship which unites every permanent homogeneous group against all outsiders with a powerful sentimental bond, are naturally selected traits of the human creature, and the group unity which they cement is primitive man's most powerful defense against hostile beasts and hostile men. Even animals show these feelings and also the higher quality of altruism and mutual helpfulness. And the group of primitive men in which the members helped each other most effectively would tend on that account to lose fewer of its members by misfortune, to come through famines and other crises

---

[1] The subject of social control has received classic treatment in the work of that title by Professor Edward Alsworth Ross.

less reduced, to increase, and to drive out or exterminate the alien groups of less sympathetic human beasts with which it came in contact. By this process nascent humanity became increasingly humane. The natural sentiment of anger and craving for revenge has also contributed largely to primitive social order. It was not worth while for the strong to carry robbery and abuse of the weak too far. If the weak were sufficiently angered, though he died for it he would have his vengeance, and the pleasure or gain of abusing him was not worth the trouble. Besides anger can bide its time and lurk, and the strongest, if hated by many weak, would lead a comfortless and perilous life in the clan. By virtue of these natural human traits savages commonly live in a degree of sociability, good fellowship, and mutual helpfulness often described as on the whole equal to that of civilized communities.

But while the natural traits of sociability, partisan loyalty, altruism, anger, and sense of justice, suffice to maintain a tolerable state of society in primitive groups, they do not answer that purpose in a developed civilization. This failure is due mainly to the short-sightedness of the social instincts. They vary in efficiency inversely as the square of the distance. To speak literally they naturally depend upon immediate sense-perception or at least upon vivid ideation of the good to be sought and of the evil to be shunned or abated, and upon direct and obvious causal connection between the result, and the conduct by which the result is produced. In the complex life of developed societies conduct often has results that are not direct but remote, and the causal connection between action and its consequences is not always obvious but may be obscure. The most momentous consequences are often unintended, but none the less to be reckoned with, and they fall upon victims so remote from the personal observation of the actors that no sympathy is stirred by their suffering and no instinctive benevolence is awakened by the sense of their possible advantage. Thus the dairy owner whom nothing could induce to strangle with his own hands a single helpless baby, yet slaughters innocents like Herod, because he does not see the suffering of those babies or their mothers and does not clearly see and can refuse to admit the relation between his conduct and their death. Real-estate promoters who on no account would turn their hands to murder, offer for rental, tenements whose character doubles the death rate among the tenants, and resist laws that would prevent deadly and contagious diseases. For the same reason the passage of laws for the safeguarding of machinery and industrial processes, that would annually prevent untold suffering and many deaths, has until recently been generally resisted by employers, and kind fathers and mothers have opposed the passage of laws against destructive child labor. Protective legislation in general when once passed has been peculiarly difficult to enforce. The trust magnate who is lavishly generous to his coachman and to all those with whom he has personal relations and who could not imagine himself stealing the stocking hoard of a workman or teacher or small tradesman, ruins the weak by the heartless use of inside information and by the "manipulation" of the value of securities into which other men have put the painfully accumulated savings on which their hopes depend. The corrupt politician who makes the passage and enforcement of good laws difficult, who undermines the very foundations on which the health, prosperity and welfare of · society so largely rest, is frequently a "big-hearted good fellow" who does not have to counterfeit the cordiality which he expresses to the people of his ward or to the acquaintances he makes in his district, who distributes Christmas turkeys and corrupt "favors" with a pleasurable sense of generosity, and is intensely loyal to the partisans of his own gang.

This is the application of the principle previously stated that the social instincts have been developed, and have their characteristic sphere of operation within "personal groups." But in civilized society we are bound together interdependently in cities, states, and nations which are far too vast to be personal groups. Relationships in developed societies are largely impersonal, and the most serious consequences of conduct are largely remote, deferred and in any given instance problematical. Large-scale sinning is apt to be long-range sinning, from which the native sentiments do not adequately deter.[1]

While we thus see that instinct fails to repress the conduct that is most harmful to developed societies it is even more essential to observe the additional fact that instinct fails to elicit the conduct that is most necessary to the welfare and progress in developed societies. The fundamental social duties of the member of an advanced society are largely of the sort in which his single act produces no visible result but is only one of a multitude of similar acts all of which are necessary in order to produce a result far larger than individual endeavor can compass. This coöperation which is essential in civilized society is not secured by untaught native sentiment.

The social emotions perform an inestimable service in sweetening personal relationships within the family, the clan, the circle of friendship, and they are also the foundation for that larger virtue which has power to prevent the monstrous destruction of life's values which is invited by our organized interdependence in higher societies, as well as power to elicit the coöperation upon which waits the fulfillment of the mighty possibilities of good which such organization creates. The problem of civilization is to secure a virtue which is moved and guided, not merely by the consequences of conduct which immediate sense-perception recognizes, but also by the vaster consequences which instructed reason discerns.

Even in the simple relationships of savage society the social

---

[1] In the foregoing statement lies one of the fundamental objections to philosophical anarchism. The other is contained in the discussion of private vengeance, on pages 611 and following. The philosophical anarchist would leave the maintenance of social order and justice to the operation of individual instincts. This might result in a nearer approach to justice than has existed under some of the worst despotisms. It does secure a rude approach to justice in small and undifferentiated societies. But few, if any, save those who are influenced by revulsion against the severer forms of tyranny, have faith in the rule of instinct or "natural order," in a vast and highly evolved society. In government, as elsewhere, the rule of instinct furnishes the prototype of which the rule of reason is the riper counterpart, according to the law (if law it be) of the three stages of social evolution. Compare paragraphs 3, 8 and 9 in section begun on page 571.

instincts do not provide against more or less frequent and destructive outbreaks of the individualistic instincts. And hence we see idyllic sociability and sympathy side by side with fiendish acts; while beyond the circle of partisanship cruelty is the unchallenged rule of conduct.

Every society that has made any considerable progress has begun to cultivate crops or otherwise modify material nature, and every such society has also begun to modify the natural social order by elements of social control. In an advanced society where gigantic opportunities for evil invite destructive conduct from which no instinctive impulse restrains, where inestimable values are to be won by coöperative endeavor to which no instinctive impulse prompts, where there are many necessary positions of trust, each with its own demands upon the individual, where duties and also privileges which others are required to respect are unequally divided among social classes, where great differences in wealth are defended and made secure, the turbulent current of human impulse is dammed up or redirected by dikes and channels that have been laid out by careful engineering and that require incessant labor to keep them in repair. "We are prone to forget that civilization is a *tour de force,* so to speak, a little hard-won area of order and self-subordination amidst a vast wilderness of anarchy and barbarism that are with difficulty held in check and are continually threatening to overrun their bounds."[1] In times of peace and in well-bred society the course of life runs on so smoothly that it resembles the unjarring movement of the earth on its axis and in its orbit, and it may never occur to the mind that cataclysmic forces are held in bonds by the unremitting gravitation of social control.

The Principles of Social Control.—(a) *The two aspects of social reality.* Human activity must be judged from two standpoints: first, as an end; second, as a means. First, considered as an end, conscious activity is an experience which may be either good or bad in itself; second, considered as a means, every activity, whether it be knowing, feeling,

[1] *The Unpopular Review,* ii, No. 3, p. 132.

or overt deed, has a tendency to lead to further experience, good or bad, for the actor, and for his associates. When viewed with reference, not to its value as an end, but to its effects as a means, activity is usually called either "work" or "conduct."

The ultimate aim of social control and of all rational endeavor is to secure the completest and most harmonious realization of good human experience, regarded as an end in itself. But to this end it is necessary also to secure good conduct. The purpose of social control, therefore, is to prevent activities which do not bear the test of reason and to elicit those which do bear that test, when all activity is judged both with reference to its own intrinsic value, and with reference to its total effect upon other values, that is, both as experience and as conduct.[1]

(b) *The two types of social control.* In its pursuit of this aim society relies upon two types of social control: first, control by sanctions; second, control by social suggestion, sympathetic radiation and imitation. The word sanction is here used in the legal sense of proffered reward or threatened punishment. The teacher with the birch rod in his hand controls by sanction, the boy-scout master whom the young scouts admiringly imitate controls chiefly or wholly by the second method. The effects as well as the methods of the two forms of control are in two respects notably different. First, sanctions elicit or repress particular actions while the second type of control is adapted to establish general dispositions; second, the former is control from without while the latter is control that is adapted to become enthroned within and in so far as reason and sentiment adopt the principles of control it becomes not a law of bondage but a law of liberty.

The Perversion of Social Control.—Society has no interests aside from the interests of its members. "The social welfare," like "the social mind" is only a figure of speech. The fact referred to by that phrase is that the permanent welfare of many is of greater importance than the temporary

---

[1] Compare article by present writer in *American Journal of Sociology*, xviii, p. 470.

welfare of a single one. But the welfare of the many is not secured if, on the whole, the welfare of individuals is sacrificed. Society must beware of hedging in the activities of its members with avoidable restrictions, and cramping their minds into "safe" but sterile courses. It must elicit the powers of its members and emancipate their understandings.

We have already had various occasions to observe that some of the controlling ideas fostered by the influential are likely to be those which maintain the existing situation and serve the purposes of the ruling class rather than the masses, and also that ideas arise in the mind in response to the need of eliciting or repressing conduct, and are thereafter believed and disseminated without due regard for their truth, and that, in a degree and for a time, a society may even be ennobled by errors and illusions.[1] Of this the extremist and most naïve example is the creed held by Job's comforters, and many since, to the effect that the good man cannot suffer nor the wicked man prosper in this world. We still have our cherished illusions, but in an inquiring age we can hardly hope permanently to maintain a control by illusions. We may as well strike straight and boldly at the verities, and make our method of social life an "adaptation" to the actual conditions of existence.

Success or failure in the attempt to unite control with enlightenment will depend in part on whether men will be adequately influenced by consideration of values not their own, so as to be guided in conduct by some regard for all the interests which they perceive their conduct to effect, that is to say it depends on whether reason can either dominate instinct, or *enlist the responses of instinct* in service of wider aims. It depends yet more upon whether the sentiments of enthusiasm and detestation formed in the minds of those who see the remote and diffused consequences of conduct, and imbibed during untempted youth, and approved in hours of calmness, will be strong enough to reënforce reason in the thick of action. It depends also upon whether the pressures of

---

[1] Compare Ross: Social Control, p. 305 *seq.*

social approval and disapproval will adequately supplement private conscience. The success of the experiment of human society depends upon converting life into team work—into a coöperative enterprise. Fears and illusions have failed to bring this about save to a very limited and unsatisfactory degree. The world is inevitably committed to the experiment of uniting *control* with enlightenment.

The motives of enlightenment are not yet enshrined in symbols, shibboleths, and accepted maxims and in poetry, art and religion. But they may be in the era next before us, and may prove the method of a nearer approach to the fulfillment of possibilities that have thus far seemed always to be just beyond the reach of human attainment.

Not Law But Personality Is the Ultimate Basis of Social Order.—Without in the least underestimating the importance of aiming directly at the repression of crime, we shall see, if we correctly apprehend the facts of social life, that it is far, very far, more important to raise the moral grade of those who never go to prison. Humanized wants, reliability, devotion to social service, and freedom from perverting egoism, would not only secure the passage and enforcement of laws and the diminution of crime, but also the realization of the positive aims of associative activity—the fulfillment of life's inestimable possibilities of good. Nothing else will secure these ends. The slow dragging centuries will continue to drag and the destiny of humanity go unfulfilled in spite of all the progress in science and industry, unless there be commensurate progress in morality. In so far as society creates the individual it must create individuals who possess the traits or dispositions which experience has shown to be essential to the general welfare. The most fundamental task of social control is to take the bundle of instincts and propensities which each individual brings into the world and so cultivate it that it will develop into a disposition to those activities which will yield the highest correlation between individual satisfaction and social service.

The First of the Essential Virtues—Reliability.—It behooves us to inquire what are the essential traits in such a disposition. There may be numerous traits that are highly desirable for all citizens, and particular traits which are useful in particular walks of life, but there are a very few which age-long experience has demonstrated to be the universal essentials.

The first of these is honesty or reliability. It is possible for a society to prosper, more or less, where there is much dishonesty, provided there is also a considerable amount of honesty, but the degree to which its prosperity and advancement can be carried will depend upon the degree to which honesty preponderates over dishonesty, reliability over unreliability in every walk of life. It has been argued by a distinguished writer that lying, under exceptional circumstances and from a kind motive, is justified. But if the rule were once adopted that one may lie in exceptional cases and for a kindly purpose, how much faith could we put in pleasant words, and how could any deep anxiety be relieved by favorable reports? He who has once been known to depart from the truth has impaired the credit of all that he thereafter says. The more need he has of credence and the more emphatically he asseverates the more his statements are likely to be discounted. His words are like the blows of a phantom, having no weight or substance. The man who has the courage to speak sincerely where a person of loose veracity would have equivocated acquires a weight which nothing else can impart. Honesty or reliability while it is largely a matter of speaking truth is quite as really a matter of acting so as to make our promises true—carrying out the expectations which others have been given reason to form in fulfilling promises, both those which have been written or verbally expressed and those which have been implied. The doctrine of "implied contract" which runs through the law, runs also through life. He who officially counts a vote is pledged in honor to count it as it was cast; he who assumes a position of trust or engages to do a job is pledged in honor to the fulfillment of the responsibility assumed.

The average normal human animal is born with a tendency to craft. Sympathetic feeling may keep him truthful in most of his dealings with his own pals and partisans, and shrewdness and caution will make him economize lies, and native sense of moral beauty and ugliness may cause him more or less to prefer truth to deceit where he is disinterested. But seldom, if ever, is one adequately equipped by nature with honesty, in the sense of detestation for falseness as such, when it is advantageous, or zeal for truth in dealing with those whom he is trying to beat in a game or an election or one with whom he is driving a bargain or even at the cost of comfort and convenience, especially if dealing with a stranger. And yet a splendid "sense of honor" can somewhat readily be acquired. The problem is to communicate to the young by sympathetic radiation, a sense of honor which their elders already have acquired, just as language which is native to no one is the social heritage of normal children who grow up in a developed society.

Control of Animalism.—The second of the traits which experience has shown to be essential to proper membership in a developed society is the control of animalism. Every normal human being has certain appetites in common with the animals. These are not evil in themselves but necessary. Men must eat and drink and rest if they are to live, and they must propagate if society is to continue. But man has learned to pervert the natural impulses with intoxicants and with sexual indulgence which is not confined to a breeding season or to mating as with wild beasts, nor by the requirements of social experience. And man is adapted for other satisfactions which are capable of indefinitely greater prolongation and of inestimable value, but which will be forfeited and destroyed unless the animal propensities are confined within the limits set by a social order which experience has shown to be necessary. Though passion may clamor against the verdict, the experience of the race has proved, if anything in life is proved, that the highest happiness of individuals and the welfare of society require the monogamous family, built on mutual love and trust, and the limitation of sexual indulgence by either sex within the bounds of wedlock. Moreover, there must be no need of zenana walls, but men and women must have acquired an honor that can be trusted in free association. The male, who in youth may understand far better than the female the nature of the impulses involved, should have a sense of honor which makes him the defender of innocence against the perilous advances that lead toward the slippery incline which ends in an abyss.

The multitudes who escape this peril do so not by a gift of nature but by virtue of an acquired trait, a sentiment stronger than instinct, inculcated by society, as a result of countless bitter lessons. Though in well-reared characters the defenses are built so high and strong, still society must rebuild them with every generation; because desire for physical pleasure is so strong and because social tolerance can make anything seem right. Every society has still some customs that are like low weak places in the dikes.

The Third Essential Trait.—The third essential trait of civilized man is steadiness in endeavor. The savage and the child tire quickly of work. Work requires as much courage and grit as war and is less prompted by instinct than war. Not to flinch before an uninviting task when there is a good reason for doing it, to order time and things and errant impulses, is a power which society has to impart to its youthful members by example and training, a process in which it is necessary to enlist the resolute coöperation of those who are in the process of their education. For lack of this acquired power we have an army of slovens, paupers, ne'er-do-wells, tramps, criminals, ruined sons of rich fathers, and gifted failures.

The Social Spirit.—The fourth and the last to be here enumerated of the traits which are indispensable qualifications in the members of a developed society is justice or "the social spirit." The word "justice" is consciously applied both to a subjective trait and to the conduct in which that trait is expressed. Justice is conduct guided by reason as distinguished from conduct guided merely by instinctive impulses. The reasoning which is the foundation of justice has for its major premise the fact that the values of life are real by whomsoever experienced: they are real not only in the experience of the actor and the actor's family and partisans, but also in the experience of persons entirely outside his habitual "we." Instinct and sentiment have been prone to act often as if suffering and joy, ruin and fulfillment were not realities to be taken into account when they were in the experience of persons of another nation; often, likewise, when they were in the experience of persons in the same nation but of another social class, sect, or party, and often even when they were in the experience of persons in the same nation, sect, and party but not in one's own family. We have in fact been prone to ignore the reality of these values when they were in the experience of persons in one's own family but not in one's very own experience.

The Reasonableness of Good Conduct.—The "golden rule" does not mean that we should feel the same instinctive prompting to act in the interest of others that we have to act in our own, but it means that life in society cannot be lived on a merely instinctive level. It means that we should estimate at par the values of every life we touch. Our responsibility for those values is in proportion to our power over them. One's power over his own life is greater than over any other, and his responsibility to realize the joy and worth of his own life is proportionally greatest. One's power over the lives of his own family is normally vastly greater than over the lives of any other persons, and his responsibility for them proportionally greater. But his responsibility for all the human interests that he does or can affect, though not so great, is just as real and is proportionate to his power over them. The demand of reason is that he should so spend his energies as to produce the greatest net increase of human values, whether those values are realized in his own experience or in the experience of others.

This is the "law of sacrifice." There is no virtue in sacrifice for its own sake. No one has any right to engage in conduct which on the whole is a sacrifice of human values, and for that very reason it will at times be his reasonable duty to prefer his own greater future good to the indulgence of the moment, and to prefer the greater good of the group to the lesser good of himself. The soldier does not die for the sake of death but for the sake of life, the life of his nation. No reasonable being is asked to sacrifice for the sake of sacrifice but for the sake of the joy and worth of other time or other lives, or for the prevention of evil greater than the hurt of the sacrifice.

It has been argued by certain writers with great emphasis and eloquence that duty, and especially sacrifice, cannot be supported by reason, that if reason were the sole guide every actor would regard only the values to be realized in his own experience, and life would be a warfare of unmitigated individualism. Some have added that life ought to be such a warfare and others that we ought to depend upon the guidance of some transcendental faculty which sanctions sacrifice and duty. But the real trouble is, not that reason denies the interests of others, but that instinct disregards them. Reason admits that the interests of others are, if not as important to me, at least as important to others and as real as my own, and if so then to disregard them entirely is unreasonable to the extent of disregarding some of the facts of the case, facts which even instinct by no means entirely disregards. It is not impartial reason but the extremest of all biases that allows one to act as if a part of the interests affected by his conduct had no reality. If reason is allowed to speak it affirms that all the interests which one affects have equal reality though not an equal appeal to impulse.

Reasoned justice includes every virtue. It is not only negative, forbidding the infliction of injuries, it is positive, summoning every human being to promote every interest that he can affect in the exact measure of its worth, except as he is excused from promoting some interests by the fact that his net contribution to human welfare will be increased by applying his powers in the promotion of certain particular interests rather than in attempting the promotion of all interests and in the promotion of those which in the long run and in the sum total he can most affect rather than of those which he can affect less. It allows no man to form his ambition with indifference to the social effect of his conduct.

It summons each of us to subordinate his own interest when-ever by so doing he can secure the realization of other interests which in their sum are greater. This justice is honesty which is willing to admit the facts of life and to acknowledge the effects of our own conduct. It is fair play which is willing to abide by the laws which we try to enforce upon others. Its rule is: I for one will so play my part that if all played their part in the same spirit the good possibilities of society would be fulfilled.[1] When the declaration of reason evokes response of sentiment it becomes "the social spirit" which would make of human life one vast coöperative enterprise in which each participant, while receiving from society a million times more than he can repay, is not indifferent to fulfilling his own share of the common work. This is that love which is "the greatest thing in the world," and "the fulfilling of the law."

It seems to be a law of evolution that the highest traits develop last; in ethics society has not yet fully reached the "culture stage" of evolution. But individuals have already reached this stage, and have demonstrated that it is not beyond human attainment. The line between the sheep and the goats, the good citizen and the bad, is the sincere adoption of this ideal rule as the guide of life. This is the ethical ideal of Christ and of all the great prophets of the most advanced civilizations.

The requirements of justice seem categorical; that is, they seem to be arbitrary commands rather than conclusions of reason, because at the moment when one must obey he is often incapable of the reasoning that justifies them. In the heat of the occasion short-sighted views, immediate interests, urgent desires that inhibit countervailing reflection, fill up the attention. No man is fit for life who has not some settled

---

[1] This is the principle of Kant: "In all cases I must act in such a way that I can at the same time will that my maxim should become a universal law." Kant based this requirement upon the majesty of an abstract conception. We base it upon the law of cause and effect work-ing out matter-of-fact results in human experience. "The Philosophy of Kant, as Contained in Selections from His Own Writings," selected and translated by John Watson. Macmillan, 1894, p. 230.

principles that will guide him in the thick of action, even though impulse for the moment blinds him to the justice of these principles, and he chafes against their control.

The five principal agencies of social control are: (1) law, institutionalized in the state; (2) religion, institutionalized in the church; (3) education, institutionalized in the family and the school; (4) public opinion, institutionalized in moral codes and the press; (5) art, ceremony, and manners. It will be observed that the great institutions of society except the economic institutions are agencies of control. This is in accordance with the fact that the great means of welfare are two, namely: first, wealth; and second, human conduct. And the task of securing the necessary body of adapted and correlated activity is even greater and more difficult than the task of producing sufficient wealth.

CHAPTER XXXII

CRIME AND ITS CAUSES

The Law as an Agency of Social Control.—Law attempts to control by sanctions and in practice its sanctions are nearly always penalties and not rewards. So long as this is true, the law is serviceable for the repression of conduct that is socially condemned, rather than for eliciting serviceable conduct. It is easy and cheap to inflict pain and deprivation, but it is by no means impossible to grant inexpensive rewards, especially in the form of distinctions such as significant badges and titles. Distinctions appeal to one of the deepest interests of human nature, which is a natural fulcrum for social control. And the gratification of this instinct is to nearly all human beings one of the greatest possible sources of satisfaction. Meritorious conduct in war has long been recognized by medals and rank, but for promoting peaceful achievement this means has thus far been little utilized. We have been so obsessed with our notion of the power of the economic motive that we have comparatively overlooked another spring of action which is apt to move all normal men from the savage, who after his most elementary needs for food and warmth have been rudely satisfied can with difficulty be stirred to action by purely economic motive but who will endure any toil and sell his life in struggling for the glory of taking scalps, to the modern millionaire, who with every material want satisfied, still sacrifices other pleasures, his health, and sometimes life itself to keep his place in the race for success.

Penal law is a deterrent and compelling agency of immense usefulness and with long experience it has been adapted to the compulsion of not a few necessary actions as well as to the repression of a great number of objectionable actions. It is the strong indispensable outwork of social defense. If only one in twenty obeyed the law from fear of penalty yet so small a proportion, if set free from all restraint, would be enough to inaugurate a reign of anarchy.

Vice, Sin, Immorality, Tort and Crime.—Vice is action injurious to the actor and offset by no social gains; it brings its own penalty according to the natural operation of the laws of cause and effect. It is seldom injurious to the actor alone, and society may be compelled to forbid it in order to prevent the injury which vice inflicts on the associates of the vicious.

The word "sin" carries two connotations. The one formerly most prominent was the idea of a violation of divine law, the other is the thought of a disclosure of baseness or other evil trait in the character of the actor. Vice is self-injury. Sin is self-disclosure.

Immorality is a violation of the maxims which embody the lessons of group experience and tradition as to the essentials of conduct.

Tort is the infliction of injury for which damage may be recovered by civil process in the absence of any contract. Such damage may be inflicted for example by libel or trespass. The injurious action may or may not be a crime.

Crime is the violation of law. To drive on the left side of a city street in New York is a crime but not naturally a vice, a sin, or an immorality; ingratitude is a sin but not a crime. In Canada it is a crime to drive on the right side of the street; in one state it is a crime to carry a revolver or to sell whiskey; in another state neither of these acts is a crime. Law determines what acts are crimes. In free and adequately enlightened communities crimes would be immoralities by virtue of having been made crimes. And a good test of the enlightenment of a community is the degree in which it has succeeded in identifying and branding as criminal the actions that harm it most. The tendency is to make actions criminal in proportion as they excite disgust or anger, rather than in proportion to the harm they do. Thus to commit a rape seems "more criminal" than habitually to practice seduction. The evil acts of unshorn, ill-clad, ignorant thieves are sooner recognized as crimes than those of immaculately tailored manipulators of values and promoters of bubble investments. And crimes against a particular victim who is visualized both by the criminal and by the public indicate a more perverted nature, and are more quickly execrated than the long-range crimes of the quack medicine vender, employer of child labor, and maintainer of the conditions which cause occupational diseases and accidents, although by far the greater harm may be wrought by actions of the latter type. "A scientific penology will graduate punishments primarily according to the harmfulness of the offense to society, and secondarily according to the attractiveness of the offense to the criminal." [1]

The severer crimes are termed felonies, and are usually punished by death or by imprisonment in a state institution for a term of years. Misdemeanors are minor crimes, and are usually punishable by fine, or by imprisonment in a municipal or county jail for months or days, or by both. As the law defines crime, so also it determines which crimes shall be treated as felonies, and which as misdemeanors. What in one state is a felony in another may be a misdemeanor.

Classes of Crimes.—Crimes may be classified with reference either to the object or to the subject of the action. With reference to the object of the action they are:

1. *Crimes against order.* To prevent confusion and to secure the aims of general welfare, definite methods of procedure must be carried out. In crowded thoroughfares there must be an understanding as to the side of the street to be taken by vehicles going in a given direction; at crossings the policeman's signal must be obeyed; automobiles must be lighted at night; marriages must be licensed, solemnized, and recorded in some authorized manner; elections must be conducted in accordance with a system.

Crimes against legal rights and privileges may properly be regarded as against the social order.

2. *Crimes against property, such as theft, arson, and malicious mischief.*

---

[1] Ross: Social Control, p. 110.

3. *Crimes against persons,* such as assault, rape, mayhem, and murder.

With reference to the subject of the action crimes are classified as:

1. *Crimes by accident.* A teamster may be on the wrong side of the road because his horse has become unmanageable, or one may kill another because a gun unexpectedly goes off. The act objectively considered is in violation of law; the question to be decided is as to the state of the subject of the action: was he free from guilty volition?

2. *Crimes of reformers and would-be reformers.* These are persons who believe that the social condition is wrong and that the way to right it is to violate law. Here fall a large part of the political crimes, and crimes of labor agitators.

3. *Crimes of passion or sudden impulse.* These may be the acts of occasional criminals presently to be defined, yet the criminal degenerate and the criminal by education are by far more likely than others to commit crime under the spur of some violent passion.

4. *Premeditated crimes.*[1]

Classes of Criminals.—Criminals are classified in a variety of ways. The following classification is useful:

1. *Insane criminals.*

2. *Degenerate criminals.* Persons not insane in the usual acceptance of the term, but who, either as a result of inborn abnormality, or as a result of their mode of life, are without the psychophysical adaptations that enable most other men, in an ordinary environment, to escape careers of crime.

3. *Criminals by education.*

4. *Occasional criminals.* Men who commit crime in reaction to an unusual occasion, who may never have committed crime before and may never do so again.

Is There a Criminal Type?—The great Italian criminologist Cæsar Lombroso won a considerable number of adherents to the theory that practically all who commit serious crimes, or who follow careers of crime, are lacking the psychophysical organization that is required by orderly civilized life, and

---

[1] Other than reformers' crimes.

that in nearly all cases the presence of this lack reveals itself in outward and visible abnormality of face, head, and body. There is now hardly any scientific authority who sustains the view in this extreme form. Yet we have recognized in our classification the existence of criminal degenerates. The following psychophysical defects conduce to crime:

1. *Defective altruism.* Some persons appear to be born abnormally lacking in this trait of higher social animals. A boy who sets on fire the petticoats of his baby sister and then throws her out of a second-story window is not a normal human being. The annals of crime reveal cases of hideous insensibility to the sufferings of others, of which it would seem that a well-constituted orang-outang would be incapable

2. *Lack of sensibility* to social approval and disapproval. This sensibility is an instinct that plays a leading part in enabling society to adapt its constantly rising generations for membership in the social body. It has been said of the born criminal that he cannot blush. With these, however, are often confused those who have a normal responsiveness to the admiration and contempt of their fellows, but who aspire to secure the admiration of criminals, and not of well-regulated citizens, who are ambitious to count in the world but whose world is the world of crime, and who in other environment might have pursued, with the same ardor, respectable callings.

3. *Lack of imaginative and esthetic idealism.*

4. In another connection we have studied the difference between *fractional response* with peripheral control and total response with central control. Fractional response corresponds to a defect which may be due either to heredity or to inadequate rearing. When due to hereditary defect it may result from either excess or defect of qualities that should more nearly balance each other, or from general stupidity. When due to lack of rearing it results from the absence of the guiding sentiments, interests, and principles, socially acquired, which are essential to the normal control of conduct.

5. *General neurasthenia and undervitalization* is one of the most frequent causes of crime. The man whose feet drag,

who lacks natural cheer, hope, daring, evenness of temper, and capacity for a protracted course of endeavor, is likely to find his way to the police station.

6. *Feeble-mindedness.* The feeble-minded may be in good general health, they may be sociable, sympathetic, and sensitive to praise or blame, but they exhibit the symptoms of fractional response because there is not enough clear mentality to hold in vivid consciousness the principles which guide normal conduct. Not all who exhibit fractional response are feeble-minded, but all feeble-minded exhibit what in a normal person would be called fractional response. They fall behind in school, tend to give up the expectation of respectability, and are with great ease duped and led by any designing person.

Causes of Crime.—The causes of crime may be classified under three heads: (1) heredity; (2) acquired traits; (3) environment.

1. *Heredity.* Concerning heredity but little need be added to that which has just been said in discussing the question of a criminal type. The natural appetites are not in themselves bad. Even the hunting instinct, to which bullying and cruelty are attributed, certainly once had its proper place in human life and may have it still; and there is hardly any natural prompting that could be omitted from man's equipment without serious loss. Man's characteristic difficulty is not depravity but complexity. A prompting which is good in its place is only one factor in a whole that must not be disarranged and to which each part must be in orderly subordination. It is the very richness of man's endowment that makes it so easy for him to make a mess of it all. And this destruction is all the easier in the case of men who are born deficient in general vigor and soundness of balanced capacity, or who have any of the specific defects referred to in discussing the question of a "criminal type."

It is stated that at Elmira Reformatory during a long period for which figures are known, 13.7 per cent. of inmates had insane or epileptic heredity; and that of 233 prisoners at Auburn, New York, 23.03 per cent. were clearly of neurotic origin. One European investigation found 195 out of 266 criminals affected by diseases that are "usually hereditary," and another found morbid inheritance in 46 per cent. of criminals. An investigator who examined nearly 4,000 German criminals in a prison of which he was director found insane, epileptic, suicidal, and alcoholic heredities predominant. Still another investigator reports that he finds among the parents of 184 criminals only 4 to 5 per cent. quite healthy. With reference to such figures it is essential to bear in mind that in the case of a very large percentage of persons who never go to prison some ancestor could be found who had one of those defects that are often inherited; and it is equally important to remember that investigators are prone to find what they are looking for. But after all allowances are made it is safe to say that one of the causes of a considerable proportion of crime is general inborn defectiveness, or some special excess or defect in the natural predispositions, that invites an overthrow of the orderly balance in action that fits into a place in civilized society. There seems to be good ground for the belief, common among social workers, that as a class, though with many exceptions, honest men are stronger and better endowed than criminals, and, moreover, that criminals are stronger and better endowed than paupers. This refers to sedentary paupers, not to migratory hoboes. "Crime, as compared with pauperism, indicates vigor." "Criminal careers are more easily modified by environment, because crime, more especially, contrived crime, is an index of capacity, and wherever capacity is found, there environment is most effective in producing modifications of career." [1]

2. *Acquired Characteristics.* The treatment of this subject in Chapter XVI, "Acquired Population Traits and Public Health" should be recalled. Drugging is of special and sinister importance in this connection. Chloral has been added to

---

[1] These words are from Dugdale (The Jukes, pp. 16, 47, 49, etc.), who found that among the 540 members of one degenerate family, crossing with better blood produced children, who in the same wretched environment, tended to become criminals, while the full-blooded Jukes were not criminals but paupers.

alcohol as a means by which men render themselves reckless as criminals and finally shatter their nervous constitution. Drugging is almost inseparable from professional prostitution. It helps to create the appearance of cheer, to deaden sensibility to suffering, and to hasten death. According to the relatively conservative estimate of Professor Henderson, drink is one of the causes of 50 per cent. of the crimes, the chief cause of 31 per cent., and the sole cause of 16 per cent. Sexual perversion as an acquired trait was not mentioned in the earlier chapter referred to, but must here be recognized as the cause of a variety of crimes, including certain atrocious murders; by choking and by slashing mutilations that cause the blood to flow.

More serious in causing crime than any of the more positive and specific acquired traits is the negative failure to have developed the general adjustment to orderly and civilized life which we have called normal second nature, and which includes the four traits enumerated in the preceding chapter: honesty; temperance, in the broad sense; steadiness in effort; and justice. The "hardened criminal" has acquired instead a second nature of toughened maladaptation to normal civilized existence. His habits, sentiments, ideas, his "world view," are perverted. His standard of self-respect from his youthful experiences in his boy gang may be the idea of a swaggering, bullying, vice-indulging tough; his conception of glory and success may be embodied in safe-cracking and police evasion; he may believe all virtue, save personal kindness and loyalty between pals, to be hypocrisy, a part of a universal game of craft which he plays in his own way. Such a man is a "criminal by education."

3. *Environment and Crime.* The reader who recalls the discussion of heredity in Chapter XIII will realize that bad heredity is to some degree a result of bad environment of the parents. The neurasthenia due to stunted youth, drunkenness, and other acquired physical defects are far more the results of bad environment. Most significant of all as causes of crime are the bad psychic effects of social molding, which make what we have just called the criminal by education.

(a) *Failure of the family* may be offset by other social influences, but the frequency of serious consequences from such failure illustrates the importance of that primary institution. At times practically the only hope for the child is to be transplanted from the environment of an evil family. Wines asserts that "few criminals are reared in the atmosphere of mutual help, subordination, and sacrifice, which large families of living children imply." Rylands found that of 107 boys committed to the Park Row Industrial School, Bristol, in five years only 56 had both parents living. Of all the boys and girls committed to industrial schools in Great Britain in 1885 only 41.2 per cent. had both parents living and able to take care of them, while of the other 58.8 per cent. one or both parents were dead or criminal or had deserted their children.

Among the serious causes of crime must be enumerated: orphaning; break-up of homes by divorce or by desertion by the father; imprisonment of the father; employment of both parents and consequent lack of oversight and home atmosphere; bad housing that makes the home a mere den or resting-place to be escaped as much as practicable; and the ruin of homes by drink and vice. Hunger seldom makes a thief of an honest man, but poverty diminishes the chance that a boy will be reared into honest manhood equipped for success in an honorable career. To these domestic causes must be added the loss of influence over their children by immigrant parents whose broken English, quaint dress and old-world ways prevent them from being looked up to as examples by their sons and daughters, because the latter are unable to discriminate between such externals and the essentials of personality. It is important to note that it is not the immigrants themselves, reared in the established order of old-world communities, that swell our criminal statistics, but their children reared in the slums of American cities and towns and loosed from parental control because of the break in the continuity of social traditions.[1] Finally child labor takes boys and girls out of the

---

[1] For explanation of appearance of criminality among the immigrants themselves see p. 244.

home and makes them more or less independent economic units before their characters are formed, and often throws them into a corrupting environment.

(b) *Bad company* usually waits just outside the door of the evil or inadequate home. And in the boys' gang, in the schoolyard and in the rendezvous the same propensities to imitate those who have prestige in the group and to emulate the standards of the group continue their work. The well-known tendency for ideals, even when ideals have been formed, to hide themselves in the crowd, and the tremendous urge of the desire to stand well with the crowd, mold the unformed boy or girl with a pressure which he or she may see no reason to resist, and is not likely to resist unless as a result of some other social influence. The greater the energy and the greater the social amenability, which in another environment would manifest itself as conscientiousness and approved ambition, the swifter may be the destruction, if the group standards which appeal to these instincts are destructive standards. Bad company lies in wait with the lure of sociability and instinctive appeals, not only for those who issue from inadequate homes, but for most youths. And in the worse sections instruction in vice and crime is abundantly and gratuitously provided.

(c) *Lack of education* is usually enumerated as one of the serious causes of crime which may be classed as environmental. What has already been said of the criminal by education shows plainly that education in the deepest sense is not all a matter of the schools or formal instruction, but what is meant under this third head is formal education by schooling and by apprenticeship. The high percentage of illiteracy among criminals means not so much that illiteracy causes crime as that both illiteracy and crime result from the same conditions; that those who lack the home influences which insure good schooling, and run the streets instead, are the very ones most likely to enter careers of crime. Truancy is recognized as a vestibule to crime. Yet mere illiteracy cannot be looked upon as a cause of crime. Neither does a knowledge of arithmetic and geography sensibly diminish criminal propensities; it may make a boy less likely to become a highwayman or a burglar, but more likely to become a forger or defaulter. A great class of offenses, and probably the most dangerous class both economically and socially, are not the crimes of the ignorant; such, for example, are bribery, misrepresentation of news, adulteration, grafting, jerry-building, ruining competitors by cut-throat methods, etc., etc. However, without exaggerating the relation between illiteracy and morality we may well observe that the influence of teachers is usually salutary, and the reading habit is a defense against misused leisure, while history and literature, if it is literature worthy of the name and not the nickel thriller or the yellow daily, are the moral equivalent of good company. It is highly probable that the schools will at some time design their work with deeper insight into social requirements and that they will then do more toward the prevention of crime than they now accomplish, as well as more toward the positive development of social resources.

That education which results from apprenticeship to some calling that will both discipline to steady industry and afford a way of making an honest living is an important preventive of crime, and the lack of a trade is a negative cause of crime.

(d) *Social disorganization,* the failure of any of the great social organizations to function in proper adjustment, may be a cause of crime; particularly to be noted here are failures of the state and the industrial organization.

(1) Political disorganization of a radical sort appears in the "spoils system." The spoils system promotes such practices as bribery at elections and falsification of counts and returns, crimes that strike at the vitals of democracy and public welfare. Bribery of councils and legislatures has sometimes been practiced and even defended by men of standing, on the ground that it is a practical necessity in the existing state of legislatures and councils. That attitude on the part of such men is the surest way to continue the evil. The spoils system and political corruption in general gives the public an education in the anti-social spirit, the essence of which is the sacrifice of broader to narrower and more selfish interests.

Politicians are given tremendous publicity and at least the adventitious prestige which publicity confers. For that reason corruption in political life is peculiarly contagious. Professor Henderson remarks that "the local boss has more influence over the ideals accepted by the youth of his district than Washington or Lincoln." When appointing power is guided by political considerations and legislators vote according to anti-social motives, it is natural that many adopt a world view of which the major premise is the faithlessness of man.

One of the greatest promoters of crime resulting from bad politics is the shameful complicity with panders, pickpockets, and criminals in general, on the part of the officials who are employed and sworn to protect the public against crime. The abuse, so often exposed, still continues, and we do not seem to command sufficient morality in political life to rid us of these contemptible traitors to public trust. The temptation exists because of the opportunity for concealment where concealment is for the interest of all the parties acquainted with the facts.[1] And the evil is so systematized that the individual is tempted to shift his own responsibility to other shoulders. The dishonor of the offense is so dastardly that its continuance is a disgrace to our whole civilization.

(2) *Bad business* as well as bad politics is a source of public corruption. We learn too frequently of scandals in insurance, railroading, and other fields of high finance. The two forms of success most brought to public attention are success in big business and success in politics, and it is a calamity when from both issue the impressions that cause the spread of that world view which has for the central article of its creed the faithlessness of men—a world view which affects the character of many who never become criminals. The moral responsibility of conspicuous sinners is great. It is proper that they should be exposed; but the appetite of newsreaders for scandal is so great and leads to such a shaking-out of soiled linen, while decency gets no advertising, that

---

[1] Lincoln Steffens: The Shame of Cities. McClure, Phillips & Co., 1904. C. H. Parkhurst: Our Fight with Tammany. Scribners, 1895.

all faith in virtue might be undermined if most of us did not encounter it constantly in life's intimate relationships.

Industrial disorganization is promotive of crime in a variety of other ways. It is a cause of poverty and the evil consequences of poverty. It occasions the violence and disorder of strikes. Of all the incidents of industrial disorganization unemployment is perhaps the most promotive of crime. The laborer out of a job, whether he merely loafs or prosecutes, half despairing, the daily search for a job, is in a bad way. Savings are eaten up, the physical condition is likely to deteriorate, the temptation to drink is increased, habits of vagrancy are easily set up, the outlook upon life is likely to become stolid or discouraged or hostile. To men in this condition crime offers an interest and a reward.

(3) *The obliteration of the neighborhood* in great cities is a form of social disorganization. The neighborhood is one of the natural primary groups. It is natural for every man to have a public outside the home, which he may indeed defy, but which appreciates his successes, respects his worth, and effectively sets its face against him if he departs from the path of propriety and rectitude. In the anonymity of the city the neighborhood is dissolved. Acts from which the villager would be deterred by shame are brazenly committed in the concealment of "the city wilderness." Moreover, enough persons of every good or evil sort may be found in the city so that the criminal can consort with those who do not condemn, but even applaud his crimes.

The lack of domesticity, the unmarried condition of many men, is a state of social disorganization. Traits and conditions that tend toward crime tend also to prevent marriage, and the absence of the restraints, responsibilities, interests, aims, and satisfactions that center in a home is itself a condition favorable to criminality.

(4) The eleven million *negroes* in this country may be said to live in a state of partial social disorganization and this helps to make their rate of criminality higher than that of any other equal number of people. They are not members in full and regular standing in American society. Disgrace

is less disgraceful, and high standing less attainable to them because of their anomalous position. It is necessary for white people to recognize that negroes are not all alike and to treat the intelligent, capable, and virtuous among them with appropriate consideration. But it is still more necessary for negroes to learn to value the esteem and respect of members of their own race and for their own churches and social circles to discipline irregularities with greater severity, so that there shall be careers for negroes as negroes and both ambition and disgrace will exert their full power irrespective of the attitude of white men. Social separateness of the black race does not necessarily mean discrimination against the black race. It tends rather to diminish unkind discrimination against individuals. Wherever negroes seek social contact for the sake of social contact, and claim recognition of the equality of their race, this contact and recognition are denied. Wherever they entirely resign such claims their progress is watched with eager and hopeful friendliness, and right-minded white people are entirely ready to admit that many a black man is the superior of very many whites and that every such black man is entitled to special respect. The friction, social disorganization, and lack of repression of vice and crime, and lack of stimulus to honest endeavor are partly due to the lack of an established *modus vivendi* accepted by both races. Such a *modus vivendi,* to be stable and acceptable, must be honest, free alike from unwarranted claims on the one side and from unwarranted assumption and blindness on the other.

The Extent of Crime.—There can be no doubt that the amount of crime in the United States is excessive. It is customary to quote appalling statistics as to the increasing number of arrests. Yet it is by no means certain that the more serious forms of crime are increasing in frequency. Drunkenness and the crimes due to drunkenness have fallen off. Yet the number of arrests on account of liquors has temporarily increased in some localities because of the increased stringency of the laws to be enforced against intoxication as well as against the traffic. Carrying firearms, gambling, and various forms of disorder once went unforbidden in states which now treat these acts as crimes. Increase in the number of arrests may be a sign of progress, though it would show a more advanced stage of progress if harmful acts were not only forbidden but so effectively prevented that arrests should become few.

The cost of the arrest, trial, and maintenance of criminals is about one-tenth of the total burden of state taxation and, excepting that for education, is the heaviest item of state expenditure. If we could add the expenditures for such purposes by municipalities, states and nation, and to that add the loss and damage inflicted upon society by crime and criminal habits, the total financial cost would probably reach into the billions.[1] The personal and social losses and indirect damages are of course incalculable. The number of persons in prisons and reformatories in the United States on July 1, 1922, was 163,889.[2] The number of habitual criminals at large was far greater.

Drill is right in remarking that crime is a sensible measure of pathological conditions existing in society. More accurately still they are a measure of recognized symptoms of the social diseases. It may be quite another matter to diagnose those diseases. And practices not yet branded as crimes and the fact that they are not so recognized and prohibited may reveal even more serious social derangement or immaturity.

---

[1] E. H. Sutherland: Criminology, p. 65 seq.
[2] Ibid., Ch. II.

CHAPTER XXXIII

CRIME AND ITS TREATMENT

The Motive of Punishment.—The treatment of crime may be divided into two parts: first, the detection, arrest, trial, and acquittal or conviction; second, the treatment of the criminal after conviction. The former may be called criminal procedure, the latter penology. The phrase "criminal procedure" is usually applied only to so much of the first of these two as pertains to the method of conducting trials.

The dictum of ex-President Taft that "the administration of criminal law in all the states of this Union is a disgrace to civilization," is echoed by many students of the subject. The absurdity and inefficiency of our criminal procedure is almost worthy of comparison with procedure in the old English courts of chancery which Dickens pilloried. It is so needlessly slow and cumbersome that the courts of great cities fall years behind their docket, and so uncertain of reaching just decisions that most competent witnesses agree that criminals guilty of homicide are more likely to escape through the tangled meshes of its obsolete technicalities than to be convicted.[1] The chief though not the only reason for this is the fact that the original motive of criminal procedure has become uncertain of itself, and no wiser motive has clearly established itself in the public mind.

Development of Criminal Procedure.—The original motive in the treatment of offenders was that crude vengeance, the usefulness of which in maintaining the instinctive, natural

---

[1] According to Graham Taylor in *The Survey* of February 23, 1915, page 535, a man arrested for serious crime in Chicago "stands only about one chance out of five of ever getting into the criminal court," and "anyone charged before the court with felony stands about one chance in thirty of going to the penitentiary or reformatory."

order of primitive societies, has been commented upon. The danger of free vengeance is not only that it may wreak itself upon the innocent but also that the angry avenger will limit the harm he inflicts only by the bitterness of his own hate and the heat of his own fury, so that the original culprit, after vengeance has been taken upon him, feels, and all his friends join in the feeling, that it is now his turn to take rightful vengeance. And after he in his turn has satisfied his resentment, his first offense has been much exceeded and the original victim and all his friends feel that they have a right to renewal of vengeance even greater than that which they first exacted. Thus free vengeance tends to make matters worse and worse and to embroil the clan in permanent and destructive feuds. When the attempt has failed to moderate the vengeance of angry men to such a point that the culprit will accept the penalty as just and let the quarrel drop, the hopeless tendency of free vengeance to engender feuds leads to the second and greater reform by which chieftains seek to suppress private revenge. Then, "Vengeance is mine, I will repay," is the claim of every wise and strong ruler. At this point we find the criminal procedure of all peoples that have risen out of savagery to barbarism and the earlier stages of civilization. In this stage the offended party goes before the judge to "demand vengeance against his adversary." And the purpose of the court is to inflict such penalties that the injured party and the bystanders will feel that "justice has been done" and will be content to abstain from private revenge. "Retributive justice" means such severity as group feeling at the given stage of progress can witness with satisfaction. Now arises the institution of *compositio,* or *wergild,* that is, the complainant may be content to sell his right to vengeance for a price. Cupidity is pitted against hate. Originally, if he insists upon his pound of flesh he cannot be compelled to take gold. Group opinion sympathizing with the aggrieved will not tolerate such denial of the natural rights of hate. But the influence of authority is in favor of substituting redemption for penalties that kill or maim the fighting men of the clan. And both authority and group opinion insists that the redemption demanded shall not be excessive. A very angry man, it is admitted, must be allowed a good round sum in lieu of the satisfaction of his rage. Accordingly a higher payment was exacted by the law when the criminal was caught red-handed than when there had been time for the anger of his victim to cool. Moreover, a powerful man, a nobleman with seven sons to take up his quarrel, was allowed a richer redemption than could be collected by a weak man whose right to avenge himself was not so substantial a possession.

Until comparatively recent times this has been the legal conception, and more recently it has been the theological conception of "justice." But as reason has increasingly tempered instinct in the conduct of individual and social life, men have come to feel that the infliction of one injury does not necessarily constitute a ground for the infliction of another addition to the sum of human suffering, even upon the perpetrator of the first offense, and that some fallacy is involved in the ancient defense of severity for the mere satisfaction of "retribution." [1] Moreover it is more clearly realized that even if we do not go so far as to say that "to understand all is to pardon all," still it must be admitted that every crime has a "natural history," and is likely to have been the expression of a heredity for which the perpetrator was not responsible and of an unfortunate youth for the conditions of which he was not responsible. In fact the old motive of retribution has broken down as a basis for the enforcement of criminal law; and this is one fundamental cause of our deplorable laxity in its enforcement.

The sociologist is sometimes violently, but falsely, accused of standing sponsor for this laxity. It is true that sociological

---

[1] In the development of Hebrew teaching on the subject of sin and crime there have been three stages: first, moderate your vengeance, an eye for an eye; second, leave vengeance to the rulers; third, "love your enemies, do good to those who despitefully use you, forgive as you hope to be forgiven." All higher barbarians have risen to the second stage; and that instinctive attitude is more congenial to ordinary humanity than the third stage, which harbors no resentment and justifies severity only by the reasonable hope of preventing greater evil, or producing good either to the guilty or to others.

investigation makes it clear that "every crime has a natural history," as does every other social reality. And this knowledge is the chief agent in dissolving the old instinctive motive for retribution. It is true also that the sociologist stands for reformatory as well as merely punitive treatment of criminals. But the sociologist says that if reason is able to modify the instinctive motive for the punishment of crime it is also able to establish a rational motive; that the rational motive for the punishment of crime is not vengeance or retribution, but the protection of society; and that reason calls not for a further reduction of severity in the treatment of crime,[1] but on the contrary it demands a notable increase in the swiftness and certainty of punishment; and that punishment guided by the motive of protection to society will be far wiser than punishment guided by the spirit of vengeance or retribution, for it will mete out its severities not in proportion to the power of the criminal and the crime to awaken instinctive repugnance rising from primitive race experience or ancient prejudice but in proportion to its harmfulness to society and its attractiveness to the criminal under present conditions. It will not let the pretty woman, and the well-tailored society man who is guilty of impersonal wholesale crimes, go free, while emptying its vials of wrath upon the unshorn victim of evil social conditions, in whose breast may still be kindled the flame responsive to noble ideals if once they can be clearly presented to him.

The sociologist may add that the deterrent power of punishment depends far more upon its certainty than upon its severity. The instinctive motive for the punishment of offenders called for severity; but the growing opposition to that motive has destroyed the certainty of punishment, and has provided a maze of defenses to protect the accused against the severities of retributive law, until it has created the probability of his entire escape. The further progress of reason will not only

---

[1] Ex-President Roosevelt may be quite right in saying that as long as brave and noble men are required to lay down their lives for the public safety there can be no reasonable refusal to take the lives of certain classes of criminals as a means of promoting that safety.

supply a new and adequate motive for severity, namely, regard for public safety, but will also sweep away the cumbrous impediments to swiftness and certainty of procedure, and substitute efficient methods of intelligent, speedy, and far less uncertain detection and punishment of offenders.

Trial by Jury.—Two principal considerations appear to have guided the development of English and American criminal procedure: first, a desire to protect suspected persons against the summary wrath of angry accusers and precipitate magistrates, the main reliance for this protection being upon the jury; and second, a desire to avoid perversion of justice through the befuddlement of juries. These two purposes have found expression in rules like these:

There must be a jury who will be open to the purely human appeal. Instead of assuming neither guilt nor innocence, everything must be consistent with the assumption of innocence. In general a unanimous verdict of the jury is necessary for conviction. No witness can be allowed to tell what has been reported to him, but must confine his testimony to what he has himself directly observed. No testimony against the general character of the accused can be introduced; the prosecutor and the witnesses must confine themselves strictly to the specific action accurately described in the indictment, unless the defense has first attempted to prove good general character, in which case the prosecution may introduce testimony in rebuttal to that claim. The accused cannot be required to testify. If at the end it can be shown that in the course of a trial any of the numerous rules of procedure have been broken, the accused may ask for a new trial, and if retrial is granted, the severity of the penalty adjudged at the first trial may be diminished but cannot be increased, while on the other hand the prosecutor cannot appeal from an acquittal; it is final.

This system has become cluttered by technicalities, and with the breakdown of the motive of vengeance or retribution to which it is adapted it has far too many facilities for the escape of the guilty.

Should the jury be retained? Some students of this subject are of the opinion that the jury should be abolished. Its original purposes can hardly be said now to exist. If a bench of three judges were substituted for the jury most if not all of the hindrances to the taking of testimony which now hedge in our criminal procedure could safely be removed. Even "hearsay evidence," which is sometimes of great value, when both of the speakers involved are of high character and intelligence, might be admitted before a bench of judges specially trained in the sifting and weighing of evidence. The objection to examining the prisoner, who is likely to be incomparably the most important of all witnesses, would be removed before judges who understood the tricks of lawyers and knew how to avoid being misled by the confusion of a witness anxious for his own safety. The jury is composed of men of no special training for the task or experience in it, chosen by lot from a list of names from which the names of doctors, lawyers, ministers, and most others of special, proved intelligence, as well as names of day laborers, have been omitted. These untrained juries are likely to be swayed by the skill and eloquence of lawyers, so that there is much reason in the saying that "the able advocate has greater influence than the merits of the case." The winsome or pathetic appearance of the accused, the dramatic incident in the courtroom, the striking fact connected with the case that takes possession of attention to the practical exclusion of considerations more essential to a proper decision, the fluctuating attention with which untrained minds follow testimony and argument, continue to render the verdicts of juries a doubtful foundation for justice or for social defense. The juror can accept a bribe with little danger of detection, and he has no reputation as a judge to maintain.[1]

The Training of Criminal Lawyers.—Whether we permanently retain the jury or not it is evident that subordinating the motive of retribution to that of social protection, and changing the purpose of procedure from merely identifying the perpetrator of an act, to discovering the character of a man,

---

[1] Parmelee: Anthropology and Sociology in Relation to Criminal Procedure, chap. x.

will necessitate marked changes from the historic practices of the courts.

In the first place those responsible for the decisions to be reached must be trained not only in the law, which defines crimes and penalties and the method of conducting trials, but also in anthropology, sociology, and the psychology of testimony. That is to say, they must be expert in identifying the causes of crime, and able to distinguish between the different classes of criminals. There should ultimately be employed by the state, criminal anthropologists or psychiatrists, who should pass upon cases of suspected insanity or criminal abnormality, instead of either ignoring such peculiarities, or, in case they are urged as defenses, depending on the decision of judges who are trained only in the law and who base their decisions on the testimony of psychiatrists chosen and paid by the contending parties. Criminal law should constitute a profession distinct from civil law and all who deal with criminals should have had a special training for that service. Even policemen should have been instructed as to what they should look for when gathering evidence. And it would be desirable for every criminal lawyer after his schooling to spend a period of residence at a penal institution, as young physicians do at a hospital, familiarizing himself with the types of cases with which he must later deal. Theoretically the trial should be a scientific investigation aiming to get at the truth about the accused person, and free from the spirit of either attack or defense toward him. Practically, however, the bias of personal sympathy on the one hand, and of professionalism as representing the accusing public on the other, is so nearly sure to creep in, and the mental difficulty if not impossibility of pursuing evidence for conflicting theories with equal attention and eagerness is such that the practice of having both a prosecutor and a defender seems to be the only way to insure adequate presentation of the facts. But for the sake of fairness to rich and poor who come under the suspicion of the law, the defender as well as the prosecutor should be provided by the public. These officers might be appointed to serve for alternate periods as defenders and then as prosecutors. Every judge in a criminal court should have had experience as a criminal lawyer, both as a prosecutor and as a defender.

Individualization and Criminal Procedure.—Under our present system of procedure any indefiniteness or irregularity in the indictment may secure the release of the prisoner, even though the testimony has afforded complete evidence of his guilt. And the whole purpose of the trial is to answer but one question: Is this man guilty of the charge? This was all the knowledge wanted so long as retribution was the motive. But under the new motive of social protection the inquiry would be: Is this man dangerous to society; if so how dangerous? Why is he so, by inborn and incurable disposition or by reason of acquired bent? How can he be treated with reasonable assurance of preventing further injury to society from his acts, and of restoring him to useful membership in society, if that be feasible, while at the same time applying such swift and certain punishment as to deter others from the commission of crimes like his?

The knowledge that a man has committed a single act is far from being sufficient basis for the wise treatment of his case. Two acts that are outwardly and legally the same may be vastly different as expressions of the character and dangerousness of the actor. One may be the act of a professional thief engaged in the regular pursuit by which he sustains himself in a life of debauchery, the other may be the only crime of a devoted husband and father hard-pressed by temporary unemployment, or the prank of a misguided joker, or the first offense of an endangered youth. And it is impossible for us to measure out a precise quantity of suffering demanded by retributive justice. The law of one state may allow twice as long an imprisonment as that prescribed by another state for the same act. And thirty or ninety days in jail to one may be a brief sojourn in a public rest cure with all expenses paid, a subject for jocose remarks among boon companions; to another the same sentence may mean the blasting of a career. Not an act but a man would be the object of inquiry by criminal procedure if it were guided by rational rather than instinctive motives. Instead of barring all inquiry into

the general character of the accused, except under certain
specified conditions, the court would always proceed to the
investigation of the general character. And the prisoner, who
of all persons has knowledge of the facts which the court
must learn, would be required to testify. Our present procedure allows a certain departure from absolute rigidity by
such provisions as that in some cases the indictment may
specify whether the action is the first offense, and that the
court may have discretion within certain limits as to the sentence to be imposed upon one who has been convicted of an
act defined, but still the inquiry is strictly limited to this: Is
the accused guilty or not guilty of a specific action that has
been legally defined as a crime and against which, when proved,
a specific penalty, defined within limits, must be denounced
by the court? That our present judicial machinery is totally
inadequate to the purpose of individualization in the treatment
of crime is the natural result of the fact that it has not been
developed for any such purpose.

Individualization After Conviction.—Such expert investigation of the native and acquired traits, and social past of criminals would disclose the absurdity of treating them all alike
after convictions.

A large proportion of first offenders, as the experience of
some states shows, can safely be released under suspended
sentence, provided sufficient intelligence is exercised in selecting those who are to be accorded such treatment, and provided the probationers are continuously supervised by adequately competent officers of the court. The probationers
should be required to be regular at their employment, and to
make periodical reports to the probation officer, very probably
each to the very lawyer who had defended him and who would
be in an intimate and confidential relation well calculated to
promote personal helpfulness. If at any time the conduct and
spirit of a probationer became unsatisfactory he could be
sent to a penal institution in execution of the original sentence, without retrial. In this way, judging from such experience on the point as we already have, about 85 per cent. of
these adult probationers, whose sentence had been suspended,

would entirely escape prison experience because they would never again show themselves dangerous to society.[1]

At the opposite extreme, born criminals and some who now are acquitted and set at liberty on the ground that they are "not responsible," would be permanently confined at such labor as they were able to perform. The fact that a given criminal was "not responsible for his acts" may have been a logical ground for releasing him so long as "retribution" was the motive for incarceration, but it becomes one of the strongest grounds for his permanent detention as soon as we adopt "the protection of society" as the motive for the incarceration of criminals. At the same time punishment for the sake of deterrence is without warrant in the case of those who have not sufficient reason and self-control to be governed by regard for consequences. Those of the same class who remain at liberty cannot be deterred from crime by the penalties suffered by those who have been convicted. And in cases of absolute inability to be governed by regard for consequences, no strictly penal element in their treatment would be justified. But the feeble-minded, congenitally perverted, and all irresponsible criminals, should be kept in humane but permanent confinement.

The great majority of criminals by education should be subjected to reformatory treatment.

Reformatory Treatment.—Reformatory treatment requires the indeterminate sentence, educational measures, gradation, and conditional release.

The indeterminate sentence is an indispensable part of any satisfactory system for the reformation of criminals. The criminal does not usually want to be reformed. But it is

---

[1] The Indiana Board of Charities states that if the prisoners paroled during the year 1912 "had remained in prison their maintenance for one year would have cost the State, at the average per capita expense, the additional sum of $1,152,555. Professor Ganet in the *Journal of the American Institute of Criminal Law and Criminology*, March, 1915, estimates that the parole system has saved to the States of the Union in which it is in force more than $10,000,000, or more than five times what it has cost, and that the earnings of the men on parole have had a value of not less than $30,000,000."

necessary that he apply himself to the activities that will help to reform him: he must study lessons and learn to work. There is just one motive that can be depended on to call forth the activities that will help to transform him, namely, the hope of release. Let him know that his release is conditioned upon making a certain record and accomplishing certain results and he will almost always apply himself with all the powers he possesses. After his reading and discussions and contact with prison officials have fixed his attention upon views of life different from those by which his criminal career had been actuated he may begin to coöperate with the efforts made in his behalf, not merely out of hope for release, but out of desire to prepare himself for an honest career. Unless this spirit can be awakened there is little or no hope of genuine reform. Those men who have had least contact with normal society and whose world view has therefore been utterly perverted, are not seldom the very ones who, when they catch sight of a practicable entrance to a better way of life and are convinced that there is such a thing as sincere virtue, adopt the better way with a zeal that is akin to the idealism of unsullied youth.

The educational measures applicable to men who have been convicted of crime cannot be extensively discussed here, and if they could they would fall properly under a later topic: education is a supplement to the law, rather than a part of its control by sanctions. Law besides deterring men by threat of the penalties to be swiftly and certainly meted out to offenders, exercises the compulsion necessary to force unwilling adults into a school adopted to their reform.

By "gradation" of prisoners is meant the practice of separating the prison population into classes, one of which may wear stripes, live in hard quarters, eat the simplest fare, and perform irksome tasks, while others are admitted to better privileges, the classification depending upon the behavior and progress of the individuals. This is a supplement to the indeterminate sentence as a motive, but will not serve as a substitute for it.

Provisional release is the next step in the system. Experienced prison officials acquire notable proficiency in distinguishing between genuine reform and artful and diligent pretense. Nevertheless, they cannot be certain that every man who has acquired a given proficiency in assigned tasks and who professes with apparent sincerity the desire for an honest life has ceased to be dangerous to society. Such men may be provisionally released. If their conduct is not satisfactory they should be recommitted without trial. But if they are regular at their work, unobjectionable in their practices and companionships, and punctual in their reports, then surveillance may be relaxed. And after the lapse of a sufficient time they might be formally rehabilitated by legal ceremony, as is the practice in France.

The judge who has presided at the trial of a criminal (or one of the judges in case it became the practice to have more than one) has special knowledge of the case and has assumed responsibility for the propriety of the treatment prescribed by the sentence. It is proposed that such a judge shall be one of those who have a voice in determining when the time for release and then for rehabilitation has come. An official of the reformatory institution where the prisoner has been should have a voice in the decision. And it is argued that a third person having no professional connection with the case should also have membership in the board to which this decision is intrusted.

It should be made sure either by the probation officer to whom the released prisoner is paroled or by some other person that there is employment for him. In many states a voluntary organization now secures in advance the dates at which prisoners are to be discharged, enters into relation with the men before their release, and assists them in making a new start in the world.

It is sometimes objected that reformatory treatment is not sufficiently deterrent. The prisoner's health is restored by medical care, proper diet, and physical training, his education is promoted, and the objector declares that he is better off than the honest laborer outside prison walls. To this it may be replied that there is no reason why life in a reforma-

tory may not be sufficiently penal; and that deprivation of
liberty is in itself a penalty which most men regard with dread
and that release from a reformatory can be had only after
submission to an exacting régime. So exacting is it and at
first so repugnant to lawless loafers who have acquired no
habits of regulated application that "the worst men prefer to
be sent to a prison organized on the old plan." [1] The system
of individualization just described, especially the indeterminate
sentence, is possibly the greatest deterrent from careers of
professional crime. In spite of the earlier release of some,
the average prison term is longer under the indeterminate sentence than under the definite sentence, on account of the prolonged retention of professional criminals. In every great
American city there are men who follow no honest calling
and whom the police recognize on the street as professional
criminals. But these men cannot be arrested save when there
is evidence of some specific crime, complete enough to make
conviction probable, and after arrest they can be convicted and
punished, not as professional criminals, but only for the
specific act named in the indictment. The sentence may indeed be lengthened upon the second and third conviction, but
upon release the criminal is turned loose to resume his illicit
profession. When a man is punished again and again for the
same crime it is obvious that the penal treatment which he
has received has not been such as to secure the protection of
society. Under a system of individualization, the period of
incarceration can be utilized for purposes of reëducation and
the establishment of habits of regular industry, and release
takes place only after satisfactory progress in this reëducation
accompanied by evidence of a reformed disposition. Moreover, release is not unconditional but the state insists upon
the pursuit of an honest calling and upon proper habits
and associations, and will recommit the offender without
retrial if his conduct is such as to convince the proper authority that his continued liberty is a menace to the public
safety.

[1] Wines: Punishment and Reformation. Crowell and Co., 1895,
p. 225.

The Jail.—All students of this subject agree in denouncing the stupidity and the demoralizing effects of the jails in which misdemeanants are confined. The ordinary county jail is regarded as probably the most efficient school of crime ever devised.

Here prisoners spend their thirty or sixty or ninety days in idleness, usually supplied with tobacco and cards, entertaining each other with such conversation as their character prompts. Here the vicious and hardened impart their outlook upon life, as well as specific lessons in vice and crime, to endangered youth, to first offenders, and often even to innocent accused persons and detained witnesses. In most counties there is not enough money available and not a sufficient number of prisoners, to seem to justify spending the money that would be required to secure adequate discipline, regular industry, and some educational and reformatory influences. These things are provided for felons who have graduated from our jails but not for misdemeanants. It would be a great gain if misdemeanants were committed to workhouses properly administered and supervised by the state and located at such intervals as local conditions require. Possibly in some of the most sparsely settled states this will for a time be impracticable. The objection of the labor unions to convict labor has weight when the labor is for the benefit of a contractor, but not when it is part of a policy necessary to the common good.

Other Suggestions.—It has been suggested that convicts in penitentiaries and in the proposed workhouses be paid something for their labor so that they may have the feeling of an honest dollar, so that they may leave the place of confinement with a little money truly earned, and especially in order that those with families may be made to contribute something toward their support during the period of confinement.

In several of the chief American cities, including New York and Boston, fines may be paid in installments, so that men need not so often be committed for non-payment of fine to jails where they cannot pay, and where they are demoralized, and so that misdemeanants may keep themselves instead of being kept by the city or county.

It is argued that an acquitted person be indemnified for the costs to which he has been put and the loss of his time, and that a person proved to be innocent, after serving a sentence, have financial redress.[1]

It is argued that since the law exists to protect the citizens, the person injured by a crime should benefit by the fine collected, and that a thief should be compelled to make good the loss his act has caused, if necessary out of wages earned in confinement.

Juvenile Courts.—Most of the recommendations above discussed for individualizing the treatment of accused persons have been adopted in a larger part of the United States in the treatment of juvenile delinquents.

Inestimable as are the advantages of juvenile court methods in turning aside endangered youth from courses of crime "the chief significance of the juvenile court movement is that in breaking away from the old procedure it is preparing the way for a new procedure for adults as well as for juveniles."[2]

Juvenile courts were first established in large cities, but later certain states[3] have authorized all county judges in dealing with prisoners under eighteen years of age to suspend the ordinary rules of criminal procedure and adopt the juvenile court methods; and have authorized every county board to appropriate funds to pay the salary of a probation officer appointed by the court. Such appropriations can be justified in the eyes of county officials on the ground of immediate economy alone, for they save the cost of criminal prosecution and it is less expensive to have juvenile delinquents at school

[1] John E. Schuyler, released from prison in New Jersey, Dec. 23, 1915, after eight years' imprisonment for a murder, of which he had been convicted on circumstantial evidence, and which another man finally confessed, had lost $13,040 in wages and costs. There was no way in which he could recover a dollar.

[2] Maurice Parmelee: Anthropology and Sociology in Relation to Criminal Procedure. Macmillan, 1908, p. 176.

[3] Illinois was the first state to pass such a law.

under the care of a probation officer than to keep them in jail.[1] And when we take into account the criminal careers averted, the cost of detective and police service, and of prison terms rendered unnecessary, the depredations prevented, and the boys saved, the argument cannot be resisted by a mind conversant with the facts.

The principles of juvenile court procedure are as follows: (1) The object is not to punish a specific act but to understand the case and devise treatment calculated to prevent the beginning or continuance of a criminal career. (2) There is no prosecution but rather an investigation, the state seeking facts both favorable and unfavorable to the accused, and the probation officer and the judge assuming the relation of friends and advisers having no tolerance for evil conduct but desiring to save the child from evil conduct and so from its consequences. (3) Where there is reasonable hope of cooperation from the endangered child probation is granted under the supervision of an officer of the court. (4) The investigation is extended to the social environment of the child and an effort made to improve it by enforcing laws relating to child labor, school attendance, parental non-support, neglect contributory to delinquency, etc. (5) There is avoidance of publicity and of all association with criminals. To prevent criminal association and the criminal stigma no child should be sent to jail. In the larger cities and towns a special place of detention for juvenile delinquents is provided, the influences of which are intended to be helpful instead of debasing.

The good effect of the juvenile court often reaches to the gang from which the boy comes. A new attitude on the part of the boys is developed toward law and government no longer represented solely by the uncomprehending policeman, the street boy's hereditary foe. Even the policeman himself

---

[1] It is reported that during a certain period 454 cases were brought before the juvenile court of Denver at a cost of $14,648, which otherwise would have come under regular criminal court procedure at a cost of $105,455.60, and that in three years the saving by this means was $288,000.

may catch some new ideas concerning the treatment of boys. And the boys through association with the judge and the probation officer have opportunity to catch the view of a civilized and even a public-spirited life policy which often they otherwise would fail to get.

War.—War is not crime because there is no authority competent to make and enforce criminal laws against the acts of nations. Except for this difference war is crime raised to the nth power.

War is instinctive action. The instinct of partisanship, which on one side is loyalty and devotion, on the other side bigotry and hate, the instinct of dominance which makes the strong love to assert their strength over rivals, and the instinct of pugnacity urge nations to war.

The very same instincts urge tribes and clans to feuds and strong and assertive individuals to broils. Feuds and broils are condemned by popular sentiment and almost suppressed in civilized society because there is a power strong enough to discipline individuals and clans.

If there were an authority powerful enough to discipline the nations it would certainly make criminal laws which would punish the violation of treaties and the warlike invasion of territory. Every reason against private perfidy and violence holds good against war. War is not the expression of reason but of instinct, and there is no such thing as civilization on the level of reasonless instinct. As chieftains punished broils because they weakened the group, so an authority capable of legislating for the nations would punish wars because they weaken the international society of the civilized world. The periodic destruction of wealth by war postpones the time when universal plenty will extend to every normal life. The resources consumed by war would suffice to finance every plan of progress, that is now postponed.[1]

---

[1] "Many men keep in their minds some particular piece of possible expenditure which they think to be needed, and against which as a 'margin' they balance alternative expenditure. I sometimes use for this purpose the 5,000 children who, in the poorer parts of London,

Most great wars are fratricidal. The worst wars and the worst misunderstandings, prejudices and hatreds bred by war are as a rule between strong nations closely akin. The ultimate struggle for world supremacy is to be between the pioneering white race, and the prolific, patient, deft, disease-resisting, light-feeding yellow race. A European war is like the feuds between the Saxon kings which made them the prey of the Danes, and the inter-tribal hostility of the Indians which made them unable to resist the early feeble colonies of whites in North America. We wonder at their folly but we are governed by the same instincts. All great nations are brave; it is silly vanity for any one of them to claim unique excellence in this respect. Triumph and predominance in the final balance between the peoples of the earth as to their participation in coming history, whether won by warlike or by peaceful competition, will not be decided by mere physical courage and pugnacity but by other qualities, including reasonable wisdom.

The saying of Dr. Wines that "crime is imbecility, and it is as impossible to regard it with intellectual respect as it is to regard it with moral approval," is equally true of war. In the words of another writer, "Since two nations find it impossible to destroy their own treasures and slaughter their own sons, they accomplish the same result by exchanging work," and so they "take the sword and perish by the sword."

The crimes of individuals, of highwaymen and pirate, often show strategy and courage. And what boy is beyond finding pleasure in tales of outlaw deeds? War has the zest of action at terrific intensity. It is an intoxication of instinctive life, and is as tempting as strong drink. Men are born savages as truly as they are born naked. We delight in tales of battle,

are at any given moment kept away from school and confined to their frowsy living rooms by ringworm. If the state were willing to incur the necessary expense ringworm could be completely stamped out in England, and the present reason why it is not stamped out is that we have preferred to spend on dreadnoughts the money which might have been given in subsidies for local medical treatment." Wallas: The Great Society, p. 168. This is a small and marginal item in the program of amelioration.

and glorify the warrior in song and story. Moreover, the partisanship of the individual soldier frequently shows more of beautiful devotion than of hideous prejudice and hate; and it is the devotion that orators and poets celebrate, while they would let us forget the prejudice and hate. But devotion, strategy, courage, and grim constancy of determination are required in peaceful social life, without the foolish bigotry of prejudice and without the hate. And even wrath and hate, if they are good or necessary, can find sufficient scope without the orgy of war. In peace all the greater strength of devotion, courage, and constancy is required, because these qualities are not stimulated by an intoxication of excited passion. The percentage of men who are morally unequal to the demands of peace indicates that these demands of peace are hard and high. The commonest life cannot be well lived without the silent practice of heroic virtues.

Nations tempted to war defend and glorify war and need to feel a world sentiment condemning it, just as the ruffianly savage whom the chief suppressed gloried in his depredations until he felt the weight of group opinion and the strength of the chieftain's hand. Individuals, dynasties, and nations can usually believe that what they mightily want to do is right. It often requires only a slim show of reason to convince desire of its own justification. The nations that hoped to profit by war, whose circumstances powerfully aroused the instinctive urgency to fight, have not wished to believe that war was wrong, or that it could be avoided. The classes that have had social control in the nations of Europe have maintained a cult of war, which holds that war is on the whole a normal and desirable expression of human strength and virtue, that its occurrence is inevitable, and that the greatness and even the safety of every nation require the nations to go armed like the men in a lawless mining camp. The last item in this cult may be true so long as the first two are believed. This creed taken as a whole is in part a survival from a more brutal past and in part an instance of the power of social control to mold public sentiment and belief. It contains only enough elements of plausibility to make its falsehood dangerous. It is the existence of this cult that has done most to create a situation which ought to be the final *reductio ad absurdum* of war, a situation in which vast populations, made up for the most part of peaceable, loveable, and industrious individuals, whose best instincts are far more violated than expressed thereby, are forced unwillingly and in self-defense to enter into a terrific struggle to destroy each other. As yet war is inevitable, but this in our day is due only in a subordinate degree to the fact that fierce instincts and economic rivalry are not balanced by good will and reason; it is due more to the fact that the past reign of force has left unstable boundaries of states and a heritage of hate and fear. Most of all, war is inevitable to-day because men think it so and have devised the mechanism of war instead of the mechanism of peace. If the nations get enough of war so that they break the spell of this erroneous creed and set their hearts on peace, they will have no difficulty in finding abundant reasons to prove that war is wrong or in devising a program for the promotion of peace.

That program, however, must itself be in some degree warlike. Those nations that propose to establish peace must arm as the policeman does, and may even invade, as the policeman does when provided with a warrant to search and seize. A coalition of nations adequate to command the respect of the world and strong enough to punish a criminal nation must undertake to act as the ally of any nation that is obliged to defend itself against robbery and murder. It could also announce itself as the ally of any nation that was ready to submit its dispute to adjudication and abide by the result, as against an opposing nation that refused to accept the legal settlement of its dispute. An international public sentiment expressed in such a coalition could establish a world peace. It is hard to see that any other means could accomplish that infinitely to be desired end. The accomplishment of that end alone can justify the right of mankind to its self-chosen title of *homo sapiens*. There ought soon to be such a coalition of nations in the new world, pledged to the proposition that there shall never be another international war in this hemisphere.

Such a coalition must set itself against the aggrandizement of the strong by forcible acquisition of new territory, and must exercise its power to secure the drawing of national boundaries with reference to ties of blood and of culture, the only method that will conduce to peace and happiness. Future conquest of territory must be by a method that can be more effective than war and wholly beneficial; namely, by peaceful migration of members of the expanding and dominating race and by the spread of the ideas and sentiments and enlightened practices which such a race originates.

The exercise of force by a strong coalition, though it be the main agency in the establishment of peace among the nations, is not the only agency that will play a part. That result will depend also upon growth of the international public opinion that regards perfidy and violence by a nation as ignominious. And in part it will depend upon the developed individuality of the modern cosmopolitan, a type of individuality that is being developed through the same agencies that in any department of human action have already improved the ratio of sane reason and right sentiment to bigotry, passion, and folly. Ultimately the cult of war, in so far as it is an artificial cult, will be dispelled, and there will be a custom of settling international questions by law. Then war will violate the "group-expectation" of the world, and will be as bad form as a broil between gentlemen.

Those who prove the impracticability of a condition in which nations will be as peaceable and as law-abiding as individuals have become, are in a position like that of those who proved the impracticability of democratic government, of the abolition of slavery, of railroads, and of every great project that has ever broken with the past.[1]

---

[1] The section beginning on p. 648 is an essential part of the discussion of war.

CHAPTER XXXIV

RELIGION, PUBLIC OPINION, AND POLITICS AS AGENCIES OF SOCIAL CONTROL

Legal Religion.—When studying the evolution of religion we saw that religion originally had no connection with righteousness. Even to this day legal religion spends its heaviest thunderings upon the enforcement of observances and other strictly religious requirements and sets an absurdly low estimate upon "mere morality." In its origin religion was simply a way of avoiding the disfavor and securing the favor of unseen powers by means of "ritual." Men had little or no thought that the unseen beings would be pleased with socially beneficent conduct. We have seen also how naturally fear of the wrath or desire for the favor of the spirits of departed ancestors became a means of enforcing tribal customs and group morality, and how the ruling chief or patriarch or prophet was prone to threaten not only the sanctions of his own wrath but also those of the offended deities, and to promise rewards which living rulers could not bestow. In this way legal religion became a bulwark of earthly sovereignty and all of the chief means of social control were consolidated in the hands of one ruling class. This has been the case until the recent popular demand for separation between church and state. Indeed it is so still to a considerable degree in all monarchical countries with "established" churches. Of this Russia is the extreme example, but even democratic England preserves decided remnants of this consolidation of earthly and divine authority. Where this is true the powerful influence of the church mingles suggestions of loyalty to an earthly ruling class with the very prayers of the people, and a Tory Heaven blesses dutiful adherence to the existing régime. In very early stages of social development the sanctions of religion were mostly, if not wholly, anticipated in this earthly life. The religious and obedient were to prosper in basket and in store, their flocks should be free from murrain, their corn from blight and mildew, their fig-trees should not cast their unripe figs, they should divide the spoil of their enemies, and their descendants should possess the land. Even here and now many a Bible is put in the trunk with the same feelings that led the savage to take along his fetish; men refrain from field work on Sunday for fear their crops will suffer if they break the holy day, and contributions are made to religious causes in the belief that business prosperity will be promoted thereby. There are better reasons for thus acting.

The belief in immortality was undoubtedly fostered in part because of its possibilities as an engine of social control. When to hopes and fears for this brief life there were added the most terrific threats that imagination could devise of sufferings to be eternally endured, there was a form of sanction that gave pause to the fiercest passions, and could turn the medieval baron into an anchorite. There is no doubt that among the effects of these fears there has been more or less good. Some drunkards have been turned from their cups; the hand of cruelty and the practice of fraud have sometimes been stayed. Year after year the number of illegitimate births in the poorest and most ignorant but most Catholic counties of Ireland is only half what it is in the most prosperous and enlightened counties of Scotland.

It is no part of our task to raise the question what among all the teachings of religions concerning the hereafter is to be believed. But we must observe the tremendous power which belief in religious sanctions in time and eternity have had and still have. They have one incalculable advantage over every other form of control by sanction, namely, the offender does not have to be "caught." They control secret acts, for the eye "that seeth in secret" cannot be avoided or deceived. Moreover, unlike the other forms of control by sanctions, legal religion has as great a hold upon the rich and powerful as upon the poor and weak. The court of heaven cannot be defied by the mighty, bribed by the rich, or evaded by the cunning. This form of control, while still of great importance, tends to play a diminishing rôle. While the religion of fear, especially in its cruder forms, lessens in power, there are other aspects of religion which in an atmosphere of growing intelligence may show a more lasting vitality. The religion of love dreads to violate a prized relationship with an unseen Friend. And the religion of loyalty causes the worshiper to feel himself a co-worker in a Divine system of things. The religion of fear represses sins, but the religion of love and loyalty ennobles the inner springs of life and calls forth a devotion of service.

Public Sentiment.—Another form of control by sanctions remains to be considered, and it is probably the most powerful as well as the most original of all, namely, control by the sanctions of public sentiment. This is one of the instinctive elements in natural social order.

It becomes an element of conscious social direction not only in that the expression of social approval and disapproval is sometimes prompted by desire to affect conduct but also and especially, in that the molding of public sentiment by leaders and by the folk-sense, is guided by a knowledge of its power over the conduct of individuals. Reformers, prophets, priests, and all persons in authority, and also the folk-sense of the multitude are canny in their efforts to mold prevailing sentiment into approval toward beneficial conduct and into hostility toward the conduct which is feared. Practically every one of us in the expressions of approval and disapproval with which common conversation is highly spiced exercises a power that may surpass the power of the ballot in enforcing the public will and also in shaping the public will. This is the most democratic of all forms of government. This direct pressure of public sentiment exercises control over the conduct of every member of society. Yet democratic as it is, even this agency of control can be turned into a bulwark of class privilege through the activity of those who control the education of public sentiment. However, there is not one of us but may have a voice in molding public opinion, and the expressions of most of us are in some degree influenced by a dim or vivid consciousness that we exercise this power. Public sentiment is largely an expression of emotional likes and dislikes, rather than of rational judgments, but it is also an expression of practical fears and hopes. We all condemn the conduct that seems likely to imperil our interests, while we praise the conduct that promises us benefits.

The sanctions of public sentiment unlike those of law, as law is now administered, include rewards equally with punishments; therefore, this agency has power not only to repress bad conduct, but also to elicit the conduct that is socially desired.

And the power of public sentiment is stupendous. Even the law depends for its efficiency upon the force of public sentiment. Not only is it true that without public sentiment convictions are difficult or impossible to secure, and laws likely to become "dead letters" but even when conviction has taken place the fact that conviction carries with it social condemnation is what chiefly gives to legal penalties their sting. "Thirty days in jail" has a social significance vastly more deterrent than the deprivation of comfort and liberty. Success is in general largely the gift of our associates, and depends upon our taking the courses which they approve, and failure is the penalty of their condemnation. Moreover, we are so constituted that our happiness or our misery are directly conditioned by the attitude of our fellows. Affection and respect make a man rich, of whatever else he may be deprived; without them, though possessed of every other good, he is in bitter poverty. Complete withdrawal of respect, esteem, and recognition affect us as the frosts of autumn affect the flowers, but when they are given us all our powers unfold and blossom like flowers in the sunshine of spring.

Besides the fact that it has power as great to elicit good conduct as to repress the bad, public sentiment, as an agency of control, has this further advantage over the law, that it requires no doubtful, difficult, and expensive process of conviction.

The clumsy and uncertain hammer of the law comes down upon certain of the most outstanding faults, but the pneumatic pressure of group sentiment enters into the recesses and crevices of conduct. It presses lightly upon small derelictions, and overwhelms great sins with its ruinous weight. It even finds its way within our own bosoms and becomes the voice of conscience.

Yet it is not a perfect agency of control because it is sometimes foolish and never altogether wise. It has the power to elicit any form of service up to the very measure of human possibility. Men will "seek glory e'en at the cannon's mouth." It can repress instincts, evoke heroism, turn the ambition of men toward art, literature, science, and constructive statesmanship. But it may shower its rewards instead upon the prize-fighter, the soubrette, the boss, and the successful speculator. It may stone the prophets, and damn its benefactors with faint praise. It may rage at harmless offenses against custom like vegetarianism, long hair, or bloomers, while customary grossness goes unrebuked, and familiar sins unpunished. Moreover, it may be servile before the rich and great. It hushes its condemnation if the liaison is that of a prince, and toward the rich sybarite and the successful slave of mammon its smile does not freeze into the merited frowning scorn and its cordiality is not transmuted into the cold shoulder of ostracism. And in the populous city the common sinner escapes the visitations of public sentiment under the cloud of anonymity, or seeks sociability in a circle of his own kind. And the control of public sentiment is baffled when responsibility is not individualized, but spread out over a "board of directors" or an administrative "department."

However, public sentiment remains the most original and pervasive and probably also the most powerful of all the agencies of social control by sanction. It is capable of progressive development, as the experience of ages becomes crystallized in definite judgments, incorporated into the "common-sense"; as newly developed possibilities of good and evil become more generally understood; as the general level of personality is raised by the agencies of education; and as the method of organization gives increasing definiteness and publicity to social responsibility.

Politics in the Light of Sociological Principles.—The principles of sociology are applicable to politics as to all other forms of social activity. Politics, whatever else it may be, is primarily a method of social control. Political control in its characteristic form is control by sanctions. Political activity may be directed toward other aims than the preservation of social order by the operation of sanctions, but even when directed toward economic or educational ends its peculiar effectiveness depends upon the fact that it is founded upon the police power, the power to control by sanctions which renders possible the collection of taxes, and the enforcement of other requirements.

A democratic state is an independent political society, organized to promote the interest of its members through the exercise of sovereignty. All the legal powers of minor political units as cities, rest back upon the sovereign power. Sovereignty is that power which no other power within the state can successfully oppose.

Politics, like agriculture, medicine, and the other great practical arts, made progress by the method of trial and error, before there was any fundamental science by which it could be guided. But political institutions are evolved,[1] and political movements take place, in accordance with the causal principles elaborated by sociology. Without attempting here to make any detailed applications of sociological principles to political phenomena two remarks may be made.

1. In the deepest sense, *the real constitution of a state* is not a written document, but an actual situation created by prevalent ideas and sentiments. Some of these ideas form institutions; others are of a more fleeting or irrational character. It is constitutionality as tested by this pervasive but subtle and complex unwritten constitution (of opinions and sentiments) that sets the bounds and prescribes the methods of successful legislation. It is the amendment of this un-

---

[1] Compare Part iii, "Social Evolution."

written constitution that is the fundamental reform. The written constitution of the United States is that of an aristocratic confederacy; the unwritten constitution has become modified into that of a federal union of far more democratic character. If England had a written constitution it would be that of a monarchy, but though it has a king and lords, by virtue of its unwritten constitution it is politically the most democratic country in the world. The written constitution of Mexico and of the troubled South American republics are modeled after that of the United States, but it is the unwritten social constitution that really governs, or fails to govern, and these in such republics are vastly different from that of the United States. It is the study of this social constitution and the method of its life—for it is a living thing, that is, a thing composed of activities, and constantly evolving —that can make our political knowledge more than empirical.

Laws grow; they are not made, save in a limited sense. There were laws long before there were constitutional assemblies or legislatures. And the statesman is like the gardener who cultivates and reaps a crop, more than he is like a mechanic who fashions what he will. There is much truth, if some exaggeration, in the simile which compares the legislator to the grammarian who does not make the laws of languages but discovers, states, and helps to enforce the laws which usage makes. It is true that legislators are among the leaders of the people, and law is one of the agencies for forming public opinion, but it is only one; and it is more an instrument for carrying public opinion into effect. It is a part of the function of intelligent legislators to ally themselves with the wisest and best leaders of the people. Good legislation in general sets down only that which largely has become, or is on the point of becoming, the will of the social sovereign.[1] But there is often division and opposition among

---

[1] "The idea that institutions (legislative enactments) can remedy the defects of society and that social changes can be effected by decrees, is still generally accepted, and the social theories of the present day are based upon it. The most continuous experience has

unrelated individual is a mere splinter. Professor Royce[1] is right in saying that man is contented only in loyalty to something bigger than himself. And what is bigger than man? Men. There is not a social situation from a dinner party to a senate in which there are not possibilities of good waiting to be realized but depending for their realization upon the loyalty of each member to social aims. The centaur or the satyr, the being with but half-developed humanity, may content himself without the supremacy of the social spirit—but not man, full grown, and it is man full grown whose needs and possibilities must be considered in the formation of a social program of education. Man can never grow to the full stature of humanity, except when life is animated by devotion to an aim that is big enough to be worth sacrificing for, worth living and dying for. This is the redeeming feature of war, that men see something at stake that is worth devotion. But there is always that at stake which is worth devotion if we were so instructed as to see. War, especially modern war, is mainly negative and men die to save their nation from destruction. Peace is positive and men live to bring their nation to fulfillment. But construction of good does not appeal to instinct as do destruction and defense; and so constructive peace must depend for motive less on instinct, and more on reason and enlightenment. By mere instinct men will not give themselves to produce gradual good, as they will to prevent sudden destruction, and do not know that the word truly spoken at cost, often counts more for the good that is worth dying for than the bullet bravely sped, and that the sacrifices of a devoted ambition are more heroic than sudden and bloody death. The coöperative enterprise of social life is the great summons to ennobling devotion. To make this plain to the common-sense of the people, as the summons of war is plain, is the highest aim of education.

The preceding paragraphs have been devoted to the idea that the virtues are essential to the complete self-realization of the individual. Now conversely we proceed to observe that *interests, appreciations, and powers, though primarily they*

[1] Josiah Royce: The Philosophy of Loyalty. Macmillan Co., 1908.

are developed capacities for individual experience, are also essential to society.[1] All education is the eliciting of activity. Sanctions suppress and mold from the outside; but education displaces objectionable conduct by evoking sentiments and ideas hostile to evil and promotive of good. A bane and peril of education is that it may insist that suggested ideas and radiated sentiments shall be given back untinged by individual reaction, and that it may produce a standardized output of imperfect reflections and echoes of accepted social activities, instead of developing power and individuality. The principle that all education is elicitation of activity should guide our educational methods. It is obvious that developed powers on the part of individuals are essential to the general welfare and progress of society. Without them the good intentions of the social spirit would be futile. But it is also to be noted that developed interests and appreciations though less obviously so, are no less truly essential to society. There is no little truth in the view of Professor Patten that man lives at first in a pain economy. That is to say, his activity is called out mainly in efforts to ward off hunger, cold, mysterious disease, hostile beasts, and more hostile men; such pleasures as he enjoys are mainly those connected with the functioning of the instincts necessary to survival. Later, having subdued nature to his uses, he enters upon a pleasure economy, in which the motive of his activity is not the avoidance of pains but the securing of pleasures. Various peoples have entered upon a pleasure economy, for a brief period of glory, only to sink rapidly into decay. The lasting welfare and progress of a society which has entered upon a pleasure economy depends in part upon the strength of its virtues, but it depends also and perhaps still more upon the popularization of the innocent and ennobling pleasures. Such pleasures are found especially in athletic sports, in society, in science, in the arts, and in literature. Why is it that on Monday morning so many more men than on other

---

[1] Spencer: Principles of Ethics. Appleton and Co., 1901, Vol. 1, chap. ii, "Egoism versus Altruism"; and chap. xii, "Altruism versus Egoism."

days are missing from their places in shop and factory and so many more are in jails and hospitals? It is because the common man has had some leisure to do as he pleased, and he pleased to do what was not good for him. The pitiful thronging of men on Saturday nights from the pay-window to the saloon, the brothel, the tawdry, inartistic show or the dingy tobacco-reeking loafing place, the barrenness, and the blasting curse of leisure, the leisure that should be a crowning blessing, must be combated by the popularization of better pleasures. The leisure of common men is rapidly increasing and the problem of pleasure is becoming fuller and fuller of the possibilities of good and of the possibilities of evil. The "higher" pleasures are not to be regarded merely as safeguards, substitutes for "lower" and more dangerous delights. They are essential parts of life. Yet beauty has also a survival value, else how could the predisposition to enjoy it have been evolved? The perception of beauty in nature is an instance of adaptation to environment. A happy person, a barefoot farmer's lad whistling down the lane, usually does not know why he is happy. Beauty when felt creates an atmosphere, a psychic climate, favorable to growth and vigor. The sense of beauty is, like conscience, developed and directed by culture, but made possible by a foundation in instinctive predisposition. Its survival value is not biological alone but spiritual also, as the church has not failed to perceive. Goethe declared that art saved his soul. But the sense of beauty is not to be valued merely as favorable to health, survival, or even as a means of saving the soul, but for its own sake. It is one of the ultimate human experiences that are good in and of themselves. And so are all the pleasures in their due measure and subordination to the whole of life. But at this point we are interested by the proposition that the development of tastes is important not only to the individual, but also to society, and is an essential factor in the program of social control. The fitness of men to occupy a place in society, as well as the worth of their lives to themselves, depends in no small degree on what they have learned to like. Ruskin was not far wrong in declaring that education consists in causing people to like what they ought to like.

The foregoing statements concerning tastes require to be especially applied to the development of intellectual interests. Pleasure is not a thing apart from activity or functioning; it is to be found in the satisfaction of every predisposition. The last of the "general" predispositions, namely, the predisposition to curiosity and mental activity (in the narrow sense of the word "mental") has its pleasures as well as any of the others.

The hungry mind will occupy itself with something, even if it be nothing better than puzzles in the back of the weekly paper, or trivial gossip. And so long as we are interested we have pleasure. Two old men gossiping may be poor, rheumatic, without honors or high hopes, but they are not without pleasure so long as they are interested. The mind's appetite is greatest for knowledge about our own kind, and what an infinite supply for this hunger is available: in the newspaper, biography, published correspondence, anecdotes and reminiscences, descriptive travels, folklore, and history of the people of more than a score of centuries, descriptions of the teeming summoning present of which we are a part, with all its suffering and hopes and possibilities, and to supplement all, the winsomely recorded lives of the characters of fiction who have such absorbingly interesting traits and experiences. But we are interested also in the world of material realities, in the ancient records of the rocks, in the seas and harbors, rivers and mountains, in the beasts and birds and fishes and the trees and flowers. Even one of their countless subdivisions like the bees, as Maeterlinck found, affords unfailing interest for much of the pleasure time of a whole life. The mysteries of nature as they are half unraveled in the laws of the fundamental physical sciences find innumerable illustrations. Then there are the material works of man, a world of fascinating wonders. And above and beneath and through it all run the deep questions of philosophy.

There is no necessity that the life of any normal human being should revolve in a petty orbit, from the work-bench to the dinner-table, to the barber-shop, to bed and back to the work-bench. One need not have developed all the interests, but he is impoverished indeed if he have no interest to which he turns with zest when leisure comes. Developed interests, like other developed tastes, are not only an antidote to degrading and destructive allurements, they are a positive addition to life's pleasure and worth. They enable man to live in a big world and an ennobling world, instead of a petty and degrading one.

Moreover, they enlarge man's powers. His powers are like sleeping giants until interest arouses them and calls them forth. We hear a great deal about interest as an aid to the learning process, as if learning were the end and interest only a means. It would be at least as near the truth to regard knowledge as a means to developing and satisfying interests, and developed interests as the end. If not the aim, at least one chief aim of education is to enable men to live interested lives, for it is interested lives that have both power and worth.

Power, in so far as power can be acquired by formal education, is mainly encouragement to confident self-expression, balanced but not overbalanced by socially acceptable standards of self-criticism plus stimulating interests plus useful habits of thought and action plus knowledge. An educated man is first a man who has the four virtues not only as clear judgments but also as established enthusiasms and detestations; second, he is one who is enriched with developed tastes and interests; third, his virtues and his tastes and interests must have been exercised into a framework of orderly and practical habits; fourth, in acquiring the first three, especially in acquiring tastes and interests he will have gathered considerable knowledge, and he ought also to have special knowledge of how to do some useful work. If he has all four of these he has powers and his life will have worth both to himself and to society.

The Variability of Individuals and of Society.—By finding out all we can about the causation that molds life, sociology makes it plain that the factors in that causation are numerous.

The influential and well-to-do classes that mold popular opinion are prompted by pride to assume and teach that they are what they are because of inborn excellence. Indeed, what man is so poor as not to be proud and to set up for himself a similar claim? Self-consciousness is partisan and we have strong individual pride, a considerable family pride, more or less national pride, and a weak pride in our whole culture-group. Partisan pride is strongest when we can shut out others with the clearest boundary. Sociology makes it clear that the tendency for us as individuals to shut out others in explaining to ourselves whatever excellences we claim, has gone vastly too far. It is also possible to go too far in the opposite direction and so to undervalue the importance of inborn traits as virtually to attribute everything to environment. That is not the attitude of sociology which gives as full weight to the hereditary psychophysical causes as it does to all the others. The familiar question, which makes the man, heredity or environment, is as unreasonable as it would be to ask which makes the steam, water or fire, or to ask which makes the farmer's crop, the soil and climate which nature furnishes or the planting and cultivation of the husbandman. Neither alone could accomplish the result.

The art of education like the art of agriculture deals with growing things. Though agriculture has been practiced and discussed for so many ages, and enlists the imperious bread-and-butter interests, yet it is only now becoming scientific. We have already observed that in the opinion of the agronomists the yield of American corn lands could be doubled by the application of the lessons of science, and that it is equally within the truth to say that the harvest of life for the people of America could be doubled if the possibilities with which they are endowed by nature were brought to approximate realization. For this it is not enough to make the benefits of present methods in education more nearly universal, as Ward so impressively advocated, important as that is. It is essential to introduce into our education guiding principles which have been only dimly apprehended and applied. Heredity sets the limits within which individual development can vary. By all means let us do what we can by the program of eugenics, by selective regulation of immigration, and by promotion of public health, to improve the biological quality of population. But after all is done we shall have the problem of making the most of the latent possibility of each rising generation just as the farmer has the problem of securing the largest yield and highest conservation of his land. And as the same land may yield little or much and that which it yields may be corn, alfalfa, or weeds, so the same population may yield Periclean achievement and levels of character which we know only by rare but blessed instances, or futility and deviltry.

Within the limits set by birth, individuality is a social product. Without education by social contacts there would be no such thing as individuality as we understand that term. Social contacts begin to be educative among the higher animals. Social relations not only determine that there shall be self-consciousness, but even more certainly they determine what the nature of the self-thought shall be. We inherit contrasting instincts, instincts of competition and of coöperation, of self-assertion and of loyal self-subordination. Social contacts have power to determine whether the self-thought, to which both spontaneously and voluntarily a man's acts conform, shall be one of swaggering self-assertion, of more refined self-aggrandizement, or predominantly one of service. The self-thought is complex; social contacts determine the nature of the elements which it contains. And the further development of personality is largely a reaction between the self-thought already established and the subsequent stream of social suggestion.

Without social contacts we should have no language and no need of any, for we should be about equally destitute of thoughts requiring the medium of words and of the words in which to formulate thoughts. We should be dumb brutes. We should be more heathen than any heathen. Each hour of civilized life is a social heritage. Any one of us would find it hard to name one definite thought, desire, or any element of conscious life aside from sense perception and the functioning of his animal organism of which he can say: "this is mine by virtue of my inborn gifts alone; I owe it to no associate."

However highly the biological mechanism of life may be developed, that alone cannot make men and women. Men and women are social products.

By social evolution there have been developed languages, religions, moral conceptions and conscience codes, sciences, mechanic arts, methods of political and judicial organization, and all customs and institutions. Social evolution still goes on and shows no signs of abatement. Instead, social progress makes further progress possible. The work of thousands of investigators of electricity from Thales down culminates in the discovery of Hertzian waves; this discovery becomes the property of the world, and hundreds of laboratories thereupon become tense with the possibility of wireless telegraphy. Each social mutation that takes place in the mind of a Marconi is the culmination of a process of social evolution, and when added to the common stock becomes a starting-point for new advance. The elements of previous progress enter into fertile combination and give birth to new progeny of ideas or sentiments.

Education has for its business to make each individual born into the world an heir of all the ages. Each is born naked of soul as of body; rich, if rich at all, only in possibilities. Each begins at the very commencement of social progress. Some advance only a little way in their three-score years and ten. Many are molded in youth by contact with those who are not bearers of the ripened culture of the ages. The character of society to-day and its possibilities of progress depend upon the degree to which the social store becomes the possession not of a few fortunates, but of all.

With all regard for material causes of social effects and for all due qualifications, there remains great truth in the saying of Comte that "ideas rule the world or throw it into chaos." The most needed reform in the world of education is a more adequate idea of the variability of individuality, of the fact that the harvests a life may yield are as various as the crops that an acre may bear. A boy born in the corn belt and inheriting one hundred and sixty acres of its black soil is likely to become a farmer; if born with identical endowments on an island off the coast of Maine there is likelihood that he would become a fisherman or a sailor; if born with those same endowments in Turkey and seeing only Turks he would have been a Turk, have spoken the Turkish language and believed in Mohammedanism and polygamy. Jerry Macaulay during half his life was a king of toughs and terror of the police; during the latter part of his life he was a saint and a savior to his kind. Both men were in Jerry Macaulay all the time; one was evoked by his early contacts, later another influence called out the other man. The often quoted statement of Goethe that he never heard of a crime that he himself might not have committed, did not mean, I think, merely that he felt such evil instincts within him, but that he caught a glimpse of the great truth that with other social contacts he would have been another man. As the insight of his genius caught a glimpse of the fact of biological evolution before the scientists had demonstrated it, so also he glimpsed this great conclusion before the facts of comparative sociology had made it stand forth in its momentous dimensions. Of the traits that make Christ the Savior one of the chief was his power to discover the unrealized possibilities in man. In the publican he saw the apostle, and in the Magdalen he saw the saint. It is only as education is guided by similar vision that it can accomplish its saving mission and fulfill the larger destiny to which it is called.

Sociology reveals the variability of human life, not only, as just indicated, by pointing out the numerous and variable causes by which it is molded, but also by comparing the heterogeneous effects that actually issue. Comparative sociology breaks up "the illusion of the near." Men who had grown up in the vast steppes and had no conception of mountains or forests or sea would have a clear and definite conception of nature. And if told of vegetation towering a hundred feet into the sky they would either regard it as magical or treat with laughter or indignation such an insult to their knowledge concerning the limits to variation set by nature. Similarly it is necessary for us to learn that "human nature" determines only within wide limits what men shall regard as beautiful, what things they shall desire, what ambitions they shall pursue, or what they shall regard as right or wrong. That is to say, it leaves undetermined, save by wide limits, what their character and content of life and personality shall be. We have seen that human nature does not prevent men from seeing beauty in yellow cheeks and eyes aslant and blackened teeth and feet deformed to lumps and beards dyed in bright colors, or from regarding the eating of a dead parent's body as a seemly mark of respect; that social influence does more than human nature to determine musical preference for a bedlam of squawks, squeals, clangs, and bangs, or for simple melodies, or for the intricate harmonies and subharmonies of Wagner; that birth from a rake who is called a duke, or ability to pound an opponent's face, may at one time and place set a man higher in social regard than virtue coupled with ordinary or even extraordinary usefulness, and at other times and places have no such power; that social molding can build consciences that approve not only of slavery, as did many of the most Christian and most charming people in America till recently, and polygamy, as Abraham and a majority of the wise and good men of the past have done, but also infanticide, human sacrifice, killing the aged, and wife-lending, as a duty of hospitality; "that the mores can make anything seem right."

The degree of achievement is more dependent upon heredity than the directions of effort, of interest, of enthusiasm, and of character.[1] Birth largely determines which individuals shall go further than others in achievement, and whether any in a given group shall attain the highest ranges of accomplishment, but society has more to do with deciding whether its members go as far and as high as their nature allows, and

---

[1] "The important moral traits seem to be matters of the direction of capacities and the creation of desires and aversions by environment to a much greater extent than the important qualities of intellect and efficiency." Thorndike: Educational Psychology, p. 45.

above all, society has more to do in deciding the direction in which its activities flow.

Education the Chief Agency of Social Control.—The direction of ambition is socially determined. We want to be winners at the game that is being played. The small boy's springtime obsession for marbles is gone long before fall, because "the boys aren't playing marbles any more." The Indian who dreamed and longed and risked his life to hang scalps at his belt, or the Igorrot who measures his success by the number of skulls over his door, or the Kafir or Thibetan whose standard of greatness and mainspring of endeavor is the size of his herd, or the American toiling to make a high score at the dollar-piling game and to support his wife in competitive ostentation, have not selected these goals as an expression of their own independent individuality. The operation of the same principle of the molding of personal ambition by social radiation caused the Spartans to despise money. The swift advance of Germany from the foot to the head of great European powers has been due largely to the fact that achievement in science has been a goal of ambition of her most gifted sons, so that by her application of science to industry and government she has been able to redemonstrate the truth that knowledge is power. A traveler in Florence asked one of the curly-headed, great-eyed urchins of its streets what he would like to be when he grew up, and the boy replied, "A sculptor." Now, Florence has sculptors, though not all of her sculptors are great. A street boy in an American city would not have answered so; he might have said that he wanted to become pitcher for the White Sox, or boss of the ward. Jane Addams says that in a ward chiefly inhabited by workingmen there was difficulty in replacing a corrupt boss by an honest workingman as its aldermanic representative, because the people wanted to vote for a man who was a success. Where the soubrette, the boss, the money-maker, represent success, soubrettes, bosses, and money-makers will be produced. Why did the Spartan boy let the fox gnaw his vitals without giving a sign, and why did Spartan soldiers commit suicide because they had not perished with their comrades on the battlefield?

What was it that made Spartans out of Greeks whose name elsewhere became a synonym for self-indulgence? Grit was the social ideal in Sparta. Whatever society adequately appreciates, society will get, up to the very limits of human possibility, whether it be prizefighters, money-kings, scientists, or constructive statesmen. No other reform is so fundamental as a shifting of emphasis in social valuations. Ambition in a given population or in a given individual may be drawn out in any one of various directions. Its direction and its power are not fixed by "human nature," but are matters of education.

Society must impart to its members tastes, interests, ambitions, and a set of moral detestations and moral enthusiasms strong enough to inhibit instincts and to elicit zeals—detestations and enthusiasms that are not inborn and that embody the lessons of race experience respecting the conduct of life. Nature does not give us a conscience any more than it gives us a language, but only the capacity to acquire one; social evolution and education must do the rest. The task of order and progress is not only to erect the towering structure of social organization out of individual units, but also to make the bricks of which alone such a structure can be built.

Education and Progress.—The principle of the wide variability of each individual within the limits set by nature—the fact that there is in each normal child a generous assortment of unrealized possibilities inviting any one of numerous careers, including material for devil and saint, savage or social flower, the truth that interests, tastes, ambitions and conscience vary in response to social conditions as really as language and as widely as the contrast between the Chinese or Algonquin language and our own—this momentous principle is one of the words which sociology has for the guidance of education, as important as its teachings concerning the method by which personality is socially formed and elicited. It is a principle of which common-sense perceives only a dim fragment and the proportions of which are disclosed by comparative and genetic sociology. As common-sense sees only a flat and stationary earth till science makes its disclosures, so common-sense sees a too fixed and too limiting "human nature." We know what we are but none of us knows what we might have been and none dares set limits to that which society may become. Only for a moment or two on the dial of time has man been able to leave written records. Just now electricity was known only as a destructive power, or a tiny curiosity that would move pith balls. Science has begun to make discoveries in the realm of the racial life itself. We have learned that "one man is no man" that "the individual is an abstraction," a thing that can be thought of apart from others, but that cannot so exist; that individuals are social products, and that the business of education is not merely to impart a little knowledge or teach a trade, but also and chiefly to build personalities. Human life is the most variable of all natural phenomena.

To accept the present condition of society as final would be to surrender to pessimism. Complacency that believes only what it likes to believe may protest against such fearful estimates of the progress thus far attained by humanity as have been recorded by Huxley and Wallace; but no one who knows our world as it is can willingly accept the present stage of social evolution as a stopping-place. And none who survey the past and the hole of the pit from whence we were digged need fear to hope. After a study of comparative sociology and the method of social causation we shall be slow to say that anything is forbidden by the limits of human nature. The psychophysical nature of mankind does set limits, but they are very wide apart. The unformed infants that intrust themselves to society are such material that if a single generation could be raised ideally the world would lurch forward further than it will climb in centuries. The trouble is that each generation has to be reared by the society into which it is born. Their rearing is society's supreme responsibility. This responsibility must be comprehended. It must enlist the energies of society's best and wisest to the end that every member of the new generation shall share as fully as may be the fruits of all the progress that divides us from our naked, groping, savage ancestors, and that prepares for the still better day that is to be. Not only is it as well within the bounds of scientific practicability to double the average worth of human lives as to double the harvest of our cornfields, but with that done we shall have created new collective possibilities and rendered practicable programs of organization and progress that are beyond the range of human second nature as it is molded by the society of the present.

CHAPTER XXXVI

EDUCATIONAL AGENCIES OUTSIDE THE SCHOOL

The Family.—Among educational agencies the family stands first. When at its best, the power of the family to give to personality its character and content is comparable rather with all other agencies combined than with any other single agency. But it is often far from its best. Social workers often find the delinquent and imperiled child in a home that seems to be the child's most dangerous enemy. And the assertion of parental claims upon the child may be the stubbornest obstacle to its welfare. At such a time the school, the supervised playground, the social settlement, and the juvenile court appear as the true friends of the child and the reliable educational agencies. But it would be absurd to judge the family by the instances in which it fails to discharge its function. The fact that abnormality of the family is so often the cause of juvenile misconduct emphasizes the importance of that function.

The power of the family rests partly upon sanctions, rewards, and punishments, but far more upon social suggestion, sympathetic radiation, and imitation. The greatness of this power is due to three well-known principles of social psychology: first, the naïveté and suggestibility of the child. The empty mind of the child has at first nothing to oppose to whatever ideas are presented, and it has no prejudice against whatever sentiments are radiated by its associates. Second, the principle of repetition. Even the well-fortified mind, stored with accepted tastes, approvals, and beliefs, is so susceptible to the effects of repetition as to give rise to the popular remark that it is only necessary to say a thing often enough in order to have it believed. The child in the home is subjected for years to a repetition of the same impressions.

Third, the principle of prestige. Elders have tremendous natural prestige with the young. This prestige may be lost, but it is easily retained, and in the self-respecting family it is reënforced by group pride and partisanship and by affection.

From all this it follows that in a normal household the mind of the child, its second nature, is born of its parents as truly as its body. Very early and perhaps even before he enters the schoolroom at six, the influence of the family has determined for the child and in the majority of cases for life whether he is to be Catholic or Protestant, Methodist or Presbyterian, standpatter or progressive, whether he is to use refined or degraded speech, be truthful or deceiving, a self-seeker or animated by the social spirit.

Save in a very subordinate degree it is not by precept that parents and other elder members of the family mold the children in the home. It is by daily speech and conduct; it is by the comparison between promise and performance, between words spoken before the face of a neighbor and behind his back, by self-control or lack of it in a thousand little emergencies, by the unstudied table talk, by the pleasures sought and enjoyed, by the trend of ambition.

The family in the discharge of this function must take account of the other agencies of education and coöperate with the school, the play of the children, and the church. The juvenile literature provided by the home is one of the chief agencies of education and may go far toward developing tastes, interests, sentiments, and a habit of intellectual life that will enrich all the after years.

The mother who reads to her children at bedtime in that half-hypnotic hour may build into their personality the best she knows or is or can find in the world's life. The death rates in scientifically managed foundling asylums furnish an amazing demonstration of the inadequacy of any substitute for the watchful individual care of a mother for her baby's physical life. Babies do not come in litters because one is enough to exhaust the care of a mother. And only the solicitude of individual love suffices. Even if science should succeed in providing successfully for the physical care of babies

in batches, there would remain the more exacting task of motherhood in the development of individuality. It is a task in which many mothers fail, but one in which no other agency can succeed as mothers can. No advantages of the so-called emancipation of woman can compensate society for diminished efficiency in mother-work, which is more important than any other special calling or profession.

There are a few things that have been settled, not by discussion and theory, but by the experience of peoples, not once for all but thousands of times for all, and one of these is the high social expediency of maintaining inviolate the monogamous family. But if any persist in discussing this as though it were still open to question they must not discuss it from the point of the two contracting parties alone, still less as if these two were merely cheerful animals, ignorant of life's higher values and of life's weighty responsibilities. They must discuss it with reference to four sets of interests: (1) the interests of the two contracting parties, man and woman being equally regarded. (2) Next to be considered are the interests of the children for whose bodies and souls the married pair assume responsibility. The family does not exist merely for purposes of selfish indulgence, either on the carnal or the esthetic and intellectual level; it unites duty and sacrifice with the most priceless joys, and there is no relation in life where the shirking of obligation is more to be condemned and despised. To estimate a plan of domestic organization by anything else more than by its effect upon offspring is to prostitute the institution of the family from its natural purpose. It was the interest of parents in their offspring more than the interest of men and women in each other that originally gave to the family its permanence and solidarity. It is founded upon race-preserving instinct as well as upon individualistic instinct, and if now its basis is to become rational instead of instinctive, reason must regard both these aims. (3) Other interests to be considered are those of the declining generation, which is always present in society and to which the marrying pair will sometime belong. The question what to do with the aged is a more or less puzzling one. The peaceful nook in the chimney corner in an atmosphere created by the grateful love of well-nurtured children is the best solution thus far devised. But while the duty of parents to children is primary and voluntarily assumed by all who bring children into the world, the duty of children to parents is secondary, and only those parents who have done their duty by their children can claim as a right, dutifulness from their children. Thus far the only way to make old age a period of ripe content and not of wretchedness for mankind in general is to establish the family in such solidarity that it will bear the strain of demands upon filial devotion. (4) The interests of society are to be considered. Society as a whole has a colossal stake in its domestic institutions. Society must insist that the family shall be of a type which affords great motives to every kind of productive endeavor which develops reliability of personal character and habits in men and women, which tends to secure stability in these domestic functional groups and above all one calculated to rear for society successive generations of citizens of the highest individual development.

Marriage is a product of both biologic and social evolution, the expression both of instinct and also of reason and sentiment. The awakening of the instinct requires only the presence of a normal member of the opposite sex of suitable age in the absence of any inhibiting cause. Therefore strange and undesirable matches occur because it is accidental propinquity that has made the selections. Before the mind adds its consent to instinct and the whole nature consents to love, two sets of considerations should be regarded: first: health, and inborn gifts of head and heart; second, congenial social development which shapes the habits, tastes, interests, ambitions, and ideals. Money and other things, however desirable, are vastly secondary to these personal considerations. Marriage should be based upon a love strong enough to make service a joy and to elicit upon occasion willing and silent sacrifice for the beloved. Ideals do not come true of themselves, but two who thus love, who each steadily deserve the absolute trust of the other, and who sincerely and persistently aim to make the best come true in marriage, may safely reckon upon deep and lasting joys.

Divorce.[1]—The foregoing discussion of the function of the family, together with the facts previously stated concerning the relation between family disruption and crime, emphasize the importance of the subject of divorce.

In the United States about one in every twelve marriages ends in divorce, and the ratio is much higher in some states. This condition of things has come into existence within the last generation and a half. In Switzerland, the European country that most nearly approaches us in this respect, the proportion of marriages ending in divorce is only about three-sevenths as great; in France, which stands next, it is a little more than one-third as great, and in England and Wales it is only about one-thirtieth as great.

There are two sides to this problem. There ought to be release from cruelty, drunkenness and brutal infidelity. Increase in divorce is due in part to a heightened estimate of the individual, and a proper increase of individual liberty. It is an accompaniment of the social emancipation and greater economic opportunity of woman. On the other hand there is a boundary beyond which liberty degenerates into license. Excessive laxity here may be a sign and cause of social decay. Divorce usually implies serious defect of character on the part of one or the other of the parties, or at least sad blundering.

Unquestionably the divorce laws of some of our states render separation so easy as to invite hasty and ill-considered matches. Laws that fail to require a considerable interval between the issuance of a marriage license and celebration of the ceremony have a similar effect. The lack of conformity between the marriage and divorce laws of different states of this Union gives rise to undesirable complexity and confusion.

Among the poor mere desertion largely replaces divorce. In certain American cities special "courts of domestic relations" deal with cases of desertion and non-support. Legal penalties

---

[1] See G. E. Howard: History of Matrimonial Relations. University of Chicago Press, 1904, Vol. iii, chs. xvii and xviii.

"suspended during good behavior" prove effective as motives to reform. A probation officer aids the judge to develop character in the erring parties and rehabilitate breaking families.

The divorce rate is about four times as high among childless couples as among those with children. The lack of domesticity already commented upon as a characteristic of urban life, the obliteration of the neighborhood in the city and exacting standards of economic display are contributory causes of divorces. Above all the lack of the ennobling life policy of social team work is the greatest cause of matrimonial failure, as of other social evils, while the development of such a life policy as a distinct social tradition and as an individual motive is the only radical cure.

Art and Play.—Among the primary groups the neighborhood stands next to the family. But during the impressionable years of childhood the neighborhood means, largely if not chiefly, the play group. Children learn a large part of the evil that they know from each other. Children are by nature little savages. It is of great social importance to get a civilized being into the group of little savages. And the civilized being can be *persona grata* in that company. The unsupervised city playground is comparatively deserted, while the supervised playground is thronged, for the knowledge of games is a social heritage to be taught by one who already knows, and the children can teach each other but few games; and without supervision the big boys are likely to break up the play that is attempted. The play leader who knows more about the very things that interest them than the children do, who excels them in sports, who gives them the time of their lives, easily gains great prestige with them.

The fundamental lessons of social life are readily learned on the playground. The cat, the panther, and the wolf learn their arts of life in play. We recognize that for animals play is nature's training-school. It is no less so for man. Active and vigorous play is the normal means of developing the muscles, heart, lungs, and digestive organs. It is also a means of developing the mind and nerves, alertness, resourcefulness, and self-command. Moreover, the play of children is social and is nature's opportunity for development of the social powers and virtues. Happiness, the common welfare, the success of the game, are dependent on observance of rules, on playing fair, on admitting your own fouls. The big boy must learn to stand in line and let the little boys have their turns. By supervised play children learn from experience that civilized life is far happier for all concerned than savagery. It turns out that even for the bully bullying has not so durable and satisfying charms as fair play. The bully is easily made to satisfy his sense of importance by becoming the guardian of order. On the supervised playground the grown-up world becomes the ally of childhood in its pleasures. And the regulations of the grown-up world become intelligible. Not seldom the playground actually transforms the incipient tough into an ally of the police. And where malicious mischief, petty pilfering, and juvenile vice had abounded the properly conducted playground has had the power to spread about itself an oasis of comparative immunity from juvenile delinquency. It cannot give brains to the feeble-minded, nor replace all the other agencies of social education. But it demonstrates the fact that children are provided with both the more individualistic and animal and the more human and social instincts, and that the latter respond to the proper natural elicitations. Yet we allow it to remain true that thousands grow up without a chance of acquiring a normal conception of social coöperation, its requirements, and its advantages.

The introduction into our schools of participation in self-government, with pupils as mayor, police, and council, and a teacher as court of last resort, has proved a means of developing social responsibility and the social virtues and of giving vivid instruction in the elements of politics. The pupils when intrusted with a share in discipline are more likely to be over-severe than to be lax with one another.

Play used to be regarded as characteristically the affair of children. But athletics, mountain-climbing, and the like are affairs of men. Moreover, play is not a matter of bodily activity alone; art is play, music is play, literature is play, science may be play. Play is any activity in which we engage because we like to.[1] It is the free play of our powers. In their free activities, their play, men are prone to rise high or to sink low.

To open avenues of normal pleasure is one of the measurelessly important social aims, and that not only as a substitute and preventive for destructive pleasures, but for the sake of the joy of life. The commercial amusement business, like the grocery and clothing business, ministers to a great inherent need. And the men who engage in it have as good a right as any to do so with idealism and the sense that they are discharging a highly important public function. And society should insist on pure pleasures as it insists on pure food and competent medical practice. When we contemplate the thousands who when the evening whistles blow, pour out of our factory gates weary and irked and hungry for happiness, and remember the cheerlessness of their homes, the little that has been done to awaken in them elevating tastes, and the character of the solicitations that surround them, the wonder is, not that there is so much vice among the poor but that there is so much decency. The paucity of their opportunities for the satisfying and elevating employment of leisure has been as appalling as the former omnipresence of the saloon. In nearly all cities we still tolerate the saloon, and afford no adequate substitute for it. And over the saloon we tolerate with averted faces the brothel and their close seconds and allies in infamy, the low dance hall and degenerate theater.

Play must be in line with our instincts or predispositions. The sex instinct is powerful, universal, requires no education to develop it and it costs very little to arouse it. Hence the appeal to this instinct is the most profitable form of commercialized play. Of this fact full advantage is taken by the theater and in recent times by literature. This commercialization of sex suggestion and display is intolerable.

The instinct is a useful and necessary inheritance from our animal ancestors. Its abuse is perfidy to the sacred trust we owe to posterity. Moreover, it threatens perpetually to

---

[1] For completer definition of play see p. 365.

break the bounds that must be set for it if society is to escape degeneracy and to continue to advance upon a human level. This instinct will take all the liberty that society allows it. Our grandmothers were shocked at the waltz; to-day we think of the return to the waltz and two-step as an austere reform. Society can make anything seem right, even to Roman orgies. There is constant pressure to make society draw the line nearer and nearer to the edge of the precipice; as manners grow too lax the function of the chaperon increases and finally come zenana walls. The freedom of the sexes to enjoy friendship without conscious or obvious intrusion of any physical element is conditioned upon honor and idealism and restraint. There ought to be abundant unembarrassed association between the youth of the two sexes. It is a shame to any society when this becomes difficult. To purge the speech of men and literature and the theater and the dance of every needless play upon an element in life which takes fire at suggestion and threatens to consume the social fabric is a thing greatly to be desired; and so likewise is the revival of old and the invention of new social pastimes where youths and maidens may freely mingle without offense to idealism or propriety.

The theater embodies a great and precious art. It ought to be institutionalized; which does not mean that of necessity it ought to be taken under public ownership, as is in part the case in some countries of Europe, but that it ought to be adopted as an approved and treasured element in our civilization. And because we treasure it we shall insist that it be not degraded but fulfill its possibilities. Those who are allowed for profit, to take to themselves the tremendous power of publicity, must be held to social accountability. As society progresses in the recognition of the things that hurt it most, the murderous crime of evil suggestion will come to be identified and branded. If one compares the numbers who attend the theater in a great city with the numbers who attend church, and realizes the effectiveness of dramatic representation, he will be able to appreciate the social importance of the theater. The moving picture show in spite of the possibilities of improvement is a tremendously valuable addition to the resources of civilization, a foe to the saloon and other baser pleasures, with great possibilities of positive good.

Athletic sports appeal directly to instincts that are especially strong in men; they are among the most effective foes of evil. Because of their universal appeal they are available for the young and the uneducated as well as the most cultured. They develop the body and also the powers and virtues, and are an inestimable addition to the sum of human happiness.

Gambling also appeals directly to an inborn propensity. But its mischievous results cause it to be one of the few things that are almost universally condemned by the thoughtful. A plausible argument can be made for almost every tempting thing, but experience has the final word. Games of cards should not be condemned because they have been used and still are used by some as a means of gambling. That is somewhat like the judgment of those who once condemned the violin because it was used to furnish music at indecorous dances. It is true that any game that is good, that is to say, very enjoyable, may lead some who are weak or who lack serious interests to spend upon it too large a portion of their time and energies.

The primary quality of good literature, good art, and all other good play, is that it is enjoyable. That is its frank purpose and in that it rejoices. The business of art is to please and not to teach. Yet when art becomes degenerate and portrays disease and vice it does not say frankly, "these are the things that please me," but as if its function were to teach, its apology is, "these things are real, the truth demands their portrayal." Science must go where art need not follow. It is quite true that what art portrays it should portray truly. Moreover, it may even portray vice, disease, perfidy and cruelty as parts of a whole picture that includes other elements in proportion and perspective. But it always chooses for portrayal that which gives pleasure to the artist and his patrons. Art, like eating, is always selective. And when it selects vice and faithlessness for the pleasure it takes in vice and the preference it has for unexacting standards of duty, then it becomes part and parcel of vice and perfidy.

There is great occasion to desire more art and play and more general and liberal participation in their pleasures. But art and all play must so fit into the scheme of life that it does not destroy more pleasure than it adds; otherwise it is on the whole bad and to be excluded. There is no good thing that cannot be debased and perverted. Literature, art, and other play in its essential nature is not only innocent, but it is a functional part of the unity of life; it is priceless in itself, and makes life stronger and better in all of its departments.

Manners and Ceremony as Agencies of Control.—Manners are properly described as "minor morals," and ceremony has been called the earliest form of government, the original material from which both morality and law have been differentiated. According to Professor Sumner the whole life of most savage and barbarous peoples may be regarded as a ritual, minutely regulated by pressure of the public opinion of the group and fear of the divinities, which together enforced the customary forms of procedure. Ceremony becomes a matter of taste or sentiment and the violation of it is therefore shocking or hideous. Like other matters of taste it is variable, that which is shocking to one group or one age exciting no disapproval in another.

Ceremony continues to play a large rôle in the lives of the civilized. It regulates dress and the manners of daily intercourse as well as weddings and funerals and the conduct of assemblies. Happiness may be quite as deeply affected by the constant personal contacts which are regulated by ceremony and manners as by the occasional matters that are controlled by law. Etiquette is a means of securing the desired relations between the sexes, as well as between the young and their elders. Moreover, it is not only the ceremony which serves as a defense against intrusion and a regulator of intercourse in daily life, which is an agency of government, but so also is the ceremony of occasions. The wedding which takes place in the office of the justice of the peace among files of bad debts and tittering bystanders is less likely to be the commencement of a permanent and honored union than one which is accompanied by flowers and music and the forms of the church. Life is governed quite as much by appeals to the sentiments as by appeals to the reason, and ceremonies are the forms of speech and action, which serve as an expression and as a provocative of these sentiments which are felt to befit and to ennoble the conduct of life.

Ceremony is art in conduct. It resembles the art which renders beautiful houses, furniture, carpets, draperies, and other objects of use. We may despise it as artificial, and indeed, like other forms of human excellence, it may be abused; but as long as we prefer Chippendale chairs to stumps to sit upon in our homes, we shall have reason to prefer that conduct which gratifies esthetic sensibility and both expresses and tends to elicit the sentiments of civilized beings and to regard undiscriminating contempt for ceremony as an evidence of imperfect adaptation to human society.

The Press as an Agency of Social Control.—The press is as essential to the democratic control of activity in a great nation as nerve fibers to the control of activity in a vertebrate animal. Without it a democracy of a hundred millions would be like a vast jelly-fish, inert and certain to fall to pieces. Public opinion is dependent upon publicity, and no other medium of communication is adequate to make a vast population into one public. On the other hand, a society composed of capable, intelligent, and reliable individuals who have the means of prompt and pervasive intercommunication, is practically certain to become a true democracy. If the many can think and act together they are more powerful than any tyrant or oligarchy. The degree of their freedom and power to promote their interests by organized coöperation, will be directly proportional to two things: first, the intelligence and reliability of the individuals; second, the adequacy of their means of intercommunication.[1]

---

[1] C. H. Cooley: Social Organization. Scribners, 1909, Part II; and chap. 12 of Part III.

Walter Bagehot: Physics and Politics. Appleton, 1875, chap. v.

The more democratic forms of modern legislation increase our dependence upon the press. Primary election laws convert all the voters into members of nominating assemblies. Candidates must find a way to address these vast assemblies, and this they do chiefly through the press. The cost of this renders primary election laws, in a degree, undemocratic, and creates one argument for official organs maintained at public expense, or payment by public funds for announcements in privately owned papers by candidates whose petitions have been officially accepted, and the limitation of expenditure of private funds by candidates. The popular initiative and referendum and recall also greatly increase the dependence of social welfare upon the mediation of the press. Switzerland simplifies legislation by a wise coöperation between administrative officers and the press. Instead of having countless bills presented to the legislative body by its members, the administration is expected to present to the legislature a bill for any needed law, and if it fails to do so upon any important subject, although any member of the legislature has the right to offer a bill, in practice in such a case the legislature instructs the administration to prepare the bill. Custom requires each bill to be published in the official gazettes well in advance of the legislative session at which it is to be acted upon. Thus public opinion is intelligently formed in advance. The legislature meets two or three times a year for a session usually continuing not more than three weeks to perform a task so simplified and clarified as to involve "no more strain and anxiety than the meeting of a board of directors."

The importance of the press as a means of social control is by no means confined to its power as the agency of democratic politics. We have seen that besides government, the other most powerful agency of control by sanctions is the pressure directly exerted by public opinion and sentiment. Public opinion controls by keeping constantly before the mind the idea that certain courses of action will be rewarded with reputation, respect, and friendship, while other courses of conduct will be punished with ostracism, hatred, and contempt. The ideas we have concerning public opinion, like those we have of law, both define the nature of the acts that will be rewarded and punished, and fix the degree of recompense anticipated. It is the idea a man has concerning public opinion that governs him. Hence, whatever spreads abroad the idea that society is lax in its standards and negligent in its responses, reduces its control over its members, and whatever spreads the idea that society is exalted and exacting in its standards and emphatic in its condemnations and approvals, enhances its control.

At this point the press assumes a stupendous responsibility. It has the vice of the gossip systematized, commercialized, and multiplied by the powers of the telegraph, printing-press, and mails. It is the unusual that has "news value." One embezzler or bigamist makes news, but ten thousand honest cashiers or faithful husbands make none. Crime and scandal receive a thousandfold disproportionate prominence. In so far as the impression is created that vice and crime are practiced and condoned by a larger proportion of society than do in fact practice and condone them, and the impression that the execration of wickedness is weaker than it really is, the effect is to undermine the controlling power of public opinion and to make society tend to become as black as it is thus painted. Evils ought to be reported, but not with conspicuous headlines or extended or gloating details. The activities constantly being put forth to improve society ought to receive much fuller public recognition. The depraved like to believe and do believe that the world is worse than it is. The good tend to suppress knowledge of evil, to advertise goodness, and to create a social expectation of regular and approved conduct. If this expectation were not on the whole justified society would go to perdition. It should be true and all men should know that it is true that anti-social conduct can count on social execration and that socially beneficial conduct can count on social approval and appreciation. This is one of the two chief means of control by the sanctions of reward and punishment.

Nor is this all. Besides being the essential medium of democratic government and besides giving form and weight to the sanctions of public opinion, the press exercises another form of social control, a control that is not dependent upon sanctions but results directly through social suggestion, sympathetic radiation, and imitation. Without regard to what the government may do or what others may do to us or think about us, each one has an inner stream of ideas and sentiments which is the essence of life, and the control of which is the individual's prime concern if he wishes to make something of himself, and is society's deepest concern in its attempts to control its members. Into this inner current of life the press pours a constant stream. Thus the press heightens or allays business depressions, popularizes recreations, inflames or cools the passions of war, defines the secret ambitions that direct the energies of men, braces or relaxes the moral demands that men impose upon themselves, and foments or allays the jealousies that separate social classes, and gives to attention its bent. Attention is the determinant of conscious life. That which occupies the attention of men is that which, as conscious beings, they are, and is that which they will do; while that which has no place in their attention is for them as if it were not.

If the press has such power over society then the press itself must be controlled. But the press must also be free. Experience has demonstrated that the suppression of honest opinion is perilous, that the essence of freedom is freedom of thought and expression, and that if we lose confidence that on the whole and in the long run, reason and right sentiment will respond with fairness and good sense to adequate presentation of all interests, then we lose confidence in democracy. There are two means which may contribute toward the adequate control of the press without unduly limiting its freedom. One is to disseminate higher standards of public demand and of professional ethics with reference to the character of the press; the other is to make sure that both sides of every great issue are advocated adequately and above board. To this end several expedients have been proposed:

1. Every newspaper should be required to publish promi-

nently the names of its actual owners, so that the power they exercise may not be dissociated from responsibility and so that the interests that are finding expression in each periodical may be recognized. Nothing is easier than to distort the facts by suppressing portions of them, to deprive the public of information which it has a right to demand, and to warp opinion according to the dictates of personal and party interests.

2. It is held that if it is desirable to endow educational institutions it would be desirable to endow periodicals which purvey intelligence to the masses who are out of school, that such periodicals would be free from the pressure of the great advertisers on whom ordinary papers depend for their income and that they would attract the disinterested service of men as impartial in their devotion to the truth and to the public weal as are found in the service of any university.

3. The experiment has been tried, although inadequately, of a municipal newspaper, the columns of which are open equally to rival candidates, and opposing parties, and to which every member of the city government has access for the advocacy of measures or the exposure of abuses.

4. It is desirable that it become a recognized conventionality of good editorial practice to publish signed articles from advocates of opposing sides of every great issue. As a rule people read papers that give expression to the opinions and sentiments with which they agree and see little of the statements of fact and of argument which might modify their own prejudices. It is difficult, and speaking broadly, impossible for writers to do justice to the opinions and interests to which they are opposed, and equally honest and good men hold opposing views. Particularly in the great struggle of class interests it is of the highest importance that both sides should be heard. The papers present the arguments before the bar of public opinion, which is the court of last resort. And here as in other courts, frank advocacy of both sides is indispensable to justice. This practice would add immensely to the interest of a paper, and in time it may become a matter of editorial ethics and of public demand.

The Church.—In earlier centuries the control of the church was exercised mainly through the hope and fear of the external sanctions of reward and punishment. But the church has always been, and to-day is mainly, an agency for disseminating ideas and evoking sentiments which shape the inner springs of conduct.

The experience of the past leaves it at least very doubtful whether an adequate system of social control without religion is possible. Religion is of three types:

First is the religion of fear. Second is the religion of unconscious pragmatism, that is to say religion which adopts, exalts and disseminates ideas because they work well. Such ideas are believed because they prove to be inspiring or consoling or to have the power to repress or elicit conduct. The religion of unconscious pragmatism abounds in cherished ideas concerning that which is beyond the range of human knowledge or objective test. Third is social religion, or the religion of humanity, or the religion of service. Elements of all three kinds combine readily into one creed. Religion of the third type, at least, is on the increase.

"There is no one belief or set of beliefs which constitutes a religion. We are apt to suppose that every creed must teach a belief in a god or gods, in an immortal soul, and in a divine government of the world. The parliament of religions which lately met in Chicago, announced in its preliminary call these elements as essential to the idea of religion.

"No mistake could be greater. The religion which to-day counts the largest number of adherents, Buddhism, rejects every one of these items.[1] The Jewish doctrine of the Old Testament, the Roman religion of the time of Julius Cæsar, and many others have not admitted the existence of a soul or the continuance of the individual life after death. Some believe in souls but not in gods; while a divine government is a thought rarely present in savage minds."[2]

So great has been the social rôle of the church that Dean

---

[1] See T. Rhys Davids, "Indian Buddhism," Hibbert Lectures, p. 29, and in first series of American Lectures on the History of Religions.

[2] Brinton: Religions of Primitive Peoples, p. 28.

Stanley was prompted to declare that all history is ecclesiastical history. To-day, however, some believe that the church is obsolescent. There are weighty facts which seem to support this belief. The mere number of communicants is not a final test. A social movement may fade away without diminishing in numbers save in the last stage, somewhat as the ice in a lake without diminishing in area softens and finally, in a night, disappears in water. But there are two considerations that seem to give proof that the church is not in obsolescence but only in transition and that the church will be a permanent necessity of highly developed social organization:

First, individuals need to create for themselves and for each other a spiritually helpful environment; that is, an environment in which ideas and sentiments which ennoble life are communicated and heightened by social suggestion and sympathetic radiation so as to give stable character to the subconscious set. We must recall [1] that the same human organism may be set to play any tune from "The Messiah" to "The Devil's Hornpipe," that potentially man has as many stories as a skyscraper and he needs an elevator if he wishes to live on the highest level, that man is like a watch that must be wound up or it is sure to run down, like an engine propelled by storage batteries that must frequently be recharged, that, in literal phraseology, human life is the most variable of phenomena and that it is a matter of cause and effect, and we can expect the best effects in character and work and worth, only on condition of supplying the necessary conditions. And these conditions are largely to be found in the regular currents of social suggestion and radiation with which we surround ourselves. The church stands for the deliberate endeavor to seek and supply the social conditions essential to the highest life.

Religion is based upon discrimination, which recognizes the ideas and sentiments that are found by experience to lift life to its highest level. Conversion is a readjustment of attention, bringing into the middle of the stage in our mental drama the ennobling ideas and sending away from the spot-

[1] Compare passage beginning on page 299.

light of attention the ideas that drag life down. Every adult has a multitude of ideas stored in memory but makes habitual daily use of a few, and these give to life its character. Instinctive propulsions and the suggestions of the general social environment are sure to thrust themselves forward, but the ideas that differentiate man from his less evolved progenitors and tend to raise him above the commonplace must be diligently brought to mind. Attention is to life what seeds are to a garden. The religious man selects some of his seeds and does not allow his garden to be entirely wind-sown. The religious man is one who discriminates between the ideas that give life dignity and worth and those which drag life down or anchor it to mediocrity, and who takes the necessary pains to keep the ennobling ideas in the fore-front of his attention.

This description, however, is true not so much of religions as they have been as of religion as it must be if it is to be a permanent element in advancing civilization. Historically religions have contained many debasing elements and slighted the most ennobling elements in the life of the peoples by whom they were believed. And every religion tends to become laden with trivial non-essentials.

Second, the church appears to have a permanent function not only as an agency of individual development for its members but also as the organ for giving effective social expression to purely ethical aims. Society needs one organization with no commercial ends to seek, no axes to grind, in order to direct, foster, and focus the ethical opinions and sentiments of the community upon every question that has an ethical significance as well as to organize practical activities in promotion of ethical aims. The peril is that the church may become an end unto itself and in seeking its life lose it.

To deserve perpetuity and power by effectively discharging the two social functions to which reference has been made the church is perhaps as really, if not as badly, in need of a reformation as it was in Luther's day.[1] Whether we will

---

[1] Both Catholics and Protestants may agree that in Luther's day there was need of reformation however they may disagree concerning the changes that then actually took place.

or no, this is a time of transition in the history of the church. For the sake of the first of its two functions, the church needs to restore the emphasis to the simple essentials that constituted the message of Jesus,[1] and that are the common property of all branches of the Christian church. The fact that about so large a portion of their creeds equally Christian people differ as they do is experimental demonstration of the non-essential character of these divisive doctrines. The instinct of partisanship leads each religious body to exaggerate those features of creed or practice which distinguish it from other sects. Moreover, those items of creed that stand most in need of defense are likely to be defended most, and the teachers of a sect often affirm with special emphasis that unless men believe the doctrines that are most likely and fittest to be disbelieved they have no religion, and so excommunicate the most honest and intelligent. There is hope of a great world-wide religious revival. Even in countries like Germany and France, where Christianity has so far lost its power over the life of the present, there is such a hope. This is because there is increasing prospect that Christianity will divest itself of its incubus of outgrown, man-made creed and observance, and stand forth in its essential simplicity and power.

For the sake of the second of its two functions the reformation which the church requires must lead toward more practically efficient organization. The first reformation broke up the catholicity, that is, the unity of the church; the second reformation, whether it comes slowly or rapidly, should restore a far broader catholicity than the first destroyed, ultimately and ideally uniting the right-minded of every nation of mankind in humanity's common enterprise, the establishment of the kingdom of God.

At present the church is handicapped by an irrational but fortunately declining sectarianism which has no adequate logical ground in the present, but a sentimental ground in the partisan loyalties which it perpetuates, and a basis in still narrower self-interests. Here as elsewhere group loyalty ap-

---

[1] Adolph Harnack: What Is Christianity? Tr. Putnams, 1901. A statement by the most famous living biblical scholar.

peals to the powerful instinct of partisanship, which on the inside is devotion but on the outside is blind misunderstanding and divisiveness. It is the same instinct which makes both patriotism and war and breaks down the wider international coöperation upon which the ultimate civilization depends. The church confronts the universal social problem of widening the circle of coöperation, in part by subordinating instinct to reason, which as truly as instinct is a predisposition of man, and in part by recognizing broader relationships so that they will enlist the instinct of coöperation.

In the country denominationalism largely destroys the dignity and the power of the church, and substitutes divisiveness and feebleness for unity and strength. Sixteen country meeting-houses within a radius of three miles, and fifty-two country meeting-houses in sight from a single belfry illustrate the *reductio ad absurdum* of inefficiency. A thousand souls do not form too large a parish. Of one hundred and twenty-nine rural communities recently investigated in Illinois twenty-five had more than one English-speaking Protestant church each, where the Protestant population, children and all, was but two hundred or less than two hundred per church, and where at least one of the churches was receiving home-missionary aid. In the presence of endangered youth in factories and slums, thronging immigrants, millions of neglected negroes, and other pressing needs and urgent opportunities home-missionary funds are squandered to maintain the denominational rivalries of groups of feeble, struggling churches, where one church might well accomplish far more.

In the city the effects of denominationalism are as bad. Where two hundred thousand immigrants move into an urban district half a score of churches move out. In proportion as the church is needed in an urban district it withdraws, seeking its life to lose it. Miles of city streets in the quarters inhabited by laborers are innocent of a Protestant church, while in the aristocratic districts churches face each other across the same thoroughfare. The whole city should be divided into geographic parishes, and the church of each parish should be strong with the strength of the united church of the whole city.

The second of these two reforms which are required by the church is dependent upon the first. The union or effective coöperation of sects will never come about by the triumph of the speculative doctrines of one of them over the others. Men will gradually moderate their respective assumptions of infallibility, yet with respect to matters of speculation, inference, and interpretation, equally good men will continue to differ. They should be free to differ without impairing their standing in the church. The only basis for a practicable union or efficient coöperation is not a creed but a purpose. The personal ideal and the social purpose of Christianity are the common property of all Christians. To the student of sociology it is an impressive fact that with Jesus the sole test of discipleship was *service* in obedience to the purpose to bring in throughout the world and in each particular situation the Kingdom of Human Fulfillment, in which God's will should be accomplished upon earth and the coming of which his followers are bidden to make the first of all their prayers.

BIBLIOGRAPHY

The following list necessarily omits many books that might with propriety have been mentioned, including a part of those to which allusion has been made in the text, and a great number which are available for use in connection with intensive courses in special divisions of sociology. Some of the books contain matter on more than one of the topics under which the list is classified.

It is desirable to have a selection of books placed where all members of the class can browse among them. The required reports on supplementary reading should be in part on definite assignments, but in part also on matter chosen by the student himself as a result of his own exploration among the books placed on reserve for the course. The footnotes to the text will be of assistance in making specific assignments.

STATISTICS AND METHOD

Bailey, W. B., *Modern Social Conditions.* 377 p. illus. New York, 1906.

Bouglé, C. C. A., *Les Sciences sociales en Allemagne; les méthodes actuelles.* 2nd ed., 172 p. Paris, 1902.

Bowley, A. L., *An Elementary Manual of Statistics.* 215 p., diagrams. London, 1910.

Brinton, W. C., *Graphic Methods for Presenting Facts.* xii, 371 p. illus. New York, 1914.

Durkheim, Émile, *Les règles de la méthode sociologique.* xxiv, 186 p. Paris, ed. of 1907.

Elderton, W. P., and Elderton, E. M., *Primer of Statistics.* vii, 86 p. illus. London, 1912.

Giddings, F. H., *Inductive Sociology.* 302 p. New York, 1901.

King, W. I., *The Elements of Statistical Method.* xxiv, 278 p., tables, diagrams. New York, 1912.

Mayo-Smith, Richmond, *Statistics and Sociology.* xvi, 399 p. New York, 1896.

Newsholme, Arthur, *Elements of Vital Statistics*. 326 p. London, 1899.

Pearson, Karl, *The Grammar of Science*. 518 p. London, 1911.

Robinson, L. N., *History and Organization of Criminal Statistics in the United States*. 104 p. Boston, 1911.

Seignobos, Charles, *La Methode Historique Appliqué aux Sciences Sociales*. ii, 322 p. Paris, 1901.

Spencer, Herbert, *The Study of Sociology*. 426 p. New York, 1873.

U. S. Census Bureau, *American Census Taking*. 34 p. illus. Washington, 1903.

——*Marriage and Divorce*, 1867-1906. 2 vols.

——*Mortality Statistics*. 1913.

——*Prisoners and Juvenile Delinquents*. Bul., 1910.

——*Statistical Atlas of the United States*. 99 p., plates. Washington, 1914.

——*Thirteenth Census* (1910) *Abstract*—with supplement for your own state.

U. S. Children's Bureau, *Birth Registration*. 20 p. incl. chart. Washington, 1914.

——*Handbook of Federal Statistics of Children*. Bul., Washington, 1914.

Webb, A. D., *New Dictionary of Statistics*. xi, 682 p. London, 1911.

Wundt, Wilhelm, *Methodenlehre, Zweite abtheilung, Logik der Geisteswissenschaften*. vii, 643 p. Stuttgart, 1895.

Yule, G. U., *Introduction to Theory of Statistics*. xiii, 376 p. illus. London, 1911.

GEOGRAPHIC AND BIOLOGICAL CONDITIONS AND EUGENICS

American Academy of Medicine, *Physical Bases of Crime, A Symposium*. Papers and Discussion Contributed to the thirty-eighth annual meeting of the American Academy of Medicine, Minneapolis, June 14, 1913. 188 p. Easton, Pennsylvania, 1914.

Barr, M. W., *Mental Defectives—Their History, Treatment and Training*. x, 17-368 p., liii plates. Philadelphia, 1904.

Buckle, H. T., *Introduction to the History of Civilization in England*. xlviii, 915 p. New York, 1863.

Conklin, E. G., *Heredity and Environment in the Development of Men.* xiv, 533 p. illus. Princeton, 1915.

Davenport, C. B., *Heredity in Relation to Eugenics.* iii-xi, 298 p., front., illus., chart. New York, 1911.

Dugdale, R. L., *The Jukes,* 4th ed., v, 120 p. New York, 1910.

Ellis, H. H., *Man and Woman.* 4th ed., 488 p. illus. London, 1904.

——*Sex in Relation to Society.* xvi, 656 p. Boston and New York, 1912.

——*The Task of Social Hygiene.* xv, 414 p. Boston, 1912.

Fisher, Irving, *National Vitality, Its Wastes and Conservation.* p. [619]-751, diagram. Senate document No. 419, Washington, 1910.

Galton, Francis, *Natural Inheritance.* ix, 259 p. illus. London and New York, 1889.

Goddard, H. H., *Feeble-Mindedness, Its Causes and Consequences.* xii, 599 p. illus., plates. New York, 1914.

Gross, Hans, *Criminal Psychology.* xx, 514 diagrams. Boston, 1911.

International Congress on Hygiene and Demography, 5th, Washington, 1912, *Transactions.* 6 vols. Washington.

Jennings, H. S., *Behavior of the Lower Organisms.* xiv, 366 p. illus. New York, 1906.

Loeb, J., *Comparative Physiology of the Brain and Comparative Psychology.* v-x, 309 p. illus. New York, 1900.

Lombroso, Cesar, *Criminal Man.* (Summarized by his Daughter.) xx, 322 p. illus. New York, 1911.

MacDonald, Arthur, *Man and Abnormal Man, Including a Study of Children.* 780 p. illus. Washington, 1905.

McDougall, William, *An Introduction to Social Psychology.* vii-xv, 355 p. Boston, 1909.

Mill, H. R., *The International Geography.* xx, 1088 p. illus., maps, diagrams. London, ed. of 1903.

Morgan, C. L., *Habit and Instinct.* 351 p. front. London and New York, 1896.

Newsholme, A., *The Declining Birth-rate.* 7-60 p. incl. tables. London, New York, 1911.

Parker, G. H., *Biology and Social Problems.* xix, 130 p., plates. Boston and New York, 1914.

Parmelee, Maurice, *The Science of Human Behavior.* xvii, 443 p. illus., plates. New York, 1913.

Pearson, C. H., *National Life and Character; a Forecast.* vi, 381 p. London, ed. of 1913.

Punnett, R. C., *Mendelism.* xiv, 192 p. illus. New York, 1911.

Semple, E. C., *Influences of Geographic Environment.* xvi, 683 p.; maps, bibliography at end of each chapter. New York, 1911.

Thomas, W. I., *Sex and Society.* vii, 325 p. Chicago, 1907.

U. S. Census Bureau, *Blind Population of United States,* 1910. ——*Insane and Feebleminded in Institutions.* 1910.

Walter, H. E., *Genetics.* xiv, 272 p. illus., plates, diagrams. New York, 1913.

Weissmann, August, *Essays upon Heredity.* 2 vols., diagrams. Oxford, 1892.

IMMIGRATION AND RACE

Antin, Mary, *They Who Knock at Our Gates.* x, 142 p., plates. Boston, 1914.

Baker, R. S., *Following the Color Line; An Account of Negro Citizenship in the American Democracy.* xii, 314 p. illus. New York, 1908.

Balch, E. G., *Our Slavic Fellow Citizens.* xx, 536 p. illus., charts, plates, portraits, maps. New York, 1910.

Baskerville, Beatrice C., *The Polish Jew, His Social and Economic Value.* 5 p. 1., 336 p. double map. New York, 1906.

Burgess, Thomas, *Greeks in America.* xiv, 256 p., illus. Boston, 1913.

Cable, G. W., *The Negro Question.* 173 p. New York, ed. of 1890.

Commons, John R., *Races and Immigrants in America.* iii-xiii, 242 p., illus. New York, 1907.

Fairchild, H. P., *Immigration, A World Movement and Its American Significance.* xi, 455 p. New York, 1913.

Hall, Prescott E., *Immigration and Its Effects upon the United States.* 393 p. New York, 1906.

Hapgood, Hutchins, *The Spirit of the Ghetto.* 311 p., front., illus. New York, 1902.

Jenks, J. W., and Lauck, W. J., *The Immigration Problem.* xvi, 496 p. incl. tables. New York, 1912.

Lord, Eliot, Trenor, J. J. D., and Barrows, S. J., *The Italians in America.* ix, 268 p. illus. New York, 1906.

Mecklin, J. M., *Democracy and Race Friction.* xi, 273 p. New York, 1914.

Roberts, Peter, *The New Immigration; A Study of the Industrial and Social Life of Southeastern Europeans in America.* xxi, 386 p. illus. New York, 1912.

Ross, E. A., *The Old World and the New.* 327 p. New York, 1914.

Southern Sociological Congress *Addresses.* 1st 387 p. Nashville, 1912. 2nd 702 p. Nashville, 1913. 3rd 227 p. Nashville, 1914.

Stone, A. H., *Studies in the American Race Problem.* xxii, 555 p. New York, 1908.

U. S. Immigration Commission, *Abstract of Reports.* 2 vols. Washington, 1911.

Washington, B. T., and DuBois, W. E. B., *The Negro in the South; His Economic Progress in Relation to His Moral and Religious Development.* 222 p. Philadelphia, 1907.

Weatherford, W. D., *Present Forces in Negro Progress.* 191 p., illus., maps, bibliography. New York, 1912.

Whelpley, J. D., *The Problem of the Immigrant.* 295 p. London, 1905.

Woodruff, C. E., *Expansion of Races.* xi, 495 p. incl. tables. New York, 1909.

CITY, COUNTRY, AND POPULATION PRESSURE

Anderson, W. L., *The Country Town.* 307 p. New York, 1906.

Ashenhurst, J. O., *The Day of the Country Church.* 208 p. New York and London, 1910.

Bailey, L. H., *The Country Life Movement.* xi, 220 p. New York, 1911.

——*The State and the Farmer.* xii, 177 p. New York, 1913.

Bonar, James, *Malthus and His Work.* 432 p. London, 1885.

Bookwalter, J. W., *Rural Versus Urban; their conflict and its causes.* viii, 292 p. New York, 1911.

Butterfield, K. L., *Chapters in Rural Progress.* ix, 251 p. Chicago, 1908.

——*The Country Church and the Rural Problem.* ix, 153 p. Chicago, 1911.

Carney, Mabel, *Country Life and the Country School.* xxi, 405 p. illus. Chicago, 1912.

Commission on Country Life, *Report.* 150 p. New York, 1911.

Cubberley, E. P., *Rural Life and Education.* xiv, 367 p. illus. New York, 1914.

Fiske, G. W., *The Challenge of the Country*. xiii, 283 p., front., plates, plan. New York, 1912.

Foght, H. W., *The American Rural School, Its Characteristics, Its Future and Its Problems*. xxi, 361 p. illus., maps, plans, plates. New York, 1910.

Gillette, J. M., *Constructive Rural Sociology*. xiii, 301 p. New York, 1913.

Godfrey, Holles, *The Health of the City*. xvi, 372 p. New York, 1910.

Howe, F. C., *European Cities at Work*. xiv, 370 p. New York, 1913.

——*The Modern City and Its Problems*. x, 390 p. New York, Chicago, Boston, 1915.

Housing, National Conference on, *Proceedings*. 1911-1914.

Jewett, F. G., *Town and City*. iii-viii, 272 p. illus. New York, 1906.

Kellog, P. U. (Editor), *The Pittsburg Survey*. 6 vols. New York, 1910.

   Vol. 1. Butler, E. B., *Women and the Trades*. 1909.

   Vol. 2. Eastman, Crystal, *Work Accidents and the Law*. 1910.

   Vol. 3. Fitch, J. A., *The Steel Workers*. 1910.

   Vol. 4. Byington, M. F., *Homestead, the Households of a Mill Town*. 1910.

   Vol. 5. Pittsburgh District Civic Frontage. 1914.

   Vol. 6. Wage Earning Pittsburg. *The Gist of the Survey*. 1914.

Kellog, P. U., and others, *The Social Survey*. 62 p. New York, 1912.

Knorr, George W., *Consolidated Rural Schools and Organization of a County System*. 99 p. illus., incl. tables, diagrams. U. S. Dept. Agriculture Bul. 232.

Lunn, Henry S., *Municipal Lessons from Southern Germany*. viii, 139 p. illus. London.

Malthus, T. R., *The Principle of Population*. 3 vols. London, 1909.

Massachusetts, Agricultural College, Amherst, *A Selected Bibliography on Rural Social Science*. 11 p. Massachusetts Agricultural College, 1911.

McKeever, William A., *Farm Boys and Girls*. xviii, 326 p., xxxii plates. New York, 1912.

Myrick, Herbert, *How to Coöperate*. 349 p., illus., tables. New York, 1891.

Perry, C. A., *Wider Use of the School Plant*. xiv., 423 p., plates. New York, 1910.

Plunkett, Sir Horace, *The Rural Life Problem of the United States.* xi, 174 p. New York, 1911.

Powell, E. P., *The Country Home.* 382 p., front., 21 plates. New York, 1905.

Strong, Josiah, *The Challenge of the City.* xiv, 332 p., front., illus., 11 plates. New York, 1907.

Van Hise, Charles R., *The Conservation of Natural Resources in the United States.* xiv, 413 p. illus., maps, charts, tables, xvi plates. New York, 1912.

Veiller, Lawrence, *Housing Reform.* vii-xii, 213 p. incl. forms. New York, 1910.

Ward, E. J., *The Social Center.* x, 359 p. New York, 1913.

Wilcox, D. F., *The American City.* vii, 423 p. New York, 1904.

Wilson, Warren H., *The Church of the Open Country.* xiv, 238 p., plates, 3 parts. New York, 1911.

——*Quaker Hill—A Sociological Study.* 168 p., 2 maps. New York, 1907.

Woods, R. A. (Editor), *The City Wilderness.* vii, 319 p., maps, plans, diagrams. Boston and New York, 1898.

POVERTY AND CHARITY

Abbott, Edith, *Women in Industry.* 408 p. New York, 1910.

Adams, T. S., and Sumner, H. L., *Labor Problems.* xv, 579 p. New York, 1905.

Bolen, G. L., *Getting a Living.* 769 p. New York, 1903.

Booth, Chas., *Labor and Life of the People in London.* 5 vols. London, 1892.

Brooks, John Graham, *The Social Unrest.* 394 p. New York, 1903.

Chapin, R. C., *Standard of Living Among Workingmen's Families in New York.* xv, 372 p. New York, 1909.

Conynton, Mary, *How to Help.* x, 367 p. New York, 1909.

Davenport, H. J., *Value and Distribution.* xi, 582 p. Chicago, 1908.

Dawson, W. Harbutt, *Social Insurance in Germany.* xi, 283 p. London, 1912.

Devine, Edward T., *Misery and Its Causes.* xi, 274 p. New York, 1909.

——*The Principles of Relief.* vi, 495 p. New York, 1914.

Ely, R. T., *Property and Contract in Their Relations to the Distribution of Wealth.* 2 vols. New York, 1914.

Fowle, T. W., *The English Poor Law.* 175 p. London, ed. of 1900.

Frankel, L. K. and Dawson, M., *Workingmen's Insurance in Europe.* xviii, 477 p. New York, 1910.

Henderson, C. R., *Dependent, Defective and Delinquent Classes.* 2nd ed., 397 p. Boston, 1901.

——*Industrial Insurance.* 2nd ed., viii, 429 p. Chicago, 1911.

——and others, *Modern Methods of Charity.* Bibliography, 713 p. New York, 1904.

Hollander, J. H., *The Abolition of Poverty.* iii, 122 p. Boston, 1914.

Hunter, Robert, *Poverty.* 302 p. New York, 1905.

Kellor, F. A., *Out of Work. A Study of Employment Agencies.* 292 p. New York, 1904.

King, W. I., *Wealth and Income of the People of the United States.* xxiv, 278 p. New York, 1915.

Kirkup, Thomas, *History of Socialism.* 4th ed., 436 p. New York and London, 1909.

Lee, Joseph, *Constructive and Preventive Philanthropy.* x, 242 p. New York, 1902.

MacLean, A. M., *Wage-Earning Women.* xv, 202 p. New York. 1910.

McLean, F. H., *Formation of Charity Organization Societies in Smaller Cities.* 51 p. New York, 1910.

Minimum Wage Boards. Report of Massachusetts Commission. Boston, 1912.

Money, L. G. C., *Insurance versus Poverty.* 396 p. London, 1912.

More, L. B., *Wage Earners' Budgets.* x, 280 p. New York, 1907.

Nearing, Scott, *Income.* xxvii, 238 p. New York, 1915.

Richmond, M. E., and Hall, F. S., *A Study of Nine Hundred and Eighty-five Widows Known to Certain Charity Organization Societies.* 83 p. New York, 1910.

Richmond, M. E., *The Good Neighbor.* 159 p. Philadelphia, 1908.

Rowntree, B. S., *Poverty—A Study of Town Life.* 3rd ed. xxii, 452 p. London, 1902.

Ryan, J. A., *A Living Wage.* 348 p. New York, 1912.

Schloss, D. F., *Insurance Against Unemployment.* 132 p. London, 1909.

Seager, H. R., *Social Insurance: A Program of Social Reform.* 175 p. New York, 1910.

Spahr, C. B., *The Present Distribution of Wealth in the United States.* 2nd ed., 184 p. New York, 1896.

Spargo, John, *The Bitter Cry of the Children.* xxiii, 337 p. illus. New York, 1906.

Solenberger, A. W., *One Thousand Homeless Men: A Study of Original Records.* xxiv, 374 p. New York, 1901.

Squier, L. W., *Old Age Dependency in the United States; a Complete Survey of the Pension Movement.* xii, 361 p. New York, 1912.

Streightoff, F. H., *The Distribution of Incomes in the United States.* 171 p. New York, 1912.

Sutherland, William, *Old Age Pensions.* x, 227 p. London, 1907.

Thompson, J. J., *Social Insurance.* 105 p. Chicago, 1914.

U. S. Census Bureau, *Benevolent Institutions.* 1910.

——*Insane and Feebleminded in Institutions.* 1910.

——*Paupers in Almshouses.* 1910.

U. S. Labor Commission, *Reports.*

Warner, A. S., *American Charities.* Revised by Coolidge. Bibliography. 510 p. New York, 1908.

Webb, Sidney and Beatrice, *The Prevention of Destitution.* vi, 348 p. London, 1911.

Willard, J. F. (Josiah Flynt), *Tramping with Tramps.* 398 p. New York, 1901.

SOCIAL EVOLUTION

Bancroft, H. H., *Native Races of the Pacific States of North America.* 5 vols. illus. New York, 1875.

Boaz, Franz, *The Mind of Primitive Man.* x, 294 p. New York, 1911.

Brinton, D. G., *Races and Peoples.* 313 p., maps, illus. Philadelphia, 1901.

——*Religions of Primitive Peoples.* xiv, 264 p. New York, 1897.

Chapin, F. S., *An Introduction to the Study of Social Evolution.* xxii, 306 p. illus. New York, 1913.

Churchward, Albert, *The Origin and Evolution of Primitive Man.* 860 p., 46 plates. London, 1912.

Codrington, R. H., *The Melanesians.* xv, 419 p. illus. Oxford, 1891.

Cox, Sir G. W., *The Mythology of the Aryan Natives.* 2 vols. London, 1878.

Crawley, E., *The Mystic Rose, A Study of Primitive Marriage.* xviii, 492 p. New York, 1902.

Cushing, F. H., *Zuñi Folk-Tales.* 474 p. illus. New York, 1901.

Dellenbaugh, Frederick S., *The North Americans of Yesterday.* xxvi, 487 p. illus. New York, 1901.

Deniker, J., *The Races of Man.* xxiii, 610 p. illus. London, 1900.

Dewey, J., and Tufts, J. H., *Ethics.* xiii, 618 p. New York, 1908.

Espinas, Alfred, *Des Sociétés Animales.* 2nd ed., 309 p. Paris, 1878.

Forrest, J. D., *Development of Western Civilization.* xii, 406 p. Chicago, 1907.

Frazer, J. G., *The Golden Bough. A Study in Magic and Religion.* 3rd ed., 10 vols. London, 1907-1913.

Frobenius, Leo, *The Childhood of Man.* xviii, 504 p. illus. Philadelphia, 1909.

Grosse, E., *The Beginnings of Art.* (Trans.), xiv, 327 p. illus. New York, 1907.

Haddon, A. C., *Evolution in Art.* 364 p. illus. London, 1895.

——*Magic and Fetichism.* viii + 98 pp. London, 1906.

Hirn, Y., *Origins of Art.* 331 p. London, 1900.

Hobhouse, L. T., *Morals in Evolution.* xiv, 415 p. New York, 1900.

Hollis, A. C., *The Masai—Their Language and Folklore.* xxviii, 359 p. Oxford, 1905.

Howard, G. E., *History of Matrimonial Institutions.* 3 vols. Chicago, 1904.

Howitt, A. W., *The Native Tribes of South-East Australia.* xix, 819 p. illus. London, 1904.

Ihering, Rudolph, von (Trans. by Drucker), *The Evolution of the Aryan.* xviii, 412 p. London, 1897.

Joly, N., *Man Before Metals.* 365 p. illus. New York, 1883.

Keane, A. H., *Ethnology.* xxx, 442 p. Cambridge, 1896.

Kidd, Dudley, *Kafir Socialism.* xi, 286 p. London, 1908.

——*The Essential Kafir.* xv, 435 p., 100 plates. London, 1904.

——*Savage Childhood. A Study of Kafir Children.* xvi, 314 p., 32 pl. London, 1906.

Kropotkin, P. K., *Mutual Aid—A Factor of Evolution.* xix, 348 p. New York, 1902.

LaFarge, Paul, *The Evolution of Property.* vi, 174 p. London, 1894.

Lang, Andrew, *Myth, Ritual and Religion.* 2 vols. London, 1887.

Letourneau, Charles, *Property: Its Origin and Development.* 401 p. London, 1907.

——(Trans. by Trollope), *Sociology Based on Ethnology.* 608 p. London, 1881.

Letourneau, Charles, *The Evolution of Marriage and of the Family*. 373 p. New York.

Mason, O. T., *Woman's Share in Primitive Culture*. 295 p. illus. New York, ed. of 1907.

Morgan, L. H., *Ancient Society*. 560 p. New York, 1877.

Nassau, R. H., *Fetichism in West Africa*. xvii, 389 p., 12 plates. New York, 1904.

Nieboer, H. J., *Slavery as an Industrial System*. (Bibliography.) xxvii, 474 p. The Hague, 1900.

Powell, J. W., *Annual Reports of the Bureau of Ethnology*. Washington. From 1879.

Ratzel, F., *The History of Mankind*. 2 vols. London, 1896.

Réclus, Élie, *Primitive Folk*. xiv, 339 p. London, 1891.

Ripley, W. Z., *The Races of Europe: A Sociological Study*. 2 vols. illus., maps. New York, 1899.

Rivers, A. Lane (Fox Pitt), *The Evolution of Culture*. 232 p. Oxford, 1906.

Rivers, W. H. R., *Kinship and Social Organization*. vii, 96 p.

——*The History of Milanesian Society*. 2 vols. Cambridge, 1914.

——*The Todas*. xviii, 755 p. illus. London, 1906.

Romanes, G. J., *Mental Evolution in Animals*. 411 p. New York, 1884.

——*Mental Evolution in Man*. 452 p., plate. New York, 1889.

Roth, W. E., *Ethnological Studies Among the N. W. C. Queensland Aborigines*. xvi, 199 p., xiv plates. Brisbane, 1897.

Skeat, W. W., *Malay Magic*. xiv, 685 p. London, 1900.

——and Blagden, Charles Otto, *Pagan Races of the Malay Peninsula*. 2 vols. plates. London, 1906.

Smith, W. R., *Kinship and Marriage in Early Arabia*. xiv, 322 p. Cambridge, 1885.

——*Lectures on the Religion of the Semites*. xiv, 507 p. London, ed. of 1901.

Spencer, Baldwin, and Gillan, F. J., *The Native Tribes of Central Australia*. xx, 671 p. illus. London, 1899.

——*The Northern Tribes of Central Australia*. xxxv, 784 p. illus. London, 1904.

Spencer, Herbert, *Descriptive Sociology*. 8 vols. London, 1873-1910.

Sumner, W. G., *Folkways*. v, 692 p. extensive bibliography. Boston, 1911.

Thomas, W. I., *Source Book for Social Origins*. Invaluable bibliographies. Chicago, 1909.

Todd, A. J., *The Primitive Family as an Educational Agency*. ix, 251 p. bibliography. New York, 1913.

Tylor, E. B., *Primitive Culture*. 4th ed., 2 vols. Boston, 1903.

Vierkandt, A., *Natür Völker und Kultur Völker*. xi, 497 p. Leipzig, 1896.

Webster, Hutton, *Primitive Secret Societies*. xiii, 227 p. New York, 1908.

Westermark, Edward, *Origin and Growth of Moral Ideas*. 2 vols. London, 1906, 1908.

——*The History of Human Marriage*. xx, 644 p., bibliography. London, 1894.

CRIME AND SOCIAL CONTROL

Addams, Jane, *Democracy and Social Ethics*. ii, 281 p. New York. Ed. of 1913.

——*Newer Ideals of Peace*. xviii, 247 p. New York. Ed. of 1911.

——*The Spirit of Youth and the City Streets*. 3-162 p. New York, 1914.

Aschaffenburg, Gustav, *Crime and Its Repression*. xxviii, 331 p. diagrams. Boston, 1913.

Baldwin, R. N., *Juvenile Courts and Probation*. xii, 3-308 p. illus. New York, 1914.

Barker, J. M., *The Saloon Problem and Social Reform*. vii, 212 p. Boston, 1905.

Bentley, A. F., *The Process of Government*. xv, 501 p. Chicago, 1908.

Bernaldo De Quirós, C., *Modern Theories of Criminality*. xxvii, 249 p. Boston, 1911.

Block, I. S. (Trans. by Lang), *The Future of War*. lxxix, 380 p. illus. Boston, 1903.

Boies, H. M., *The Science of Penology*. xvii, 459 p. New York, 1901.

Booth, Mrs. Maude B., *After Prison, What?* 290 p. New York, 1903.

Brandt, Lilian, *Family Desertion: Five Hundred and Seventy-four Deserters and Their Families*. 64 p. New York, 1905.

Breckinridge, Sophonisba (Editor), *The Child in the City*. xiii, 502 p., plates. Chicago, 1912.

Breckinridge, Sophonisba P., and Abbott, Edith, *The Delinquent Child and the Home*. x, 355 p. illus. New York, 1912.

Brockway, Z. R., *Fifty Years of Prison Service*. xiii, 437 p. illus. New York, 1912.

Calkins, Raymond, *Substitutes for the Saloon*. xvi. 397 p. Boston, 1901.

Clopper, E. N., *Child Labor in City Streets*. ix, 280 p. New York, 1912.

Devon, James, *The Criminal and the Community*. xxi, 348 p. London, 1912.

Economic Aspects of the Liquor Problem. An Investigation Made for the Committee of Fifty. ix, 182 p. Boston, 1905.

Ellis, H. H., *The Criminal*. 4th ed., xxx, 440 p., front., illus., plates. New York, 1910.

Ellwood, C. E., *The Social Problem*. xii, 255 p. New York, 1915.

Fernald, J. C., *The Economies of Prohibition*. xvi, 9-515 p. New York, 1890.

Ferri, Enrico, *Criminal Sociology*. xx, 284 p. New York. Ed. of 1900.

Folks, Homer, *The Care of Destitute, Neglected, and Delinquent Children*. 142 p. New York, 1902.

Garofalo, Baron R. (Trans. by R. W. Millar), *Criminology*. xl, 478 p. Boston, 1914.

Hart, H. H., *Preventive Treatment of Neglected Children*. x, 419 p. illus. New York, 1910.

Henderson, C. R., *Correction and Prevention. Russell Sage Foundation*. 4 vols. illus. New York, 1910.

Hobson, J. A., *The Social Problem*. x, 295 p. New York, 1901.

Holmes, J. H., *The Revolutionary Function of the Modern Church*. xi, 264 p. New York, 1912.

Jenks, J. W., *Citizenship and the Schools*. ix, 264 p. New York, 1906.

Keely, Edward, *The Elimination of the Tramp*. ix, 111 p. New York, 1908.

Keller, A. G., *Societal Evolution*. xi, 238 p. New York, 1915.

Kelley, Florence, *Some Ethical Gains Through Legislation*. x, 341 p. New York, 1905.

Kneeland, G. J., *Commercialized Prostitution in New York City*. xii, 334 p. illus. New York, 1913.

Lichtenberger, J. P., *Divorce—A Study in Social Causation*. 230 p., diagram, charts. New York, 1909.

Lombroso, Cesar, and Ferrero, William, *The Female Offender.* xxvi, 313 p. plates, portraits. New York, 1900.

MacDonald, Arthur, *Criminology.* x, 416 p. New York, 1893.

Mangold, G. B., *Problems of Child Welfare.* xv, 522 p., bibliography. New York, 1914.

McConnell, R. M., *Criminal Responsibility and Social Constraint.* vi, 339 p. New York, 1912.

Mitchell, C. A., *Science and the Criminal.* xiv, 240 p. illus. Boston, 1911.

Mitchell, Dr. Kate, *The Drink Question, Its Social and Medical Aspects.* 256 p. London, 1896.

Morrison, W. D., *Crime and Its Causes.* x, 236 p. London, 1891.

——*Juvenile Offenders.* xx, 317 p. New York, 1897.

Mosby, T. S., *Causes and Cures of Crime.* iii-x, 354 p., front., illus., plates. St. Louis, 1913.

Osborne, T. M., *Within Prison Walls.* 327 p. New York, 1914.

Parkhurst, C. H., *Our Fight with Tammany.* vii, 296 p. New York, 1895.

Rauschenbusch, Walter, *Christianity and the Social Crisis.* xv, 429 p. New York, 1908.

——*Christianizing the Social Order.* xii, 493 p. New York, 1914.

Ross, E. A., *Social Control.* xii, 463 p., bibliography. New York, 1912.

Russel, C. E. B., and Rigby, L. M., *The Making of the Criminal.* xvi, 362 p. London, 1906.

Scott, C. A., *Social Education.* xi, 289 p. Boston, 1908.

Tarde, Gabriel, *Penal Philosophy.* xxxii, 581 p. Boston, 1912.

Taylor, Graham, *Religion in Social Action.* xxxv, 279 p. New York, 1913.

True, R. C., *The Neglected Girl.* 143 p.; *Boyhood and Lawlessness.* 215 p. In one vol. New York, 1914.

Vice Commission of Chicago, *The Social Evil in Chicago.* 399 p., 1911.

Ward, L. F., *Applied Sociology.* xviii, 381 p., 4 maps, chart. Boston, New York, 1906.

Warner, H. S., *Social Welfare and the Liquor Problem.* 274 p. Chicago, 1913.

Williams, Edward Huntington, *The Walled City—A Story of the Criminal Insane.* 263 p., front., plates. New York, 1913.

Wines, F. H., *Punishment and Reformation.* xi, 339 p. illus., plans. New York, Boston, 1895.

GENERAL THEORY, SOCIAL CAUSES, AND ESSENTIAL NATURE OF SOCIETY

Achelis, Th., *Sociologie*. 148 p. Leipzig, 1899.

Adams, Brooks, *The Law of Civilization and Decay*. New York, 1895.

Bagehot, Walter, *Physics and Politics*. 224 p. New York, 1898.

Baldwin, J. M., *The Individual and Society, or, Psychology and Sociology*. 3rd ed. 13, 210 p. New York, 1906.

——*Social and Ethical Interpretations in Mental Development*. xiv, 574 p. New York, 1897.

Blackmar, F. W., and Gillen, J. L., *Outlines of Sociology*. viii, 586 p. New York, 1915.

Bogardus, E. S., *An Introduction to the Social Sciences*. An analytical bibliography. 206 p. Los Angeles, 1913.

Bouglé, C., *Les Idées Égalilaires*. 249 p. Paris, 1899.

Brinton, D. G., *The Basis of Social Relations*. 204 p. New York, 1902.

Carver, Thomas Nixon, *Sociology and Social Progress*. 810 p. New York, 1905.

Caullet, Paul, *Éléments de Sociologie*. 356 p. Paris, 1913.

Comte, Auguste (Trans. by Martineau), *The Positive Philosophy* —freely translated and condensed. 2 vols. London, 1853.

Cooley, C. H., *Human Nature and the Social Order*. viii, 413 p. New York, 1902.

——*Social Organization*. xvii, 426 p. New York, 1909.

Crozier, John Beattie, *Civilization and Progress*. 4th ed. xxxi, 464 p. London, 1898.

Davis, M. M., *Psychological Interpretations of Society*. 260 p. New York, 1909.

Dealey, J. Q., *Sociology, Its Simpler Teachings and Application*. Bibliography. 405 p. New York, 1909.

——and Ward, L. F., *Textbook of Sociology*. xxv, 326 p. New York, 1905.

Durkheim, Emile, *De la division du travail social*. Ed. 2. 416 p. Paris, 1902.

Eleutheropulos, A., *Soziologie*. xii, 236 p. Jena, 1904.

Ellwood, C. A., *Sociology in Its Psychological Aspects*. xiii, 416 p. Bibliography. New York, 1912.

Ellwood, C. A., *Sociology and Modern Social Problems*. Revised and enlarged. 394 p. New York, 1913.

Fairbanks, Arthur, *Introduction to Sociology*. 3rd ed. xii, 307 p. New York, 1901.

Fiske, John, *Outlines of Cosmic Philosophy*. 2 vols. Boston, ed. of 1902.

Fite, Warner, *Individualism*. xix, 301 p. New York, 1911.

Fouillée, Alfred, *La science sociale contemporaine*. xiii, 424 p. Paris, 1904.

Gehlke, C. E., *Emile Durkheim's Contributions to Sociological Theory*. 188 p. New York, 1915.

Giddings, F. H., *Elements of Sociology*. xi, 353 p. New York, 1900.

——*Readings in Descriptive and Historical Sociology*. xiv, 553 p. New York, 1906.

——*The Principles of Sociology*. 3rd ed. xxvi, 476 p. New York, 1896. Bibliography.

Greef, Guillaume de, *Introduction à la Sociologie*. 2 vols. Paris, 1911.

——*Transformisme social*. xxxii, 500 p. Paris, 1901.

Gumplowicz, Ludwig, *Der Rassenkampf*. viii, 376 p. Innsbrück, 1909.

——*The Outlines of Sociology*. 229 p. Philadelphia, 1899.

Hobhouse, Leonard T., *Social Evolution and Political Theory*. ix, 218 p. New York, 1911.

Howard, G. E., *General Sociology*. An Analytical Reference Syllabus (classified bibliography). 86 p. Lincoln, Neb., 1907.

Lamprecht, Karl, *What is History?* ix, 227 p. New York, 1905.

Lane, M. A., *The Level of Social Motion*. An Inquiry into the Future Conditions of Human Society. ix, 577 p. New York, 1902.

Le Bon, Gustav, *The Crowd*, xii, 219 p. New York, 1901.

Loria, Achille, *The Economic Foundations of Society* (Trans. by Keasbey). xiv, 385 p. New York, 1899.

Mackenzie, J. S., *An Introduction to Social Philosophy*. xv, 454 p. Glasgow, 1895.

Novicow, J, *Conscience et volonté sociales*. 380 p. Paris, 1897.

——*Les Luttes entre sociétés humaines*. 2nd ed. 761 p. Paris, 1896.

——*Limites et mechanisme de l'association humaine*. 113 p. Paris, 1911.

Odin, Alfred, *Genèse des grandes hommes*. 2 vols. Paris, 1895.

Patten, S. N., *The New Basis of Civilization.* xii, 220 p. New York, 1907.

——*Theory of Social Forces.* 151 p. Philadelphia, 1896.

Ratzenhoffer, Gustav, *Die Sociologische Erkenntnis.* xii, 372 p. Leipzig, 1898.

——*Soziologie.* xv, 231 p. Leipzig, 1907.

Roberty, E. de., *Nouveau programme de sociologie.* 268 p. Paris, 1904.

——*Sociologie.* 3rd ed. 232 p. Paris, 1893.

——*Sociologie de l'action.* xi, 355 p. Paris, 1908.

Rogers, J. E. T., *The Economic Interpretation of History.* xvii, 547 p. New York, 1889.

Ross, E. A., *Foundations of Sociology.* xiv, 410 p. New York, 1905.

——*Social Psychology.* xvi, 372 p. New York, 1908.

Saleeby, C. W., *Sociology.* 123 p. London, n. d.

Seligman, E. R. A., *The Economic Interpretation of History.* ix, 166 p. New York, 1902.

Sighele, Scipio, *La Foule Criminelle.* 2nd ed. 300 p. Paris, 1901.

——*Psychologie des Sectes.* 231 p. Paris, 1898.

Simmel, Georg, *Soziologie.* 782 p. Leipzig, 1908.

Small, A. W., *Adam Smith and Modern Sociology.* ix, 247 p. Chicago, 1907.

——*General Sociology.* xiii, 739 p. Chicago, 1905.

——*The Meaning of Social Science.* vii, 309 p. Chicago, 1910.

Spencer, Herbert, *The Principles of Sociology.* 3 vols. New York, 1901.

Stuckenberg, J. H. W., *Introduction to the Study of Sociology.* 3rd ed., 336 p. New York, 1905.

——*Sociology, The Science of Human Society.* 2 vols. New York, 1903.

Tarde, Gabriel, *La Logique Sociale.* xvi, 466 p. Paris, 1898.

——*Les Transformations du Pouvoir.* x, 266 p. Paris, 1899.

——*Social Laws* (Trans. by Warren). xi, 213 p. New York, 1899.

——*The Laws of Imitation* (Trans. by Parsons). xxix, 404 p. New York, 1903.

Tönnies, Ferdinand, *Gemeinschaft und Gesellschaft.* xxx, 294 p. Leipzig, 1887.

Veblen, Thorstein, *The Instinct of Workmanship.* ix, 355 p. New York, 1914.

——*The Theory of the Leisure Class.* viii, 400 p. New York, 1911.

Wallas, Graham, *Human Nature in Politics.* xvi, 302 p. Boston, 1909.

——*The Great Society.* xii, 383 p. New York, 1914.

Ward, Lester F., *Dynamic Sociology.* 2 vols. New York, 1883.

——*Outlines of Sociology.* xii, 301 p. New York, 1904.

——*Psychic Factors of Civilization.* xxiii, 369 p. Boston, 1893.

——*Pure Sociology.* xii, 607 p. New York, 1903.

Waxweiler, Emile, *Esquisse d'une sociologie.* 306 p. Brussels, 1903.

Worms, René, *Philosophie des sciences sociales.* 3 vols. Paris, 1903-1907.

JOURNALS, ETC.

American Journal of Sociology, Chicago. Bi-monthly. From 1895.

Annals of the American Academy of Political and Social Science, Philadelphia. Bi-monthly from 1890.

Bliss, W. D. P., *Encyclopedia of Social Reform.* New York, 1908.

Journal of the American Institute of Criminal Law and Criminology. From 1900.

Proceedings of the American Prison Association. From 1887.

Proceedings of the National Conference of Charities and Corrections. Annual from 1876. (Guide to the same—Johnson, Alexander; Guide to the Study of Charities and Corrections, Indianapolis, 1908).

The Survey (replacing *Charities and the Commons*). New York, weekly. From 1909.

The Sociological Review (replacing *Sociological Papers*), London. From 1908.

Revue Internationale de Sociologie, Paris. From 1893.

L'Année Sociologique from 1898.

INDEX

An exponent [²] means that the citation does not begin till the second or last third of the page. No exponent is used where there is a heading to aid the eye.

Names of authorities are printed in *italics*.